The Impact of International Organizations on International Law

The Impact of International Organizations on International Law

By

José E. Alvarez

BRILL
NIJHOFF

LEIDEN | BOSTON

Library of Congress Cataloging-in-Publication Data

Names: Alvarez, Jose E., 1955– author.
Title: The impact of international organizations on international law / by
    Jose E. Alvarez.
Description: Leiden; Boston: Brill/Nijhoff, [2017] | Series: Collected
    courses of the xiamen academy of international law, ISSN 1875-4678 |
    Includes bibliographical references and index.
Identifiers: LCCN 2016032431 (print) | LCCN 2016032606 (ebook) | ISBN
    9789004328396 (hardback : alk. paper) | ISBN 9789004328457 (pbk. : alk.
    paper) | ISBN 9789004328402 (E-book)
Subjects: LCSH: International law. | International agencies.
Classification: LCC KZ3410 .A448 2017 (print) | LCC KZ3410 (ebook) | DDC
    341—dc23
LC record available at https://lccn.loc.gov/2016032431

Typeface for the Latin, Greek, and Cyrillic scripts: "Brill". See and download: brill.com/brill-typeface.

ISSN 1875-4678
ISBN 978-90-04-32845-7 (paperback)
ISBN 978-90-04-32840-2 (e-book)

This paperback is also published in hardback under ISBN 978-90-04-32839-6.

Contents

Preface and Acknowledgements

This monograph grows out of an invitation to present the general course at the Xiamen Academy of International Law. While those 15 one hour lectures were originally delivered in the summer of 2013, the expanded version here updates the material that I originally presented to approximately 100 students. These students, principally from the Asian region, had varying backgrounds in the field. They included novices studying law for the first time and young academics already teaching international law. Their probing questions and intense interest are, I hope, reflected here.

The subject of how institutionalization has affected the making, the interpretation, the contents, and the effect of international law is one that has long interested me—long before I wrote *International Organizations as Law-Makers* (OUP 2005). I have been teaching on this subject since January 1989 when I first taught a course on international organizations at the George Washington University School of Law. Numerous distinguished colleagues at a number of schools since—from my co-teacher the late Oscar Schachter at Columbia Law School to my colleague at Michigan Law School, Eric Stein—profoundly shaped my work. Throughout, they, and the hundreds of students from whom I have learned much over the years, have taught me that the proliferation of international organizations is not an unalloyed good. Although the UN system is often celebrated as a major element in international law's narrative of progress, these institutions, like the states that produced them, are flawed bureaucracies. They are, like Paul Vermeulen's famous "Broken Chair" which faces the Palais des Nations in Geneva, solid exemplars of humanity's idealism but wobbly sites to deploy in expanding the domain of the rule of law. Like Vermeulen's Chair, the UN system's effort to promote rule of law seems to be missing a leg—namely that part of the rule of law that insists that its rules apply to the law-makers themselves. For this reason, I thought it appropriate to portray Vermeulen's Chair on the cover of this book. The artist's original intent was to hold UN members' feet to the fire and force them to confront the dire consequences of the use of anti-personnel mines. The conclusion of the Ottawa Treaty was the occasion for the Chair's original installation in 1997 and the Treaty on Cluster Munitions was the subject of the Chair's subsequent re-dedication ten years later. Today, the Chair exemplifies the UN system's ambitious and not always successful treaty-making and broader law-making efforts over the years. This is my attempt to make some sense of those efforts—and particularly the paradox that the international community's attempts to advance the promises of legal positivism can themselves pose threats to it.

Transforming these lectures to the written page required the encouragement and assistance of many people. I am grateful to Professor Cheng Chia-Jui of Soochow University School of Law for suggesting the topic, extending the original invitation, and for encouraging the completion of this much-delayed monograph—all in his capacity as Secretary-General of the Curatorium for the Xiamen Academy. I particularly want to acknowledge NYU students Adam Gordon, Charles Kopel, Andrew Larkin, Sumeya Mulla, Ian Murray, Nastasja Suhadolnik, Kaveri Vaid, and Simon Williams for their research assistance; Rachel Jones, my faculty assistant, who kept all of us in line and on schedule; and the Belle S. and Irving E. Meller Fund for International Law at NYU. I am particularly grateful, as always, to my spouse, Susan Damplo, for tolerating many lost weekends along the way.

CHAPTER I

Legal Positivism and its Discontents

The ideal model of legal positivism, described in the first section of this chapter, remains the dominant framework for understanding pubic international law. It assumes that: (1) international law emerges from the consent of states; (2) international law, like all law, is distinct from natural law, morality, or politics; (3) international lawyers deploy distinctive sources and use arguments that, as is common to science, can be defended and verified; and (4) the international legal system is closed off from others.[1] Legal positivism presumes a distinction between inquiries pursued by non-lawyers, like sociologists and historians, and the "scientific" appraisal of what the law is undertaken by lawyers. It presumes that law applies irrespective of social aims, public policy, or moral standards. For all these reasons, it is said that law and lawyers enjoy qualities absent from political advisers. A finding by a credible authority such as a judge that a rule of law applies has a legitimating quality because it can be defended on the basis of delimited legal arguments—that is the narrow evidence and methods of proof permitted under the law.

This monograph is an effort to suggest how the rise of international organizations (IOs), including international institutionalized adjudicators, challenges all of these tenets.

---

1 *See, e.g.,* JOSÉ E. ALVAREZ, INTERNATIONAL ORGANIZATIONS AS LAW-MAKERS 46 (2006) (quoting H.L.A. Hart, *Positivism and the Separation of Law and Morals*, 71 HARV. L. REV. 593, 601–602 n. 25 (1958)). For an exemplar of the application of these legal positivism tenets, see GENNADY M. DANILENKO, LAW-MAKING IN THE INTERNATIONAL COMMUNITY (1993). Many of the leading teaching texts and treatises currently utilized around the world, particularly in Latin America, Russia and Eastern Europe, and Asia, including China, adhere to these central tenets or presume their validity. *See infra* note 51 and accompanying text. At the same time given differences among legal positivists, the model or elements of legal positivism outlined here is an ideal type in the sense used by Max Weber. It is a generalized rubric deployed for didactic purposes derived from the views espoused by legal positivists generally. *See* ALVAREZ, *supra* at 45 (citing MAX WEBER, THE THEORY OF SOCIAL AND ECONOMIC ORGANIZATION 89 n. 5 (A.M. Henderson & Talcott Parsons trans., 1947)). Due in part to the rise of international organizations, some international law scholars question at least some of the tenets of legal positivism outlined here. For examples of such contestations, see José E. Alvarez, *Positivism Regained, Nihilism Postponed*, 15 MICH. J. INT'L L. 747 (1994) (reviewing DANILENKO, *supra*).

1   The Mainstream: Legal Positivism

The teaching of public international law has not caught up with its practice. Although there are now innumerable challenges to the lauded tradition of legal positivism, that conception of what "law" is (and is not) continues to exercise a powerful grip on the imagination of many public international law teachers around the world. This is surprisingly true even for the United States where the study of national law has long been dominated by realist, functionalist, and inter-disciplinary perspectives that are at odds with a positivist fascination with rules. A gulf continues to exist between how national law and international law are discussed and taught. In the U.S., the teaching of national law usually means a focus on institutions, including courts, and the law-making process generated within these bodies. In common law jurisdictions, like the U.S. and Canada for example, law students begin their studies by examining the historical role of common law courts in England. They learn how common law developed through the need to apply rules to particular facts and how judges rely on prior resolutions on similar facts by other judges (thereby developing the practice and preference for "precedent" known as *stare decisis*). They are taught why such precedents proved appealing to individuals who did not want to be accused of inventing the law in the course of applying it to settle disputes, and who often found that the most well-articulated rationales of the law were those propounded by fellow judges.[2]

In the U.S., the study of law also involves more generally examining the three branches of government: the executive, legislature, and judiciary. It requires studying the interactions between: the chief executive and the Congress in enacting and enforcing the law, various levels of courts that exist in hierarchical relation to one another and interpret that law, and diverse governmental agencies that are delegated power by the executive and legislative branches of government to issue regulations on specific topics (for example, finance, commerce, health, and the environment).

Courses in U.S. law schools emphasize institutions and institutionalized processes. U.S. constitutional law examines the process of constitutionalization, and in particular, how the Supreme Court managed to turn a slight document, drafted in the eighteenth century and amended only sporadically since, into a blueprint to run a complex modern society. That course and others tell

---

2   For a persuasive application of these insights to explain why the arbitrators in the Iran-U.S. Claims Tribunal turned to prior arbitral caselaw for authority, see Patrick M. Norton, *A Law of the Future or a Law of the Past? Modern Tribunals and the International Law of Expropriation*, 85 Am. J. Int'l L. 474 (1991).

the story of the "humanization" of American law, that is, how all three branches of government, particularly U.S. state and federal courts, transformed the first ten amendments of the U.S. Constitution, its bill of rights, into a charter for protecting the human rights of the peoples of the United States. Further, students are taught how that process led to the creation of foundational structural principles that are not expressly stated in the Constitution like "judicial review" and the "separation of powers." U.S. courses on "administrative" law study how executive agencies have developed an extraordinarily intricate regulatory state, and the equally complex statutes and caselaw that attempt to make such agencies accountable to Congress and ultimately to the people. U.S. administrative law addresses in particular the requirements for transparency of agency action, including public access to government documents through the *Freedom of Information Act*, rules for permitting notice and comment on proposals for agency actions, and the deferential doctrines that apply to review of agency action when these are challenged in court. The "public law" curriculum of U.S. law schools covers the specific challenges posed by the acts of government authorities, whether at the municipal, state, or federal level. The "private law" curriculum—addressing the relations between private parties involving their contracts, torts, and property interests—is also taught from the perspective of institutions. To the extent black letter rules are taught, the stress is on understanding them in their institutional context, on the assumption that the student is better off knowing how and why these rules change rather than what the current rules happen to be. The emphasis of the curriculum is on the manner in which a court, an executive agency, or a legislative body handles legal rights, focusing on how these distinct venues influence the nature of these rights, the evidence that is required to be preserved for presentation to relevant institutional decision-makers, and the rules of procedure that would be applied.

The approach taken by traditional public international law teachers tends to be different. Traditional teachers, steeped in legal positivism, highlight how international law differs from national law because it lacks institutions. Students of international law often begin their studies by learning that there is no global sovereign, executive, legislature, or court with compulsory and hierarchical jurisdiction—and, of course, no global police to enforce inter-state rules. They are taught to be leery of making domestic analogies when it comes to the "anarchic" world of states subject only to "islands" of law. From the outset, the teaching of international law tends to focus on rules, not institutions. If the traditional international law professor makes analogies to national law, she is careful to note that, despite superficial resemblances, the UN Security Council is not "the executive branch," the UN General Assembly is not a "legislature" charged with making law, and talk of a "judiciary" hardly makes sense since even the International Court of Justice (ICJ) can only exercise its power to issue a binding ruling when states consent to its contentious jurisdiction.

Positivist teachers go out of their way to explain that since few IOs have been delegated any power to issue legally binding "regulations," it is wrong to compare them to government agencies at the national level. Although students are made aware that international courts exist and have recently proliferated, these are traditionally described as modes of "dispute settlement" and not as institutions for global governance.[3] IOs that aspire to universal participation are sharply distinguished from a regional entity like the European Union (EU), which has the capacity to make law directly enforced by a European Court. The doctrine of direct effect and supremacy of European Union law are seen as unique to an organization that is on its way to becoming a pseudo state. EU law is treated as fundamentally different from general public international law as the latter penetrates the domestic sphere only insofar as permitted by national law (and a national constitution). The typical student of international law is taught early on that Article 2(7) of the UN Charter contains a fundamental limit, namely, that there is a sacred realm of "domestic jurisdiction" outside the reach of global IOs (and courts or tribunals). As noted later in this chapter, while a growing number of scholars and some international law teachers resist the positivist mainstream, their views are viewed with suspicion within the invisible college of international lawyers.[4]

The traditional international lawyer finds comfort in rules, not institutions. She starts with the premise that the principal actors and subjects are states that are only loosely and imperfectly governed by inter-state rules. These rules are

---

3   See, e.g., J.G. MERRILLS, INTERNATIONAL DISPUTE SETTLEMENT (3d ed. 1998). But see KAREN J. ALTER, THE NEW TERRAIN OF INTERNATIONAL LAW (2014)(enumerating the alternative functions of international courts).

4   See, e.g., MÓNICA GARCÍA-SALMONES ROVIRA, THE PROJECT OF POSITIVISM IN INTERNATIONAL LAW 1 (2013) (noting that positivism is "the basis of the mainstream school of international law today"). Some contemporary positivists call themselves "formalists," see, for example, JEAN D'ASPREMONT, FORMALISM AND THE SOURCES OF INTERNATIONAL LAW (2011). On the concept of the "invisible college," see generally Oscar Schachter, The Invisible College of International Lawyers, 72 NW. U. L. REV. 217 (1977–78). This influential description of the epistemic community of public international law scholars remains apt today insofar as it describes the closely interwoven world of international lawyers, many of whom are trained within a small number of elite academic institutions and share considerable commonalities of points of view. For a critical view of the implications, see David Kennedy, The Politics of the Invisible College: International Governance and the Politics of Expertise, 5 EUR. HUM. RTS. L. REV. 463 (2001).

rudimentary (and only rarely fully effective) efforts to tame the "S" word, that is, sovereignty.[5] In this view, international rules exist on a horizontal, not vertical, plane. Any control they assert on states occurs horizontally—as between consenting states—and not top down, as commands to states imposed against their will. Inter-national rules permit co-equal sovereigns to co-exist with one another peacefully, but only when these sovereigns agree to be so ruled.

The traditional approach to the study of public international law starts, and all too often sadly ends, by examining the international "sources" of law as codified in Article 38 of the Statute of the ICJ. Those under the sway of legal positivism examine institutional processes such as international courts only insofar as they tell us something about those positivist sources. In the beginning, the typical student is taught Article 38: the alpha and omega of the international rule system. According to this positivist totem, those who apply international law need to limit their gaze to: "(a) international conventions, whether general or particular, establishing rules expressly recognized by the contracting states; (b) international custom, as evidence of a general practice accepted as law; (c) the general principles of law recognized by civilized nations; (d) (...) judicial decisions and the teachings of the most highly qualified publicists... as a subsidiary means for the determination of rules of law."[6]

To the positivist, the underlying premises of Article 38 are as important as its text. Article 38 assumes that the sources of law apply exclusively between, and arise only from the action of, states *inter se*. It presumes that these, the only sources of international obligation, are derived from the consent of states. Treaties must be "expressly recognized" under (a), custom must be "accepted" under (b), and general principles must be "recognized" under (c). These three sources are distinct and are not subject to a clear hierarchy. Since nothing in Article 38 indicates that treaties are superior to custom or vice versa, it is assumed that the one that emerges later in time as between the two governs. Article 38 is silent on how these sources may intermingle, emerge one from the other, or exist atop one another, such as treaty above custom, but it suggests that each of the three has a distinct evidentiary basis. We find a treaty when a genuine compact among nations exists, custom when it can be demonstrated that there is state practice accepted as law, and general principles when these are recognized (presumably within the national laws) of "civilized" nations. Further, as Article 38(2) indicates, lawyers and judges on the ICJ "determine"

---

5   *See, e.g.*, Louis Henkin, *That "S" Word: Sovereignty, and Globalization, and Human Rights, Et Cetera*, 68 FORDHAM L. REV. 1 (1999).

6   *See* Statute of the International Court of Justice art. 38(a)–(c), Apr. 18, 1946, 59 Stat. 1055, 33 U.N.T.S. 933.

these rules based on certain delimited forms of evidence, particularly judicial decisions and the writings of highly qualified publicists or scholars. Article 38 is careful to distinguish the latter two mere evidentiary materials from the preceding actual sources of international obligations. The implication is that "determining" the existence and presumably the meaning of international obligations is a scientific enterprise, whereby an objective observer such as a judge on the ICJ can be expected to apply evidence to facts and arrive at an objective conclusion that can be verified by the analysis of others working on the basis of the same rules. In this way judges and lawyers generally can be expected to reach the same results—as do scientists—and unlike moralists who rest their more speculative conclusions on "natural law" or religious beliefs, these results are not subject to refutation.[7] On this view, the role of an international judge or arbitrator is mechanical. He or she is charged with finding facts, determining the applicable source of law, and applying the latter to the former as if applying a mathematical equation such as $A + B = C$.[8] The positivist views the task of lawyering as a science, not an art subject to discretion likely only to produce un-lawyerly disagreement and therefore to discredit the would be rule applier or interpreter. It is the exercise of this scientific skill that distinguishes the contribution of the lawyer in the foreign office from the political adviser.

These distinctions are only encouraged by the second part of Article 38 which enables the Court to decide a case "*ex aequo et bono*"—but only if the litigating parties expressly agree. That states can consent to permit the court to decide a dispute on the basis of non-legal and equitable considerations only

---

7   Indeed, the history of international legal thought is usually depicted, at least by Western scholars, as a drawn out struggle between naturalist and positivist conceptions—with the latter eventually emerging victorious. *See, e.g.*, WERNER LEVI, CONTEMPORARY INTERNATIONAL LAW: A CONCISE INTRODUCTION 6–13, 17–18 (2d ed. 1991); Samantha Besson, *Sources of International Law, in* THE PHILOSOPHY OF INTERNATIONAL LAW 165 (Samantha Besson & John Tasioulas eds., 2010); Benedict Kingsbury & Benjamin Straumann, *State of Nature Versus Commercial Sociability as the Basis of International Law: Reflections on the Roman Foundations and Current Interpretations of the International Political and Legal Thought of Grotius, Hobbes, and Pufendorf, in* THE PHILOSOPHY OF INTERNATIONAL LAW *supra*; Richard Collins, *Classical Legal Positivism in International Law Revisited, in* INTERNATIONAL LEGAL POSITIVISM IN A POST-MODERN WORLD (Jörg Kammerhofer & Jean d'Aspremont eds., 2014).

8   This approach leads some scholars to suggest that the most effective international judge—and court—treats judicial interpretation as a tool to serve the needs of the states. *See, e.g.*, Eric A. Posner & John C. Yoo, *A Theory of International Adjudication*, 93 CAL. L. REV. 1 (2005) (arguing that the most effective international judges are those who see themselves as the "agents" of the state "principals" that established their court).

emphasizes that the alternative—deciding on the basis of international law—is limited to the three sources spelled out in the rest of Article 38. A decision on the basis of equity means going outside the three sources and the legitimate scientific endeavor involving their application.[9] Examples of states giving permission to adjudicators to decide a matter *ex aequo et bono* are naturally rare because states are not usually willing to permit their disputes to be resolved on such open-ended terms; the rarity of the authorized exercise of *ex aequo* powers is seen as a back-handed tribute to the virtues of positivist sources and the positivist method.

For the traditional positivist international lawyer, Article 38 affirms another fundamental tenet of faith: legal obligations either exist or they do not. There is a clear binary between black letter law (*lex lata*) and the progressive development of the law that may be normatively desirable but that has not yet occurred (*lex ferenda*). When black letter rules of law exist, they are binding by definition. There is no spectrum of legal authority wherein some legal rules are more or less binding than others. Article 38 sources are subject to a strict black/white dichotomy of bindingness with no shades of grey. This is, after all, what distinguishes a "rule of law" from other concepts, like a "rule" of politics, a moral injunction, or mere comity. To this end, manuals for teaching international law routinely illustrate the point by noting that the politesse of addressing a state representative as "your excellency" is not a rule of law but only a norm of civility entailing no legal sanction if violated.[10] A rule of law is thus only something that falls into the respective boxes of Article 38 (a), (b), or (c) and a lawyer is one who uncovers it. This also explains the meaning of "state responsibility." While it is acknowledged that the sources of international law do not frequently provide for a clear remedy in an international court of law or an enforceable sanction for their violation, they are distinguished from non-law insofar as their violation, considered to be an "internationally wrongful

---

9   For an arguable example, see Int'l Sch. Services, Inc. v. NICIC, 9 Iran-U.S. Cl. Trib. Rep. 187, 199 (1985) ("As an exercise of its equitable discretion, the Tribunal finds that the Claimant's recovery should be reduced...").

10   In U.S. casebooks, the distinction between a mere application of comity and the use of binding custom and the positivist approach to distinguishing between the two is often illustrated the U.S. Supreme Court's ruling in The Paquete Habana, 175 U.S. 677, 694 (1900) (finding that a customary rule prohibiting the capture of private fishing vessels in the course of war, originally arising as a rule of "comity, courtesy or concession" developed into a settled rule of international law by the general assent of civilized nations).

act," triggers the legal responsibility of states, even if such a claim can only be made through diplomatic protest and not in a court of law.[11]

For the true positivist, the absence of a world government limits the analogies that can be drawn from national law. The structure of the international system and the dearth of genuine processes for governance require looking at state consent as its crucial foundation. The need for state consent drives the preoccupation not only with the three "sources," but also with how these are described and found, as well as their content and modes of interpretation. In the sections that follow, I examine what legal positivism, treated as a Weberian "ideal" type,[12] has to say about the three sources in Article 38. Thereafter, this chapter compares the legal positivism model with the reality of modern international organizations.

1.1   *Positivist Treaties*

While by its own terms, Article 38 is only a direction to the judges of the ICJ as to the choice of law that they are authorized to apply, most international law students are typically taught that Article 38 is much more than that.[13] Article 38 is not, they are told, merely an optional choice of law clause that applies to one particular dispute settlement mechanism. It enumerates the *only* legitimate sources of legal authority. To be an international lawyer means to apply only these three sources and not to be distracted by an oxymoron such as "soft law."[14]

---

11   Articles on Responsibility of Statutes for International Wrongful Acts, *in* Rep. of the Int'l Law Comm'n, 53rd Sess., Apr. 23–June 1, July 2–Aug. 10, 2001, UN Doc. A/56/10/2001; GAOR, 56th Sess., Supp. No 10 (2001) [hereinafter Articles on State Responsibility], *reprinted in* JAMES CRAWFORD, THE INTERNATIONAL LAW COMMISSION'S ARTICLES ON STATE RESPONSIBILITY: INTRODUCTION, TEXT AND COMMENTARIES 61 (2002) [hereinafter ILC COMMENTARY].

12   The ideal type as defined by Weber is a generalized rubric within which an indefinite number of particular cases may be classified. *See* WEBER, *supra* note 1, at 13.

13   *But see* Onuma Yasuaki, *The ICJ: An Emperor Without Clothes? International Conflict Resolution, Article 38 of the ICJ Statute and the Sources of International Law, in* 1 LIBER AMICORUM JUDGE SHIGERU ODA 191, 195–203 (Nisuke Ando et al. eds., 2002) (arguing that the "norms of adjudication" contained in Article 38 should not be regarded as definitive norms of conduct for an international society that lacks a court with compulsory jurisdiction).

14   *See, e.g.,* JAN KLABBERS, AN INTRODUCTION TO INTERNATIONAL INSTITUTIONAL LAW 183 (2d. ed. 2009) (criticizing the idea of "soft law"); DANILENKO, *supra* note 1, at xv, 14–15. *Compare* Prosper Weil, *Towards Relative Normativity in International Law?*, 77 AM. J. INT'L L. 413 (1983) (objecting to relative normativity) *with* Martha Finnemore &

To the faithful positivist, treaties are like contracts, with the only differences being that international rather than national law governs treaties, states or other state-approved international legal persons are their only parties, and no consideration is required. Treaties are like contracts because even when they are multilateral and not merely bilateral instruments, they reflect particular consensual bargains between the negotiating parties. Like contracts, they are reciprocal bargains reached between persons that the law sees as equal and concluded on the basis of an uncoerced exchange.[15] Like contracts, they are reciprocal tit-for-tat deals where State A desires X and State B desires Y, but since both seek to achieve goal Z, they are prepared to give up a little in order to achieve what they want. Treaties reflect the particular desires of those who negotiate them and bind only those states that adhere to them. They are unlike, for example, legislation that applies to all subjects of the law. Like contracts under national law, where common rules of contract exist without respect to different subject matter or the number of parties, common default rules exist for treaties. For the positivist, these default rules, now contained in the Vienna Convention on the Law of Treaties (VCT), are so important that all states have agreed to them and they have therefore become general rules of custom. Under the VCT—irrespective of whether a treaty establishes a boundary, provides for the bilateral extradition of certain criminal suspects, or establishes an organization like the UN, except insofar as the treaty parties have expressly agreed otherwise—all treaties are subject to the same rules regarding conclusion, ratification, and interpretation.[16]

The rules of the VCT, including those in Articles 31 and 32 regarding treaty interpretation, emphasize the consensual basis of all treaties. Those rules emphasize the need for interpretations based on the plain meaning of the text, including its (narrowly defined) "context" and "object and purpose."[17] By privileging text, context, object, and purpose, these rules define treaties as discrete compacts between particular parties. They indicate that irrespective of whether the instrument under review is a bilateral investment treaty between the U.S. and Argentina or the UN Charter, the "scientific" interpretative process

Kathryn Sikkink, *International Norm Dynamics and Political Change*, 52 INT'L. ORG. 887 (1998) (describing the impact and proliferation of soft norms).

15   *See* Vienna Convention on the Law of Treaties, art. 51, *opened for signature* May 23, 1969, 1155 U.N.T.S. 331 [hereinafter VCT] (invaliding consent to a treaty obtained through coercion of representative of a state); *id.* art. 52 (rendering a treaty void if it is procured by the threat or use of force in violation of the UN Charter).

16   *Id.* art. 18.

17   *Id.* art. 31.

is the same, as is the interpretative goal: to determine and give effect to the intention of the parties to the treaty. Treaty interpretation is not about advancing the goals or interests of anyone other than the state parties to the compact. It is not about advancing the goals of the "international community," or about securing any other goals outside the object and purpose sought by the creators of the contract no matter how socially or politically desirable. This is what distinguishes a genuinely objective legal interpretation from one that is biased or unscientific.

While it is often said that Article 32 of the VCT[18] discourages resort to the negotiating history of a treaty,[19] practicing lawyers know that this is rarely the effect of that provision.[20] Article 32 licenses such an inquiry to "confirm" the meaning achieved by using the techniques spelled out in Article 31—and not only when ignoring the negotiating history leads to a result that is ambiguous, absurd, or unreasonable. As Julian Mortensen has argued, the drafters of the VCT did not set out to discourage recourse to the negotiating history.[21] Rather, they presumed that reliance on it was legitimate. The text and perhaps the original intent of Article 32 itself are consistent with examining the "object and purpose" of a treaty. Article 32 serves as a license to search for the intent of the original parties. On this view, there is no contradiction between what Articles 31 and 32 demand of a treaty interpreter as both permit a search for the intention or perceived intention of the drafters of a treaty. Note that this does not necessarily give rise to a "strict" or literal interpretation over an "expansive" or teleological one. It merely suggests that either of these is possible, provided the strict or teleological interpretation is grounded in a good faith effort to discern whether either of those (or something in between) was contemplated by the parties when the treaty was concluded or by their subsequent agreement(s)

---

18   *Id.* art. 32 ("Recourse may be had to supplementary means of interpretation, including the preparatory work of the treaty and the circumstances of its conclusion, in order to confirm the meaning resulting from the application of article 31, or to determine the meaning when the interpretation according to article 31: (a) leaves the meaning ambiguous or obscure; or (b) leads to a result which is manifestly absurd or unreasonable.").

19   *See, e.g.,* Julian Davis Mortenson, *The Travaux of Travaux: Is the Vienna Convention Hostile to Drafting History?*, 107 Am. J. Int'l L. 780 (2013).

20   *See* Jan Klabbers, *Interpretation as the Continuation of Politics by Other Means*, Opinio Juris, (Mar 2, 2009, 2:15 PM), *at* http://opiniojuris.org/2009/03/02/continuation/ ("I cannot think of a serious lawyer who would not at least have a look at some of the preparatory work to bolster her conclusion or, if necessary, reconsider her conclusion, regardless of whether an interpretation without the preparatory works would lead to ambiguous or absurd results.").

21   Mortenson, *supra* note 19.

relating to the treaty over time.[22] For these reasons, the VCT rules generally encourage interpretations specific to the treaty in question. The central rule in Article 31 (1) of the VCT and the residual recourse contemplated with respect to supplemental materials in Article 32 do not encourage generalized interpretations across treaty regimes. They presume, on the contrary, that each treaty ought to be interpreted in light of its text, context, and specific negotiation history.[23] The principle of *pacta sunt servanda* in Article 26 requiring compliance with treaties "in good faith," also seeks to accomplish this result.[24]

The VCT's state-centric rules are directed at giving effect to the freely expressed desires of states. Reflecting the positivist tenet that states are the only true "subjects" of international law, they essentially make states the emperors of their compacts. For the strict positivist, the ordinarily applicable rules of treaty interpretation offer little room to consider the desires of non-state actors—whether these are international civil servants within IOs or members of international civil society represented by NGOs—unless these are filtered through the expressed wishes of the party states.[25] The VCT rules also

---

22   *See generally* Rep. of the Int'l Law Comm'n, 65th Sess., May 6–June 7, July 8–Aug. 9, 2013, 12, U.N. Doc. A/68/10; GAOR, 68th Sess., Supp. No. 10 (2013) ("Subsequent agreements and subsequent practice under articles 31 and 32 may assist in determining whether or not the presumed intention of the parties upon the conclusion of the treaty was to give a term used a meaning which is capable of evolving over time.").

23   But note the potential, discussed further *infra*, for more open-ended possibilities provided under Article 31(3)(c) of the VCT. VCT, *supra* note 15, art. 31(3)(c) (enabling resort to other "relevant rules of international law among the parties"). Some have argued that this rule, which allows interpreters to consider law outside the four corners of the treaty in question, is a tool for the "systemic integration" of international law. *See, e.g.*, Campbell McLachlan, *The Principle of Systemic Integration and Article 31(3)(c) of the Vienna Convention*, 54 INT'L & COMP. L. Q. 279 (2005). *See also* Bruno Simma & Theodore Kill, *Harmonizing Investment Protection and International Human Rights: First Steps Towards a Methodology, in* INTERNATIONAL INVESTMENT LAW FOR THE 21ST CENTURY: ESSAYS IN HONOUR OF CHRISTOPH SCHREUER 678 (Christina Binder et al. eds., 2009) (proposing that article 31(3)(c) of the VCT be used to integrate human rights principles into the interpretation of investment protection treaties).

24   VCT, *supra* note 15, art. 26 ("Every treaty in force is binding upon the parties to it and must be performed by them in good faith").

25   Indeed, this is the *de facto* result produced within the WTO Dispute Settlement as it is more likely to accept and consider *amicus* briefs when attached to a WTO Member's submissions or when these are adopted by the parties. *See* James Durling & David Hardin, *Amicus Curiae Participation in WTO Dispute Settlement: Reflections on the Past Decade, in* KEY ISSUES IN WTO DISPUTE SETTLEMENT: THE FIRST TEN YEARS 225, 230 (Rufus Yerxa & Bruce Wilson eds., 2005).

imply that treaties have specific meanings that are discerned once the intent of their negotiators is scientifically determined. There is a status quo quality to these rules, as there is to the treaties they purport to govern. Moreover, these default rules are difficult to overcome. The VCT rules governing *lex specialis* and the International Law Commission's attendant commentaries essentially put the burden on the party that seeks to deviate from the default rules of the VCT to prove that in the specific case a contrary rule was intended.[26]

Subject to the narrow exceptions in Article 31(3),[27] the interpretation rules also assume that treaties have static meanings that do not change over time, even in the face of the changing needs of the "international community of states." The proper interpretation of treaties, whatever their nature or subject matter and whether embedded in an institutional setting or not, drive us back to the intent formed at their formation—except where the state parties have consented to change through their joint and mutual subsequent agreement,[28] through the subsequent practice of all the state parties,[29] or where the state parties have agreed to other relevant rules of international law that should also prove applicable given their consent to them.[30] Thus, although the VCT rules of interpretation permit treaties to evolve over time, any changes remain formally within the control of their state parties, as suited to the bedrock principle of consent. The rest of the VCT similarly elevates the role of state consent. Consider Article 34 (the general rule indicating that a treaty only binds its parties and not third parties) which affirms state consent,[31] Article 35 (which provides that a third party is only bound by obligations imposed by a treaty if

---

26   Articles on State Responsibility, *supra* note 11, art. 55 & note (4) ("For the *lex specialis* principle to apply it is not enough that the same subject matter is dealt with by two provisions; there must be some actual inconsistency between them, or else a discernible intention that one provision is to exclude the other.").

27   VCT, *supra* note 15, art. 31(3) ("There shall be taken into account, together with the context: (a) Any subsequent agreement between the parties . . . (b) Any subsequent practice in the application of the treaty which establishes the agreement of the parties regarding its interpretation; (c) Any relevant rules of international law applicable in the relations between the parties.").

28   *Id.* art. 31(3)(a).

29   *Id.* art. 31(3)(b).

30   *Id.* art. 31(3)(c). *But see* discussion at *supra* note 23 about contemporary efforts to reinterpret the scope of the interpretative license accorded under this rule.

31   VCT, *supra* note 15, art. 34 ("A treaty does not create either obligations or rights for a third State without its consent.").

it expressly consents to it),[32] and Article 28 (ensuring that absent a different intention expressly stated in a treaty, the latter only has prospective effect).[33] At the same time, the VCT rules emphasize the separation of this source of international obligation from national law and its institutions and courts. To this end, Article 27 of the VCT tells us that a state's internal law is irrelevant with respect to a treaty obligation, and that once a treaty is duly ratified by a state under the procedures for accession, it is irrelevant whether the ratifying state has properly followed its own internal procedures for entering into a treaty.[34] In all these respects, treaties are grounded in the ideal model of legal positivism.

1.2   *Positivist Custom*

The positivist is also clear-eyed about the state-centric and consensual nature of custom. This source of law differs from treaties because it is unwritten, and for that reason requires some effort to uncover the mutual, but sometimes unexpressed, consent of states to be bound. Two types of evidence of state consent are required: objective state practice and the more subjective *opinio juris*. State practice requires a scientific counting of the numbers of states actually engaged in particular action, such as preventing the targeting of civilians for harm during a war. For general custom to exist, the practice must be found among a sufficiently high number of states so that it is reasonable to presume that it is generally performed by all, or that no significant portion of states would dispute the existence of a particular custom. While complete uniformity of conforming practice by all states is neither practical nor essential, it is desirable to find that nearly universal state practice actually exists or can be presumed. The search for sufficiently generalizable practice is greatly facilitated by the license to treat omissions as cognizable practice. Still, the practice of states must be accompanied by evidence that ideally is separately demonstrated: namely evidence that those states who engaged in the relevant

---

32   *Id.* art. 35 ("An obligation arises for a third State from a provision of a treaty if the parties to the treaty intend the provision to be the means of establishing the obligation and the third State expressly accepts that obligation in writing.").

33   *Id.* art. 28 ("Unless a different intention appears from the treaty or is otherwise established, its provisions do not bind a party in relation to any act or fact which took place or any situation which ceased to exist before the date of the entry into force of the treaty with respect to that party.").

34   *Id.* art. 27 ("A party may not invoke the provisions of its internal law as justification for its failure to perform a treaty."). *But see* art. 46 (requiring a violation to be "manifest" and concern an internal rule of fundamental importance that would be objectively evident to other states).

practice did so out of a sense of legal obligation and not because of comity or another non-legal rationale. The scientific method of finding custom requires, in other words, convincing evidence of genuine agreement among states comparable to that found more readily and concretely expressed in a treaty.

Examples of searches for the elements of positivist custom by tribunals would include the significant decision of the ICJ affirming that sovereign immunity is indeed a recognized principle of customary international law.[35] Another example of the search for custom in a wholly different sub-field is *Glamis Gold v. United States*, a ruling of the arbitral investor-state tribunal of the North American Free Trade Agreement (NAFTA).[36] That decision involved the application of Article 1105 of the NAFTA, which guarantees investors of the three state parties "fair and equitable treatment."[37] The tribunal had to decide on the meaning of customary law since the NAFTA parties had issued a joint interpretation of their agreement indicating that Article 1105 "prescribes the customary international law minimum standard of treatment of aliens as the minimum standard of treatment to be afforded to investments of investors of another party."[38] The *Glamis* tribunal rejected arguments by the claimant investors that this customary standard had evolved and no longer required proof (as had been decided by a prior arbitral tribunal) that a state engaged in "shocking" or "egregious" conduct.[39] The arbitrators in *Glamis* reaffirmed the need to search for actual state practice and *opinio juris* and not merely rely on opinions rendered by prior arbitral tribunals. It found that while the old arbitral decision of *Neer v. Mexico* had properly applied the traditional practice and *opinio juris* criteria, subsequent investor-state arbitrators could not be relied upon for accurately finding the customary international standard of treatment since they had sometimes been guided by the "autonomous" texts of treaties for specific investment protection (which may have required "fair and

---

35   Jurisdictional Immunities of the State (Ger. v. It.), 2012 I.C.J. 99, ¶ 55 (Feb. 3) (stating that "the existence of a rule of customary international law requires that there be 'a settled practice' together with *opinio juris*," the Court explored state practice through national courts, the legislation of those states dealing with immunity, claims to immunity advanced by states before foreign courts and the statements made by states).

36   Glamis Gold v. United States, Award (NAFTA Ch. 11 Arb. Trib. June 8, 2009), *at* http://www.state.gov/documents/organization/125798.pdf.

37   North American Free Trade Agreement, U.S.-Can.-Mex., Dec. 17, 1992, 32 I.L.M. 289, Art. 1105 (1993).

38   Glamis Gold, *supra* note 36, ¶ 599.

39   *Id.* ¶¶ 600–616 (referring to Neer v. United Mexican States, No. 136 (U.S.-Mex. General Claims Comm'n Oct. 15, 1926), *reprinted in* 21 AM. J. INT'L L. 555 (1927)).

equitable treatment" not connected to the customary standard) and not by the application of the two requisites of custom.[40]

That tribunal implicitly affirmed the distinctions made in Article 38 of the Statute of the ICJ, between the three "primary" sources of international obligation and mere "secondary evidence" of such sources in judicial opinions or the writings of scholars. The *Glamis Gold* tribunal indicated that arbitral rulings were not themselves evidence of state practice or *opinio juris* of states.[41] It therefore declined to follow rulings, like that in *Tecmed v. Mexico*, which it suggested had applied a specific text of a treaty as an autonomous standard instead of the proper requisites of custom.[42]

1.3   *Positivist General Principles*

Positivist international lawyers have had difficulties explaining the meaning and consensual rationale for the general principles of law identified in Article 38(1)(c). They have disagreed on what general principles are, where to find them, and even whether this source of international obligation is really distinguishable from, or just an effort to generalize from, the other two sources of law, particularly custom.[43] Oscar Schachter has summarized disagreements over the nature of general principles. He noted that the concept might encompass five different ideas:

---

40   *Id.* ¶¶ 606–611. For a view that even the Neer case did not objectively apply the two requisites of custom but reflected a "permissive and loose concept of customary law," see Jean d'Aspremont, *International Customary Investment Law: Story of a Paradox*, 10 (Amsterdam Law School Legal Studies Research Paper No. 2011–19, Aug. 25, 2011).

41   Glamis Gold, *supra* note 36, ¶¶ 598–611.

42   *Id.* ¶ 610, citing Técnicas Medioambientales Tecmed, S.A. v. The United Mexican States, ICSID Case No. ARB (AF)/00/2, Award, ¶¶ 4, 155 (May 29, 2003), *at* http://ita.law.uvic.ca/documents/Tecnicas_001.pdf.

43   *See, e.g.,* OSCAR SCHACHTER, INTERNATIONAL LAW IN THEORY AND PRACTICE 50–55 (Developments in International Law Ser. No. 13, 1991). Indeed, this confusion is suggested by some judicial rulings that seem to merge this source with custom by finding "general principles of customary international law." *See, e.g.,* Prosecutor v. Tadic, Case No. IT-94-1-I, Decision on Defence Motion for Interlocutory Appeal on Jurisdiction, ¶ 125 (Int'l Crim. Trib. For the Former Yugoslavia Oct. 2, 1995) ("State practice shows that general principles of customary international law have evolved with regard to internal armed conflict also in areas relating to methods of warfare."). A blurring of the categories of custom and general principles of law may also occur when courts turn to the same evidentiary sources, namely national laws or practices, to find both.

(1)   The principles of municipal or internal national law as recognized by "civilized nations";

(2)   General principles of law "derived from the specific nature of the international community";

(3)   Principles intrinsic to the idea of law and basic to all legal systems (that is, as arising from the rule of law);

(4)   Principles "valid through all kinds of societies in relationships of hierarchy and coordination"; or

(5)   Principles of justice founded on "the very nature of man as a rational and social being."[44]

Recognizing these conceptual difficulties, Ian Brownlie argued that the category of general principles demonstrates that a "rigid categorization of sources" is inappropriate.[45] Brownlie noted that certain purported examples of general principles—namely the principles of consent, reciprocity, equality of states, finality of awards and settlement, the legal validity of agreements, good faith, domestic jurisdiction, and the freedom of the seas—are in reality abstract derivations from the mass of treaty and customary rules that are no longer directly connected with state practice, but are undoubtedly supported by the other two sources.[46]

Given these difficulties it should be no surprise that traditional positivists downplay this third source of law, usually suggesting that the list of legitimate general principles is quite short and resort to the concept insignificant. Most traditional legal treatises focus on Schachter's first category, wherein general principles are derived from a comparative law search for those few universally accepted concepts that can be found within the world's diverse legal systems. The general consensus around Schachter's first category may be due to fear that his other four categories come perilously close to collapsing the distinction between positivism and natural law altogether. The quest for general principles consistent with the tenets of legal positivism has therefore produced a very narrow number of approved general principles. Those most commonly cited in international legal treatises include laches, *res judicata*, *lex posterior derogat prior*, *lex specialis derogat generalis*, estoppel and acquiescence, *ex*

---

44   SCHACHTER, *supra* note 43, at 50.

45   IAN BROWNLIE, PRINCIPLES OF PUBLIC INTERNATIONAL LAW 37 (8th ed. 2012).

46   *Id.*

injuria jus non oritur, the duty to mitigate damages, and the prohibition on *non liquet.*[47]

As is suggested by the frequent resort to terms known even to ancient systems of law on this list, the premise is that the number of general principles needs to remain small because we must be careful, as with respect to treaties and custom, to limit this source to only those concepts that states generally and genuinely accept. But there is another reason for the positivist resistance to this third source: locating the basis of state consent for general principles is not an easy task. To the extent that general principles are found in the least controversial of Schachter's categories—namely through a comparative law exercise involving a search through municipal legal orders—such principles are generally applied with respect to private law disputes in national courts over real property, contracts, or torts, at a considerable remove from the inter-state plane upon which much of international law operates. On what basis can a positivist assert that states have expressed their consent that such principles, even those limited ones enumerated, should apply to their inter-state disputes? For some positivists, this suggests that despite the text of Article 38, general principles do not truly exist as a distinct source of international obligation, but are mere derivations from the others.[48] Those positivists who accept this third source of law contend that the implicit consent from states emerges from the very fact that their courts find it impossible to ignore these general principles when applying the law. To the extent that one accepts this rationale for "implicit consent," it would seem that Schachter's categories tend to collapse into one another, insofar as we appear to be deriving general principles under category one because they belong to his categories three, four, and/or five. Of course, a legal positivist would still insist that these general principles are based on "scientifically" derived or observed facts discovered in the real world, and not a priori assumptions of what morality or natural law demands.

---

47   *See generally* Malcolm N. Shaw, International Law 98–105 (6th ed. 2008); Malcolm D. Evans, International Law 108–109 (3d ed. 2010); Antonio Cassese, International Law 190–194 (2d ed. 2005); Jan Klabbers, International Law 34–35 (2013).

48   *See* Brownlie, *supra* note 45.

2   The Institutional Challenge to Positivism

This section begins to consider how the "move to institutions"[49] which began in earnest with the establishment of the League of Nations and continues today at least with respect to the proliferation of venues for international adjudication is a challenge to legal positivism. While other sections below describe the institutional challenges posed to the specific sources in Article 38, this section considers more generally how the turn to institutions in the twentieth and twenty-first centuries has undermined the core positivist tenets that international law: (1) emerges from the consent of states; (2) is distinct from natural law, morality, and politics; (3) deploys distinctive sources and arguments unique to legal science; and (4) is a closed logical system.

At the outset, one objection needs to be met head on: are not these core tenets of the Weberian ideal type of legal positivism outdated straw-men? Aren't most legal positivists today less willing to tie themselves to the positivist mast and more likely to describe themselves as "enlightened positivists" of the twenty-first century? Evidence for the last proposition might be sought in the 1999 volume of the *American Journal of International Law* (AJIL), which purported to canvass modern "methodological approaches" to international law. That issue described legal positivism as only one of the possible methodological approaches and the sole representative of positivism contained in that volume, a contribution by Bruno Simma and Andreas Paulus, offered a picture of "enlightened positivism" that differs in several respects from the descriptions of positivist sources in the previous sections above.[50]

But Simma and Paulus postulated their "enlightened" view precisely because the more rigid version of positivist sources propounded by others for decades, including by Russian scholars like Danilenko and Tunkin, was no longer tenable given contemporary realities. Their version of enlightened positivism, however prevalent in some contemporary scholarly circles, has not reached legions of law students from all around the world who continue to be taught international law in ways that adhere closely to the legal positivism ideal type described above. Most of them are, I suspect, not as familiar with the more "enlightened" version propounded by Simma and Paulus (which might be called "positivism lite"). A survey of some of the leading teaching texts used in Latin America, Russia and Eastern Europe, as well as Asia, tends to support this

---

49   *See generally* David W. Kennedy, *The Move to Institutions*, 8 CARDOZO L. REV. 841 (1987).

50   Bruno Simma & Andreas L. Paulus, *The Responsibility of Individuals for Human Rights Abuses in Internal Conflicts: A Positivist View*, 93 AM. J. INT'L L. 302 (1999).

conclusion.[51] Even in the United States, home to the various inter-disciplinary and competing methodologies canvassed in the 1999 AJIL volume, positivism remains the lingua franca of the field—and indeed legal positivism is the starting point for leading critiques of the field.[52]

2.1 The Reality of Institutionalization

Consider how different our conception of international law would be if, instead of starting with the Article 38 sources of law, law students embarked on its study by examining the bureaucratic charts of existing international organizations, such as the elaborate ones that enumerate the many human rights related

---

51 Lauri Mälksoo, *International Law in Russian Textbooks: What's in the Doctrinal Pluralism?*, 2 GÖTTINGEN J. INT'L L. 279, 290 (2009) ("[T]he Russian doctrine of international law remains largely positivist and oriented towards textual interpretation; if necessary, willing to bend the contested rule or historical event favorably towards one's own state rather than against it."); ANTONIO CASSESE, INTERNATIONAL LAW (2d ed. 2004); TAHIRIH V. LEE, CHINESE LAW: SOCIAL, POLITICAL, HISTORICAL AND ECONOMIC PERSPECTIVES 13–17 (1997) (discussing the attitudes of Chinese international law scholars towards the Article 38 sources of international law); WANG TIEYA, INTERNATIONAL LAW (1995); DIEZ DE VELASCO, MANUEL. INSTITUCIONES DE DERECHO INTERNACIONAL PÚBLICO 113 (15th ed. 2005). As for Western Europe, it is revealing that the leading treatise by Brownlie, *supra* note 45, devoted only 33 pages to international organizations even in a recent edition. Europe is also the home of sterling defenses of legal positivism periodically on offer. *See, e.g.,* D'ASPREMONT, *supra* note 4. To be sure, the emphasis on a legal positivist approach may be a matter of convenience. *See, e.g.,* Florian Hoffman, *Teaching General Public International Law, in* INTERNATIONAL LEGAL POSITIVISM IN A POST-MODERN WORLD 349 (Jörg Kammerhofer & Jean d'Aspremont eds., 2014). Moreover, some leading international treatises even in Europe appear to be breaking free of the positivist frame. *See, e.g.,* MALCOLM SHAW, INTERNATIONAL LAW 33 (7th ed. 2014) ("[T]he gradual sophistication of positivist doctrine, combined with the advent of new approaches to the whole system of international relations, has broken down this exclusive emphasis and extended the roles played by non-state entities, such as individuals, multinational firms and international institutions."); MARTIN DIXON, TEXTBOOK ON INTERNATIONAL LAW (7th ed. 2013) (noting that Article 38 does not provide a complete list of the matters which the Court can consider and that "old conceptions about the nature of statehood and sovereignty have had to be re-thought in light of a revitalized international judicial system and a widespread perception that a shrinking and complex world *needs*, rather than just *chooses*, an effective international legal order.").

52 Martti Koskenniemi's critical engagement with "the structure of international legal argument" prominently engages with each of the positivist tenets enumerated above; indeed the positivist doctrine of sources, the vagaries of treaty interpretation, and the dialectics of custom form core elements of that text. MARTTI KOSKENNIEMI, FROM APOLOGY TO UTOPIA: THE STRUCTURE OF INTERNATIONAL LEGAL ARGUMENT (2d ed. 2005).

organs and committees operating just within the United Nations,[53] or Barbara Woodward's "Outline of Framework of Global Governance."[54] Woodward's enumeration of "global governance" institutions, includes, for the UN Security Council alone, four subsidiary bodies (the Military Staff Committee, the UN Monitoring, Verification and Inspection Committee for Iraq (UNMOVIC), three standing committees, and the Peacebuilding Commission), two *ad hoc* bodies (the Governing Council on the UN Compensation Commission, and the Counter-Terrorism Committee), two ad hoc international criminal tribunals (the International Criminal Tribunal for the former Yugoslavia (ICTY) and the International Criminal Tribunal for Rwanda (ICTR)), eleven sanctions committees, and six working groups.[55]

Woodward's list of the UN GA entities is even more extensive: apart from a large number of subsidiary organs, it includes four boards, six commissions, seventeen categories of main committees (with innumerable sub-committees), three councils, and six categories of working groups.[56] And what if the basic international law course were to commence with the synoptic chart produced by the Project on International Courts and Tribunals which enumerates the numerous judicial and quasi-judicial forums for addressing international disputes, prosecuting international crimes, or dealing with allegations of human rights abuses?[57] That synoptic chart is only one possible way of categorizing the "international judiciary" through a basic division between "permanent" courts or tribunals capable of issuing binding judgments and those frequently ad hoc bodies that only issue non-binding "views." Alternatively, students could be asked to examine Karen Alter's table of twenty four permanent international courts, which she distinguishes on the basis of whether these engage in "dispute settlement," "enforcement," "administrative review," or "constitutional

---

53   *See, e.g.*, U.N. Office of the High Commission for Human Rights, The United Nations Human Rights System: How to Make It Work For You, 21 UNCTAD/NGLS/2008/2 (2008), *at* http://www.un-ngls.org/IMG/pdf/Final_logo.pdf; U.N. Department of Public Information, U.N. System Organizational Chart (August 2013), *at* http://www.un.org/en/aboutun/structure/org_chart.shtml.

54   BARBARA WOODWARD, GLOBAL CIVIL SOCIETY IN INTERNATIONAL LAWMAKING AND GLOBAL GOVERNANCE: THEORY AND PRACTICE app. B (2010).

55   *Id.*

56   *Id.*

57   *The International Judiciary in Context*, THE PROJECT ON INTERNATIONAL COURTS AND TRIBUNALS (Nov. 2004), *at* http://www.pict-pcti.org/publications/synoptic_chart/synop_c4.pdf.

review."[58] Or consider the possible result if, in addition, students were steered away from formal brick and mortar institutions to more episodic institutional phenomena, whether Meetings of the Parties (MOPs) under some environmental treaties,[59] or Woodward's separate listing enumerating the nine major global UN conferences held from 1990 to 1996?[60]

Whether these lists have properly classified the sub-organs or courts they have identified is not important here. The point is not whether we agree or disagree with Alter when she contends, for example, that the Andean Tribunal of Justice can accurately be described as a "constitutional" body. Nor is it important for the purposes here to agree with Woodward's categorization of the outcome of certain UN conferences, such as her contention that the Declaration on the Survival, Protection and Development of Children produced by the 1990 World Summit should be seen as "soft law."[61] These lists and tables begin to suggest that law at the global level cannot and should not be described as existing in a state of anarchy with only occasional islands of inter-state voluntary cooperation, when the rare conjunction of inter-state mutual consent coincides sufficiently to produce treaty or custom. Woodward, Alter, and other scholars who study what legal positivists would criticize as another oxymoron, "global governance," remind us of the reality of institutionalization that has occurred over the course of the past one hundred years, while the myopic gaze of many international lawyers remains fixed on rules rather than on the dramatic changes in how those rules (and other norms) are being fashioned, interpreted, and applied—and by whom.

Woodward's "governance" framework and Alter's analyses of the legal and political impact of courts and tribunals suggest that, as with respect to the study of national law, history matters. While it may still be correct to call the international legal system a rudimentary one as compared to ever more complex national legal systems, it is no longer accurate to portray it as a world of opaque billiard balls of interacting states subject to few global or regional institutions or forms of adjudication. On one count (by the Union of International

---

58   Karen Alter, *The Multiple Roles of International Courts and Tribunals, in* INTERDISCIPLINARY PERSPECTIVES ON INTERNATIONAL LAW AND INTERNATIONAL RELATIONS: THE STATE OF THE ART, 345–355, fig. 14.3 (Jeffrey L. Dunoff & Mark A. Pollack eds., 2012). *See also* ALTER, *supra* note 3, at 161–282.

59   Robin R. Churchill & Geir Ulfstein, *Autonomous Institutional Arrangements in Multilateral Environmental Agreements: A Little-Noticed Phenomenon in International Law*, 94 AM. J. INT'L L. 623 (2000).

60   WOODWARD, *supra* note 54, app. F (including the number of states and NGOs participating in each of these conferences, along with outcomes).

61   *Id.* at 439.

Associations in 2012), there were 1,839 IOs as of 1999, as compared to 37 in 1909.[62] The number of treaties has also proliferated along with IOs. The number of treaties registered at the UN at the end of each decade from the 1950s through the 2010 was 4,318; 5,106; 8,146; 9,461; and 9,809.[63] By the end of 2014, the number of UN registered treaties had grown to 52,050.[64]

Despite some evidence that the level of interest in concluding ambitious multilateral treaties in the modern era has cooled,[65] there is an ever-rising "density" of legalization around the world. While the sheer numbers of UN registered treaties do not tell us whether these are more or less significant than those that have come before, the fact remains that many treaties are not only registered at the UN—which is after all strongly encouraged under the UN Charter's Article 102—they are negotiated there or within the auspices of other IOs. Contemporary negotiations of treaties, at least multilateral ones, are now conducted with the assistance of these organizations, under organizational rules, and often in familiar organizational venues with predictable procedural rules like UN conferences. The venue for the negotiation of treaties often matters; it has an impact on the content, method of negotiation, extent of non-state and state participation, and the likelihood of certain post ratification procedures.[66] The institutionally negotiated treaties of the modern age are not the bilateral compacts that inspired the positivist model. They include multilateral efforts at global legislation, instruments that enable dynamic reinterpretations of treaty terms, as well as the constitutive instruments of international organizations, courts, and arbitral mechanisms. Moreover, as Woodward's summary of the outcomes of major UN conferences indicates, global institutions are no longer exclusively focused on producing the two principal sources of law in Article 38. If we focus on the products of institutions, we will discover the fact that the production of "soft law" instruments now exceeds the production of treaties—and that the former may sometimes have the same or even greater effects on the actual behavior of states and others than do "hard" treaties.[67]

---

62   *See* Kal Raustiala, *Institutional Proliferation and the International Legal Order*, *in* Interdisciplinary Perspectives, *supra* note 58, at 296.

63   *Id.* at 307.

64   U.N. Office of Legal Affairs, Treaty Section, Statement of Treaties and International Agreements Registered or Filed and Recorded with the Secretariat, ST/LEG/SER.A/809 (Jul. 2014).

65   Woodward, *supra* note 54, at 307–308.

66   *See* Alvarez, *supra* note 1, at 273–400.

67   *See generally* Dinah Shelton, Commitment and Compliance: The Role of Non-Binding Norms in the International Legal System (2000); Andrea K.

To be sure, the level of institutionalization in the world is not equally dis-tributed. Not all regions have shown an equal enthusiasm for turning to deep institutional integration through regional IOs or regional international courts and tribunals. As Karen Alter indicates, the Asian region remains relatively less institutionalized, especially with respect to international courts.[68] While this does not suggest that Asians—who continue of course to participate in the UN system and international financial organizations including the World Bank's International Center for the Settlement of Investment Disputes (ICSID) and the World Trade Organization (WTO)—ignore the institutionalization of the world, it surely indicates that there are east/west and north/south aspects to institutionalization. The turn to institutions does not have equal participants and is surely producing winners and losers.

At one time, when the prospect of international organizations was in the distant horizon, the institutionalization of law (and especially the prospect of international courts) was seen as the culmination of a "progressive narrative" in which global peace would be achieved through functionalist organizations for piecemeal cooperation.[69] Today's students of global governance acknowledge, on the contrary, that institutions may be instruments of state power and not necessarily vehicles for attaining the laudatory goals of "the international com-munity." The powerful use institutions to enhance their power or to distance themselves from organizations—the better to exercise more unilateral forms of control. When it comes to participating in international adjudication, two of the leading powers of the world—the U.S. and China—share comparable atti-tudes. These veto-wielding nations on the UN Security Council are exception-ally well positioned to deploy that body's unique enforcement and legislative powers. At the same time, both of these powerful states remain outside of the

---

BJORKLUND & AUGUST RENISCH, INTERNATIONAL INVESTMENT LAW AND SOFT LAW (2012).

68   *See* Alter, *supra* note 58, at 347, fig. 14.1. Indeed, although ASEAN has become more insti-tutionalized over time and seemingly has acquired the status of an international legal person, it has exercised its treaty-making capacity in limited fashion. *See* Hao Duy Phan, *ASEAN's Legal Personality and its Treaty-Making Power*, International Organizations Law Review (forthcoming).

69   *See, e.g.,* ALVAREZ, *supra* note 1, at 26–28 (discussing the work of David Mitrany and other scholars). For an account of how the "functionalist" perspective on international organi-zations has contributed to this progress narrative, see Jan Klabbers, *The EJIL Foreword: The Transformation of International Organizations Law*, 26 EUR. J. INT'L L. 9, 36–39 (2015). *See also* RUSSELL A. MILLER & REBECCA M. BRATSPIES, PROGRESS IN INTERNATIONAL LAW (2008) (consisting of essays on the general progressive vision within international law).

ICJ's compulsory jurisdiction and both are wary of acceding to the jurisdiction of that Court even with respect to particular treaties (as both countries habitually file reservations to ICJ referral clauses).[70] Neither country is a party to a regional human rights court such as those in Africa, the Americas, and Europe, and both remain outside the Rome Statute establishing the International Criminal Court (ICC). Further, although China, unlike the United States, is a party to the Law of the Sea Convention, its actions before the International Tribunal for the Law of the Sea at this writing suggests that it may regard itself as not subject to the jurisdiction of that Tribunal.[71] Both states are, however, subject to the adjudicative mechanisms in the trade and investment regimes and face the prospect of trade disputes in the WTO and arbitral investor-state claims.[72] At least to that extent, neither of the world's two most powerful states can afford to ignore developments in the greater world of international adjudication. While both countries exercise the rare privilege of having one of their nationals sit as a permanent judge on the ICJ, both recognize that they cannot afford to ignore the "jurisprudence" produced by international courts and tribunals since it may affect their interests even when they remain aloof from using the ICJ (or the ICC) except when it suits their own agendas. Accordingly, both China and the U.S. have appeared voluntarily before the ICJ to assert

---

70   *See, e.g.*, Convention on the Elimination of Discrimination Against Women, Declaration of China, *opened for signature* Mar 1. 1980, 1249 U.N.T.S. 13, *at* https://treaties.un.org/pages/viewdetails.aspx?src=treaty&mtdsg_no=iv-8&chapter=4&lang=en. ("The People's Republic of China does not consider itself bound by paragraph 1 of article 29 of the Convention."); Convention on the Prevention and Punishment of the Crime of Genocide, Ratification by the United States of America, Nov. 25, 1988, S. EXEC. REP. No. 99–2 (1985), at 26–27, 1518 U.N.T.S. 344, Annex A, No. 1021 (entered into force for the United States Feb. 23, 1989), *at* https://treaties.un.org/doc/Publication/UNTS/Volume%201518/v1518.pdf ("[B]efore any dispute to which the United States is a party may be submitted to the jurisdiction of the International Court of Justice under this article, the specific consent of the United States is required in each case.").

71   *See, e.g.*, Luke Eric Peterson, *Philippines-China UNCLOS Arbitration Moving Forward Without Chinese Participation*, KLUWER ARB. BLOG (Jun. 10, 2015, 10:46 PM), *at* http://kluwerarbitrationblog.com/blog/2013/08/28/an-update-on-the-philippines-china-unclos-arbitration/.

72   Indeed, the United States, which has faced nearly 20 investor claims under NAFTA, is a frequent respondent in investor-state dispute settlement. *See* U.S. DEP'T OF STATE, *Cases Filed Against the United States of America*, *at* http://www.state.gov/s/l/c3741.htm (compiling case reports on NAFTA Investor-State Arbitrations filed against the U.S.); *See also* INTERNATIONAL CENTRE FOR SETTLEMENT OF INVESTMENT DISPUTES, *Search ICSID Cases*, *at* https://icsid.worldbank.org/ICSID/FrontServlet?requestType=CasesRH&reqFrom=Main&actionVal=ViewAllCases.

their views—as in that Court's proceedings on Kosovo—and both have voted in the Security Council in favor of referring a situation to the ICC.[73]

As Woodward's list of governance institutions, Raustiala's treaty numbers, and Alter's enumeration of international courts illustrate, the proliferation of IOs and institutionalized international adjudicators is historically unprecedented. IOs, because they usually have the capacity to create subsidiary bodies and may also create independent institutions, breed. They generate other organizations and become ever more complex bureaucracies—layers of agencies—over time.[74] As any student of bureaucracy knows, the motivations of bureaucrats, their desire to preserve or expand their domains vis-à-vis other bureaucrats, or to work together in networks that share expertise, may lead to actions that are not entirely congruent with the goals and motivations of the governments that delegate authority to them. The study of the international legal process is today, therefore, also the study of bureaucratic paralysis and politics.

While Article 29 of the UN Charter equips the Security Council with the authority to establish "subsidiary" organs as "necessary for the performance of its functions,"[75] few of those present at the creation of the UN would have predicted that the Security Council would use this power to establish independent criminal courts, operations to engage in "peacekeeping" (a term that does not appear in the Charter), more complex (and sometimes coercive) "peace operations" to combat internal insurgencies, to administer a state, and even to conduct elections. Nor would they have predicted the rise of multiple sanctions regimes including some that would impose so-called "smart sanctions" directly on named individuals and organizations to prevent terrorism or the proliferation of weapons of mass destruction.[76] Today's Security Council bears little resemblance to the global police force to prevent inter-state aggression foreseen back in 1945 in the wake of German and Japanese aggression. As is further addressed in Chapter II, the Council's delegated authority to a diverse number of entities engaged in numerous "state building" tasks demonstrate its

---

73   See Written Statement of the United States of America, Accordance with International Law of Unilateral Declaration of Independence in Respect of Kosovo, Advisory Opinion, 2010 I.C.J. 141 (Apr. 17, 2009), at http://www.icj-cij.org/docket/files/141/15640.pdf; Written Statement of the People's Republic of China, id. (Apr. 16, 2009), at http://www.icj-cij.org/docket/files/141/15611.pdf. See also S.C. Res. 1970 (Feb. 28, 2011) (referring the situation in Libya to the ICC).

74   See Paul C. Szasz, The Complexification of the United Nations System, 3 MAX PLANCK U.N.Y.B. 1 (1999).

75   U.N. Charter, art. 29.

76   See, e.g., ALVAREZ, supra note 1, at 174–176.

wide discretion to respond to (undefined) "threats to the peace" under Article 39 as it sees fit and without clear legal limitation. It also demonstrates its wide capacity to establish subsidiary organs, delegate tasks to the UN Secretariat (which it charged with, for example, drafting the statute for the ICTY), or call on experts of all kinds. The Security Council's diverse actions in the post-Cold War period when it musters a veto-proof majority and sufficient support among its non-member members suggests that the protection accorded the "domestic jurisdiction" of states under Article 2(7) may be feeble indeed.[77]

As Woodward's enumeration of UN bodies also suggests, the Security Council is a timid progenitor of subsidiary bodies as compared to the GA. The latter has had a voracious appetite for producing subsidiary organs under its standing authority under Article 22 of the UN Charter.[78] There is a complex set of 10 bureaucracies established by the GA with respect to such topics as human rights, UN financing, development and rule of law assistance, and other forms of technical education (including with respect to international law). Indeed, the sheer number of GA entities dealing with human rights (including reporting mechanisms, quasi-judicial treaty bodies, *ad hoc* or other committees, and working groups), give credence to those who would claim, such as Ruti Teitel, that international law is now engaged in a project at odds with its formerly "inter-national" nature, namely the construction of "humanity's law."[79]

Whether or not one agrees with Teitel's re-branding of the field, no one would deny that the GA has institutionalized and mainstreamed human rights and given ever-greater precision to what these "rights" are, and that this achievement would have surprised those who drafted the UN Charter. The references to human rights in the UN Charter, in its preamble, and the purposes in Articles 1, 55, and 56, contained no hard enforceable obligations on UN members. Article 55 merely urges states to "promote" human rights and Article 56 "pledges" joint and separate action without more specificity.[80] Those who drafted the Charter rejected a plea to include a bill of rights (as contained in the U.S. Constitution) and the Charter's vague references to "human rights" fell far short of indicating their content. The principal drafters of the Charter were

---

77   *Id.* at 169–183 (discussing the impact of the Security Council on the "shrinking domain" of the prohibition on interference with domestic jurisdiction contained in Art. 2(7)). Of course, the prohibition on interference with states' domestic jurisdiction under Art. 2(7) does not apply to "enforcement action."

78   U.N. Charter, art. 22 ("The General Assembly may establish such subsidiary organs as it deems necessary for the performance of its functions.").

79   *See* RUTI G. TEITEL, HUMANITY'S LAW (2011) (arguing that a paradigm shift in the international legal order has occurred involving a change from an emphasis on state security to a human-being centered approach).

80   U.N. Charter, arts. 55–56.

not anxious back in 1945 to impose any more specific human rights obligations onto themselves. The United States was handicapped by a *de facto* system of apartheid, particularly in its southern states. In 1945, Britain and France retained colonies whose peoples did not enjoy the same rights as their citizens. And, of course, the then Soviet Union maintained a Gulag of political prisoners. The story about how the Charter's feeble references to rights became a "human rights revolution" has been told elsewhere.[81] For our purposes, it is yet more evidence of how, contrary to the traditional manner of interpreting treaties under the VCT, the UN Charter has been transformed in ways not foreseen by its text, its "object and purpose," or anything in its negotiating history.

Woodward's framework begins to suggest how expansively, and at times unpredictably, the charters of IOs generally—and not only the UN's—have been interpreted over time. In defiance of positivist expectations, the "original" intent contained in the respective *travaux préparatoires* of these IO charters have imposed few limitations.[82] Woodward's list also suggests that global institutionalization has not been cabined to inter-state organizations established by traditional treaties. Her framework for "global governance" includes, as does the Global Administrative Law (GAL) project, "hybrid" or "global public-private" partnerships, including the World Commission on Dams, the Kimberly Process certification scheme on conflict diamonds, and the Extractive Industries Transparency Initiative.[83] The world is now governed, at least in part, by "trans-governmental networks," like the Basel Committee on Banking Supervision (which features the participation of nations' central banks) and the Financial Action Task Force; "private business organizations" like the Paris Club; the International Chamber of Commerce and the Trilateral Commission; and NGOs like Human Rights Watch.[84] And global governance cannot be understood without considering other associations, like the G-7 or G-20, as well.

---

81   *See, e.g.*, THE HUMAN RIGHTS REVOLUTION: AN INTERNATIONAL HISTORY (Akira Iriye et al. eds., 2012).

82   *See, e.g.*, GUY SINCLAIR, TO REFORM THE WORLD (forthcoming 2016) (examining case studies of the evolution of UN peacekeeping, technical assistance at the ILO, and the World Bank's turn to "governance" as involving informal charter amendment in all three organizations).

83   WOODWARD, *supra* note 54, at 29; Benedict Kingsbury, Nico Krisch & Richard B. Stewart, *The Emergency of Global Administrative Law*, 68 LAW & CONTEMP. PROBS. 15 (2005); Benedict Kingsbury & Nico Krisch, *Introduction: Global Governance and Global Administrative Law in the International Legal Order*, 17 EUR. J. INT'L L. 1 (2006).

84   WOODWARD, *supra* note 54, at 21–22. *See also* ANNE-MARIE SLAUGHTER, A NEW WORLD ORDER (2005).

While the focus of this monograph is on inter-state organizations created by treaty and not on hybrid or non-state entities, contemporary IOs share many qualities with less formal or hybrid bodies and often work alongside them. In defiance of positivist assumptions, neither states nor formal inter-state organizations monopolize the process of international law-making.[85] Today, in addition to IOs, trans-governmental networks, hybrid public-private entities, and other non-state actors feature prominently in a number of jurisprudential international law frameworks.

Nor should it be assumed that any of these diverse institutions for global governance are lone rangers acting within self-enclosed silos. As Bruno Simma has persuasively shown, entirely self-contained regimes do not exist.[86] Despite the relative independence and autonomy encouraged by distinct venues and forms of expertise, IOs, trans-governmental networks, hybrid and private institutions, including NGOs, interact and often work together or at cross-purposes. They engage in cooperative ventures to produce Article 38 sources of law (like the Tobacco Framework Convention[87] which is a product of the World Health Organization and the WTO working together in a joint public health measure that would not unduly disrupt the goals of the free trade regime) as well as innovative "soft law" instruments like the many identified in Woodward's chart of global conferences at the UN global conferences. Today's international lawyers also need to broaden their vision to study the interactions among these entities, including by examining interlocking "regime complexes" in and outside the UN system that pool expertise to work on a particular topic.[88]

As is clear from the inclusion of wholly private business entities and NGOs in Woodward's lists, the "legalization" of the world is no longer (if it ever was) wholly state-centric. A world where 1,378 NGOs were accredited to the Preparatory Committee for the 1992 Rio Conference on the Environment and Development (which ultimately led to the adoption of six treaties and three instruments of so-called "soft law"), and where the parallel NGO Forum involved the participation of 2,400 representatives and 17,000 people—as

---

85   *Compare Civil War and International Law, in* ANTONIO CASSESE, THE HUMAN
       DIMENSIONS OF INTERNATIONAL LAW: SELECTED PAPERS 110–127 (2008) (concluding
       that entities other than states contribute only marginally to the making of international
       law).

86   *See* Bruno Simma, *Self-Contained Regimes*, 16 NETH. Y.B. INT'L L. 111 (1985).

87   WHO Framework Convention on Tobacco Control, *adopted on* May 21, 2003, 2302 U.N.T.S.
       166, *at* http://apps.who.int/iris/bitstream/10665/42811/1/9241591013.pdf.

88   For an example of work on "regime complexes," see Kal Raustiala & David G. Victor, *The
       Regime Complex for Plant Genetic Resources*, 58 INT'L ORG. 277 (2004). On the resulting
       opportunities for forum-shopping, see Raustiala, *supra* note 62.

compared to only 172 states participating at the time—is a place where states face some law-making competition.[89] Nor is non-state involvement limited to the making of "soft law." Non-state actors have been influential in the evolution of formal law as well, such as the Landmines Convention and the Rome Statute for the ICC.[90]

2.2   *The International Judiciary*

As is further discussed in Chapter V, the proliferation of international courts makes it clear that states are no longer (if they ever were) the sole interpreters and enforcers of international law. By the end of 2011, the world's 24 permanent international courts had issued, by one count, more than 37,000 binding legal rulings.[91] After the European Court of Justice (ECJ) and the European Court of Human Rights (ECtHR), the next most active courts, based on number of rulings, were the Andean Tribunal (2,197 rulings), the Organization for the Harmonization of Corporate Law in Africa (OHADA) (569 rulings), the Inter-American Court of Human Rights (239 rulings), and the WTO (with 117 GATT-era rulings and 176 WTO-era rulings).[92]

Even a cursory look at many of these rulings suggests that judges and arbitrators are not mere technicians mechanically applying the law. Contrary to positivist assumptions, the truth is that international adjudicators, like their domestic colleagues, exercise considerable discretion, even when purporting to apply the positivist rules of treaty interpretation. Further, the product of this

---

89   *See* Steve Charnovitz, *Two Centuries of Participation: NGOs and International Governance*, 18 MICH. J. INT'L L. 183, 265 (1997); ANNA-KARIN LINDBLOM, NON-GOVERNMENTAL ORGANIZATIONS IN INTERNATIONAL LAW 480–481 (2005). Indeed, as states have become aware of the power of non-state actors, they have sometimes undertaken efforts to counter that power. For an example, see Elin Enge & Runar Malkenes, *Non-Governmental Organizations at UNCED: Another Successful Failure?, in* GREEN GLOBE YEARBOOK OF INTERNATIONAL CO-OPERATION ON ENVIRONMENT AND DEVELOPMENT 25, 27 (Helge Ole Bergesen & Georg Parmann eds., 1993) ("[B]y the penultimate meeting, as the bargaining became heated . . . all governments agreed to close the doors, and the NGOs frequently suffered the humiliation of being turned out . . . the governments introduced a new type of forum: 'informal informals'—too informed for NGOs to participate, but indeed where the decisions were made.").

90   *See generally* Kal Raustiala, *NGOs in International Treaty-Making, in* THE OXFORD GUIDE TO TREATIES 158–160 (Duncan B. Hollis ed., 2012).

91   Alter, *supra* note 58, at 348 (noting that before the end of the Cold War there were only five permanent international courts in addition to the European Court of Justice and the European Court of Human Rights and that 88 percent of the 37,000 binding rulings had been issued since 1989).

92   *Id.* at 349.

discretion—adjudicative rulings—are increasingly public and are themselves becoming, *de facto* if not *de jure*, a source of law. The ever growing body of international judicial/arbitral "case law," now the most pervasive source of authority cited by judges and arbitrators, increasingly merits as much attention as the other formal sources in Article 38.[93] Further, a whole body of inquiry involves examining why international judges and arbitrators are delegated authority to decide international disputes, to determine whether states are violating the rights of individuals or investors, or to prosecute crimes. There is considerable evidence that states delegate these powers not in the expectation that their adjudicators will behave as their agents—as essentially diplomats in robes— but in the expectation that formal adjudication is valuable precisely because it is distinct from diplomacy. They delegate such authority because judges or arbitrators are perceived to be "independent" or "impartial" trustees of the rule of law who can be expected to deploy their own agency and not merely follow the orders of states.[94] Increasingly international lawyers (and political scientists who study law) are becoming aware that judges and arbitrators need to be considered as international actors in their own right who are capable of exercising some autonomy from the states that established their tribunals.

Some of the evidence stems from the authority that is increasingly given to international adjudicators. According to Karen Alter, 84 percent of the permanent international courts that she examines have at least partial compulsory jurisdiction, while 64 percent allow private actors to initiate litigation, and 52 percent grant access to institutional actors, such as certain international civil servants of IOs.[95] International judicial processes, particularly newer courts or arbitration processes, empower not only judges and arbitrators, but also other entities authorized to initiate dispute settlement including private investors, businesses, or individuals. Increasingly, these "new styled" courts or tribunals also empower NGOs which are permitted to participate at least by filing amicus briefs.[96] In addition, to the extent such adjudicative mechanisms involve other actors, such as independent prosecutors, defense attorneys, clerks or others employed to assist international judges or arbitrators (such

---

93   For an example, see Ole Kristian Fauchald, *The Legal Reasoning of ICSID Tribunals – An Empirical Analysis*, 19 EUR. J. INT'L L. 301 (2008) (noting that ICSID tribunals tend to follow an interpretative approach steeped in the common law, rather than the civil law tradition).

94   Karen J. Alter, *Agents or Trustees: International Courts in Their Political Context*, 14 EUR. J. INT'L RELATIONS 33 (2008).

95   Alter, *supra* note 58, at 348.

96   *See* Chapter V *infra*.

as a substantial number of Geneva-based lawyers employed to assist wto panelists or its Appellate Body), there are other actors, beside the adjudicators themselves, whose actions and motivations need to be considered to truly understand the process by which modern international law gets made. This means, as is addressed in Chapter v, looking to the actions of the office of the ICC's prosecutor for example and not only to the rulings of its judges.[97]

Once we see international courts as institutions, it is to easier to appreciate that, like the UN itself, these bodies exercise diverse functions beyond "dispute settlement" narrowly construed that respond to the (changing) desires of their many stakeholders. Chapter v examines how these go far beyond the role assigned to them by positivists, namely the resolution of inter-state disputes.[98] As with respect to IOs, the relationship *among* international courts and tribunals has also become a worthy object of study, as for those who claim that the emerging "international judiciary" empowers itself through cross-judicial dialogues that produce "global governance" alongside "judicialization."[99]

International lawyers now have to consider the possibility that despite the absence of an established hierarchy among these courts and tribunals or an agreed doctrine of precedent comparable to the common law notion of *stare decisis*,[100] a less formal but no less real *jurisprudence constante* may be evolving among judges and arbitrators within discrete regimes. Investor-state arbitrators rely on other investor-state rulings, wto panels and its Appellate Body cite to their own rulings, regional human rights courts rely on their prior precedents, and particular international criminal courts rely on their own prior

---

97   For a general study of how interpretation by ICs and organizational officials make law, *see* INGO VENZKE, HOW INTERPRETATION MAKES INTERNATIONAL LAW (2012).

98   *See* Alter, *supra* note 58; José E. Alvarez, *What are International Courts For? The Main Functions of International Adjudication, in* THE OXFORD HANDBOOK OF INTERNATIONAL ADJUDICATION, 158 (Cesare Romano, Karen J. Alter & Yuval Shany eds., 2014); *see also* Samantha Besson, *Legal Philosophical Issues of International Adjudication: Getting Over the* Amour Impossible *Between International Law and Adjudication, in* THE OXFORD HANDBOOK OF INTERNATIONAL ADJUDICATION, *supra.*

99   *See, e.g.,* Anne-Marie Slaughter, *Judicial Globalization,* 40 VIRG. J. INT'L L. 1103 (2000); Alec Stone Sweet, *Judicialization and the Construction of Governance,* 32 COMP. POL. STUD. 147 (1999). Much of this literature has been inspired by developments within the European Union. *See, e.g.,* Joseph H.H. Weiler, *The Transformation of Europe,* 100 YALE L.J. 2403 (1991); MARTIN SHAPIRO & ALEC STONE SWEET, ON LAW, POLITICS & JUDICIALIZATION (2002); ALEC STONE SWEET, THE JUDICIAL CONSTRUCTION OF EUROPE (2004).

100 *See, e.g.,* Statute of the International Court of Justice, *supra* note 6, art. 59.

decisions, for example.[101] This reality has encouraged fears that international law may be "fragmenting" not only because of the proliferation of law-making formal and informal by IOs and their bureaucracies, but also because of the interpretive decisions made by international adjudicators.[102]

2.3   *The Return of Domestic Analogies*

As international law penetrates more deeply into domestic legal systems and international institutional forums interact with regulatory agencies within states, the line between international and national law blurs. It is increasingly less tenable to maintain that at the international level we have no counterparts to the three branches of national government. There are increasing collaborations between those who study institutions at both the international and national levels. Scholars of "humanity's law" increasingly study how rights talk has transformed both. Constitutionalists, many of whom are inspired by the institutionalization and judicialization of European law, look to national and EU constitutional frameworks to enhance their understanding of how international adjudicators, whether in the WTO or other regimes, behave.[103] Some, inspired by Albert O. Hirschman's work, examine how exit, voice, and loyalty operate within national *and* international organizations.[104] GAL scholars look to the national administrative state for relevant models with which to understand and reform global organizations and international tribunals.[105]

---

101   *See, e.g.*, Fauchald, *supra* note 93.

102   Fears of interpretative fragmentation have led to recommendations to ameliorate it, as by the International Law Commission (ILC). International Law Commission, Fragmentation of International Law: Difficulties Arising from the Diversification and Expansion of International Law, Report of the Study Group on the Fragmentation of International Law, UN Doc. A/CN.4/L.682 (2006) (finalized by Martti Koskenniemi). For some, fragmentation threatens not only the coherence of the law but also the unity of Schachter's "invisible college" of international lawyers. *See* Santiago Villalpando, *The Invisible College of International Lawyers" Forty Years Later*, (Eur. Soc. Int'l L. Conference Paper Series, No. 5/ 2013), *at* http://papers.ssrn.com/sol3/papers.cfm?abstract_id=2363640. *But see* Martti Koskenniemi & Päivi Leino, *Fragmentation of International Law? Postmodern Anxieties*, 15 LEIDEN J. INT'L L. 553 (2002) (suggesting that fears that international law is fragmenting are overstated).

103   *See, e.g.*, DEBORAH Z. CASS, THE CONSTITUTIONALIZATION OF THE WORLD TRADE ORGANIZATION (2005); Joost Pauwelyn, *The Transformation of World Trade*, 104 MICH. L. REV. 1 (2005). *See also* Laurence Helfer & Anne-Marie Slaughter, *Toward a Theory of Effective Supra national Adjudication*, 107 YALE L. J. 273 (1997).

104   *See generally* ALBERT O. HIRSCHMAN, EXIT, VOICE AND LOYALTY (1970). *See, e.g.*, Pauwelyn, *supra* note 103.

105   Kingsbury & Krisch, *supra* note 83.

As discrete international legal regimes deepen, they come to hold greater interest to those who study the same subject at the national level, whether it is the law governing labor or family relations.[106]

Greater interaction between IOs and national courts means that domestic analogies to common law or civil law courts become more relevant. As is discussed in a later chapter, the fact that the text of the UN Charter does not include a formal principle of judicial review entitling any court, including the ICJ, to review the legality of any actions of the Security Council does not mean, it turns out, that the Council is entirely free of legal constraints or able to ignore international or national courts. The Security Council's counter-terrorism sanctions programs involving Al-Qaida and the Taliban[107] have been indirectly subject to judicial review by the ECJ and by some national courts.[108] In addition, since the end of the Cold War, the Security Council has added more "enforcement" tools to its toolbox: it has turned to the use of specially designed international criminal courts to handle perceived threats to the peace, added the goal of achieving "transitional justice" to its agenda, and has now twice resorted to referring situations to the International Criminal Court.[109] And the Council now needs to consider the rapidly expanding domain of international criminal law that its own actions have engendered. As noted in Chapter V, the Council's ICC referrals have led to greater interactions between the ICC's prosecutor and the Council—and may yet produce decisions from that Court (as with respect to the limits imposed under the Council's referrals) that may surprise the Council. Even the world's foremost political body may yet find itself operating within some of the rule of law constraints that have long operated within national legal systems.

As more IOs, from the UN to the global financial institutions, take on actions designed to promote the "rule of law" and "good governance" generally, both

---

106   *See, e.g.,* Cynthia Estlund & Seth Gurgel, *Will Labour Unrest Lead to more Democratic Trade Unions in China?, in* CHINA AND ILO FUNDAMENTAL PRINCIPLES AND RIGHTS TO WORK (Roger Blanpain, Yifeng Chen & Ulla Liukkunen eds., 2014).

107   *See* S.C. Res. 1267 (Oct. 15, 1999); S.C. Res. 1333 (Dec. 13, 2000).

108   *See* Joined Cases C-402/05 P & C-415/05 P, Kadi v. Council, 2008 ECR I-6351 (reported by Mila Zgonec-Rolej at 103 AM. J. INT'L L. 305 (2009)) (overturning the implementation of Security Council resolutions 1267 & 1333 by the Council of the European Union); Joined Cases C-584/10 P, C-593/10 P, & C-595/10 P, Commission v. Kadi, ¶¶ 131–134 (Eur. Ct. Justice July 18, 2013). On national court cases involving the Council's sanctions measures, see, for example, Antonios Tzanakopoulos, *Domestic Court Reactions to UN Security Council Sanctions, in* CHALLENGING ACTS OF INTERNATIONAL ORGANIZATIONS BEFORE NATIONAL COURTS 54 (August Reinisch ed., 2010).

109   *See* Chapter II *infra.*

stakeholders and participants increasingly recognize the need to require reciprocal acceptance by these organizations that the rule of law and good governance also applies to them. A Security Council that has defended its actions on the basis of the need to promote the "rule of law," now comes under pressure to provide greater transparency, participation, and reason-giving. As is addressed in a later chapter, the Council, like many international organizations engaged in law-making, is not exempt from pressures to be more accountable—particularly as increasing numbers of governments have come under comparable pressures. The actions of IOs, including interactions between the Security Council and the General Assembly not anticipated given the explicit limits ostensibly imposed under Article 12(1) of the Charter,[110] have prompted comparisons to "checks and balance" that function at the domestic level. The Council has had to be mindful, for example, of the shadow of the GA's potential interference, which Article 12(1) has failed to prevent, as well as criticisms stemming from the "16th vote" at the Council, namely the media and elements of "international civil society." As is suggested by the GA's actions granting observer state status to Palestine which enabled Palestine's ability to access the ICC,[111] the Council's "primary" jurisdiction over international peace and security is not what it once was. Even when the veto in the Council prevents that body from taking action on major issues—such as Palestine—some other organization, in this instance the GA and the ICC, may step into the vacuum. The deliberative powers of forums once disparaged by positivists as mere "talk shops" incapable of binding action (like the GA or a multitude of human rights committees and special rapporteurs) have to be considered in any evaluation of the UN's effectiveness (or lack thereof). Of course, the power of deliberation has long been a staple framework for describing or explaining how national norms are dispersed, interpreted, and enforced.[112]

---

110   U.N. Charter, art. 12(1) (indicating that the GA should not make any recommendation on a dispute or situation being considered by the Security Council). *But see* Legal Consequences of the Construction of a Wall in the Occupied Palestinian Territory, Advisory Opinion, 2004 I.C.J. 136, ¶¶ 27–28 (July 9) (implicitly suggesting that article 12(1) is dead letter law given that its interpretation has evolved and the accepted practice of the GA is consistent with this growth).

111   G.A. Res. 67/19 (Nov. 29, 2012). *See also* United Nations, Depository Notification, Rome Statute of the International Criminal Court (Jan. 6, 2015), *at* https://treaties.un.org/doc/Publication/CN/2015/CN.13.2015-Eng.pdf; Press Release, The Prosecutor of the International Criminal Court, Fatou Bensouda, Opens a Preliminary Examination of the Situation in Palestine (Jan. 16, 2015), *at* http://www.icccpi.int/en_menus/icc/press%20and%20media/press%20releases/Pages/pr1083.aspx.

112   *See generally* IAN JOHNSTONE, THE POWER OF DELIBERATION (2011).

Thanks in large part to institutionalization, international lawyers are now considering questions that have long preoccupied scholars of national law and national judiciaries. As noted, international lawyers, like their domestic colleagues, are taking a closer look at the roles performed by international judges and arbitrators, examining how or why reliance on "precedent" emerges even when it is not formally required or when adjudicators in one institutional setting engage in cross-regime "boundary crossings.[113] Other domestic analogies, long derided by positivists, are re-emerging.

For a small but increasing number of international law scholars, the absence of a world government does not mean that is meaningless to address forms of global "governance" or its implications on the Hegelian state.[114] The absence of a single chief executive does not preclude the possibility that some institutional organs, most prominently the Security Council, but possibly others, are exercising some kind of "executive" function. The absence of *a* global parliament does not mean that global legislation as such does not exist. *De facto* global rules exist. These include the Security Council's counter-terrorism sanctions (which are imposed on all states to compel them to combat terrorists or global anti-corruption rules); human rights norms endorsed by states that emerge from, for example, the views of 10 UN treaty bodies, expert bodies or special rapporteurs; fundamental labor law standards proclaimed by the ILO; the WHO's rules to prevent the transmission of global health threats; or ICAO regulations on civil aviation. Global law or its functional equivalent is also now emerging, albeit in fits and starts—as promoted, interpreted, or enforced by a number of other IOs.

Moreover, the absence of compulsory jurisdiction by a single hierarchically superior court does not mean that the prospect of transnational judicial "enforcement" action, including joint actions by international and national courts, is a chimera—not in a world where 24 permanent international courts or tribunals exist, alongside a myriad of additional entities that issue quasi-judicial opinions such as UN human rights treaty bodies.

Domestic analogies are especially prevalent among those who discuss the "humanization" or "constitutionalization" of international law or GAL. "Humanity's law" stresses the revolutionary impact for both national governments and the world order once we insist that legal constraints exist on

---

113   José E. Alvarez, *Beware: Boundary Crossings*, 17 World Inv. & Trade 171 (2016).

114   *See, e.g.*, Eyal Benvenisti, *Sovereigns as Trustees of Humanity: On the Accountability of States to Foreign Stakeholders*, 107 AM. J. INT'L L. 295 (2013).

how states treat their own citizens.[115] There is but a small step from a government's responsibility to protect its nationals under a national constitution to the concept of a "responsibility to protect" whereby a state that fails in that essential duty is deemed to waive core "sovereign" rights under international law. Constitutionalists explore how certain treaties (like the UN Charter or the "WTO's constitution") have been subject to interpretative methods that, while distinctly at odds with those authorized by the VCT, are not unfamiliar to those who interacted with national constitutions.[116] GAL scholars explain how certain international regimes (or their adjudicators) are engaging in forms of supra-national review over the internal actions of governments in ways that are reminiscent of the actions taken by national administrative agencies.[117] GAL scholars argue that those who seek to impose the global rule of law should themselves adhere to the rule of law values that we have come to expect from administrative agencies in well-ordered states. They urge, as do administrative law scholars within the U.S. who address regulation by federal government agencies, that more accountability be required for institutions of global governance, from the WTO to the World Bank to investor-state arbitrations. To this end, they urge greater transparency of organizational actions, greater participation and access to non-state actors, enhanced reason-giving by IO actors (including judges and arbitrators), and greater capacity for review of IO action.[118] GAL scholars, along with a recently formed group of principally German scholars,[119] see organizations like those of the UN system as "public" law forums that need to be responsive and accountable to a broader group of stakeholders beyond the highest government officials of states and need to include individuals, businesses, and NGOs. This breaks from the state-centricity of legal positivism.

2.4   *From Static Rules to Process*

As a result of the proliferation of IOs and institutionalized adjudicators, international legal scholars are focusing more on *process* and not merely rules. This

---

115   TEITEL, *supra* note 79.

116   *See, e.g.*, ALVAREZ, *supra* note 1, at 65–108.

117   Kingsbury & Krisch, *supra* note 83; *see also* INSTITUTE FOR INTERNATIONAL LAW AND JUSTICE, NEW YORK UNIVERSITY SCHOOL OF LAW & IRPA, ISTITUTO DI RICERCHE SULLA PUBBICA AMMINISTRAZIONE, GLOBAL ADMINISTRATIVE LAW: CASES, MATERIALS, ISSUES (Sabino Cassese et al. eds, 2d ed. 2008)).

118   *See, e.g.*, EYAL BENEVISTI, THE LAW OF GLOBAL GOVERNANCE (2014).

119   *See, e.g.*, THE EXERCISE OF PUBLIC AUTHORITY BY INTERNATIONAL INSTITUTIONS (Armin Von Bogdandy et al. eds., 2010).

emphasis yields some controversial propositions about the positivist under-standing of Article 38 sources.

What is perhaps most evident—and perhaps most troubling to the positivist—is that the elaboration, interpretation, and enforcement of inter-national obligations are no longer confined to the actions of states inter-se. International legal obligations are now often partly created, interpreted, and enforced by non-state actors and may be intended to produce direct effects on non-state actors as well. The consent of states as a basis for all international obligations is increasingly attenuated. How much have states truly consented when an IO purports to exercise an implied power nowhere indicated in its charter, where members' obligations result from their failure to "opt out" of IO rules, where weighted voting enables decisions to be taken over minority oppo-sition, or where some modes of governance are preferred precisely because they sideline state consent?[120] Moreover, even where state consent remains a vital element in finding that an international obligation applies, in many insti-tutional contexts that "consent": is found in the failure of states to act (omis-sions), is justified on the basis of ambiguous delegations of authority, or is the product of consent given long ago by a far different group of states under very different circumstances. While it is true, for example, that UN Charter drafters accorded the Security Council judicially unreviewable and apparently limit-less authority to take legally binding decisions, they did not consent in 1945 (and in all probability never even contemplated) the varied menu of Council actions undertaken by that body particularly since the end of the Cold War.[121]

The three sources of international obligation enumerated in Article 38 no longer exhaust the rules that international lawyers need to consult to effec-tively and credibly advise clients—whether states, NGOs, or multinational cor-porations (MNCs). Today, clients and their lawyers need to look at the varied work-product of many organizations. These include codes of conduct for busi-nesses; resolutions by IO organs; commission or expert committee reports; the "views" or advisory opinions of judicial, quasi-judicial, or arbitral interpreters; opinion letters issued by IO general counsels; and myriad other documents. These varied products, whether or not formally binding and whether or not violations of them would constitute "international wrongful acts" triggering state responsibility, produce a number of legal effects. The professional codes

---

120 For these and other examples, see Nico Krisch, *The Decay of Consent: International law in an Age of Global Public Goods*, 108 AM. J. INT'L L. 1 (2014); Laurence R. Helfer, *Monitoring Compliance with Unratified Treaties: The ILO Experience*, 71 Law & Contemp. Probl. 193 (2008).

121 *See* Chapter 11 *infra*.

of responsibility under which lawyers operate would seem to require providing advice about such instruments or hortatory rulings, especially when an organizational venue exists to examine "compliance" with these instruments or when these may be enforced through other methods, including by market actors who take into account a client's "compliance" with them.

Moreover, even those who believe that Article 38 continues to be an accurate description of the "true" sources of international legal obligation can scarcely ignore the changes in those sources that have emerged in the age of institutions. Today's treaties are often not the positivist contracts of old. The ways these treaties are negotiated, interpreted, and enforced have been inescapably altered by the rise of organizations and the proliferation of adjudicative venues.[122] The interpretation of treaties nestled in institutions is not as static as positivists assume. Such treaties, including IO charters, are subject to a more fluid approach to the traditional rules of treaty interpretation. As noted in Chapters II and III dealing with the actions taken by the contemporary Security Council and General Assembly, there are innumerable examples of the UN Charter's "evolving" or teleological interpretations over time. Chapter IV tells a comparable story with respect to some select UN system organizations, while Chapter V enumerates how some international adjudicators have been enablers to the same end.

Dynamic forms of interpretation are not limited to IO charters. Much the same can be said with respect to other institutionally grounded treaties, from older documents like the International Covenant on Civil and Political Rights to more recent ones like the Rome Statute of the ICC. These efforts are most often portrayed as consistent with Articles 31 and 32 of the VCT through various tactics, such as treating "subsequent practice" of the parties as including subsequent practice by IO organs or even by secretariat officials, deference to presumptive treaty intent over reliance on the original travaux, and generous resort to "relevant rules of international law among the parties." Treaties subject to institutionalized mechanisms for interpretation, whether by institutionalized adjudicators or by IO general counsels, are more likely to be beneficiaries of a canon of interpretation that privileges the securing of (changing) institutional goals, even at the expense of adherence to the plain meaning of the treaty's text.

General principles have also not emerged unscathed amidst today's institutions. To the chagrin of positivists who would relegate this source to the margins or limit such principles to a handful of examples, recourse to general principles is now more frequent. As international courts and tribunals prolif-

---

122   See ALVAREZ, *supra* note 1, at 273–400 (enumerating the ways the turn to IOs have changed the negotiation, interpretation, and enforcement of treaties).

erate and interpreters' need to fill gaps in the law increases, there appears to be increasing resort to general principles of law and new conceptions of what these are.[123] Indeed, some public law scholars, anxious to draw closer domestic analogies between how international and national law permits states to engage in permissive regulation in the public interest, would make even greater use of general principles—and draw increasingly specific conclusions from their use—as part of a project to elaborate a more closely integrated "public law" for states.[124]

The impact of IOs on custom is more complicated. Custom has become more or less important depending on the institution or regime. In cases where the regime avoids reliance on customary law and makes clear that its rules are *lex specialis*, custom takes a back seat or even disappears. This is arguably the case in the WTO where, except insofar as the Dispute Settlement Understanding incorporates the customary rules of treaty interpretation, only the GATT covered agreements are subject to dispute settlement.[125] For those focused on such regimes, custom appears to be of decreasing relevance. But customary international law may, on the contrary, become even more important in institutionalized settings where adjudicators are called upon to invoke it either as an independent source of obligation or because the relevant treaty calls for its application.[126] In such cases, customary law is likely to be found and interpreted in ways that are not consistent with positivist premises. As discussed in Chapter V, this is the case in the international investment regime where investor-state arbitrations often rely on customary law—but also resort to non-positivist "short cuts" in its elaboration and interpretation.[127] Modern custom today, where it appears at all, seems less about the actual practice of

---

123 For examples of the increasing resort to general principles in the context of international adjudication, see Chapter V *infra*. For a critical look at the use of general principles in international criminal law, see Neha Jain, *Comparative International Law at the ICTY: The General Principles Experiment*, 109 AM. J. INT'L L. 486 (2015).

124 *See, e.g., International Investment Law and Comparative Public Law—An Introduction, in* STEPHAN W. SCHILL, INTERNATIONAL INVESTMENT LAW AND COMPARATIVE PUBLIC LAW 3, 29–35 (2010).

125 This may explain why some prominent specialists in trade law, like Joel Trachtman, have become convinced that customary law is of increasingly little significance. *See* Joel Trachtman, *The Obsolescence of Customary International Law* (Oct. 2014), *at* http://papers.ssrn.com/sol3/papers.cfm?abstract_id=2512757.

126 *See, e.g.,* José E. Alvarez, *A BIT on Custom*, 42 NYU J. INT'L L. & POL. 17 (2009).

127 *See, e.g.,* D'ASPREMONT, *supra* note 4. *See generally* MICHAEL P. SCHARF, CUSTOMARY INTERNATIONAL LAW IN TIMES OF FUNDAMENTAL CHANGE: RECOGNIZING GROTIAN MOMENTS (2013) (detailing case studies (all in institutionalized settings) where customary law developed rapidly or through "Grotian moments").

states or their explicit articulations for their actions and more about organizational substitutes for direct state action (such as General Assembly resolutions or the views expressed by prior international courts or tribunals).[128]

Consider again the arbitral decision in *Glamis Gold*, often cited in support for a traditional (positivist) application of custom.[129] The question posed to that tribunal was whether the "international minimum standard" applicable under the doctrine of state responsibility under customary law is a dynamic and evolving standard that bars arbitrary measures by an investor host state and requires that state to protect the legitimate expectations of an investor. The tribunal appeared to endorse the U.S. government's position that proof of custom requires recourse to state practice and *opinio juris* and not mere reliance on prior arbitral decisions. The tribunal declared that "[a]scertaining custom is necessarily a factual inquiry, looking to the actions of States and the motives for and consistency of these actions."[130]

A closer examination of the criteria used by the *Glamis Gold* tribunal to prove the existence of custom belies this statement. The tribunal appeared to agree with the U.S. that custom was not an evolving standard; it found that violation of the international minimum standard still required egregious or shocking treatment by a state. At the same time, the tribunal found that what was deemed to be "shocking" had indeed evolved. It found that the customary international minimum standard as applied was not a static doctrine. To reach this conclusion, neither the U.S. as respondent nor the tribunal cited anything by way of actual state practice in support. The U.S. simply argued that its view of custom was supported by a number of older arbitral decisions.[131] The tribunal relied on those same decisions and identified categories of "concordant practice" (generally consisting of the language for treaty ratification, statements of governments, model BITs, and pleadings) without elaborating or relying on any examples for these in its legal conclusions.[132]

---

128   *See, e.g.*, SCHARF, *supra* note 127; *see also* Chapter V *infra*.

129   *See supra* text accompanying notes 36–42.

130   Glamis Gold, *supra* note 36, ¶ 607.

131   *Id.* ¶¶ 598–618 (citing *Neer, supra* note 39); S.D. Myers Inc. v. Canada, Partial Award (NAFTA Ch. 11 Arb. Trib. Nov. 13, 2000), *at* http://www.italaw.com/sites/default/files/case-documents/ita0747.pdf; Int'l Thunderbird Gaming Corp. v. Mexico, Award (NAFTA Ch. 11 Arb. Trib. Jan. 26, 2006), *at* http://italaw.com/documents/ThunderbirdAward.pdf; ADF Group Inc. v. United States, ICSID Case No ARB(AF)/00/1, Award (Jan. 6, 2003), 6 ICSID Rep. 470 (2004); Mondev Int'l, Ltd. v. United States, ICSID Case No. ARB(AF)/99/2, Award (Oct. 11, 2002), 42 I.L.M. 85 (2003).

132   Glamis Gold, *supra* note 36, ¶¶ 602–603.

The *Glamis Gold* ruling did not use or cite any actual practice of states. Ironically, a decision that seems on its face to rebuke other investor-state arbitrators for turning to caselaw instead of actual state practice and *opinio juris* largely rested its own conclusion on an arbitral decision, namely *Neer v. Mexico*. The arbitrators in *Glamis Gold* were apparently content to rely on that precedent as having properly applied actual state practice and *opinio juris*.[133] Of course, a traditional positivist would question this shortcut to determining customary law, particularly given questions that have been raised with respect to whether *Neer* itself purported to address the general international minimum law standard or a much narrower set of circumstances, and whether it relied on actual evidence of general state practice or *opinio juris* regarding that general standard.[134] Moreover, *Glamis Gold's* other relevant legal findings with respect to the meaning of the customary standard—namely its finding that what constitutes "shocking" treatment has evolved since the decision in *Neer* and further, that bad faith by the government need not be proven to show a violation of the international minimum standard—were also based on the tribunal's examination of particular lines of arbitral decisions and not on any actual investigation of state practice.[135]

In short, even this decision by an investor-state tribunal reflects not a reversion to positivism, but evidence of a countertrend. *Glamis Gold* seems to involve disagreement over *which line of arbitral precedents* one should rely upon for purposes of proving custom, rather than fundamental disagreement with the modern trend of treating arbitral decisions as a substitute for a factual inquiry into state practice and *opinio juris*. If so, *Glamis Gold* is not at odds with other recent investor-state decisions which routinely rely on other arbitral decisions for authority.[136] If investor-state arbitral decisions are any indication, the subsidiary "judicial opinions" mentioned in Article 38(2) of the statute of the ICJ may have come to displace the positivist core sources in Article 38(1). Despite its appearances, the *Glamis Gold* decision is very much the modern product of the institutionalization of international investment law.

But the challenge to positivist tenets brought by the turn to institutions does not stop there. To the horror of traditional positivists, some dare to suggest that the binding force of international obligations is no longer subject to a simple on/off switch. The legally binding quality of much of contemporary

---

133   *Id.* ¶ 616.

134   *See* Jan Paulsson & Georgios Petrochilos, *Neer-ly Misled?*, 22 ICSID Review 242–257 (2007). For a somewhat different critique, see D'ASPREMONT, *supra* note 4.

135   Glamis Gold, *supra* note 36, ¶ 616.

136   Fauchald, *supra* note 93.

international law now seems to lie along a spectrum of authority. As is suggested by the very conception of "soft law" or "informal" law, some forms of institutionalized law are harder or softer than others along a number of criteria. As is the case with much of the recent work of the ILC (and with respect to all of the topics on its current agenda) that seeks to produce draft articles or studies in lieu of negotiated treaties,[137] the line between *lex lata* and *lex ferenda* is blurring. Nor is this the only blurring that is taking place. As international institutions develop and increase their mandates (as bureaucracies often do), they engage in not only the making of law, but also its interpretation, application and enforcement. This blurs the lines dividing legislators, enforcers, and interpreters.

All of this threatens the positivist "closed logical system" that presumes legal rules exist irrespective of social aims, public policy, or morality. Given the flow of politics in our international organizations, and the interplay between law and politics in the process by which international organizations are generated and interpreted, the contemporary international lawyer needs to recognize the interplay between law and politics. Although the Security Council is undoubtedly a political organ that is the antithesis of an expert body charged with the scientific codification and progressive development of the law like the ILC, it is, as will be clear from the following chapter, as engaged in global law-making as is the ILC or any international court.

2.5   *From Process to Inter-disciplinarity*

The study of institutions and institutional processes encourages the crossing of disciplinary divides. More international legal scholars are now trying to learn from those studying the behavioral attributes of organizations and the cultures in which bureaucrats are embedded. They are reaching for insights from economists, anthropologists, sociologists, and political scientists because they need them to explain a world that cannot be fully explained by legal positivism's focus on rules.

There are myriad contributions that non-legal disciplines are making to the understanding of our increasingly institutionalized field. As is suggested by Alter's efforts to determine the effects of the turn to institutionalized adjudication,[138] political scientists may be more inclined to tackle questions that cut across specialized adjudicative venues. Whereas increased specialization

---

137   *See* Santiago Villalpando, *Codification Light: A New Trend in the Codification of International Law at the United Nations*, 8 (2) ANUÁRIO BRASILEIRO DE DIREITO INTERNACIONAL (BRAZILIAN Y.B. INT'L L.) 117 (2013).

138   *See supra* note 58.

within international law means that foreign investment lawyers, for example, are more likely to look to investor-state precedent and not decisions reached by the Law of the Sea Tribunal, non-lawyers may be less reticent to cross the disciplinary divides within international law itself. It is up to a political scientist like Alter to point out to lawyers that a "paradigm" shift towards greater judicialization and "altered politics" in its wake may be occurring.[139] Of course, states discovered that they can "forum-shop" among institutionalized adjudicators, including national courts, long ago.[140]

Non-legal disciplines, like sociology, are also more likely to address institutions as such. They are more likely to highlight, for example, the "path dependency" or other pathologies shared by bureaucrats.[141] Other disciplines are more likely to examine the role of politics, personality, ethnicity, ideology, or economics (including the roles of public choice and game theory) that affects these institutions, including institutionalized adjudicators. Those focusing on history may be better positioned to see the role of personalities and ideology in the development of UN peacekeeping under Dag Hammarskjöld or the expansion of the World Bank's mandate under Ibrahim Shihata, for example.[142] Other disciplines, not beholden to legal positivism, are more likely to examine with a fresh eye phenomena that appear to have a legal impact, even if they do not fit these into the constraints of traditional Article 38 sources. Those less beholden to positivism and its state-centricity are more likely to examine the

---

139 ALTER, *supra* note 3, at 335–365.

140 A number of ICJ advisory opinions, for example, might be seen as disguised forms of contentious disputes that failed to reach the Court. *See, e.g.,* Legal Consequences of the Construction of a Wall in the Occupied Palestinian Territory, *supra* note 110; Accordance with International Law of the Unilateral Declaration of Independence in Respect of Kosovo, Advisory Opinion, 2010 I.C.J. 403 (July 22). For a contemporary example of forum-shopping, see Argentina's resort to the Law of the Sea Tribunal to secure the release of a military vessel that was seized under orders from Ghana courts acting at the behest of a holder of Argentina's sovereign debt in ARA Libertad (No. 20) (Arg. v. Ghana), Case No. 20, Order of Dec. 15, 2012, *at* http://www.itlos.org/index.php?id=222&L=1AND1%3D1.

141 *See, e.g.,* Michael N. Barnett & Martha Finnemore, *The Politics, Power and Pathologies of International Organizations,* 53 INT'L ORG. 699 (1999).

142 *See, e.g.,* ANNE ORFORD, INTERNATIONAL AUTHORITY AND THE RESPONSIBILITY TO PROTECT 3–6 (2011) (discussing the significant role UN Secretary General Dag Hammerskjöld played in the evolution of UN peacekeeping); SINCLAIR, *supra* note 82 (historical case studies of the impact of institutional actors on the evolving interpretation of organizational charters).

significant roles of non-state actors[143] or to empirically assess their impact.[144] For all these reasons, the insights of non-lawyers may be vital to producing better descriptions, better jurisprudential explanations, and ultimately better prescriptions for reform. It may take, in other words, a non-lawyer to better explain to lawyers the world lawyers have constructed.

Fortunately, thanks to the institutionalization of international law, there is more two-way traffic among legal and non-legal disciplines.[145] Of course, the prospect and reality of inter-disciplinarity is not an unalloyed good. As a number of critics of u.s.-styled inter-disciplinarity point out, legal scholars who seek to learn from political science or other fields may, whether consciously or not, become tools of particular ideological agendas.[146] This was suggested long ago with respect to some adherents to the so-called McDougal-Lasswell or Yale School of international law whose public science approach to international law, tinged with realpolitik, seemingly led to conclusions that coincided with the policy positions of the u.s. government during the Cold War.[147] And positivists have added their own complaint: when lawyers attempt to engage in political science or when political scientists engage with law, the result is often bad political science or bad lawyering or both.[148] We need not settle the merits of inter-disciplinarity here. It is sufficient to recognize that one of the impacts of the turn to institutions has been to encourage, for good or bad, such work. Like it or not, the presumed positivist divide between what

---

143 *See, e.g.,* MARGARET E. KECK & KATHRYN SIKKINK, ACTIVISTS BEYOND BORDERS: ADVOCACY NETWORKS IN INTERNATIONAL POLITICS (1998).

144 *See, e.g.,* BETH A. SIMMONS, MOBILIZING FOR HUMAN RIGHTS: INTERNATIONAL LAW IN DOMESTIC POLITICS (2009).

145 *See, e.g.,* Jeffrey L. Dunoff & Mark A. Pollack, *Reviewing Two Decades of IL/IR Scholarship: What We've Learned, What's Next, in* DUNOFF & POLLACK, *supra* note 58, at 663.

146 *See* James C. Hathaway, *America, Defender of Democratic Legitimacy?,* 11 EUR. J. INT'L L. 121, 128–131 (2000). *See also* Vera Gowlland-Debbas, *The Limits of Unilateral Enforcement of Community Objectives in the Framework of UN Peace Maintenance,* 11 EUR. J. INT'L L. 361, 380 (2000) (expressing a preference for the "pure theory of law" over more open-ended sociological exercises focused on ends not means); Jan Klabbers, *The Relative Autonomy of International Law or The Forgotten Politics of Interdisciplinarity,* 1 J. INT'L L. & INT'L RELATIONS 35 (2005) (arguing that interdisciplinarity is a "politically charged activity").

147 *See* Hathaway, *supra* note 146, at 127 (arguing that the Yale School approach "depletes international law of the certainty required for meaningful accountability" and "is too readily exploited by powerful states anxious to disguise their particularist agendas as compelled by, or at least consistent with, international law.").

148 *See* James Crawford, *Remarks,* 97 AM. SOC'Y INT'L. L. PROC. 321 (2003) (criticizing the theme of an annual meeting of the American Society of International Law, "The Politics of International Law," for tackling matters that did not take advantage of lawyers' peculiar expertise).

lawyers and others do, premised on the greater legitimacy ostensibly generated by the "scientific" positivist enterprise, is breaking down.

3   Caveats

This monograph, like my earlier book, is not intended to celebrate the turn to institutions.[149] As noted in that book, the reality of IOs can be examined from a variety of perspectives: functionalism, realism, liberal theory, critical theory, and international relations theories such as constructivism.[150] None of these perspectives are explicitly premised on a normatively positive evaluation of what IOs or international adjudicators accomplish but many of them, such as Alter's account of the "new terrain" of judicialized international law, describe these institutions in evolutionary terms—as part of a progress narrative where politics is increasingly displaced by the "rule of law."[151] This premise is resisted here.

A close look at IOs or international courts fails to conclusively demonstrate that they have made the world a better place, truly enhanced the hold of the rule of law over powerful actors, or necessarily made tangible progress on achieving even the much narrower goals sought by designers of particular organizations or courts—whether to rid the world of aggression, increase respect for human rights, prosecute war criminals, enhance the safety of civil aviation, improve the rights of workers, or avoid the trans-boundary crossing of disease. It has not been proven that the more IOs, international courts, or international civil servants we have, the better off the planet will be. Indeed, to the extent that domestic analogies are useful, the comparison to national legal orders with highly organized state institutions, whether Hitler's Germany, Stalin's U.S.S.R., the Khmer Rouge's Cambodia, or Mao's China, yields cautionary lessons about what happens when we turn to strong governmentally controlled organizations to achieve ostensibly "progressive" purposes.

It is the quality of institutions—and whether they are *not* so powerful that they can evade the rule of law—and not the sheer number of them that

---

149   ALVAREZ, *supra* note 1, at xix.

150   *Id.* at 17–45. *See also* Klabbers, *supra* note 69 (analyzing the rise and fall of functionalism).

151   *See supra* note 69. *See, e.g.,* ALTER, *supra* note 3, at 344 (arguing that the turn to international courts "is a good thing for democracy because like all actors, governments and ICs [International Courts] can make decisions that are bad, wrong, poorly reasoned, and worth ignoring. ICs' outside and legal voice provides a different perspective in political debates, one that privileges law and helps shore up the positon of those domestic actors who want to see predetermined and principle-based goals and objectives realized.").

matters. It may be the case, as is discussed in the last chapter of this monograph, that even though the turn to institutions has radically changed what
"sovereignty" means, the sovereign state needs to remain a bulwark against
over-bearing IOs and international adjudicators. There may be such a thing as
"too much" global governance, at least with respect to certain regimes (including some that are now showing signs of sovereign backlash or strains due to
perceived lack of accountability).[152]

It is surely the case as well that in some instances the world has too little
global governance despite the proliferation of IOs and international courts
and tribunals. Although Chapter II surveys what might be called the Security
Council's "greatest hits," and highlights the creative use by that body of the
vague powers accorded to it under the Charter, contemporary observers might
be more inclined to address the Council's never ceasing failures and prominent
omissions. The Council has, after all, failed: to secure the arrests of criminal
suspects whose prosecutions it has encouraged, to do more than issue ineffective "condemnations" of actions (whether by Assad, Obama, or Putin) that
objectively ought to have triggered Chapter VII sanctions, to authorize peacekeeping troops or other experts to many of the world's worst conflicts, and to
deal with undoubtedly serious "threats to the peace" such as floods of hapless
refugees dying on the high seas, the security threats posed by climate change, or
even the use of chemical weapons by states on their own peoples. If one measures the effectiveness of the Council by its ability to keep the peace, its central purpose as the police force for the world, there is something fundamental
askew when, by the UN's own calculation, the level of global conflicts has led
more than 60 million persons to be forcibly displaced from their homes by the
end of 2014, the largest number of asylum seekers, refugees, or displaced persons in the 65-year history of the UNHCR.[153] Moreover, even when the Council
has mustered the political will to act, as with respect to imposing sanctions on
certain alleged terrorists, its capacity to follow through and successfully implement its actions has been repeatedly questioned. Similarly, although Chapter
III discusses the General Assembly's creative exercise of its more deliberative
powers, there again, one might emphasize that body's abundant failures to act
(or to act forcefully enough), including its refusal to challenge the Council when
it should have done so, whether by more determined efforts to give voice to
views not heard within the 15-member Council or through renewed attention

---

152   *See, e.g.*, Klabbers, *supra* note 69, at 65–74.
153   United Nations High Commissioner for Refugees, World at War: Global Trends 2014,
      2 (2015). *See also* Chapter III *infra*.

to the Assembly's residual powers over peace and security (including under the seemingly defunct Uniting for Peace Resolution).[154] What the Assembly has managed to do under its "hortatory" powers can be seen as a glass half full: imagine all those Assembly resolutions that have not been passed because of the inability to muster the political will of enough UN member states—from advisory questions never posed to the ICJ to subsidiary investigatory bodies never established (including by the often reticent UN Human Rights Council). Much the same could be said of other IOs discussed in these pages. Indeed, Chapter III's examination of the WHO's International Health Regulations ends with a short account of the organization's most recent failure: namely its inability to use its collective powers to stem the spread of Ebola before thousands lost their lives in a pandemic that affected some of the poorest countries in the world.

Nor can we be overly sanguine about the subject of this monograph's Chapter V: institutionalized international adjudicators. These can only render rulings to the extent their jurisdiction is triggered and even when judicial or arbitral decisions are issued, the targets of those rulings, usually states, do not always comply.[155]

Many of these complexities—including the interactions between formal IOs and other hybrid or private institutions—are beyond the scope of this monograph. This is a narrower effort to understand the impact of IOs on the law, and what that tells us about the most dominant framework for understanding international law, namely legal positivism. But even on this score, caveats are

---

154   Uniting for Peace, G.A. Res. 37(V) (Nov. 3, 1950) (enabling the Assembly to meet in emergency session should the Council, for "lack of unanimity" fail to "exercise its primary responsibility for the maintenance of international peace and security" and enabling that body to recommend that states take peacekeeping actions); *see also* Larry D. Johnson, *"Uniting for Peace": Does it Still Serve Any Useful Purpose?*, AM. J. INT'L L. UNBOUND (July 15, 2014, 12:02 PM); Frederic L. Kurgis, *He Got it Almost Right*, AM. J. INT'L L. UNBOUND (July 16, 2014, 11:26 AM); Ieva Mulina, *What Does the Uniting for Peace Resolution Mean for the Role of the UN Security Council?*, AM. J. INT'L L. UNBOUND (July 17, 2014, 1:20 PM); Stefan Talmon, *The Legalizing and Legitimizing Function of UN General Assembly Resolutions*, AM. J. INT'L L. UNBOUND (July 18, 2014, 11:32 AM); Boris N. Mamlyuk, *Uniting for "Peace" in the Second Cold War: A Response to Larry Johnson*, AM. J. INT'L L. UNBOUND (July 21, 2014, 12:24 PM). *See generally* ALVAREZ, *supra* note 1, at 126–127. *See also* Chapter III *infra*.

155   *See, e.g.*, CONSTANZE SCHULTE, COMPLIANCE WITH DECISIONS OF THE INTERNATIONAL COURT OF JUSTICE (2004); Aloysius P. Llamzon, *Jurisdiction and Compliance in Recent Decisions of the International Court of Justice*, 18 EUR. J. INT'L L. 815 (2007).

in order. The core tenets of classical legal positivism are, as argued here, under threat and, in some scholarly circles, in retreat, even while positivism remains the dominant framework. No one has yet come up with a single over-arching model or perspective to displace positivism—whether grounded in rules or institutions. Indeed, the absence of a clear alternative to positivism poses, as addressed in the last chapter of this monograph, a difficult challenge for the international rule of law. Those who contend that international organizations are effectively law-makers have yet to clarify what precisely international law is if it is not one of the three sources of law identified in the ICJ's Article 38.[156] Moreover, the effects of institutions on the sources of Article 38, even if they are acknowledged to be pervasive, should not be presumed to be normatively desirable.

The impact of IOS on legal positivism and its sources is not necessarily a progress narrative. Even assuming that more law is desirable (in itself a questionable proposition), IOS may not have generated a greater number of treaties, rules of custom, or general principles than would otherwise have occurred in a world that would have produced them in response to technological developments or other needs in any case. Of course, even assuming that the turn to institutions, including for purposes of adjudication, has generated more law within distinct regimes (such as peace and security, human rights, or trade), the rules that have emerged are not necessarily better than what preceded them.[157] Moreover, in some cases the turn to IOS has not resulted in more formal law. The fact that multilateral treaties now tend to be negotiated within IO auspices may help to explain some successful treaty negotiations and may even help explain high ratification rates for some of these (e.g., certain counter-terrorism conventions), but IOS and their bureaucracies might also be blamed for some treaty failures, such as the OECD's failed 1998 effort to secure a Multilateral Investment Agreement or the WTO's collapsed DOHA Round.[158] Treaty

---

156   For expressions of this complaint, see, for example, Jan Klabbers, Book Review, 3 INT'L ORG. L. REV. 153 (2006) (reviewing JOSÉ E. ALVAREZ, INTERNATIONAL ORGANIZATIONS AS LAW-MAKERS (2006)); D'ASPREMONT, *supra* note 4, at 195–220.

157   *See, e.g.,* R.E. Hudec, *The New WTO Dispute Settlement Procedures: An Overview of the First Three Years,* 8 MINN. J. GLOBAL TRADE 1, 5 (noting the relatively high level of compliance with GATT rulings in the pre-WTO era).

158   *See, e.g.,* Alvarez, *supra* note 1, at 365–370; Gabriella Blum, *Bilateralism, Multilateralism, and the Architecture of International Law,* 49 HARV. INT'L L. J. 323 (2008). Moreover, even when IOS engage in formal treaty making at the global level, their efforts may prove to be less effective than informal, non-treaty efforts undertaken by others. The Pope's Encyclical on Climate Change, issued in 2015, for example, may come to have a more dramatic effect on global efforts to control climate change than anything yet done within the UN. POPE FRANCIS I, ENCYCLICAL LETTER LAUDATO SI' OF THE HOLY

negotiations that require reaching a consensus among over 100 states may explain treaty outcomes that appeal to the "lowest common denominator," as Bruno Simma once pointed out.[159] And although courts and arbitrators sometimes may be finding (or even creating) more rules of custom or applicable general principles, this does not mean that they are doing so with due regard for the views of all states, even when IO shortcuts, like IO sponsored treaties or resolutions, are deployed to this end. Even a widely supported multilateral treaty endorsed by an IO or a General Assembly resolution may not reflect the genuine views of states that faced regional or hegemonic pressures to vote in favor of adopting either, for example. Normative judgments about the quality of legal products produced in the age of IOs and international courts are beyond the scope of this monograph.

No one should assume that the turn to "soft law" or more generally to alternatives to Article 38 sources elicits greater compliance with such norms. It does not take much imagination to see instances where states (or others) turn to alternatives to hard treaty or avoid inclusion of a dispute body with the capacity to issue binding rulings within a treaty precisely because they want to avoid hard pressures to comply with the norm in question. The turn to institutionalized "deliberative" or "managerial" efforts to secure compliance may be an interesting alternative to the positivist preoccupation with methods that compel states to recognize the bindingness of legal commitments, but sometimes such "soft" enforcement efforts may be exactly what realists and legal positivists fear: efforts to obfuscate, postpone, or avoid the rule of law altogether.

Caveats are also needed with respect to section 2 above concerning the institutional challenge to positivism. As noted, the "reality of institutionalization" discussed in part 2.1 has not reached all parts of the world. Important hold-outs remain with respect to prominent international courts, including the US and China. Moreover, not all formal IOs, even where they exist, have exercised their delegated (or implied) powers. ASEAN is a very different regional organization than is the European Union, after all.[160]

FATHER FRANCIS ON CARE FOR OUR COMMON HOME (May 24, 2015), *at* http://w2.vatican.va/content/dam/francesco/pdf/encyclicals/documents/papa-francesco_20150524_enciclica-laudato-si_en.pdf.

159   Bruno Simma, *Consent: Strains in the Treaty System, in* THE STRUCTURE AND PROCESS OF INTERNATIONAL LAW, 485 (R.St.J. McDonald & Douglas M. Johnston eds., 1983).

160   *See, e.g.,* STEFANO INAMA & EDMUND W. SIM, THE FOUNDATION OF THE ASEAN ECONOMIC COMMUNITY: AN INSTITUTIONAL AND LEGAL PROFILE (2015); PARUEDEE NGUITRAGOOL & JÜRGEN RÜLAND, ASEAN AS AN ACTOR IN INTERNATIONAL FORA: REALITY, POTENTIAL AND CONSTRAINT (2015).

Part 2.2's description of the "international judiciary" should not be taken to imply greater unity among the world's diverse international judges and arbitrators than actually exists. As Chapter V addresses, international adjudicators, from ICJ judges to investor-state arbitrators, do not share a common vision of what their roles are. Some adjudicators believe that their function is to preserve the status quo among the disputing parties and that they should therefore settle disputes on the narrowest possible terms, and be circumspect about making more statements of law or fact than absolutely necessary. This includes, for example, some judges on the ICJ who have suggested that even the advisory jurisdiction of that Court should be deployed to resolve concrete inter-state disputes and not to make broad and "speculative" proclamations on the state of the law.[161] Not all international adjudicators would agree that their court or tribunal should legitimately "make" law, serve a constitutional function, "regulate" states, or be a vehicle for any other form of "global governance."

In addition, as Chapter V demonstrates, when international courts are perceived as being unduly activist, states may demur or engage in 'sovereign backlash' directed at such courts or tribunals. Further, even though scholars might judge the effectiveness of international adjudicators on the basis of their capacity to be impartial and therefore serve as "trustees" (and not the mere agents of states), the politicized ways by which most judges or arbitrators are selected tells a different story. It suggests that states may not fully agree.[162] Some states seem inclined, based on the persons that they propose to serve as adjudicators, to appoint persons who are closer to diplomats in robes than to "trustees" (or servants) of the rule of law. Indeed, empirical attempts to measure the extent to which international adjudicators deviate from the positions of the governments that nominate them, the regions from which they come from, or the legal cultures of which they are a part have not yielded uniform results in support of their impartiality or lack of bias.[163] Given the fact

---

161   See, e.g., Legality of the Use by a State of Nuclear Weapons in Armed Conflict, Advisory
       Opinion, 1996 I.C.J. 66, 88 (July 8) (separate opinion of Judge Oda).

162   See, e.g., RUTH MACKENZIE ET AL., SELECTING INTERNATIONAL JUDGES (2010).

163   See, e.g., NINA-LOUISA AROLD, THE LEGAL CULTURE OF THE EUROPEAN COURT OF
       HUMAN RIGHTS, (2007); Erik Voeten, Politics, Judicial Behavior, and Institutional Design,
       in THE EUROPEAN COURT OF HUMAN RIGHTS BETWEEN LAW AND POLITICS, at 61
       (Jonas Christoffersen & Mikael Rask Madsen eds., 2011), Erik Voeten, International Judicial
       Independence, in DUNOFF & POLLACK, supra note 58, at 421; Erik Voeten, International
       Judicial Behavior, in ROMANO ET AL., supra note 98, at 550; Abhinav Chandrachud,
       Diversity and the International Criminal Court: Does Geographic Background Impact
       Decision Making?, 38 BROOK. J. INT'L L. 487 (2013); Eric A. Posner & Miguel F.P. de
       Figueiredo, Is the International Court of Justice Biased?, 34 J. LEGAL STUD. 599 (2004);

that no international judge or arbitrator has a life appointment, and most are beholden to states for their initial nomination or prospects for re-election, adjudicative biases may arise merely from the manner in which these courts are established.[164] Of course, to the extent international adjudicators come from national judiciaries or from national legal cultures where biases or even corruption issues are endemic, these tendencies may find their way to international bodies as well.

Similarly, sections 2.3, 2.4, and 2.5 above should not be taken to mean that domestic analogies are always useful, that understanding legal rules can be ignored in favor of studying the international legal process that generates their creation, or that lawyers need to cede their expertise to other disciplines. These sections illustrate important new dimensions to the study of international law but cautionary notes are needed here as well.

The domestic analogues emphasized by section 2.3 should not come at the expense of recognizing the unique features of the international legal system. That "system," to the extent it is a single system at all and not a series of discrete regimes, does not always have a domestic counterpart. Domestic legal concepts (such as the U.S. conception of the "separation of powers" applicable under its Constitution) need "translation" prior to export;[165] domestic analogues cannot be simply transplanted to individual IOs or applied by an international tribunal to a treaty regime without attention to institutional context.[166]

Section 2.4's attention to process has not displaced black letter law or the need to focus on positivist sources. Despite the rise of more "dynamic" forums for re-interpreting international rules (including treaties), the core meaning of these rules, particularly when they were originally the hard-won result of reaching consensus among diverse states, are often hard to dislodge or re-interpret precisely because of the sheer weight (and sunk costs) of that

Eric Voeten, *The Impartiality of International Judges: Evidence from the European Court of Human Rights*, 102 AM. PO. SCI. L. REV. 417 (2008); Erik Voeten, *The Politics of International Judicial Appointments: Evidence from the European Court of Human Rights*, 61 INT'L ORG. 669 (2007); Vera Shikhelman, *Geopolitics and Culture in the United Nations Human Rights Committee*, AM. J. INT'L L. (forthcoming 2015).

164   *See, e.g.*, Leigh Swigart & Daniel Terris, *Who are International Judges?, in* ROMANO ET AL., *supra* note 98, at 619.

165   For comparable insights with respect to the "domestication" of international law, see Karen Knop, *Here and There: International Law in Domestic Courts*, 32 N.Y.U. J. INT'L L. & POL. 501 (2000).

166   *See, e.g.*, Alvarez, *supra* note 113.

consensus. International norms have a certain "stickiness" precisely because of the absence of a single *legitimate* legislative process.[167]

Finally, the appeal of other disciplines, the subject of section 2.5, has an upper limit: it cannot or should not come at the expense of the close analytical examination of the legal work products of IOs and international adjudicators that lawyers do best.[168]

---

167   For examples of the strained efforts by international lawyers to take into account the "legislative" actions taken by the Security Council, see, for example, Martti Koskenniemi, *The Police in the Temple Order, Justice and the UN: A Dialectical View*, 6 EUR. J. INT'L L. 325 (1995); Stefan Talmon, *The Security Council as World Legislature*, 99 AM. J. INT'L L. 175 (2005), Eric Rosand, *The Security Council as "Global Legislator": Ultra Vires or Ultra Innovative?*, 28 FORDHAM INT'L L.J. 542 (2004).

168   *See, e.g.*, José E. Alvarez, *Global Judicialization Revisited*, 109 AM. J. INT'L L. 677 (2015) (reviewing KAREN J. ALTER, THE NEW TERRAIN OF INTERNATIONAL LAW: COURTS, POLITICS, RIGHTS (2014) and critiquing Alter's failure to closely engage with the underlying judicial and arbitral rulings).

The UN Charter Over Time: The Contemporary Security Council

1   What is the UN Charter for?

According to its text, the UN Charter establishes an organization designed to solve economic, social, cultural, or humanitarian concerns and to promote and encourage respect for human rights (Article 1(3)). But the foremost purpose of the UN, given pride of place in Articles 1(1) and (2) as well as in the leading paragraph in its preamble, is to "save succeeding generations from the scourge of war." The "scourge" referenced—World War II—reminds us that the Charter is a historical and not just a legal text, designed to correct the perceived shortcomings of the prior League of Nations. The UN Charter drafters sought to establish a world body that, unlike the League, could respond to inter-state threats like those posed by the Nazis and the government of Emperor Hirohito.[1] Correcting the League's "birth defects" meant, among other things, encouraging all states to become UN members (universality)[2] and discouraging states from leaving the organization voluntarily.[3] For our purposes here, the most important "corrections" were threefold: including a legally binding prohibition

---

1 *See* U.N. Charter art. 53(1)–(2), art. 107. For a discussion of the failures of the League with respect to international peace, see, for example, HANS J. MORGENTHAU, POLITICS AMONG NATIONS 290 (4th ed. 1967) (discussing the League's inability to apply collective enforcement, Japan's departure from the League, and the expulsion of the USSR).

2 *See* U.N. Charter art. 2(6), arts. 4–6 and the absence of a withdrawal clause. These provisions sought, within the limits of a traditional treaty which cannot bind non-parties, to reach even non-members (art. 2(6)), to set relatively low standards for UN membership (art. 4), and relatively high thresholds for suspension or termination of membership (arts. 5, 6). *But see* THE CHARTER OF THE UNITED NATIONS: A COMMENTARY 342–352 (Bruno Simma et al. eds., 3d ed. 2012) [hereinafter CHARTER COMMENTARY] (discussing how the pressures of the Cold War brought about a less liberal interpretation of the threefold criteria for membership in art. 4 and its "aspiration to absolute universality" with respect to UN participation).

3 CHARTER COMMENTARY, *supra* note 2, at 354–355 (discussing Indonesia's attempt to withdraw from the organization and the absence of a withdrawal clause in the Charter). These efforts were motivated by the failure of the League to prevent the departure of certain members whose absence proved fatal to that organization's efforts to prevent WWII.

© KONINKLIJKE BRILL NV, LEIDEN, 2017 | DOI 10.1163/9789004328402_003

on the threat or use of force against another state,[4] establishing a credible collective security system whereby the world's police powers would enforce that prohibition,[5] and granting that body (the Security Council) primacy over the organization's other organs or other organizations.[6]

Unlike the League, the Charter embraces a rudimentary separation of functions between its principal organs—namely the Security Council, the General Assembly, the Secretariat, the Economic and Social Council (ECOSOC), and the International Court of Justice (ICJ).[7] Under the League of Nations Covenant, two organs were afforded undemarcated responsibilities with respect to crucial international peace and security concerns. By contrast, the Charter clearly put the Security Council in the driver's seat with respect to such matters while leaving all the other functions of the organization (suggested by the broad purposes and principles in Articles 1 and 2) in the hands of the General Assembly and ECOSOC. Accordingly, the "primary" responsibilities accorded to the Council had negative as well as positive aspects. The Council was essentially limited to addressing threats to the peace, both imminent and likely, while the Assembly was given primary responsibility for all

---

4   U.N. Charter art. 2(4). This is to be contrasted with the League's far more ambiguous demands that states settle their disputes peacefully. *See, e.g.*, D.W. Bowett, The Law of International Institutions 17–22 (4th ed. 1981); Ruth Wedgwood, *The Fall of Saddam Hussein: Security Council Mandates and Preemptive Self-Defense*, 97 Am. J. Int'l L. 576, 584 (2003) (describing the UN Charter as an attempt to overcome the failures of Wilson's League of Nations and its covenant of inaction).

5   Although the words "collective security" do not appear in the Charter's text, this was clearly the point of according the Security Council the power to render legally binding decisions (art. 25) and requiring it to "function continuously" (art. 28(1)) so that it can respond promptly and effectively (art. 24). *See* Sebastian von Einsiedel et al., *Introduction*, The UN Security Council in the Twenty-First Century 3–5 (Sebastian von Einsiedel et al. eds., 2016); Oscar Schachter, *The Charter's Origins in Today's Perspective*, 89 ASIL Proc. 45 (1995); José Alvarez, *Legal Perspectives, in* The Oxford Handbook on the United Nations 58 (Thomas G. Weiss & Sam Daws eds., 2007).

6   Thus, the Council was given "primary responsibility for the maintenance of international peace and security" (art. 24) while the Assembly was instructed to defer to the Council on such matters. *See* U.N. Charter art. 11(2) (limiting the Assembly to "recommendations" on such matters and directing it to refer requests for action to the Council); U.N. Charter art. 12(1) (stating that the Assembly "shall not make any recommendation" with respect to disputes or situations over which the Council was exercising its functions). The Council's powers with respect to peace and security also prevail over enforcement actions by regional organizations. *See* U.N. Charter, art. 53(1).

7   *See, e.g.*, José E. Alvarez, International Organizations as Law-Makers 109–111 (2006).

other Charter functions. Thus, the Charter indicates that the Council's "specific powers" were those "laid down in Chapters VI, VII, VIII, and XII."[8]

The text of the Charter suggests that its drafters were willing to delegate to the Council the extraordinary capacity to render legally binding decisions on all UN members—all the more unusual given the Council's limited membership and the P-5 veto powers over such decisions—on the condition that such actions would be taken only with respect to (hopefully rare) instances in which inter-state aggression loomed as a threat to the security of nations. The "sovereign equality" principle proclaimed in the Charter itself was made subject to the exceptional power of 15 Council members to bind the whole membership on the premise that such power would be exercised only when the Council was acting on behalf of the whole in pursuant of collective security. To this end, the capacity of the Council to take the actions foreseen in Chapter VII was characterized in its title as "action with respect to threats to the peace, breaches of the peace, and acts of aggression." Nothing in the Charter text envisions or authorizes the Council to act outside the context of peace and security.[9] Indeed, even when the Charter addresses less forceful actions by the Council, under Chapter VI, that too is in the context of the Council's diverse roles to encourage or facilitate the "pacific settlement of disputes" (as the title of that chapter indicates). Accordingly, to the extent the Charter authorizes the Council to make "law"—at least to the extent that we are willing to call its capacity to impose legally binding obligations on members law-making—that delegation of authority is restricted under the terms (and apparent intent) of

---

8   U.N. Charter art. 24(2).

9   This is arguably what the injunction in art. 24(2)—indicating that in discharging its functions, the Council "shall act in accordance with the Purposes and Principles of the United Nations"—intends to achieve. See also U.N. Charter art. 25 (obliging members "to accept and carry out the decisions of the Security Council in accordance with the present Charter"). The only possible exception might be the Council's powers under Chapter XII, which established the International Trusteeship System. However, given the close connection between the handling of trusteeships and the prospect for international disputes leading to potential threats to the peace, even those parts of Chapter XII that anticipate Council action might be seen as an essential part of that body's primacy over peace and security. See U.N. Charter art. 84 (recognizing the duty of the administrative authority to ensure that trust territories play their part in the maintenance of international peace and security). This is also suggested by art. 83 which recognizes that while the Council retains responsibility for "strategic areas" and "security matters" involving trusteeships, the Trusteeship Council would perform functions "relating to political, economic, social, and educational matters in the strategic areas." See also U.N. Charter arts. 85, 87–88, 91 (entrusting the Trusteeship Council, as authorized by the General Assembly and working with ECOSOC, with key functions on non-strategic areas).

the Charter to the "law-making" needed to respond to the threats to the peace foreseen by the victims of German and Japanese aggression who drafted it.

Once we comprehend that a principal purpose of the Charter was to accord the victors of WWII certain restrictive powers over others because only they had the military capacity to do so, it becomes easier to understand the structure of the Council, its voting provisions and procedures, and most significantly, its powers. The P-5 needed to be specifically identified under Article 23 because they were, at the time, the most credible military powers. They were accorded powers jointly as well as individual vetoes (Article 27) on the premise that they all needed to agree to make their judgments on collective security credible and to make any subsequent enforcement action effective. The SC was given discretion to decide whether and when an (undefined) threat or breach of the international peace[10] occurs because the P-5 needed such broad discretion to be enticed to join the collective security system and to assume their assigned duties under it, any more defined lists of aggressive acts would have risked under-inclusion, and they thought that the plain meaning of the prohibition in Article 2(4) was clear.[11]

To advance these military ends, the Charter required all Council members be represented at all times (Article 28(1)). The P-5 were given the extraordinary power, when joined by only four others on the Council, to compel others to comply with its edicts, in short, because it was assumed that such Council decisions would be restricted to those absolutely needed to protect the territorial integrity or political independence of states. The delegation of power to the Council reflected a decision to take a "calculated risk" that when foundational sovereign rights are threatened—and only then—it was better to cede power to five Council hegemons (subject to a possible informal veto if the other non-permanent members of the Council could not be convinced to provide the four additional votes).[12]

---

10 Notably, neither "threats" nor "breaches" of the peace were legal terms of art prior to the Charter while acts of aggression presumably included the "crimes against peace" adjudicated at Nuremberg. Charter of the International Military Tribunal—Annex to the Agreement for the Prosecution and Punishment of the Major War Criminals of the European Axis ("London Agreement") art. 6(a), Aug. 8, 1945, *at* http://www.refworld.org/docid/3ae6b39614.html.

11 *See, e.g.*, Arthur Mark Weisburd, *The War in Iraq and the Dilemma of Controlling the International Use of Force*, 39 TX. INT'L L. J. 521, 547 (2004) (noting that "the drafters assumed that the rule to be imposed by the Charter was straightforward: states are, in all circumstances, forbidden to use force against one another").

12 *Id.* at 546. *See generally id.* at 544–547 (describing the underlying assumptions made by those who designed the Charter's collective security scheme).

Accordingly, the Council was accorded the exclusive power to determine "threats" to and "breaches" of the peace as well as "acts of aggression" under Article 39. It was understood that Council-authorized force would be consistent with the Charter and would not be subject to the prohibition on states *inter se* in Article 2(4). The Council was also given similarly broad discretion with respect to how it could respond to aggressive inter-state security threats, through hortatory or binding measures designed to prevent aggravation of the situation (Article 40), through any other actions "not involving the use of armed force" (Article 41), or through use of force otherwise "necessary to maintain or restore international peace and security" (Article 42). This collective security scheme was further fortified by requiring UN members, in anticipation of any UN forces required by the Council under Article 42 directed by the P-5's Military Staff Committee under Article 47, "to make available to the Security Council, on its call and in accordance with a special agreement or agreements" their armed forces or other forms of assistance (Article 43).[13] Anticipating that the Council's "enforcement" tools, including any sanctions it might impose on those states that threaten the peace, could require the violation of treaties, the Charter included a provision making it clear that in the event of "conflict" between members' obligations under the Charter and their other treaty obligations, their Charter obligations would prevail.[14]

The Council's powers as anticipated by the text of the Charter also need to be understood in the wider context of what the Council was not charged with undertaking. As noted, the Assembly, not the Council, is authorized to address "any matters within the scope of the present Charter" (Article 10), and such matters may include questions relating to international peace and security

---

13   As is well known, no such military agreements have ever been concluded. *See generally* NIKOLAI WESSENDORF, THE CHARTER OF THE UNITED NATIONS: A COMMENTARY 2137 (Bruno Simma et al. eds., 3d ed. 2012) (explaining the reasons why this is so, including disagreements within the Military Staff Committee on the number of troops each permanent member should make available, locations where they would be stationed, and other disagreements over support options and troops strength, all of which foreshadowed the reluctance of states to commit to such agreements). *See also* ROSALYN HIGGINS, PROBLEMS AND PROCESS: INTERNATIONAL LAW AND HOW WE USE IT 263 (1995). *See also infra* § 3.

14   U.N. Charter art. 103. *See* CHARTER COMMENTARY, *supra* note 2, at 2114–2116 (comparing art. 103 to the comparable provision in the League of Nations Covenant). The Charter drafters rejected an alternative formulation which would have enabled the Charter to prevail over "any other international obligations to which they are subject," suggesting a reluctance to explicitly include customary international law. CHARTER COMMENTARY, *id.*, at 2116.

(Article 11(2)). The trade-off in the Charter is clear: the Council, accorded the power to render legally binding decisions, is given this power only in a narrow sphere; the Assembly, given a far wider range with respect to subject-matter, is generally given only the power to recommend.

This delineation of functions and corresponding powers is also broadly consistent with the vision, suggested by the Charter's sparse provisions relating to UN specialized agencies in Chapter IX, that the UN would preside over an interconnected system of specialized agencies with responsibilities as accorded in their basic instruments over "economic, social, cultural, educational, health, and related fields" (Article 57). Consistent with the pre-Charter world of international administrative unions, these Charter provisions anticipated that the principal responsibilities to secure the broad Charter goals relating to such fields would rest with these other organizations, defined along functionalist terms,[15] and brought into UN "relationship" through treaties entered into between ECOSOC and those specialized agencies (Articles 57, 63). Responsibility for "international economic and social co-operation," the title of Chapter IX, was accordingly "vested" in the General Assembly and ECOSOC, not the Council (Article 60).

With the exception of the Council's powers under Chapter VII, the UN Charter as written is a relatively conservative document that is exceedingly deferential to the sovereign powers retained by states. With the important exceptions of the ban on the use of force and the requirement that UN members must respect the Council's decisions with respect to sanctioning rogue nations that violate that prohibition, the Charter imposes very few other substantive obligations on its members. These include the vague injunctions: to fulfill in good faith their Charter obligations (Article 2(2)), to peacefully settle their disputes (Article 2(3)), to assist the organization and not assist those that are targeted for UN action (Article 2(5)), to bear the expenses of the organization as apportioned by the General Assembly (Article 17), to accept and carry out the decisions of the Council made under the Charter (Articles 25, 48), to comply with decisions of the ICJ in any case to which it is a party (Article 94), to respect the independence of the UN secretariat (Article 100), to abide by their Charter obligations over their conflicting treaty obligations (Article 103), and to recognize certain privileges and immunities of the organization and UN representatives within their territories (Article 105).

---

15   On the functionalist premises of international organizations law more generally, see Jan Klabbers, *The EJIL Foreword: The Transformation of International Organizations Law*, 26 EUR. J. INT'L L. 9 (2015).

The sovereignty-protective nature of the Charter is also reflected in its hesitation to intrude on the "domestic" affairs of states. The negotiations at Dumbarton Oaks and San Francisco that led to the Charter are notable for what their negotiators rejected. These included proposals to give the General Assembly or the ICJ the explicit authority to provide authoritative interpretations of the Charter or to include Charter duties on members to submit their international legal disputes to the ICJ.[16] The negotiators even rejected a modest proposal to accord the organization international legal personality and not merely the capacity to be treated as a person in national courts.[17] Also rejected were far-reaching and prescient proposals to include a "bill of rights" within the Charter itself like those included in some national constitutions, including the U.S. Constitution.[18]

Although the Charter opens with the ringing "we the peoples of the United Nations," the "peoples" of the world are scarcely mentioned in the rest of its text. While Articles 2(4) and (7) address specific rights of sovereign states (namely territorial independence, political independence, and domestic jurisdiction), the "human rights" mentioned in the Charter's preamble and Articles 1(3), were not given specific content.[19] Unlike the obligation not to threaten or use force in Article 2(4), states only pledged "to take joint and separate action" to achieve the undefined human rights mentioned (Article 56) while the organization itself agreed to only "promote" them (Article 55). Nothing in the Charter suggests that the Council's Chapter VI or VII powers—designed to

---

16   ALVAREZ, *supra* note 7, at 74–81.

17   *See, e.g., id.* at 129–139 (discussing how the UN achieved recognition as an international legal person as a result of the ICJ's Advisory Opinion in Reparation for Injuries).

18   *See, e.g.,* Canadian Charter of Rights and Freedoms, Part I of the Constitution Act, 1982, being Schedule B to the Canada Act, 1982, c.11 (U.K.); U.S. CONST. amends. I–X.

19   This is not to suggest that these vague Charter references, a departure from the League of Nations silence on human rights, are without significance. Even under a strict positivist reading of the Charter, these references can be interpreted as transforming human rights, once a matter of domestic concern, into a topic that is proper for UN and further treaty consideration. *See, e.g.,* HERSCH LAUTERPACHT, INTERNATIONAL LAW AND HUMAN RIGHTS 147 (1950) (noting that the Charter provisions on human rights "figure prominently in the statements of the Purposes of the United Nations" and that members have a "legal obligation to act in accordance with these Purposes . . ."). At the same time, the suggestion that human rights are suited to "joint and separate action by states" was taken by some to mean that the subject was left within the prerogative of each state. For this classical understanding of the protection of human rights, see GEORG SCHWARZENBERGER, POWER POLITICS: A STUDY OF WORLD SOCIETY 462 (3d ed. 1964).

protect the integrity of states and to protect states from each other—includes the authority to tackle the human rights of persons inside them.[20]

Not surprisingly, for the first four decades of its existence, the Council largely avoided human rights issues.[21] Of course, the relatively weak provisions on human rights in the Charter are easy to explain historically: all of the most influential drafters of the Charter (the u.s., the ussr, the uk, and France) had little interest in creating an organization charged with effective human rights enforcement. In 1945, the United States was contending with *de facto* apartheid (particularly within its southern states) directed at African-Americans, the ussr had in place a Gulag filled with political prisoners and was facing its own difficulties with ethnic or linguistic minorities, and the uk and France still retained colonies whose populations did not enjoy the same rights as did uk or French nationals.[22]

2   The UN Charter as Positivist Instrument

On its face, the Charter satisfies the expectations of legal positivists. It is an inter-state pact based on and limited by the consent of states and designed to protect their interests as sovereigns. Even the few substantive legal obligations that it imposes on states, including its prominent prohibition on the use of force, are designed to protect sovereign rights. As noted in the prior section,

---

20   Indeed, to this day, as Ian Johnstone points out, "if a member of the Security Council wants to act on human rights, it must make the case that the action is for the purpose of maintaining international peace and security." *See* Ian Johnstone, *The Security Council and International Law, in* THE UN SECURITY COUNCIL IN THE TWENTY-FIRST CENTURY, *supra* note 5, at 783.

21   *See, e.g.,* UNITED NATIONS SECURITY COUNCIL IN THE AGE OF HUMAN RIGHTS 6 (Jared Genser & Bruno Stagno Ugarte eds. 2014). *See also* Juergen Dedring, *Human Security and the UN Security Council, in* CONFLICT AND HUMAN SECURITY: A SEARCH FOR NEW APPROACHES OF PEACE-BUILDING 45, 46–47 (2004).

22   2 THE OXFORD COMPANION TO AMERICAN POLITICS 506 (David Coates ed., 2012) (noting that during the drafting of the Charter, Roosevelt, Truman, and their advisors well understood the power of senators in the South where "discrimination and even lynchings" against African Americans was prevalent); THOMAS BUERGENTHAL, INTERNATIONAL HUMAN RIGHTS IN A NUTSHELL 22 (2d ed. 1995) (noting that the principal powers at the close of WWII did not see it as within their political interests to "draft a Charter that established an effective system for the protection of human rights . . . [as] the Soviet Union had its Gulag, the United States its de jure racial discrimination [and] France and Britain their colonial empires").

its clearest exception to sovereign equality—the privilege accorded the P-5 and other members of the Council's 15—arises out of necessity: the need to establish effective police action to protect states' territorial integrity and political independence. Indeed, as Tom Dannenbaum has argued, the Charter's drafters understood the third trigger for Council action, acts of aggression, as effectively a "crime against sovereignty"—that is, a crime that is triggered by infringement of a state's or of a political collective's rights.[23] To this extent the Charter can be understood as a military pact no less than, say, NATO's Atlantic Charter; it is all about protecting, not diminishing, the power of states.

As would be predicted of an inter-state pact imposing only those reciprocal contractual obligations that states have an interest in offering to one another, the Charter accords pride of place to the principles of "sovereign equality" (Article 2(1)), while also reassuring member states that but for the Council's enforcement power, the UN is barred from "intervening" in their "domestic jurisdiction" (Article 2(7)).

This state-centric Charter does not establish a government with delegated law-making power. No such general power is accorded to the Council or any other organ. Unlike the constitutions of states, it establishes no legislature, executive branch, or judiciary authority with preordained jurisdiction. The same is true of the UN specialized agencies with which it is authorized to conclude relationship agreements.[24] The GA can only make recommendations, the SC can only take enforcement power against those states that threaten other states, the UN Secretariat can only administer to the needs of UN members, and the ICJ is not given any jurisdiction to render a legally binding decision against any state absent its prior and express consent.[25] Indeed, the Charter itself affirms, in Article 2(7), that nothing in it requires members to submit

---

23   Tom Dannenbaum, *Why Have We Criminalized Aggressive War?* 126 YALE L.J. (forthcoming 2017) (criticizing what the author considers to be the dominant view of the crime of aggression). As Dannenbaum points out, the most influential effort to justify this perspective remains Michael Walzer's JUST AND UNJUST WARS: A MORAL ARGUMENT WITH HISTORICAL ILLUSTRATIONS (1977).

24   ALVAREZ, *supra* note 7, at 71–72. *See also* Chapter IV *infra* on the WHO.

25   Statute of the International Court of Justice art. 36(1), Apr. 18, 1946, 59 Stat. 1055, 33 U.N.T.S. 933 [hereinafter ICJ Statute]. Indeed, it was the U.S. and the USSR that adamantly opposed the grant of compulsory jurisdiction to the Court and others ceded to their opposition. *See* Sean D. Murphy, *The United States and the International Court of Justice: Coping with Antinomies, in* THE SWORD AND THE SCALES: THE UNITED STATES AND INTERNATIONAL COURTS AND TRIBUNALS 46, 61 (Cesare P.R. Romano ed., 2009). *See also* RUTH B. RUSSELL & JEANNETTE E. MUTHER, A HISTORY OF THE UNITED NATIONS CHARTER: THE ROLE OF THE UNITED STATES 1940–1945, 884–890 (1958).

disputes involving their "domestic jurisdiction" to settlement under the Charter, and nothing in Chapters VI or VII suggests that the SC has the power to compel states to submit their disputes to the ICJ against their will.[26] Nor is there anything in the Charter granting anyone judicial review authority over its enforcer of the peace, namely the Council. If this is a "constitution," it is an extremely enfeebled version of one.

As a positivist would expect, the Charter is an instrument of, by, and for sovereigns. It is intended, as the Permanent Court of International Justice suggested in the Wimbledon case, to enhance, not detract from, state authority.[27] And it is not just the Charter's collective security scheme that reflects state-centricity. By establishing a trusteeship system, alongside an affirmation of the right of self-determination, it was anticipated that the UN would become (as it did) the foremost enabler (or maker) of states in history, particularly (but not only) by encouraging and promoting decolonization and thereafter welcoming the emerging states into an organization designed to accord them protection.

The Charter leaves the positivist sources of international law intact, neither adding to nor detracting from the list of sources originally governing the predecessor Permanent Court of International Justice and replicated in Article 38 for the ICJ.[28] Article 38 of the ICJ Statute affirms the three positivist sources as traditionally understood.[29] With the exception of the priority rule of Article 103 enabling the SC to take effective enforcement despite existing treaties, the Charter is just another treaty among equals. It does not claim exception from or nor does it seek special rules for its interpretation. Of course, Article 38 does not claim any special distinction for the Charter of which it is a part, does not indicate that SC or GA resolutions are additional sources of law, and does not

---

26   Indeed, art. 33(1) affirms that states retain discretion over the choice—from negotiation to adjudication—of the "peaceful means of their own choice" when it comes to settling their disputes.

27   Case of the S.S. Wimbledon, 1923 P.C.I.J. (ser. A) No. 1, at 25 ("The Court declines to see in the conclusion of any Treaty by which a State undertakes to perform or refrain from performing a particular act an abandonment of its sovereignty. No doubt any convention creating an obligation of this kind places a restriction upon the exercise of the sovereign rights of the State, in the sense that it requires to be exercised in a certain way. But the right of entering into international engagements is an attribute of State sovereignty.") *See also* Jan Klabbers, *Clinching the Concept of Sovereignty: Wimbledon Redux*, 3 AUSTRIAN REV. INT'L & EUR. L. 345, 364 (1998) (finding that the Wimbledon court had managed to make a virtue out of a vice, that is, the need for states to conclude treaties).

28   Statute of the Permanent Court of International Justice art. 38, Dec. 16, 1920, 1926 P.C.I.J. (ser. D) No. 1.

29   *See* Chapter I *supra*.

even mention such organizational work products within its "subsidiary" means for determining the rules of law. Nor does Article 38 suggest that ICJ decisions have any privileged position among the "judicial decisions" that it mentions, alongside the views of scholars, as "subsidiary means."

The Charter does not even delegate general authority to the organization or its organs to conclude treaties. Even in this respect, its delegations of power are hedged and tentative. The treaty making powers identified in the Charter are limited to those that seem indispensable to fulfilling the core Charter purposes previously described. Thus, the Charter anticipates only the conclusion of relationship agreements with UN specialized agencies (Article 63) and military agreements between itself and members (Article 43).[30] Nothing in the Charter delegates authority to the SC or the GA to intervene with respect to how or when states conclude treaties. There is nothing entitling either UN organ to interpret existing or future treaties, whatever the topic; nothing permitting these bodies to amend them; and, of course, nothing enabling UN bodies to force states to conclude or ratify them. While the Charter's drafters may have anticipated that the UN would be a convenient negotiating venue to conclude treaties as well as other forms of diplomatic business, there is nothing to suggest that the resulting harvest of treaties concluded under UN auspices would be any different in content, form, or effect than treaties that pre-existed the birth of the UN. The Charter assumes that states would retain the freedom to decide whether or not to ratify a treaty, and that the parties to treaties negotiated at the UN would retain complete control over subsequent interpretation and enforcement.

The Charter does not otherwise disturb the centrality of positivist consent.[31] There is no authority granted to any organ of the UN to enact or otherwise influence the making of customary law or the process for deriving general principles of law. The Charter's text leaves those sources and the positivist tenets underlying them intact. Its only entry into such questions innocuously provides that the GA can "initiate studies and make recommendations" thereby encouraging the progressive development and codification of international

---

30   Notably, even art. 105(3), dealing with privileges and immunities of the organization and anticipating the need to conclude treaties for this purpose, appears to anticipate treaties among UN members (and not with the organization) for this purpose.

31   *See, e.g.,* Vienna Convention on the Law of Treaties art. 34, *opened for signature* May 23, 1969, 1155 U.N.T.S. 331 [hereinafter VCT] ("A treaty does not create either obligations or rights for a third State without its consent."). *See also* JAN KLABBERS, INTERNATIONAL LAW 24 (2013) ("[I]nternational law is often deemed a positivist system in that rules are created by consent of the states themselves, and do not flow from elsewhere.").

law (Article 13(1)), a task that had earlier been performed by a Committee of Experts created by the League of Nations prior to the UN. Accordingly, this last was not a novel League "correction."[32]

The Charter is also timid in affirming the rights of the organization itself vis-à-vis the "real" subjects of international law, namely states. As noted, despite the urgings of some during the course of its negotiation, the Charter does not affirm the international legal personality of the organization and only mentions UN privileges and immunities in the territory of members (Article 105).[33] Nor does the Charter, despite its oblique reference to non-member states (Article 2(6)) or its attempt to secure its primacy over treaties (Article 103), purport to establish itself as the *de facto* constitution of the world, hierarchically superior to all law national or international. On the contrary, it presumes that its rules, like those in any treaty, bind only UN member states—and not non-members, other international organizations, NGOs, or individuals.[34]

In other respects as well the Charter accords with the positivist tenets described in Chapter I. The Charter's reference to two ostensibly different activities—the progressive development and codification of international law (Article 13(1))—endorses the traditional dichotomy between black letter existing rule, which by definition is binding, and sought-after policy prescription which is not. The Charter accepts its members' need for firm guidance as to what they are urged to do versus what they must do. It carefully distinguishes hortatory recommendations from binding decisions by using these two terms and by using "shall" when it means to impose an obligation (e.g., Article 2(2)–(7)) and the use of other language when it intends to indicate discretion (e.g., its suggestion that the Assembly "may discuss" matters in Article 10). Similarly the Charter's drafters drew a clear distinction between legally binding judgments of the ICJ (pursuant to its contentious jurisdiction once state consent is demonstrated), which states must respect and the Security Council can enforce (Article 94), and mere non-binding "advisory" opinions issued by that Court in response to questions posed by the GA, the SC, or by other IOs (Article 96).

The UN Charter is, in short, a positivist instrument that relies on state consent; imposes limited obligations on states and respects their primacy; clearly distinguishes between binding and non-binding (or discretionary) actions for

---

32   United Nations, Documents on the Development and Codification of International Law, 41 AM. J. INT'L L. SUPP. 29, 102–103 (1947).

33   *See supra* note 17.

34   But art. 2(6) obliquely suggests that the organization, not non-member states, has a duty to ensure that non-members act in accordance with the principles in art. 2.

members and the organization; incorporates and reaffirms Article 38 positivist sources of law and the clear distinction that rules of law need to be distinguished from the demands of politics; and makes no suggestion that alternative conceptions of the rules of international law are appropriate or that alternatives sources of international obligation exist for states or for itself.

• • •

The rest of this chapter focuses on select Chapter VII actions of the Security Council to explore how far that body—and the organization—has come from the original conception of the Charter outlined above and in section 1. As Table A and the graphic Chart B vividly illustrate, Council Chapter VII resolutions have grown exponentially in the contemporary period, with the dramatic growth most apparent if one compares the SC's first 43 years (corresponding roughly to the Cold War years) to the 25 years since the end of 1989.

In 1990, the Council relied explicitly on Chapter VII in 27 percent of the total number of Council resolutions passed that year. Since then, it has never gone below that annual percentage.[35] Indeed, the total number of Chapter VII resolutions it adopted in 2011 alone (43) equals the number of Chapter VII resolutions it adopted in total from 1946–1989.[36] In 2011, over 65 percent of the Council's resolutions invoked Chapter VII, and the total percentage of Chapter VII resolutions relative to the number of annual resolutions adopted have since then stayed above 50 percent. This trend continued on track through 2015. As Table A indicates, in 2015, the Council adopted 38 resolutions that relied on Chapter VII out of a total of 68, yielding a percentage of 56.

---

35   Table A refers only to those resolutions in which the Council has invoked in the text of the resolution Chapter VII as the source of its authority. As is well known, the Council has, on occasion, adopted other resolutions that include at least some provisions that may have been intended to be legally binding but do not rely explicitly on Chapter VII. *See, e.g.,* Johnstone, *supra* note 20, at 775–776 (discussing the difficulties of interpreting in particular contexts some of the Council's operative words, such as "calls upon," "decides," "demands," or "requires," and citing as an example Secretary-General Boutros-Ghali's difficulties in interpreting whether Council Resolution 242 was or was not legally binding). Accordingly, Table A and Chart B likely understate the numbers of Council resolutions that were intended to be legally binding decisions notwithstanding the absence of an explicit Chapter VII reference. *See also* Chapter V *infra* (discussing ICJ and Article 25).

36   LORAINE SIEVERS & SAM DAWS, THE PROCEDURE OF THE UN SECURITY COUNCIL 389–392 (4th ed. 2014) (noting that the Council adopted 43 Chapter VII resolutions in the 1946–1989 period as compared to 558 such resolutions from 1990–2013).

TABLE A   *Chapter VII Resolutions Adopted by the Security Council as of Feb. 23, 2016**

Year	Number of Security Council Resolutions	Chapter VII Resolutions	Percentage of Chapter VII Resolutions
1990	37	10	27%
2000	50	14	28%
2009	48	23	48%
2010	53	32	60.3%
2011	66	43	65.2%
2012	53	32	60.3%
2013	47	24	51%
2014	63	32	51%
2015	68	38	56%
2016	6	4	67%

** Between 1946–1989, the Council adopted 22 resolutions which explicitly cited Chapter VII. From 1990–2013, the Council adopted 558 of Chapter VII resolutions.[37]

CHART B

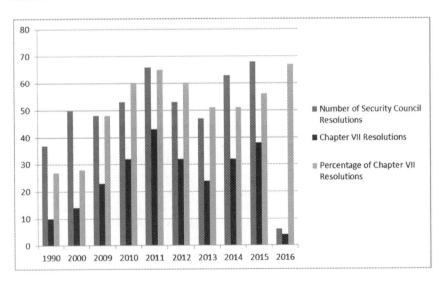

---

37   LORAINE SIEVERS & SAM DAWS, THE PROCEDURE OF THE UN SECURITY COUNCIL 389–392 (4th ed. 2014).

These numbers suggest that the many commentators who argue that the contemporary Security Council is at an impasse comparable to the worse days of the Cold War are overstating the case. Despite the growing number of vetoes exercised by one or more of the P-5 over recent years (which includes a fairly new trend of joint Russian-Chinese vetoes over the 2007–2014 period),[38] there has been a remarkable change in the post-Cold War practice of the SC: 90 percent of its resolutions since 2001 have been adopted by consensus.[39] And these numbers suggest something else: the Council is deploying Chapter VII in ways that the drafters of the Charter would not have anticipated and that are not consistent with the positivist conception of the Charter described above. A positivist interpretation of the Charter, according primacy to its plain meaning, object and purpose, and context, would not have predicted that over the past quarter century—during which the world was not threatened with or engulfed in a world war and the numbers of inter-state conflicts have been vastly overtaken by purely intra-state conflicts—the Council would have seen fit to engage the Charter's collective security scheme 578 times, and yet that is the number of Chapter VII resolutions adopted by the Council from 1990 through 2013.

This chapter goes behind the numbers to describe the Council's post-Cold War flexibility and adaptability.[40] As the select examples of Council actions in this chapter illustrate, the SC has now acted as enforcer of the law not just enforcer of the inter-state peace, as *de facto* legislator and not just collective "cop," and on occasion, even as adjudicator of disputes.[41] The Council has managed to innovate in ways that would have astounded the Charter's drafters (or anyone who reads the Charter as a positivist text) despite political conflicts among the P-5 that some compare to the worst days of the Cold War, the absence of the anticipated Article 43 military agreements, a moribund Military Staff Committee under Article 47, and the Charter's restrictions on the subject matter over which the SC has authority. The basic grand bargain struck within the Charter—relatively unconstrained Council power but only over necessary

---

38   Sebastian von Einsiedel, David M. Malone & Bruno Stagno Ugarte, The UN Security Council in an Age of Great Power Rivalry at 3 (UN Univ. Working Paper Series, No. 4, 2015) (enumerating six such joint vetoes over this period as compared to only such joint veto in the preceding 36 years).

39   *Id.* (including a table indicating the numbers of Council vetoes over the 1987–2014 period). According to this data, whereas 15 vetoes were cast in the 6-year period of 1987–1990, only 6 were cast in 2011–2014.

40   *But see* Einsiedel et al., *supra* note 5, at 1, 3–5 (describing the Council's creative use of its powers, particularly under Chapter VI, even during the Cold War period).

41   The point has also been made by many others. *See, e.g.*, Johnstone, *supra* note 20.

responses to discrete (hopefully rare) inter-state threats to the international peace—has essentially come undone. The Council has now found "threats" to the international peace where there is no plausible claim of the existence of an inter-state aggressive act, and, often, where the perceived threat has no clear geographic or temporal limit. It has taken measures in response to such threats that were not contemplated by the Charter's drafters and that are fundamentally at odds with the positivist conception of the Charter described above. Along the way, the Council's actions have had an impact not only on the interpretation of the UN Charter but also on general international law.

But this chapter does not argue that the extraordinary number of Chapter VII resolutions passed or the innovative nature of many of them is *ultra vires*. On the contrary, the point here is that the SC's innovations have, for the most part, not drawn such criticism. What is extraordinary is how few of the SC's actions—with the exceptions of some of its sanctions programs that have prompted serious human rights complaints—have drawn the ire of international lawyers. Although the targets of the Council's actions (such as Iraq) have sometimes objected, the Council's departures from the Charter's text, structure, and original purpose have largely been accepted by UN members as a whole. When the Council has been criticized, most often the complaint is based on its efficacy or its inactions, not the legality of what it has done. There has been general acquiescence in the Council's practice and, more importantly, in the underlying premise that the UN Charter (and perhaps other IO charters) should not be interpreted as ordinary compacts subject to the traditional positivist rules of interpretation, but as "living" or dynamic instruments of governance capable of adapting to changing circumstances.[42] This begins to suggest how far international law in the age of IOs has deviated from positivism's central tenets.

At the same time, the innovations canvassed in this chapter, like those examined in Chapter III with respect to the GA, Chapter IV (the WHO and other UN specialized agencies), and Chapter V (international courts), pose accountability challenges that have not yet been fully satisfied and that are explored in Chapter VI. The departures from legal positivism that these chapters highlight are not necessarily to be celebrated. Indeed they may explain why many see international law (and not only IOs) as suffering from an existential crisis.[43]

---

42   For a thorough historical exploration of this thesis, encompassing three case studies involving UN peacekeeping, ILO assistance, and the World Bank's governance activities, see Guy Sinclair, To Reform the World (forthcoming 2016).

43   *See, e.g.*, Joel P. Tractman, *The Crisis in International Law*, 44 Case W. Res. J. Int'l L. 407 (2011); Martti Koskenniemi, *The Fate of Public International Law: Between Technique and Politics*, 70 Mod. L. Rev. 1, 4–9 (2011).

IOS' contribution to the undermining of legal positivism and its formal sources may help to explain a perceived recent decline in resort to multilateral treaties or customary law,[44] and why some argue that increasing reliance on the third Article 38 source, general principles of law, is not a viable or credible solution.[45] These challenges, along with alternative frameworks for understanding how IOS impact international law, are introduced in Chapter VI.

3   The Council and the "Contracting Out" of Force: Iraq

The Council's response to Iraq's invasion of Kuwait is often depicted as a case where the UN Charter "worked as intended." To be sure, there was nothing innovative about the Council's initial reaction to Iraq's August 2, 1990 invasion of Kuwait. Council Resolution 660, proclaiming that inter-state invasion to be a breach of international peace and security and demanding Iraq's immediate withdrawal from Kuwait under Charter Articles 39 and 40, was a straightforward application of the Charter's text and fully in accord with the collective security scheme it envisions.[46] The same might be said for the next Council resolution, which decided, under Chapter VII and "in accordance with Article 51," to impose a number of trade, financial, and weapons embargoes on Iraq as anticipated by Article 41.[47] But even that resolution contained a few provisions that gave positivist appliers of the Charter pause:

---

44   *See, e.g.*, Joost Pauwelyn et. al, *When Structures Become Shackles: Stagnation and Dynamics in International Lawmaking*, 25 EUR. J. INT'L L. 733 (2014) (contending that formal international law is stagnating in terms of quantity and quality and is being superseded by "informal international lawmaking"); Agora, The End of Treaties?, AJIL UNBOUND (April 18, 2014) *at* https://www.asil.org/blogs/end-treaties-online-agora; Joel P. Tractman, *The Growing Obsolescence of Customary International Law*, in CUSTOM'S FUTURE: INTERNATIONAL LAW IN A CHANGING WORLD 172 (Curtis Bradley ed., 2016).

45   Neha Jain, *Comparative International Law at the ICTY: The General Principles Experiment*, 109 AM. J. INT'L L. 486 (2015) (criticizing the resort to general principles by international criminal tribunals).

46   S.C. Res. 660, U.N. Doc. S/RES/660 (Aug. 2, 1990). A full account of the Council's involvement with the Gulf War of 1990, the subject of a vast literature, is not attempted here. For a more detailed account, see, for example, Weisburd, *supra* note 11.

47   S.C. Res. 661, pmbl., para. 6, ¶¶ 3–4, U.N. Doc. S/RES/661 (Aug. 6, 1990).

1.   Resolution 661 appears to blur the Council's own authority to respond to a threat to the peace under Articles 39 and 41 with Kuwait's right to individual and collective self-defense under Article 51. From the start, the Council failed to make clear whether it was in charge as collective enforcer of the peace or whether it was simply granting permission to Kuwait and its defenders to resort to self-defense as anticipated by the "until" clause under Article 51.

2.   The Council was not content with simply responding to the threat to the peace. It affirmed, as part of its decisions in Resolution 661 that the goal was "to restore the authority of the legitimate Government of Kuwait,"[48] thereby making what some might see as a quasi-legislative or judicial finding that exceeds its "police" powers.

3.   The Council's decision to apply sanctions to "all States" as opposed to all members suggests that it could directly impose obligations on non-parties to the Charter.

4.   The Council's sanctions were to be directly applied, as determined by a subsidiary sanctions committee established for this purpose, to all companies, including public utilities, within Iraq or Kuwait, and to individuals within any other states, such as to prevent payments to persons within Iraq or Kuwait, with the exception of monies for medical or humanitarian purposes.[49]

5.   The Council "called on" all states, including non-UN members, to abide by Council sanctions and to breach, as necessary, any private contracts or licenses.[50]

Innovations (1) and (2) above proved crucial to the Council's succeeding actions in the course of the Gulf: they legitimated, as is further discussed below, the sc's "contracting out" of force as opposed to using the UN force anticipated by Articles 42, 43, and 47. Innovations (3), (4), and (5), obviously intended to enhance the effectiveness of the multilateral sanctions imposed on Iraq, were at odds with the standard positivist principle that treaties do not impose duties on non-parties. Innovation (4) pierced the veil of state sovereignty to impose obligations directly on non-state actors within states, while (5) seemed to use Charter Article 103 to justify breaching private contracts and licenses and not just pre-existing treaties. Moreover, the Council assumed a power to establish a subsidiary body that could be delegated authority to take significant deci-

---

48   *Id.* ¶ 2.
49   *Id.* ¶¶ 4–6.
50   *Id.* ¶ 5.

sions on how or when to apply these intrusive measures, including when to apply the humanitarian exceptions it creatively carved out from its otherwise comprehensive sanctions.[51]

These innovations were just the start of many others rendered in the course of and subsequent to the Gulf War. Resolution 665, the Council's initial invocation of the use of force, authorized member states "cooperating with the Government of Kuwait" to undertake "measures commensurate to the specific circumstances" to halt and inspect cargoes heading to Iraq and Kuwait.[52] This "contracting out" of the use of force to particular states,[53] rendered necessary by the absence of Article 43 agreements, was also the expedient used in the crucial Resolution 678 which authorized the same group of states to "use all necessary means to uphold and implement resolution 660 (1990) and all subsequent relevant resolutions and to restore international peace and security in the area."[54]

As with respect to its preceding resolutions on Iraq, the underlying legal authority for Resolution 678 is ambiguous. As Oscar Schachter has suggested, this resolution, consistent with either Article 51 or 42, might reflect a new Council power under "Article 42 and one half."[55] Others have argued, precisely for the same reasons, that Resolution 678 enjoyed "precarious legitimacy."[56] Given the lack of sympathy for Iraq's actions, however, it was largely left to Iraq (and its very few friends) to argue that "contracting out" the use of force was not permitted under the Charter, that in the absence of genuine UN force

---

51   Note that while the Resolution 661 sanctions committee formally consisted of all members of the Council, according to reliable reports, day to day decisions as to whether, for example, a particular shipment of medical goods should be permitted to proceed toward Iraq and unload its goods were typically made by the President of the sanctions committee or whomever was the (monthly) President of the SC. Thus, potentially life or death decisions were effectively delegated to one Council member's representative.

52   S.C. Res. 665, ¶ 1, U.N. Doc. S/RES/665 (Aug. 26, 1990).

53   See, e.g., Jules Lobel & Michael Ratner, Bypassing the Security Council: Ambiguous Authorizations to Use Force, Cease-Fires and the Iraqi Inspection Regime, 93 AM. J. INT'L L. 124, 125 (1999) (contending that the contracting out model leaves states with a wide discretion to exercise control over hostilities and that such States may seek the Security Council resolutions in conflict with its aims and objectives or the view of its members).

54   S.C. Res. 678, ¶ 2, U.N. Doc. S/RES/678 (Nov. 29, 1990).

55   Oscar Schachter, United Nations Law in the Gulf Conflict, 85 AM. J. INT'L L. 452, 457–463 (1991).

56   See Burns H. Weston, Security Council Resolution 678 and Persian Gulf Decision-Making: Precarious Legitimacy, 85 AM. J. INT'L L. 516, 518 (1991). See also John Quigley, The Privatization of Security Council Enforcement Action: A Threat to Multilateralism, 17 MICH. J. INT'L L. 249 (1996).

directed by the Military Staff Committee it was illegal for the Council to simply hand over the waging of the conflict to states led by the United States, that the Charter anticipates either a recommendation or a decision but not an "authorization" that effectively leaves it to individual states to decide when or whether to deploy force, that the Council failed to make a determination on whether peaceful means were futile or had been exhausted as Article 42 anticipates, and that contracting out in this instance was merely a pretext for a regime change or other illegitimate goals. Although widely praised as establishing a "New World Order" in which the Charter's collective security scheme was finally able to work, Resolution 678 led to an outcome radically at odds with what was originally contemplated: a devastating war waged entirely under the control of the United States and its allies with no supervision, requirements of transparency, or a "sunset" clause, which left serious accusations of violations of international humanitarian law unaddressed, and where the Council re-emerged only after the conflict was over.[57]

Of course, the SC's turn to contracting out the use of force was not, by 1990, a complete invention. The Council had previously authorized the UK and Northern Ireland to intercept oil tankers destined for Southern Rhodesia[58] and had also recommended that members furnish assistance to South Korea to repel the armed attack on that country without referring to Article 42 or 43.[59] Those resolutions also delegated to others enforcement action. Although the legality of those "contracting out" precedents had divided positivist from more pragmatic interpreters of the Charter, by the time Iraq invaded Kuwait, the Council's prior practices served to legitimate "contracting out" in the view of most observers.[60]

---

57   *See, e.g.,* FREDERIC L. KIRGIS, INTERNATIONAL ORGANIZATIONS IN THEIR LEGAL SETTING 662–666 (2d ed. 1993); U.N. Secretary-General, Report of the Secretary-General on the Work of the Organization, U.N. Doc. A/461/1, 3 (1991) (suggesting the need for serious reflection on whether "the mechanisms required for the Council to satisfy itself that the rule of proportionality in the employment of armed force is observed and the rules of humanitarian law applicable in armed conflicts are complied with").

58   S.C. Res. 221 (Apr. 9, 1966).

59   S.C. Res. 83 (Jun. 27, 1950).

60   *But see* HANS KELSEN, RECENT TRENDS IN THE LAW OF THE U.N.: A SUPPLEMENT TO "THE LAW OF THE UNITED NATIONS" 932–937 (1951) (arguing that the framers of the Charter seemed to exclude the possibility of action except through armed forces made available to the UN under art. 43 agreements). For a counter, see, for example, THOMAS M. FRANCK, RECOURSE TO FORCE: STATE ACTION AGAINST THREATS AND ARMED ATTACKS 26 (2002) ("[T]extuallly, Article 42 can stand on its own feet and it now may be said to do so as a result of Council practice."). *See also* Rosalyn Higgins, *A General*

After the conflict was over, the significance of the wording in Resolution 678 authorizing force "to restore international peace and security in the area" became clearer. That language, credited to u.s. State Department lawyers who replicated the wording used in Resolution 83 authorizing the use of force in Korea, provided the justification for later arguments that the Council had authority not only to drive an aggressor out of Kuwait, but also to compel Iraq after the war to implement in full all the Council's prior resolutions, and to direct Iraq to take numerous other actions to maintain into the future the security needs of the broader "area."[61] These arguments supported the Council's adoption of Resolution 687, informally called the "mother of all resolutions." The innovations of that resolution, the subject of much scholarship and controversy, need only be briefly summarized here.[62]

By it terms, Resolution 687 required Iraq, under Chapter VII: to accept a demarcation of its contested border with Kuwait; to destroy, remove, or render harmless, under intrusive UN and IAEA supervision, various weapons systems (including certain ballistic missiles that were not illegal); to accept all financial liability for all direct damage, including environmental damage and depletion of natural resources, resulting from its invasion; to accede to the Council's designated mechanism for determining these liabilities (the UN Commission) and to allocate payment from Iraq's oil revenues; to take all necessary measures to renounce all claims pending in all national courts where the underlying performance for such claims was affected by Resolution 661 and subsequent resolutions; and to renounce terrorism—all while remaining subject to a comprehensive trade embargo that would ultimately endure for longer than a decade.[63] The sheer intrusiveness of Resolution 687 led some to suggest that Iraqi sovereignty had been put in "receivership" subject to that country's demonstrating to the Council's satisfaction that it would remain at peace with its neighbors.[64] Others suggested that the Council had in effect

Assessment of United Nations Peace-Keeping, in UNITED NATIONS PEACE-KEEPING: LEGAL ESSAYS 1–14, 3 (Antonio Cassese ed., 1978).

61   s.c. Res. 83 (June 27, 1950).

62   s.c. Res. 687 (Apr. 8, 1991).

63   For a more thorough description of Resolution 687, see Pascal Teixeira da Silva, _Weapons of Mass Destruction: The Iraqi Case_, in THE UN SECURITY COUNCIL: FROM THE COLD WAR TO THE 21ST CENTURY 205 (David Malone ed., 2004).

64   The legal and policy merits divided commentators. _Compare_ Oscar Schachter, _supra_ note 55 (suggesting that the Council was within its rights when it comes to handling a proven aggressor) to José Alvarez, _Legal Unilateralism_, in WARS ON TERRORISM AND IRAQ: HUMAN RIGHTS, UNILATERALISM, AND U.S. FOREIGN POLICY 201 (Margaret E.

"criminalized" Saddam Hussein's regime.[65] Human rights groups criticized the decade of comprehensive economic sanctions which followed, which had an impact on the most vulnerable within Iraq, including women and children, while Iraq's elites and government officials seemed able to evade their impact.[66] Resolution 687's quasi-judicial proclamation that Iraq was financially liable for the consequences of the Gulf War led to the largest claims commission ever established at the international level, the first of its kind under the Council's Chapter VII authority.[67] The UN Compensation Commission processed some 2.68 million claims from 80 countries, including 200,000 business claims, with an aggregate amount of claims sought totaling $352.5 billion.[68]

Although Iraq had no choice but to accept the terms of Resolution 687,[69] the arguments it and others advanced against the legality of many of its provisions

---

Crahan et al. eds., 2004) (discussing complaints that Resolution 687 was comparable to the war-guilt clause in the Treaty of Versailles).

65   *See, e.g.*, Allain Pellet, *Can a State Commit a Crime? Definitely, Yes!*, 10 EUR. J. INT'L L. 425, 433 (1999).

66   *See, e.g.*, Human Rights Watch, Letter to UN Security Council (Jan. 4, 2000), *at* http://www .hrw.org/legacy/press/2000/01/iraq-ltr.htm. *See also* Human Rights Watch, Explanatory Memorandum Regarding the Comprehensive Embargo on Iraq (Jan. 4, 2000), *at* https:// www.hrw.org/news/2000/01/14/explanatory-memorandum-regarding-comprehensive-embargo-iraq. Indeed, revulsion against Iraqi countrywide sanctions ultimately led to the more targeted "smart" sanctions of Resolution 1267 and its progeny which as discussed *infra* § 7 raised problems of their own.

67   *See* S.C. Res. 692 (May. 20, 1991) (establishing the details of the compensation fund and commission). *See also* Norbert Wühler, *The United Nations Compensation Commission: A New Contribution to the Process of International Claims Resolutions*, 2 J. INT'L ECON. L. 249, 251 (1999).

68   CHRISTOPHER S. GIBSON ET AL., WAR REPARATIONS AND THE UN COMPENSATION COMMISSION: DESIGNING COMPENSATION AFTER CONFLICT xxxi (2015); David D. Caron & Brian Morris, *The United Nations Compensation Commission: Practical Justice, Not Retribution*, 13 EUR. J. INT'L L. 183, 187 (2002).

69   Resolution 687 required Iraq's consent. *See* S.C. Res. 687, ¶ 33 (Apr. 3, 1991). Iraq complied, sending letters of acceptance on April 6, 1991. *See* Identical Letters Dated 6 April 1991 from the Permanent Representative of Iraq to the United Nations Addressed Respectively to the Secretary-General and the President of the Security Council, UN Doc. S/22456 (1991) [hereinafter S/22456]. The effects of this "consent," obviously under protest and under threat of continued action by the coalition partners, can be debated. It might be argued that Iraq was obligated to accept the terms of Council resolutions by virtue of the Charter and its UN membership. *See* U.N. Charter arts. 25, 48(1). *But see* JAMES D. FRY, LEGAL RESOLUTION OF NUCLEAR NON-PROLIFERATION DISPUTES 122 (2013) (recognizing the Charter's authority but contending that Resolutions 1441 and 687 appear to be devoid of genuine Iraqi consent).

are a telling reminder of the Council's innovations. For critics of Resolution 687, there was nothing in Chapter VII authorizing the Council to take either "legislative" actions (such as ordering Iraq to "reaffirm unconditionally" its obligations under certain treaties)[70] or "judicial" actions (such as the effective imposition of a border or financial liabilities irrespective of Article 36(3) of the Charter which anticipates that legal disputes should be referred by the Council to the ICJ).[71] Iraq also protested that the restrictions on access to or the use of weapons that were perfectly legal and that were not imposed on others in the region threatened its rights to self-defense and its right to sovereign equality under the Charter.[72] In an argument that would come back to haunt the Saddam regime, Iraq also complained about the seemingly open-ended terms of Resolution 687, which by affirming the continuing power of the Council's prior resolutions, appeared to give the Council continuing authority without a time limit to renew the use of force whenever it (or perhaps those states that had originally responded to 678) wished to do so, notwithstanding the bar of Article 2(4).[73] As the Council's sanctions wore on, Iraq and others also argued that the continuation of Resolution 687's comprehensive trade sanctions violated human rights and international humanitarian law, imposed a form of collective punishment on generations of Iraqis, and constituted an illegal reprisal.[74] Of course, it was the sheer intrusiveness of the weapons inspections conducted by the UN Monitoring, Verification and Inspection Commission (UNMOVIC) and the International Atomic Energy Agency (IAEA), requiring

---

70   S.C. Res. 687, *supra* note 69, ¶ 11 (addressing the Treaty on the Non-proliferation of Nuclear Weapons).

71   Iraq also complained that the Council-ordered UN Compensation Commission scheme, by restricting Iraq's ability to contest the claims brought, was unfair and violated the principle of the equality of arms. It also complained that the basis of the financial liability imposed by the Council, in particular the inclusion of liability for environmental damage, exceeded what was required under international law. *See* Dr. Riyadh Al-Qaysi, Under-Secretary of the Ministry of Foreign Affairs, Statement Before the Twenty-Second Session of the Governing Council of the United Nations Compensation Commission on the Request of the Government of Iraq Filed on 27 July 1996 (Oct. 14, 1996) in U.N. Doc. S/1996/893 (Oct. 31, 1996); S/22456, *supra* note 69.

72   *Id.*

73   *Id. See also* 1991 U.N.Y.B. 194–195, 208–210. For Iraqi criticism of boundary demarcation portion of resolution 687 and S-G's implementation of it, see Letter from the Minister for Foreign Affairs of Iraq to the Secretary-General (Apr. 23, 1991), in U.N. Doc. S/22558, annex II.

74   For scholarly commentary on S.C. Res. 687, see, for example, David J. Bederman, *Collective Security, Demilitarization and 'Pariah' States*, 13 EUR. J. INT'L L. 121, 127 (2002) (noting that the language of Resolution 687 "eerily resonates" with that of the Treaty of Versailles).

Iraq to grant unprecedented access to sensitive sites within its territory, that was perhaps the most innovative—if not always effective—aspect of the "mother of all resolutions."[75]

Twelve years later, Iraq's worse fears were realized when the United States and a few of its allies argued that Resolution 678 together with Resolution 687 indeed left Iraq open to their continued use of force, even without additional Council authorization.[76] This proposition, which had been previously used to justify more limited uses of force and threats to deploy force in response to Iraq's alleged breaches of 687 by the United States or the UK,[77] was put to the test in debates over the meaning of Resolution 1441.[78] That resolution, passed at the insistence of the U.S., claimed that Iraq was not abiding by Resolution 687's weapons inspection regime and found Iraq to be in "material breach" of the Council's earlier resolutions, but fell short of authorizing a renewed use of force against Iraq despite U.S. and UK attempts to include such wording.[79] In lieu of such authority, Resolution 1441 opted to give Iraq one "final opportunity to comply" with the weapons regime it was charged with violating, promising "serious consequences" should it fail to do so.[80]

Despite the SC's rejection of U.S. (and UK) attempts to secure an immediate authorization to use force (this time to topple Saddam Hussein's regime) in the context of Resolution 1441, the United States and its *ad hoc* "coalition of the willing" relied on Resolution 1441's determination that Iraq was in "material

---

75   *See, e.g.*, Michael A. Lysobey, *How Iraq Maintained Its Weapons of Mass Destruction Programs: An Analysis of the Disarmament of Iraq and the Legal Enforcement Options of the United Nations Security Council*, 5 UCLA J. INT'L L. & FOREIGN AFF. 101 (2000) (arguing that Iraq's nondisclosures in 1997–1998 constituted "material breaches" of the requirements of Resolution 687).

76   *See* William H. Taft IV & Todd E. Buchwald, *Preemption, Iraq, and International Law*, 97 AM. J. INT'L L. 557 (2003) (articulating the legal justification offered by the Legal Adviser of the U.S. Department of State and the Assistant Legal Adviser for Political-Military Affairs of the U.S. Department of State); *see also* William H. Taft IV, Remarks Before National Association of Attorneys General (Mar. 20, 2003), *at* http://www.state.gov/s/l/2003/44408 .htm. For a digest of U.S. government views preceding and after Resolution 1441, see Sean D. Murphy, *Contemporary Practice of the United States Relating to International Law*, 96 AM. J. INT'L L. 956, 956–62 (2002); Sean D. Murphy, *Contemporary Practice of the United States Relating to International Law*, 97 AM. J. INT'L L. 203, 203–305, 419–432, 681–683 (2003).

77   For a thorough account of these incidents prior to adoption of Resolution 1441, see Weisburd, *supra* note 11, at 523–526.

78   *See* S.C. Res. 1441 (Nov. 8, 2002). For a thorough airing of the potential meanings of Resolution 1441 in the context of the ensuing Gulf Conflict, see Agora, *Future Implications of the Iraqi Conflict*, 97 AM. J. INT'L L. 553 (2003).

79   *See* Weisburd, *supra* note 11, at 527.

80   S.C. Res. 1441, *supra* note 78, ¶¶ 2, 13.

breach" of prior Council resolutions, particularly Resolutions 678 and 687, as the legal basis for launching a second Gulf War in 2003.[81] The language of "material breach" in Resolution 1441, of course invokes the key term used in Article 60 of the Vienna Convention on the Law of Treaties (VCT) which permits the suspension of a treaty by a treaty party specially affected by such a breach and even permits termination of the treaty if the rest of the treaty parties so agree.[82] Few international lawyers outside the U.S. were persuaded by these purported justifications, and most saw the resulting conflict, which resulted in the toppling of the Hussein regime and the occupation of Iraq by coalition forces, as an illegal war not authorized by the SC.[83]

---

81   Weisburd, *supra* note 11, at 531 n. 92 (citing letters from Australia, the UK, and the U.S. to the UN reporting their military operations against Iraq and offering their justifications). *See also* Taft & Buchwald, *supra* note 76; Michael Matheson, Remarks at the Proceedings of the American Society of International Law on The Challenge of Non-State Actors: Legal Authority for the Possible Use of Force Against Iraq (Apr. 4, 1998), in ASIL PROC. 137 (1998) ("In the U.S. Government's view, there is a continuing right to use force [to respond] to such [material] breaches regardless of whether there is further [Security Council] authorization to respond."); *see also* Letter dated 20 March 2003 from the Permanent Representative of the United States of America to the United Nations Addressed to the President of the Security Council, U.N. Doc. S/2003/351 (Mar. 21, 2003). For Iraq's reaction to the charges of "material breach" in Resolution 1441, see, for example, Letter dated 23 November 2002 from the Minister for Foreign Affairs of Iraq addressed to the Secretary-General, U.N. Doc. S/2002/1294 (Nov. 25, 2002) (arguing the determinations in the resolution were baseless and being used to justify US "aggression").

82   VCT, *supra* note 31, Art. 60. But as many scholars noted, the analogy seems inapt in this context. Even assuming that Iraq was materially breaching Resolution 687, that Resolution was not itself a treaty and is not formally subject to art. 60. To the extent the contention is that Iraq was in material breach of the Charter, art. 60 would demand that only the state specially affected by the material breach would have the right to suspend the treaty—that is the Charter—in response. But no one was suggesting that the UN Charter, including its Art. 2(4), was thereby suspended vis-à-vis Iraq, what was being suggested was that Iraq's breach revived the Council's prior authorization to use force, given 12 years earlier, in Resolution 678. Most regarded this as implausible. *See, e.g.,* Weisburd, *supra* note 11, at 531–541 (canvassing and dismissing arguments that use of force continued to be justified under Resolutions 678 or 687, could be based on Resolution 1441, or could otherwise be legally justified). But see Christopher Greenwood, *International Law and the Pre-emptive Use of Force: Afghanistan, Al-Qaida, and Iraq*, 4 SAN DIEGO INT'L L. J. 7, 26–35 (2003) (emphasizing that Resolution 678 authorized force not only to liberate Kuwait but to restore peace and security in the region).

83   *See, e.g.,* Weisburd, *supra* note 11; International Commission of Jurists, ICJ Deplores Move Towards a War of Aggression on Iraq (Mar. 18, 2003), *at* http://www.icj.org/icj-deplores-moves-toward-a-war-of-aggression-on-iraq/; *Iraq War Illegal, says Annan*, BBC NEWS, (Sept. 16, 2004), *at* http://news.bbc.co.uk/2/hi/middle_east/3661134.stm; Dutch

Although the sc did not authorize the second Gulf War, for many its failure to prevent an invasion that, after weapons of mass destruction were not found, was deemed to be both unwise and illegal was a blow to optimistic post-Cold War hopes that a "new world order" based on the UN's collective security regime had finally arrived.[84] But while the sc failed to stop the invasion of Iraq in 2003, the absence of express UN authorization for it was cited by many states as justification for rejecting requests to participate in or to financially contribute to that operation. Thanks at least in part to the Council's actions (and inactions), the second Gulf War, unlike the first, was perceived as a far more unilateral operation in which the u.s. and the UK in particular bore the full brunt of the financial and other costs.

The story of the sc and Iraq would not be complete without consideration of Resolutions 1483 and 1546 in which the Council was forced to deal with the consequences of the demise of the Hussein regime. Resolution 1483 recognized the reality that the u.s. and the UK were in fact occupiers of Iraq after Operation Iraqi Freedom.[85] At the same time, that resolution went beyond the settled law regarding the rights and duties of military occupations by according the u.s. and the UK an apparent license to remake Iraqi laws and transform that country's institutions as necessary in order to pave the way for democracy.[86] As commentators have recognized, this seems inconsistent with the 4th Geneva Convention and the Hague Regulation with respect to the law

---

Committee of Inquiry on Iraq, States-General of the Netherlands, Rapport Commissie van Onderzoek Besluitvorming Irak [Report of the Commission of Inquiry on Iraq] 527 (2010), *at* http://vorige.nrc.nl/multimedia/archive/00267/rapport_commissie_i_267285a .pdf; Severin Carrell & Robert Verkaik, *War on Iraq was Illegal, Say Top Lawyers*, THE INDEPENDENT, May 25, 2003, *at* http://www.robincmiller.com/art-iraq/b58.htm.

84   Even if the arguments in favor of the use of force against Iraq based on prior sc resolutions were unconvincing, some blamed the sc in part for not imposing any kind of restriction on the use of force in those resolutions and clarifying the matter. The sc has occasionally passed resolutions whose continuing authority is premised on that authority being renewed by the full vote of the Council. For a fuller account of the changing fortunes of the Council before and after the second Gulf conflict, see Einsiedel et al., *supra* note 5.

85   s.c. Res. 1483 (May 22, 2003). For a fuller discussion see ALVAREZ, *supra* note 7, at 181–183, 214–217. Resolution 1483 was thought to be needed to settle doubts as to who was in a position of effective authority within Iraq. It was not justified or seen as granting the Council's post-hoc permission for the use of force even if such after the fact legal authorization were indeed possible under the Charter.

86   s.c. Res. 1483, *supra* note 85, ¶ 8.

of occupation as well as customary law.[87] That law does not authorize occupiers to change the occupied country's laws or institutions, except as necessary to fulfill the occupying powers' humanitarian duties, for security purposes, and to maintain an orderly government of the territory. Resolution 1483 seemed to license a new kind of occupation regime, best suited to an organization that, as is addressed elsewhere in this monograph, sometimes suggests that it is in the business of promoting the rule of law and democracy.[88] For the U.S. and the UK, Resolution 1483 was a useful tool to legitimize the transformation of Iraqi institutions, including adoption of market reforms. As the British Secretary of State for Foreign and Commonwealth Affairs indicated in 2004:

> The various measures of economic reform undertaken by the Coalition Provisional Authority have been undertaken within occupation law, as supplemented by Security Council Resolution 1483 ... Occupation law does indeed constrain the capacity of an Occupying Power to carry out economic reform.... Legislation to achieve economic reform is permissible under occupation law within ... limits. That position is supplemented by Security Council Resolution 1483, and in particular paragraph 8(e) which envisages assistance to the people of Iraq for the promotion of economic reconstruction.[89]

---

87   Geneva Convention Relative to the Protection of Civilian Persons in Time of War art. 64, Aug. 12, 1949, 75 U.N.T.S. 28 [hereinafter Geneva Convention]; Convention (IV) Respecting the Laws and Customs of War on Land & Annex: Regulations concerning the Laws and Customs of War on Land, Preamble, art. 43, *opened for signature* Oct. 18, 1907, 36 STAT. 2277, 2280, reprinted in 2 AJIL SUPP. 90, 92 (1908) [hereinafter Hague Reg.].

88   David J. Scheffer, *Beyond Occupation Law*, 97 AM. J. INT'L L. 842, 847–848 (2003) (noting that occupation law does not anticipate wholesale change in the occupied state's laws and institutions and does not encourage or facilitate prolonged occupation but is intended to permit only those measures for public order and safety); *see generally* EYAL BENVENISTI, THE INTERNATIONAL LAW OF OCCUPATION (2d ed. 2012). As is further addressed in Chapter VI, all UN bodies, including the Secretary-General, the SC, and the GA, have endorsed the idea that one of the UN's goals is to promote democracy as well as the rule of law. *See, e.g.*, 2005 World Summit Outcome, G.A. Res. A/60/L.1, ¶¶ 134–37 (Sept. 15, 2005), *at* http://www.globalr2p.org/media/files/wsod_2005.pdf. Indeed, according to one study, the SC has passed 69 resolutions from 1998–2006 referring to the "rule of law." *See* JEREMY MATAM FARRALL, UNITED NATIONS SANCTIONS AND THE RULE OF LAW app. 3, tbl. A (2007).

89   FOREIGN AFFAIRS COMMITTEE, FOREIGN POLICY ASPECTS OF THE WAR AGAINST TERRORISM, 2003–04, H.C. 441-I ¶ 81.

Resolution 1483 reflected the desires of the U.S. and the UK in another respect: it recognized the rights of Iraq's occupiers but did not establish any independent UN mechanism to assure that they complied with the rest of occupation law.

Resolution 1546, adopted in 2004, is of a piece with Resolution 1483.[90] It too seems to depart from the formerly settled rules governing occupation. According to Article 42 of the 1907 Hague Regulations, the end of occupation is determined by examining facts on the ground, that is, whether in fact a state's territory is no longer under the authority of a hostile army.[91] Resolution 1546, by contrast, determined in advance and by fiat that the occupation of Iraq would end by June 30, 2004.[92] When that date arrived, however, Iraq seemed as much under effective occupation as before since 161,000 foreign troops not subject to Iraqi authority remained in the country.[93] In another departure from settled law, Resolution 1546 authorized the Multi-National Force (MNF) in Iraq to take all necessary means to contribute to that country's security, including authorizing "internment" (that is, detention without charge or trial) if necessary for imperative reasons of security.[94] As a result, between June 28, 2004 and Dec. 31, 2008, British forces in southern Iraq, as part of the MNF, interned persons under this authority, even though this otherwise would have been in violation of Art. 5(1) of the European Convention of Human Rights (which had been found by the ECtHR applicable to persons detained by British forces in Iraq) and to Article 9 of the ICCPR.[95] The highest British court, in Al Jedda v. Secretary of State for Defence, found that Resolution 1546 in fact exempted the UK from these human rights treaty obligations, only to have the European Court of Human Rights come out against it.[96]

---

90   S.C. Res. 1546 (June 8, 2004).

91   *See* Hague Reg., *supra* note 87, art. 42; BENVENISTI, *supra* note 88.

92   S.C. Res 1546, *supra* note 90, ¶ 1.

93   *See, e.g.*, MICHAEL E. O'HANLON & IAN LIVINGSTON, BROOKINGS INSTITUTE, IRAQ INDEX: TRACKING VARIABLES OF RECONSTRUCTION & SECURITY IN POST-SADDAM IRAQ 22 (Jan. 26, 2010), *at* http://www.brookings.edu/~/media/Centers/saban/iraq-index/index20100126.PDF.

94   *Id.* ¶ 10.

95   Convention for the Protection of Human Rights and Fundamental Freedoms art. 5(1), Nov. 4, 1950, E.T.S. No. 5, 213 U.N.T.S. 222; International Covenant on Civil and Political Rights art. 9, Dec. 16, 1966, G.A. Res. A/21/2200, 999 U.N.T.S. 171.

96   R (on the application of Al-Jedda) v. Sec. of State for Defence, [2007] UKHL 58, [2008] 1 AC 332 (appeal taken from Eng.) [hereinafter Al-Jedda I]; Al-Jedda v. United Kingdom [GC], 2011-IV Eur. Ct. H.R. 305 [hereinafter Al-Jedda II]. For further discussion of these cases, see Erika de Wet, *Holding the United Nations Security Council Accountable for Human Rights Violations Through Domestic and Regional Courts: A Case of "Be Careful What You Wish For?", in* SANCTIONS, ACCOUNTABILITY AND GOVERNANCE IN A GLOBALISED

The Iraq saga highlights one of the curious feature of the SC's contracting out of force: it delegates to others what the Charter anticipates would be undertaken under UN auspices and by the joint efforts of all members of the P-5 under the Military Staff Committee but still permits the Council to determine the terms of the subsequent peace. Of course, the Council has resorted to the contracting out of force on numerous occasions since, including to protect civilians from attack in Libya,[97] to protect the interests of maritime traders against pirates,[98] and to authorize a robust "intervention brigade" in the Congo.[99]

WORLD, 143, 160–161 (Jeremy Farrall & Kim Rubenstein eds., 2009); Erika de Wet, *Holding International Institutions Accountable: The Complementary Role of Non-Judicial Oversight Mechanisms and Judicial Review*, in THE EXERCISE OF PUBLIC AUTHORITY BY INTERNATIONAL INSTITUTIONS: ADVANCING INTERNATIONAL INSTITUTIONAL LAW (Armin von Bogdandy et al. eds., 2010).

97   S.C. Res. 1973 (Mar. 17, 2011). *See* discussion *infra* § 10.

98   S.C. Res. 1816, pmbl. (June 2, 2008) (determining Somalia's lack of capacity to interdict pirates and secure its sea lanes constitutes a threat to international peace); *id.* ¶ 7 (authorizing an international flotilla of some 20 countries cooperating with the Somali federal government to enter the territorial waters of Somalia and use "all necessary measures" to repress acts of piracy and armed robbery at sea); S.C. Res. 1851, ¶ 6 (Dec. 16, 2008) (extending mandates of the cooperating states to allow "all necessary means that are appropriate in Somalia for the purpose of suppressing acts of piracy and armed robbery at sea); S.C. Res. 1950 (Nov. 23, 2010) (reauthorizing states to intervene in acts of piracy by Somali pirates). As with many other contemporary threats to the peace, the SC has also turned to criminalization and incapacitation or other preventive measures. It urged states to change their laws to prevent the illicit financing of piracy and the laundering of proceeds, to cooperate with Interpol and Europol on investigations, and of course to investigate and prosecute those who finance, plan, organize or profit from pirate attacks off the Somali coast. *Id.* ¶¶ 13, 16 & 17; *see also* S.C. Res. 2015 (Oct. 24, 2011); S.C. Res. 2020 (Nov. 22, 2011); S.C. Res. 2077 (Nov. 21, 2012)]; S.C. Res. 1976 (Apr. 11, 2011) (comprehensive resolution towards capacity building needs of Somalia and the region to conquer piracy). For analysis of these piracy actions and their origins, see Clive Schofield & Robin Warner, *Horn of Troubles: Understanding and Addressing the Somali "Piracy" Phenomenon*, in DEEP CURRENTS AND RISING TIDES: THE INDIAN OCEAN AND INTERNATIONAL SECURITY (John Garofano & Andrea J. Dew eds., 2013); INT'L CHAMBER OF COMMERCE INT'L MAR. BUREAU, PIRACY AND ARMED ROBBERY AGAINST SHIPS: 2008 ANNUAL REPORT 26 (2009); Helmut Tuerk, *Piracy and the Law of the Sea, in* REGIONS, INSTITUTIONS, AND LAW OF THE SEA: STUDIES IN OCEAN GOVERNANCE 493 (Harry N. Scheiber & Jin-Hyun Paik eds., 2013); Mario Silva, *Somalia: State Failure, Piracy, and the Challenge to International Law*, 50 VA. J. INT'L L. 553 (2010).

99   S.C. Res. 2098, pmbl., ¶¶ 9, 10 & 12 (Mar. 28, 2013) (finding that the internal conflicts and humanitarian crisis within parts of the DRC constitute a threat to the peace and extending the mandate of MONUSCO to enable that peacekeeping operation to protect civilians,

4   The Council as Extradition Tool

The 1988 bombing of Pan Am flight 103 over Lockerbie, Scotland and the 1989 bombing of Union de Transport Aéries flight 772 over Niger, jointly resulting in the deaths of approximately 441 persons, generated a number of Council resolutions in 1992 aimed at "illegal activities directed against international civil aviation," that is, international terrorism.[100] The first, Resolution 731, made no mention of Chapter VII and urged the Libyan government "to provide a full and effective response" to the requests made by the authorities in France, the U.S., and the UK, that Libya surrender for trial in their national courts two men who they believed to be working for Libyan intelligence, Abdel Basset Ali al-Megrahi and Lamen Khalifa Fhimah.[101] Libya had rejected such requests and had announced that it would undertake its own investigation provided it was accorded cooperation from the U.S., France, and the UK, and claimed

---

"neutralize" armed groups through a new "intervention brigade," monitor the implementation of the arms embargo, and support national and international judicial processes). Of course, this was not the first time that the Congo was the focus of "robust" peacekeeping at the outer edges of that concept. *See, e.g.*, Certain Expenses of the United Nations (Article 17, Paragraph 2 of the Charter), Advisory Opinion, 1962 I.C.J. 151 (July 20). The SC has repeatedly turned its attention to the DRC in more recent times. *See, e.g.*, S.C. Res. 1807 ¶¶ 1, 11 & 13 (Mar. 31, 2008) (authorizing a ban on arms and related material applicable to all non-governmental entities and persons in the country, certain travel restrictions, an assets freeze for certain categories of entities, and smart sanctions on individuals, including leaders of Congolese militias receiving foreign support and those accused of serious violations of international humanitarian law (including the recruitment of child soldiers)). *See also infra* § 8.

100   S.C. Res. 731 pmbl. (Jan. 21, 1992) (condemning the bombing and noting that the investigations conducted by the French, U.S., and UK authorities "implicate officials of the Libyan Government").

101   *Id.* ¶ 3. See also Letter dated 20 December 1991 from the Permanent Representative of France to the United Nations Addressed to the Secretary-General, U.N. Doc. S/23306 (Dec. 31, 1991); Letter dated 20 December 1991 from the Permanent Representative of the United Kingdom of Great Britain and Northern Ireland to the United Nations Addressed to the Secretary-General, U.N. Doc. S/23307 (Dec. 31, 1991); Letter dated 20 December 1991 from the Permanent Representative of the United States of America to the United Nations Addressed to the Secretary-General, U.N. Doc. S/23308 (Dec. 31, 1991); Letter dated 20 December 1991 from the Permanent Representative of France, the United Kingdom of Great Britain and Northern Ireland and the United States of America to the United Nations Addressed to the Secretary-General, U.N. Doc. S/23309 (Dec. 31, 1991); Letter dated 23 December 1991 from the Acting Permanent Representative of the United States of America to the United Nations Addressed to the Secretary-General, U.N. Doc. S/23317 (Dec. 23, 1991).

that it was entitled to do so itself, without surrendering the suspects, under the Montreal Convention for the Suppression of Unlawful Acts Against the Safety of Civil Aviation (Montreal Convention).[102] Faced with Resolution 731, Libya filed identical applications in the ICJ against the U.S. and the UK citing the Montreal Convention as the basis of jurisdiction and its claims.[103] Libya asked the Court for, among other things, provisional relief in the form of orders enjoining the U.S. and the UK "from taking any action against Libya calculated to coerce or compel Libya to surrender the accused individuals to any jurisdiction outside of Libya" pending resolution of the dispute at the ICJ.[104] Libya argued that it had already taken steps to comply with its Montreal Convention obligations by submitting the case to its own competent authorities and that SC interference was therefore contrary to international law.[105] During the oral hearings on Libya's claim for provisional orders, the U.S. and the UK argued that the Court should decline jurisdiction over the case since the SC's seizure of the dispute made the Montreal Convention either irrelevant or inapplicable.[106]

Three days after ICJ oral arguments, however, and prior to the issuance of the Court's opinion, the SC took far more decisive action. It passed Resolution 748, which, citing for the first time Chapter VII, imposed a civil aviation and arms embargo on Libya, while reaffirming "that, in accordance with the principle in Article 2, paragraph 4 of the Charter ... every State has the duty to refrain from organizing, instigating, assisting or participating in terrorist acts in another state or acquiescing in organized activities within its territory directed towards

---

102 *See* Montreal Convention for the Suppression of Unlawful Acts Against the Safety of Civil Aviation, art. 7, Sept. 23, 1971, 974 U.N.T.S. 177 (obligation to prosecute or extradite) & art. 11 (contracting states shall afford to one another assistance in connection with criminal proceedings).

103 *Id.* art. 14 (disputes concerning the interpretation and application of Convention to be submitted to arbitration and failing that to the ICJ).

104 *See* Request for the Indication of Provisional Measures of Protection Submitted by the Government of the Socialist People's Libyan Arab Jamahiriya, Mar. 3, 1992, ¶ 7(a), *at* http://www.icj-cij.org/docket/files/89/13253.pdf. Although the Libyan request for provisional relief does not mention U.S. and UK actions at the SC, it was clearly intended to prevent those governments from taking any action in that body to secure multilateral economic sanctions.

105 Questions of Interpretation and Application of the 1971 Montreal Convention Arising from the Aerial Incident at Lockerbie (Libya v. U.S.), Provisional Measures, 1992 I.C.J. 3, ¶¶ 36–39, (Apr. 14) [hereinafter Libya v. U.S.]; Questions of Interpretation and Application of the 1971 Montreal Convention Arising from the Aerial Incident at Lockerbie (Libya v. U.K.), Provisional Measures, 1992 I.C.J. 114, ¶¶ 36–39 (Apr. 14) [hereinafter Libya v. U.K.].

106 Libya v. U.K., *supra* note 105, ¶ 24; Libya v. U.S., *supra* note 105, ¶¶ 25–29.

the commission of such acts, when such acts involve threat or use of force."[107] The Council decided that Libya "must now comply without any further delay" with the sc's prior demands that it respond to the requests to surrender its two nationals.[108]

Back at the ICJ, the sc's adoption of a binding Chapter VII resolution appeared to make the decisive difference. The very brief majority opinion denying Libya's request for provisional relief by a vote of 11 to 5, turned on the Court's finding that "both Libya and the United States, as Members of the United Nations, are obliged to accept and carry out the decisions of the Security Council in accordance with Security Council Resolution 748," with the Court noting that that Council obligations prevail over the Montreal Convention under Article 103 of the Charter.[109] The Court did not close the door to eventual review should the matter proceed to the merits, indicating only that it was not called upon "at this stage ... to determine definitively the legal effect of Security Council resolution 748" but only that it was not appropriate to indicate the provisional relief that Libya was seeking.[110] It was left to the more fulsome separate opinions of a number of the ICJ judges to address more directly the underlying issues left unresolved by the majority's opinion. A number of the ICJ judges would have been prepared to consider the merits of Libya's claims—and to test whether the sc was in fact acting in accord with international law—if the sc was still in Chapter VI rather than Chapter VII mode and had not taken a binding decision, and if the Court's jurisdiction had been grounded in general international law and not just the Montreal Convention.[111]

---

107   s.c. Res. 748, pmbl., ¶ 6 (Mar. 31, 1992). The sc sanctions on Libya were later strength-ened in 1993 when the sc adopted Resolution 883. In that resolution, the sc, again using Chapter VII, extended the aviation sanctions imposed earlier by requiring the closure of all Libyan Arab Airlines offices within all states and imposing financial freeze orders on funds owned or controlled by the Libyan government. *See* s.c. Res. 883, ¶¶ 3, 6 (Nov. 11, 1993). Significantly, that Resolution did not include what was arguably the most potent type of sanction against Libya: it did not apply the freeze to funds derived from the sale of oil. *See* s.c. Res. 883, ¶ 4.

108   s.c. Res. 748, *supra* note 107, ¶ 1.

109   Libya v. u.s., *supra* note 105, ¶ 42.

110   *Id.* ¶ 43.

111   *See, e.g.,* Libya v. u.s., *supra* note 105 (declaration of Vice-President Oda). For criticism of the view that the ICJ might be able to interfere and second guess the Council when it is seized of a dispute but has not crossed the Chapter VII threshold, see Michael W. Reisman, *The Constitutional Crisis in the United Nations,* 87 AM. J. INT'L L. 83 (1993). For a suggestion that this ICJ's decision constitutes a weak form of "judicial review" in the

Although its request for provisional measures was rejected, Libya won a tactical victory when, on Feb. 27, 1998, the ICJ subsequently rejected the U.S. and the UK's preliminary objections to jurisdiction and admissibility. The Court rejected, 13 to 2, their objections that no dispute actually existed or was inadmissible under the Montreal Convention, and it rejected, 12 to 3, U.S. and UK objections that even if the Convention was applicable it was "superseded" by the SC's Chapter VII sanctions under its Resolutions 748 and 883.[112] The majority upheld the Court's jurisdiction and found Libya's claims admissible because at the time Libya applied to the Court the SC had only adopted Resolution 731 and had not yet taken binding decisions under Chapter VII.[113] The Court also rejected arguments that the Council's later Chapter VII resolutions rendered Libya's claims under the Montreal Convention "moot." The majority found that this objection to its continuing to hear the case would force the Court to address the merits of the case; that is, it would force it to decide at a preliminary stage in the proceedings whether Libya's rights under the Montreal Convention were incompatible with Resolutions 748 and 883 and also to decide whether those obligations prevail over the Montreal Convention under Articles 25 and 103 of the Charter.[114]

For Judge Schwebel, the U.S. judge, the majority ruling in favor of retaining the case on the merits was simply incompatible with the absence of judicial review power over the SC. According to Judge Schwebel:

---

form of dicta not unlike that assumed by the U.S. Supreme Court in Marbury v. Madison, see Thomas M. Franck, The "Powers of Appreciation": Who is the Ultimate Guardian of UN Legality?," 86 AM. J. INT'L L. 519 (1992) (drawing on especially the separate opinion by Judge Shahabuddeen who speculated about whether there were any limits on the Council's powers of appreciation as well as Judge Weeramantry's dissent which was skeptical of the proposition that the SC could discharge its "variegated functions free of all limitations"). *See also* José E. Alvarez, *Judging the Security Council*, 90 AM. J. INT'L L. 1 (1996).

112   Questions of Interpretation and Application of the 1971 Montreal Convention Arising from the Aerial Incident at Lockerbie (Libya v. U.S.), Preliminary Objections, Judgment, 1998 I.C.J. 115, ¶ 40 (Feb. 27) [hereinafter Libya v. U.S. Prelim. Obj.]; Questions of Interpretation and Application of the 1971 Montreal Convention Arising from the Aerial Incident at Lockerbie (Libya v. U.K.), Preliminary Objections, Judgment, 1998 I.C.J. 9, ¶ 37 (Feb. 27) [hereinafter Libya v U.K. Prelim. Obj.].

113   Libya v U.K. Prelim. Obj., *supra* note 112, ¶ 44; Libya v. U.S. Prelim. Obj., *supra* note 112, ¶ 43. The Court specifically rejected U.S. claims that by seizing the Court, Libya was attempting to "undo the Council's actions." *See* Libya v. U.S. Prelim. Obj., *supra* note 112, ¶ 40.

114   Libya v. U.S. Prelim. Obj., *supra* note 112, ¶ 49; Libya v U.K. Prelim. Obj., *supra* note 112, ¶ 50.

Judicial review could have been provided for at San Francisco...but both directly and indirectly it was not in any measure contemplated or enacted...Proposals which in restricted measure would have accorded the Court a degree of authority, by way of advisory proceedings, to pass upon the legality of proposed resolutions of the Security Council in the sphere of peaceful settlement—what came to be Chapter VI of the Charter—were not accepted. What was never proposed, considered, or, so far as the records reveal, even imagined, was that the International Court of Justice would be entrusted with, or would develop, a power of judicial review at large, or a power to supervene, modify, negate or confine the applicability of resolutions of the Security Council...[115]

We will never know what the ICJ would have decided with respect to the merits of Libya's claims—whether it would have reviewed the SC's resolutions for legality and under what standard even if its analysis was restricted to those cognizable under the Montreal Convention—because, in the wake of the ICJ's 1998 decision to proceed to hear Libya's case despite the U.S. and UK objections, the UK persuaded the U.S. to accept a Libyan compromise. Under the agreement struck between the three states, the two Libyan suspects would be transferred for trial but not to the U.S. or the UK: they would be tried in a neutral country by a panel of Scottish judges.[116] Pursuant to that agreement, al-Megrahi and Fhimah were transferred to The Netherlands on April 6, 1999 where they were tried under Scottish criminal law. On Jan. 31, 2001, Al-Megrahi was convicted of murder and sentenced to life imprisonment in Scotland but the charges against Fhimah were deemed "not...proved."[117] Two years later, the U.S., the UK, Libya, and the families of those killed in the Lockerbie bombing entered into an agreement whereby Libya accepted responsibility for that bombing and paid $10 million in compensation to each of the families.[118] The proceedings at the ICJ were subsequently discontinued and the SC agreed to lift the sanctions on Libya on Sept. 13, 2003.[119]

---

115 Libya v. U.S. Prelim. Obj., *supra* note 112 (dissenting opinion of Judge Schwebel), at 168.

116 Agreement Concerning a Scottish Trial in the Netherlands, U.K.–Neth., Sept. 18, 1998, 43 U.K.T.S. 2.

117 Her Majesty's Advocate v. Al Megrahi, ¶ 86 (2001) J.C. (Scot.).

118 For a general account of the Lockerbie cases, see Michael P. Scharf, *The Lockerbie Model of Transfer of Proceedings, in* 2 International Criminal Law: Multilateral and Bilateral Enforcement Mechanisms 521–527 (Cherif M. Bassiouni ed., 2008).

119 *See* S.C. Res. 1506, ¶ 1 (Sept. 12, 2003); Jeffrey L. Dunoff et al., International Law: Norms, Actors, Process: A Problem-oriented Approach 915–916 (3d ed. 2010).

In retrospect, the Council's imposition of sanctions on Libya in 1992–1993 accomplished a number of things: the sanctions compelled Libya to comply with U.S. and UK demands that it surrender two alleged Libyan terrorists whom authorities in those countries had charged with terrorism; thwarted a possible decision by the ICJ that, it was feared, could "second-guess" the Council by engaging in judicial review over it; and encouraged ongoing state-to-state negotiations that ultimately resulted in an unprecedented criminal trial under Scottish law conducted in The Netherlands.[120] By all these measures, the Council's actions were a success.[121] But this was a success that was built on a number of Council innovations that, at least when originally taken, were not uniformly praised as in conformity with the law of the Charter.[122]

In that instance, the Council was responding, in 1992, to a threat to the peace that had occurred in 1988 and 1989, where there was no evidence that the subject of the Council's actions—the two Libyan suspects—posed a continuing threat to the international peace. The SC appeared to be saying that Libya's failure to transfer the alleged terrorists was itself a threat to the peace. If so, the SC seemed to be acting less like the global police force anticipated by the Charter than as an adjudicator which had determined that the demands for the surrender of suspects issued by some members of the P-5 were meritorious and should be enforced. But in this instance, the SC encountered a third intervening actor waiting in the wings: the ICJ. Libya's resort to the Court appeared to have affected at least the timing of the Council's actions. It is hard to believe that but for the Court, the SC would have crossed over into Chapter VII when it did. Moreover, it seems likely that the Court's 1998 decision to retain jurisdiction over the case encouraged the compromise that was finally reached among the parties and triggered the end of the Council's and the ICJ's involvement in the case. As legal commentary has since pointed out, in that instance the ICJ's

---

120   S.C. Res. 748 (Mar. 31, 1992).

121   For a generally positive assessment, see IAN HURD, AFTER ANARCHY: LEGITIMACY AND POWER IN THE UNITED NATIONS SECURITY COUNCIL 137–170 (2007).

122   See, e.g., ENHANCING THE RULES OF LAW THROUGH THE INTERNATIONAL COURT OF JUSTICE 59 (Giorgio Gaja & Jenny Grote Stoutenburg eds., 2014) (arguing that the Security Council acted as a judge in ruling on the responsibility of a State and imposing sanctions related to this responsibility was an "excès de pouvoir"); see also Libya v. U.K.: Prelim. Obj. supra note 112, ¶ 33 (dissenting Opinion of Judge ad hoc El-Kosheri); Bernhard Graefrath, Leave to the Court What Belongs to the Court: The Libyan Case, 4 EUR. J. INT'L L. 204 (1993). For a more general assessment of how the SC and scholars should examine the challenges raised by the SC acting as "judge," see Ian Johnstone, Legislation and Adjudication in the UN Security Council: Bringing down the Deliberative Deficit, 102 AM. J. INT'L L. 275 (2008).

judges introduced the possibility that someday it or perhaps another international or national court would opine that the sc, even when acting under
Chapter vii, is subject to some legal limits, despite the primacy accorded to its
decisions under Article 103.[123]

Resolutions 731, 748, and 883 are, most obviously, precursors to the Council's
numerous post-9/11 reactions to acts of terrorism—and not just to the classic
inter-state aggression that Article 2(4) anticipates.[124] In that instance, the sc
transformed itself into an agent for extradition.[125] In the end the sc's innovations with respect to the Lockerbie case—and Libya's creative resort to the
icj in response—inspired a novel diplomatic solution that bridged the worlds
of international and national criminal justice. The competing pressures of
Council action/icj threat ultimately drove the state parties to a compromise
that few would have foreseen at the outset but that, in retrospect, seems close
in spirit to some of the Council's later hybrid approaches to achieving international criminal justice, the subject of the next section.

5   The Council and *Ad Hoc* War Criminal Tribunals

In 1993, the Council found an additional tool for maintaining international
peace and security: *ad hoc* criminal tribunals. The story of how the sc came
to establish first the icty and one year later the ictr has been ably told elsewhere and requires but short summary here.[126] In order to establish these
tribunals pursuant to Chapter vii the sc had first to cross the threshold of
Article 39. It did so by finding that "flagrant violations of international humanitarian law" occurring within the territories of the former Yugoslavia and
Rwanda constituted threats to the international peace and that "in the particular circumstances" restoration and maintenance of peace requires establishment of an international tribunal to prosecute the responsible parties as
a tool that would contribute to halting such violations and effectively redress-
ing them.[127]

---

123   *See, e.g.*, Alvarez, *supra* note 111.

124   This is particularly true since at the time when the sc was initially seized with the
      Lockerbie case it was not entirely clear whether the alleged terrorists had been directed
      by the Libyan government.

125   For further analysis of this institutional arrangement, see for example, Donna Arzt, *The
      Lockerbie "Extradition by Analogy" Agreement: "Exceptional Measure" or Template for
      Transnational Criminal Justice?*, 18 Am. U. Int'l L. Rev. 208 (2002).

126   Richard Ashby Wilson, Writing History in International Criminal Trials
      24 (2011). *See also* Alvarez, *supra* note 7, at 172, 176–177.

127   s.c. Res. 827, pmbl., para. 3 (May 25, 1993); s.c. Res. 955, pmbl., para. 4 (Nov. 8, 1994).

The justifications offered for turning to Chapter VII to establish the ICTY were summarized in the Secretary-General's report that was annexed to Resolution 827. According to the Secretary-General, the Council was empowered to establish the tribunal because the alternatives—conclusion of a treaty or action by the General Assembly—would simply take too long or offered no guarantees that they would prove effective if relevant states proved unwilling to cooperate. The SC could and should act because it could do so quickly and could use its binding enforcement power. The Secretary-General stressed that the tribunal would be "circumscribed in scope and purpose," would not be a permanent court,[128] and its jurisdiction would be limited to prosecuting existing international crimes that would not violate the principle of *nullum crimen sine lege*.[129] With respect to the SC's legal authority for establishing the tribunal, the Secretary-General pointed out that the Council had established "subsidiary organs for a variety of purposes" under Resolution 687 with respect to Iraq and that:

> In this particular case, the Security Council would be establishing, as an enforcement measure under Chapter VII, a subsidiary organ within the terms of Article 29 of the Charter, but one of a judicial nature. This organ would, of course, have to perform its functions independently of political considerations; it would be subject to the authority or control of the Security Council with regard to the performance of its judicial functions. As an enforcement measure under Chapter VII, however, the life span of the international tribunal would be linked to the restoration and maintenance of international peace and security in the territory of the former Yugoslavia, and Security Council decisions related thereto.[130]

---

128   U.N. Secretary-General, Report of the Secretary-General Pursuant to Paragraph 2 of the Security Council Resolution 808, ¶ 12, U.N. Doc. S/25704 (May 3, 1993) [hereinafter S-G Report, Res. 808].

129   *Id.* ¶ 34.

130   *Id.* ¶ 28. The ICTY itself had occasion to revisit the legal authorities under which it was established in the course of deciding the first defendant's objections to that Court's jurisdiction. *See* Prosecutor v. Tadić, Case No. IT-94-1-I, Decision on Defence Motion for Interlocutory Appeal on Jurisdiction, (Int'l Crim. Trib. For the Former Yugoslavia Oct. 2, 1995) [hereinafter Tadic]. In that case, Tadic attempted to argue without success that the Council had no power to establish such tribunals given the lack of authority in the Charter. Similar challenges before the STL have also been unsuccessful. *See* Decision on the Defence Challenges to the Jurisdiction and Legality of the Tribunal, Ayyash and others (STL-11-01/PT/TC) (Special Trib. For Lebanon July 27, 2012); Decision on the Defence Appeals Against the Trial Chamber's 'Decision on the Defence Challenges to the Jurisdiction and Legality of the Tribunal', Ayyash and others (STL-11-01/PT/AC/AR90.1),

Notably, in the cases of the ICTY and ICTR, the Council delegated to the UN Secretariat the drafting of statutes to establish these tribunals in The Hague and in Arusha respectively.[131] In doing so, the SC was resurrecting the long-sought ideal, in abeyance since Nuremberg, that international crimes should be heard by an international court.[132] The draft statutes produced by the Secretary-General, subsequently incorporated into the respective Chapter VII Council resolutions establishing the two tribunals, were the product of wide consultation with member states, interested NGOs, and comments received from the International Committee of the Red Cross (IRC) and other expert associations of lawyers.[133] The specific language included in the statute reflected a number of texts proposing such courts, including those proposed by the International Law Commission (ILC) and the International Law Association.[134] Under the statute for the ICTY, essentially replicated a year later when the Council established the ICTR, both tribunals enjoyed jurisdictional "primacy over the national courts of all states," including over the courts in the nations where the crimes took place.[135]

As is addressed in Chapter V of this monograph, notwithstanding the contention that the ICTY and the ICTR were merely applying long-established crimes, the two tribunals' subsequent case law contributed immensely to international criminal law. Even though both statutes contained definitions of war crimes, crimes against humanity, and genocide (ostensibly drawn from relevant treaty and customary law), these definitions left many interpreta-

---

Appeals Chamber (Oct. 24, 2012). For a critique of the STL decision, see José Alvarez, *Tadić Revisited: The Ayyash Decisions of the Special Tribunal for Lebanon*, 11 J. INT'L CRIM. JUS. 291–302 (2013). Notably, in the Tadic case, the ICTY's Appellate Body suggested that the General Assembly, which had established an administrative tribunal to decide UN employee disputes, also had the power to establish courts under its power to establish "subsidiary organs" under Charter Article 22. Tadić, *supra* at ¶ 15.

131 S.C. Res. 827 (May. 25, 1993) (establishing the ICTY); S.C. Res. 955 (Nov. 8, 1994) (establishing the ICTR).

132 In 1989, the GA tasked the ILC with drafting a statute for such an international court. *See* G.A. Res. 44/39 (Dec. 4, 1989). *See also* Affirmation of the Principles of International Law Recognized by the Charter of the Nuremberg Tribunal, G.A. Res. 95/1, U.N. Doc. A/64. Add.1 (Dec. 11, 1946).

133 *See, e.g.*, S-G Report, Res. 808, *supra* note 128, ¶¶ 13–14.

134 *Id.* ¶ 17.

135 Statute of the International Criminal Tribunal for Rwanda arts. 8(2), S.C. Res. 955, annex (Nov. 8, 1994), 33 I.L.M. 1598 (1994) [hereinafter ICTR Statute]; Statute of the International Criminal Tribunal for the Former Yugoslavia, Art. 9(2), S.C. Res. 827, annex (May 25, 1993), 32 I.L.M. 1203 (1993) [hereinafter ICTY Statute].

tive gaps to be filled. This was true particularly since, but for Nuremberg (which never even addressed the crime of genocide which was only defined via treaty in 1948), and a handful of national prosecutions, there had been very little judicial guidance as to the meaning of these crimes, the legal forms of co-participation in them, or the relevant international rules of criminal procedure.[136] Whether or not the Council foresaw the consequences, it is now clear that contemporary international criminal law would have remained in a rudimentary state but for the establishment of these tribunals and the steady accretion of relevant precedents that they produced. Indeed, but for the Council's actions in 1993 and 1994, in all likelihood the International Criminal Court would probably not have emerged scarcely a decade later.[137] Even the provisions of the ICC's Rome Statute that differ from the corresponding ones in the ICTY's and ICTR's respective statutes—such as the ICC's turn to complementarity instead of primacy with respect to national courts—can best be explained as considered reactions to the experience gained from the preceding *ad hoc* tribunals.[138]

The establishment of the two *ad hoc* tribunals also revived conversations and sometimes heated debates, not seen since Nuremberg, about the relative merits of handing over responsibility for prosecuting international crimes to international judges located outside the territories where the crimes were committed and having little direct connection to the local laws or national judges where the crimes were committed.[139] Debates also ensued over whether the *ad hoc* tribunals were focusing equal attention on prosecuting all persons from the respective countries, irrespective of whether they were Hutu or Tutsi, Croat or Serb.[140] With respect to Rwanda there were considerable tensions, particularly initially, over the ICTR's assertion of primary jurisdiction given

---

136   See, e.g., Theodor Meron, War Crimes Law Comes of Age 228–242 (1998); Theodor Meron, The Making of International Criminal Justice: A View From the Bench: Selected Speeches 239 (2011).

137   See also Chapter v infra.

138   Rome Statute of the International Criminal Court art. 17, July 17, 1998, 2187 U.N.T.S. 90 (providing that cases are inadmissible in the ICC where the case is being investigated or prosecuted by a state that has jurisdiction over the case). For a discussion on how some of the experiences of the ICTY and ICTR led to provisions in the Rome Statute, see, for example, Leena Grover, *A Call to Arms: Fundamental Dilemmas Confronting the Interpretation of Crimes in the Rome Statute of the International Criminal Court*, 21 Eur. J. Int'l L. 543, 549–553 (2010).

139   See, e.g., José E. Alvarez, *Rush to Closure: Lessons of the Tadić Judgment*, 96 Mich. L. Rev. 2031, 2039–2040, 2095 (1998); José E. Alvarez, *Crimes of States/Crimes of Hate: Lessons from Rwanda*, 24 Yale J. Int'l L. 365, 415–416 (1999).

140   Alvarez, *Rush to Closure, supra* note 139, at 2039.

that its Tutsi-led regime was only too willing to prosecute the Hutus deemed responsible for the vast bulk of the crimes within that Court's jurisdiction.[141] In parts of what was the former Yugoslavia as well as in Rwanda, the two tribunals have been viewed with some skepticism, even though to the surprise of many of their initial critics the two tribunals managed to arrest and try all those it had indicted.[142] Over time, the financial implications of the two *ad hoc* tribunals and the considerable time they have taken to complete trials and appeals have also generated controversy.[143]

---

141   Alvarez, *Crimes of Hate, supra* note 139, at 393; *see also* Christine M. Venter, *Eliminating Fear Through Recreating Community in Rwanda: The Role of Gacaca Courts*, 12 Tex. Wesleyan L. Rev. 577, 580 (2007) (referring to the international community's condemnation of Rwandan "show trials" and public executions); Emily Amick, *Trying International Crimes on Local Lawns: The Adjudication of Genocide Sexual Violence Crimes in Rwanda's Gacaca Courts*, 20 Colum. J. Gender & L. 1 (2011) (noting the one-sidedness of Tutsi prosecutions and discussing the appropriateness of local gacaca courts for trying crimes of sexual violence).

142   Press Release, President Meron congratulates the ICTR on 20th anniversary (Nov. 7, 2014), *at* http://www.icty.org/sid/11573 ("Since its inception 20 years ago, the ICTR has indicted 93 individuals and has sentenced 61 of these individuals for genocide, war crimes, and crimes against humanity."); Bringing Justice to Thousands of Victims and Giving them a Voice, *at* http://www.icty.org/sid/324#bringing (noting that the ICTY has indicted 161 accused for crimes committed against many thousands of victims during the conflicts in Croatia (1991–1995), Bosnia and Herzegovina (1992–1995), Kosovo (1998–1999) and the Former Yugoslav Republic of Macedonia (2001)). For a description of public opinion polls on the ICTY among locals, see Dr. Mladen Ostojic, Between Justice and Stability: The Politics of War Crimes Prosecutions in Post-Milošević Serbia 112 (2014) (noting that despite the ICTY's relative success, public opinion polls carried out throughout the 2000s show that local populations mistrusted the ICTY and that people generally believed that the Court was biased against their community). *See also* Organization for Security and Co-operation in Europe, Public Opinion Survey on Attitudes towards the ICTY and Domestic War Crimes Trials (Dec. 8, 2009), *at* http://www.osce.org/serbia/40751.

143   The financial consequences of the tribunals were especially controversial in years such as 2004 when the two tribunals' annual expenditures consumed roughly 15 percent of the UN's annual budget. *See* U.N. Secretary-General, The Rule of Law and Transitional Justice in Conflict and Post-Conflict Societies, ¶ 42, U.N. Doc. S/2004/616 (Aug. 23, 2004); *see also* Ralph Zacklin, *The Failings of Ad Hoc International Tribunals*, 2 J. Int'l Crim. Jus. 541, 541–545 (2004) ("[T]he ICTY and ICTR have grown into enormous and extremely costly bureaucratic machines that outstrip or rival in size many of the specialized agencies of the United Nations, and dwarf core offices and departments of the UN Secretariat."). *But see* David Wippman, *The Costs of International Justice*, 100 Am. J. Int'l L. 861, 872 (2006) (noting that the high costs of the ICTY in comparison to U.S. domestic law enforcement

The Council's establishment of the Special Court of Sierra Leone (SCSL) in 2000 relied on the ICTY and ICTR precedents but was unique in a number of respects. Under Resolution 1315 that tribunal was established as a result of an agreement, requested by the Council, between the UN Secretary General and the government of Sierra Leone.[144] It is representative of what have been called a "second generation" of country-specific internationalized "hybrid" criminal tribunals established, at least partially, in reaction to the criticisms of the ICTR and ICTY and responsive to the particularized concerns of different contexts.[145]

While the SCSL enjoys primacy over national prosecutions in Sierra Leone, as a product of a treaty between the UN and Sierra Leone whose negotiation was delegated to the Secretary-General, it lacks the power possessed by the ICTY and the ICTR to assert primacy over national courts of third states, and it cannot, on its own accord, attempt to order the surrender of an accused located in such third states.[146] In addition, the SCSL differs from the ICTY and ICTR insofar as it is a genuine hybrid in terms of its core personnel: unlike those tribunals, its judges, at both the trial and appellate levels, include international judges elected by the GA, as well as judges appointed by the Sierra Leone

can be attributed to a variety of factors including the length and complexity of international criminal trials).

144   *See* S.C. Res. 1315, ¶ 1 (Aug. 14, 2000); Agreement between the United Nations and the Government of Sierra Leone on the Establishment of a Special Court for Sierra Leone, U.N.–Sierra Leone, Jan. 16, 2002, 2178 U.N.T.S. 137 [hereinafter U.N.–Sierra Leone Agreement]; *see also* Agreement between the United Nations and the Government of Sierra Leone on the Establishment of a Residual Special Court for Sierra Leone, Aug. 11, 2010, with annexed Statute of the Residual Special Court for Sierra Leone (the essential remaining functions of the SCSL are now performed by the Residual Special Court for Sierra Leone (RSCSL) as the SCSL was officially closed on Dec. 2, 2013).

145   Other tribunals in addition to the SCSL and the SCL not explored here include the Extraordinary Chambers in the Courts of Cambodia, the War Crimes Chamber in the Court of Bosnia and Herzegovina, the East Timor Special Panels, and the Kosovo Regulations 34 and 64 Panels. William A. Schabas, *International Criminal Courts, in* THE OXFORD HANDBOOK OF INTERNATIONAL ADJUDICATION 207–208 (Cesare Romano et. al eds., 2013).

146   Statute of the Special Court for Sierra Leone arts. 1–8, Jan. 16, 2002, 2178 U.N.T.S. 145 [hereinafter SCSL Statute]. *See also* U.N. Secretary-General, Establishment of a Special Court for Sierra Leone, ¶ 10, U.N. Doc. S/2009/915 (Oct. 4, 2000) (noting that the court lacks primacy over national courts in third states); WILLIAM A. SCHABAS, THE INTERNATIONAL CRIMINAL TRIBUNALS: THE FORMER YUGOSLAVIA, RWANDA AND SIERRA LEONE 58–59 (2006) (noting that like the two *ad hoc* tribunals, the SCSL is free to appeal to the Security Council to assist it in executing orders and also shares a relationship with the UN as a result of its mode of creation).

government.[147] Its subject matter jurisdiction is also a hybrid—it has jurisdiction over violations of international humanitarian law and crimes against
humanity, but also for crimes under Sierra Leonean law.[148] Despite these
important differences, the SCSL is linked to the ICTY and ICTR in terms of
applicable substantive law. The SCSL's judges are supposed to be guided by the
decisions of the appeals chamber of the ICTY and the ICTR and are directed to
apply the rules of procedure of the latter except as are amended by its judges.[149]

Resolution 1315 was concluded in the wake of a number of prior steps by
the government of Sierra Leone required under the Lomé Peace Agreement,
which required, among other things, the creation of national truth and reconciliation process.[150] That Lomé Agreement included a note by the signature
of the representative of the Secretary-General indicating his understanding
that its amnesty provisions would not apply to the international crimes of
genocide, crimes against humanity, war crimes, and other serious violations
of international humanitarian law.[151] Resolution 1315 significantly "recalls"
this statement in its preamble.[152] In doing so, the SC appeared to endorse the
legal conclusion, affirmed later by the SCSL in a decision on jurisdiction, that
the Lomé Agreement did not authorize an amnesty for international crimes.[153]
Some have seen a greater significance in this and other Council actions that

---

147   SCSL Statute, *supra* note 146, arts. 12–13.

148   *Id.* art. 5 (containing provisions from Offences Relating to the Abuse of Girls under the
      Prevention of Cruelty to Children Act, 1926, Offences Relating to the Wanton Destruction
      of Property under the Malicious Damage Act, 1861).

149   *Id.* art. 20(3) ("The judges of the Appeals Chamber of the Special Court shall be guided
      by the decisions of the Appeals Chamber of the International Tribunals for the former
      Yugoslavia and for Rwanda. In the interpretation and application of the laws of Sierra
      Leone, they shall be guided by the decisions of the Supreme Court of Sierra Leone.").

150   Peace Agreement Between the Government of Sierra Leone and the Revolutionary
      United Front of Sierra Leone art XXVI, July 9, 1999, U.N. Doc. S/1999/777 annex (July 12,
      1999) [hereinafter Lomé Agreement].

151   *See* S.C. Res. 1315, *supra* note 144, pmbl., ¶ 5 ("Recalling that the Special Representative
      of the Secretary-General appended to his signature of the Lomé Agreement a statement
      that the United Nations holds the understanding that the amnesty provisions of the
      Agreement shall not apply to international crimes of genocide, crimes against humanity,
      war crimes and other serious violations of international humanitarian law.").

152   *Id.*

153   Prosecutor v. Kallon, Case Nos. SCSL-2004-15-AR72(E) & SCSL-2004–16-AR72(E), Decision
      on Jurisdiction (Mar. 13, 2004) [hereinafter Lomé Decision]. The Kallon decision is the
      first ruling by an international criminal tribunal that unequivocally found that amnesties
      provided within a separate agreement are not a bar to the prosecution of international
      crimes before international or foreign courts.

affirm the need for international criminal accountability or assert that forms of transitional justice are needed to restore or maintain international peace and security. It is possible to interpret Resolution 1315, albeit addressed to "the particular circumstances of Sierra Leone,"[154] as suggesting that general amnesties for established international crimes are no longer valid either under the Charter or perhaps emerging customary international law.[155]

The experience of the SCSL suggests that even when an international court is established via a separate treaty, the Council may still be tempted to intercede with respect to that Court's operation—and perhaps depart from customary international law. When it became impossible to try Charles Taylor in the SCSL because of potential threats to regional stability, peace, and security, the Council, acting under Chapter VII, passed Resolution 1688. That Resolution took note that under the Agreement between the UN and Sierra Leone, the SCSL was authorized to exercise its functions away from its seat and that The Netherlands was willing to host the SCSL and allow the premises normally used by the ICC to detain and try Taylor.[156] Accordingly, acting under Chapter VII, the Council determined that the SCSL would retain exclusive jurisdiction over Taylor during his transfer to and presence in The Netherlands.[157] In doing so, the Council facilitated Taylor's trial in The Hague and formally precluded The Netherlands from exercising its own jurisdiction over Taylor when it might have been able to do otherwise under customary international law principles

---

154   S.C. Res. 1315, *supra* note 144, pmbl., ¶ 7.

155   For a debate in the literature on the legality of amnesties, see Michael P. Scharf, *The Letter of the Law: The Scope of the International Legal Obligation to Prosecute Human Rights Crimes*, 59 LAW & CONTEMP. PROBS. 41, 58–59 (noting several concerns with the reasoning that there is a customary international law duty to prosecute crimes against humanity); John Dugard, *Dealing with Crimes of a Past Regime: Is Amnesty Still an Option?*, 12 LEIDEN J. INT'L L. 1001, 1003–1004 (1999) (noting that it is doubtful whether international law has reached the stage of prohibiting amnesties, but that it is moving in this direction); *see also* Mark Freeman & Max Pensky, *The Amnesty Controversy in International Law, in* AMNESTY IN THE AGE OF HUMAN RIGHTS ACCOUNTABILITY: COMPARATIVE AND INTERNATIONAL PERSPECTIVES 42 (Francesca Lessa & Leigh A. Payne eds., 2012) (offering a critical reconstruction on the amnesty debate). *See also* Lomé Decision, *supra* note 153, ¶¶ 71–72 (noting that the amnesties granted by the Sierra Leone government cannot extend to international crimes subject to universal jurisdiction). *But see* LOUISE MALLINDER, AMNESTY, HUMAN RIGHTS AND POLITICAL TRANSITIONS: BRIDGING THE PEACE AND JUSTICE DIVIDE 19 (2008) (noting that by some measures states have increased their resort to amnesties).

156   S.C. Res. 1688, pmbl., para. 3, ¶ 2 (June 16, 2006).

157   *Id.* ¶ 7.

of universal jurisdiction or passive personality.[158] As is discussed further in Chapter VI, although the SCSL was yet another *ad hoc* tribunal operating alongside the permanent ICC, its decisions can sometimes raise systemic questions about general international criminal law no less than those issued by the ICC.

The Council's establishment of another hybrid criminal court, the Special Tribunal for Lebanon (STL) illustrates other Council innovations. In that instance, while Lebanon and the UN had concluded an agreement to establish the STL, the agreement proved controversial within the Lebanese parliament which delayed giving its consent. In response, the Council, acting under Chapter VII, decided that the Lebanon-UN agreement in question, annexed to its resolution, would enter into force as of June 10, 2007 unless the Lebanese government provided notification before that date.[159] In the absence of such notification, the STL came into being as a result.[160] Accordingly, while the STL was the subject of separate treaty as was the Special Court of Sierra Leone, the latter was established by Council fiat no less than the ICTY or ICTR.[161] Resolution 1757 in effect set an ultimatum for Lebanon to ratify a treaty and when the deadline passed effectively imposed the provisions of that treaty on that country.[162]

---

158   S.C. Res. 1688, *supra* note 156.

159   Agreement between the United Nations and the Lebanese Republic on the Establishment of a Special Tribunal for Lebanon, U.N.–Lebanon, Feb. 6, 2007, 2461 U.N.T.S. 257 [hereinafter UN-SL Agreement] and Statute of the Special Tribunal for Lebanon, S.C. Res. 1757 annex (May 30, 2007) [hereinafter STL Statute].

160   U.N. Secretary-General, Report of the Secretary-General Submitted Pursuant to Security Council Resolution 1757, ¶ 3, U.N. Doc. S/2007/525 (Sept. 4, 2007).

161   Indeed, this aspect of Resolution 1757 led five Council members to abstain. Russia's statement was quite pointed: "The arrangement chosen by the sponsors is dubious from the point of view of international law. The treaty between the two entities—Lebanon and the United Nations—by definition cannot enter into force on the basis of a decision by only one party. The constituent documents for the Tribunal, imposed by a unilateral decision of a United Nations body—that is, a Security Council resolution—essentially represents an encroachment upon the sovereignty of Lebanon. We do not believe that the establishment of a special tribunal by decision of the Council under Chapter VII of the Charter is warranted. There is no basis for a reference to Chapter VII in the draft resolution." *See* U.N. SCOR, 62nd Sess., 5685th mtg. at 5, U.N. Doc. S/PV.5685 (May 30, 2007).

162   As discussed above, Resolution 687 contained comparable impositions of a treaty on a target state but in that instance Iraq had been the subject of UN-authorized use of force and was, for all practical purposes, deemed an aggressor nation that posed a continuing threat to the international peace (at least in the judgment of the Council). No such determination was made with respect to Lebanon.

The mode of establishment for the STL is not its only controversial feature. Unlike the other criminal tribunals, the STL's jurisdiction covers a single event: the 2005 assassination of former Prime Minister Hariri and 22 others.[163] Its jurisdiction over attacks between Oct. 1, 2004 and Dec. 12, 2005 must be "connected" and be of a nature and gravity similar to the Hariri attack.[164] Unlike the SCSL, which is charged with atrocities committed during the course of an approximate 11-year civil war subject to some temporal limits, the STL may end up holding a single trial.[165] Not surprisingly, for its critics, the STL is the most prominent example of the Council's resort to "selective" justice.[166] It is also unique within Council-generated *ad hoc* criminal courts insofar as it does not enjoy jurisdiction over any international crimes but only over acts of "terrorism, crimes and offences against life and personal integrity," including criminal participation and conspiracy, under the Lebanese criminal code.[167] In this instance, what makes this tribunal "international" is not the law that it applies or the crimes over which it has jurisdiction, but that it was established through the SC, that all its judges and officials are not from Lebanon, that part of its funding comes from the UN, and that its seat is, as with respect to a number of other international courts, in The Hague.[168] The STL is also unusual (and controversial) insofar as it purports to have authority to conduct trials in the absence of the accused.[169] This was a concession to reality insofar as it was assumed that some of the alleged perpetrators might be in Syria.[170]

---

163   STL Statute, *supra* note 159, art. 1.

164   *Id.*

165   *Id.*

166   *See, e.g.*, David Tolbert, *Introduction: A Very Special Tribunal, in* THE SPECIAL TRIBUNAL FOR LEBANON: LAW AND PRACTICE 2–3 (Amal Alamuddin et al. eds., 2014).

167   *See* STL Statute, *supra* note 159, art. 2. The sui generis nature of the STL is indeed recognized by many scholars. *See, e.g.*, Nidal Nabil Jurdi, *The Subject-Matter Jurisdiction of the Special Tribunal for Lebanon*, 5 J. INT'L CRIM. JUS. (2007).

168   *See* JUDGES OF THE SPECIAL TRIBUNAL FOR LEBANON, *at* http://www.stl-tsl.org/en/about-the-stl/biographies/judges-of-the-special-tribunal-for-lebanon (describing the presence of four Lebanese judges and seven international judges). Article 5 of the STL Agreement provides that 51 percent of the expenses of the Tribunal are to be borne by voluntary contributions from States and 49 percent by Lebanon. *See* Giorgio Tortora, *The Financing of the Special Tribunal for Lebanon, Cambodia and Lebanon, in* THE REALITIES OF INTERNATIONAL CRIMINAL JUSTICE 120 (Dawn L. Rothe et al. eds., 2013).

169   STL Statute, *supra* note 159, art. 22. *See* Paola Gaeta, *Trial in Absentia before the Special Tribunal for Lebanon, in* THE SPECIAL TRIBUNAL FOR LEBANON: LAW AND PRACTICE 230 (Amal Alamuddin et al. eds., 2014) (canvassing the procedure for holding a trial in absentia and addressing the human rights implications).

170   A decision has been taken to hold a trial presently before the STL in absentia. *See* Prosecutor v. Ayyash, Case No. STL-11-01/I/TC, Decision to Hold Trial in Absentia (Feb. 1, 2012).

If the STL is seen as the relevant precedent, the Council's turn to creating criminal courts as tools to handle threats to the peace is no longer restricted to tribunals charged with prosecuting international crimes. On the other hand, the fact the STL was established by the SC may have helped to convince its judges that even though the STL is formally limited to adjudicating crimes under Lebanese law, it can also make pronouncements concerning international law.[171] In a decision that astounded some observers given its potential implications, the STL's Appeals Chamber handed down a landmark ruling in response to its prosecutor's request for guidance on its sealed indictments. That Appeals Chamber, in a ruling signed by Presiding Judge Antonio Cassese, opined that there now existed a customary international law offense of "terrorism" consisting of the following key elements:

> (i) the perpetration of a criminal act (such as murder, kidnapping, hostage-taking, arson, and so on), or threatening such an act; (ii) the intent to spread fear among the population (which would generally entail the creation of public danger) or directly or indirectly coerce a national or international authority to take some action, or to refrain from taking it; (iii) when the act involves a transnational element.[172]

The Chamber's resort to international law was useful insofar as it permitted the STL to go beyond Lebanese law and declare that attacks committed using rifles or handguns, and not weapons that are more likely to endanger the general

---

171   See Michael P. Scharf, *Special Tribunal for Lebanon Issues Landmark Ruling on Definition of Terrorism and Modes of Participation*, ASIL INSIGHTS (Mar. 4, 2011), *at* http://www.asil .org/insights/volume/15/issue/6/special-tribunal-lebanon-issues-landmark-ruling-defini tion-terrorism-and (noting that the STL's Appeals Chamber read the crime of terrorism under Lebanese law and its gaps in light of international law which is presumed to be applicable). Scharf also points out the Presiding Judge of the Appeals Chamber at the time, Antonio Cassese, was a prominent international law scholar who was instrumental in some of the leading decisions issued by the ICTY in its early days. *See id.* n. 3.

172   Case No. STL-11-01/I, Interlocutory Decision on the Applicable Law: Terrorism, Conspiracy, Homicide, Perpetration, Cumulative Charging ¶¶ 83, 85 (16 February 2011) (noting that "although it is held by many scholars and other legal experts that no widely accepted definition of terrorism evolved in the world society because of the marked difference of views of some issues, closer scrutiny reveals that in fact such a definition has gradually emerged") [hereinafter Interlocutory Decision]. *See, e.g.,* Nidal Nabil Jurdi, *The Crime of Terrorism in Lebanese and International Law, in* THE SPECIAL TRIBUNAL FOR LEBANON: LAW AND PRACTICE 230 (Amal Alamuddin et al eds., 2014) (commenting on the findings of the Appeals Chamber on a definition for a customary international crime of terrorism).

population, are nonetheless within that Court's jurisdiction over terrorism.[173] As commentators have pointed out, this is the first time that an international tribunal has decided that terrorism is a general crime under international law and purported to define it.[174]

Moreover, even though the STL drew support for its conclusion on applicable custom from the over one dozen multilateral counter-terrorism conventions now in force and the preambles in numerous GA and SC resolutions, the STL's three-pronged definition of the ostensible customary crime of terrorism encompass actions far beyond the specific attacks that are now covered by, for example, the ICAO-generated counter-terrorism conventions cited by the STL (which impose obligations to extradite or prosecute individuals who, for example, hijack planes or bomb international airports).[175] Along the way, the STL noted that since Article 3 of the STL Statute on principles of liability was based on the Statutes of the ICTY and ICTR, "it reflects the status of customary international law as articulated in the case law of the *ad hoc* tribunals."[176] It is unclear whether these STL interpretations of what it considers to be customary law will have consequences on how the international community criminalizes terrorist acts and on continuing efforts to negotiate a comprehensive agreement on terrorism within the General Assembly.[177]

6   The Council and the "Right to Democracy"

Resolution 940 from 1994, another instance in which the Council "contracted out" the use of force as has become its usual practice, is worthy of special

---

173   Interlocutory Decision, *supra* note 172, ¶¶ 59, 138 & 145.

174   Scharf, *Special Tribunal, supra* note 171.

175   *See, e.g.*, Protocol for the Suppression of Unlawful Acts of Violence at Airports Serving International Civil Aviation, Dec. 22, 1990, 1589 U.N.T.S. 474; *see generally* United Nations, United Nations Actions to Combat Terrorism: International Legal Instruments, *at* http://www.un.org/en/terrorism/instruments.shtml (last visited Feb. 16, 2016); *see also* Scharf, *Special Tribunal, supra* note 171 (noting that under existing counter-terrorism conventions numerous attacks or acts of sabotage other than the use of explosives, including cyberattacks or acts of psychological terror not involving physical injury, are not covered).

176   Interlocutory Decision, *supra* note 172, ¶ 206. As Scharf, *Special Tribunal, supra* note 171, indicates, the STL ruling also "clarified" that joint criminal enterprise liability existed for the crime of terrorism at least where the co-perpetrators were acting pursuant to a common design and possess the same criminal intent and act like aiders and abetters.

177   The G.A.'s efforts were encouraged by the 2005 World Summit Outcome document, G.A. Res. 60/1, ¶ 85 (Oct. 24, 2005).

attention because its impetus was the plight of refugees heading towards Florida. Those Haitian refugees were fleeing the chaos that ensured after a military coup toppled President Aristide who had been elected under a UN supervised election that the organization had proclaimed to be "free and fair."[178] Resolution 940 was groundbreaking insofar as it marked the first time that the United States had sought UN authorization for the use of force within its own hemisphere and it was innovative insofar as the purpose of the intervention was to replace one regime with another.[179] In it the Council authorized "member States to form a multilateral force ... to use all necessary means to facilitate the departure from Haiti of the military leadership ... [and] the prompt return of the legitimately elected President and the restoration of the legitimate authorities of the government of Haiti."[180] To be sure, the Council attempted to reassure those who were understandably nervous about the precedent being set by its action by noting "the unique character of the present situation in Haiti and its deteriorating, complex and extraordinary nature, requiring an exceptional response."[181]

Resolution 940 targets the very heart of sovereignty: the legitimacy of a state's government. In this case, the Council branded one government illegitimate and authorized the restoration of another. To be sure, the UN had an exceptional stake in this instance since it had supervised the underlying election results that the coup leaders failed to respect. Yet this was not a situation where the Council was acting in response to one country invading another as with Iraq and Kuwait. Nor was the Council acting in response to a terrorist act that might engender retaliation, as with respect to Lockerbie and Libya. The threat to the peace in this instance seemed to be the internal human rights situation within Haiti and the plight of those on the high seas seeking refuge.

---

178 S.C. Res. 940 (Jul. 31, 1994). *See also* MAX HILAIRE, WAGING PEACE: THE UNITED NATIONS SECURITY COUNCIL AND TRANSNATIONAL ARMED CONFLICTS 60 (2015).

179 DAVID MALONE, DECISION-MAKING IN THE UN SECURITY COUNCIL: THE CASE OF HAITI, 1990–1997 at 110 (1998). While the U.S. had intervened militarily on many occasions in Latin America on the premise that its actions were authorized by a regional organization (as with respect to Grenada or Cuba during the Cuban Missile crisis) or was required for individual or collective self-defense (the use of force in Nicaragua or Panama), this was the first time that it sought Council permission.

180 S.C. Res. 940, *supra* note 178, ¶ 4.

181 *Id.* ¶ 2. This would not be the last time that the SC would attempt, through specific language, to limit the precedential effects of its actions. *See, e.g.,* S.C. Res. 2098, *supra* note 99, ¶ 9 (Mar. 28, 2013) (authorizing an intervention brigade in the DRC "on an exceptional basis and without creating a precedent or any prejudice to the agreed principles of peacekeeping").

At the same time, the implicit threat may have been to the credibility of the UN itself, which had so recently affirmed the legitimacy of the Aristide government after a lengthy effort supervising its election.

While the "unique" nature of the Council's action was emphasized in the text of Resolution 940 (at the apparent request of China) it was not difficult to see this resolution as the culmination of many actions by the Security Council, the General Assembly, and the Secretariat to promote the "right to democracy" as affirmed in, for example, Article 25 of the International Covenant on Civil and Political Rights and Article 21 of the Universal Declaration of Human Rights.[182] Resolution 940 emerged in the midst of growing UN involvement in election assistance and supervision throughout the globe and some resistance to institutionalizing this form of assistance from states like Cuba and China, particularly within the General Assembly.[183] In this instance the Council proved willing to defend the results of a UN election by force.

In the end, however, no force was actually needed. While the United States had recruited nineteen countries with a total of 2000 troops for the envisioned multilateral force, when word arrived that military aircraft were on route to Haiti, the coup leaders agreed to leave.[184] As a result, the multilateral force, along with a small monitoring team from UNMIH, deployed smoothly without resistance. This seems to be an instance in which the threat or shadow of Council action proved as effective as the real thing. Ultimately, the UNMIH operation ended in June 1996, several months following the elections and was replaced by the United Nations Support Mission in Haiti (UNSMIH) with a

---

182 Thomas Franck, *The Emerging Right to Democratic Governance*, 86 AM. J. INT'L L. 46, 72–73 (1992) (stating that the Haiti election mission "may be understood as the first instance in which the United Nations, acting at the request of a national government, intervened in the electoral process solely to validate the legitimacy of the outcome"). *But see* Susan Marks, *What Has Become of the Emerging Right to Democratic Governance?*, 22 EUR. J. INT'L L. 507 (2011) (reviving the debate spurred by Franck's 1992 article and examining four different ways of considering the significance of an emerging right to democratic governance: legitimacy, security, development, ideology).

183 *Compare* Enhancing the Effectiveness of the Principle of Periodic and Genuine Elections, G.A. Res. 48/131 (Feb. 15, 1994) to G.A. Res. 49/140, ¶ 2 (March 9, 1995) (commending the electoral assistance provided by the United Nations) with Respect for the Principles of National Sovereignty and Non-Interference in the Internal Affairs of States in their Electoral Processes, G.A. Res. 49/180 (March 2, 1995); *see also* Strengthening the Role of the United Nations in Enhancing Periodic and Genuine Elections and the Promotion of Democratization, G.A. Res. 66/163, U.N. Doc. A/66/163 (Apr. 10, 2012).

184 MALONE, *supra* note 179, at 111–112.

mandate extending through July 31, 1997.[185] However, the security situation deteriorated and in 1999, following resistance by China in the Security Council for UN operations in Haiti due to ties between Haiti and Taiwan, the GA authorized a drastically reduced follow-up mission, the International Civilian Support Mission (MICAH), which succeeded the UN Civilian Police Mission in Haiti (MIPONUH).[186] As a result of these multiple peacekeeping operations charged with different purposes, Haiti has come to be seen by many as under "UN occupation." This helps to explain why it has become an important test case for UN accountability concerns, as is discussed in Chapter VI.

Seen against the wider backdrop of UN election assistance, Resolution 940 is another example of the ever-shrinking domain of "domestic jurisdiction" under Article 2(7) thanks to the practices of UN organs. In authorizing force in defense of democracy, Resolution 940 exemplifies how the organization has deviated from the original sovereign-protective premises that gave rise to the Charter. While UN supervised elections are always conducted at the request of a government, thus deflecting some of the sovereignty concerns, states may be compelled by external circumstances and may request this assistance due to heavy outside pressures, including the need to appear legitimate and receive conditional aid. There may also be serious questions as to who is authorized to "consent" to election assistance. In the case of Haiti, candidate Aristide, in exile at the time, consented to election assistance and sought UN assistance when his regime was toppled.[187]

The UN's positive responses to requests by states for election assistance and the experiences gained in the course of this provide considerable insights into just how intrusive such a choice by a government can prove to be. To be effective, UN election assistance does not occur on the day of an election. It is not merely a matter of counting the ballots fairly. It ordinarily requires a UN presence many months prior to an election and considerable UN involvement (sometimes in conjunction with a broader peacekeeping force) that

185   S.C. Res. 1063 (June 28, 1996). The mandates of UNSMIH were extended in S.C. Res. 1085 (Nov. 29, 1996) and in S.C. Res. 1086 (Dec. 5, 1996).

186   G.A. Res. 54/193 (Dec. 17, 1999). For a thorough overview of the Haitian situation and the Council response, see generally DAVID MALONE, THE UN SECURITY COUNCIL: FROM THE COLD WAR TO THE 21ST CENTURY 476–477 (2004); UNITED NATIONS, YEARBOOK OF THE UNITED NATIONS 2001, 249 (2003).

187   UNITED NATIONS PEACEKEEPING, HAITI: BACKGROUND: SUMMARY, at http://www .un.org/en/peacekeeping/missions/past/unmihbackgr1.html; G.A. Res. 46/7, pmbl. (Oct. 11, 1991) (noting Aristide's October 3 request to the Security Council).

seeks to ensure the structural fairness of the electoral system.[188] This is evident in Resolution 1671, which authorized the European Union to deploy a force to support the UN Organization Mission in the Democratic Republic of the Congo (MONUC) during the electoral period in that country, and Resolution 2090 which addressed the roles and tasks given to the UN Office in Burundi for an election that was not scheduled to take place until 2015.[189] In the Congo, MONUC was authorized to "take all necessary measures" to stabilize the situation in the country, including to protect civilians under imminent threat of physical violence.[190] In Burundi and in other countries such as in Côte d'Ivoire, where the UN was called upon to provide election assistance, this has often involved: receiving assurances, including through changes made to local laws, that certain groups are not discriminated against; setting up comprehensive voter registration procedures that address such sensitive questions as the voting rights of refugees, political prisoners, and nomadic populations; and assuring public order and security for all phases of the process, including primaries and post-election transition. It has also involved external supervision of the conditions imposed on candidature, access to media and fairness in reporting, opportunities for public participation in campaigns, settling questions about fair districting and the neutrality of the supervising mechanisms, adequate polling procedures, and opportunities for contesting the results of an election.[191]

---

188   See, e.g., THOMAS M. FRANCK, FAIRNESS IN INTERNATIONAL LAW AND INSTITUTIONS 105–124 (1998) (noting how far the rules for monitoring elections evolved in practice in the Nicaraguan elections where the UN Observer Mission (ONUVEN) established to verify the electoral process in Nicaragua, did not merely monitor voting, but observed the voting and established its own projection of results and actively observed the activities of the Supreme Electoral Council in drafting and implementing new laws that applied to nominating, campaigning, and related activities, including also mediating disputes between candidates).

189   See S.C. Res. 1671 (Apr. 25, 2006) (authorizing the deployment of the MONUC in the Congo); S.C. Res. 2090 (Feb. 13, 2013) (extending the mandate of the United Nations Office in Burundi (BNUB) until 15 February 2014 and laying out a six-point support agenda for the Office including those for the run-up to the 2015 elections); S.C. Res. 2137 (Feb. 13, 2014) (extending the mandate of BNUB until December 31, 2014).

190   S.C. Res. 1671, supra note 189, ¶ 8.

191   See, e.g., S.C. Res. 2090, supra note 189; S.C. Res. 2137, supra note 189. See also S.C. Res. 2162 (Jun. 25, 2014) (encouraging reconciliatory agreements between the Government of Côte D'Ivoire and political opposition to strengthen the rule of law and make reforms on the legal framework for elections in preparation for the Oct. 2015 elections and further extending the mandate of the United Nations Operation in Côte D'Ivoire to include supporting the national authorities in stabilizing the security situation in the country, with a special attention to providing support for the provision of security through the 2015

In an extreme case such as the UN Transitional Authority in Cambodia (UNTAC), election assistance may involve UN takeover of the functioning of government entities pending elections that can be certified as free and fair by international observers.[192] Even without such a massive UN presence, sensitive political issues must be confronted. Thus, in the Burundian situation, for example, the Council addressed the need to promote dialogue between political actors within that country in order to strengthen the independence and capacity of the judiciary and parliament, to support efforts to fight impunity through transparent, independent, and impartial transitional justice mechanisms, as well as to promote and protect human rights. That resolution highlights the intrusive state-building transformative aspects of UN efforts more generally, including when the organization is tasked to assist with an election.[193]

7   The Council's "Smart" Sanctions

Following considerable human rights criticisms over Council-authorized comprehensive economic sanctions on Iraq under Resolution 687, the Council

---

presidential election); S.C. Res. 2190 (Dec. 15, 2014) (extending the mandate of the United Nations Mission in Liberia (UNMIL) to justice and security initiatives including also to provide electoral support such as the facilitation of access to report areas and creating an atmosphere conducive to a peaceful election through the UNMIL Radio).

192   S.C. Res. 745 (Feb. 28, 1992). For a close look at the complex work of, in effect, administrating Cambodia as allocated to UNTAC under the Cambodia settlement agreements, see Steven R. Ratner, *The Cambodia Settlement Agreements*, 87 AM. J. INT'L L. 1 (1993). In earlier periods, including in the late 1990s, it was not uncommon for the SC to authorize intrusive UN "transitional administrations" or "state-building" exercises that were designed at least partly to provide enable the successful conduct of elections. *See, e.g.*, SIMON CHESTERMAN, YOU, THE PEOPLE; THE UNITED NATIONS, TRANSITIONAL ADMINISTRATION AND STATE-BUILDING (2004). Significantly, the new edition of a leading book surveying the actions of the SC omits the chapter on such efforts, noting the SC is "highly reluctant to repeat the experience of assuming executive authority over entire territories, as it had done in Kosovo, East Timor, and Eastern Slavonia in the late 1990s." *Preface*, The UN SECURITY COUNCIL IN THE 21ST CENTURY PREFACE, xi, *supra* note 5.

193   For an examination of the changing fortunes of the Council's "democracy promotion" efforts over time, compare Gregory H. Fox, *Democratization*, *in* THE UN SECURITY COUNCIL: FROM THE COLD WAR TO THE 21ST CENTURY 69, *supra* note 63, to Francesco Mancini, *Promoting Democracy, in* THE UN SECURITY COUNCIL 235, *supra* note 5. Recent Council actions involving election assistance include S.C. Res. 2065 (Sept. 12, 2012) (Sierra Leone) and S.C. Res. 2186 (Nov. 25, 2014) (Guinea-Bissau).

turned to "smart" sanctions designed to affect only designated individuals and organizations. The purpose of these sanctions varies. Some target individuals who are alleged to have committed terrorist acts or grave violations of international humanitarian law, others target government officials implicated in weapons of mass destruction, while yet others are at one remove from direct threats to the international peace but are directed at those engaged in, for example, the illicit exploitation of natural resources that contributes to escalating internal conflicts. As of February 2016, the Council had 15 such sanctions regimes in place, with delegated sanctions committees for each presiding over "consolidated lists" of named individuals or organizations that, once named by a member of the Security Council, are denied access to international travel, face freezes on their bank accounts, and, of course, are barred from securing access to arms.[194]

Smart sanctions began with the creation of a Sanctions Committee under Resolution 1267 charged with monitoring states' compliance with sanctions imposed on members of the Taliban.[195] Subsequent Council resolutions have expanded the categories of individuals and organizations under that resolution to include members of al-Qaida and "assorted" groups.[196] Other resolutions target other groups and persons for comparable "smart" sanctions. Those now subject to UN smart sanctions include foreign terrorist fighters recruited by the Islamic State in Iraq and the Levant (ISIL) and the Al-Nusrah Front (ANF), as well as persons from North Korea, Libya, Liberia, and the Congo; they include private individuals as well as government officials, state entities,

---

194   UNITED NATIONS, UNITED NATIONS SECURITY COUNCIL SUBSIDIARY ORGANS: SANCTIONS, *at* https://www.un.org/sc/suborg/en/sanctions/information (providing overview of current sanctions regimes committees targeting Somalia and Eritrea, ISIL and al-Qaida, Iraq, Liberia, the Democratic Republic of Congo, Côte d'Ivoire, Sudan, North Korea, Libya, Guinea-Bissau, the Central African Republic, Yemen, South Sudan Lebanon (concerning the assassination of Prime Minister Hariri) and individuals associated with the Taliban); *see generally* FARRALL, *supra* note 88 (noting that since the birth of the UN, the Security Council has acted upon its Art. 41 sanctions powers to create twenty-five UN sanctions regimes.).

195   S.C. Res. 1267 (Oct. 15, 1999).

196   S.C. Res. 2161 (June 17, 2014) and particularly 2199 (Feb. 12, 2015) make clear that the al-Qaida sanctions under S.C. Res. 1267 also include those "associated with al-Qaida," including ISIL and ANF. *See* S.C. Res 2199, ¶¶ 1, 2. Significantly, that resolution targets direct and indirect oil trade associated with these terrorist groups and directs that smart sanctions (including freeze orders) should be imposed on oil producers who engage in such transactions and are therefore supporters of terrorism. *Id.* ¶¶ 1–3.

and even Somali pirates.[197] The precise sanctions that states are required to impose on designated persons and entities are well illustrated by Resolution 1390 (directed at al-Qaida and the Taliban):

> The Security Council ... Decides that all States shall take the following measures ...
>
> (a) Freeze without delay the funds and other financial assets or economic resources of these individuals, groups, undertakings and entities, including funds derived from property owned or controlled, directly or indirectly, by them or by persons acting on their behalf or at their direction, and ensure that neither these nor any other funds, financial assets or economic resources are made available, directly or indirectly, for such persons' benefit, by their nationals or by any persons within their territory;
>
> (b) Prevent the entry into or the transit through their territories of these individuals, provided that nothing in this paragraph shall oblige any State to deny entry into or require the departure from its territories of its own nationals and this paragraph shall not apply where entry or transit is necessary for the fulfilment of a judicial process or the Committee determines on a case-by-case basis only that entry or transit is justified;
>
> (c) Prevent the direct or indirect supply, sale and transfer, to these individuals, groups, undertakings and entities from their territories or by their nationals outside their territories, or using their flag vessels or aircraft, of arms and related materiel of all types including weapons and ammunition, military vehicles and equipment, paramilitary equipment, and spare parts for the aforementioned and technical advice, assistance, or training related to military activities.[198]

The Council has also turned to smart sanctions to deal with individuals or entities that have been found to contribute to "destabilizing forces" within the Central African Republic (CAR) that have led to a "cycle of violence and retaliation" including serious violations of international humanitarian law and human rights law.[199] Those resolutions target individuals that engage, for

---

197   *Id.*; s.c. Res. 2094 (Mar. 7, 2013); s.c. Res. 1874 (Jun. 12, 2009); s.c. Res. 2087 (Jan. 22, 2013); s.c. Res. 1970 (Feb. 26, 2011); s.c. Res. 1521 (Dec. 22, 2003); s.c. Res. 1533 (Mar. 12, 2004). *See also* s.c. Res. 2178 (Sept. 24, 2014).

198   s.c. Res. 1390 ¶ 2(a)–(c) (Jan. 16, 2002).

199   s.c. Res. 2134, pmbl. (Jan. 28, 2014). *See also* s.c. Res. 2127 (Dec. 5, 2013); s.c. Res. 2198 (Jan. 29, 2015).

example, in "diamond smuggling and other forms of illicit natural resource exploitation, including wildlife poaching."[200] In these cases, the Council has turned to Chapter VII to address not only those who are alleged to have engaged in acts that are themselves threats to the peace but also those who are seen as contributing to such threats, including by providing "material support" to terrorism, committing violations of international criminal law, or engaging in other actions that destabilize governments or regions. Resolution 2127, like Resolution 940, connects the dots between threats to the peace and the law and order associated with stable governments.[201]

The Council's smart sanctions programs are an illustration of how organizations "learn" over time. As noted, the turn to "smart" or targeted sanctions was in part a response to criticisms of the Council's prior comprehensive economic embargoes, particularly its twelve-year long effort to sanction Iraq.[202] The Council's "learning" also occurs within a single sanctions regime. Thus the original al-Qaida resolutions imposed under Resolution 1267 have been repeatedly

---

200   s.c. Res. 2134, *supra* note 199, ¶¶ 30–42 and particularly ¶ 37(d) (obligating states to impose sanctions on individuals and entities "providing support for armed groups or criminal networks through the illicit exploitation of natural resources, including diamonds and wildlife and wildlife products, in the CAR"). *See generally* s.c. Res. 2127, *supra* note 199 ("Reiterating its condemnation of the devastation of natural heritage and noting that poaching and trafficking of wildlife are among the factors that fuel the crisis in the CAR"); s.c. Res. 2136 (Jan. 30, 2014) ("Recalling the linkage between the illegal exploitation of natural resources, including poaching and illegal trafficking of wildlife, illicit trade in such resources, and the proliferation and trafficking of arms as one of the major factors fuelling and exacerbating conflicts in the Great Lakes region of Africa" and imposing sanctions on individuals or entities supporting armed groups in the DRC through illicit trade of natural resources, including gold or wildlife as well as wildlife products).

201   s.c. Res. 2127, *supra* note 199, ¶¶ 14–15. Like many comparable sc efforts that rely heavily on fact-finding on the ground, the factual determinations made in s.c. Res. 2127 owe much to the Secretary-General's preceding report based on a technical assessment mission dispatched to the CAR from Oct. 27–Nov. 8, 2013 and submitted to the Council pursuant to the Council's request in s.c. Res. 2127. U.N. Secretary-General, Report of the Secretary-General on the Central African Republic Submitted Pursuant to Paragraph 22 of Security Council Resolution 2121 (2013), U.N. Doc. S/2013/677 (Nov. 15, 2013). That report also highlights the "pervasive breakdown in law and order" in parts of the CAR. *Id.* ¶ 9.

202   *See, e.g.,* Durson Pekson, *Better or Worse? The Effect of Economic Sanctions on Human Rights*, 46 J. PEACE RES. 59 (2009) (citing evidence that broad economic embargoes cause more human rights damage than do more selective sanctions). *See generally* NICHOLAS TSAGOURIAS & NIGEL D. WHITE, COLLECTIVE SECURITY: THEORY, LAW AND PRACTICE 221–223 (2013).

modified over time.[203] Resolution 1452, responding to some early complaints of smart sanctions, carves out financial assets that a relevant state deems are necessary for basic expenses, such as food, rent or mortgage, medicines and medical treatment, taxes, insurance premiums, and public utility fees, so long as these are not rejected by the sanctions committee.[204]

The Council's smart sanctions regimes are also an example of the "administrative" turn in how IOs govern themselves and others.[205] The Council's smart sanctions efforts involve a great deal more than passing a single resolution. They involve the ongoing staffing, supervising, and coordinating of an extensive bureaucracy of UN-based counter-terrorism monitoring bodies, such as the Analytical Support and Sanctions Monitoring Team under Resolution 1267 and its progeny, as well as the efforts of that monitoring body to improve countries' compliance with the 1267 sanctions. The Council's implementation efforts include "carrots" and not just the "sticks" implicit in all Chapter VII decisions (namely the threat that the SC will apply secondary Chapter VII sanctions on countries that are unwilling or unable to comply with the principal SC sanctions). The "carrots" include the possibility of technical and other assistance to enable states to make their internal agencies adapt their procedures to the new rules. The SC and its monitoring bodies thus become engaged in the scrutiny of and advice to immigration officials, financial regulators, security and law enforcement officers, and many others inside states, all of whom need to be convinced to adopt the intrusive, time-consuming and sometimes technically complex actions to make the smart sanctions as effective as they are "smart."

---

203   As has been enumerated in detail by Farrall, the SC has frequently modified its sanctions regimes and has also revisited the rules governing the mandates of its sanctions committees. *See* FARRALL, *supra* note 88, app. 3, tbls. D & E.

204   S.C. Res. 1452, ¶¶ 1(a), 3(a) (Dec. 20, 2002). This resolution also permits exclusion of "extraordinary expenses" requested by the relevant state provided these are approved by the Committee. *Id.* ¶¶ 1(b), 3(b). This replaced the Council's earlier approach whereby the sanctions committee decided, on a case-by-case basis, whether to extend make exceptions on the ground of unspecified "humanitarian need." *See* S.C. Res. 1267, *supra* note 195, ¶ 4(b).

205   *See generally* Benedict Kingsbury & Lorenzo Casini, *Global Administrative Law Dimensions of International Organizations Law*, 6 INT'L ORG. L. REV. 319 (2009) (contending that IOs share many features of global administrative law (GAL)). *See also* Sabino Cassese, *A Global Due Process of Law?*, in VALUES IN GLOBAL ADMINISTRATIVE LAW 17 (Gordon Anthony et al. eds., 2011); Simon Chesterman, *Globalisation and Public Law: A Global Administrative Law*, in SANCTIONS, ACCOUNTABILITY AND GOVERNANCE IN A GLOBALIZED WORLD 75 (Jeremy Farrall & Kim Rubenstein eds., 2009).

This involves continuing efforts by states and relevant UN officials to decide on "best practices" with respect to, for example, the implementation of the humanitarian exceptions identified in Resolution 1452 above or to implement consistent rules on what it means to freeze the financial assets of not only listed persons but "funds derived from property owned or controlled, directly or indirectly, by them or by persons acting on their behalf or at their direction" as indicated in Resolution 1390.[206] It involves, in short, the UN's involvement in national administrative law. It also means coordinating with the advice or information being given to states or the UN by many other entities, both inside the UN and external to it, including the Financial Action Task Force (FATF).[207] To these ends, the 1267 monitoring committee is charged with reporting on and making recommendations regarding implementation, engaging in case studies, conducting in depth explorations of issues raised by the 1267 committee, and submitting work plans to that committee.[208]

The Council's smart sanctions programs, as is well known, have been subject to strong criticisms advanced by human rights NGOs, the General Assembly, member states, and the UN's own Special Rapporteurs.[209] When the Council

---

206   See S.C. Res. 1390, *supra* note 198, ¶ 2(a). These are but two of the many interpretative questions. As suggested by Resolution 1390 quoted above, states need consistent guidance on what is covered "paramilitary equipment" or what to prohibit under "technical advice, assistance, or training related to military activities." *Id.* ¶ 2(c).

207   See, e.g., S.C. Res. 1617, ¶ 7 (urging states to implement the standards in the FATF's Forty Recommendations on Money Laundering and the FATF's Special Recommendations on Terrorist Financing), ¶ 8 (requesting that the Secretary-General work with Interpol to assist the 1267 sanctions committee), ¶ 12 (urging cooperation with the Counter-Terrorism Committee (CTC) established under Resolution 1373) & ¶ 13 (urging cooperation with the Resolution 1540 committee) (July 29, 2005).

208   See, e.g., S.C. Res. 1904, annex I (Dec. 17, 2009) (containing the enumerated activities of the Monitoring Team for the Al-Qaida and Taliban sanctions).

209   See, e.g., Press Conference, Martin Scheinin, UN Special Rapporteur on Human Rights and Countering Terrorism (Oct. 22, 2008), *at* http://www.un.org/press/en/2008/081022_Scheinin.doc.htm ("[T]he Organization's terrorist listing procedures did not meet due process requirements of fair trial."); Thomas Hammarberg, Council of Europe Commissioner for Human Rights, Human Rights in Europe: No Grounds for Complacency 255 (Apr. 2011), *at* http://www.coe.int/t/commissioner/source/prems/HR-Europe-no-grounds-complacency_en.pdf; Kenneth Roth, Human Rights Watch, UN: Sanctions Must Protect Due Process (March 3, 2002), *at* https://www.hrw.org/news/2002/03/03/un-sanctions-rules-must-protect-due-process; Islamic Human Rights Council, Economic Sanctions as Human Rights Violations: International Law and the Right to Life (May 14, 2013), *at* http://www.ihrc.org.uk/publications/briefings/10518-economic-sanctions-as-human-rights-vio

puts an individual on its consolidated list for 1267 sanctions, the effect is dramatic. Designated persons lose access to their bank accounts and are effectively barred from inter-state travel. They are also stigmatized publically by the world's most well known international body as being guilty of the bad acts that these resolutions condemn. These resolutions cause, as they are intended to, material hardship. Targeted persons may lose their jobs; their children and spouses, even if not themselves named in the Council's lists, may suffer the consequences of the "terrorist" or other stigmas no less. NGOs, including fragile charities operating in some of the world's poorest countries, may be forced to close. To their critics, the SC's turn to smart sanctions avoids doing harm to innocent collective publics at the expense of imposing on individuals and organizations what are in effect criminal sanctions without benefit of trial.[210]

As originally conceived, the 1267 sanctions program anticipated no remedy for those who argued that they were wrongly targeted for sanction. There was no formal "de-listing" mechanism other than the prospect (never publically announced) that those objecting to the SC's smart sanctions could appeal to their governments and have them approach the SC for redress. Eventually, some of those targeted found lawyers, and legal challenges began to emerge in national courts, regional courts like the European Court of Human Rights (ECHR) and the European Court of Justice (ECJ), and UN human rights bodies such as the ICCPR committee.[211]

---

lations-international-law-and-the-right-to-life; Evelyn Leopold, *UN al-Qaeda Sanctions Said to Violate Rights*, REUTERS, June 23, 2006 (citing Danish foreign minister's criticisms to the Security Council); G.A. Res. 59/191 (Dec. 20, 2004) (welcoming dialogue between the Security Council and the Office of the High Commissioner for Human Rights on "giving due regard to the promotion and protection of human rights in the ongoing work pursuant to the relevant Security Council resolutions relating to terrorism").

210 Jared Genser & Kate Barth, *Targeted Sanctions and Due Process of Law, in* THE UNITED NATIONS SECURITY COUNCIL IN THE AGE OF HUMAN RIGHTS, *supra* note 21, at 195; SECURING HUMAN RIGHTS? ACHIEVEMENTS AND CHALLENGES OF THE UN SECURITY COUNCIL 106, 173–174 (Bardo Fassbender ed., 2011); Bardo Fassbender, *Targeted Sanctions Imposed by the UN Security Council and Due Process Rights: A Study Commissioned by the UN Office of Legal Affairs and Follow-up Action by the United Nations*, 3 INT'L ORG. L. REV. 437 (2006); Iain Cameron, *UN Targeted Sanctions, Legal Safeguards and the European Convention on Human Rights*, 72 NORDIC J. INT'L L. 159, 161 (2003). *See generally* GUGLIELMO VERDIRAME, THE U.N. AND HUMAN RIGHTS: WHO GUARDS THE GUARDIANS? (2011); Johnstone, *supra* note 122, 294–299.

211 International Covenant on Civil and Political Rights Human Rights Committee, Views of the Human Rights Committee Under Article 5, Paragraph 4 of the Optional Protocol to the International Covenant on Civil and Political Rights, U.N. Doc. CCPR/C/94/D/1472/2006 (Dec. 29, 2008) [hereinafter ICCPR Views]. *See generally* Peter Hilpold, *UN Sanctions Before the ECJ: The Kadi Case, in* CHALLENGING ACTS OF INTERNATIONAL ORGANIZATIONS

The most prominent judicial challenge led to two judgments by the European Court of Justice in the Kadi case.[212] In that case, the ECJ found the sanctions as applied to Mr. Kadi and implemented under European Union legislation illegal under European human rights law. The ECJ found fault in European states' failures to accord fair process to those designated for sanction and that this denial resulted in violations of Kadi's rights to an effective remedy; it also found that implementing the financial sanctions as directed by the SC violated Kadi's rights to property.[213] The failings highlighted by the ECJ were endemic to the SC sanctions regime as it then existed. Since the SC did not require members of the sanctions committee (most often the U.S. and the UK) to provide detailed facts to substantiate their request for a listing, and no such public evidence was otherwise available, it was difficult for states implementing the Council's orders to be in a position to inform the individual or entity subject to a freezing order or a travel ban as implemented under national law or EU law the basis for their being listed. This meant that individuals had no real opportunity to present their side of the case, even if a forum was available to them in national court. SC sanctions committees, and states faithfully implementing their mandates against designated persons and entities, rely on information supplied by Council members' secretive security agencies. In the U.S., that is the Office of Foreign Assets Control (OFAC) which argues, like other security agencies, that requiring disclosure of the underlying reasons for listing someone would undermine national security, including the identity of informants.[214]

BEFORE NATIONAL COURTS (August Reinisch ed., 2011). On national court cases involving the Council's sanctions measures, see generally Antonios Tzanakopoulos, *Domestic Court Reactions to UN Security Council Sanctions, in* CHALLENGING ACTS OF INTERNATIONAL ORGANIZATIONS BEFORE NATIONAL COURTS 54 (August Reinisch ed., 2011).

212   Joined Cases C-402/05 P & C-415/05 P, Kadi v. Council, 2008 E.C.R. I-6351 (overturning the implementation of Security Council resolutions 1267 & 1333 by the Council of the European Union) [hereinafter Kadi I], reported in 103 AM. J. INT'L L. 305 (2009); Joined Cases C-584/10 P, C-593/10 P, & C-595/10 P, Commission v. Kadi, 2013 E.C.R. 518 ¶¶ 131–134 (July 18, 2013) [hereinafter Kadi II]. Indeed, the Kadi decisions may be influencing some national courts. *See, e.g.*, Abdelrazik v. Canada (Minister of Foreign Affairs), [2010] 1 F.C.R. 267 (Can.) (finding that Resolution 1267 does not authorize Canada to bar reentry to a Canadian citizen).

213   *See* Kadi I, *supra* note 212, ¶¶ 334–337 & 369–372; Kadi II, *supra* note 212, ¶ 132; *see also* ICCPR Views, *supra* note 211.

214   *See, e.g.*, Per Cramér, *Recent Swedish Experiences with Targeted UN Sanctions: The Erosion of Trust in the Security Council, in* REVIEW OF THE SECURITY COUNCIL BY MEMBER STATES 85, 88, 90–91, 94–95 (Erika de Wet et al. eds., 2003).

In response to the Kadi case and other judicial challenges as well as widespread criticisms from many other quarters, the Council began modifying its smart sanctions procedures as applied to al-Qaida under Resolution 1267 and its progeny.[215] Under SC Resolution 1617, states proposing names to be listed to the 1267 committee must provide a "statement of the case" indicating the reasons for their proposal which could be used by the sanctions committee to answer queries from states whose nationals or entities have been included on the consolidated list.[216] Significantly, that Resolution also permitted the Committee to release this information to others on a case-by-case basis.[217] The SC adopted a delisting procedure under Resolution 1730.[218] In a series of later resolutions the SC implemented a sunset clause linked to an ombudsperson procedure to examine what is done in the Council's name and to make delisting recommendations.[219]

Under the existing framework, which applies only to the list of persons and entities associated with ISIL and al-Qaida,[220] the ombudsperson, is empowered to receive petitions from individuals listed in the al-Qaida Sanctions list, collect information from the person and relevant states, and make recommendations to the SC as to whether or not to delist individuals.[221] The Ombudsperson procedure remains a diplomatic and intergovernmental process where the final decision to delist or not rests with the SC.[222] If the ombudsperson recommends delisting, this occurs within 60 days unless all members

---

215   As discussed *infra*, the smart sanctions procedures applicable in other contexts remain largely the same although the SC has clarified and arguably expanded the humanitarian exceptions that apply with respect to all of them. *See, e.g.*, S.C. Res. 2206, ¶¶ 11, 12(a) (March 3, 2015) (allowing humanitarian exceptions to travel bans, asset freezes); S.C. Res. 2140, ¶¶ 12(a), 16(a) (Feb. 26, 2014) (same).

216   S.C. Res. 1617, *supra* note 207, ¶¶ 4–5.

217   *Id.* ¶ 6.

218   S.C. Res. 1730 (Dec. 19, 2006).

219   S.C. Res. 1988 (June 17, 2011) (permitting individual delisting requests and calling for a system of regular review and splitting the list of persons and entities subject to sanctions and setting out a delisting procedure), S.C. Res. 1989 (June 17, 2011) (renewing the Ombudsperson's term and requesting a report on recommended delistings), & S.C. Res. 1904 (Dec. 17, 2009) (establishing Office of the Ombudsperson).

220   S.C. Res. 1988 *supra* note 219, ¶ 1; *see also* United Nations Security Council: Subsidiary Organs, Focal Point for Delisting, *at* https://www.un.org/sc/suborg/en/sanctions/delisting [hereinafter Focal Point for Delisting].

221   S.C. Res. 1904, *supra* note 208, ¶¶ 20–21 & annex II.

222   *Id.* annex II, ¶¶ 10–14.

of the sanctions committee disagree or, if the question is brought to the full Council, the Council blocks the delisting.[223] This unique procedure applies only to the consolidated list associated with al-Qaida (and now ISIL) and not to the many other smart sanctions committees in place.[224]

The Ombudsperson procedure has not, however, mollified all critics. It certainly falls short of the independent judicial review process that Kadi II envisions.[225] In addition, the SC's choice to limit that process to the al-Qaida Sanctions list has raised questions about why due process rights apply only to some but not all individuals and entities targeted by the Council. Some have also suggested the SC's focus on the Taliban for potential delisting is not motivated by genuine human rights concerns but realpolitik: removing some of those associated with Afghanistan coincides with the "reconciliation" process being pursued by the U.S. and the Kabul government. Thus, although Mr. Kadi himself has, after many years finally been delisted, the challenges that his case highlighted and the Council's reactions to them remain works in progress.[226] As is further addressed in Chapter VI of this monograph, the challenges posed by the SC's smart sanctions are perhaps only the most prominent example of the broader "accountability gap" that many see emerging as IOs engage in more "governance" activities.[227] The tensions generated by Resolution 1267 and its progeny are also a reminder of the continued interactions between the contemporary Council and human rights, even if such connections were not clearly foreseen in the Charter.[228]

The Council's North Korea sanctions program is not directed at terrorism. In January 2003, North Korea announced its decision to withdraw from the

---

223   S.C. Res. 1989, *supra* note 219, ¶ 23.

224   *See* Focal Point for Delisting, *supra* note 220.

225   Kadi II, *supra* note 212, ¶ 96 (describing shortcomings in the Ombudsman's powers noted by Kadi).

226   *See, e.g.,* Grant L. Willis, *Security Council Targeted Sanctions, Due Process, and the 1267 Ombudsperson,* 42 GEO. J. INT'L L. 673 (2011) (arguing that new procedures do not satisfy the international legal guarantees of due process rights afforded to listed individuals); Craig Forcese & Kent Roach, *Limping into the Future: The U.N. 1267 Terrorism Listing Process at the Crossroads,* 42 GEO. WASH. INT'L L. REV. 217 (2010) (claiming that the reform of the 1267 listing process will not satisfy domestic expectations of due process).

227   *See generally* Laurence Boisson de Chazournes & Edouard Fromageau, *Balancing the Scales: The World Bank Sanctions Process and Access to Remedies,* 23 EUR. J. INT'L L. 963 (2012) (addressing the due process gaps raised by the World Bank's "black-listing" policies with respect to entities charged with engaging in corruption).

228   *See, e.g.,* ALVAREZ, *supra* note 7, at 174–181.

Nuclear Non-Proliferation Treaty (NPT).[229] If that notice were deemed to be legally effective, North Korea would no longer have been a party to the NPT as of April 10, 2003.[230] When that country conducted a nuclear weapons test in October 2006, the SC demanded that North Korea retract its withdrawal announcement and "return to the treaty."[231] In Resolution 1718, the Council, acting under Chapter VII, decided that North Korea had to "act strictly in accordance" with the obligations under the NPT.[232] While the Council did not force North Korea to rejoin the NPT, it prescribed that treaty's obligations on that country by incorporating these into its Chapter VII decisions.[233] Stefan Talmon explains these resolutions as creating an "NPT-like" regime that imposed Chapter VII obligations based on North Korea's threats to the peace.[234] One could also see these resolutions as in effect imposing a treaty on a non-party. This also appeared to be the case when, in Resolution 1718, the Council also imposed the obligations under the IAEA Standards Agreement that North Korea and the IAEA had entered bilaterally in January 1992 but which had ceased to have effect when North Korea withdrew from the NPT.[235] These Council decisions prompted charges of hypocrisy, the application of double standards, and improper selectivity in arguable violation of the rule of law and sovereign equality insofar as the Council had not reacted the same way when India and Pakistan conducted their own nuclear weapons tests back in May 1998.[236]

---

229 Statement, Korean Central News Agency of the DPRK (Jan. 10, 2003).

230 Treaty on the Non-Proliferation of Nuclear Weapons art. XX, March 5, 1970, 729 U.N.T.S. 169.

231 S.C. Res. 1718, ¶ 6 (Oct. 14, 2006) (deciding that North Korea has to "act strictly in accordance" with the obligations applicable to the parties under the NPT); S.C. Res. 1874, *supra* note 197, ¶ 26 (June 12, 2009) (establishing a Panel of Experts to assist the Security Council Committee); S.C. Res. 2087 (Jan. 22, 2013) (condemning North Korea's ballistic missile technology in violation of the sanctions imposed).

232 S.C. Res. 1718, *supra* note 231. The SC reiterated this determination in S.C. Res. 1874, *supra* note 197.

233 *See, e.g.*, S.C. Res. 1874, *supra* note 197, ¶ 8.

234 Stefan Talmon, *Security Council Treaty Action*, 62 REVUE HELLÉNIQUE DE DROIT INTER-NATIONAL 65–116 (2009). For a discussion on whether there is an international prohibition on nuclear testing, see, for example, Lisa Tabassi, *The Nuclear Test Ban: Lex Lata or de Lege Ferenda?*, 14 J. CONF. & SEC. L. 309, 310 (2009).

235 S.C. Res. 1718, *supra* note 231, ¶ 6.

236 These earlier tests had led only to Council condemnations. *See* S.C. Res. 1172 (June 6, 1998). *See also* Michael Krepon, *Looking Back: the 1998 Indian and Pakistani Nuclear Tests' Arms Control Today*, ARMS CONTROL ASSOCIATION (May 2008), *at* http://www.armscontrol.org/print/2982; James Fry, *Dionysian Disarmament: Security Council WMD Coercive*

The resulting North Korean sanctions resolutions combined distinct demands on different entities. As noted, they targeted North Korea as a state not only by imposing treaty-like obligations on it but also by demanding that its government suspend certain weapons-related activity (such as suspending its development of ballistic weapons) that was not illegal under any treaty.[237] The resolutions also imposed requirements on all member states. These third parties were told that they had to prevent the supply of weapons and technology of various kinds as well as luxury goods to North Korea, and had to cooperate in inspecting cargo to and from that state.[238] Finally all member states were required to impose financial asset freezes and travel restrictions on those named individuals and organizations listed by the North Korea sanctions committee.[239]

In Resolution 1874, the Council imposed additional demands on North Korea. These included requirements to take transparency measures with respect to the IAEA that went beyond any imposed under the IAEA Safeguards Agreement.[240] The SC also imposed an additional arms embargo on the country.[241] In Resolution 2087, the Council itself, not the relevant sanctions committee, identified four individuals and six entities (including a bank and trading corporations located in North Korea) that would be subject to its asset freeze.[242]

It is important to recognize the innovative nature of the SC's multiple smart sanctions, only some of which are addressed here. In some instances, the relevant resolutions adopt both traditional targeted sanctions with effects directly on states or their governments (as would be suggested by the text of Article 41 of the Charter when it mentions "economic relations") and smart sanctions targeting individuals and other non-state entities directly. In doing so, the SC appears to be acting as if it were a court judging (probable?) guilt or innocence and imposing penalties accordingly—but without the elements that rule of law states associate with the judicial process, namely independent judges acting on evidence that is accessible to the defendant who is thus able to mount

---

Disarmament: WMD Coercive Disarmament Measures and their Legal Implications, 29 MICH. J. INT'L L. 197 (2008).

237 S.C. Res. 1718, *supra* note 231, ¶ 5.

238 *Id.* ¶ 8.

239 *Id.*

240 S.C. Res. 1874, *supra* note 197, ¶ 8 ("Decides that the DPRK ... shall provide the IAEA transparency measures extending beyond [the IAEA Safeguards Agreements's] requirements.").

241 *Id.* ¶ 10.

242 S.C. Res. 2087, *supra* note 231. As noted, these individuals are not subject to the ombudsperson procedure described above that is applicable to the Taliban.

a defense against state action based on that evidence. Further, unlike the situations discussed above with respect to Iraq or on Libya after Lockerbie, smart sanctions, while more limited in their scope, are not limited to one country's or one region's nationals or companies. When the SC resorts to these sanctions, it can act directly on individuals of any nationality and its reach can be global. Moreover, since many of the SC's smart sanctions are motivated by endemic problems—such as the ever-changing terrorist threat posed by new entities like ISIS or their access to WMDS—they are likely to continue indefinitely. Unless the Council imposes a sunset clause, dismantling an existing sanctions regime requires nine votes on the Council, including the concurring votes of the P-5.[243] Not surprisingly, few SC smart sanctions programs have been discontinued.[244]

8   The Council's Global "Legislation"

Scholars have generally defined legislative acts as having four essential characteristics: they are unilateral in form, create or modify some element of a legal norm, are directed at all relevant actors, and are capable of repeated application over time.[245] By these standards, the SC has to date adopted global legislation in at least three prominent instances, in Resolutions 1373, 1540, and 2178.[246] These general directives by the Council under Chapter VII are not like

---

243   ALVAREZ, *supra* note 7, at 176. *See generally* Jared Genser & Kate Barth, *supra* note 210, at 229.

244   *See* FARRALL, *supra* note 88. Students of bureaucracy would not be surprised if some of these sanctions programs last longer than may be warranted by the underlying threat to the peace that they are intended to resolve—at least to the extent bureaucrats and experts gain useful employment from their continuance.

245   *See generally* Frederic L. Kirgis, *The Security Council's First Fifty Years*, 89 AM. J. INT'L L. 506, 520 (1995) (quoting EDWARD YEMIN, LEGISLATIVE POWERS IN THE UNITED NATIONS AND SPECIALIZED AGENCIES (1969)).

246   S.C. Res. 1373 (Sept. 28, 2001); S.C. Res. 1540 (April 28, 2004); S.C. 2178, *supra* note 197. *See, e.g.,* Paul C. Szasz, *The Security Council Starts Legislating*, 96 AM. J. INT'L L. 901, 903 (2002); Ian Johnstone, *The Security Council as Legislature, in* THE UN SECURITY COUNCIL AND THE POLITICS OF INTERNATIONAL AUTHORITY 80 (Bruce Cronin & Ian Hurd eds., 2008); THE SECURITY COUNCIL AS GLOBAL LEGISLATOR (Vesselin Popovski & Trudy Fraser eds., 2014); Anna Hood, T*he United Nations Security Council's Legislative Phase and the Rise of Emergency International Law-Making, in* LEGAL PERSPECTIVES ON SECURITY INSTITUTIONS (Hitoshi Nasu & Kim Rubenstein eds., 2015). *But see* Martti Koskenniemi, *The Police in the Temple: Order, Justice and the UN: A Dialectical View*, 6 EUR. J. INT'L L. 325 (1995) (warning of the consequences should the SC be used as something more than the police power that it was meant to be).

the North Korean and most of the other resolutions discussed above. They are not directed against a specific target state and not intended to change that state's behavior. They do not result from a finding that a target state is itself threatening the international peace but from a more generalized finding that terrorism, access to WMDs, and foreign terrorist fighters are threats to the peace that require collective measures applicable to all states jointly and individually. As might be expected, these efforts—along with other SC efforts that appear to be intended to make law—have been very controversial. The literature on the first two instances—Resolutions 1373 and 1540—is substantial and requires but brief summary here.[247]

In Resolution 1373, passed shortly after 9/11, the SC condemned those acts and reaffirmed that "such acts, like any act of international terrorism, constitute a threat to international peace and security."[248] Acting under Chapter VII, the Council decided to require all states to take relatively specific legal actions to prevent the financing of terrorist acts, to criminalize such financing, and to freeze any such funds.[249] As many commentators have noted, in passing this resolution the SC was undoubtedly reacting to and endorsing the International Convention for the Suppression of the Financing of Terrorism that had been adopted by the General Assembly in 2000.[250] When Resolution 1373 was adopted, only a handful of states had ratified that Convention.[251] The SC took in effect a shortcut around the arduous process of securing treaty ratification while encouraging states to ratify that instrument.[252] Resolution 1373 and later resolutions built upon it obligated states to change their laws insofar

---

247   See, e.g., José E. Alvarez, Hegemonic International Law Revisited, 97 AM. J. INT'L L. 873 (2003); Ilias Bentekas, The International Law of Terrorist Financing, 97 AM. J. INT'L L. 315 (2003); Eric Rosand, Security Council Resolution 1373, the Counter-Terrorism Committee, and the Fight Against Terrorism, 97 AM. J. INT'L L. 333 (2003); Johnstone, supra note 122.

248   S.C. Res. 1373, supra note 246, pmbl.

249   Id. ¶ 1.

250   G.A. Res. 54/109, annex (Feb. 25, 2000); see, e.g., Jane Stromseth, The Security Council's Counter-Terrorism Role: Continuity and Innovation, 97 ASIL PROC. 41, 43 (2003).

251   As of September 2001, only 4 countries had ratified the Convention (though over 40 had signed it). See Status as at 22-02-16: International Convention for the Suppression of the Financing of Terrorism, UNITED NATIONS TREATY COLLECTION (Feb. 23, 2016), at https://treaties.un.org/pages/ViewDetails.aspx?src=TREATY&mtdsg_no=XVIII-11&chapter=18&lang=en.

252   See, e.g., Martin Scheinin, A Comment on Security Council Res. 2178 (Foreign Terrorist Fighters) as a "Form" of Global Goverance, JUST SECURITY (Oct. 6, 2014), at https://www.justsecurity.org/15989/comment-security-council-res-2178-foreign-fighters-form-global-governance (praising Resolution 1373 for getting states on board with that Convention and noting that it has obtained ratification by 186 parties).

as necessary to, for example, deny safe haven to terrorists, prosecute those who finance terrorist acts, cooperate with other states engaging in relevant criminal investigations, and adopt effective border controls and controls on travel documents to prevent the transnational movement of terrorists.[253] As with the bureaucratic systems put in place under smart sanctions, Resolution 1373 enabled the Council to establish the new international administrative law on terrorist financing.

In Resolution 1540, the SC expanded on the license it had seized previously with respect to treating terrorist acts even when committed by non-state actors as threats to the peace, to formally declare that "the proliferation of nuclear, chemical and biological weapons, as well as their means of delivery, constitutes a threat to international peace and security."[254] Taking note of the multilateral treaties aimed at eliminating or preventing the proliferation of such weapons of mass destruction (WMDs), the Council took aim at filling gaps in those treaty obligations insofar as these did not sufficiently address state obligations to prevent WMD access to non-state actors, particularly given the potential of their use in terrorist acts.[255] Accordingly, that resolution obligated states, under Chapter VII, to refrain from any support to non-state actors seeking access to WMDs and to prevent such actors from developing or transporting WMDs; to this end, it directed states to take and enforce effective measures to establish effective physical protection measures to prevent the proliferation of WMDs.[256] As with respect to its smart sanctions resolutions, both Resolution 1373 and 1540 established separate sub-committees of the Council charged

---

253   S.C. Res. 1373, *supra* note 246, ¶ 2. Indeed, given the similarities with the obligations imposed under Resolution 1373 and those under the United States' Patriot Act, it was suggested that the SC's implementation effort was in effect an effort to "export" that U.S. law as a model to the world. This effort to "launder" U.S. law by stamping it with the UN stamp of approval was criticized by human rights groups insofar as it was a SC license for authoritarian governments to crack down on dissent under the guise of combatting terrorism. *See, e.g.*, Alvarez, *supra* note 247, at 876 & n. 18.

254   S.C. 1540, *supra* note 246, pmbl.

255   *See, e.g.*, George Bunn, *Enforcing International Standards: Protecting Nuclear Materials From Terrorists Post 9/11*, ARMS CONTROL ASSOCIATION: ARMS CONTROL TODAY (Jan. 1, 2007), *at* https://www.armscontrol.org/act/2007_01-02/Bunn (noting that the NPT, while calling for safeguards to prevent the diversion of nuclear material to the making of nuclear weapons, does not impose comparable safeguards or IAEA review over physical protection of such material to prevent theft or sabotage).

256   S.C. Res. 1540, *supra* note 246, ¶¶ 1–3.

with receiving states' reports indicating their implementation and compliance with the two sets of Council edicts.[257]

Both resolutions have had arguable impacts on treaty and custom.[258] In both instances the Council turned to Chapter VII as a shortcut to arduous treaty making processes. Both of these resolutions can be seen, at least in part, as efforts by the Council to impose by fiat obligations previously contained in treaties—as did the North Korean resolutions on North Korea and Resolution 687 on Iraq. To the extent these resolutions increased the number of states that were effectively subject to obligations contained in treaties, the domain of those treaty regimes in fact increased beyond their ratifying parties. But, as in the instances involving North Korea and Iraq, the Council did not stop there. It turned to Chapter VII to overcome treaty gaps and to impose additional or somewhat different obligations from those contained in existing treaties even with respect to treaty parties.[259] In addition, because in both of these instances the SC put in place a number of mechanisms to attempt to assure that states comply with its edicts, Resolutions 1373 and 1540 can also be seen as complements to the underlying treaties' mechanisms for enforcement or implementation.[260]

Of course, what makes Resolution 1373 and 1540 different is that in these instances the SC was not focusing on one state at a time but on all of them.[261] Because of this generality, as well as the Council's efforts in both cases to connect its actions to the Charter and its prohibitions on use of force, the SC is

---

257   *Id.* ¶ 6. See also ALVAREZ, *supra* note 7, at 196–198, 205–217.

258   *See also* ALVAREZ, *supra* note 7, at 205–217.

259   *See, e.g.,* Alvarez, *supra* note 247, at 874–875 (noting differences between the Convention on Terrorist Financing and Res. 1373).

260   The state reports generated under both resolutions have, of course, yielded considerably more information on the extent to which states implement these resolutions as well as the corresponding obligations under the International Convention on the Suppression of Terrorist Financing and the NPT. *See, e.g.,* Lars Olberg, *Implementing Resolution 1540: What the National Reports Indicate,* ACRONYM INST. FOR DISARMAMENT DIPL. (May 1, 2006).

261   As Ian Johnstone has pointed out, the SC makes law in other ways, as when it determined that Iraq had illegally invaded Kuwait, or when it imposes legal obligations on one target—it has done with respect to Iraq, UNITA in Angola, or the RUF in Sierra Leone for example. Of course, the SC's authorizations to establish transitional administrations in Kosovo and East Timor—which were given the power to "exercise all legislative and executive authority"—are also, as he points out, law-making on a sovereign scale. Johnstone, *supra* note 20, at 774–776.

likely to have a potential impact on the underlying customary law that the Charter affirms.[262]

In these instances the SC was suggesting that terrorist acts, including those involving WMDs, were criminal acts requiring the kind of preventative measures (e.g., to deny access to financing or WMD material) that states routinely take to prevent other criminal activity. The resolutions also make clear that states are now required to make such acts crimes, requiring prosecution of not only those who commit terrorism but those who facilitate it by providing them with funds or weapons.[263] It is possible that these resolutions will convince states that these actions are all part of the customary crime of terrorism. But that may not be their only impact on the law. In the preamble to Resolution 1373, adopted a few weeks after 9/11 when the U.S. was clearly and publicly preparing to use force against Afghanistan, the SC reaffirmed "the inherent right of individual or collective self-defense as recognized by the Charter of the United Nations as reiterated in resolution 1368."[264] For some commentators, this reference, coupled with the same preamble's affirmation that all states have "the duty to refrain from organizing, instigating, assisting or participating in terrorists acts . . . or acquiescing in" such acts, seemed to authorize the U.S. to take its anticipated action against the Taliban regime and not merely use force against terrorist bases located in Afghanistan.[265]

As discussed, the Charter's drafters assumed that "armed attack" for purposes of Article 51 or the inherent right of self-defense meant an attack by one state against another—such as Germany's against Poland or Japan attacking the U.S. base at Pearl Harbor. Indeed, in 1986, the ICJ, in the Nicaragua case, held that only the "most grave forms of the use of force" constitute an armed attack and these could not be "mere frontier incidents"; that court also opined that a victim state could not resort to force in response to attacks by

---

262   We leave for another day whether these resolutions may have an impact on treaty law in other respects. Does Resolution 1540's expansion of the obligations of states under the NPT and its expansion of the powers of the IAEA have a permanent effect on the underlying treaties in question for example? This seems an academic question insofar as resolution 1540 reaches all states irrespective of whether they are parties to the NPT, but what if the SC were to dismantle its 1540 regime? Would those otherwise responsible for compliance with the NPT and the IAEA revert to their prior practices, or have the underlying treaties changed, along with the relevant "practice of the parties"?

263   *See generally* COUNTER-TERRORISM STRATEGIES IN A FRAGMENTED INTERNATIONAL LEGAL ORDER: MEETING THE CHALLENGES (Larissa van den Herik & Nico Schrijver eds., 2013).

264   S.C. Res. 1373, *supra* note 246, pmbl.; S.C. Res. 1368, pmbl (Sept. 12, 2001).

265   *See, e.g.*, Alvarez, *supra* note 247.

non-state actors unless those actors were effectively controlled by the territorial state.[266] The ICJ has affirmed its view that an armed attack triggering self-defense requires inter-state force and does not extend to the acts of terrorists whose conduct is not imputable to the territorial state in which they operate in its opinions in Oil Platforms, the Congo Case, and its Advisory Opinion on the Israeli Wall.[267] There seem good reasons for this view. If a rebel group or terrorist is physically located in the territory of another state, and that state is not in control of that group, to use force against that state for terrorist acts by such actors would seem to violate the equality of states. Moreover, keeping a tight rein on states' ability to turn to self-defense helps avoid slippery slope arguments that would threaten peace. Columbia or Mexico could be subject to the use of force for the acts of its international drug traffickers in neighboring countries; Russia would be deemed responsible for acts of the Russian mafia, and so on. In the Nicaragua case, the ICJ found that even the supply of arms and other support to groups within a state did not constitute an armed attack; the Court suggested that the U.S. could not use force against Nicaragua even if Nicaragua was arming rebels in El Salvador.[268] It also found that the U.S. was not responsible for the violent acts of the Contras within Nicaragua unless it was shown that the U.S. exercised "effective control" over them.[269]

By contrast, the Council's apparent endorsement of self-defense in the wake of 9/11 suggests three very different rules. It implies that terrorist violence at least of the scale of 9/11 constitutes an armed attack; that a state's assistance to, harboring of, or acquiescence to such acts within its territory authorizes defensive use of force against that state and not just non-state actors within it; and that the state victimized by terrorist armed attack has a continued right to respond with proportionate force so long as the continued threat of terrorism

---

266   Military and Paramilitary Activities in and Against Nicaragua (Nicar. v. U.S.), 1986 I.C.J. 14, ¶¶ 195, 253 (June 27) [hereinafter Nicaragua].

267   Legal Consequences of the Construction of a Wall in the Occupied Palestinian Territory, Advisory Opinion, 2004 I.C.J. 136, ¶¶ 27–28 (July 9) [hereinafter Wall Advisory Opinion]; Armed Activities on the Territory of the Congo (Dem. Rep. Congo v. Uganda), 2005 I.C.J. 168, ¶¶ 29–31, 48–50 (Dec. 19) [hereinafter Congo v. Uganda]; Case Concerning Oil Platforms (Iran v. U.S.), 2003 I.C.J. Rep. 161, ¶¶ 61–64 (Nov. 6) [hereinafter Oil Platforms]; Nicaragua, *supra* note 266. For a critical analysis on the I.C.J. jurisprudence related to armed attack, see Christian J. Tams, *Swimming with the Tide, or Seeking to Stem It? Recent ICJ Rulings on the Law of Self-Defence*, 18 REVUE QUÉBÉCOISE DE DROIT INT'L 275, 286 (2005); Theresa Reinold, *State Weakness, Irregular Warfare, and the Right to Self-Defense Post 9/11*, 105 AM. J. INT'L L. 244 (2011).

268   Nicaragua, *supra* note 266, ¶¶ 230, 236.

269   *Id.* ¶ 115.

continues. The arguments for these changes in the Charter and the underlying customary law require but short summary here. Those defending the new rules would argue that the old rules restricting armed attack to inter-state actions were adequate for a world that faced inter-state aggression or at worst state terrorism—by Iraq, Syria, Libya, Iran, Cuba, North Korea, or even France with respect to its attack on Greenpeace's Rainbow Warrior.[270] But restrictions on the use of defensive force when a single non-state act kills, as on 9/11, nearly 3000 people—a number that is higher than U.S. casualties in the War of 1812, the U.S.-Mexican War, or the Japanese attack on Pearl Harbor in 1941—threaten to turn, it is said, the UN Charter into a suicide pact.[271] Given the threats posed by non-state actors, especially when they might be armed with WMDs, it is argued that states cannot afford to wait until these clandestine attacks are demonstrably imminent—in the way that inter-state force was triggered only when the aggressor state's armies are gathered at the border poised to attack.[272]

Those suggesting that rules governing the use of force and self-defense have changed also point to the context in which Resolutions 1368 and 1373 were adopted. They point out that the day after the 9/11 attacks the U.S. informed the Council that it had been a victim of an armed attack.[273] For its part, NATO, for the first time in its history, invoked Article 5 of the North Atlantic Treaty, indicating that NATO members had determined that an armed attack had occurred against one of its members, thereby invoking the rights of that collective

---

270   *See, e.g.,* Roger S. Clark, *State Terrorism: Some Lessons from the Sinking of the "Rainbow Warrior",* 20 RUTGERS L.J. 393 (1989).

271   In addition, it is estimated that the 9/11 attacks cost the US economy over $650 billion. *See* MICHAEL P. SCHARF, CUSTOMARY INTERNATIONAL LAW IN TIMES OF FUNDAMENTAL CHANGE: RECOGNIZING GROATIAN MOMENTS 191–192 (2013). Of course, as is well known, al-Qaida attacks after 9/11 included the November 2003 truck bombings in Istanbul (injuring 700 and killing 58); the March 2004 train bombings in Madrid (injuring 1800; killing 191) and the July 2005 train and bus bombings in London (injuring 700; killing 56), to cite only three of the most prominent incidents. Karl Vick, *Al-Qaeda's Hand in Istanbul Plot,* THE WASHINGTON POST (Feb. 13, 2007); *Spain Train Bombing Fast Facts,* CNN (March 11, 2015); July 7 2005 *Bombings Fast Facts,* CNN (July 13, 2015).

272   The vast literature debating these issues includes Thomas M. Franck, *Terrorism and the Right of Self-Defense,* 95 AM. J. INT'L L. 839, 840 (2001); Mary Ellen O'Connell, *Dangerous Departures,* 107 AM. J. INT'L L. 380 (2013); NOAM LUBELL, EXTRATERRITORIAL USE OF FORCE AGAINST NON-STATE ACTORS (2010).

273   Statement of Ambassador James B. Cunningham, U.S. Deputy Representative to the United Nations, Transcript of the 4370th meeting of the Security Council, at 7, U.N. Doc. S/PV.4370 (September 12, 2001) (indicating that the US would respond and make "no distinction between the terrorists . . . and those who harbor them.").

security organization.[274] The OAS took a similar stance.[275] On October 7, 2001, just days after the adoption of Resolution 1373, the U.S. informed the Council that it had launched Operation Enduring Freedom in Afghanistan.[276] Those claiming that the rules of force now permit defensive action against non-state terrorist threats pointed to the relative lack of protest or condemnation by states in response to U.S. actions in Afghanistan as well as the numerous actions taken by other states in response to terrorist acts by non-state actors since 9/11.[277]

As noted in Chapter III, these three alleged new rules with respect to defensive force in the age of terrorism have not been endorsed by the General Assembly and continue to be resisted by many scholars.[278] They have not, as noted, yet been endorsed by the ICJ or other courts. And interestingly, they do not appear to have been clearly endorsed by other more recent Council resolutions. This uncertainty and lack of firm determinacy may be characteristic of what this author has called "hegemonic international law"—that is "law" as applied by an entity that is essentially controlled by the P-5 "hegemons" where those actors have an interest in retaining discretion to act without clarifying the rules that may apply to others.[279]

But these resolutions, as well as the many others that the SC has adopted to combat various forms of terrorism, may be having an impact on international

---

274   Press Release, Statement by the North Atlantic Council (Sept. 12, 2001), *at* http://www.nato.int/docu/pr/2001/p01-124e.htm.

275   Organization of American States Permanent Council Res. 797 (Sep. 19, 2001).

276   Letter from the Permanent Representative of the U.S. to the U.N. addressed to the President of the Security Council, Oct. 7, 2001, U.N. Doc. S/2001/946; *see generally* SCHARF, GROTIAN MOMENTS, *supra* note 271, 152–156 (2013).

277   SCHARF, GROTIAN MOMENTS, *supra* note 271, at 204–205 (citing examples including Turkish strikes against PKK sites in northern Iraq and a Colombian airstrike against FARC officials in Ecuador).

278   *See, e.g.,* John Cerone, *The Legality of the Killing of Osama Bin Laden,* 107 ASIL PROC. 47 2013 (questioning whether the rules on the use of force have evolved in the post-9/11 world and in particular, whether the U.S. invasion of Afghanistan and the international community's response brought a change in customary law or a novel, authoritative interpretation of the UN Charter). *See also* Tom Ruys, *The Meaning of "Force" and the Boundaries of Jus ad Bellum: Are "Minimal" Uses of Force Excluded from UN Charter Article 2(4)?,* 108 AM. J. INT'L L. 159 (2014); SCHARF, GROTIAN MOMENTS, *supra* note 271, 183–210 (doubting whether a "Grotian moment" has yet occurred to change the relevant customary rules on use of force in the wake of 9/11).

279   But, as Martti Koskenniemi has suggested, both "deformalisation" and reliance on hegemonic law may be characteristic of the modern age and not only the SC. Koskenniemi, *supra* note 246, at 78–80 and 83–88. *See also* Chapter VI *infra.*

law apart from its rules governing the use of force. The Council's repeated condemnations of terrorism make it hard to deny that whether or not terrorist acts by non-state actors constitute an "armed attack," they are, without any doubt, threats or breaches of the peace under Article 39.[280] As noted, the Council has repeatedly suggested that under international law, terrorist acts are illegal, indeed criminal, actions having no justification, including self-determination. Its resolutions, as noted, have also repeatedly suggested that such non-state acts within a state's territory can be attributed to the host state, at least for purposes of state responsibility, if the state provides a safe haven or even merely acquiesces in such activity.[281] According to Resolution 1566, "criminal acts...[c]ommitted with the intent to cause death or serious bodily injury, or taking of hostages, with the purpose to provoke a state of terror in the general public or in a group of persons or particular persons...are under no circumstances justifiable by considerations of a political, philosophical, ideological, racial, ethnic, religious or other similar nature...." and states now also have an obligation under international law "to find, deny safe haven and bring to justice...any person who supports, facilitates, participates or attempts to participate in the financing, planning, preparation or commission of terrorist acts or provides safe havens."[282]

In accordance with these affirmations of law, the Council has repeatedly urged or called upon states to ratify numerous counter-terrorist conventions, many of which were negotiated under the auspices of ICAO and address more specific terrorist acts, such as those involving hijacking or bombing of planes or threats to international airports. These invocations and states responses to them may make it increasingly likely that some or all of these are obligations even for states that are not parties to the underlying counter-terrorism con-

---

280   *See, e.g.*, S.C. Res. 1267, *supra* note 195, pmbl. ("Reaffirming its conviction that the suppression of international terrorism is essential for the maintenance of international peace and security").

281   If this is the case, these rules on state attribution would make a state responsible in at least some contexts not encompassed by the ILC's Articles on State Responsibility. International Law Commission, Draft Articles on State Responsibility arts 4–11, reprinted in THE INTERNATIONAL LAW COMMISSION'S ARTICLES ON STATE RESPONSIBILITY: INTRODUCTION, TEXT AND COMMENTARIES, at 61 (James Crawford ed., 2002). To this extent the actions of the SC and the GA may be contributing to *lex specialis* rules governing attribution in the context of terrorism but that is only one way to consider the potential interplay between the Security Council and the residual rules on state responsibility. *See* Vera Gowlland-Debbas, *The Security Council and Issues of Responsibility*, 105 ASIL PROC. 348 (2011).

282   S.C. Res. 1566, ¶ ¶ 2–3 (Oct. 4, 2004).

ventions—either because these obligations now emerge under the UN Charter itself or under general customary law.[283] As a practical matter, however, the SC's (and General Assembly's) condemnations of "terrorism" without more detail as to what the term means undermines the likely impact on the law.[284]

The most recent example of Council-generated global legislation is Resolution 2178, introduced by President Obama at a special session of the Council attended by heads of state.[285] That resolution repeats the condemnations of terrorism contained in prior resolutions but focuses attention on the recruitment of "foreign terrorist fighters" to join entities such as ISIL and ANF. It revisits the obligations originally imposed on all states under Resolution 1373 to prevent the transborder movement of terrorists and expands or reinterprets those duties by demanding that member states "shall, consistent with international human rights law, international refugee law, and international humanitarian law, prevent and suppress the recruiting, organizing, transporting or equipping of individuals who travel to a State other than their States of residence or nationality for the purpose of the perpetration, planning, or preparation of, or participation in, terrorist acts or the providing or receiving of terrorist training, and the financing of their travel and of their activities."[286]

Resolution 2178 differs from 1373 and 1540 in one critical respect: in this instance the Council was not acting to impose obligations in an existing treaty. There is no foreign fighter convention and no such treaty is under negotiation. This resolution is therefore an even more definitive step by the Council towards ignoring or bypassing positivists' most revered and legitimate method for generating new international obligations: the time-consuming negotiation, ratification, and implementation of a new treaty. To critics of this approach and

---

283   Thus, it might be argued that a state that harbors non-state terrorists within its borders and does nothing to prevent their continued threats on others, is in violation of Art. 2(4) of the Charter even if such an act does not amount to an "armed attack" sufficient to trigger self-defense.

284   There is a wealth of literature on the Council's lack of guidance in providing a definition of terrorism. Indeed, by the time the SC passed Resolution 1566, many if not most states already had in place counter-terrorism laws with more specific definitions. See GLOBAL ANTI-TERRORISM LAW AND POLICY (Victor V. Ramraj et. al eds., 2012). On the other hand, the wealth of domestic laws might constitute the "state practice" that traditional positivists seek for the establishment of custom.

285   S.C. Res 2178, *supra* note 197.

286   *Id.* ¶ 5. *See also id.* ¶ 8 (deciding that all members must "prevent the entry into or transit through their territories of any individual about whom that state has credible information that provides reasonable grounds to believe that he or she is seeking entry into or transit through their territory" for the prohibited purposes).

Council-generated global law generally, the resolution was "worse—indeed far worse—than Resolution 1373 from the perspective of the international rule of law."[287] This criticism of the Council has a domestic as well as international dimension. If a state, including the u.s., can turn to the sc to impose legally binding obligations, this bypasses the often difficult hurdles to securing legislative approval of a treaty common to democratic states, therefore short changing the national rule of law.[288] For their part some international lawyers see these actions as violating the international rule of law insofar as nothing in the Charter permits the sc to make general law.[289]

But another aspect of Resolution 2178 has not led to comparable criticism. Whereas 1373 did not anticipate the human rights critiques that the Council's counter-terrorism measures, including smart sanctions, would unleash,[290] Resolution 2178 shows what the sc has learned from over a decade of such criticisms. That resolution includes what is now standard language in many of the sc's later counter-terrorism resolutions: a clear statement that all measures that states take to counter terrorism must "comply with all their obligations under international law, in particular international human rights law, international refugee law, and international humanitarian law" and that efforts to comply with such obligations and to combat terrorism are complimentary insofar as both signal "respect for the rule of law."[291]

Resolution 2178 is, of course, part of a broader coalition effort, now involving some 60 countries, to use force against ISIL, especially within Iraq and in parts of Syria. Iraq and the u.s. in particular have justified their use of force against ISIL as individual and collective self-defense permitted under Article 51.[292] Resolution 2178 has been applauded as part of a "holistic, multi-

---

287   Scheinin, *supra* note 252. Of course the sc, as noted, bypassed treaty negotiations in establishing the ICTY and the ICTR.

288   This accusation is one complaint us critics have of the deal with Iran on nuclear weapons reached in June 2015. That deal, as approved by the sc, will not be treated as a formal treaty subject to the usual legislative approval of at least the u.s.

289   Koskenniemi also argues that the sc's composition and mode of operation undermines the claim that it is a legislative body. Koskenniemi, *supra* note 246, 326–327.

290   Indeed, Res. 1373, *supra* note 246, ignored the references to nondiscrimination, human rights, humanitarian law, or the rights of extradited persons contained in the International Convention for the Suppression of Financing of Terrorism. *See* International Convention for the Suppression of the Financing of Terrorism, *supra* note 251, arts. 6, 9, 15, 17 & 21.

291   s.c. Res. 2178, *supra* note 197, pmbl.

292   *See* Letter from the Permanent Representative of Iraq to the United Nations addressed to the President of the Security Council, UN Doc. S/2014/691 (Sept. 22, 2014); Letter from

national approach to arresting and then reversing that group's gains."[293] Like 1373 and 1540, it is not hard to see how Resolution 2178 suits the interests of the P-5—and might therefore be either praised or condemned as another example of "hegemonic international law." According to top counterterrorism officials, some 3000 Europeans have traveled to fight in Iraq and Syria while over 100 Americans have done so; it is feared that such individuals, with European or U.S. passports, may return home to commit individual terrorist attacks and indeed some have already done so.[294] Of course, much of the burden for enforcing the new travel and immigration restrictions anticipated by this resolution will fall on gateway states like Qatar and Turkey that will need to take political decisions at the highest levels and make considerable adjustment to internal laws and practices if this resolution is to prove effective.[295]

9   The Council's New "Tool": The ICC

The Council's interactions with the International Criminal Court, whose Rome Statute came into force on July 1, 2002, were initially hostile. Since three members of the P-5 (China, Russia, and the U.S.) did not ratify that Statute and show no intentions of doing so, that hostility is quite understandable. Accordingly, in Resolutions 1422 and 1487 from 2002–2003, the Council passed resolutions to exempt, a year at a time, UN peacekeepers from states that were not parties to the Rome Statute from investigations or prosecutions in the ICC.[296] These Council efforts, passed at a time when the Bush Administration in the U.S. was engaging in a number of actions to sideline the ICC or at least make it impossible for U.S. nationals to be brought before it,[297] were taken pursuant to

---

the Permanent Representative of the U.S. to the U.N. addressed to the Secretary-General, UN Doc. S/2014/695 (Sept. 23, 2014).

293 Zachary Goldman, *The Foreign Fighter Resolution: Implementing a Holistic Strategy to Defeat ISIL*, JUST SECURITY (Sept. 29, 2014).

294 *Id.*

295 *Id.*

296 S.C. Res. 1422 ¶ 1 (July 12, 2002); S.C. Res. 1487 ¶ 1 (June 12, 2003). Both Resolutions expressed the Council's intent to "renew the request … under the same conditions each 1 July for further 12-month periods for as long as may be necessary." S.C. Res. 1422, *supra*, ¶ 2; S.C. Res. 1487, *supra*, ¶ 2.

297 This included controversial treaty negotiations conducted around the world between the U.S. and ratifiers of the Rome Statute, arguably as permitted by Art. 98 of the Rome Statute, whereby both states exempted U.S. nationals from being transferred to the ICC. *See* Markus Benzing, U.S. *Bilateral Non-Surrender Agreements and Article 98 of the Statute*

Article 16 of the Rome Statute which permits the SC to request that the Court defer investigations or prosecutions for a renewable period of 12 months.[298] But it was not entirely clear whether Article 16, which permits the Council acting under Chapter VII to defer particular investigations or prosecutions before the Court, was really intended for this purpose.[299] By the time 1422 came up for renewal in Resolution 1487, the prospect of perpetual SC deferrals for all future peacekeeping operations was controversial and it drew three abstentions (by France, Germany, and Syria).[300] The next year, when even the UN Secretary General appeared critical, the proposed resolution was withdrawn. While these deferrals were in place, they provided, to critics of the Council, a potent example of its selectivity when it comes to the enforcement of international criminal law and international humanitarian law.

A couple of months later, Resolution 1497, in which the Council exempted from ICC jurisdiction "current or former officials or personnel" involved in UN peacekeeping operations in Liberia from non-Rome party states, was even more controversial.[301] In this case, the Council determined that such persons were subject to the "exclusive jurisdiction" of the troop-contributing states, and purported to do so on a permanent basis and not merely for the 12-month period anticipated under the ICC's Article 16. This Council action, just seven weeks before Liberia ratified the Rome Statute, seemed to be a direct challenge to the Court's jurisdiction that was not authorized by anything in its Statute.[302]

---

of the International Criminal Court: An Exercise in the Law of Treaties, in 8 MAX PLANCK Y.B. UNITED NATIONS L. ONLINE 187 (2004); David Scheffer, Article 98(2) of the Rome Statute: America's Original Intent, 3 J. INT'L CRIM. JUS. 333–353 (2005). See also 2002 Supplemental Appropriations Act for Further Recovery from and Response to Terrorist Attacks on the United States, Pub. L. No. 107–206, §§ 2001–2015, 116 Stat. 820 (2002) [hereinafter American Servicemembers' Protection Act] (authorizing the President to use "all means necessary" to secure an American servicemember detained by the ICC); Sean D. Murphy, American Servicemembers' Protection Act, 96 AM. J. INT'L L. 975 (2002).

298 Rome Statute, supra note 138, art. 16.

299 See, e.g., Carsten Stahn, The Ambiguities of Security Council Resolution 1422, 14 EUR. J. INT'L L. 85–104 (2002).

300 Voting Records, United Nations Bibliographic Information System, at http://unbisnet. un.org:8080/ipac20/ipac.jsp?profile=voting&index=.VM&term=sres1487.

301 S.C. Res. 1497 ¶ 7 (Aug. 1, 2003). See, e.g., Marco Roscini, The Efforts to Limit the International Criminal Court's Jurisdiction over Nationals of Non-Party States: A Comparative Study, 5 LAW & PRAC. INT'L CTS. & TRIBS. 495, 504 (2006) (assessing the legality of the Security Council's "multilateral strategy" in all three of the resolutions pertaining to the jurisdiction of the ICC).

302 See Rome Statute, supra note 138, art. 12(2) (providing for ICC jurisdiction where a crime is committed within the territory of an ICC member state or by one of its nationals).

Given these precedents, many were surprised when the Council, on a divided vote but without the veto of a Permanent Member, referred the situation in the Sudan to the ICC in Resolution 1593, and six years later followed suit with a unanimous vote in favor of referring the situation in Libya to the ICC.[303] In both of these instances the SC deployed a new tool at its disposal: namely the power the Council acquired through the Rome Statute's Article 13(b) providing the ICC with jurisdiction if "a situation" involving one or more of the crimes within that Court's statute (namely genocide, crimes against humanity, or war crimes) "is referred to the Prosecutor by the Security Council acting under Chapter VII of the Charter of the United Nations."[304]

In these instances, the Council acted under Chapter VII. In both instances it adhered to strikingly similar language in doing so. Each resolution decided that the Libyan and Sudanese authorities respectively were required to cooperate with the Court and to provide it all necessary assistance but that non-Rome Party states owed no such obligations; each indicates that the resulting expenses would not be borne by the UN but by the parties to the Rome Statute; and each imposed certain other temporal constraints on the referral.[305] Both resolutions also borrowed from the text of Resolution 1497 insofar as each decided "that nationals, current or formal officials or personnel from a State outside [Libya or the Sudan] which is not a party to the Rome Statute ... shall be subject to the exclusive jurisdiction of that State for all alleged acts or omissions arising out of or related to operations in [Libya or Sudan] established or authorized by the Council," unless such exclusive jurisdiction has been expressly waived by the state.[306]

Many have praised these SC referrals for showing the Council's unexpected embrace of the ICC, particularly since its referral of the Libyan situation was supported by a unanimous vote.[307] It is remarkable that non-parties to the

---

Resolution 1497, which does not refer to art. 16 of the Rome Statute, appears to be based squarely on the SC's Chapter VII authority (and therefore on art. 103 of the Charter with respect to conflicting treaties).

303   S.C. Res. 1593 (Mar. 31, 2005); S.C. Res. 1970, ¶ 4 (Feb. 26, 2011).

304   Rome Statute, *supra* note 138, art. 13(b).

305   S.C. Res. 1593, *supra* note 303, ¶¶ 1, 2 & 7. That resolution referred the situation in Darfur since 1 July 2002. *Id.* ¶ 1. In the case of Libya, Resolution 1970 refers the situation in Libya only as of Feb. 15, 2011. S.C. Res. 1970, *supra* note 302, ¶¶ 4–8.

306   S.C. Res. 1593, *supra* note 303, ¶ 6; S.C. Res. 1970, *supra* note 303, ¶ 6.

307   Voting Records, United Nations Bibliographic Information System, *at* http://unbisnet .un.org:8080/ipac20/ipac.jsp?session=145L2V66546A0.48445&menu=search&aspect= power&npp=50&ipp=20&spp=20&profile=voting&ri=1&source=~%21horizon&index= .VM&term=sres1970&x=0&y=0&aspect=power.

Rome Statute like the U.S., Russia, China, and India all approved of sending the Libya situation to the ICC, with only Russia merely abstaining as opposed to voting in favor in both instances. These actions suggest that the ICC has now become part of the SC's regular toolbox to deal with threats to the peace, even though such referrals will presumably remain rare. But as a number of commentators have pointed out, these referrals are not an unmitigated boon for the ICC's legitimacy of the ICC or for advocates of international criminal accountability.[308]

The SC's ICC referrals are a mixed blessing for the Court's and its prosecutor's independence. While both the ICC prosecutor and the pre-trial chamber of the Court retain their formal independence and could, for example, refuse to bring forward investigations of particular individuals that the SC might have had in mind when it referred the underlying situations, the limits imposed by the SC put both prosecutor and Court in a peculiar position. But for the SC's referrals, the ICC would not have jurisdiction of crimes in these non-Rome Party States. This means that the SC referred complex situations of ongoing conflict within two African states to the Court in instances where the countries involved would not be expected to cooperate, where politically risky and expensive investigations in high risk environments would be necessary, and where it was likely that controversial high level indictments (including of then sitting presidents) would be likely. It surely could not have escaped the SC's attention that these referrals would only exacerbate perceptions that the ICC was overly preoccupied with Africa and insufficiently attentive to crimes committed elsewhere. Moreover, the Council referred these expensive situations (which would likely involve a number of trials and considerable investigations within fragile or dangerous states) while refusing to pay itself for the resulting expenses—despite Article 115(b) of the Rome Statute which clearly anticipates that UN funds should be used for expenses incurred due to referrals by the SC.[309] While the financial aspects of these referrals can be explained by U.S. national legislation which bars U.S. payments to the Court,[310] this aspect of the referrals underscored the Council's exceptionalist approach to international criminal justice.[311]

---

308   *See, e.g.,* Joseph M. Isanga, *The International Criminal Court Ten Years Later: Appraisal and Prospects*, 21 CARDOZO J. INT'L & COMP. L. 235, 287 (2013) (noting that referrals may seem politicized).

309   Rome Statute, *supra* note 138, art. 115b.

310   American Servicemembers Protection Act, *supra* note 297.

311   *See, e.g.,* Isanga, *supra* note 308; William A. Schabas, *Victor's Justice: Selecting "Situations" at the International Criminal Court*, 43 J. MARSHALL L. REV. 535 (2010); *see also* Margaret M.

The time limit imposed on the Libyan referral was subject to similar complaints. The SC's insistence that the ICC could not look at crimes committed prior to February 15, 2011 prevents, conveniently, a fuller inquiry about some of the underlying crimes—inquiries that might have implicated at least the financial assistance provided by some prominent Western states that had, in recent years, increasingly seen Colonel Qadaffi as a possible ally in the "war" on al-Qaida.[312] While it remains possible that the ICC could resist some of the limits imposed by the SC,[313] these referrals threaten to turn the Court into a "mere" tool of diplomacy.

Skepticism about these referrals has also arisen due to what the SC has done, or more accurately, not done after sending these difficult situations to the Court. Although both resolutions directed the ICC prosecutor to report back to the Council every six months, the prosecutor's subsequent pleas for Council cooperation or assistance in securing enforcement of the Court's requests for suspects or evidence has not produced any follow-up enforcement actions by the SC to date.[314] Further, as noted, since non-Rome Statute states have no obligation to cooperate with the Court or its prosecutor, several members of the P-5 were not under any pressure to use Chapter VII to assist the Court's handling of cases that would not be before the Court but for the SC's action. Worse still, the innovation in these referrals—to provide that crimes committed by non-Rome Party States's nationals are within those states' "exclusive jurisdiction"—demonstrated how the SC could use its newfound ability to refer cases to the ICC as a convenient tool to achieve what some of its members could not

---

de Guzman, *Choosing to Prosecute: Expressive Selection at the International Criminal Court,* 33 MICH. J. INT'L L. 265 (2012) (addressing accusations that the prosecutor's selection of cases has been political).

312   *See, e.g.,* Luc Côté, *Independence and Impartiality, in* INTERNATIONAL PROSECUTORS 404 (Luc Reydams et al. eds., 2012); Ronli Sifris, *Weighing Judicial Independence Against Judicial Accountability: Do the Scales of the International Criminal Court Balance?,* 8 CHI.-KENT J. INT'L AND COMP. L. (2008); Adejoke Babington-Ashaye, *Politicizing the International Criminal Court: Redefining the Role of the United States Security Council in the Age of Accountability,* 108 ASIL PROC. 301 (2014).

313   It has been argued, for example, that SC efforts to cut back on the ICC's normal jurisdiction by excepting nationals of non-Rome Statute States might not be "in accordance with the provisions of this Statute" under the chapeaux of the Statute's Art. 13 and that phrase conditions the acceptance of SC's referrals. To the extent the ICC were to take this courageous or foolhardy stance, this too might be seen as a form of "judicial review" over the SC.

314   That is with the exception of occasional and perfunctory references to the need for cooperation by the Libyan government with the ICC. *See, e.g.,* S.C. Res. 2040, pmbl. (Mar. 12, 2012); S.C. Res. 2095, pmbl. (Mar. 14, 2013); S.C. Res. 2144, pmbl. (Mar. 14, 2014).

achieve during the Rome Statute's negotiations.[315] Resolutions 1593 and 1970
thus have a double effect: they make Sudanese and Libyan nationals subject to
the ICC jurisdiction over certain crimes while making sure that neither the ICC
nor any court other than the courts of Russia, China, or the U.S. respectively,
have jurisdiction over Russian, Chinese, or American nationals who might
commit such crimes in the Sudan or Libya.

For all these reasons, the SC's two referrals to the ICC are hardly unadorned
endorsements of the ICC or expressions of faith in the principle that international criminal accountability applies equally to all nations and all individuals.
With "friends" like the Council dumping selectively the hardest cases on the
Court without paying for them, who needs enemies? When the ICC's prosecutor responded to the Council's referrals by (predictably) investigating and
eventually indicting Colonel Qadaffi and President al-Bashir, the Council did
not respond to his and others' requests for assistance in securing evidence or
later with the arrests of these individuals. No Chapter VII actions were directed
at, for example, African countries who failed to send President al-Bashir to The
Hague for trial when given the chance. To the contrary, at one point, under
pressure from the African Union and having achieved its immediate goals for
South Sudan, the Council even considered deferring the situation in the Sudan
under Article 16 of the Rome Statute.[316] These inactions arguably suggest that
the SC treats the ICC as yet another political tool that can be traded away if it
is politically expedient. Indeed, some criticized the Libyan referral in particular as essentially a tool to delegitimize a regime that some members of the SC
wanted to eliminate.[317]

But when it comes to its contribution to international criminal justice,
there is another side to the SC's ledger. As noted, but for the SC's establishment of the ICTY and ICTR there probably would not be an ICC to discuss.
Further, many of the Chapter VII efforts discussed in this chapter stem from
the Council's concerns with the commission of international crimes and violations of international humanitarian law. Its smart sanctions regimes, as well

---

315   The provision of exclusive jurisdiction means that nationals from non-ICC states, even
      if they commit international crimes that are otherwise within the jurisdiction of that
      Court, would be immune from ICC jurisdiction. It also means, presumably, that no state
      could attempt to assert jurisdiction, including universal jurisdiction, over such nationals.
      Neither assurance was, of course, provided under the Rome Statute.

316   Security Council Report, Update Report No. 4: Sudan (July 28, 2008), *at* http://www.secu
      ritycouncilreport.org/update-report/lookup-c-glKWLeMTIsG-b-4381649.php.

317   *See, e.g.,* Frédéric Mégret, *Practices of Stigmatization*, 76 L. & CONTEMP. PROBS. 287, 297
      (2013).

as its more obvious legislative efforts in 1373 and 1540, can be seen as part of a global effort to criminalize certain terrorist acts.[318] In addition, it cannot be said that the SC has done nothing to enforce international criminal law. The Council's inaction following its Sudan and Libyan referrals can be compared to its efforts elsewhere, including Resolution 2098's establishment of an "intervention brigade" in the Congo.[319] This appears to be the first serious Council enforcement action directed, at least in part, at supporting the ICC's prosecutorial efforts. That resolution, which followed a series of prior SC resolutions addressing international crimes and the possibility of ICC intervention in the DRC,[320] authorized MONUSCO to take "all necessary measures" to protect civilians, ensure the protection of UN personnel, and work with the government of the Congo to identify threats to and ensure the protection of civilians from violence, including all forms of sexual and gender based violence.[321] While condemning the mass rapes reportedly committed by the Congo's own armed forces (the FARDC), the SC approved that government's efforts to arrest those responsible and to cooperate with the ICC to uphold criminal accountability. A clear target of that resolution are the "destabilizing" activities of the 23 March Movement (M23) and other Congolese and foreign armed groups (including the Lord's Resistance Army) operating in Eastern Congo who have been allegedly responsible for extrajudicial executions, arbitrary arrests, and mass rapes as well as systematic recruitment and use of children for armed conflict there. Accordingly, the resolution authorized MONUSCO and its new Intervention Brigade to "arrest and bring to justice those responsible for war crimes and crimes against humanity ... including through cooperation with States of the region and the ICC."[322] That resolution also requested the Congolese government to "arrest and hold accountable those responsible for war crimes and crimes against humanity in the country, including Sylvestre Mudacumura, and

---

318   For an interesting discussion of how the culmination of all of these efforts has "created the rudiments of a system of international criminal justice," see James Cockayne, *Unintended Justice: The United Nations Security Council and International Criminal Governance, in* INTERNATIONAL AND COMPARATIVE CRIMINAL JUSTICE AND URBAN GOVERNANCE: CONVERGENCE AND DIVERGENCE IN GLOBAL, NATIONAL AND LOCAL SETTINGS 41 (Adam Crawford ed., 2011).

319   *See* Part 3 *supra.*

320   *See, e.g.,* S.C. Res. 2098, *supra* note 99, ¶ 19; S.C. Res. 2053, pmbl & ¶ 13 (June 27, 2012).

321   S.C. Res. 2098, *supra* note 99, ¶ 12.

322   *Id.* ¶ 12(d).

stresses the importance to this end of regional cooperation, including through cooperation with the ICC."[323]

These are not the only other references to the ICC in the SC's recent practice. Since 2012, there has been a steady increase in the number of SC resolutions that explicitly refer to the ICC even though the SC has only referred the Sudan and Libyan situations to that Court. In 2012, there were nine resolutions with ICC references dealing with four countries: Mali, the DRC, Ivory Coast, and Libya; by 2013, that number had risen to ten, and by 2014, the SC had mentioned the ICC in fourteen resolutions involving those same countries along with Burundi and the CAR.[324] The Mali resolutions for 2012, for example, suggested that some acts

---

323   *Id.* ¶ 21. The SC has continued to express interest in the DRC and the pursuit of ICC investigations and prosecutions. *See* S.C. Res. 2147, pmbl. & ¶¶ 4, 24 (Mar. 28, 2014); S.C. Res. 2137, *supra* note 189, ¶ 11.

324   *See* S.C. Res. 2085 (Dec. 20, 2012) (regarding the situation in Mali); S.C. Res. 2071 (Oct. 12, 2012) (same); S.C. Res. 2056 (July 5, 2012) (same, focusing on Mali's World Heritage Sites); S.C. Res. 2068 (Sept. 19, 2012) (concerning children in armed conflict); S.C. Res. 2078 (Nov. 28, 2012) (encouraging cooperation between the ICC and the DRC government); S.C. Res. 2053 (June 27, 2012) (same); S.C. Res. 2062 (Jul. 26, 2012) (authorizing an investigation of Côte d'Ivoire); S.C. Res. 2045 (Apr. 26, 2012) (stressing that Ivorian perpetrators be brought to justice including before the ICC); S.C. Res. 2040 (Mar. 12, 2012) (recalling referral of Libya situation); S.C. Res. 2127 (Dec. 5, 2013) (noting that certain events in the Central African Republic may amount to Rome Statute crimes); S.C. Res. 2121 (Oct. 10, 2013) (same); S.C. Res. 2101 (Apr. 25, 2013) (encouraging Côte d'Ivoire to cooperate with the ICC); S.C. Res. 2112 (July 30, 2013) (expanding the Prosecutor's investigation in Côte d'Ivoire); S.C. Res. 2122 (Oct. 18, 2013) (saying that the ICC has strengthened the fight against impunity for serious crimes against women and girls); S.C. Res. 2106 (June 24, 2013) (recalling sexual violence offences in the Rome Statute); S.C. Res. 2100, U.N. Doc. S/RES/2100 (Apr. 25, 2013); S.C. Res. 2098 (Mar. 28, 2013) (welcoming the DRC's cooperation with the ICC); S.C. Res. 2095 (Mar. 14, 2013) (recalling referral of the situation in Libya to the ICC); S.C. Res. 2090 (Feb. 13, 2013) (recalling that Burundi is a party to the Rome Statute); S.C. Res. 2175 (Aug. 29, 2014) (recalling criminalization of intentional attacks against civilians); S.C. Res. 2171 (Aug. 21, 2014) (emphasizing the importance of the fight against impunity); S.C. Res. 2150 (Apr. 16, 2014) (recognizing the contribution of the ICC to the fight against impunity); S.C. Res. 2143 (Mar. 7, 2014) (same); S.C. Res. 2174 (Aug. 27, 2014) (recalling referral of the situation in Libya to the ICC); S.C. Res. 2144 (Mar. 14, 2014) (same); S.C. Res. 2164 (June 25, 2014) (noting ICC investigation in Mali); S.C. Res. 2162 (June 25, 2014) (welcoming the transfer of an Ivorian suspect to the ICC); S.C. Res. 2153 (Apr. 29, 2014) (encouraging Côte d'Ivoire to cooperate with the ICC); S.C. Res. 2149 (Apr. 10, 2014) (noting that certain acts in the Central African Republic may violate the Rome Statute); S.C. Res. 2134 (Jan. 28, 2014) (same); S.C. Res. 2147 (Mar. 28, 2014) (encouraging the DRC to cooperate with the ICC); S.C. Res. 2136 (Jan. 30, 2014) (regarding ICC operations in the DRC); S.C. Res. 2137, *supra* note 189 (recalling that Burundi is a party to the Rome Statute).

committed in that country "may amount to crimes under the Rome Statute" and called upon AFISMA to support "national and international efforts, including those of the International Criminal Court, to bring to justice perpetrators. . . ."[325] With respect to the Ivory Coast that year, to give another example, the SC took note of that country's acceptance of the ICC and the opening of an ICC preliminary investigation into crimes and urged a quick response by that government to cooperate with the ICC.[326] By 2014, the SC was directing MINUSCA, as part of its mandate, to "support, as feasible and appropriate" Malian government efforts to bring to justice perpetrators taking into account that country's self-referral to the ICC.[327] And by 2014, the SC was "welcoming . . . the transfer of Charles Blé Goudé, former leader of the Young Patriots, to the ICC. . . ."[328] In other cases, the SC seemed to be gently prodding a Rome Party state to referral itself to the Court.[329] Still, but for the two referrals to the Court which invoked Chapter VII, none of these other references involve the application of Chapter VII.[330]

10   The Council and "Human Security"

This chapter's examination of SC resolutions began with Resolution 678 where, despite that resolution's innovations, the SC was resorting to force in exactly the type of situation foreseen by the Charter: a classic case where one state invaded another and tried, as Germany had, to acquire its territory. By the time the Council reached its most prominent recent recourse to the contracting out of force, Resolution 1973 authorizing force in Libya in 2011, it was reacting to an internal conflict that threatened human security.[331] The Council of today responds most often to civil wars, other internal conflicts, internal breakdowns of law and order, and threats posed by non-state actors. All of these situations

---

325   S.C. Res. 2085, pmbl. & ¶ 19 (Dec. 20, 2012). *See also* S.C. Res. 2071, *supra* note 324, pmbl.; S.C. Res. 2056, *supra* note 324, ¶ 16.

326   S.C. Res. 2062, *supra* note 324, pmbl. & ¶ 12; S.C. Res. 2045, *supra* note 324, pmbl.

327   S.C. Res. 2164, *supra* note 324, ¶ 13(b)(vi).

328   S.C. Res. 2153, *supra* note 324, pmbl.; S.C. Res. 2162, *supra* note 324. pmbl.

329   *See, e.g.,* S.C. Res. 2137, *supra* note 189, pmbl. ("recalling" that Burundi is a party to the ICC and "has undertaken obligations to fight impunity for crimes falling within the jurisdiction of the Court, and emphasizing that the International Criminal Court is complementary to the national criminal jurisdictions").

330   *See supra* note 324.

331   S.C. Res. 1973, *supra* note 97. Paul R. Williams & Colleen (Betsy) Popken, *Security Council Resolution 1973 on Libya: A Moment of Legal and Moral Clarity*, 44 CASE W. RES. J. INT'L L. 225 (2011).

involve threats to the "peoples" mentioned in the Charter that, as discussed above, largely disappear in the rest of the Charter's text. Increasingly, through many of the resolutions discussed in sections 3–9 above, the SC has become as much a protector of human beings located inside states as it is of sovereign governments.

Resolution 1973 was, in many respects, emblematic of this fundamental change in the SC's purpose. In that case, the Council, having referred the situation of Libya to the ICC in an earlier resolution, went a step further. Acting under Chapter VII, it authorized member states that have notified the Secretary-General (namely NATO member states) "to take all necessary measures . . . to protect civilians and civilian populated areas under threat of attack in [Libya], including Benghazi, while excluding a foreign occupation force of any form on any part of Libyan territory. . . ."[332] Having authorized a limited recourse to force to protect civilians, that resolution also demanded an immediate establishment of a cease-fire and a complete end to violence and all attacks on civilians, established a ban on all flights in Libyan air space and a ban on the operation of Libyan aircraft over any state's territory except as otherwise approved, permitted cooperating member states to enforce the flight ban over Libyan airspace with all necessary means, authorized inspections at seaports and airports to enforce its arms embargo on Libya, and expanded the asset freeze and travel bans previously imposed on designated Libyan nationals and entities.[333]

Resolution 1973 encapsulated much of the Council's recent activity. It showed a Council willing to treat certain select internal human rights threats as a threat to the peace irrespective of whether those spill over into borders and impact on other states, as was arguably the case with respect to Haiti in Resolution 940.

Moreover, this Resolution, as well as Resolution 1970, reiterated "the responsibility of the Libyan authorities to protect the Libyan population."[334] This appears to be the first instance where the Council invoked the R2P principle as the raison d'etre for the invocation of its Chapter VII powers.[335]

---

332   S.C. Res. 1973, *supra* note 97, ¶ 4.

333   *Id.* ¶¶ 1, 6, 8, 17, 19–21. The resolution also includes an annex identifying two additional individuals that would be subject to the travel ban and another 7 individuals and 5 entities that would subject to the asset freeze.

334   *Id.* pmbl.

335   Michael W. Doyle, *Law, Ethics, and the Responsibility to Protect*, in THE ETHICS OF ARMED HUMANITARIAN INTERVENTION 201 (Don E. Scheid ed., 2014) (noting that the Libyan resolution gave "teeth" to the R2P principle and that this was only the third time since the principle was adopted that it was invoked to enforce the protection of civilians). *See also* Catherine Powell, *Libya: A Multilateral Constitutional Moment?*, 106 AM. J. INT'L L. 298

Resolution 1973, together with Resolution 1970, shows the Council treating a human rights threat that is the product of the current leadership of a country as criminal activity that needs to be subject to criminal law enforcement (hence the referral in Resolution 1970 to the ICC), while, at the same time, treating the government's actions as requiring a military response—namely aerial "protection of civilians," enforcement of a no-fly zone (as with respect to Iraq prior to the U.S. led invasion of 2003), and enforcement of an arms embargo through intrusive inspections of vessels and aircraft bound to or from Libya. This resolution might be read as the culmination of the human rights revolution.[336]

Like the SC's referrals to the ICC, progressive international lawyers applauded the SC's move, with some suggesting that this was finally the moment when the R2P principle was transformed from political or moral precept into a legal code of conduct embedded in the Charter to be enforced by Chapter VII if necessary.[337] For some this seemed like the Council's clear endorsement of the core idea that a state's right to enjoy its sovereignty is conditioned on not slaughtering their own people or committing serious international crimes against them. Yet, like many of the Council's actions, Resolution 1973 manifested a more ambiguous message. It showed a latent respect for "sovereignty." Although it ultimately resulted in massive aerial bombings that lead to the collapse of the Qaddafi regime—and indirectly to the killing of Colonel Qaddafi himself[338]—its text was not a license for such actions. The contracting out of force was considerably more circumscribed than the "all necessary means" licensed in Resolution 678; moreover, unlike that resolution, which anticipated action to restore and maintain international peace and security,

---

(2012) (arguing "that the Security Council's invocation of RtoP in the midst of the Libyan crisis significantly deepens the broader, ongoing transformation in the international law system's approach to sovereignty and civilian protection").

336   *See generally* RUTI G. TEITEL, HUMANITY'S LAW (2011) (discussing R2P among other developments as demonstrating a normative shift in the international legal order from prioritizing state security to protecting human security).

337   R2P has generated a substantial literature. *See, e.g.*, Carsten Stahn, *Responsibility to Protect: Political Rhetoric or Emerging Legal Norm?*, 101 AM. J. INT'L L. 99 (2007). As affirmed in the 2005 World Outcome document, it seemed to authorize the SC, but not individual states acting unilaterally, to "take collective action, in a timely and decisive manner . . . including under Chapter VII . . . should peaceful means be inadequate and national authorites are manifestly failing to protect their populations from genocide, war crimes, ethnic cleansing and crimes against humanity." G.A. Res. 60/1, *supra* note 177, ¶ 139.

338   Human Rights Watch, Death of a Dictator: Bloody Vengeance in Sirte (2012), *at* https://www.hrw.org/report/2012/10/16/death-dictator-bloody-vengeance-sirte.

the goals of the cabined use of force in Resolution 1973 were limited to the protection of civilians through aerial interdiction and aerial bombing. Rather than regime change, the resolution sought only to "facilitate[e] dialogue to lead to the political reforms necessary to find a peaceful and sustainable solution."[339] As with respect to Haiti in Resolution 940 and many other Council efforts, there was also a suggestion that the exceptional measures being authorized with respect to Libya were being undertaken with the consent of the legitimate government as well as the consent of the most relevant regional organization, namely the Council of the League of Arab States (which had called for the imposition on a no-fly zone and the establishment of safe areas to protect civilians).[340]

On closer inspection, Resolution 1973 is not the ringing endorsement of the R2P principle that it appears to be. It is the typically ambiguous Council Resolution—filled with compromises to bridge over politically fraught divides—that can be read differently by different observers. It is, depending on one's perspective, either destructive or respectful of sovereignty, totally within the positivist licenses given to the SC in the Charter or a radical step towards establishing a far more robust "constitution" protective of the forgotten "peoples" in the Charter's preamble. These conflicting perspectives may be reflective of divides within the SC itself, where, it has been suggested, China and Russia were caught off guard by the regime change that occurred in the wake of Resolution 1973 and have since resisted comparable "humanitarian" interventions, including in Syria.[341]

At the same time, the SC has not been reticent about referring to R2P. In Resolution 1674, one of a series of contemporary SC resolutions addressing the protection of civilians in armed combat,[342] for example, the SC reaffirmed the

339   S.C. Res. 1973, *supra* note 97, ¶ 2.
340   Council of the League of Arab States, The Outcome of the Council of the League of Arab States Meeting at the Ministerial Level in its Extraordinary Session on the Implications of the Current Events in Libya and the Arab Position (Mar. 12, 2011), *at* http://responsibilitytoprotect.org/Arab%20League%20Ministerial%20level%20statement%2012%20march%202011%20-%20english(1).pdf. The veneer of state consent was supplied by the then current Libyan ambassador to the UN who called for the Council to authorize force for the humanitarian purposes stated in Res. 1973. Colum Lynch, U.N. *Votes to Impose Sanctions on Qaddafi*, THE WASHINGTON POST (Feb. 26, 2011).
341   *See, e.g.*, Sebastian von Einsiedel, David Malone & Bruno Stagno Ugarte, *Introduction, in* The UN SECURITY COUNCIL IN THE 21ST CENTURY, *supra* note 192, at 2.
342   For a history of how this regular SC agenda item came to be and how that achievement connects more broadly with the SC's adoption of the concept of "human security" originally invoked in the 1994 Human Development Report of the UNDP, see Dedring, *supra* note 21, ch. 3.

relevant paragraphs of the 2005 World Summit Outcome Document on R2P and emphasized "the responsibility of States to comply with their relevant obligations to end impunity and to prosecute those responsible" international crimes.[343] Indeed, since the adoption of the World Outcome Summit document, there appear to have been over 40 explicit references to R2P in SC resolutions.[344] Putting debates over R2P to one side, Ruti Teitel and others may well be correct that the best way to understand the SC's "humanitarian" turn, that is, its increasing preoccupation with dealing with the underlying causes of internal conflicts, including the commission of serious crimes, violations of human rights, and even animal poaching—and combatting impunity for any of these—is to see these as a shift from protecting states qua states to protecting persons inside them, that is from protecting state security to protecting human security.[345] If this is true, this would indeed be a fundamental change in the basic Charter as it was understood by those present at the creation— and as it would be understood by a legal positivist.

Like R2P, "human security" is a contested term in both scholarly and UN circles. In the 1994 Human Development Report, the concept encompassed threats in seven areas: economic security, food security, health security, environmental security, personal security, community security, and political security.[346] For Canadian diplomats who encouraged the SC to take human security seriously, particularly during Canada's two year term on the Council in 1999–2000, the term meant protecting civilians during armed conflict, building UN capacities for peace support operations, conflict prevention, and "governance and accountability" (which meant focusing on improving the accountability of public and private sector institutions in terms of democracy and human rights).[347] Japanese diplomats at the time sought a simpler formulation: human security was "the preservation and protection of life and dignity of individual human being . . . [it] can be ensured only when the individual is

343   S.C. Res. 1674, ¶¶ 4, 8 (Apr. 28, 2006).

344   See The Global Centre for the Responsibility to Protect, UN Security Council Resolutions Referencing R2P, at http://www.globalr2p.org/resources/335.

345   TEITEL, supra note 336.

346   United Nations Development Project, Human Development Report 1994, at http:// hdr.undp.org/sites/default/files/reports/255/hdr_1994_en_complete_nostats.pdf. Personal security sought to protect people from physical violence, whether from state or non-state actors; community security aimed at protecting traditional communities, including minorities; political security looked to protecting human rights.

347   Dedring, supra note 21, at 48.

confident of a life free of fear and free of want."[348] Despite the differing empha-
ses, the term—and the proposition that the Charter generally should be read
to protect human security—migrated from UNDP and its development focus,
to the General Assembly, Secretariat, and the SC.[349] Although a Secretary-
General Report on Human Security in 2010 was careful to distinguish R2P (and
its inclusion of using force if prevention proves futile) from "human security"
(which does not envisage the use of force),[350] it is doubtful that all members of
the SC are inclined to draw such distinctions.

What seems clear, even from the selective instances surveyed in this chapter, is that the SC is increasingly (re)defining threats to the peace to include
the fulsome list of "security" threats to human life that are typically included
within the concept of "human security."

The SC has now seen threats to the peace and has acted under Chapter VII
in response to: internal conflicts not involving inter-state aggression; threats
by an existing government to commit violent acts against civilians; threats of
violence or acts of violence (even if isolated) committed by non-state actors
(particularly when cast as "terrorism"); the failure of national authorities to
prevent or to prosecute perpetrators of serious international crimes, including
war crimes; a military coup that topples a UN supervised election and prompts
refugees to take to the high seas; the failure of a state to transfer alleged terrorists to another state that seeks to prosecute them; attempts by anyone, state or
individual, to develop weapons of mass destruction; acts of or threats of piracy;
and state failures to control the travel of foreign terrorist fighters. Indeed, presumably taking its cue from the need to protect "health security," in 2014 the SC
for the first time crossed yet another line: it declared a health crisis (Ebola) to
constitute a threat to international peace and security.[351]

---

348   *Id. See also* Franklin Delano Roosevelt, President of the U.S., Four Freedoms Speech
       (Jan. 6, 1941).
349   *See, e.g.*, U.N. Secretary-General, Report of the Secretary-General: Human Security, U.N.
       Doc. A/64/701 (Mar. 8, 2010) (submitted pursuant to ¶ 143 of the 2005 World Summit
       Outcome, G.A. Res. 60/1).
350   *Id.* ¶ 23.
351   S.C. Res. 2177, pmbl. (Sept. 18, 2014). This was not the first time, however, that the SC had
       discussed a health issue as a security matter. *See* Security Council Report, In Hindsight:
       The Security Council and Health Crises (Oct. 2014), *at* http://www.securitycouncilreport
       .org/monthly-forecast/2014-10/in_hindsight_the_security_council_and_health_crises
       .php?print=true (discussing SC discussions on AIDs in 2000–1 and other pandemics in
       2011).

As is clear from the many examples in this chapter, the SC's chosen means to deal with its ever expanding concept of "threat" has been as diverse as would be expected of any public authority attempting to deal with human security threats broadly understood. A SC that needs to address threats to people inside states and not merely threats to their governments has seen fit to go beyond the limited inter-state remedies anticipated in Articles 41–42. It has, accordingly, resorted to: authorizing only specific types of force targeting particular organizations or groups of states; establishing international criminal tribunals on a case-by-case basis; creating other adjudicative mechanisms for such things as the demarcation of borders and the settlement of claims; ordering sanctions to be imposed directly on certain designated individuals or entities; compelling national courts to dismiss certain claims otherwise within their jurisdiction; compelling states to enter into or to comport themselves as if they were parties to certain treaties; requiring states to implement domestically certain international obligations including those imposed by international human rights and international humanitarian law; imposing detailed state reporting requirements on a wide variety of "administrative" issues; referring specific situations to the independent International Criminal Court; and engaging in transitional administrations of territories pending an election or plebiscite. Through these transformative actions the SC has redefined its role—and has redefined the Charter order.

CHAPTER III

The Contemporary General Assembly

1   The Assembly and the Sources of International Law

The formal powers of the UN General Assembly expressly accorded under the Charter are sparse. The Assembly has the authority to discuss any matter within the scope of the Charter or relating to the powers and functions of any UN organs and to make recommendations to members or to the Council on such matters (Art. 10). Its power to discuss and to recommend specifically includes questions relating to the maintenance of international peace and security, so long as any of its recommendations do not involve matters that are subject to "disputes" or "situations" over which the Security Council is exercising its functions (Art. 11(1) and (2) and Art. 12(1)). It has the right to call the Council's attention to situations likely to endanger international peace and security (Art. 11(3)). It can initiate studies and make recommendations to, among other things, encourage the development and codification of international law and assist in the realization of human rights (Art. 13(1)(a) and (b)). It can recommend measures to peacefully adjust situations (including those involving violations of the Charter) that threaten friendly relations among nations (Art. 14). It approves the UN's budget which anticipates that expenses of the organization shall be borne by UN members as these expenses are apportioned by the Assembly (Art. 17(1) and (2)). Procedurally, the Charter anticipates that "important questions" (some of which are specified) require a two-thirds majority of the Assembly, while all other questions require only a simple majority (Art. 18(2) and (3)). Like the Council, the Assembly is also given the power to establish subsidiary organs (Art. 22). The Assembly can also consider draft conventions submitted to it by ECOSOC.[1]

These Charter provisions suggest that the Assembly is not empowered to be a law-maker except insofar as it adopts what might be called "internal" UN law.[2] No one questions, for example, the Assembly's legal power to establish,

---

1   ECOSOC is empowered to make recommendations, initiate studies, and undertake reports with respect to a number of issues, including human rights. *See* U.N. Charter art. 62(1) & (2). It is also authorized to "prepare draft conventions for submission to the General Assembly, with respect to matters falling within its competence." *Id.* art. 62(3).

2   JOSÉ E. ALVAREZ, INTERNATIONAL ORGANIZATIONS AS LAW-MAKERS 121 (2006). On the blurred distinctions between "internal" and "external" law, see ALVAREZ, *supra*, at 122–156

with full legal effect, a subsidiary organ under Art. 22 or to take legally binding decisions by majority vote on what is an "important question" requiring a
two-thirds vote under Art. 18(3). Moreover, certainly after the ICJ rendered
its opinion in Certain Expenses, no one questions the Assembly's "tax"
power under its capacity to approve and apportion the expenses of the organization under Art. 17.[3] At the same time, the positivist argues that these decisions are limited to the "internal" realm. The Assembly makes internal rules
for the organization, but these rules do not have "external effect" on the "real"
sources of law—treaties, custom, and general principles. And even those critical of positivism's constraints do not deny that most Assembly resolutions
are exactly what the Charter anticipates: hortatory declarations expressing
the opinions of those UN members who voted in favor of them having political but no legal effect. Positivists are clearly correct when they point out that
the drafters of the UN Charter knew the difference between conferring the
power to render binding "decisions" (see Articles 25, 39, 41, 42, and 48) and
delegating the power only to "recommend" or to discuss (see Articles 10–14).
Commentators are not entirely wrong when they write that the Assembly is
the world's "talk shop," a place to vent "hot air."[4]

But this is not the end of the story. Faced with how governments, national
courts, international tribunals, and quasi-judicial bodies (like UN human rights
committees) have used Assembly resolutions in the real world, even some erst-
while positivists have accepted the premise that some Assembly resolutions
may have legal effects. They have sought to explain this, not surprisingly, by
attempting to re-cast some Assembly efforts within the sources of obligations
recognized in Article 38 of the ICJ's Statute, namely as a species of treaty or
customary obligation or as evidence of general principles of law.

Under the first (treaty) approach, some Assembly efforts to interpret the
UN Charter are seen as the functional equivalent of the "subsequent practice"
of the UN's treaty parties under the Vienna Convention on the Law of Treaties
(VCT)'s Article 31(3)(b) or as de facto "subsequent agreements" among those
parties under its Article 31(3)(a).[5] Accordingly, the 1986 U.S. Restatement on

---

(canvassing examples of instances in which internal decisions have had impacts on the
general law).

3 Certain Expenses of the United Nations (Article 17, Paragraph 2, of the Charter), Advisory
Opinion, 1962 I.C.J. 151 (July 20). See also ALVAREZ, supra note 2, at 122–129.

4 See, e.g., Nick Bryant, World Leaders Flock to UN General Assembly, BBC NEWS, Sept. 22, 2014,
at http://www.bbc.com/news/world-us-canada-29284682.

5 See, e.g., ALVAREZ, supra note 2, at 87–92 (discussing the ICJ's use of "subsequent practice" in
its Certain Expenses opinion).

the Foreign Relations Law of the United States indicates that some Assembly resolutions that purport to interpret particular provisions or phrases in the UN Charter (such as the meaning to be given to "self determination" or to "inherent self defense") may come to secure such an authoritative effect.[6] Some scholars support this conclusion based on the Charter's negotiating history insofar as the UN's drafters appeared to agree that Charter interpretations reached by UN organs in the course of their activities were authoritative when they secured members' general acquiescence.[7] More controversially, others have argued that some GA resolutions may constitute, in of themselves, binding inter-state compacts that happen to be manifested in the form of a resolution.[8] Those who take this position are presumably inspired by the fact that under customary international law, states may be bound by commitments that are not in written form, are not called "treaties," and may even be unilateral in nature.[9]

An alternative basis for according Assembly resolutions binding status turns to customary law. Some scholars and adjudicators have accepted the contention that particular Assembly resolutions (or portions of them) have, over time, come to reflect state practice and/or *opinio juris* and can be treated as proclamations of customary law.[10] The narrowest way to reach this

---

6   *See* RESTATEMENT (THIRD) OF THE FOREIGN RELATIONS LAW OF THE UNITED STATES § 103 Reporter's Note 2 (1987) [hereinafter RESTATEMENT] ("Declarations interpreting a charter are entitled to considerable weight if they are unanimous or nearly unanimous and have the support of all the principal members.").

7   ALVAREZ, *supra* note 2, at 74–91 (describing discussions during the Charter's negotiations and the conclusions reached by early Charter commentators such as Louis Sohn).

8   BLAINE SLOAN, UNITED NATIONS GENERAL ASSEMBLY RESOLUTIONS IN OUR CHANGING WORLD 65–66 (1991) ("[T]he text of a resolution may itself constitute an agreement among the Member States or even contain a unilateral declaration of an individual state.").

9   *See* Vienna Convention on the Law of Treaties art. 2(1)(a), *opened for signature* May 23, 1969, 1155 U.N.T.S. 331 [hereinafter VCT] (anticipating that treaties need not be designated as such); art. 3 (recognizing the possibility of treaties not in written form and not between states so long as these are recognized as treaties under customary law); Nuclear Tests Case (N.Z. v. Fr.), 1974 I.C.J. 457, ¶ 46 (Dec. 20); Nuclear Tests Case (Austl. V. Fr.), 1974 I.C.J. 253, ¶ 43 (Dec. 20) (finding that a unilateral statement can constitute a binding commitment).

10 This appears to be the approach cautiously taken in the Draft Conclusions emerging within the ILC's current topic dealing with the "Identification of customary international law." According to the ILC, while a finding of custom requires identifying two separate elements, state practice and *opinio juris*, the former needs to be "primarily the practice of states" but "[i]n certain cases, the practice of international organizations also contributes to the formation, or expression, of rules of customary international law." *See* International

conclusion is to argue that a UN resolution like the Universal Declaration of Human Rights, for example, though originally intended to be a mere "standard of achievement," through the subsequent practice and *opinio juris* of states independent of the resolution itself (such as repeated invocations of that declaration or rights therein in diplomatic correspondence or in briefs filed by states in national or international courts), has been transformed into customary law. The Charter basis for this contention is admittedly thin; the Charter anticipates under Article 13(1)(a) that the Assembly plays a role in the progressive development and codification of international law. But to the extent Assembly resolutions are merely cited as *additional evidence* to support a finding of custom, no Charter basis would be needed to produce such effects; even a declaration adopted by a group of experts or by NGOs if followed by distinct evidence of state practice and *opinio juris* could come to be seen as an expression of custom. Arguably those who refer today to the Universal Declaration of Human Rights as customary law are merely being insufficiently precise: what they mean is that the declaration generated the seed for what became a customary rule thanks to the distinct actions and expressions of *opinio juris* by the real law-makers, namely states.

The ICJ's Article 38 is not necessarily inconsistent with this conclusion at least insofar as one is entitled to assume that judicial opinions and the views of scholars, identified in 38(1)(d), are not the exclusive ways to identify rules of custom, and that Assembly resolutions are another such subsidiary form of evidence. Another common way of reaching the same conclusion, the contention that General Assembly resolutions (and possibly those of other IOs) "crystalize" custom, is not particularly threatening to positivist tenets if all that is meant is that once the Assembly suggests something is a rule of custom,

---

Law Commission, Identification of Customary International Law, Interim Report by the Chairman of the Drafting Committee, ILC 66th Sess., at 8 (Aug. 7, 2014) [hereinafter ILC Report]. Draft Conclusion 6 also includes, as "forms of practice," "acts in connection with resolutions of international organizations or international conferences." ILC Report, at 13. The ILC's cautious approach is clear in its Draft Conclusion 13, which states that a "resolution adopted by an international organization... cannot, of itself, create a rule of customary international law," but "may provide evidence for establishing the existence and content of a rule of customary international law or contribute to its development." Draft Conclusion 12 provides that a provision in such a resolution "may reflect a rule of customary international law if it is established that the provision corresponds to a general practice that is accepted as law (*opinio juris*)." *Id.*

that conclusion inspires a search for actual state practice and *opinio juris* to confirm that conclusion.[11]

More threatening to positivist tenets is the proposition, also suggested in the U.S. Restatement, that on some occasions since "the practice of states...includes what states do in or through international organizations," some General Assembly resolutions *may in and of themselves* constitute "state practice" (or perhaps *opinio juris*) and are therefore entitled to be considered as customary law (and not mere subsidiary evidence of its possible existence requiring complementary evidence of actual state practice).[12] This is but a short step to the more controversial contention, sometimes found in connection with General Assembly resolutions on issues where state practice is understandably absent or scarce, that some resolutions are "instant custom."[13]

Others have suggested that there is nothing to prevent a state from incorporating as part of its national law, a particular Assembly resolution or parts of one, and that, if enough states do the same, IO resolutions may come to be treated as general principles of law.[14] Of course, to the extent that an Assembly

---

11   *See, e.g.,* RESTATEMENT, *supra* note 6, § 103 cmt. c (noting that declaratory pronounce-
      ments in international organizations "provide some evidence of what the states voting for
      it regard the law to be. The evidentiary value of such resolutions is variable").

12   *Id.* § 102 Reporter's Note 2. The Restatement also expands this conclusion to international
      conferences, "especially those engaged in codifying international law" which "provide
      occasions for expressions by states as to the law on particular questions. General con-
      sensus as to the law at such a conference confirms customary law or contributes to its
      creation." *See also* ILC Report, *supra* note 10, at 7 (Draft Conclusion 4).

13   *Compare* MICHAEL P. SCHARF, CUSTOMARY INTERNATIONAL LAW IN TIMES OF
      FUNDAMENTAL CHANGE: RECOGNIZING GROATIAN MOMENTS 123–137 (2012) (dis-
      cussing the effects of the 1963 Declaration of Legal Principles Governing the Activities
      of States in the Exploration and Use of Outer Space) and RESTATEMENT, *supra*
      note 6, § 102 Reporters' Note 2 *with* GENNADY M. DANILENKO, LAW-MAKING IN THE
      INTERNATIONAL COMMUNITY 97–98 (1993) (criticizing the idea of "instant custom" as
      fundamentally inconsistent with the fundamentals of that source). While the ILC's Draft
      Conclusions issued to date do not suggest that there can be any such thing as "instant cus-
      tom" and specifically deny that IO resolutions can by themselves create custom, they also
      state that IO resolutions may constitute evidence of state practice and *opinio juris. See* ILC
      Report, *supra* note 10, at 17 (noting that the Draft Conclusions do not recognize "instant
      custom"); International Law Commission, Identification of Customary International Law,
      Text of the Draft Conclusions Provisionally Adopted by the Drafting Committee, 67th
      Sess., May 4–June 5, July 6–June Aug. 7, UN Doc. No. A/CN.4/L.869 at 3 (Draft Conclusion
      12(1)) (July 14, 2014).

14   This assumes that general principles emerge from a comparative law search for common
      principles found in national law, perhaps the most common definition of such principles

resolution is accepted under one (or more) of the traditional sources, there is nothing to prevent a treaty interpreter, including a judge, from turning to such a resolution to interpret a treaty that refers to customary law or to support an interpretation of the treaty in the context of a "relevant rule of international law applicable among the parties" under Article 31(3)(c) of the VCT. At least to this extent, IO resolutions that come to be seen as reflections of custom may influence treaty interpretation.[15]

Under one or more of these justifications some positivists have come to treat some UN General Assembly resolutions as legally binding even though Article 10 of the Charter only anticipates the issuance of "recommendations."[16]

But there are those who find the effort to pour the work-product of the Assembly—never fully anticipated when Article 38 was drafted—into that article's traditional vessels of obligation to be an arid, artificial, or misconceived enterprise. For some, the General Assembly is a *sui generis* body whose composition, legitimacy, and authorized capacity to engage on issues accords it implicit authority to take legally binding decisions whenever this leads to general acceptance.[17] Other scholars, less invested in adhering to the firm positivist divide between law and non-law, are content to label some Assembly resolutions as "soft law"—thereby suggesting that their legally binding authority may exist along a spectrum or vary by context or subject matter.[18]

---

among legal scholars. *See* OSCAR SCHACHTER, INTERNATIONAL LAW IN THEORY AND PRACTICE 50–55 (1991). See Chapter I, § 1.3, *supra*.

15   International Law Commission, Fragmentation of International Law: Difficulties Arising from the Diversification and Expansion of International Law: Report of the Study Group of the International Law Commission, 58th Session, May 1–June 9, July 3–Aug. 11, U.N. Doc. A/CN.4/L.682 (Apr. 13, 2006), as corrected U.N. Doc. A/CN.4/L.682/Corr.1 (Aug. 11, 2006) (finalized by Martti Koskenniemi) [hereinafter ILC Fragmentation Report].

16   *See, e.g.*, PHIL C.W. CHAN, CHINA, STATE SOVEREIGNTY AND INTERNATIONAL LEGAL ORDER 95–96, n. 132 (2015).

17   To the extent that the legal status of Assembly resolutions is grounded in the "unique" status of the UN General Assembly, this view may preclude or at least avoid the question of the legal status of other IO resolutions or of other resolutions adopted in IO conferences. This is not the route taken, at least so far, by the ILC, which has treated all of these resolutions as on par with one another. *See supra* note 10.

18   *See, e.g.*, Alan E. Boyle, *Some Reflections on the Relationship of Treaties and Soft Law*, 48 INT'L & COMP. L. Q. 901 (1999); Richard A. Falk, *On the Quasi-Legislative Competence of the General Assembly*, 60 AM. J. INT'L L. 782 (1966).

As the different (and not always consistent) positions taken even by conservative forums like the ILC or within the 1986 U.S. Restatement on Foreign
Relations suggest, the legal status of General Assembly resolutions remains
a contentious, if oft-debated, matter. Adjudicative bodies, international and
national, have cited to UN General Assembly resolutions as authority for interpretations of treaties (including the UN Charter) as well as in support of findings of custom; in doing so, they have not always clarified their rationales.
The practice of arbitral and judicial bodies suggests that the authority of an
Assembly resolution turns on evidentiary or factual context, including the text
of the resolution (e.g., whether it indicates in its preamble that it is intended
to provide an interpretation of the UN Charter or to codify customary law),
the title of the resolution (e.g., whether it is a "declaration" or other solemn
undertaking),[19] whether the resolution as a whole or the relevant provision
within it was adopted by consensus or by a separate vote (and if the latter,
whether there was sufficient consensus in favor among the generality of states,
including those specifically affected), whether the negotiating history of the
resolution or relevant provision indicates an intent to confer binding authority, and whether the past practice of the Assembly has treated other resolutions on the same subject matter as authoritative.[20]

A leading illustration involves the old controversy over whether customary international law supports what the U.S. calls the "Hull Rule" (after the
response given by then Secretary of State Cordell Hull to the Mexico's claim
that it could expropriate properties belonging to U.S. citizens without providing compensation). Under the Hull Rule, allegedly a rule of custom,
governmental nationalizations or expropriations of alien property require
the payment of prompt, adequate, and effective compensation.[21] As is well
known, the General Assembly adopted competing resolutions on this subject.
Under the 1962 resolution on "Permanent Sovereignty over Natural Resources,"
the Assembly took the position that such cases require the payment of appropriate compensation in accordance with international law, with the U.S. government arguing that, in its view, this entailed prompt, adequate, and effective

---

19   *See, e.g.*, RESTATEMENT, *supra* note 6, § 102 Reporters' Note 2 (quoting UN, Office of Legal
       Affairs, Use of the Terms "Declaration" and "Recommendation", U.N. Doc. E/CN.4/L/610
       (1962)).

20   *See generally* THE CHARTER OF THE UNITED NATIONS: A COMMENTARY 92 (Bruno
       Simma et al. eds., 3d ed. 2012) [hereinafter CHARTER COMMENTARY] ("[T]he interpreta-
       tive effect of the General Assembly's practice depends on subject-matter, wording, con-
       nection to the terms of the Charter, and voting results of a resolution.").

21   3 GREEN HAYWOOD HACKWORTH, DIGEST OF INTERNATIONAL LAW 660–665 (1942).

compensation.[22] In 1973, the Assembly, enamored with securing a "New International Economic Order," passed a resolution stating that each state was entitled to determine the amount of possible compensation and the mode of payment in such cases in accordance with national law, making no mention of international law or an international minimum standard.[23] A year later, in its Charter of Economic Rights and Duties of States, the Assembly stated that "appropriate compensation should be paid . . . taking into account its relevant laws and regulations and all circumstances that the State considers pertinent."[24] Once again, no mention was made of international law requirements in such cases. Arbitral tribunals faced with the issue have considered the authoritative effects of these Assembly efforts, and particularly whether any of these resolutions either reflect customary law or evince a change in the relevant rule. Decisions in the Iran-U.S. Claims Tribunal and arbitral tribunals considering the legality of Libya's nationalization of Western oil interests have generally affirmed the continuing validity of the Hull Rule, on the premise that of the three resolutions on point, the 1962 resolution was the only one that garnered support across north/south and east/west divides on the subject, whereas the latter two resolutions drew, at least on the matter at issue, the objection of many of the "specifically affected states" (namely home countries of the foreign investors whose properties were expropriated).[25] Some have reached the same result on the argument that while the Assembly could, in appropriate cases, modify an existing rule of custom, for that to occur there must be genuine agreement among all or most states; that is, an Assembly resolution that seeks to topple a customary rule needs to be supported by the general membership since the general agreement of states is required to establish the rule in the first place.[26]

---

22   G.A. Res. 1803, ¶ 4 (Dec. 14, 1962). For a further discussion, see JEFFREY L. DUNOFF
      ET AL., INTERNATIONAL LAW: NORMS, ACTORS, PROCESS: A PROBLEM-ORIENTED
      APPROACH 73–92 (3d ed. 2010).
23   G.A. Res. 3171(XXVIII), ¶ 3 (Dec. 17, 1973).
24   G.A. Res. 3281(XXIX), art. 2(2)(c) (Dec. 12, 1974).
25   See, e.g., Sedco, Inc. v. National Iranian Oil Company, 10 IRAN-US CL. REP. 180 (1986);
      Award on the Merits in Dispute Between Texaco Overseas Petroleum Company/California
      Asiatic Oil Company and the Government of the Libyan Arab Republic, 17 ILM 1 (1978)
      [hereinafter TOPCO]. See also Patrick M. Norton, A Law of the Future or a Law of the Past?
      Modern Tribunals and the International Law of Expropriation, 85 AM. J. INT'L L. 474 (1991).
26   See TOPCO, supra note 25, ¶¶ 80–91. For a thorough account of the various effects of G.A.
      resolutions, see Blaine Sloan, General Assembly Resolutions Revisited (Forty Years Later),
      58 BRIT. Y.B. INT'L L. 39 (1987).

Debates over how or whether Assembly resolutions should be understood within the context of the traditional sources of obligation in the ICJ's Article 38, the subject of a considerable literature, need not detain us further here.[27] It may be more important to those seeking to understand the contemporary legal relevance of the UN General Assembly to focus on the types of functions being undertaken by the Assembly. Anyone examining the output of recent Assembly sessions would be struck with the amazing range of its activity—and with the apparently few constraints that exist on it in terms of subject matter. As Rosalyn Higgins and others demonstrated even prior to the end of the Cold War—which affected the Assembly almost as much as it did the Council— the Charter's injunction against interfering with the "domestic jurisdiction" of states (Article 2(7)) has not seemed to impose many limits on the Assembly, despite occasional complaints that some resolutions are "*ultra vires*" on that ground.[28] The Article 2(7) non-interference rule, which, as noted, does not apply with respect to "enforcement action" (presumably by the Council under Chapter VII), did not prevent the Assembly from criticizing the human rights policies of Spain in the earliest days of the UN, and does not prevent resolutions critical of the human rights actions of UN members today.[29] Neither that Charter limit nor others that might be inferred from the principles and purposes of the Charter have prevented the Assembly from assuming various roles. The General Assembly has been a treaty initiator, a treaty interpreter and

---

27   *See, e.g.*, GODEFRIDUS J.H. HOOF, RETHINKING THE SOURCES OF INTERNATIONAL LAW 179 (1983); Stephen M. Schwebel, *The Effect of Resolutions of the United Nations General Assembly on Customary International Law*, 73 ASIL PROC. 301 (1979). Often scholars have been quick to acknowledge the possibility that G.A. resolutions have legal effects without resolving the tensions with Art. 38 sources. *See* Christopher C. Joyner, *U.N. General Assembly Resolutions and International Law*, 11 CAL. W. INT'L L.J. 445 (1981) ("[w]hile General Assembly resolutions are not ipso facto new sources of international law, they can contribute to the normative process of law creation."); Oscar Schachter, *The Nature and Process of Legal Development in International Society, in* THE STRUCTURE AND PROCESS OF INTERNATIONAL LAW: ESSAYS IN LEGAL PHILOSOPHY DOCTRINE AND THEORY 745, 788 (R.St.J. MacDonald & Douglas M. Johnston eds., 1983) ("It is, of course, true that such [General Assembly] resolutions are not a formal source of law within the explicit categories of article 38(1) . . . [y]et few would deny that General Assembly resolutions have had a formative influence in the development of international law in matters of considerable importance to national states.").

28   ALVAREZ, *supra* note 2, at 156–169 (noting the impact of the G.A. on the "shrinking" domain of "domestic jurisdiction"). *See also* ROSALYN HIGGINS, THE DEVELOPMENT OF INTERNATIONAL LAW THROUGH THE POLITICAL ORGANS OF THE UNITED NATIONS 61–62 (1963).

29   *See infra* § 3.

enforcer, a supplier of institutional checks and balances, a progressive developer and codifier of customary law, and, along with the Council, a gatekeeper to statehood, UN membership, or continued UN participation. This chapter will focus on three select categories of Assembly actions that illustrate the Assembly's multiple "hats": the Assembly as UN Charter interpreter, as human rights interpreter and enforcer, and as peace and security institutional actor.

2   The Assembly as Charter Interpreter

Classic examples of the Assembly's efforts to interpret the Charter are a staple of international law treatises. Two oft-cited examples are the Assembly's 1970 Declaration on Principles of International Law Concerning Friendly Relations and Cooperation Among States in Accordance with the Charter of the United Nations[30] and its Definition of Aggression from 1974.[31] These two resolutions have been repeatedly cited, by scholars and some courts, as evidence of authoritative interpretations of particular terms in the Charter, including of the meaning to be given to threats or use of force under Article 2(4), "collective or individual self defense" under Article 51, "aggression" in Article 39, and, in the case of the Friendly Relations Declaration, a number of other important Charter terms as well, such as the meaning of "equal rights" and the "self determination" of peoples in Article 1(2), "sovereign equality" in Article 2(1), or what it means to "intervene in matters which are essentially within the domestic jurisdiction" of states under Article 2(7).

In the ICJ's Nicaragua case, for example, which involved allegations that the U.S. violated customary international law prohibiting the use of force except in self-defense, the ICJ cited the Friendly Relations Declaration for the proposition that "organizing or encouraging the organization of irregular forces or armed bands ... for incursion into the territory of another State," and "participating in acts of civil strike ... in another State," constituted a *"prima facie"* violation of the customary rule against the threat or use of force "subject to the question whether the action of the United States might be justified as an exercise of the right of self-defense."[32] That decision also cited the Assembly's later

---

30   Declaration on Principles of International Law Concerning Friendly Relations and Co-operation Among States in Accordance with the Charter of the United Nations, G.A. Res. 2625 (Oct. 24, 1970) [hereinafter Friendly Relations Declaration].

31   G.A. Res. 3314(XXIX) (Dec. 14, 1974).

32   Military and Paramilitary Activities in and Against Nicaragua (Nicar. v. U.S.), 1986 I.C.J. 14, ¶ 228 (June 27) (also noting that under that resolution "participation of this kind is

Definition of Aggression for the proposition that there "appears now to be general agreement on the nature of the acts which can be treated as constituting armed attacks," noting that this includes, as the Assembly stated, "the sending by or on behalf of a State of armed bands, groups, irregulars or mercenaries, which carry out acts of armed force against another State of such gravity as to amount to 'inter alia an actual armed attack by regular forces' or its substantial involvement therein."[33]

The Assembly's Definition of Aggression has assumed renewed importance as it has now been incorporated as an essential definitional element in the amendments to the Rome Statute for the ICC negotiated at Kampala in 2010. Article 8(bis) of the Court's Statute, if approved under the procedures anticipated by the Kampala conferees, provides that the crime of aggression "means the use of armed force by a State against the sovereignty, territorial integrity or political independence of another State, or in any other manner inconsistent with the Charter of the United Nations," including through "invasion or attack by the armed forces of a State of the territory of another State, or any military occupation, however temporary, resulting from such invasion or attack, or any annexation by the use of force of the territory of another State or part thereof"; bombardment of another state; blockading the ports or coasts of another State; attacking the land, sea, or air forces or marine and air fleets of another states; use of armed forces by one state in the territory of another State by the latter State's permission but in a manner inconsistent with the conditions of entry; hosting the armed forces of another State which uses them to perpetrate an act of aggression against a third State; or the sending on behalf of a State "armed bands, groups, irregulars or mercenaries" which carry out any of the aforementioned acts.[34]

The proposed Article 8 (bis) also provides, however, that an act of aggression for purposes of criminal prosecution in the ICC needs to be an act "which, by its character, gravity and scale, constitutes a manifest violation of the

---

contrary to the principle of the prohibition of the use of force when the acts of civil strife referred to 'involve a threat or use of force'"). But the Court found that while arming and training the contras involves the threat or use of force against Nicaragua, the mere supply of funds to them, while an intervention into Nicaragua's internal affairs, "does not in itself amount to a use of force". *Id.* ¶ 228.

33   Nicar. v. U.S., *supra* note 32, ¶ 195 (citing Article 3(g) of the Assembly's Definition of Aggression and stating that this description "may be taken to reflect customary international law").

34   *See* Rome Statute of the International Criminal Court, July 17, 1998, 2187 U.N.T.S. 90. Note that Parts a–g of art. 8(bis) replicate the definition of aggression provided by the General Assembly in its Resolution 3314.

Charter of the United Nations."[35] According to "understandings" concluded at the same time issued at the Kampala conference (which may or may not influence the ICC itself in a subsequent prosecution), the definition of act of aggression in 8(bis) is only for the purpose of ICC prosecutions and should "not be interpreted as limiting or prejudicing in any way existing or developing rules of international law for purposes other than this Statute."[36] Those understandings also state that "aggression is the most serious and dangerous form of the illegal use of force" and "[i]t is understood that in establishing whether an act of aggression constitutes a manifest violation of the Charter of the United Nations, the three components of character, gravity and scale must be sufficient to justify a 'manifest' determination. No one component can be significant enough to satisfy the manifest standard by itself."[37]

Should the Art. 8(bis) amendments to the Rome Statute come into force upon the ratification by 30 or more Rome Party states as well as subsequent action by the ICC's Assembly of State Parties after Jan. 1, 2017,[38] they would produce an extraordinary *de facto* change in the operation of the UN Charter. The text of the Charter puts determinations of aggression in the hands of the Security Council, no less than other determinations anticipated under Article 39. Like threats or breaches of the peace, acts of aggression are, under the Charter, subject to the voting provisions (and the veto) in the Council.[39] The Charter does not anticipate that the Council would or could delegate its powers under Article 39 to an independent Court, much less one that did not involve the participation of all five permanent members. And yet, under the ICC amendments, the Council may not be able to exercise the primacy anticipated by the Charter.

The Kampala amendments anticipate that the Court's prosecutor should first "ascertain whether the Security Council has made a determination of an act of aggression," but under their terms, even when no such determination is made by the Council, within six months after the prosecutor notifies the

---

35   Rome Statute, *supra* note 34, art. 8(bis), ¶ 1.

36   ICC Res. RC/Res. 6, annex III, Understanding 4 (June 11, 2010).

37   *Id.* ¶¶ 6–7.

38   *See* Rome Statute, *supra* note 34, art. 15(bis), ¶¶ 2–3.

39   Indeed, the potential for overlap between art. 39 determinations, which are allocated to the Council, and violations of art. 2(4), mean that, in effect, even violations of article 2(4) that might be deemed an international wrongful act triggering state responsibility that fall short of a criminal act of aggression might require reaching agreement among at least nine members of the Council, including the P-5. This is particularly the case should any such act trigger the "until" clause in article 51 suggesting that Council notification be provided and its permission be sought prior to defensive action in response.

Council that there is reasonable basis to proceed with an aggression investigation, a pre-trial division of the court may commence such an investigation.[40] In a departure from the rest of the Rome Statute, the Kampala amendments preclude prosecutions for aggression for nationals from states that are not parties to the Rome Statute (and therefore protect, among others, nationals of Russia, China, and the U.S.).[41] Art. 8(bis) also confirms that the Council, if it manages to secure enough votes in favor, can defer an investigation or a prosecution for aggression (as it can with respect to other cases before the ICC) for 12 months at a time.[42] These assurances, while they placate some of the concerns that Council members may have, do not maintain the Charter's status quo with respect to aggression. For the Council to defer an aggression investigation or prosecution, it must be able to muster nine affirmative votes, and continue to maintain that deferral beyond 12 months it must continue to find those affirmative votes in favor. Should a permanent member of the Council fail to agree or enough non-permanent members resist, the ICC prosecution revives. This is the opposite of what the Charter now provides since in the absence of 8(bis) a determination of aggression requires the affirmative votes of nine in the Council. Accordingly, defenders of Council supremacy find the Council's capacity to defer ICC prosecutions to be a small consolation for the loss of Council control. Recall that the Council attempted for a time to use its Article 16 deferral power to preclude ICC prosecutions for any peacekeepers from a non-Rome Statute party state, including from P-5 members, but ultimately found its capacity to renew such deferrals, the subject of considerable resistance by ICC supporters and even tacitly by the then Secretary-General, politically unsustainable.[43]

The Kampala jurisdictional preconditions for aggression prosecutions are an innovative compromise between competing principles: the effort to secure criminal accountability for an international crime that has arguably existed since Nuremberg's prosecutions for "crimes against peace" and the need to retain political control over determinations crucial to peace and secu-

---

40   Rome Statute, *supra* note 34, art. 15(bis), ¶¶ 6–8.

41   For other ICC crimes, nationals from non-Rome Party states may still face prosecution to the extent they commit their crimes in Rome Party states or such crimes are encompassed by a Security Council referral to the ICC. *Id.* art. 13(b).

42   *Id.* art. 15(bis), ¶¶ 5–8 (anticipating the continued ability for the Council to defer investigations or prosecutions under article 16 of the Rome Statute).

43   S.C. Res. 1422 (July 12, 2002). For an overview, see Frederic L. Kirgis, U.S. *Drops Plan to Exempt G.I.'s from U.N. Court*, ASIL INSIGHTS (July 1, 2004), *at* http://www.asil.org/insights/volume/8/issue/15/us-drops-plan-exempt-gis-un-court.

rity within the body charged with "primary" responsibility for such determinations. This compromise may prove to be as momentous as prior *de facto* "amendments" of the Charter such as the decision to count "abstentions" as "affirmative" votes for purposes of Article 27(3), the tendency to regard the Article 12(1) limit on the Assembly as a dead letter, or the seating of the Russian Federation in place of the "USSR" despite the text of Article 23.[44] If these amendments to the ICC Statute come into effect, the *de facto* change in the Charter order will have been accomplished, as have other "evolutionary" changes in that Charter discussed here, without any formal amendment of the Charter under the arduous procedures anticipated in Article 108. The Council's veto-proof control over aggression will have been eliminated without even a majority vote (much less a consensus) decision by the General Assembly or a veto-proof vote in the Security Council, much less the ratification by two-thirds of UN members anticipated under Article 108.[45] Under the circumstances, it should surprise no one that at least two of the P-5, neither of which are Rome Party states, continue to resist these changes in the ICC Statute.[46]

Should the ICC aggression amendments come into effect, the *propio moto* powers of the ICC prosecutor, combined with the actions of a single pre-trial chamber of that court, could have dramatic effects on ongoing conflicts and the Council's efforts to settle them by quiet, behind the scenes diplomacy or Chapter VII actions. Once one or more prominent leaders to a conflict are investigated, indicted, or prosecuted for aggression, the prospect of engaging them in negotiations is likely to be dramatically affected.[47] The Kampala

---

44 ALVAREZ, *supra* note 2, at 143–149, 169–173.

45 A majority of the votes in the Assembly of State Parties would require, at this writing, some 63 states to vote in favor of the article 8(bis) and article 15(bis) amendments assuming there are 124 Parties to the Rome Statute, not including three of the Permanent Members, Russia, China, or the U.S. *See* ICC, *The State Parties to the Rome Statute, at* http://www .icc-cpi.int/en_menus/asp/states%20parties/Pages/the%20states%20parties%20to%20 the%20rome%20statute.aspx (last visited April 7, 2016).

46 *See, e.g.*, Review Conference of the Rome Statute of the International Criminal Court, Kampala, May 31–June 11, 2010, annex IX (A) IX (E), VIII (E), ICC Doc. RC/11 (2010) (statements of China, the UK and the U.S. following the adoption of RC/Res. 6 on the crime of aggression). *See generally* Harold Hongju Koh & Todd F. Buckwald, *The Crime of Aggression: The United States' Perspective*, 109 AM. J. INT'L L. 257 (2015); Bing Bing Jia, *The Crime of Aggression as Custom and the Mechanisms for Determining Acts of Aggression*, 109 AM. J. INT'L L. 569 (2015).

47 As was presumably the case with respect to high-level Libyan officials once the Security Council referred the Libyan situation to the ICC in Res. 1970. For an insightful discussion of the debate, see CHANDRA LEKHA SRIRAM, CONFRONTING PAST HUMAN RIGHTS

amendments are a dramatic step towards the position of those who contend that there is no conflict between peace and security because truly lasting peace always requires criminal accountability for those who engage in international crimes.[48] While the formation of the ICC was itself a step in this direction, its Kampala amendments would extend this principle (and policy goal) to the most political crime in the international firmament, one that has been, since the UN Charter was fashioned and under its terms, within the sole control of the Council. Of course, with or without Article 8(bis), there was always the possibility that a state would attempt to prosecute the crime of aggression and proclaim that its courts enjoy universal jurisdiction to prosecute foreign persons for that crime but such unilateral actions by states was always and remains politically unlikely. Any such attempt would be seen as tantamount to a declaration of war on the targeted official (and state). In such cases, as remains the case even under the Kampala amendments with respect to ICC prosecutions that can be halted by annual Article 16 deferrals, the Council could, if it had the votes, stop such efforts. But the Kampala amendments, by interposing the actions of an independent international prosecutor and court, considerably raise the stakes for the Council. A Council or member state that seeks to halt a unilateral prosecution by a member state faces the wrath of that member state, but a Council or member state that resists action by the ICC

VIOLATIONS: JUSTICE VS PEACE IN TIMES OF TRANSITION (2004). *See generally* Louise Arbour, Speech on the Occasion of the Inaugural Roland Berger Lecture on Human Rights and Human Dignity: Are Freedom, Peace and Justice Incompatible Agendas?, Feb. 17, 2014, *at* http://www.crisis-group.org/en/publication-type/speeches/2014/arbour-are-freedom-peace-and-justice-incompatible-agendas.aspx; Janine Natalya Clark, *Peace, Justice and the International Criminal Court: Limitations and Possibilities*, 9 J. INT'L CRIM. JUST. 521–545 (2011) (arguing that the ICC can potentially contribute to peace but only as part of a comprehensive approach to justice); PROMOTING PEACE THROUGH INTERNATIONAL LAW 323–325 (Cecilia Marcela Bailliet & Kjetil Mujezinovic Larsen eds., 2015).

48   *See, e.g.,* Luis Moreno-Ocampo, *The Role of the International Community in Assisting the International Criminal Court to Secure Justice and Accountability, in* IUS GENTIUM: COMPARATIVE PERSPECTIVES IN LAW AND JUSTICE: CONFRONTING GENOCIDE 7, 279–289 (René Provost & Payam Akhavan eds., 2010) (contending that peace and justice are complementary); U.N. Secretary-General, *The Rule of Law and Transitional Justice in Conflict and Post-Conflict Societies: Report of the Secretary-General*, ¶ 21, UN DOC. S/2004/616 (Aug. 23, 2004) (arguing that if properly pursued, justice and peace sustain one another).

risks the wrath of the international community, including an array of NGOs favoring international criminal accountability.[49]

The Kampala amendments also universalize the elements of the crime of aggression and give concrete form to the vague reference to "aggression" in the Charter. In so doing, they limit the interpretative discretion accorded to the Council. Even though Article 8(bis) purports to define the crime only for the ICC, the ICJ has already suggested, as noted, that the Assembly's definition of aggression reflected in 8(bis) constitutes customary law.[50] It is not hard to see that court—or another international or national court—treating the detailed enumeration in Article 8(bis), and its effort to distinguish aggression from other insufficiently "manifest" breaches of the Charter's Article 2(4), as authoritatively determining the meaning of state aggression for purposes of Article 39 as well as the customary crime of aggression applicable to state officials.

These effects are not dependent on actual prosecutions for aggression within the ICC. The mere existence of Article 8(bis) even prior to its enactment puts pressure on Council members to address in detail whether a specific act within Article 8(bis)(a)–(g) has occurred, and if it has not (e.g., an act of cyberterrorism) why it would still enable individual or collective self-defense under Article 51.[51] An investigation or prosecution of aggression by the ICC would

---

49   As is the case where the African Union has resisted cooperating with the ICC in the indictment of Bashir or criticisms against the South African government for not detaining Bashir during his visit to that country. *See, e.g.*, African Union, Decision on the Meeting of African Parties to the Rome Statute of the International Criminal Court (ICC), ¶ 10, AU Doc. Assembly/AU/Dec. 245 (XIII) Rev. 1 (Jul. 3, 2009) (deciding that "in view of the fact that the request by the African Union has never been acted upon, the AU Member States shall not cooperate pursuant to the provisions of Article 98 of the Rome Statute of the ICC relating to immunities, for the arrest and surrender of President Omar El Bashir of The Sudan"); Associated Press, *African Union Opposes Warrant for Qaddafi*, N.Y. TIMES, July 2, 2011, *at* http://www.nytimes.com/2011/07/03/world/africa/03african.html; Norimitsu Onishi, *Omar al-Bashir, Leaving South Africa, Eludes Arrest Again*, N.Y. TIMES, June 15, 2015, *at* http://www.nytimes.com/2015/06/16/world/africa/omar-hassan-al-bashir-sudan-south-africa.html.

50   This contention is supported by the fact that it incorporates, as noted, G.A. Res. 3314 *supra* note 31. *See* Nicar. v. U.S., *supra* note 32, ¶ 195.

51   This is distinct from the Wales Summit Declaration which proclaimed that cyber-defense is part of NATO's task of collective defense and that a cyber attack can trigger the right of individual or collective self-defense under Article 51 of the UN Charter and trigger the obligation under Article 5 of the NATO Charter to take action. *See* Press Release, NATO, Wales Summit Declaration Issued by the Heads of State and Government Participating in the Meeting of the North Atlantic Council in Wales, Sept. 5, 2014, *at* http://www.nato.int/

put pressure on the Council to take appropriate Chapter VII action (even if only a determination that a breach of the peace has occurred), and where such a prosecution or investigation has not occurred may put constraints on the scope of Council action where it is otherwise inclined to act. Consider the political impact, for example, of an announcement by the ICC prosecution that in situation X that office has found no evidence to proceed with an investigation for aggression. To what extent would the Council be free to take a different view of the facts in order to make a determination that Chapter VII action is still warranted? By elevating the Assembly's definition of aggression to a formal crime within the jurisdiction of a Court that can count on, at least formally, treaty obligations on its party states to cooperate, acts of aggression will have been transformed from politicized determinations within the sole discretion of the world's police powers to a legally defined crime subject to enumerated procedures and judicial interpretation.[52] The Kampala amendments, and the Assembly definition incorporated within it, have the prospect of fundamentally changing the council's discretion to define aggression, as well as the politics surrounding Article 39 determinations more generally.

Of course, most GA resolutions are not incorporated into a binding criminal law provision intended for criminal law enforcement, and most are not cited by international or national courts as authoritative interpretations of either the UN Charter or of customary law terms incorporated into the Charter. Most Assembly efforts to interpret the Charter, even when these are successfully implemented within the organization, are not *de facto* constitutional amendments to the Charter order but modest incremental steps that subtly affect the UN's operation. These include, for example, more routine Assembly resolutions that determine that a certain matter is or is not an "important" question for purposes of Article 18 or that innocuously reframe or reinterpret a peacekeeping mandate previously given to the Secretary-General.[53]

---

cps/en/natohq/official_text_112964.htm. This presumes that an armed attack sufficient to trigger self-defense constitutes an act of aggression; not all agree that this is necessarily the case.

52 While advocates of the ICC and the Kampala amendments argue that these developments simply return us to the prosecution of crimes against the peace at Nuremberg, obvious differences include the fact that the Security Council did not exist when Nuremberg was established and that the Atlantic Charter under which the Nuremberg tribunal was established was concluded by WWII's victors and did not involve the participation (or the financial support) of what are now 124 Rome Statute parties.

53 CHARTER COMMENTARY, *supra* note 20, at 269–270 (discussing resolutions that address whether a matter is an "important" question).

Others are more significant, like the resolution that established, under Article 22, the organization's first administrative tribunal to handle secretariat employment matters.[54] That resolution led to the establishment of an entire field of IO administrative law, has affected the operation and employee rights of a number of UN system organizations, gives particular meaning to Article 100's objective to secure an independent international civil service, and has formed the backbone for evolving notions of fair process and accountability within IOs.[55] That Assembly decision, as was implicitly recognized by the ICJ Advisory Opinion affirming the legality of the Assembly's action, was something of a stretch of the language under Article 22. That tribunal, in purpose and effect, was hardly "subsidiary" to the Assembly.[56] While the Assembly's decision in that instance (and the ICJ's opinion affirming its legality) had substantial legal effects both inside and outside the organization, and was even cited much later as demonstrating that the Assembly could have legally established the ICTY,[57] it would be an over-statement to call the Assembly's action a *de facto* amendment of the Charter.

Moreover, most Assembly efforts to interpret or re-interpret Charter provisions do not have demonstrable legal effects, at least in the short term, or for all UN member states. Even its highly regarded Friendly Relations Declaration contains interpretations of the Charter that some states have ignored.[58] Calling an Assembly resolution an "authoritative" Charter interpretation does not necessarily elicit state compliance—any more so than Assembly resolutions that

---

54   G.A. Res. 351 A(IV) (Nov. 24, 1949). That tribunal was later replaced under G.A. Res. 62/228 (Feb. 6, 2008) (establishing a two-tier formal system of administration of justice including a first instance UN Dispute Tribunal and an appellate UN Appeals Tribunal).

55   *See, e.g.*, C.F. AMERASINGHE, THE LAW OF THE INTERNATIONAL CIVIL SERVICE (AS APPLIED BY INTERNATIONAL ADMINISTRATIVE TRIBUNALS) (2d ed. 1994). The Assembly regularly revisits the topic of the "administration of justice at the UN." *See, e.g.*, G.A. Res. 66/237 (Dec. 24, 2011); G.A. Res. 64/119 (Jan. 15, 2010); G.A. Res. 69/203 (Dec. 18, 2014).

56   *See* Effect of Awards of Compensation Made by the United Nations Administrative Tribunal, Advisory Opinion, 1954 I.C.J. 47, at 59–61 (July 13).

57   *See, e.g.*, Dusko Tadic, Appellate Chamber, Case No. IT-94-1-AR72, Oct. 2, 1995, ¶ 16. *See also* Report of the Secretary-General Pursuant to Paragraph 2 of Security Council Resolution 808, ¶ 21, U.N. Doc. S/25704 (May 3, 1993) (discussing the possibility of using the General Assembly to establish the ICTY).

58   *Compare* Friendly Relations Declaration, *supra* note 30, at 123 (recognizing that Article 2(4) forbids the forceful military occupation of a state and requiring states not to recognize as legal any "territorial acquisition resulting from the threat or use of force"), *with* G.A. Res. 68/262 (Mar. 27, 2014) (declaring Russia's annexation of Crimea to be illegal but drawing the consenting votes of only 100 of the UN's 192 members).

call states' attention to their treaty obligations. The real world "bindingness" of international law is a variable thing, irrespective of whether it involves an Article 38 source or an Assembly resolution.

Determining the relative legal impact of Assembly interpretative resolutions is not a simple matter given the diffuse ways that international law is routinely enforced or implemented. Even relatively "hard" GA resolutions like its Friendly Relations Declaration and Definition of Aggression efforts are most likely to have legal effects indirectly, by influencing the discourse of states, including the justifications offered within UN bodies like the Council, states' briefs in international courts, or bilateral diplomatic demarches. But given the fact that most hard treaties are not subject to enforceable provisions enabling an international or national court's jurisdiction to compel states to comply with their terms, the relative lack of enforcement venues does not distinguish Assembly resolutions.

The most prominent (if indirect) effects of the General Assembly's (and the Security Council's) efforts to re-interpret the Charter are felt with respect to the mandate of the organization. The routine and not so routine Charter interpretations that the General Assembly engages in on a day-to-day basis reliably expand (and, at least potentially, could contract) the functions of UN organs and of the organization itself. As Jan Klabbers has argued, UN system organizations, especially the UN itself, are difficult to cabin as tools of functionalism, at least if functional organizations are defined as mere institutional repositories for achieving narrowly defined, technocratic, and apolitical tasks specifically delegated to them by state principals.[59] Functionalism so defined is not, as he points out, a good fit with the vague purposes and principles in Articles 1 and 2 of the Charter, or with the all-encompassing goals contained in its preamble. It is an even worst fit when those purposes, principles, and goals are handed over to the General Assembly to expansively (re)interpret over time.

Consider just three ways that the Assembly (sometimes aided and abetted by the Council) has expanded the reach of the organization, and its own operative activities: the concepts of "human security," "democratization," and the "rule of law."

The Assembly's re-visitations of the 2005 World Summit Outcome has led to its oft-repeated efforts to link, as "mutually reinforcing," the Charter's preamble goals to advance development, human rights, and peace and security. To this end, the Assembly has advanced the idea that the organization

---

59   Jan Klabbers, *The EJIL Foreword: the Transformation of International Organizations Law*, 26 EUR. J. INT'L L. 9, 31–33 (2015).

exists to advance "human security."[60] Since its "common understanding" of this concept embraces the rights of all persons to live in "freedom and dignity," free from "poverty", "despair," "fear," "want," and with an equal opportunity to enjoy all the above and "fully develop their human potential,"[61] this is a recipe for an organization that can, along with national governments, enact and go beyond Franklin D. Roosevelt's Four Freedoms.[62] To interpret the UN's (and the Assembly's) mandate to embrace the protection and advancement of "human security" is to transform the organization from a collective security body to a governance institution. To be sure, Assembly resolutions on human security tend to affirm that governments "retain the primary role" for securing the human security of their peoples, but they also recognize that the "international community" needs to provide "the necessary support to Governments, upon their request, so as to strengthen their capacity to respond to current and emerging threats."[63] If the UN, and specifically the Assembly, is charged with advancing all-encompassing "human security," it is hard to see what "implicit powers," i.e., operational activities, condemnatory resolutions, or authority to establish subsidiary bodies with delegated powers, are denied to it, no matter the political impact of such actions or the effect on members' residual sovereignty.

This expansive view of the "object and purpose" of the UN Charter helps to explain how the Assembly and the UN secretariat have managed to embrace a second expansive agenda in the name of promoting "democratization." The democracy-building activities of the organization, particularly its electoral assistance and supervisory activities over elections and plebiscites, has generated a substantial literature, a relatively new body of expertise, and a wide network of cooperating private contractors.[64] For a number of years the UN, with support from the Assembly, the Council, and its Secretariat, has embraced election assistance and supervision as a core function, including with respect

---

60   *See, e.g.,* G.A. Res. 66/290, ¶ 4 (Sept. 10, 2012).

61   *Id.* ¶ 3(a).

62   Franklin Delano Roosevelt, *Four Human Freedoms*, 6 HUM. RTS. Q. 384 (1984) (excerpted from President Franklin D. Roosevelt, Annual Message to Congress, 87 CONG. REC. 44, 46–47 (1941), *at* http://www.fdrlibrary.marist.edu/fourfreedoms).

63   G.A. Res. 66/290, *supra* note 60, ¶ 3(g).

64   *See, e.g.,* KIRSTEN HAACK, THE UNITED NATIONS DEMOCRACY AGENDA: A CONCEPTUAL HISTORY (2011); Caroline E. Lombardo, *The Making of an Agenda for Democratization*, 2 CHI. J. INT'L L. 253 (2001); Margaret Satterthwaite, *Human Rights Monitoring, Elections Monitoring, and Electoral Assistance as Preventive Measures*, 30 N.Y.U. J. INT'L L. & POL. 709 (1998).

to its peacekeepers.[65] So long as UN electoral assistance and democracy support comes at the "request of the Member State concerned,"[66] there appears to be little principled opposition to an activity that is not only not mentioned in the Charter but that is somewhat inconsistent with its universal membership aspirations. The UN was never, after all, intended to be a league of democracies, as were (arguably) regional organizations like the Organization of American States (OAS). Membership in the UN was not based on whether the applicant's government was the result of periodic free and fair elections. And yet the UN's electoral efforts, which to date has involved election assistance or supervision in over 100 states, has now generated a whole new sub-field of international law outlining the pre-conditions for a fair and free election.[67] To the extent public international law has given considerable content to the right of individuals to "take part in the conduct of public affairs, directly or through freely chosen representatives," the practice of the UN, and its election experts, needs to be given principal credit.[68]

---

65   *See, e.g.*, G.A. Res. 66/163 (Dec. 19, 2011).

66   *Id.* pmbl., ¶ 7.

67   United Nations Peacekeeping, Electoral Assistance, *at* http://www.un.org/en/peacekeeping/issues/electoralassistance.shtml. *See, e.g.*, Jon M. Ebersole, *The UN's Response to Requests for Assistance in Electoral Matters*, 33 VA. J. INT'L L. 91 (1992). UN electoral efforts have also led to related human rights efforts within the Assembly. *See, e.g.*, G.A. Res. 66/130, pmbl., ¶¶ 1–5 (Dec. 19, 2011) (declaring, under the Charter and treaty law, that states have a duty to enable all persons, including women, to take part in political activities, including elections). Particularly in the wake of post-Cold War hopes for a "new international order," the UN's democracy promotion efforts tempted some scholars to proclaim that there was an "emerging right to democratic governance" as a matter of general international law. *See* Thomas M. Franck, *The Emerging Right to Democratic Governance*, 86 AM. J. INT'L L. 46 (1992).

68   International Covenant on Civil and Political Rights art. 25, Dec. 16, 1966, 999 UNTS 171. *See, e.g.*, H.R.C. Res. 27/24 (Mar. 10, 2014) (resolution of the Human Rights Council on equal participation in political and public affairs); U.N. Human Rights Committee, General Comment No. 25: The Right to Participate in Public Affairs, Voting Rights and the Right of Equal Access to Public Service (Art. 25), U.N. Doc. CCPR/C/21/Rev.1/Add.7 (July 12, 1996); Gregory H. Fox, *The Right to Political Participation in International Law, in* DEMOCRATIC GOVERNANCE AND INTERNATIONAL LAW 71 (Gregory H. Fox & Brad R. Roth eds., 2000). One reason often given for the UN's democracy promotion activities is the ostensible link between democracy and peace, that is, the contention that democracies tend not to go to war against each other. *See, e.g.*, BOUTROS BOUTROS-GHALI, AN AGENDA FOR DEMOCRATIZATION ¶¶ 17–18 (1996) ("Democracy within States thus fosters the evolution of the social contract upon which lasting peace can be built. In this way,

The General Assembly has, thirdly, expansively re-interpreted its own mandate and that of the UN by embracing the need to promote and expand the "rule of law at the national and international levels." This too is the product of the 2005 World Summit Outcome,[69] and seems to emerge organically from the organization's decision to include human rights and democracy as indispensable foundations of the more peaceful, prosperous, and just world envisioned in the Charter's preamble.[70] As with respect to "human security," the Assembly's periodic resolutions on the "rule of law" lack a concrete definition of the term. Undoubtedly the Assembly has found it difficult to come up with a consensus definition for a concept that has eluded or bedeviled legal philosophers for centuries. But the absence of a definition for either the national or international rule of law has not prevented the Assembly from advancing abundant policy rationales for advancing both. Rule of law efforts are, according to the Assembly, related to but distinguishable from activities to protect human security or to advance democracy.[71] The Assembly sees the rule of law as "essential for the realization of sustained economic growth, sustainable development, the eradication of poverty and hunger and the protection of all human rights and fundamental freedoms."[72]

The Assembly's turn to rule of law has led to a steady accretion in bureaucratic activity in support of "good governance" that may sometimes work in tandem with similarly justified efforts by other IOs, especially international financial institutions. Subsidiary UN bodies include a Rule of Law Coordination and Resource Group, a Rule of Law Unit, and nearly 40 other UN entities that periodically report on progress achieved and obstacles to be overcome.[73] Rule of law has also become a relatively all-purpose rubric for branding and assessing long-established activities of the Assembly. The Assembly now sees its

---

a culture of democracy is fundamentally a culture of peace ... Democratic institutions and processes within states may likewise be conducive to peace among States.").

69   2005 World Summit Outcome, G.A. Res. A/60/L.1, ¶ 134 (Sept. 16, 2005).

70   Indeed, annual reports by the Secretary-General regularly re-cast the UN's efforts, from the earliest days of the organization, as having always been designed to strengthen the rule of law at the national and international levels. *See, e.g.*, U.N. Secretary-General, *Annual Report on Strengthening and Coordinating United Nations Rule of Law Activities: Rep. of the Secretary-General*, ¶¶ 1–6, U.N. Doc. A/64/298 (Aug. 17, 2009); U.N. Secretary-General, *Strengthening and Coordinating United Nations Rule of Law Activities: Rep. of the Secretary General*, ¶¶ 1–4, U.N. Doc. A/63/226 (Aug. 6, 2008).

71   *See, e.g.*, G.A. Res. 67/1, ¶ 5 (Nov. 30, 2012) (reaffirming that "human rights, the rule of law and democracy are interlinked").

72   *See, e.g.*, G.A. Res. 66/102, pmbl., ¶ 5 (Dec. 9, 2011).

73   *See Coordinating United Nations Rule of Law Activities* (2008), *supra* note 70, ¶¶ 1–11.

longstanding supervisory efforts, through its Sixth Committee, of the work of
the International Law Commission (ILC), for example, as another rule of law
activity. At the national level, rule of law has become a reliable vehicle justifying UN "enhanced technical assistance and capacity building" within member
states that extend far beyond international assistance rendered during an election cycle.[74] Rule of law is now an important component of the highly intrusive mandates of contemporary UN Peace Operations.[75]

The Assembly's Charter (re)interpretation efforts can also occur within the
context of often contentious resolutions that target a particular UN member
for criticism. In such cases, the specificity of the wrongful actions targeted for
condemnation, often involving alleged human rights violations committed
by the target state, may incidentally serve to interpret the Charter. Among
the many examples that might be cited are the perennial Assembly efforts to
criticize the United States for its "illegal" economic, commercial, and financial
embargo on Cuba. These Assembly resolutions over the years (at least prior to
the announcement by the Obama Administration in December 2014 that it was
seeking to re-establish diplomatic relations with Cuba and presumably seeking
to end that embargo) have drawn more and more support, along with scholarly attention.[76] Such resolutions have usually cast the U.S. Cuban embargo on
goods as an affront to the principle of "sovereign equality" as expressed in the
Charter or as wrongful interference with Cuba's "domestic jurisdiction" under
Article 2(7), thereby providing some specific content to these vague Charter
terms. As with respect to other comparable Assembly condemnation efforts,
such as resolutions declaring Israeli settlement construction and other activities in the occupied Syrian Golan to constitute the wrongful acquisition of
territory by force in violation of the Charter,[77] the authoritativeness of these
Assembly efforts may be undermined to the extent the resolutions fail to draw

---

74   G.A. Res. 66/102, *supra* note 72, ¶ 5.

75   THE UN SECURITY COUNCIL IN THE TWENTY-FIRST CENTURY (Sebastian von
      Einsiedel, David M. Malone & Bruno Stagno Ugarte eds., 2015); THE UN SECURITY
      COUNCIL: FROM THE COLD WAR TO THE 21ST CENTURY (David Malone ed., 2004).

76   Kristina Daugirdas & Julian Davis Mortenson, *United States Lifts Some Cuba Restrictions
      and Explores Possibility of Normalizing Relations, Contemporary Practice of the United
      States*, 109 AM. J. INT'L L. 415 (2015).

77   *See, e.g.*, G.A. Res. 66/19 (Nov. 30, 2011) (adopted with 119 states in favor and 7 against
      (which included Canada, Israel, Marshall Islands, Micronesia, Nauru, Palau, the United
      States) along with 53 abstentions).

the general support of UN members (and not only the ire of the state targeted for criticism).[78]

The Assembly's influence on the interpretation of the Charter may sometimes occur in subtler ways. As is addressed in Chapter II, the Security Council's invocations of "individual and collective self defense" in the immediate wake of the events in the United States on 9/11 in its Resolutions 1368 and 1373 augured new interpretations of what that term (and the concept of "armed force") means for purposes of Articles 51 and 2(4).[79] Less noticed at the time was the General Assembly's more muted reaction to 9/11. The day after 9/11, the Assembly condemned the "acts of terrorism" committed but called for international cooperation to "bring to justice the perpetrators, organizers and sponsors" and declared that those responsible for aiding, supporting, or harboring such persons would be "held accountable."[80] Whereas the Council was at the time suggesting that both terrorist perpetrators as well as their state enablers were subject to the defensive use of force,[81] the Assembly seemed to be adopting a criminal justice framework wherein both non-state terrorist and state enabler should be tried in court. Even in that instance, when the acts of terror occurred within sight of UN Headquarters and the UN missions of many of its members, the Assembly resisted the idea that terrorism, while undoubtedly a violation of the Charter, was an "armed attack" triggering force in response— even when those acts were of the scale seen on 9/11.[82] At the same time, the Assembly had adopted, as part of its interpretation of Article 2(4), the following text in its Friendly Relations resolution years before: "Every State has the duty to refrain from organizing, instigating, assisting or participating in acts of

---

78   But the lop-sided votes in favor of some of these resolutions, such as G.A. Res. 66/6 (Oct. 25, 2011) (which drew only the dissenting votes of Israel and the United States, along with only 3 abstentions), may make even these more controversial efforts to interpret the Charter legally persuasive over the long term. *See, e.g.*, Jordan J. Paust, *Ten Types of Israeli and Palestinian Violation of the Laws of War and the ICC*, 31 CONN. J. INT'L L. (forthcoming 2016).

79   *See* Chapter II *supra* § 3; José E. Alvarez, *Hegemonic International Law Revisited*, 97 AM. J. INT'L L. 873, 879–882 (2003); Michael Byers, *Terrorism, the Use of Force and International Law After 11 September*, 51 INT'L & COMP. L. Q. 401 (2002).

80   G.A. Res. 56/1, ¶ 3 (Sept. 12, 2001).

81   *See* S.C. Res. 1368, pmbl., ¶ 3 (Sept. 12, 2001); S.C. Res. 1373, pmbl., ¶ 4 (Sept. 28, 2001).

82   Scholars and policy-makers have long debated whether any and all uses of force violate Art. 2(4) and whether if so, all such acts triggers self-defense actions in response. *See, e.g.*, TOM RUYS, ARMED ATTACK AND ARTICLE 51 OF THE UN CHARTER: EVOLUTIONS IN CUSTOMARY LAW AND PRACTICE (2010).

civil strife or terrorist acts in another State or acquiescing in organized activities within its territory directed towards the commission of such acts, when the acts referred to in the present paragraph involve a threat or use of force."[83] As noted in Chapter II, the Council apparently drew from this paragraph in its preamble to Resolution 1373 wherein it also noted states' duties to avoid even acquiescence in organized terrorist acts by non-state actors within its territory.

As noted in Chapter II, S.C. Res. 1373, even while going beyond what the Assembly was recommending in terms of a reaction to 9/11, relied on the Assembly's interpretation of what the link between non-state terrorist act and host state needed to be in order to constitute a Charter (and perhaps customary) violation.

Significantly, since 9/11, despite numerous other terrorist acts, with one possible exception, the Council has not invoked Article 51 in response to them. Instead, it too has adopted language comparable to that used by the Assembly in the immediate wake of 9/11.[84] Whether terrorist acts, depending on scale or gravity, should be seen as "armed attacks" sufficient to trigger individual and collective self-defense remains a contested point among scholars, even though a number of states, apart from the United States, appear to take this position.[85] As has become clear given debates over whether isolated attacks by ISIS on, for example, a U.S. journalist, can legally trigger self-defense actions by the U.S., scholars and policymakers continue to debate whether even "minimal" uses of force violate Article 2(4) and whether, even if they do, all uniformly trigger the right to individual or collective self- defense (subject, as always to necessity and proportionality).[86] One might reconcile the Assembly's paragraph above from its 1970 Friendly Relations resolution with its muted reaction to 9/11 as concluding that a state that acquiesces (as the Taliban regime

83   Friendly Relations Declaration, *supra* note 30, annex (Oct. 24, 1970).

84   *See, e.g.,* S.C. Res. 2195, ¶ 4 (Dec. 19, 2014) (referring to the prosecution of terrorist acts); S.C. Res. 1530, ¶¶ 1–3 (Mar. 11, 2004) (condemning the ETA bombing of Madrid and urging all states to "cooperate actively in efforts to find and bring to justice the perpetrators, organizers and sponsors of this terrorist attack"). *But see* S.C. Res. 2249, ¶ 5 (Nov. 20, 2015) (calling on states "to take all necessary means" to prevent and suppress terrorists acts by ISIL in the wake of attacks in Paris and elsewhere).

85   For the tip of the iceberg on these debates, see Sean D. Murphy, *Terrorism and the Concept of "Armed Attack" in Article 51 of the UN Charter*, 43 HARV. INT'L L. J. 41 (2003); Thomas. M. Franck, *Terrorism and the Right of Self-Defense*, 94 AM. J. INT'L L. 839 (2001); TOM RUYS, ARMED ATTACK AND ARTICLE 51 OF THE UN CHARTER: CUSTOMARY LAW AND PRACTICE.

86   *See, e.g.,* Tom Ruys, *The Meaning of "Force" and the Boundaries of the Jus ad Bellum: Are "Minimal" Uses of Force Excluded from UN Charter Article 2(4)?*, 108 AM. J. INT'L L. 159 (2014).

arguably did in Afghanistan both prior to and subsequent to 9/11) with terrorist actions within its border directed at other states violates Article 2(4),
commits a threat or breach of the peace under Article 39 and interferes with
a state's domestic jurisdiction, but that neither of these Charter violations is
sufficient, in and of itself, to permit the invocation of individual or collective
self-defense against that state.[87] Whether or not one agrees with this view, to
the extent the law (and interpretation of relevant state practice) remains contested, the Assembly's reluctance to deploy the terminology used in Council
Resolutions 1368 and 1373—which might be seen as Assembly interpretation
by omission—plays some role in that contestation.

To be sure, many (perhaps most) of the Assembly's grandiose efforts to (re)
interpret the Charter are appropriately seen as mere rhetorical flourishes that
do not shape the law. The contextual inquiries required for an accurate assessment of the probable legal impact of Assembly action is not a simple matter of
counting up the votes in favor of it. To be sure, the absence of general support
(needed to establish customary law or general acquiescence in Charter interpretation through subsequent practice) may be evident in the divided vote
taken upon its adoption. Many Assembly resolutions, including some that are
perennial favorites, brought to a vote on an annual basis with slight modifica-
tion, result in highly divided votes, often along north/south lines. Resolution
66/159 of 2012, one of a series promoting "a democratic and equitable international order" is a good example. That resolution purports to interpret the
crucial Purposes of the organization under Articles 1 and 2, including what it
means to "respect" the principle of "equal rights and self determination of peoples," along with other Charter terms such as "sovereign equality," "territorial
integrity and political independence," and non-intervention in domestic jurisdiction.[88] It defines the "democratic and equitable international order" that it
seeks to achieve as one that requires the realization of, among other things:

> The promotion and consolidation of transparent, democratic, just and
> accountable international institutions in all areas of cooperation, in par-
> ticular through the implementation of the principle of full and equal par-
> ticipation in their respective decision-making mechanisms...[89]
> and

---

87   *But see* Mary Ellen O'Connell, *Lawful Self-Defense to Terrorism*, 63 U. PITT. L. REV. 889,
      904 (2002) (arguing that the attacks of 9/11 justify U.S. use of force against non-state
      terrorist bases in Afghanistan but not its use of force directed at toppling the Taliban
      regime).

88   G.A. Res. 66/159 (Dec. 19, 2011).

89   *Id.* ¶ 4(g).

> The promotion of a free, just, effective and balanced international infor-
> mation and communications order, based on international cooperation
> for the establishment of a new equilibrium and greater reciprocity in the
> international flow of information, in particular correcting the inequali-
> ties in the flow of information to and from developing countries . . .[90]

This effort to draw the support of Western democracies as well as of those
UN members that seek establishment of a "New World Information and
Communications Order"[91] failed. For Western democracies like the United
States, with a tradition of seeing freedom of expression as an individual right
free of government intervention, talk of securing, through *governmental*
action, a "balanced" flow of information runs counter to human rights.[92] Not
surprisingly, that resolution was adopted only after a recorded vote of 130 to 54
with 6 abstentions, with the negative votes drawn from mostly Western states.[93]

At the same time, even such General Assembly "failures" may not be entirely
useless to an international adjudicator. A resolution like 66/159 may be useful
to an objective observer (scholar or court) as demonstrating the *lack of consensus* on such matters rather than an authoritative Charter interpretation. Many
other Assembly re-interpretation efforts, adopted over the negative or abstaining votes of some regional or ideologically defined block of states, may suggest
the same conclusion.[94] A resolution that shows fundamental disagreements
over what it means to have a "democratic and equitable international order,"
may drive a court or quasi-judicial body, charged with interpreting customary
human rights norms, away from an effort to ground its conclusions on Article
28 of the Universal Declaration of Human Rights (which suggests entitlement

---

90   *Id.* ¶ 4(j).

91   *See generally* The MacBride Commission, International Commission for the Study of
      Communication Problems, Many Voices, One World (1980), *at* http://unesdoc.unesco.
      org/images/0004/000400/040066eb.pdf.

92   Indeed, the U.S. withdrew from UNESCO during the Reagan administration as a result
      of concerns that it was impeding the free flow of information. *See* Letter from George
      Schultz, Secretary of State, to Amadou-Mahtar M'Bow, Director-General of UNESCO
      (Dec. 28, 1983), *reprinted in* U.S. Dep't of State, American Foreign Policy Current
      Documents, Document 93, at 282–283 (1983). For a historical overview of this resistance,
      see THOMAS L. MCPHAIL, GLOBAL COMMUNICATION: THEORIES, STAKEHOLDERS
      AND TRENDS 55–63 (4th ed. 2013).

93   For more recent resolutions on the subject of the "Promotion of a Democratic and
      Equitable Order," with a similar voting pattern, see G.A. Res. 67/175 (Dec. 20, 2012); G.A.
      Res. 68/175 (Dec. 18, 2013).

94   *See, e.g.,* G.A. Res. 66/155 (Dec. 19, 2011) (on the "Right to Development").

to a "social and international order in which the rights and freedoms set forth in this Declaration can be fully realized").[95]

Finally, the mere fact that an Assembly resolution achieves adoption by consensus does not mean that it was subject to sober reflection and due consideration by the top lawyers of UN member states back in their respective capitals and duly approved by their superiors at the highest level, the UN's general counsel, or by representatives of states charged with examining the draft text in, for example, the Assembly's Sixth Committee. The context of a resolution matters—at least as much as context does with respect to interpreting the significance of the practice of states. Just as we would not treat the off-the-cuff remarks of a foreign minister or other state official as definitive evidence of that state's view of customary law or its considered view of the proper interpretation of a treaty, it would be wrong to ignore the fact that, for example, a particular Assembly resolution was treated upon adoption by all or most concerned as a political statement of no intended import on the law.

3   The Assembly as Human Rights Interpreter and Enforcer

The remarkable trajectory of the Charter's brief and oblique references to "human rights" has been told elsewhere and needs no repetition here.[96] The Assembly's prominent role in developing the "rights" encompassed by the references in Articles 55 and 56 of the Charter, that can be recognized as required under customary international law or *jus cogens*, or that can be seen as within the scope of an increasingly large number of global human rights conventions negotiated under its auspices, has been amply demonstrated by other scholars.[97] As is well known, the Assembly's approval of the Universal Declaration of Human Rights in 1948 as a mere "standard of achievement" initiated a human rights revolution that has, to date, led to nine core human rights conventions most of which have been ratified by relatively high number of states.[98] Most of these human rights treaties were originally the object of

---

95   Universal Declaration of Human Rights art. 28, G.A. Res. 217(III)A (Dec. 10, 1948).

96   *See, e.g.,* IAN CLARK, INTERNATIONAL LEGITIMACY AND WORLD SOCIETY 132–152 (2007); HERSCH LAUTERPACHT, INTERNATIONAL LAW AND HUMAN RIGHTS 147 (1950).

97   *See, e.g.,* Thomas Buergenthal, *The Evolving International Human Rights System,* 100 AM. J. INT'L L. 783, 785–790 (2006).

98   Oona A. Hathaway, *Fighting the Law War: The United Nations Charter in the Age of the War on Terror, in* CHARTER OF THE UNITED NATIONS: TOGETHER WITH SCHOLARLY

attention within ECOSOC which were subsequently approved as declarations attached to Assembly resolutions.[99] It has also led to perennial and oft-repeated statements by the Assembly suggesting that many, if not all, the rights contained in its Declaration of Human Rights should now be seen as universally applicable customary norms.[100]

The Assembly's actions on human rights are the most common example of the Assembly's role as treaty initiator.[101] Apart from its continued role as treaty convener,[102] the Assembly has repeatedly sought to encourage states to

---

COMMENTARIES AND ESSENTIAL HISTORICAL DOCUMENTS 218–219 (Ian Shapiro & Joseph Lampert eds., 2014); U.N. Office of the High Commissioner for Human Rights, *The Core International Human Rights Instruments and Their Monitoring Bodies*, at http://www.ohchr.org/EN/ProfessionalInterest/Pages/CoreInstruments.aspx.

99 *See* U.N. Charter, art. 62(3) (providing that ECOSOC "may prepare draft conventions for submission to the General Assembly, with respect to matters falling within its competence"); International Convention on the Elimination of All Forms of Racial Discrimination, *opened for signature* Dec. 21, 1965, G.A. Res. 2106 (XX), 660 U.N.T.S. 195; International Covenant on Civil and Political Rights, *opened for signature* Dec. 16, 1966, G.A. Res. 2200A(XX), 999 U.N.T.S. 171 [hereinafter ICCPR]; International Covenant on Economic, Social and Cultural Rights, *opened for signature* Dec. 19, 1966, G.A. Res. 2200A(XXI), 993 U.N.T.S. 3 [hereinafter ICESCR]; Convention on the Elimination of All Forms of Discrimination against Women, *opened for signature* Dec. 18, 1979, G.A. Res. 34/180, 1249 U.N.T.S. 13 [hereinafter CEDAW]; Convention Against Torture and Other Cruel, Inhuman or Degrading Treatment or Punishment, *opened for signature* Dec. 10, 1984, G.A. Res. 32/62, 1465 U.N.T.S. 85; Convention on the Rights of the Child, *opened for signature* Nov. 20, 1989, G.A. Res. 44/25, 1577 U.N.T.S. 3; International Convention on the Protection of the Rights of All Migrant Workers and Members of their Families, *opened for signature* Dec. 18, 1990, G.A. Res. 45/158, 2220 U.N.T.S. 3; International Convention for the Protection of All Persons from Enforced Disappearance, *opened for signature* Dec. 20, 2006, G.A. Res. 61/177, 2716 U.N.T.S. 3; Convention on the Rights of Persons with Disabilities, *opened for signature* Mar. 30, 2007, G.A. Res. 61/106, 2515 U.N.T.S. 3. For an interactive list of ratification numbers or these treaties, *see* U.N. Office of the High Commissioner for Human Rights, Status of Ratification Interactive Dashboard, *at* http://indicators.ohchr.org.

100 Thus, the Assembly repeatedly states that it is guided by "the fundamental and universal principles enshrined in the Charter of the United Nations and the Universal Declaration of Human Rights." *See, e.g.*, G.A. Res. 60/153 (Dec. 16, 2005) and G.A. Res. 58/181 (Dec. 18, 2013).

101 *See generally* ALVAREZ, *supra* note 2, at 273–337 (discussing the impact IO treaty negotiations may have on the process of treaty making and the content of treaties).

102 *See, e.g.*, G.A. Res. 66/138 (Dec. 19, 2011) (adopting optional protocol for individual complaints procedure for Rights of Child convention). For a listing of declarations and conventions contained in General Assembly resolutions through 2013, see http://www.un.org/documents/instruments/docs_subj_en.asp?subj=32.

ratify human rights conventions that were adopted under its auspices or by a conference that it convened. Particularly with respect to human rights treaties that it played a role in approving, the Assembly takes the view that the more ratifiers the better. These efforts may reflect awareness that universal or near universal ratification makes it more likely to assert that the underlying rights in these treaties are required as a matter of custom—and can therefore be asserted even with respect to non-parties. The Assembly also has not been reticent about returning to the texts of previously adopted human rights conventions to affirm or buttress the sometimes contested interpretations of the rights contained in them by others (such as the respective UN human rights committees charged with issuing formally non-binding views) or to advance more novel interpretations being urged by human rights advocates.

Typical examples include the Assembly's repeated efforts to tackle the problem of "trafficking in women and girls." In a series of resolutions, the Assembly has sought to bring the issue within the domain of a number of human rights treaties that do not explicitly deal with trafficking, such as the International Covenant on Civil and Political Rights and the Covenant on Economic, Social and Cultural Rights,[103] to add considerable detail to the bare and vague obligations under some treaties, like CEDAW, that simply require states to take "all appropriate measures" to suppress trafficking,[104] and to suggest inter-regime connections for the sake of greater effectiveness.[105] These resolutions recast the obligations of states as embracing an "obligation to exercise due diligence to prevent, investigate and punish perpetrators of trafficking in persons, and to rescue victims as well as provide for their protection," noting that "not doing so violates and impairs or nullifies the enjoyment of the human rights and fundamental freedoms of the victims."[106] This is an expansive interpretation of the relevant duties in many of the underlying human rights conventions, which address only the duties of states to "respect" or "ensure" the underlying treaty or, as does CEDAW, only require states (ambiguously) to take "all appropriate

---

103   G.A. Res. 63/156, ¶ 26 (Dec. 18, 2008); G.A. Res. 67/145, ¶ 37 (Dec. 20, 2012) (inviting state reports under the two covenants to include information and statistics on trafficking as part of the national reports required under those two treaties); G.A. Res. 69/149, ¶ 44 (Dec. 18, 2014).

104   See, e.g., G.A. Res. 69/149, supra note 103, ¶¶ 23–24 (enumerating a number of measures to strengthen the regime at the national, regional, and international levels and calling on governments to criminalize trafficking activities).

105   See, e.g., id. pmbl. (drawing connections between a number of human rights conventions and treaties focusing on the suppression of trafficking, transnational organized crime, and smuggling of migrants, as well as prior resolutions issued by the Assembly itself, the Human Rights Council, and other 10 bodies).

106   Id. pmbl., ¶ 9. See generally ALVAREZ, supra note 2, at 164–166.

measures."[107] Along the way, the Assembly provides relevant human rights committees under these treaties, advocates before such committees, and members of international civil society more generally that file shadow reports in response to state reports, alternative ways to view the underlying human rights at stake. An example is provided by the Assembly's 2008 resolution on sex trafficking. That resolution suggests to opponents of trafficking that it is, simultaneously, an act that violates individuals' rights not to be discriminated against; an act that violates the rights of states to be secure; a crime under treaties that criminalize money-laundering or encompass other forms of transnational crime; and a violation of international labor law.[108] Each of these frames implicates a distinct legal regime with distinct approaches to interpretation and implementation. That resolution also makes the case that the organization itself, including its peacekeepers, is not immune from responsibilities to combat and deal with trafficking.[109] This is particularly important insofar as the texts of human rights treaties typically do not address the violations that IOs may commit, presumes rights violations are only committed by states, and limits ratification to states.[110]

Assembly efforts to re-interpret human rights treaties may focus attention to a newly emerging (or newly acknowledged) problem or an ignored vulnerable group whose needs are not explicitly recognized in the underlying treaties. Examples of this effort include a recent slate of Assembly resolutions dealing with the plight of "the girl child." These resolutions focus in great detail on difficulties that have been the subject of a number of major UN conferences convened after the adoption of relevant instruments such as the Rights of the Child Convention or CEDAW. These resolutions often reflect ideas or goals contained in platforms for action adopted at such conferences. Resolution 66/140, for example, identifies many examples of forms of discrimination that are particular to the girl child, including: less access to education, nutrition, physical and medical care, female infanticide and other forms of abuse and violence, forced marriage, and female genital mutilation. That resolution re-interprets treaty obligations in light of these realities. Attentive to the fact that the various human rights treaties that might be relevant to state obligations focus on different rationales, that resolution goes to great lengths to identify the underlying rights of the girl child that are routinely violated as breaches

---

107   *See, e.g.*, CEDAW, *supra* note 99, arts. 5–8, 10–13, 16.

108   G.A. Res. 63/156, *supra* note 103.

109   *Id.* ¶ 25. As is discussed in Chapter VI *infra* § 3, this is significant concern given the accountability (or rule of law) challenges facing IOs, including UN peacekeepers.

110   *See, e.g.*, U.N. Office of Legal Affairs, Treaty Section, Summary of Practice of the Secretary-General as Depository of Multilateral Treaties, UN Doc. ST/LEG/7/Rev. 1 at 28, ¶ 98.

of the right to equality, privacy, dignity, life, health (including rights to "repro-ductive health"), education, or economic opportunity.[111] These interpretative efforts may sometimes go beyond the views of the underlying human rights committees and are in fact partly directed at spurring those committees to re-dress their prior omissions. Such resolutions may also go behind the commit-tees to address directly the implementation efforts that states are required to take under the respective treaties. Resolution 66/140, for example, is quite clear that, in the Assembly's view, the relevant treaties demand culturally or socially intrusive demands on ratifiers. It urges all states, for example,

> to enact and strictly enforce laws to ensure that marriage is entered into only with the free and full consent of the intending spouses, and, in addi-tion, to enact and strictly enforce laws concerning the minimum legal age of consent and the minimum age for marriage where necessary, and to develop and implement comprehensive policies, plans of action and pro-grammes for the survival, protection, development and advancement of the girl child in order to promote and protect the full enjoyment of her human rights and to ensure equal opportunities for girls, including by making such plans an integral part of her total development process...[112]

As with respect to resolutions on trafficking, that resolution also recognizes corresponding obligations on the UN itself, including the need for all military, police, and civilian personnel involved in UN operations to fully respect and ensure the rights of woman and children.[113]

The Assembly's efforts to expand the categories of persons that need to be protected by human rights norms or to add operationally relevant details as to what protecting such persons actually means, now include attempts to protect others at one remove from the typical human rights victim, such as human rights defenders.[114] Those resolutions declare that the obligation to respect, protect, and ensure rights to freedom of expression and association

---

111   G.A. Res. 66/140 (Dec. 19, 2011).

112   *Id.* ¶ 18. Assembly resolutions with respect to human rights, particularly with respect to the treatment of women, frequently make demands on states to alter politically or cultur-ally sensitive national institutions or practices. For another example, see G.A. Res. 66/130, *supra* note 67, ¶ 6 (directing states to review the differential impact of their electoral sys-tems on the political participation of women and urging adoption of measures to elimi-nate prejudices based on stereotyped roles for men and women in the political sphere).

113   G.A. Res. 66/140, *supra* note 111, ¶ 34.

114   *See, e.g.,* G.A. Res. 66/164, ¶¶ 4–5 (Dec. 19, 2011) (seeking to make sure that the right to "ensure" human rights includes protecting those who seek to defend the rights of oth-ers). That resolution responds to reports on the subject by the Special Rapporteur of the

include oversight over government registration of civil society organizations and efforts to make sure that any such regulations, if they exist, are "transparent, non-discriminatory, expeditious, inexpensive, allow for the possibility of appeal" and otherwise in accordance with human rights norms.[115] Those resolutions also defend the right to peaceful protest without being subject to force or arbitrary detention or arrest, and urge states to take "appropriate measures" to avoid impunity for attacks, threats, or acts of intimidates committed by either state or non-state actors against human rights defenders.[116]

While it is often said that the Assembly "crystalizes" human rights, these examples help to explain more concretely the kinds of contributions that some Assembly resolutions make or seek to make to the law. At their best, Assembly resolutions lead to more creative human rights lawyering. They may inspire new demands on states or make us see from a fresh perspective the kinds of harms inflicted on individuals. They may even inspire a new human right. Consider, for example, Res. 66/137 containing the innocuous sounding "UN Declaration on Human Rights Education and Training." That declaration expands the right to access to knowledge and data by applying it to knowledge about the law of human rights. The idea is simple: no one can be expected to exercise rights that they do not know they have. In this instance the Assembly is suggesting that states owe a duty to be transparent about the human rights treaties that they have entered into.

The Assembly's attention and action may also expedite acceptance of a relatively new right. Res. 66/172, for example, affirming a number of rights owed to migrants, identifies migrants' rights to communicate with their consular officials in cases of arrest as affirmed by the ICJ in a series of cases that found the U.S. to be in violation of the Vienna Convention on Diplomatic Relations.[117] While in those decisions, the ICJ did not declare that the right to have one's consulate notified in case of arrest on foreign soil to constitute a "human right" as opposed to a right owed to other states as a matter of diplomatic law, the Assembly's attention to this in the course of affirming other rights of migrants may accelerate acceptance of the view that this state duty, owed to the foreign individuals who are arrested, is part of the panoply of rights that foreigners have long enjoyed under the customary law owed to aliens and human rights.

Human Rights Council. *See* G.A. Res. 66/164, ¶ 2. For another example, see G.A. Res. 68/181 (Dec. 18, 2013) (protecting women human rights defenders).

115   G.A. Res. 66/164, *supra* note 111, ¶ 5.

116   *Id.* ¶¶ 6, 8.

117   G.A. Res. 66/172, pmbl., ¶ 4(g) and ¶¶ 8–9 (Dec. 19, 2011).

As with respect to many Assembly efforts to interpret the Charter, many of the Assembly's human rights efforts are at best aspirational efforts. As noted, this is most likely to be true where the relevant resolution draws a significant number of abstentions.[118] The same might be said with respect to an Assembly resolution that achieves consensus but, one suspects, exceeds the political will of the Assembly or most members to take it seriously. This might be said, for example, with respect to GA Res. 64/292 which declares that there is a human right to water, and calls upon states and international organizations to provide financial resources and engage in capacity-building and the transfer of technology to scale up world-wide efforts to provide safe, clean, accessible, and affordable drinking water and sanitation for all.[119] It seems doubtful that states are willing to accept such obligations, however worthy. Yet even this highly aspirational resolution has been seen by some as a major achievement which, by reinforcing the international community's interest in access to water, suggests a new *erga omnes* right that can and should be realized by a collective duty to cooperate.[120] Only time will tell whether this pebble, cast into the water by the Assembly, will eventually generate ripples of real world effect.

Perhaps the most visible Assembly actions with respect to human rights are those that purport to judge particular states or their particular human rights practices. Few of these "name and shame" resolutions achieve consensus but are passed on the basis of a recorded vote over dissents or abstentions. As the divided votes during the 66th session of the Assembly in 2012 with respect to GA Res. 66/6 (seeking to end the US embargo on Cuba), 66/19 (condemning Israeli occupation of Syrian Golan), 66/46 (affirming the ICJ's opinion on Nuclear Weapons), 66/174 (condemning North Korea for human rights violations), 66/175 (condemning Iran for same), 66/176 (condemning Syria for same), and 66/230 (condemning Myanmar for same) demonstrate, these condemnations are among the most controversial actions that the General Assembly takes. Despite widespread agreement among scholars and most UN members that the Assembly is not violating Article 2(7) when it criticizes states for human rights violations, even today the states targeted by such resolutions may

---

118   *See, e.g.,* G.A. Res. 66/155, *supra* note 94 (attempting to bridge, albeit not entirely successfully, continuing North/South divides with respect to the inseparability thesis between ICCPR and ICESCR and the right to development with a recorded vote of 154 in favor, 6 opposed and 29 abstentions).

119   G.A. Res. 64/292, ¶¶ 1–2 (July 28, 2010).

120   For considerations of the legal status of a right to water, see INGA T. WINKLER, THE HUMAN RIGHT TO WATER: SIGNIFICANCE, LEGAL STATUS AND IMPLICATIONS FOR WATER ALLOCATION 37, 175 (2014).

argue that the Assembly is wrongly interfering in their domestic jurisdiction.[121] Others object to the selectivity of the Assembly's actions, such as its decisions to single out Israel for criticism but not others.[122]

Despite these objections, these condemnatory resolutions may play an influential role in courts or other venues charged with interpretation of relevant law, no less than more traditional general human rights resolutions. The Assembly, as political a body as is the Council, is under no legal obligation to be consistent in its criticism of states. To the extent it is not even-handed in how it judges states, this undercuts its political credibility but not necessarily the plausibility of the legal conclusions rendered in the course of those judgmental resolutions that majorities in the Assembly support. To the extent such resolutions have a legal impact, it is not because of their general acceptance but because what they condemn ends up being a persuasive interpretation of the law.

The Assembly's oft-visited condemnation of the U.S. embargo on Cuba, noted above, may be persuasive evidence that U.S. efforts to make its sanctions applicable to companies located outside the U.S. (including subsidiaries of U.S. companies incorporated abroad) violate customary international law principles governing a state's jurisdiction to prescribe its law outside its territorial jurisdiction, for example.[123] The United States' vehement opposition to these resolutions may not persuade a judge or arbitrator should the matter ever be litigated, particularly if U.S. assertions of extraterritorial jurisdiction have drawn the persistent criticism of the majority of states and the U.S. has become isolated in its opposition, as seems clear from the dwindling opposition to condemning the U.S. on this ground over time. Consider what would happen if the United States and Cuba were to enter into an arbi-

---

121   Press Release, General Assembly, Concluding Intense Session, Third Committee Approves Final Draft Resolution on Human Rights Defenders, Sending Package of 62 Texts to General Assembly, UN Press Release GA/SHC/4161 (Nov. 25, 2015) ("China's speaker regretted that in recent years, certain Western countries had used the protection of 'human rights defenders' as an excuse to interfere in the domestic affairs of developing countries.").

122   Ambassador David Pressman, Alt. U.S. Rep. to the UN for Special Polit. Affairs, Explanation of Vote on UN General Assembly Resolutions Concerning the Situation in the Middle East (Nov. 24, 2015), at http://usun.state.gov/remarks/7010 ("[W]e are disappointed that UN members continually single out Israel without acknowledging the responsibilities and difficult steps that must be taken on all sides.").

123   See generally UNITED STATES ECONOMIC MEASURES AGAINST CUBA: PROCEEDINGS IN THE UNITED NATIONS AND INTERNATIONAL LAW ISSUES (Michael Krinsky & David Golove eds., 1993).

tration agreement whereby U.S. claims on behalf of its expropriated nationals would be heard, alongside Cuban government claims for injuries caused by the U.S. embargo.[124] Would such a tribunal not consider the Assembly's legal criticisms of the U.S. sanctions in its assessment of relevant law?

Much the same could be said with respect to at least some of the Assembly's actions targeting certain Israeli actions as violations of either human rights or international humanitarian law. The Assembly (along with, on occasion the Council) has repeatedly affirmed that international humanitarian law, including the Hague and Geneva conventions and customary law regarding the treatment of occupied territory, applies to territories occupied by Israel in the West Bank, Gaza, and East Jerusalem, for example.[125] Although Israel apparently does not agree with that legal assessment,[126] the Assembly's views have been cited with approval by, among others, the ICJ, and, at least in the past, the U.S. State Department.[127] The same appears to be the case with respect to at least some other Assembly condemnations of Israeli actions, such as Israel's alleged destruction and demolition of houses in the occupied territories when such acts are not justified on the basis of military necessity.[128] It would certainly not surprise anyone if some of the Assembly and Council's resolutions criticizing, for example, the acquisition of territory by the threat or use of force,[129] or, on the Palestinian side, condemning the targeting of civilians as terrorist acts,[130]

---

124 Such an arrangement could emerge as a result of ongoing efforts to reestablish diplomatic relations and settle outstanding claims on both sides. Certainly the jurisdiction of the Iran-US Claims Tribunal, which was capable of hearing the respective claims of both governments, was an essential part of its appeal to both states.

125 Paust, *supra* note 78, n. 9.

126 *See* Israel, The Conflict and Peace: Answers to Frequently Asked Questions (Israel Min. of Foreign Affairs Nov. 2007), *at* http://www.mfa.gov.il/mfa/foreignpolicy/peace/guide/pages/israel-%20the%20conflict%20and%20peace-%20answers%20to%20frequen.aspx.

127 *See, e.g.,* U.S. DEP'T OF STATE, COUNTRY REPORTS ON HUMAN RIGHTS PRACTICES FOR 1998, THE OCCUPIED TERRITORIES 1 (Feb. 1999); Legal Consequences of the Construction of a Wall in the Occupied Palestinian Territory, Advisory Opinion, 2004 I.C.J. 136, ¶¶ 74–75, 78, 89, 98–99, 101, 117, 120–121, 124, 134, 137, 163 (July 9) [hereinafter Wall Advisory Opinion].

128 Paust, *supra* note 78, at 15–16.

129 *See, e.g.,* G.A. Res. 66/225, pmbl., ¶ 4 (Dec. 22, 2011) ("[A]ffirming the inadmissibility of the acquisition of territory by force"); S.C. Res. 1544, pmbl. (May 19, 2004) ("Reiterating the obligation of Israel, the occupying Power, to abide scrupulously by its legal obligations under the Fourth Geneva Convention relative to the Protection of Civilians").

130 *See, e.g.,* G.A. Res. 57/110, pmbl, ¶ 18 (Feb. 14, 2003) ("[C]ondemning all acts of violence and terror against civilians on both sides").

were cited in support of war crimes charges directed at either Israeli or Palestinian nationals in the ICC.[131]

4   The Assembly as Peace and Security Institutional Actor

It is well understood that the Charter does not confer "exclusive" responsibility over peace and security matters to the Council but only "primary" responsibility under its Article 24.[132] It is also clear that the Assembly has the power to discuss any matter, including those relating to peace and security, and may make recommendations to the Council and hear from states with respect to any dispute.[133] At the same time, the Charter anticipates that the Assembly may bring a peace and security matter to the Council and that when enforcement action is required, the Assembly "shall" refer the matter to the Council.[134]

Much less clear are the limits (if any) that continue to be imposed on the Assembly under Article 12(1), which by its terms precludes the Assembly from making recommendations while the Council "is exercising…the functions assigned to it in the present Charter" in respect of any "dispute or situation." This unique Charter provision, the only one that appears to delimit the respective powers of the Assembly and the Council,[135] reflects a compromise struck at the San Francisco conference between those who sought to exclude the General Assembly from making recommendations with regard to any matter relating to international peace and security and those who sought to protect the Assembly's continuing authority to act.[136] Over time, the practice of the Assembly (and to some extent the Security Council itself in acquiescing to the Assembly's practice and occasionally opening the door to Assembly action) has narrowed considerably the ostensible limits imposed under Article 12(1).

---

131   Diaa Hadid & Somini Sengupta, *Palestinians to Seek War Crimes Charges Against Israel at Hague Court*, N.Y. TIMES (June 24, 2015), *at* http://www.nytimes.com/2015/06/25/world/middleeast/palestinians-to-accuse-israel-of-war-crimes-in-international-court.html?_r=0.

132   *See, e.g.*, Wall Advisory Opinion, *supra* note 127, ¶ 26. *See also* CHARTER COMMENTARY, *supra* note 20, at 508 (citing to a number of other ICJ advisory opinions and scholars).

133   U.N. Charter arts 10, 11(1)–(2), 14, 35.

134   U.N. Charter arts. 11(2)–(3).

135   *See* CHARTER COMMENTARY, *supra* note 20, at 509 (noting that "There are no corresponding provisions clarifying the relationship between the GA or the SC and other UN organs, nor the interrelations of those other organs").

136   *Id.* at 510 (noting how the negotiators at San Francisco barred only Assembly resolutions dealing with disputes or situations before the Council).

While initially this provision was interpreted to preclude Assembly recommendations (but not discussions) when a dispute or situation was put on the Council's agenda that was not removed by the Council, it has since been interpreted to impose a ban on the Assembly only if the Council is exercising its functions "at this moment."[137] Requiring "simultaneous, actual, and active"[138] consideration of a matter that the Council has characterized as either a "dispute" or a "situation," means that the Assembly sees itself as capable of interceding on virtually any matter before the UN relating to peace and security.[139]

The weakness of the ostensible Article 12(1) limit on the General Assembly's competence was made clear in the ICJ's rejection of arguments made by Israel and others that the Court had no jurisdiction to address the question posed by the Assembly concerning the legality of the Israeli Wall because of Article 12(1). In its Advisory Opinion, the ICJ noted first that a request for an advisory opinion was not "in itself" a "recommendation" by the General Assembly "with regard to [a] dispute or situation."[140] The Court then considered that the practice of the UN on Article 12(1) had "evolved subsequently" so that "there has been an increasing tendency over time for the General Assembly and the Security Council to deal in parallel with the same matter concerning the maintenance of international peace and security."[141] The Court

---

137 *Id.* at 511 (discussing the evolution of institutional practice such that by the late 1960s the UN Legal Counsel noted that the G.A. has consistently interpreted the expression "is exercising"–which replaced the original Dumbarton Oak wording providing "being dealt with"—to mean "is exercising at this moment").

138 *Id.*

139 Thus, the authoritative commentary on the UN concludes that Article 12(1) may preclude Assembly recommendations only if these specifically contradict a Council resolution over a pending dispute or situation. *Id.* at 514. *See also id.* at 516 (noting that the G.A. has interpreted the 12(1) limit "extremely narrowly" and "has managed to assume considerable powers of discretion, which are only marginally restricted" by Art. 12(1)).

140 Wall Advisory Opinion, *supra* note 127, ¶ 25. *See also* Advisory Opinion on the Accordance with International Law of Unilateral Declaration of Independence in Respect of Kosovo, 2010 I.C.J. 141, ¶¶ 24, 41 (July 22) [hereinafter Kosovo Advisory Opinion] (finding that Art. 12(1) does not impose limits on the Assembly's powers to request an advisory opinion under Art. 96(1) of the Charter and such a request is not a "recommendation" and noting that Art. 12 does not bar all action by the Assembly in respect to threats to international peace and security "which are before the Security Council").

141 Wall Advisory Opinion, *supra* note 127, ¶ 25. The ban on making recommendations concerning a specific dispute or situation before the Council does not apply, according to the leading commentary on the Charter, to general matters involving peace and security or to "aspects of the dispute or situation not directly connected with the maintenance of or threat to the peace." CHARTER COMMENTARY, *supra* note 20, at 515.

considered the "accepted practice of the General Assembly, as it has evolved" in concluding that the Assembly did not exceed its competence in submitting its request for an advisory opinion.[142]

In affirming the Assembly's ability to request an advisory opinion from the Court on the legal status of Kosovo's declaration of independence, the ICJ went further. In that instance, the Court was faced with a situation where the Council, not the Assembly, "had been actively seized of the matter."[143] The ICJ noted that Kosovo had been the subject of Council action for "more than ten years prior to the present request for an advisory opinion."[144] The Court accepted that the Assembly was a relative late-comer to peace and security matters involving Kosovo, insofar as it has adopted only a few resolutions on the subject and the situation had not even been on the agenda on the Assembly when it requested the underlying advisory opinion—as compared to the Council, which had met to consider Kosovo on 29 occasions between 2000–2008.[145] The Court also acknowledged that the Assembly's request for an advisory opinion would necessarily involve an interpretation of Security Council Resolution 1244 (1999), but concluded that none of these considerations provide a compelling reason for the Court to exercise its discretion to refuse to answer the Assembly's request.[146]

The ICJ's advisory opinion on the Israeli Wall also had to deal with another matter that historically has been an important boost to the Assembly's capacity to deal with peace and security: its 1950 Uniting for Peace resolution. That resolution, adopted at the instigation of states such as the United States that were frustrated by the exercise of the Soviet Council veto during the Cold War, led the Assembly to establish the peacekeeping operation that was the subject of the ICJ's seminal advisory opinion in the Certain Expenses Case.[147] The operative paragraph of Uniting for Peace states:

---

142   Wall Advisory Opinion, *supra* note 127, ¶ 28.

143   Kosovo Advisory Opinion, *supra* note 140, ¶ 43.

144   *Id.* ¶ 37.

145   *Id.* ¶¶ 37–38.

146   *Id.* ¶¶ 46, 44. The Court noted that the purpose of its advisory jurisdiction was to provide guidance to UN organs that could "assist them in the future exercise of their functions," and that it was up to the Assembly to decide what to do with the Court's opinion in terms of the Assembly's next steps.

147   Certain Expenses of the United Nations (Article 17, Paragraph 2 of the Charter), Advisory Opinion, 1962 I.C.J. 151 (July 20) [hereinafter Certain Expenses]; *see* ALVAREZ, *supra* note 2, at 126.

... if the Security Council, because of a lack of unanimity of the permanent members, fails to exercise its primary responsibility for the maintenance of international peace and security in any case where there appears to be a threat to the peace, breach of the peace, or act of aggression, the General Assembly shall consider the matter immediately with a view to making appropriate recommendations to Members for collective measures, including in the case of a breach of the peace or act of aggression the use of armed force, when necessary, to maintain or restore international peace and security. If not in session at the time, the General Assembly may meet in emergency session within twenty-four hours of the request therefore: "Such emergency special session shall be called if requested by the Security Council on the vote of any seven members or by a majority of the Members of the United Nations.[148]

The Assembly's request for an advisory opinion on the Israeli Wall emerged from the Assembly's Tenth Emergency Session on Palestine, originally convened in 1997 "when the Council had been unable to take a decision on the case of certain Israeli settlements in the Occupied Palestinian Territory, due to negative votes of a permanent member" and which had continued to be convened on a "rolling" basis eleven times prior to the Court's consideration of the General Assembly's request for an advisory opinion.[149] The ICJ was urged to reject the Assembly's request for that opinion on the basis that the Assembly's action did not fulfill the requisites of Uniting for Peace, because the Security Council was never seized of a draft resolution proposing that it should request an advisory opinion from the Court on this issue, because the Council had adopted a "roadmap" for Middle East peace and continued therefore to exercise its responsibilities, and because of other procedural irregularities, including the fact the rolling Tenth Emergency Session was convened to deliberate the merits of asking for an advisory opinion at the same time that the Assembly's regular session was meeting. The ICJ rejected all these challenges, noting, as it has in the past, that resolutions of a properly constituted UN organ passed in accordance with its rules of procedure "must be presumed to have been validly adopted."[150] This presumption of legality has, of course,

---

148 G.A. Res. 377A (V), ¶ 1 (Nov. 3, 1950) (Uniting for Peace Resolution).

149 Wall Advisory Opinion, *supra* note 127, ¶¶ 31–33.

150 Wall Advisory Opinion, *supra* note 127, ¶ 35 (quoting its advisory opinion in the Namibia case from 1970). More specifically, the Court found that the requisites of Uniting for Peace were satisfied insofar as the Council had, in 2003, as a result of veto by a permanent member, failed to adopt a draft resolution concerning Israel's construction of the Wall and

facilitated considerable expansion of the Assembly's (and other UN organs') implied powers.[151]

As this example suggests, the Uniting for Peace resolution continues to be relevant today. The point is not obvious. As Larry Johnson has pointed out, much of the underlying rationale for adopting Uniting for Peace no longer appears relevant.[152] First, there is no need for a procedural tool to get the Assembly back in session to deal with an emergency. The Assembly's regular sessions are no longer restricted to the mid-September to mid-December period. An Assembly that now meets year round with virtually no break between sessions does not require calling for the "emergency sessions" anticipated in Uniting for Peace except, as Johnson points out, to make a "political point."[153] Second, given evolving interpretations of Articles 11(2) and 12(1), the Assembly no longer needs special permission either to adopt recommendations that recommend (but do not compel) actions that approximate those accorded to the Council under Article 41 and face fewer constraints on acting contemporaneously with the Council.[154] Third, if we accept that, according to the Certain Expenses opinion and the leading Charter commentary, the Assembly is only precluded from taking, under Art. 11(2), legally binding "enforcement actions," there is nothing to stop the Assembly, even in the absence of the Uniting for Peace resolution, from adopting what the resolution anticipates: "effective coercive measures" that include non-binding recommendations that states take military measures (including those anticipated by Article 42).[155] According to experienced UN observers like Johnson, Uniting for Peace, in short, is simply not needed since the Assembly can do everything that it provides without resorting to its terms.

---

       nothing in the Assembly's procedural rules precluded rolling emergency sessions even if held concurrently with the Assembly's regular sessions. *Id.* ¶¶ 31–34 (noting also that the fact that no proposal had been made to the Security Council was irrelevant to request an advisory opinion on the Wall issue).

151   ALVAREZ, *supra* note 2, at 80–81.

152   Larry D. Johnson, *"Uniting for Peace": Does It Still Serve Any Useful Purpose?*, AJIL UNBOUND (July 15, 2014), *at* http://www.asil.org/blogs/"uniting-peace"-does-it-still-serve-any-useful-purpose.

153   *Id.*

154   *Id.*

155   CHARTER COMMENTARY, *supra* note 20, at 473–475; Certain Expenses, *supra* note 147. Johnson provides an alternative justification for at least some Assembly recommendations to use force. He argues that the Assembly can recommend collective or individual self-defense actions by states that are facing an armed attack consistent with Article 51 and that such self-defense recommendations should not be considered to be "enforcement actions" that only the Council can undertake.

Why is the Uniting for Peace Resolution not superfluous? As Johnson himself acknowledges, that resolution remains potentially important politically. It is an important reminder to the Council's permanent members that their exercise of their vetoes singly or collectively may not be the final word and that the Assembly might, in reaction, focus the world's attention on the Council's paralysis through the convening of an "emergency" session. To this extent Uniting for Peace buttresses one of the Assembly's functions: to serve as the conscience of the world and induce Council police action in response to threats to the peace or, as in the Wall opinion suggests, to induce action by another politically and legally significant actor, in that instance the ICJ. One might also see Uniting for Peace, as does Henry Richardson, as a reaction to the organization's early experiences with the veto and an affirmation that the Assembly stands as a potential (albeit weak) bulwark against vetoes not deployed in "good faith."[156]

More controversially, Uniting for Peace might provide a normative hook for Assembly resolutions urging coercive actions by states in instances not justified by self-defense.[157] It has been suggested that Uniting for Peace might be used to justify Assembly recommendations on behalf of humanitarian interventions or in support of collective military responses under the principle of "responsibility to protect" (R2P).[158] While neither the principles of humanitarian intervention nor R2P anticipates Assembly permission, both of these purported justifications for the use of force are assuredly more legitimate to the extent there is an objective third party (other than the state(s) deploying force) that determines that their respective prerequisites have been

---

156   Henry Richardson, *Comment on Larry Johnson, "Uniting for Peace"*, AJIL UNBOUND (July 23, 2014), *at* http://www.asil.org/blogs/comment-larry-johnson-"uniting-peace".

157   *But see* Stefan Talmon, *The Legalizing and Legitimizing Function of UN General Assembly Resolutions*, AJIL Unbound (July 18, 2014), at https://www.asil.org/blogs/legalizing-and-legitimizing-function-un-general-assembly-resolutions (arguing that Assembly resolutions cannot displace the existing legal treaty or customary law obligations that states have and specifically cannot constitute a fundamental change in circumstances, a circumstance precluding wrongfulness, an independent legal justification, a mechanism for lawful countermeasures that would otherwise be unlawful, or a "legitimator" of otherwise unlawful actions).

158   *See, e.g.*, CHARTER COMMENTARY, *supra* note 20, at 476 (noting that Uniting for Peace serves as a reminder that the Assembly has secondary responsibilities under the Charter to respond to threats to the international peace). *But see* Johnson, *supra* note 152 (arguing that it is difficult to see how an Assembly resolution to use humanitarian force or to respond to R2P threats is compatible with Article 2(4)).

fulfilled.[159] Uniting for Peace is a procedural mechanism that attempts to ensure that "the international community," first the Council and if not it, then the Assembly, is given the opportunity to assess the need for humanitarian action rather than leaving that to unilateral determination by self-interested by states. The mechanisms anticipated by Uniting for Peace, while strictly speaking not required for an Assembly that has seemingly acquired the underlying powers on its own, are a useful tool for reducing the risk that states will use humanitarian reasons as an excuse to violate Article 2(4).[160]

Interest in the merits of Uniting for Peace and the Assembly's role in peace and security have generally revived given dissatisfactions with the Council's (in)actions and revived use of the veto, with some seeing a new "Cold War" emerging with respect to the prospects for coordinated P-5 actions. These debates are a useful reminder that the Assembly's actions on peace and security usually have multiple audiences in mind. As noted, many of the Assembly's historically significant actions with respect to peace and security are forms of institutional "checks and balances" where the Assembly seeks to spur more effective actions by the Security Council. The leading case study in this respect remains, of course, the UN's drawn out campaign against apartheid era South Africa. As all students of the organization know, the Assembly led that effort. It included condemnatory resolutions, credentials challenges, recommendations to break off diplomatic relations and boycott South African goods, and a recommended arms embargo, with the Council taking on only some of these on its own subsequent to initial Assembly action.[161]

---

159   Thus, Johnson points out the humanitarian intervention requires (1) convincing evidence generally accepted by the international community of extreme humanitarian distress on a large scale requiring immediate and urgent relief; (2) a finding that there is no practicable alternative to the use of force; and (3) that the use of force be proportionate and necessary given the humanitarian need. *See* Johnson, *supra* note 152.

160   *See* Frederic L. Kirgis, *He Got It Almost Right*, AJIL UNBOUND (July 16, 2014), *at* http://www.asil.org/blogs/he-got-it-almost-right. Kirgis also notes that some might argue that states do not violate the terms of Article 2(4) if they use force not to threaten the territorial integrity of states but, on the contrary, to protect and affirm the very purposes of the UN. Another commentator, Henry Richardson, suggests that the prohibition under Article 2(4) bars "any unilateral military intervention which has not been collectively authorized under international law in some substantive way." *See* Richardson, *supra* note 156.

161   *Compare, e.g.*, G.A. Res. 616B (Dec. 17, 1952) *with* S.C. Res. 134 (Apr. 1, 1960); G.A. Res. 1761 (Nov. 6, 1962) *with* S.C. Res. 181 (Aug. 7, 1963); G.A. Res. 3207 (Sept. 30, 1974) *with* S.C. Res. 418 (Nov. 4, 1977). *See generally* David Black, *The Long and Winding Road: International Norms and Domestic Political Change in South Africa, in* THE POWER OF HUMAN RIGHTS:

Examples of instances where the Council plays patient "good cop" to the Assembly's proactive "bad cop" are today particularly abundant when it comes to Middle East stalemates in the Council. The Council's inability to take effective action with respect to Syria's President Assad, even when his government apparently deployed chemical weapons on its people, for example, led the Assembly to condemn these actions and urge the Council to take "appropriate measures" but in addition to hint at the need for criminal accountability for "violations that may amount to crimes against humanity" and call for "an inclusive Syrian-led political transition to a democratic, pluralistic political system."[162] Other examples include GA Res. 66/14 on the exercise of the inalienable rights of the Palestinians, Res. 66/17 on peaceful settlement of the question of Palestine, Res. 66/18 on Jerusalem, and Res. 67/229 on Israeli settlements. All of these Assembly efforts, admittedly selective and arguably one-sided, go well beyond what the Council has been able to say about alleged international law violations given the vetoes exercised or threatened by some permanent members. In reacting to such Council inactions, the Assembly has multiple intended audiences in mind beyond the Council itself. These include the state or government that it targets for sanction because it threatens the peace, others in the region that it hopes to encourage to take responsive action, and much more recently, the International Criminal Court. In other cases, the Assembly may be intending to direct, support, or encourage actions by private or hybrid (public/private) actors operating outside the UN system. This appears to be the case with respect to Assembly resolutions directed at implementing the Kimberley Process Certification Scheme on "conflict diamonds," for example.[163]

As the Charter makes clear, the Assembly and the Council also share "gatekeeping" functions. The two organs are compelled by the Charter to work together to agree on granting UN membership, or to suspend or expel a UN member.[164] Given Article 4's incorporation of statehood as a necessary (if insufficient) prerequisite for UN membership, the two organs' membership decisions, though highly politicized, have influenced the law with respect to

---

INTERNATIONAL NORMS AND DOMESTIC CHANGE 78 (Stephen C. Ropp, Kathryn Sikkink & Thomas Risse eds., 1999).

162   G.A. Res. 66/253(B), ¶¶ 8, 16 (Aug. 3, 2012); see also G.A. Res. 66/253(A), ¶ 8 (Feb. 16, 2012). See also G.A. Res. 67/262 (May 15, 2013); G.A. Res. 68/182 (Dec. 18, 2013); G.A. Res. 69/189 (Dec. 18, 2014).

163   See, e.g., G.A. Res. 55/56 (Dec. 1, 2001); G.A. Res. 57/302 (April 15, 2003); G.A. Res. 66/252 (Jan. 25, 2012).

164   U.N. Charter arts. 4–6.

what a "state" is.[165] Battles over membership and other participation rights have often emerged alongside or as a reaction to peace and security issues.

Both UN organs have been as creative with respect to the exercise of their "gate-keeping" roles as they have with respect to their other powers. As became clear in the wake of the breakup of the Former Yugoslavia, both organs have been reluctant to stay within the strict confines anticipated by the Charter. Newly emerging states that were formerly part of Yugoslavia were permitted to join the organization despite considerable doubts about whether they had achieved the objective criteria of statehood, while other parts, namely Serbia and Montenegro, were subject to identically worded Assembly and Council resolutions that seemed to create a legally dubious middle category between full UN membership, suspension, and expulsion.[166] For its part the General Assembly has taken equally legally dubious (but politically expedient) actions with respect to challenging the credentials of governments whose control over territory was in no real doubt but whose actions the Assembly wished to condemn.[167] At the same time, for all the inconsistencies and political machinations of UN membership and participation decisions which were, particularly during the Cold War, often the product of peace and security concerns real or imagined, Assembly resolutions have done much to clarify that "self-determination" under the UN Charter and customary law requires at a minimum the capacity to declare independence from colonial rule.[168]

The General Assembly's decision to accord Palestine "non-member observer state" status in 2012 provides another example of the Assembly's capacity to act simultaneously on a number of fronts and have a legal impact despite its blinkered Charter powers. Resolution 67/19 is, most obviously, the Assembly's answer to the Council's refusal to accept Palestine's application to full UN

---

165   ALVAREZ, *supra* note 2, at 148–154.

166   *Id.* at 151–153.

167   *See, e.g.*, First Report of the Credentials Committee, UN Doc. A/9779 (1974); Official Records of 2281st Plenary Mtg. of the General Assembly, UN Doc. A/PV.2281 (1974) (discussing South African credentials before the Assembly).

168   *See, e.g.*, Declaration on the Granting of Independence to Colonial Countries and Peoples, G.A. Res. 1514 (Dec. 14, 1960); G.A. Res. 2625 Declaration on Friendly Relations (Oct. 24, 1970). That Declaration, as befits a proclamation adopted by states, is, as is well known, exceedingly cautious about proclaiming a right of external self-determination beyond the case of colonialism ("[N]othing in this foregoing ... shall be construed as authorizing or encouraging any action which would dismember or impair, totally or in part, the territorial integrity or political unity of sovereign and independent states.").

membership.[169] Consistent with the goals of Uniting for Peace, it is the Assembly's response to Council paralysis and/or the veto of one or more permanent members. But by branding Palestine a "state," the Assembly is signaling not only what the Council should have done but what other IOs that have yet to act should do as well. From this perspective, the resolution seeks to extend the international community's most significant gateway status, statehood, to another actor, even without extending it UN membership. To this extent, resolution 67/19 avoids or deflects the strictures of a treaty, namely Article 4 (which requires the Assembly to act only upon a (presumably previous) recommendation authorized by the Council) while simultaneously seeking to accord Palestine the rights all other states secure under customary international law. Statehood, after all, entitles its recipient to be recognized as international and national law-maker while also conferring the status to participate in international institutionalized governance.[170]

As its effusive preamble suggests, resolution 67/19 might also be seen as an essential part of the Assembly's continuing effort to intercede in one of the most intransigent (and longstanding) conflicts/threats to the peace before the UN. It is, as its preamble states, the Assembly's latest effort to promote its "two-State solution of an independent, sovereign, democratic, viable and contiguous State of Palestine living side by side with Israel in peace and security on the basis of the pre-1967 borders."[171] Consistent with the spirit of Uniting for Peace, this might be seen as the Assembly's effort to resolve a threat to international peace and security where the Council has failed. Finally, the resolution might be seen as having little or nothing to do with Palestine, which after all does not secure any tangible new rights in the Assembly as an observer-state than it previously did as a mere observer, and everything to do with criticizing Israel—as is suggested by the resolution's abundant preamblar language that, for example, addresses the need for Israel to withdraw from Palestinian territory, including East Jerusalem and the need for "complete cessation of all

---

169   *See* Security Council, Application of Palestine for Admission to Membership in the United Nations, UN Doc. A/66/371–S/2011/592 (Sept. 23, 2011).

170   For a general survey of limitations imposed under treaties requiring the participation only of "states," see Summary of Practice of the Secretary-General, *supra* note 110, at 21–28. *See also* ABRAM CHAYES & ANTONIA HANDLER CHAYES, THE NEW SOVEREIGNTY: COMPLIANCE WITH INTERNATIONAL REGULATORY AGREEMENTS 27–28 (1998) (arguing that in the contemporary world where the enjoyment of so many sovereign rights turns on IO participation, "sovereignty" now means "status," namely the ability to join and participate in IOs).

171   G.A. Res. 67/19, pmbl., ¶ 18 (Nov. 29, 2012).

Israeli settlement activities."[172] From this perspective this is essentially a condemnatory resolution in disguise. As has been suggested by critics of the resolution, viewed in context of prior Assembly actions on point, 67/19 is just one more effort to brand one party (and only one party) to this conflict a violator of international human rights and humanitarian law. These and other ambiguities of Resolution 67/19 enabled distinct groups of states to vote in favor of adopting it. Like much of what the Assembly does, these ambiguities are at least partly strategic and enable the Assembly to disclaim that it is exercising legal power even while exercising that power and expanding its mandate.

Of course, the most direct audience for this resolution, not addressed in its text but clear to all those involved in adopting or resisting it, was the International Criminal Court. Everyone involved in this effort understood that given prior statements by UN and ICC officials,[173] the Assembly's proclamation that Palestine is a "state" was intended to signal that Palestine could successfully apply and be admitted as a party to the Rome Statute for the International Criminal Court.[174] This, of course, was the most immediate result. Within 25 months of the Assembly's action, Palestine applied for and was accepted as a Rome party member, and within 14 days of that, the ICC's prosecutor announced that it was opening a preliminary investigation of crimes allegedly

---

172   *Id.* pmbl., ¶ 9.

173   Office of the Prosecutor, International Criminal Court, Situation in Palestine (Apr. 3, 2012), *at* https://www.icc-cpi.int/NR/rdonlyres/C6162BBF-FEB9-4FAF-AFA9-836106D2694A/284387/SituationinPalestine030412ENG.pdf; Summary of Practice of the Secretary-General as Depositary of Multilateral Treaties, *supra* note 110, at 21–30 (1999) (describing elements of statehood required by the UN in allowing participation in a multilateral treaty for which the Secretary-General acts as depositary).

174   When Palestine originally approached the ICC as a presumptive new party, it was met with its prosecutor's determination that it could not join the Rome State, which was restricted to "states" unless there was a UN determination that Palestine was a state. Situation in Palestine, *supra* note 173. In doing so, the ICC prosecutor appeared to be relying on the practice of the UN treaty section, that with respect to treaties that are open to "all states," it would follow the G.A.'s practice and be guided by it. *See* Summary of Practice of the Secretary-General as Depository, *supra* note 110, at 23. By the time resolution 67/19 was considered it was well understood that determining that Palestine was an observer "state" was likely to lead to a decision by the ICC's succeeding prosecutor, who had already signaled as much, that Palestine was free to join the Rome Statute. *See, e.g.,* John Cerone, *Legal Implications of the UN General Assembly Vote to Accord Palestine the Status of Observer State*, 16 ASIL INSIGHTS (Dec. 7, 2012), *at* https://www.asil.org/insights/volume/16/issue/37/legal-implications-un-general-assembly-vote-accord-palestine-status.

committed within Palestinian territory.[175] But for resolution 67/19, it is doubtful that there would be today ICC jurisdiction over crimes committed in Palestine. In this respect, that resolution is the perfect embodiment of the contemporary General Assembly: a body that formally adheres to the Charter's original intent but that sometimes manages to achieve a legal impact comparable to that of the UN's legally empowered organ, the SC.

---

175 *See* International Criminal Court, Palestine, *at* https://www.icc-cpi.int/en_menus/ icc/structure%20of%20the%20court/office%20of%20the%20prosecutor/comm%20 and%20ref/pe-ongoing/palestine/Pages/palestine.aspx.

A Contemporary Specialized Agency: The WHO

1   The Origins of the World Health Organization

States had only limited interests in cooperating internationally when it came to health matters prior to the mid-nineteenth century.[1] The story of global health law begins with the path-breaking International Sanitary Conference of 1851 and the subsequent series of diplomatic conferences that ultimately yielded many treaties relating to health and particularly infectious diseases. The catalyst for that first conference and its successors was the rise in global commerce and the outbreaks of the plague, yellow fever, and cholera that were believed to follow in its wake, as well as the need to deal with the control measures taken in response.[2] Improving the level of state surveillance over these diseases was the focus of many of these diplomatic conferences.[3] Starting with the first International Sanitary Convention of 1892, the resulting treaties adhered to the Westphalian tradition of positivist international law.[4] Those treaties were, first, state-centric: they were concluded between states seeking to control the

---

1   For accounts of legal efforts to control infectious diseases between 1851 and 1951, see DAVID P. FIDLER, INTERNATIONAL LAW AND INFECTIOUS DISEASES 21–52 (1999); David P. Fidler, *The Globalization of Public Health: The First 100 Years of International Health Diplomacy* [hereinafter *First 100 Years*], 79 BULL. WORLD HEALTH ORG. 842 (2001), *at* http://www.who .int/bulletin/archives/79(9)842.pdf; MARK W. ZACHER & TANIA J. KEEFE, THE POLITICS OF GLOBAL HEALTH GOVERNANCE: UNITED BY CONTAGION 25–38 (2008).

2   *See* NEVILLE M. GOODMAN, INTERNATIONAL HEALTH ORGANIZATIONS AND THEIR WORK 46 (2d ed. 1971); Valeska Huber, *The Unification of the Globe by Disease? The International Sanitary Conferences on Cholera, 1851–1894*, 49 HIST. J. 453 (2006); Mark Harrison, *Disease, Diplomacy and International Commerce: The Origins of International Sanitary Regulation in the Nineteenth Century*, 1 J. GLOBAL HIST. 197 (2006).

3   FIDLER, INTERNATIONAL LAW AND INFECTIOUS DISEASES, *supra* note 1, at 44–45 (enumerating the surveillance activities of the 1866, 1874, 1881, 1885, 1893, 1897, and 1902 sanitary conferences). For a more complete listing of the many international conferences on infectious disease control in the 1851–1951 period and the treaties produced by many of them, *see id.* at 22–23, Table 1.

4   *See generally* David P. Fidler, *Caught Between Paradise and Power: Public Health, Pathogenic Threats, and the Axis of Illness*, 35 MCGEORGE L. REV. 45, 58–59 (connecting the first 100 years of international health diplomacy to "the heyday of the 'Westphalian' system of international relations") [hereinafter *Paradise and Power*]. For a list of twenty treaties dealing with infectious diseases from 1892–1951, see Fidler, *First 100 Years, supra* note 1, at 1845, Table 1.

transnational spread of ostensibly infectious diseases at border entry points between them. Second, they were designed to buttress, not threaten, state sovereignty. In these arguments, states consented to only the most minimum constraints on their freedom of action consistent with achieving the mutual benefits sought. Third, the sanitary conventions were responsive to what David P. Fidler has called the "power" paradigm, insofar as the problem requiring international cooperation was the perceived exogenous threat to national security posed by "Asiatic" allegedly infectious diseases (such as plague, cholera, and yellow fever) to powerful European and North American countries (especially Britain, France, and the United States).[5]

The international health regime, such as it was at least prior to the establishment of the World Health Organization in 1948, was epitomized by the International Sanitary Convention of 1926, a successor to the International Sanitary Convention of 1892.[6] That Convention required states to notify each other if even a single case of plague, cholera, or yellow fever was discovered in their territories or if there was an "epidemic of typhus or smallpox."[7] To this end, that treaty required parties to maintain a sanitary service in and around their ports, capable of relevant surveillance and of taking the prophylactic measures foreseen by the treaty to prevent the spread of these diseases from one country to another.[8] A second set of core obligations in that treaty sought

---

5   Fidler, *Paradise & Power, supra* note 4, at 54. *See also* OBIJIOFOR AGINAM, GLOBAL HEALTH
    GOVERNANCE: INTERNATIONAL LAW AND PUBLIC HEALTH IN A DIVIDED WORLD 65
    (2005) (questioning whether, given their European origins, these conferences were truly
    international).

6   *See, e.g.*, International Sanitary Convention, Jan. 30, 1892, 1893 Great Britain Treaty Series No. 8;
    International Sanitary Convention, Apr. 15 1893, 1894, G.B.T.S. No.4; International Sanitary
    Convention, June 21 1926, 2 Bevans 545. For a general description of these conventions, see
    David P. Fidler, *From International Sanitary Conventions to Global Health Security: The New
    International Health Regulations*, 4 CHINESE J. INT'L L. 325 (2005) [hereinafter *International
    Sanitary Conventions*]; FIDLER, INTERNATIONAL LAW AND INFECTIOUS DISEASES, *supra*
    note 1, at 21–57.

7   International Sanitary Convention of 1926, *supra* note 6, art. 1.3; *see also* Pan American
    Sanitary Code, art. 4, Nov. 14, 1924, 86 L.N.T.S. 43 (requiring immediate reporting of cases of
    "plague, cholera, yellow fever, smallpox, typhus, or any other dangerous contagion liable to
    be spread through the intermediary agency of international commerce").

8   International Sanitary Convention of 1926, *supra* note 6, art. 14. The public health measures
    to be taken at border crossings were aimed at preventing the gateways for international traf-
    fic from becoming themselves "vectors of disease transmission." Fidler, *Paradise and Power*,
    supra note 4, at 56. These included measures to control rat populations and provisions for
    clean water and proper sanitation facilities for travelers. *See, e.g.*, International Sanitary
    Convention of 1926, art. 13.

to establish limits on the trade-restricting measures that states were permitted to take in response to other states' notifications of outbreaks of the specified diseases.

The maximum measures prescribed in the International Sanitary Convention of 1926 sought to balance the competing goals of protecting states from the spread of certain diseases believed to accompany international trade and travel and harmonizing the types of control measures that states could take, thereby providing greater certainty to all (particularly traders), and ensuring that these protective measures were based on scientific and public health principles—and were not imposed for pretextual reasons.[9] As Fidler suggests, conventions like these, although ostensibly universal, served "primarily the interests of the great powers" who saw themselves as vulnerable to "exotic" diseases but who, simultaneously, wanted protection from the discriminatory or politically motivated trade restrictions that had been imposed for centuries. States had, for years, imposed *cordons sanitaires*, quarantines, or requirements for "bills of health" from vessels arriving from foreign ports on the false premise that these were "necessary" health measures.[10] The International Sanitary Convention of 1926, like others of its kind, focused only on cross-border diseases of particular concern to Europe and the U.S., not the internal health conditions of other states even with respect to the particular diseases identified. These conventions sought to defuse the political disputes prompted by unjustified trade restrictive measures while also protecting the health of affected populations.[11] In short, they merged classic inter-state concerns over trade

---

9   *See, e.g.*, International Sanitary Convention of 1926, *supra* note 6, art. 15 (stipulating that "[t]he measures [of defense against infectious diseases] as provided in this Chapter must be regarded as constituting a maximum within the limits of which governments may regulate the procedure to be applied to ships on their arrival"), art. 50 (requiring states parties to "make known to the International Office of Public Hygiene what ports are open to arrivals from ports infected with plague, cholera, or yellow fever, and in particular those open to infected or suspected ships").

10   *See, e.g.*, Fidler, *Paradise and Power, supra* note 4, at 53, 57. For a detailed account of many European disputes emerging from the contested imposition of quarantines prior to the International Sanitary Conference of 1851, see, for example, Harrison, *supra* note 2.

11   Accordingly, Mark Harrison argues that while commercial pressures brought by French and British traders help to explain treaty limits on quarantines, treaty drafters were also motivated by the balance of power and the need to avoid war. He argues that the International Sanitary Conference of 1851 originated with the system of diplomacy inaugurated at the Congress of Vienna in 1815 and reflected decisions, subsequent to that conference, to pursue smaller conferences dedicated to the peaceful solution of political problems on specific topics. *Id.* at 205–209.

protectionism and the need for peaceful settlement of disputes that we now associate with the World Trade Organization (WTO) and the UN.

Institutionalizing this diplomatic calculus, particularly the surveillance activities, was a natural follow-up, and the First General International Sanitary Conference of the American Republics in 1902 formed an International Sanitary Bureau to act, "among other things, as a clearing-house for epidemiological information" received from American states.[12] By the mid-1920s, the Pan American Sanitary Bureau (PASB) (now the Pan American Health Organization (PAHO)), the Office International d'Hygiène Publique (OIHP), Office International des Epizooties (OIE), and the League of Nations Health Organization (LNHO) were in place.[13] These organizations focused on four main aspects of infectious disease control: harmonizing quarantines in light of scientific and technological advances, coordinating surveillance, providing technical assistance, and encouraging relevant research.[14] At the same time, "international health diplomacy" in the pre-WHO period also extended beyond concern for infectious diseases. It included treaties on occupational safety and health (culminating in the establishment of the International Labour Organization (ILO) in 1919), treaties to prohibit industrial or agricultural water pollution, and treaties to control international trade in narcotic drugs and alcohol.[15]

This brief history helps to explain why the UN Charter's drafters included the promotion of solutions for "health" as among the goals of the organization in Article 55(b) and why, in 1945, the San Francisco negotiators of the Charter unanimously approved the creation of a specialized health agency.[16] For those with a sense of history, it was about time to establish a single coordinating

---

12   FIDLER, INTERNATIONAL LAW AND INFECTIOUS DISEASES, *supra* note 1, at 45.

13   LAWRENCE O. GOSTIN, GLOBAL HEALTH LAW 69–70, 90–91 (2014). Fidler notes that despite the *ad hoc* nature and competing mandates of these institutions, by 1939 a "global surveillance system" had begun to take shape insofar as the cooperation among the main international health organizations "covered 90% of the world's population." FIDLER, INTERNATIONAL LAW AND INFECTIOUS DISEASES, *supra* note 1, at 46 (latter quote from GOODMAN, *supra* note 2, at 116.).

14   FIDLER, INTERNATIONAL LAW AND INFECTIOUS DISEASES, *supra* note 1, at 49.

15   *See, e.g.*, Fidler, *First 100 Years, supra* note 1, at 843–848 (including tables listing treaties on the control of narcotic drugs (Table 2, p. 845), controlling alcohol trade in Africa (Table 3, p. 846), regulating illicit trade in alcohol Table 4, p. 846), international labor standards related to occupational safety and health (Table 5, p. 847), and dealing with pollution of transboundary rivers and lakes (Table 6, p. 847)).

16   *See* United Nations History Project, Major Themes in UN History (2015), *at* http://unhistoryproject.org/themes/health-timeline.html.

global entity to replace the pre-existing institutional patchwork, as well as to settle the awkward accommodations made necessary during the inter-war period when the Paris-based OIHP co-existed with the Geneva-based LNHO.[17] Accordingly, the UN's Economic and Social Council (ECOSOC) called for a conference to consider how to create this global entity, and on June 19, 1946, 61 delegates at this conference signed the WHO Constitution.[18] Thanks to delays attributed to emerging Cold War tensions, it took more than two years for the requisite minimum number of 26 states to ratify the WHO's Constitution, and that instrument finally entered into force on April 7, 1948.

The opening provisions of the WHO's constituent instrument provided serious reasons to believe that it was indeed what advocates hoped, namely the "Magna Carta for world health."[19] Perhaps because its drafters believed that global health concerns were, by their nature, more amenable to expertise and less likely to implicate the concerns of what came to be known as "high politics," the Constitution that they drafted was, in some respects, more ambitious than the UN Charter in terms of its goals, and, some suggest, even with respect to some of the powers delegated to this more "technocratic" organization.[20] The ambitious preamble made clear the drafters' efforts to make the WHO an organizing arm for the longstanding effort to limit quarantines and the harm on trade flows while still making the world safe from the transboundary crossing of plague, cholera, and yellow fever.

That preamble opens by indicating that the WHO will not be concerned only with preventing the spread of disease but with "the physical, mental and social well-being" of people.[21] That broad vision of what "health" means is next followed by an affirmation that "enjoyment of the highest attainable standard of health" is a fundamental human right owed to all without discrimination.[22] The preamble's third paragraph affirms that this fundamental human right to

---

17   *See, e.g.*, GOSTIN, *supra* note 13, at 90–91. But, as Gostin notes, the independent status of what is now known as the Pan American Health Organization (PAHO) was preserved as that entity continues as both an independent organization and the WHO's regional office (the Americas Regional Office (AMRO)). *Id.* at 92.

18   *Id.* at 91.

19   *Id.* (quoting Thomas Parran & Frank G. Boudreau, *The World Health Organization: Cornerstone of Peace*, 36 AM. J. PUB. HEALTH 1267 (1946)).

20   David P. Fidler, *International Law and Global Public Health*, 48 U. KAN. L. REV. 1, 20 (1999) (noting the treaty-making and regulatory powers accorded to the organization in its constitution); *see generally* Fidler, *Paradise and Power, supra* note 4, at 65–72 (discussing what he calls the "paradise paradigm" in international public health).

21   Constitution of the World Health Organization, pmbl., Jul. 22, 1946, 14 U.N.T.S. 185.

22   *Id.*

complete physical, mental, and social well-being is also fundamental to maintaining peace and security among nations. The fourth, fifth, and seventh paragraphs affirm, with admirable simplicity, an interconnectedness concerning
health matters not at all apparent in prior global infectious disease control
efforts: namely the proposition that global health is not a zero sum game but
that all states benefit when states protect the health of their own inhabitants,
and that to the extent nations are prevented from doing so by inequality, this
presents a "common danger" which needs to be addressed by, among other
things, extending to all the benefits of the latest scientific knowledge. The
sixth preamblar paragraph focuses attention on the healthy development of
the child, while the eighth suggests that good health is dependent on a popu-
lace's access to information and ability to participate. And the preamble ends
with perhaps the most far-reaching proposition of all: "Governments have a
responsibility for the health of their peoples which can be fulfilled only by the
provision of adequate health and social measures."[23]

For leading commentators like Fidler, the WHO's preamble contains a
"bold, new vision of public health"—what he calls the "paradise" paradigm—
fundamentally different from the "power" paradigm that characterized the preceding 100 years of international health diplomacy.[24] Fidler makes a persuasive
case that the WHO's preamble casts the international health regime in a whole
new light, transforming it from an inter-state border patrol scheme for certain
infectious diseases to a framework for international and national governance
that merges the collective security system of the UN Charter with a human
rights regime. As he suggests, the preamble treats the provision of health as a
public good that should be supplied by governments to their populations and,
to the extent necessary, should be supplied by governments *inter se*. If the UN
Charter is the first major international legal document to clearly affirm, particularly in its Article 2(4), the right of states to be states, the WHO Constitution is
the first instrument to proclaim a holistic conception of health as a fundamental human right.[25] In suggesting that individuals hold this right and their home

---

23   *Id.*

24   Fidler, *Paradise and Power, supra* note 4, at 59.

25   *See id.* at 60–65. But note that the contemporaneous Universal Declaration of Human
     Rights, G.A. Res. 217A (III), U.N. Doc A/810 at 71, Dec. 10, 1948, mentions the right to health
     as an aspect of the right to an adequate standard of living (at art. 25.1), and the American
     Declaration of Rights and Duties of Man, O.A.S. Res. XXX, *reprinted in* 43 AJIL SUPP. 133
     (1949), affirms "the right to the preservation of . . . health through sanitary and social mea-
     sures relating to food, clothing, housing and medical care, to the extent permitted by pub-
     lic and community resources." *Id.* art. 11.

states have a responsibility to respect it—and even to supply universal and equitable access to the comprehensive health care needed to satisfy the preamble's exceedingly broad definition of health—the preamble seems a prescient precursor to far more recent developments, including the controversial R2P principle and the fulsome right to health as developed by the Committee on Economic, Social and Cultural Rights (CESCR) and UN Special Rapporteurs on the right to health.[26] In suggesting, in addition, that if states violate their own peoples' rights to health, that is not only the business of other states but a mutual threat that implicates the peace and security of all, the WHO's preamble strikes a blow against the idea (clearly implied by the preceding 100 years of international sanitary conventions) that how a government treats health inside its own borders is part of its sacrosanct "domestic jurisdiction." In suggesting the "interdependence of people's health"[27] and its connections to peace and security, the preamble is grist for the contemporary idea that "human security" licenses not only WHO action but the action of other actors charged with protecting the peace and security of nations, including the UN Security Council.[28]

The preamble also supplies clearer rationales for the voluntary (and usually modest) technical assistance that sometimes accompanied prior efforts to improve infectious disease control and surveillance. The preamble not only affirms that wealthy states have a self interest in supporting relevant technical assistance to poor nations,[29] but implies that any such redistributive duties should, to have maximum impact, apply in holistic fashion to improve the entire health systems of such states (and not just their surveillance efforts at the border) and should also include aid designed to improve the health of vulnerable groups such as children.[30]

Much (if not all) of the preamble's ambitious agenda and vision is replicated in the broad functions contained in Article 2 of the WHO Constitution's text.

---

26   *See, e.g.*, Committee on Economic, Social and Cultural Rights Committee, General Comment 14, U.N. Doc. E/C.12/2000/4 (2000); Report of the Special Rapporteur on the Right of Everyone to the Enjoyment of the Highest Attainable Standard of Physical and Mental Health, Anand Grover, U.N. Doc. A/69/299 (Aug. 11, 2014).

27   Fidler, *Paradise and Power, supra* note 4, at 64.

28   *Accord* S.C. Res. 2177 (Sep. 18, 2014), *discussed in* Chapter II *supra*. As Fidler suggests, the proposition that poor health conditions inside developing states—including infectious diseases there—can be linked to the security or other interests of more developed states (because say, healthier people are better consumers) is inconsistent with the limited purview and rationales offered of the preceding international sanitary conventions. Fidler, *Paradise and Power, supra* note 4, at 61.

29   *See* Fidler, *Paradise and Power, supra* note 4, at 62.

30   *Id.* at 62–63.

Those functions clearly encompass the key aspects of prior sanitary conventions (surveillance at the border for infectious diseases, harmonized border control measures, technical assistance designed to improve these confidence-building measures, and the convening of relevant experts to make these efforts adhere to relevant scientific and technological standards). To further these traditional goals, Article 2 anticipates that the WHO would establish international nomenclatures of diseases, standardize diagnostic procedures, develop relevant international standards, consult relevant experts, and, as in the past, propose treaties for this purpose.[31] But Article 2 does not limit the organization's coordinating, harmonization, technical assistance, or norm-setting activities to the control of specific infectious diseases at the border. On the contrary, it anticipates that the WHO would direct and coordinate activities on "international health work" generally; would assist governments at their request in strengthening "health services"; would advance work on "endemic and other diseases" (not only infectious ones); foster activities on mental health; address the ways to prevent accidental injuries; promote the improvement of "nutrition, housing, sanitation, recreation, economic or working conditions and other aspects of environmental hygiene"; promote maternal and child health and welfare; and assist in developing informed public opinion.[32] Moreover, the norm-setting functions specified extend beyond proposing unspecified conventions and agreements but also include issuing regulations and recommendations as well as performing "such duties as may be assigned" to the organization.[33] Article 2 also includes a general "catch-all" permitting the WHO to "to take all necessary action to attain the objective of the Organization."[34]

Those expecting that the rest of the WHO's Constitution would provide the organization with the extensive legal capacities needed to fulfill the exceedingly ambitious goals of its preamble and Article 2 would be disappointed, however. That Constitution does not: require states to ratify any treaties concluded within the WHO's auspices; include a precise enumeration of the fundamental rights to health that members have to respect; provide an enforcement mechanism to secure members' compliance with the fundamental right to health; require states to provide technical assistance deemed necessary by the organization; authorize or require states to intervene as necessary when their mutual interests (including with respect to peace and security) are threatened by a state's health failings; or require states to settle their interpretative disputes

---

31   *See* WHO Constitution, *supra* note 21, art. 2, ¶¶ (j), (s), (t), (u), and (k).
32   *Id.* art. 2, ¶¶ (a), (c),(g), (h), (i), (l), (m), and (r).
33   *Id.* art. 2(k).
34   *Id.* art. 2(v).

(e.g., concerning whether a state is violating the right to health or whether another state or the organization has the right to intervene if this occurs) in a binding forum. To the contrary, in most other respects the WHO's Constitution is as conservative (or about as respectful to "sovereignty") as is the text of the UN Charter.

Although the WHO Constitution adheres to the traditional tripartite division of organs and establishes a World Health Assembly consisting of all members, an Executive Board with more limited membership that meets more frequently, and a Secretariat (headed by a Director-General), these organs are, in general, not delegated authority to take binding action on members (or certainly non-members) absent their consent.[35] The powers of the Health Assembly are, subject to an important exception discussed below, essentially no different from those given to the UN General Assembly. It too can establish subsidiary organs, take recommendations, and approve the budget, for example, but that body is also authorized to "take any other appropriate action to further the objective of the Organization."[36] Although that body can adopt conventions by only 2/3 vote, such treaties do not come into force for any WHO member unless that state has accepted it "in accordance with its constitutional processes."[37] The Executive Board of 34 members from as many member states is authorized, among other things,

> to take emergency measures within the functions and financial resources of the Organization to deal with events requiring immediate action. In particular it may authorize the Director-General to take the necessary steps to combat epidemics, to participate in the organization of health relief to victims of a calamity and to undertake studies and research the urgency of which has been drawn to the attention of the Board by any Member or by the Director-General.[38]

This is the closest thing to the Security Council's Chapter VII power in the WHO's Constitution. The Director-General's and Secretariat's powers correspond closely with the corresponding provisions in the UN Charter. The Director-General is described as the organization's "chief technical and administrator officer" and the independence of the Secretariat is stressed.[39]

---

35   *Id.* arts. 9–37.
36   *Id.* arts. 18 & 23.
37   *Id.* art. 19.
38   *Id.* art. 28(i).
39   *Id.* arts. 31, 35 & 37.

The delegated powers of the WHO differ from those accorded to the corresponding UN organs in three respects. First, the Health Assembly, unlike the UN General Assembly, is specifically authorized to adopt legally binding regulations concerning: sanitary, quarantine, and "other requirements to prevent the international spread of disease"; nomenclatures with respect to disease, causes of death and public health practices; diagnostic procedures for international use; standards for biological, pharmaceutical and similar products in international commerce; and the advertising and labeling of such products.[40] While this specific enumeration of the scope of regulations cabins this delegated power, these anticipate legally binding actions beyond those in prior sanitary conventions.[41] Significantly, such regulations take effect once approved by the Health Assembly for all members unless a member chooses to opt out of them through a rejection or reservation duly notified to the Director-General.[42] This reverses the traditional rule of state consent insofar as a state that fails to express its lack of consent is presumptively bound.[43]

Second, in a move that suggests an effort to take seriously the promise that the new organization would engage with the internal health systems of states and would concern itself with whether states are satisfactorily addressing the health needs of their populations, the Director-General is given the power to establish procedures for "direct access" to relevant departments within member states as well as to non-governmental national health organizations.[44]

Third, with respect to all conventions, regulations, and recommendations adopted within the WHO, the Constitution anticipates certain reporting

---

40   *Id.* art. 21.

41   Art. 21(a), for example, regulates "other procedures" that prevent the spread of disease
      while the rest of that article includes standards for diagnostic procedures (c), standards
      for the safety of certain products in international commerce (d), and the advertising and
      labeling of certain of these products (e). *Id.*

42   *Id.* art. 22.

43   Fidler and others have argued that this represents a "radical" and "quasi-legislative"
      approach or process. *See, e.g.,* Fidler, *International Law and Global Public Health, supra*
      note 20, at 20 & n. 56. It is also important to recognize that a state's ability to file a reservation to WHO regulations does not mean that the regulations as a whole do not apply
      to the reserving state. Under the default rules governing reservations under the Vienna
      Convention on the Law of Treaties, a reservation that does not violate the object and purpose of a treaty does not preclude the continued operation of a treaty with respect to the
      reserving state. To the extent these rules apply to WHO regulations, a state that files only
      a reservation (and not a notice that it does not accept the regulation as a whole) usually
      will remain bound by that regulation subject to its reservation.

44   WHO Constitution, *supra* note 21, art. 33.

obligations on members. Under Article 20, members must notify the WHO of any actions taken with respect to WHO-generated treaties within 18 months of their adoption by the Health Assembly, and if they refuse to accept such conventions within that time limit they must inform the organization of the reasons why. In addition, the WHO's Constitution anticipates an annual report from members on actions taken with respect to treaties adopted within the organization that they have accepted as well as any recommendations and regulations adopted by the organization.[45] WHO members are also required to report "promptly" on "important laws, regulations, official reports and statistics pertaining to health ... published in the State concerned."[46]

Despite these innovations, the WHO, at least for its first 50 years, largely ignored the few powers in its Constitution that anticipated the setting of legal standards and, even when it exercised those powers by adopting its first set of health regulations, the organization continued to function within the confines set out by the prior 100 years of international health diplomacy.[47] Despite its broad powers to do so, the Health Assembly used its power to issue regulations only twice, to pass its Nomenclature Regulations in 1948 which essentially formalized long-standing rules for classifying diseases to enable cross-country comparisons on morbidity and mortality rates[48] and to adopt its set of International Sanitary Regulations in 1951 (which were later replaced in 1969 by the International Health Regulations (IHRs)).[49] As is discussed below, the latter regulations were not a significant departure from the preceding international sanitary conventions. Moreover, those who might have expected, based on prior history, that the new organization would be the focal point for continuing to negotiate and conclude a substantial number of health related conventions would have been flabbergasted by the fact that it took the Health Assembly 53 years to adopt its first treaty under Article 19. Nor has the organization, to this day, deployed its other norm-setting powers—to recommend or to issue

---

45   *Id.* arts. 20 & 62.

46   *Id.* art. 63. *See also* Fidler, *International Law and Global Public Health, supra* note 20, at 21.

47   *See* David P. Fidler, *The Future of the World Health Organization: What Role for International Law?* 31 VAND. J. TRANSNAT'L. L. 1079, 1089 (2008) (noting that the WHO was endowed with a set of international legal powers that were unprecedented in the history of international organizations but yet made minimal use of this power).

48   *See, e.g.,* GOSTIN, GLOBAL HEALTH LAW, *supra* note 13, at 111–112 (summarizing the organization's tenth edition of its International Classification of Diseases (ICD) (in use since 1994) but noting its origins in international efforts dating back to 1853 and 1893).

49   International Sanitary Regulations, 25 May 1951, 175 U.N.T.S. 214 [hereinafter ISR]; International Health Regulations, *opened for signature* Jul. 25, 1969, 764 U.N.T.S. 3 (entered into force Jan. 1, 1971) [hereinafter IHR].

regulations—to develop law consistent with the promise that there is a funda-mental human right to health. The organization that was the first to proclaim this global right, to the contrary, stayed on the sidelines as it was developed by others, including during the many years that UN members spent drafting the International Covenant on Economic, Social and Cultural Rights (ICESCR) which was opened for ratification as of 1966.[50] It took the WHO another 12 years to weigh in on the human right to health, and when it did so, it was in the form of a non-legally binding 1978 Declaration of Alma-Ata (issued at the end of the joint WHO/UNICEF International Conference on Primary Health Care) and not in the form of a treaty or regulation.[51]

As Fidler points out, the Declaration of Alma-Ata broached the broad vision and goals in the WTO Constitution's preamble but did so in the form of policy strategies for achieving "[a]n acceptable level of health for all the people of the world by the year 2000."[52] That Declaration focused on securing "primary health care" for all in accord with the expansive meaning given to health in the WTO's preamble.[53] As made manifest in the WTO's "Health for All" strategy that followed, the adoption of the Alma-Ata Declaration signaled a distinct turn in some of technical assistance policies pursued by the organization but it did not commit the organization to using its delegated norm-setting powers to engage in human rights law-making.

For much of the WHO's history, its norm-making role remained limited to passage of the 1951 ISRs, which were replaced in 1969 with the renamed IHRs. The core elements of the 1969 IHRs would not have surprised students of the preceding international sanitary conventions.[54] These regulations focused, as did those earlier efforts, on preventing the spread of certain specific diseases when these reached the borders of states. Despite periodic amendments, the

50   See International Covenant on Economic, Social and Cultural Rights, art. 12, opened for signature Dec. 19, 1966, G.A. Res. 2200A (XXI) 993 U.N.T.S. 3 [hereinafter ICESCR]. See generally Benjamin Mason Meier, Global Health Governance and the Contentious Politics of Human Rights: Mainstreaming the Rights to Health for Public Health Advancement, 46 STAN. J. INT'L L. 1, 13–38 (2010).

51   Declaration of Atma-Ata, Sept. 12, 1978, reprinted in DAVID P. FIDLER, INTERNATIONAL LAW AND PUBLIC HEALTH: MATERIALS ON AND ANALYSIS OF GLOBAL HEALTH JURISPRUDENCE 549 (2000).

52   Id. at 550. See, e.g., Fidler, Paradise and Power, supra note 4, at 71–72.

53   See Declaration of Atma-Ata, supra note 51, at 550 (including, within the core of primary health care, educational efforts, food supply and nutritional concerns, access to safe water and basic sanitation, maternal and child care, immunizations, appropriate treat-ment of common diseases and injuries, and much else).

54   See FIDLER, INTERNATIONAL LAW AND INFECTIOUS DISEASES supra note 1, at 58–65.

main features of the IHRs, which remained consistent over the two decades that they were in place, consisted of:

1. Obligations by state parties to notify other state parties of the outbreaks of even a single instance of certain specific diseases. By 1981, the IHRs, which originally covered 6 diseases (including smallpox), were amended to cover only 3: cholera, yellow fever, and plague.[55] Like pre-WHO efforts, this was obviously a confidence-building attempt grounded in a common system of surveillance to detect even a single outbreak.[56]

2. Efforts to harmonize the quarantine and isolation measures adopted by states, with the clear goal being to adopt maximum ceilings on what states could do in this respect, thereby limiting from the outset the impact on trade and providing greater predictability for traders and other stakeholders.[57]

As with respect to pre-WHO efforts, the pre-2005 IHRs envisioned the organization as being only a passive recipient of disease surveillance information supplied to it by states.[58] As with the prior sanitary conventions, this regulatory effort essentially ignored the rights of persons that were subjected to the permitted range of quarantine and isolation measures.

2   The Fall of the Old International Health Regulations

Commentators have long speculated precisely why the WHO has been historically reluctant to deploy its norm-setting powers—why, in other words, the organization stopped making law for decades once it adopted the IHRs in 1951. Fidler persuasively argues that this "neglect of law" was due, in no small part, to the kinds of people who worked in the organization. He indicates that

---

55   See ISR, supra note 49, Part V; World Health Assembly, Amendment of the International Health Regulations (1969), WHA 34.13 (May 20, 1981).

56   IHR, supra note 49, art. 3 ¶ 1 (requiring national health organizations to notify the Organization within twenty-four hours of becoming aware of a case of a disease subject to the regulations within its territory).

57   See Fidler, International Sanitary Conventions, supra note 6, at 344; IHR, supra note 49, part IV & art. 24 ("The health measures permitted by these regulations are the maximum applicable to international traffic.").

58   See, e.g., IHR, supra note 49, art. 3 (providing for the submission of notice to the organization).

the organization was dominated by a "transnational Hippocratic society" of doctors, medical scientists, and public health experts characterized by a common ethnos, while lawyers were relegated to the small Legal Council's Office to engage on administrative matters.[59] As he points out, the WHO's approach also coincided with scientific advances against the infectious diseases that had been the target of the prior sanitary conventions and adoption of the organization's "health transition" strategy to spread those advances to the developing world.[60] Given these developments, it is perhaps not surprising that science, not law, seemed crucial to improving global health.

But, as Fidler also points out, this did not mean that global health issues were not getting legal attention from others. While the WHO's attention was elsewhere, the right to health was, as noted, discussed in negotiations for the ICESCR, the balance between national regulation over health and free trade came to be addressed in Article XX of the General Agreement on Tariffs and Trade, and other forums, particularly after the 1972 Stockholm Conference on the Human Environment, generated treaties relevant to health, including on marine pollution and trans-boundary air pollution.[61]

Over time, these and other developments put pressure on the WHO to recognize that its reliance on the ISRS and later the IHRS was misplaced. What Fidler calls the "death of the classical regime"[62] represented by the old IHRS, was prompted by many factors. States gradually came to ignore the IHRS, either because the threats they addressed were no longer as significant or because transnational control over infectious diseases could be done in other ways. The eradication of smallpox and its removal from the IHRS in 1981 was only one sign of the IHRS' (and the WHO's) increasing irrelevance.[63] Starting with the Cold War, concerns over the spread of the infectious diseases specified

59   Fidler, *International Law and Global Public Health, supra* note 20, at 22–23.

60   *Id.* at 23–25 (noting how the WHO focused on applying scientific advances as the economies of countries improved and how fulfilling such demands seemed to require little from international law); *see also* Fidler, *International Sanitary Conventions, supra* note 6, at 335 (noting how improvements against infectious diseases required changes within states and how interest in the classical inter-state regime built on the sanitary conventions waned).

61   Fidler, *International Sanitary Conventions, supra* note 6, at 336–337.

62   *Id.* at 338.

63   *Id.* at 337–338. *See also* LAURIE GARRETT, THE COMING PLAGUE: NEWLY EMERGING DISEASES IN A WORLD OUT OF BALANCE 11 (1994); Lawrence O. Gostin, *International Infectious Disease Law: Revision of the World Health Organization's International Health Regulations*, 291 J. AM. MED. ASSOC. 2623 (2004); Bruce Jay Plotkin, *Mission Possible: The Future of the International Health Regulations*, 10 TEMP. INT'L & COMP. L.J. 503 (1996).

in the IHRS were increasingly eclipsed by more worrisome human security concerns such as the intentional spread of disease, new diseases not included in the IHRS, and other threats to global health. The IHRS were seen as outdated or backward looking in terms of the real risks facing states, such as the spread of HIV/AIDS or the risks to health posed by newly emerging diseases (such as malaria), pollution, or radioactive agents—none of which were covered by the IHRS' surveillance, harmonization, or technical assistance efforts. The IHRS' reliance on "maximum" measures instead of the more nuanced risk assessments being used in other forums, such as in the WTO under its SPS Agreement[64] (applicable to sanitary and phytosanitary measures) and its TBT Agreement[65] (on technical barriers to trade) was also increasingly questioned. The idea that restrictions on trade and traders should be based on the level of risk and not artificial "maximum" measures seemed more scientifically justifiable and flexible. In addition, the IHR's insistence on the reporting of a single case was seen as a recipe to license over-reaction by other WHO members, as seemed clear by the reactions to cholera in Peru and plague in India during the 1990s. Both of those cases led to massive trade restrictions costing Peru and India billions.[66] The IHRS seemed irrelevant to "Soviet secrecy concerning the Chernobyl nuclear reactor explosion, China's initial lack of candor concerning . . . SARS, the very recent interspecies crossover of a newly discovered avian influenza from birds to human beings, [and] the advent of bioterrorism."[67] Over time it became clear that the real action on global health

---

64   Agreement on the Application of Sanitary and Phytosanitary Measures, GATT Doc. MTN/
      FA II-A1A-4 (Dec. 15, 1993) [hereinafter SPS Agreement], in Final Act Embodying the
      Results of the Uruguay Round of Multilateral Trade Negotiations [hereinafter Uruguay
      Round], GATT Doc. MTN/FA (Dec. 15, 1993).

65   Agreement on Technical Barriers to Trade, GATT Doc. MTN/FA II-A1A-6 (Dec. 15, 1993)
      [hereinafter TBT Agreement], in Uruguay Round.

66   David P. Fidler, *Return of the Fourth Horseman: Emerging Infectious Diseases and
      International Law*, 81 MINN. L. REV. 771, 816 (1997) (citing David L. Heymann, The
      International Health Regulations: Ensuring Maximum Protection with Minimum
      Restriction, Address Before ABA Panel on Law and Emerging and Re-Emerging Infectious
      Diseases (Aug. 5, 1996)).

67   Gerald S. Schatz, *International Health Regulations: New Mandate for Scientific Cooperation*,
      9 ASIL INSIGHTS 23 (Aug. 2, 2005), *at* http://www.asil.org/insights/volume/9/issue/23/
      international-health-regulations-new-mandate-scientific-cooperation. *See also* David L.
      Heymann, *SARS and Emerging Infectious Diseases: A Challenge to Place Global Solidarity
      Above National Sovereignty*, 35 (5) ANNALS ACAD. MED. SING. 350 (2006) (discussing
      difficulties encountered with the first reports of SARS emerging from China). The SARS
      outbreak complicated negotiations on revising the IHR in other respects. *See, e.g.,* Fidler,
      International Sanitary Conventions, supra note 6, at 357. The prospect that the revised IHR

issues and threats was occurring (if at all) outside the WHO. In addition, since states were not getting the technical assistance from the WHO with respect to such threats, they were turning to other sources of information with respect to them (including NGOs, other networks, or the internet), or other IOs (from the WTO to the International Atomic Energy Agency (IAEA)).

For students of international organizations, the history of the old IHRs is a good illustration of what can happen when an IO or its legal instruments fail to stay current with technological developments, the functional needs of stakeholders, or developments in other forums. They also illustrate the proposition that it is very unwise to take the constituent instrument of any IO at face value. For much of the WHO's existence, that organization was not what its Constitution leads one to expect. It was not the generator of human rights norms, health conventions, or regulations suited to a holistic conception of "health."[68] It was also not an organization that was, as its preamble would suggest, actively engaged in informing public opinion and encouraging "active cooperation" of the peoples inside states; on the contrary, the WHO continued to rely, as did the sanitary conventions, on state reporting. Meanwhile, outside the WHO, states were increasingly relying on non-state sources of information to deal with emerging health threats and, increasingly, on public/private entities or other "hybrid" networks for surveillance or advice.

These concerns led the 48th WHO Health Assembly in 1995 to call for a substantial revision of the IHRs to focus on notification of events of urgent and international importance to WHO instead of disease-specific notification.[69]

---

would specifically address security threats posed by the intentional release of biological, chemical or radiological agents attracted states like the United States to the effort. *See, e.g.,* DAVID P. FIDLER & LAWRENCE O. GOSTIN, BIOSECURITY IN THE GLOBAL AGE: BIOLOGICAL WEAPONS, PUBLIC HEALTH, AND THE RULE OF LAW 138 (2007). As Fidler's history of the negotiations leading to the 2005 IHR indicates, however, specific language directed at WMDs was deleted in the final IHR which only alludes to such threats indirectly, in Art. 7's reference to an "unexpected or unusual public health event." Fidler, *International Sanitary Conventions, supra* note 6, at 365–367.

68 The comparison with other international organizations which had, on the contrary, engaged in "mission creep" by taking advantage of ambiguities in the constituent instruments may have contributed to the perception that the WHO was suffering from an "authority crisis" by at least 1987. *See* NITSAN CHOREV, THE WORLD HEALTH ORGANIZATION BETWEEN NORTH AND SOUTH 147 (2012).

69 World Health Assembly, *Revision and Updating of the International Health Regulations,* WHA Res. 48.7 (May 12, 1995); World Health Assembly, *Resolution on Communicable Diseases Prevention and Control: New, Emerging, and Re-Emerging Infectious Diseases,* WHA Res. 48.13 (May 12, 1995); World Health Organization, *The International Response*

The WHO commissioned the Swedish Institute of Infectious Disease Control
to conduct a consultation process among public health experts to define what
constitutes an urgent "international public health event" and to develop an
operational framework to be used at the country level when assessing the
importance of a public health emergency.[70] (It was during this process that
criteria were developed that ultimately led to the algorithm or "decision instrument" addressed below that is now in Annex 2 of the 2005 IHRs.[71]) According
to most observers, a fundamental catalyst that spurred the WHO to finally take
action on a total revision of the IHRs was the 2003 SARS outbreak. SARS, and
the WHO's failings in dealing with that crisis, seemed to be the final straw that
led the Health Assembly in May 2003 to instruct the WHO Secretariat to complete the revisions to the IHRs.[72]

The outbreak of SARS shone a spotlight on the failings of the IHRs and of the
WHO.[73] That outbreak highlighted what should have been clear from the WTO's
preamble: namely that as borders become more porous, and transboundary
crossing of goods and persons becomes faster and harder for any state to control
alone, there is indeed a growing global interdependence on health matters and
a pressing need for a single global institution to deal with emerging (and not just
existing) threats to health. SARS was one more piece of evidence that a nation's
failure to be legally prepared to handle internal health threats risks not only
its own economic health but has political, economic, human rights, and social
effects on many others.[74] SARS and how different states handled that outbreak

    to Epidemics and Applications of the International Health Regulations: Report of a WHO
    Informal Consultation, WHO Doc. WHO/EMC/IHR/96.1 (Dec. 11–14, 1995).

70   *See* Revision of the International Health Regulations—Progress Report, 77 WKLY
    EPIDEMIOLOGICAL REC. 157–160 (May 10, 2002); World Health Organization, *Global*
    Alert and Response Team. Global Crises—Global Solutions: Managing Public Health Emer-
    gencies of International Concern Through the Revised International Health Regulations,
    WHO/CDS/GAR/2002.4 (2002), *at* http://whqlibdoc.who.int/hq/2002/WHO_CDS_CSR_
    GAR_2002.4.pdf.

71   World Health Assembly, Revision of the International Health Regulations, Annex 2,
    WHA58.3 (May 23, 2005), *at* http://www.who.int/ipcs/publications/wha/ihr_resolution
    .pdf [hereinafter 2005 IHR]; World Health Assembly, Revision of the International Health
    Regulations, WHA56.28 (May 28, 2003).

72   World Health Assembly, Revision of the International Health Regulations, *supra* note 71.

73   *See generally* WHO, *Severe Acute Respiratory Syndrome (SARS): Status of the Outbreak and*
    Lessons for the Immediate Future (20 May 2003), *at* http://www.who.int/csr/media/sars_
    wha.pdf.

74   *See* David P. Fidler, *SARS: Political Pathology of the First Post-Westphalian Pathogen,* 31
    J.L. MED. & ETHICS 485, 486 (2003) (noting that SARS was the first post-Westphalian
    pathogen because it was the first since HIV/AIDS to pose a truly global threat and to

also suggested a need to reach deeper into states to consider their health systems generally and not only how they address points of entry. SARS pointed out the need to examine general laws and practices—including outside the health sector— to see whether a country's early warning, transparency, and accountability systems were up to the task. In that instance, China's State Secrets law, for instance, reportedly prohibited local officials from publicizing an outbreak in advance of the Ministry of Health in Beijing, resulting in fatal delays.[75] On the other hand, Singapore's Infectious Disease Act, which allowed mandatory examination and isolation—even before the WHO issued recommendations for such drastic measures—reportedly led to the home detention of some 740 people, subject to huge fines for non-compliance.[76] While Singapore's measures achieved containment of SARS more rapidly than in other places, a number of the measures taken by that government, such as keeping all children under 18 at home, were criticized as overly harsh and unlikely to be acceptable in societies with less authoritarian regimes.[77] Such questions and criticisms confronted the WHO with human rights concerns that it had long resisted. Canada's response to SARS, on the other hand, demonstrated the difficulties that federal/state systems face and the need for the WHO to address, for example, whether such states have in place procedures for coordinating and reporting across states or provinces and between such authorities and the federal government.[78] SARS, in short, made the organization more aware of the problems of decentralization attendant to federalist systems like those in Canada or the United States, and the necessity for having international health regulation that demands more intrusive actions within such states.[79]

The SARS crisis also raised awareness of the stark differences between nations with respect to compliance with WHO recommendations. Striking

---

severely challenge the emerging post-Westphalian governance system); David P. Fidler, *Revision of the World Health Organization's International Health Regulations*, 8 ASIL INSIGHTS 8 (Apr. 16, 2004), *at* http://www.asil.org/insights/volume/8/issue/8/revision-world-health-organizations-international-health-regulations. *See also* Fiona Fleck, *How SARS Changed the World in Less than Six Months*, 81 BULL. WORLD HEALTH ORG. 625 (2003).

75   *See, e.g.*, Jacques deLisle, *Atypical Pneumonia and Ambivalent Law and Politics: SARS and the Response to SARS in China*, 77 TEMP. L. REV. 193, 206 (2004).

76   *See, e.g.*, Jason W. Sapsin et. al, *SARS and International Legal Preparedness*, 77 TEMP. L. REV. 155, 158–160 (2004).

77   *Id.*

78   *Id.* at 161–162.

79   *Id.* at 162–163 (discussing the U.S. SARS measures) & 166–167 (discussing the general challenges faced by federal systems).

gaps became evident, for example, between Singapore's strict compliance with quarantines versus Toronto's legal responses targeting only fifteen persons, or either of those situations as compared to the serious difficulties encountered in getting the Taiwanese public and its health officials to comply with WHO recommendations on SARS. In Taiwan, many persons refused to register with local health authorities before traveling, others disobeyed quarantine orders, and there were even reports that some hospitals were concealing the existence of SARS cases.[80]

3   The Rise of the Revised (2005) IHRS

The World Health Assembly adopted the new IHRS on May 23, 2005 and these entered into force on June 15, 2007.[81] These legally binding regulations (henceforth 2005 IHRS or revised IHRS) reaffirm the traditional twin purposes of the previous 100 years of international health diplomacy: to protect health but also avoid interference with trade.[82] But the new IHRS, widely considered a "historic" event in the regulation of global health, wrought six distinct changes from the WHO's former approach.[83] The 2005 IHRS (1) focus on helping states

---

80   Sapsin, *supra* note 76, at 164.

81   2005 IHR, *supra* note 71. The deadline for rejection or reservations on the revised IHR was Dec. 15, 2006. As of that date, none of the WHO members had opted to reject the IHR and only two states (the United States and India) filed what were considered to be reservations. Other states had six months from the date they were notified of these reservations to object to them and only one state objected to the U.S. reservation (which dealt with U.S. federalism). Accordingly, the IHR entered into force for all states, including the U.S. and India. Bruce Plotkin, *The World Health Organization's International Health Regulations (2005)*, 101 ASIL PROC. 256, 258 (2007). As of February 2016, the 2005 IHR had 196 States parties, see WHO, *Strengthening Health Security by Implementing the International Health Regulations (2005): States Parties to the International Health Regulations* (2015), *at* http://www.who.int/ihr/legal_issues/states_parties/en/.

82   2005 IHR, *supra* note 71, at art. 2: "[T]o prevent, protect against, control and provide a public health response to the international spread of disease in ways that are commensurate with and restricted to public health risks, and which avoid unnecessary interference with international traffic and trade."

83   *See, e.g.*, David P. Fidler & Lawrence O. Gostin, *The New International Health Regulations: An Historic Development for International Law and Public Health*, 34 J.L. MED. & ETHICS 85 (2006). UN Secretary-General Kofi Annan had described the IHR revision as an important step in moving humanity toward "larger freedom" *See* UN Secretary-General, *In Larger Freedom: Towards Development, Security, and Human Rights for All: Rep. of the Secretary-General*, A/59/2005 (Mar. 21, 2005).

deal with a risk "event" determined under a risk assessment instead of specific enumerated diseases; (2) enable the organization to respond to intentional risks to global health (e.g., terrorism); (3) focus attention on internal health measures and not only national measures "at the border;" (4) are more embedded in other international law regimes, particularly human rights; (5) enable the organization to look to non-state as well as state sources of information; and (6) combine "soft" with "hard" or binding sources of obligation.

The revised IHRs enable the organization to declare a "public health emergency of international concern" (PHEIC), that is, "an extraordinary event which is determined ... (i) to constitute a public health risk to other States through the international spread of disease and (ii) to potentially require a coordinated international response."[84] Since "public health risk" is separately defined as "a likelihood of an event that may affect adversely the health of human populations, with an emphasis on one which may spread internationally or may present a serious and direct danger,"[85] the 2005 IHRs turn the WHO into a venue for addressing the health consequences posed by biological, radiological, as well as chemical agents. This expands greatly the responsibilities states incur for surveillance. Whereas the old IHRs required states to report on only three diseases, the new regulations require states to have in place "core national capacities" for surveillance and response as enumerated in Annex 1 in order to enable states to assess and notify the organization of a PHEIC as determined by its "decision instrument" in Annex 2.[86]

As would be expected under the former IHRs, the 2005 IHRs require states to develop, strengthen, and maintain "as soon as possible but no later than five years from the entry into force of these Regulations," core capacity requirements for designated airports, ports, and ground crossings, including capacities to assess travelers and disinfect cargo, and if necessary quarantine suspect travelers.[87] But Annex 1 expects the same for core capacities for surveillance and response "in all areas within the territory of the State Party;" this means establishing detection and control measures as needed at the local community

---

84   2005 IHR, *supra* note 71, art. 1.1 (Definitions).

85   *Id.*

86   As of 2012, only 42 of the 193 State Parties to the 2005 IHR had declared that they had met their core capacities to detect, assess, notify and report events, and to respond to public health risks and emergencies. *See* Director General of the World Health Organization, *Implementation of the International Health Regulations (2005): Report of the Review Committee on Second Extensions for Establishing National Public Health Capacities and on IHR Implementation*, EB136/22 Add.1 (Jan. 16, 2015).

87   2005 IHR, *supra* note 71, art. 5.1, 13.1 & Annex 1, B.2.

level, the intermediate response level, and the national level.[88] To this end, each WHO member is required to establish a National Focal Point for purposes of coordinating national action and communicating with WHO and is also obligated to develop and implement a plan of action to put in place the existing structures and resources to ensure that it has the capacities detailed in Annex 1, including the ability to generate essential information about numbers of human cases and deaths, conditions affecting the spread of the disease or other health threat, and the health measures being employed.[89]

Annex 2's "decision instrument" instructs states to follow a particular approach when their national surveillance detects certain information that may constitute a PHEIC.[90] If surveillance reveals a single case of smallpox, severe acute respiratory syndrome (SARS), or certain types of poliomyelitis or human influenza, such events shall be notified to the WHO to determine whether a PHEIC has occurred.[91] If a state detects a number of other enumerated diseases (including cholera, pneumonic plague, West Nile Fever, and Ebola), it is instructed to assess four matters: whether there is a serious public health impact, whether the event is unusual or unexpected, whether there is significant risk for international spread, and whether there is a significant risk for international travel or trade restrictions. If the state answers "yes" to two of these four questions, it should notify the WHO of the event for a possible determination of a PHEIC.[92] Finally, where states detect "any event of potential international public concern, including those of unknown cases" or diseases not otherwise identified in Annex 2, the state is also directed to the same four questions and is required to notify the organization if the answer is yes to two of those questions.[93]

Thanks to the "catch-all" category in the PHEIC "decision instrument," today an incident like a nuclear reactor meltdown presumably would be notified to the WHO, and that organization would then have the opportunity to decide whether this incident is indeed a PHEIC. Under the regulations, the WHO Director-General is given the power to determine whether, based on the information received either by states or through any other reports (including

---

88   *Id.*, art. 5(1), 13(1) & Annex 1.A. *See also* Michael G. Baker & David P. Fidler, *Global Public Health Surveillance Under New International Health Regulations*, 12(7) EMERGING INFECTIOUS DISEASES 1058, 1060 & fig. 2 (2006).

89   2005 IHR, *supra* note 71, art. 4.1 & Annex 1.A.2 & .4.b.

90   *See id.* art. 6 (Notification).

91   *Id.* Annex 2; *see also* Baker & Fidler, *supra* note 88, at 1059 & fig. 1.

92   2005 IHR, *supra* note 71, Annex 2.

93   *Id.*

those by non-state actors),[94] there is indeed a PHEIC. The Director-General is empowered to make this determination without consulting an Emergency Committee if the state where the event is occurring agrees, but if there is no consensus within 48 hours, the Director-General can declare a PHEIC after consulting, among other things, the advice of that Emergency Committee.[95] The Director-General can establish an Emergency Committee composed of experts from the IHR Expert Roster whenever he or she needs a determination about whether a PHEIC exists, needs to be terminated, modified, or extended.[96] That Emergency Committee, which can hear from the state concerned during its deliberations, is empowered to issue "temporary recommendations" once a PHEIC has been declared.[97] Such temporary recommendations, which include measures to be implemented regarding persons, baggage, or cargo, can be directed at the state party experiencing the PHEIC or other WHO parties.[98] (These should not be confused with the "standing recommendations" which the IHRs authorize to prevent or reduce the international spread of disease intended for "routine or periodic application" not involving a PHEIC.[99])

The revised IHRs intrude on sovereign decision-making at various points. As noted, the organization is now empowered to seek surveillance or other information from non-state sources and while it is obligated to secure verification of such reports before taking action on them, member states are obliged upon request to verify whether such information is correct within 24 hours.[100] Irrespective of whether an affected state chooses to cooperate, the WHO is nonetheless entitled to share information about a state obtained through non-state sources with other WHO members "when justified by the magnitude of the public health risk."[101] Under the procedures established under Article 49 of the IHRs, an Emergency Committee may recommend temporary measures and public notification of the PHEIC; the Director-General can take corresponding actions even when the state where the emergency exists resists and does not agree on those recommendations. Moreover, under Article 49(7), the state where the PHEIC exists may request termination of these measures and

---

94   *Id.* art. 9.

95   *Id.* art. 12.

96   *Id.* art. 48.

97   *Id.* art. 49.4 & .6.

98   *Id.* art. 15.

99   *Id.* art. 12 & 53. These Standing Recommendations are the product of a distinct committee, the Review Committee, established under arts. 50–53.

100   *Id.* art. 9.1 & 10.

101   *Id.* art. 10.4.

make a presentation to the Emergency Committee, but that committee (and the Director-General) is not bound to remove the measures in response.

At the same time, the revised IHRs evince considerable flexibility and are deferential to sovereignty in some crucial respects. Temporary recommendations automatically expire three months after their issuance, and while they may be modified or extended for additional periods of up to three months, they may not continue beyond the second Health Assembly after the determination of the PHEIC to which they relate.[102] While states have to develop an implementation plan to put in place the capabilities anticipated by Annex 1 within five years, they can receive an extension of two years and in exceptional circumstances may get an additional two-year extension on such implementation.[103] The 2005 IHRs also accord states considerable flexibility when it comes to settling disputes under the new regulations. Whereas the old IHRs anticipated that disputes about their interpretation or application should be submitted, if both states agree, to the International Court of Justice (ICJ), the revised regulations anticipate that disputes not otherwise settled (including through attempts by the Director-General) can be submitted, if both states agree, to arbitration under the Permanent Court of Arbitration.[104]

At the same time, the 2005 IHRs emphasize, from the outset, that states must implement them "with full respect for the dignity, human rights and fundamental freedoms of persons."[105] This greater sensitivity to human rights, manifested in the revised IHRs' numerous references to human rights,[106] is a natural outgrowth of lessons learned from the organization's prior experiences with victims of SARs and HIV/AIDs.[107] It is also likely the predictable result of the "humanization" of virtually all IOs in an age when the "human rights revolution" is producing effects across all international legal regimes.[108]

---

102   *Id.* art. 15.3.

103   *Id.* art. 5.2.

104   *Id.* art. 56.3.

105   *Id.* art. 3.1.

106   For a table listing the thirteen provisions in the revised IHRs relevant to the protection of human rights, see Fidler, *International Sanitary Convention, supra* note 6, at 368, Table 2.

107   At least seventeen countries adopted legal measures to quarantine individuals with HIV or AIDS. *See* LAWRENCE O. GOSTIN & ZITA LAZZARINI, HUMAN RIGHTS AND PUBLIC HEALTH IN THE AIDS PANDEMIC 102 (1997). For a further discussion on the human rights implications, see Katarina Tomasevski, *Health, in* 2 UNITED NATIONS LEGAL ORDER 859 (Oscar Schachter & Christopher C. Joyner eds., 1995).

108   *See generally* RUTI TEITEL, HUMANITY'S LAW (2011). For a general discussion on the interaction of these provisions with other human rights treaties, see Bruce Plotkin, *Human Rights and Other Provisions in the Revised International Health Regulations* (2005),

The need to protect the rights of travelers is now incorporated directly into the IHRs. Thus, Article 32 requires states to implement the IHRs while respecting travelers' "dignity, human rights and fundamental freedoms."[109] Article 31 prohibits "invasive medical examination, vaccination or other prophylaxis" as a condition of entry, but permits these where, for example, they are necessary to determine whether a public health risk exists.[110] Travelers who do not agree to such examinations may be forced to undergo only "the least invasive and intrusive medical examination that would achieve the public health objective."[111] The 2005 IHRs also recognize that they may clash with the rights or obligations of states under other treaties and affirm that the IHRs shall not affect the rights and obligations of any state party deriving from other international agreements and that such instruments and the IHRs "should be interpreted so as to be compatible."[112]

The 2005 IHRs suggest more general conclusions. Since an act of bioterrorism, for example, now fits into the perils covered by Article 2 of the IHRs,[113] the WHO is now partly a security organization. Its work overlaps to some extent with that of the Security Council or other counter-terrorism organizations.[114] The revised IHRs are an international security instrument—alongside others

121 PUBLIC HEALTH 840 (2007). *See also* Jeremy Youde, *Mediating Risk Through the International Health Regulations and Bio-political Surveillance*, 59 POL. STUD. 813 (2011) (noting concerns about whose human rights should be respected and the nature of those rights in light of human rights treaties).

109 2005 IHR, *supra* note 71, art. 32.

110 *Id.* art. 31.1.

111 *Id.* art. 31.2(a).

112 *Id.* art. 57.1 (noting as well that the provisions of the IHR "shall not affect the rights and obligations of any State Party deriving from other international agreements"). Art. 17, which identifies criteria for the WHO's temporary and standing recommendations, also evinces concern for their compatibility with other regimes. *See id.* art. 17(e) (urging that the Director-General consider "relevant international standards and instruments" when "issuing, modifying or terminating temporary or standing recommendations").

113 *See id.* art. 2 (proclaiming a purpose to prevent, protect against, control, and provide a public health response to the international spread of disease in ways that are commensurate with … public health risks"; notably the definition of public health risks includes those posed by intentional acts).

114 *See* discussion of S.C. Res. 2177 in Chapter II *supra*. For a discussion of the 2001 anthrax attacks and the relationship between public health responses and bioterrorism, see David P. Fidler & Lawrence O. Gostin, *The New International Health Regulations: An Historic Development for International Law and Public Health*, 34 J.L. MED. & ETHICS 85, 91–93 (2006). *See also* Fidler, *International Sanitary Conventions, supra* note 6, at 365–367 (discussing possible interactions between the 2005 IHR and the Security Council).

like the SC's counter-terrorism actions or the rules permitting access to nuclear materials in the IAEA. They constitute an early warning system for certain terrorist acts. For this reason, among others, the WHO can no longer afford to take its usual "medical-technical" approach to global health if this comes at the expense of ignoring more legalistic regimes with overlapping concerns. Further, as Article 57 of the IHRS shows,[115] the WHO is not self-contained and needs to wrestle with the possibility of conflicts with other IOs and other treaties. Of course, the WHO was always a security organization if we take seriously the broad concept of "human security" now adopted in other UN bodies. But the revised IHRS emphasize that the WHO is nestled within a larger group of IOs—the IAEA, the WTO, and human rights bodies in particular. This means that today, it would not be quite as absurd for the WHO to be legitimately concerned with the health consequences of the use of nuclear weapons—even though it was not that long ago that the ICJ opined, in an advisory opinion, that requesting the Court to give its views on the legality of such weapons exceeded its mandate in violation of the principle of speciality that governs all IOs.[116]

The revised IHRS also make clear that the WHO is now concerned with measures/institutions/developments deep inside states and not just at the border.[117] Annex 1 of the IHRS, which anticipates the existence of or building of national structures and resources to meet the minimum capacities of states, is a framework for governance. States are now being directed to establish

---

115   *See supra* note 112.

116   Legality of the Use by a State of Nuclear Weapons in Armed Conflict, Advisory Opinion, 1996 I.C.J. 66, ¶ 26 (July 8) (recognizing the wide acceptance of implied powers but noting that the WHO's powers "cannot encroach on the responsibilities of other parts of the United Nations System"). For prescient critiques of that decision, see Dapo Akande, *The Competence of International Organizations and the Advisory Jurisdiction of the International Court of Justice*, 9 EUR. J. INT'L L. 437 (1998); Michael Bothe, *The WHO Request, in* INTERNATIONAL LAW, THE INTERNATIONAL COURT OF JUSTICE AND NUCLEAR WEAPONS 103 (Laurence Boisson de Chazournes & Philippe Sands eds., 1999); Virginia Leary, *The WHO Case: Implications for Specialized Agencies, in* INTERNATIONAL LAW, THE INTERNATIONAL COURT OF JUSTICE AND NUCLEAR WEAPONS 112. The expanding mandate of the WHO now also concerns peacekeeping operations notwithstanding an absence of any direct reference to war and peace or to peacekeeping. *See* Yves Beigbeder, *The World Health Organization and Peacekeeping*, 5 INT'L PEACEKEEPING 31 (1998).

117   For a discussion of the impact of other IOs on the internal structure of states, see José E. Alvarez, *International Organizations: Then and Now*, 100 AM. J. INT'L L. 324 (2006). For a critique of the sovereignty concerns posed by the 2005 IHR, see Eric Mack, *The World Health Organization's New International Health Regulations: Incursion on State Sovereignty and Ill-Fated Response to Global Health Issues*, 7 CHI. J. INT'L L. 365 (2006).

administrative agencies that can enable them to do everything that is required under Annex 1(A)(6). This means not only the capacity "to assess all reports of urgent events within 48 hours" and "to notify who immediately," but also the ability to rapidly determine applicable control measures "to prevent domestic and international spread" of the threat, to provide logistical and "on-site assistance," to provide a "direct operational link with senior health and other officials," to directly "liaison with other relevant government ministries," to communicate efficiently with all other relevant operational agents (such as hospitals and laboratories), to establish "a national public health emergency response plan," and to provide all the above "on a 24-hour basis."[118] Scholars of Global Administrative Law (GAL) would not find it difficult to include IHRs as a form of GAL.[119] Of course, the 2005 IHRs have deep implications for how a state structures its basic health system, irrespective of whether it relies on a private system of health care or a public one. While the IHRs and their Annexes do not care whether a state relies on a system of private for-profit hospitals or not, their insistence that whatever system a state chooses must fulfill the surveillance, notification, consultation, verification, and other functions required may have implications for the health systems that states decide to hone and for their efforts to reform those systems in the future.[120]

As the foregoing implies, the WHO is now at least in part also a human rights organization. Under the IHRs, the WHO (including its Review or Emergency Committees) as well as WHO members must now consider the limits imposed by human rights on their health control measures, but they must also consider how what they do in the name of the IHRs may itself affect the right to health as a human right under, for example, the ICESCR.[121] Under the ICESCR, states are obligated to "take steps, individually and through international assistance and co-operation ... to the maximum of its available resources, with a view to achieving progressively" the right to health.[122] Under that treaty, which

---

118   2005 IHR, *supra* note 71, Annex 1(A)(6)(a–h).

119   *See* Chapter I § 2.3 (discussing elements of GAL scholarship).

120   *See generally* Fidler, *International Sanitary Conventions, supra* note 6.

121   *See* Bruce J. Plotkin, *Human Rights and Other Provisions in the Revised International Health Regulations, supra* note 108. *See also* Youde, *supra* note 108 (noting concerns about whose human rights should be respected and the nature of those rights in light of human rights treaties); Andraž Zidar, *WHO International Health Regulations and Human Rights: From Allusions to Inclusion*, 19 INT'L J. HUM. RTS. 505 (2015) (proposing greater integration of the international human rights regime into the legal framework of the 2005 IHR).

122   ICESCR, *supra* note 50, art. 2 ¶ 1 & art. 12 ¶ 1.

most members of the WHO have ratified,[123] states have recognized the "right of everyone to the enjoyment of the highest attainable standard of physical and mental health," and that this right requires states to take steps for the "prevention, treatment and control of epidemic, endemic, occupational and other diseases."[124] The ICESCR Committee has recognized that while the ICESCR did not adopt the holistic conception of health of the WHO's preamble, the right to health in the ICESCR nonetheless "embraces a wide range of socio-economic factors that promote conditions in which people can lead a healthy life, and extends to the underlying determinants of health, such as food and nutrition, housing, access to safe and potable water and adequate sanitation, safe and healthy working conditions, and a healthy environment."[125] As the ICESCR committee has noted under its influential General Comment on the right to health, that right includes "information accessibility," since the right to health is dependent on individuals' right to "seek, receive and impart [health information]."[126] That right also includes joint efforts to "make available relevant technologies, using and improving epidemiological surveillance and data collection on a disaggregated basis, the implementation or enhancement of immunization programmes and other strategies of infectious disease control."[127] The right to prevention, treatment, and control of diseases, according to that Committee, also includes "the creation of a system of urgent medical care in cases of . . . epidemics and similar health hazards, and the provision of disaster relief and humanitarian assistance in emergency situations."[128] Of course, other human rights treaties also include, implicitly or explicitly, the right to health.[129]

---

123   For a list of states parties to the ICESCR, see the Office of the High Commissioner for Human Rights' website, *at* http://indicators.ohchr.org/. For a list of WHO members, see the WHO's website, *at* http://www.who.int/countries/en/

124   ICESCR, *supra* note 50, art. 12 ¶¶ 1 & 2(c).

125   ICESCR, Committee, General Comment 14, adopted Aug. 11, 2000, E/C.12/2000/4, ¶ 4.

126   *Id.* ¶ 12.

127   *Id.* ¶ 16.

128   *Id.*

129   *See, e.g.*, International Convention on the Elimination of All Forms of Racial Discrimination, art. 5(e)(iv), *opened for signature* Dec. 21, 1965, G.A. Res. 2106 (XX), 660 U.N.T.S. 195, and CERD Committee, General Recommendation 30, ¶¶ 29, 36 (2004), U.N. Doc. CERD/C/64/Misc.11/rev.3 at 5–6; Convention on the Elimination of All Forms of Discrimination against Women, art. 12, *opened for signature* Dec. 18, 1979, G.A. Res. 34/180, 1249 U.N.T.S. 13 [hereinafter CEDAW], and Rebecca J. Cook & Verónica Undurraga, *Article 12*, *in* THE UN CONVENTION ON THE ELIMINATION OF ALL FORMS OF DISCRIMINATION AGAINST WOMEN: A COMMENTARY 311 (Marsha A. Freeman, Christine Chinkin & Beate

A state that violates its surveillance or other responsibilities under the IHRS—that is, a state that, for example, fails to establish or to implement the national focal point required under Article 4, does not notify WHO of a potential public health emergency as required under Article 6, does not develop the implementation plan for action foreseen in Annex 1, or violates temporary or standing recommendations to the detriment of the health of its population—might plausibly be seen as in violation of the ICESCR or other human rights treaties that address health, and not just its WHO responsibilities. The overlap between the goals of Article 12 of the ICESCR and the duties imposed on states under the IHRS, for example, are substantial. As the General Counsel of the WHO, Gian Luca Burci, put it: "States have the duty to take measures to prevent and control epidemic and endemic diseases. This obligation exists under Article 12 of the ICESCR, as a step to achieve the full realization of the right to health, as well as under the IHRS."[130] It would appear that state reports to the WHO and to the ICESCR provide complementary opportunities for mobilizing shame against those who fail to comply with the right to health. A state that fails to comply with or that fails to achieve within the time allotted the core capacities anticipated by Annexes 1 or 2 of the IHRS is a state that, prima facie, is in violation of the ICESCR and possibly other human rights treaties.

From another perspective, the declaration of a PHEIC pursuant to the IHRS is likely to be seen as a legitimate ground for imposing restrictions on the enjoyment of certain human rights, but perhaps not others. Under the International Convention on Civil and Political Rights (ICCPR), for example, states are permitted to derogate from certain rights when needed to address issues of "public health."[131] To the extent interpreters of the ICCPR, including

---

Rudolf eds., 2012); Convention on the Rights of the Child, arts. 23–25, *opened for signature* Nov. 20, 1989, G.A. Res. 44/25, 1577 U.N.T.S. 3, arts. 23–25, and CRC Committee, General Comment 4 (2003) U.N. Doc. CRC/GC/2003/4; African (Banjul) Charter on Human and Peoples' Rights, art. 16. Of course, health rights may also be implicated with respect to other rights enumerated in human rights treaties, as with respect to life, bodily integrity or security of the person.

130   Gian Luca Burci & Riikka Koskenmäki, *Human Rights Implications of Governance Responses to Public Health Emergencies: The Case of Major Infectious Disease Outbreaks, in* HEALTH AND HUMAN RIGHTS IN A CHANGING WORLD 516, at 517 (Michael Grodin et al. eds., 3d ed. 2013).

131   *See* International Covenant on Civil and Political Rights, art. 12, *opened for signature* Dec. 16, 1966, G.A. Res. 2200A (XXI), 999 U.N.T.S. 171 [hereinafter ICCPR]; *see also id.* art. 4 (permitting derogation from certain rights "[i]n time of public emergency which threatens the life of the nation").

the Human Rights Committee, are guided by the Siracusa Principles on the Limitation and Derogation of Provisions in the ICCPR, the proclamation of a PHEIC or other WHO actions are likely to be relevant (and may even be determinative) in deciding whether a state is in compliance with that human rights treaty. According to those principles:

> Public health may be invoked as a ground for limiting certain rights in order to allow a state to take measures dealing with a serious threat to the health of the population or individual members of the population... Due regard shall be had to the international health regulations of the World Health Organization.[132]

A state that interferes with the travel or other rights of an individual in adherence to the IHRs and temporary or standing recommendations issued pursuant to them would, at a minimum, have a defense to a claim that its measures are discriminatory in violation of the ICCPR or the ICESCR[133] or that it is taking "retrogressive" measures that are normally suspect in the context of the ICESCR.[134] While the ICESCR does not have a comparable derogation clause and does not indicate that its right to health is derogable, it is reasonable to assume that the Siracusa Principles (and by cross-reference declarations of a PHEIC) are also relevant in that context. As Burci and Koskenmäki indicate:

> The Siracusa Principles provide guidance concerning the question of when interference with human rights may be justified in order to achieve a public health goal. The Principles make clear that any limitation must be provided for by law and carried out in accordance with law; serve a legitimate aim and be strictly necessary to achieve that aim; be the least restrictive and intrusive means available; and not be arbitrary or discriminatory in the way it is imposed or applied.[135]

---

132 U.N. Economic & Social Council, Siracusa Principles on the Limitation and Derogation Provisions in the International Covenant on Civil and Political Rights, ¶¶ 25–26, U.N. Doc. E/CN.4/1985/4, Annex (1985).

133 ICCPR, *supra* note 131, art. 2(1); ICESCR, *supra* note 50, art. 2(2).

134 For a discussion of normally suspect "retrogressive" measures under ICESCR's duties for "progressive" realization of the underlying rights, see, for example, Report of the Special Rapporteur, *supra* note 26, ¶ 14.

135 Burci & Koskenmäki, *supra* note 130, at 517.

As all this suggests, there is potential synergy (as well as tension) between the IHRs and human rights instruments. The normative traffic between these regimes goes in two directions. Human rights regimes may turn to the duties imposed on states by the IHRs to clarify or elaborate some of the duties that states owe under the right to health (and perhaps other related duties such as duty to "ensure" the "right to life").[136] As Burci and Koskenmäki suggest, WHO parties who take steps to implement the IHRs are simultaneously taking steps to fulfill their duties under Article 12 of the ICESCR.[137] On the other hand, the WHO may need the human rights regimes to better understand how states (and the organization) should strike the right balance between successful prevention or control of public health threats and the respect owed to the rights of persons targeted for control measures. Quarantine, isolation, or medically intrusive measures implicate the right to liberty and security, the right to travel, the right to privacy, and the right to free consent under the ICCPR.[138]

It is too simple to say that in all cases of conflict between the IHRs and human rights regimes, human rights concerns always trump. Human rights, even fundamental ones, often have to be balanced against the rights of others. Human rights treaties include derogation clauses and some rights, such as, as noted, the right to travel within a state as well as internationally, are subject to exceptions permitting states to take measures provided by law and rendered necessary by the need "to protect national security, public order, public health ... or the rights and freedoms of others."[139] It may well be, as Burci and Koskenmäki suggest, that the broader ambit of the 2005 IHRs will inspire states to invoke new types of "emergency" derogations from the ICCPR.[140] As they indicate, even though the drafters of the ICCPR probably had political crises in mind when they drafted the Article 4 derogation clause, a "public emergency which threatens the life of a nation" can certainly describe the effects of diseases like SARs, even if there is room to doubt whether proclamation of a PHEIC should always qualify as a "public emergency" under the ICCPR.[141]

---

136   *See* ICCPR, *supra* note 131, arts. 2(1) & 6(1).

137   Burci & Koskenmäki, *supra* note 130, at 521. Burci and his co-author also argue that since the ICESCR anticipates joint as well as individual action by states, "there is arguably a collective responsibility of all States Parties to the ICESCR to cooperate in good faith with each other and with WHO in preventing and responding to the international spread of disease." *Id.*

138   ICCPR, *supra* note 131, arts. 7, 9(1), 12 & 17.

139   *Id.* art. 12(3).

140   Burci & Koskenmäki, *supra* note 130, at 520.

141   *Id.*

To be sure, other tensions between human rights and the IHR regime exist. While human rights advocates emphasize judicial mechanisms for resolving interpretative questions concerning the scope of rights, for example, the IHRS relies on the scientific expertise of WHO committees.[142] These potential conflicts exist even within the IHRS. Compare, for example, the IHRS' emphasis on the benefits of sharing scientific research including through widespread dissemination of health information to the public (which dovetails with human rights to access to information) to the IHRS' general goal to protect global health when such dissemination itself poses a threat.[143] Moreover, human rights regimes do not always impose the greater regulatory burden on states. The new IHRS include, as noted, specific temporal deadlines for compliance (albeit subject to extensions of time for states that request them) but they do not contain a principle of "progressive realization" linked to the availability of economic or other resources, as does the ICESCR.[144] Ironically, to the extent WHO members comply with the tight timetables in the IHRS for achieving their core capacities, the IHRS arguably impose a higher standard for determining whether a state complies with the right to health than would normally be the case under the ICESCR.

The openness of the revised IHRS to independent assessments based on both state and non-state sources of information is a potentially revolutionary change for an organization that, despite the gestures made to democratic governance in its preamble and the privileges it has accorded to NGOS,[145] has remained for much of its history a state-centric institution.

---

142 *Compare, e.g.*, Report of the Special Rapporteur, *supra* note 26, ¶ 17 (noting that "[o]nly an adjudicator can assess whether the right to health has been violated").

143 *See, e.g.*, David P. Fidler, *Risky Research and Human Health: The Influenza H5N1 Research Controversy and International Law*, ASIL INSIGHTS, Jan. 19, 2012, *at* http://www.asil.org/insights/volume/16/issue/2/risky-research-and-human-health-influenza-h5n1-research-controversy-and (discussing concerns over publicizing research on H5N1 undertaken in The Netherlands and the United States given the risks of bioterrorism and noting that the revised IHR do not regulate the kind of research that can take place).

144 *See, e.g.*, Fidler, *International Sanitary Conventions, supra* note 6, at 373–374.

145 *See generally* World Health Organization, Review Report, WHO's interactions with Civil Society and Nongovernmental Organizations, U.N. Doc. WHO/CSI/2002/WP6 (2002) (reporting that as of 2002, 189 NGOS had "official relations" with the WHO, *id.* at 10, meaning that they were conferred privileges such as the right to make statements during meetings of the WHO governing bodies); World Health Organization, *Mapping of WHO's engagement with non-State actors* (report provided by WHO Secretariat to Member States in response to requests for information on WHO's engagement with non-state actors) (2014), *at* http://www.who.int/about/who_reform/governance/mapping-of-

Under the 2005 IHRs, as noted, the WHO Director-General and Emergency Committees can turn for the first time to non-state sources of information and can even rely on these for taking certain actions. As a result the WHO is no longer as dependent as it was on the cooperation of states. Indeed, WHO members now face the possible burden of responding to NGOs and media reports of diseases within their borders since these have potential WHO consequences. In the age of the Internet this is a powerful disciplinary tool for the WHO to rely on for *de facto* enforcement of the IHRs.[146] Thanks to this change, the WHO is at least potentially part of a wider network of governmental, non-governmental, and hybrid outlets for health information and expertise. At the same time, this change should not be overstated. While this reliance on non-state actors may undercut the buffer of sovereignty, this may not indicate quite as dramatic a change for an organization that, from the outset, has been, as Fidler indicates,[147] dependent on an epistemic community of health care professionals within states who were likely to put the normative goal of preventing harm to global health over political (or sovereign) concerns.

Another change in international health law highlighted by the transition to the 2005 IHRs is the extent to which the regime has become less reliant on "hard" law even while expanding the reach of that law. The international sanitary conventions, as noted, were binding treaty commitments that imposed relatively precise obligations, particularly with respect to control measures permitted in response to specific enumerated diseases. The 2005 IHRs, as discussed, are also

---

WHO-engagement-with-non-State-actors.pdf?ua=1 (reporting that the WHO engages more broadly with "729 non-State actors, including 298 NGOs, 44 private sector entities, 24 philanthropic foundations and 363 academic institutions." *Id.* at 1–2.). For a description of the types of interaction and forms of participation enjoyed by these entities, *see* World Health Organization, Framework of engagement with non-State actors: Report by the Director-General, U.N. Doc. A68/5 (May 1, 2015), at ¶¶ 15–17.

146   *See* David L. Heymann, *SARS and Emerging Infectious Diseases: A Challenge to Place Global Solidarity above National Sovereignty*, 35 ANNALS ACAD. MED. SING. 350, 350 (2006) (noting that between Jan. 2001 and Oct. 2004, 39% of unverified reports of outbreaks were received from government officials while 61% "were reported from unofficial and mostly electronic sources such as the media, personal communications or NGOs"). The greater role of NGOs in the WHO aligns with general trends in other international regimes. *See* Steve Charnovitz, *Nongovernmental Organizations and International Law*, 100 AM. J. INT'L L. 348, 352–55 (2006). For a discussion on the role of non-state actors in the WHO's Framework Convention on Tobacco Control (FCTC), *see* Jeff Collin et al., *The Framework Convention on Tobacco Control: The Politics of Global Health Governance*, 23 THIRD WORLD Q. 265, 276–278 (2002).

147   *See supra* note 59, at text and note.

unquestionably "hard" legal obligations imposed under a treaty, namely the WHO Constitution. But on closer inspection, most of the specific duties that states are assuming under the new IHRs are subject to clarification or elaboration by WHO-delegated bodies or persons over time. The Director-General and the Review and Emergency Committees acquire considerable power under the new IHRs, including through the issuance of standing and temporary recommendations, and their actions may clarify precisely what national structures or procedures states need to have in place from time to time and case by case to satisfy their duties under the IHRs, including with respect to whether their core capacities under Annex 1 are satisfactory.

The revised IHRs deploy, as do other IOs, a blend of hard "binding" instruments (the IHRs themselves) with many softer instruments, including WHO recommendations. Consider, for example, the WHO's Guidance for the Use of Annex 2 of the IHRs.[148] These guidelines are directed at the national focal points and provide concrete advice on how they are supposed to assess public health events that may require notification to the WHO under the "decision instrument" contained in Annex 2. These Guidelines are "not themselves of a legally binding nature,"[149] but are intended to produce greater consistency in the application of states' legally binding notification requirements since such consistency will enhance the effectiveness of and compliance with the surveillance and response functions of the IHRs.[150] This Guidance document is also intended to instruct states on how they should implement the IHRs in different sectors at the national level.[151] Interestingly, the most prominent feature of the document is a set of 15 hypothetical factual scenarios involving everything from a toxic chemical spill, accidental exposure to anthrax in a laboratory, poisoning of a child due to a hazardous toy, to outbreaks of diseases such as cholera, measles, and bubonic plague.[152] The Guidance instrument explains the rationale for this approach as follows:

> In the absence of scientific analysis upon which to base such guidance the approach taken was to explain the role and function of the decision instrument and to describe when and how to use it. Importantly, a num-

---

148 World Health Organization, WHO Guidance for the Use of Annex 2 of the International Health Regulations (2005), U.N. Doc. WHO/HSE/IHR/2010.4 (2008) [hereinafter Annex 2 Guidance].

149 *Id.* ¶ 1.1.

150 *Id.* ¶ 2.

151 *Id.*

152 *Id.* ¶ 7.

ber of case scenarios were included to illustrate the application of the assessment criteria. Through these scenarios, the four criteria set out in the decision instrument are tested against fictional events, while applying established epidemiological and public health principles.[153]

A key lesson that can be drawn from these scenarios is the highly contextual basis for notifications to the WHO under Annex 2. The Guidance document goes to great pains to illustrate that the conditions under which a public event occurs—within a relatively secure laboratory versus during an international sports competition for example—as well as when the event is first noticed—when the first symptoms in patient number one are discovered versus after an outbreak has run its course and is contained—determine the difference between a relatively minor incident that the WHO does not need to know about and a PHEIC. The scenarios provided sometimes offer counter-intuitive lessons. It turns out that WHO notification under Annex 2 is merited in a case where a single boy is poisoned by beads in a common toy in the stream of international commerce and by a relatively small number of measles cases at an international athletic competition, but not by a significantly higher number of cases of bubonic plague in a country where such cases occur annually during the rainy summer season or a case of anthrax exposure occurring in a laboratory.[154]

For many observers (particularly those with a common law background), these scenarios seem to serve some of the functions of caselaw or of comparable hypotheticals deployed on law school examinations. By putting the law in a specific factual context, they help to define it. The WHO's scenarios, like adjudicative decisions, help to stabilize the law by giving stakeholders a better sense of what the law and regulators expect. As is addressed in the next chapter on international tribunals (whose decisions are never binding beyond the parties affected by them) the normative value of such fact-based rulings, like those contained in this WHO Guidance document, does not turn on whether these are formally legally binding.

Such WHO products are a good example of why the formally binding/non-binding nature of IO actions is not always a good indicator of effectiveness or

---

153   *Id.* ¶ 1.1.

154   *Id.* at 29–30 ("Case scenario 6: outbreak of plague – part one"), 36–37 ("Case scenario 8: cutaneous anthrax in laboratory"), 39–40 ("Case scenario 10: measles at an international athletic competition"), 44–46 ("Case scenario 13: hazardous toy").

importance.[155] In the context of a medical-technical regime like the WHO's, a Guidance document like this might have a particularly strong normative impact on decisionmakers because its scenarios resonate with the training and literature familiar to this expert community. The Guidelines' resort to factual scenarios might be more persuasive to the health care professionals to whom these are addressed than would, for example, a set of rules seeking to interpret Annex 2 without context. It is certainly plausible to contend that this Guidance document is at least as important as is the "binding" Annex 2 in fulfilling the usual expectations of public health law: that is, in generating expectations of compliance by other WHO members, assisting the overall goals of harmonization, and making the consultations/verifications more predictable. Of course the Guidance document is only one of many examples of the WHO's recourse to non-binding instruments, whether or not directly connected to the IHRS.[156] Like other IOs, the WHO also produces "studies" that, while they do not purport to have a prescriptive purpose, also provide guideposts, safe harbors, or legally compliant policy options for policymakers.[157]

More controversial is the WHO's decision to rely on comparably "soft" approaches when it comes to enforcement and implementation. Under Article 54 of the IHRS, states and the Director-General must report on the implementation of the IHRS as decided by the Health Assembly. That provision also

---

155 *See* JOSÉ E. ALVAREZ, INTERNATIONAL ORGANIZATIONS AS LAW-MAKERS 217 (2006); Lawrence O. Gostin et al., *The Normative Authority of the World Health Organization*, 129 PUB. HEALTH 854 (2015). For a discussion on the value of non-binding instruments in global health governance, see Allyn L. Taylor et al., *Leveraging Non-binding Instruments for Global Health Governance: Reflections from the Global AIDS Reporting Mechanism for WHO Reform*, 128 PUB. HEALTH, 151 (2014).

156 Thus, for example, the WHO approved in May 2011, the "Pandemic Influenza Preparedness Framework," a non-binding arrangement to facilitate sharing influenza viruses and benefits, including vaccines. Pandemic Influenza Preparedness Framework for the Sharing of Influenza Viruses and Access to Vaccines and Other Benefits, WHA Res. 64.5 (2011). Comparable soft law instruments also govern the WHO's policies towards NGOs, to cite another example. *See, e.g.*, Principles Governing Relations between the WHO and Nongovernmental Organizations, WHA Res. 40.25 (1987); WHO Executive Board, Guidelines on Interaction with Commercial Enterprises to Achieve Health Outcomes, EB107/20 (Nov. 30, 2000). *See also supra* at 53–56 (discussion of FCTC Guidelines).

157 *See, e.g.*, WHO, WTO & World Intellectual Property Organization (WIPO), Promoting Access to Medical Technologies and Innovation: Intersections between public health, intellectual property and trade, *at* http://www.wto.org/english/res_e/publications_e/who-wipo-wto_2013_e.htm (presenting policy options involving the intersection of health, trade and intellectual property where, for example, patents may serve the interest of enhancing access to medicines rather than the converse).

indicates that the Health Assembly shall periodically review the functioning of the IHRs, with the first review taking place no later than five years after their entry into force, and the WHO shall periodically conduct studies to the same end.[158] This means that while WHO members are obligated to put in place the core capacities of Annex 1, there is no WHO court imposing damages or other hard remedies if they fail to do so. In order to fulfill the expectations of Article 54 of the IHRs, the WHO has adopted another soft instrument, namely a monitoring framework that seeks:

> to give countries technical guidance in assessing the status of their IHR implementation and the development of IHR core capacities; to facilitate the reporting of States parties to the WHA required under the IHR; and to provide countries and partners with information on areas where support is needed.[159]

As this suggests, the WHO is relying on a "managerial" approach to compliance. Managerial approaches to securing compliance with international obligations, the subject of a substantial literature at the intersection of international law and international relations, rest on the assumption that states are not necessarily unwilling but may be unable to comply with their obligations or need help in figuring out precisely what those obligations are.[160] Managerialists seek to remedy these capacity deficits by relying on "carrots"—such as clarifications of the law (like the Guidance document noted above) as accompanied by technical assistance to assist states' compliance. There is, to be sure, reason to think that this is the correct model in this instance. The IHRs, after all, seek to secure goals that in most contexts are not politically controversial and that all states presumptively desire to achieve. As Fidler indicates, there is also reason to believe that the WHO's (and the IHRs') greater openness to non-state sources of information would be a potent tool (if needed) to embarrass laggard states into compliance to the extent they are unwilling as well as unable.[161]

The evidence of compliance and implementation with the WHO's 2005 IHRs, however, is considerably more mixed. Since the entry into force of the

---

158   2005 IHR, *supra* note 71, art. 54.2–54.3.

159   Implementation of the International Health Regulations (2005), WHA Doc. EB122.R3 (Jan. 24, 2008).

160   *See, e.g.,* ALVAREZ, *supra* note 155, at 316–331.

161   *See* David P. Fidler, *The UN and the Responsibility to Practice Public Health*, 2 J. INT'L L. & INT'L REL. 41, 57 (2005–2006) (describing the role of non-state actors in public health governance).

revised IHRs, the WHO secretariat has sent WHO members questionnaires designed to facilitate their reporting of IHR implementation, and these have generated reports summarizing the extent to which states have implemented the core capacity requirements. The latest such report, from 2014, indicates highly uneven rates of implementation depending on region and core capacity being assessed. Even though that report assesses national implementation based entirely on self-reported data by states, the inadequacies begin with the numbers of states that even bothered to supply such data in response to the WHO's Monitoring Questionnaire for 2013. According to that report, 77% of the countries in the African region responded to the questionnaire to begin with.[162] Even among those reporting in that region, the level of self-reported implementation of the 13 core capacities assessed ranged from a low of 23% (compared to a global average of nearly 60%) for surveillance and other responsibilities at ports of entry to a high of 70% for achieving the requisite level of laboratory capacity to test for priority health threats.[163] These disappointing rates of implementation—where only 88% of the countries reporting in the African region had even established the fundamental national focal point required and only 56% had disseminated to relevant authorities information on that focal point[164]—are particularly troubling given the dissatisfactions generated by the lack of compliance with the old IHRs. For those who think that political or other forms of opposition to the law may explain some or all of the resistance to compliance, the WHO's managerial approach resting on capacity-building carrots needs to be supplemented or even replaced by hard "sticks."[165]

These and other dissatisfactions with the 2005 IHRs and the WHO's responsiveness to global health crises have come to the surface repeatedly. An important set of critiques emerged from the organization itself, as a result of the review required by Article 54(2) of the 2005 IHRs, requiring a report by a Review Committee five years after their entry into force. That report evaluated the IHRs generally and in light of the first PHEIC to occur after the 2005 IHRs came into force, namely the global response to the influenza A (H1N1) pandemic in

162   World Health Organization, Summary of States Parties 2013 Report on IHR Core Capacity Implementation: Regional Profile, WHO/HSE/GCR/2014.10, at 1 (2014).

163   Id. fig. at 1.

164   Id. at 2.

165   See, e.g., Jennifer A. Shkabatur, A Global Panopticon? The Changing Role of International Organizations in the Information Age, 33 MICH. J. INT'L L. 159, 173 (2011) (arguing that the 2005 IHRs lack sufficient "carrots and sticks" to impel states to share unfavorable information).

2009.[166] While that report credited the revised IHRs for making the world better prepared to cope with public health emergencies and found no evidence
of malfeasance, it warned that despite the passage of five years, the IHRs were
not "fully operational and are not now on a path to timely implementation
worldwide."[167] It concluded (prophetically) that the world was "ill-prepared to
respond to a severe influenza pandemic or to any similarly global, sustained
and threatening public-health emergency"[168] and that "the fundamental gap
between global need and global capacity must be closed."[169] The experts on
that Review Committee had ample reasons for these pessimistic conclusions:
of the 194 parties to the IHRs, only 128 (66%) bothered to respond to the WHO
questionnaire on their progress in implementing the IHRs, and of those, only
58% reported having developed national plans to meet core capacity requirements, only 10% indicated that they had fully established those capacities, and
in some countries the national focal point lacked even the authority to communicate with the WHO in a timely manner.[170] The Committee accordingly
recommended greater mobilization of resources and funding to enable far better technical assistance to countries to enhance IHR related capacity building.
With respect to the H1N1 pandemic, the Committee reported numerous flaws
in how the WHO reacted and explained why, in the views of many, the WHO
vastly overstated the seriousness of the pandemic and, as a result, lost some of
its credibility.

The 2011 European E. coli outbreaks suggested comparable flaws in the
WHO's responsiveness and in the operation of the IHRs. In that instance, a
number of countries adopted control measures on trade that exceeded what
many thought were necessary and appeared to violate EU law, the revised
IHRs, and the WTO's SPS Agreement. A key lesson of that experience was that
the IHRs lacked effective tools to address a very old problem: the tendency of
some states to adopt excessive control measures with severe consequences to
trade. Some critics even suggested a need for the upper limit maximums on
permitted control measures found in the international sanitary conventions
or at least for authority to permit the organization to impose harder remedies,

---

166   Director-General, World Health Organization, Report of the Review Committee on the
       Functioning of the IHR (2005) in Relation to Pandemic (H1N1) 2009, A64/10 (May 5, 2011)
       [hereinafter 2011 Review Report].
167   Id. ¶ 16.
168   Id. ¶ 18.
169   Id. ¶ 46.
170   Id. ¶ 23.

such as those found in the WTO.[171] For others, the case highlighted the continuing possibility that states victimized by excessive or unnecessary control
measures will forum-shop their way to finding a remedy, even if this means
ignoring the WHO in deference to the WTO.[172]

But if these reactions suggested that the revised IHRs were not solving the
threat to trade flows, the next global health threat suggested that the IHRs, as
in the H1N1 case, were not sufficiently protective of public health. When a new
coronavirus emerged in Saudi Arabia in June 2012, it was not reported to the
WHO as required—until the UK did so three months later when a Qatari man
who had recently traveled to Saudi Arabia arrived at a British hospital suffering
from acute respiratory syndrome and kidney failure.[173] The new virus, named
the Middle East respiratory syndrome (MERS), accounted for 837 confirmed
cases and at least 291 deaths in 22 countries by late July 2014.[174] The spread
of MERS again highlighted the problem of uneven compliance with the IHRs.
Experts suggested that had Saudi Arabia reported the first instance of the new
disease, MERS' spread might have been more successfully contained. MERS also
demonstrated anew the IHRs' "unfounded mandates": namely their depen-
dence on a chronically underfunded organization that had recently adopted
zero growth budgeting and was increasingly relying on private sources of
funding. For critics like Gostin and Sridhar, the WHO, like some other IOs, was
burdened by its reliance on "multi-bi" sources of funding, that is money from
a small group of donors who earmark their noncore funding for specific sectors, diseases, or regions through multilateral agencies.[175] At the same time, the
revised IHRs, as another critic pointed out, "include no monies to assist states
with creating or forming surveillance systems, training personnel to oversee
such systems, or maintaining the infrastructure necessary to keep such systems

---

171   David P. Fidler, *International Law and the E. Coli Outbreaks in Europe*, 15 ASIL INSIGHTS
      (June 6, 2011), *at* http://www.asil.org/insights/volume/15/issue/14/international-law-and-
      e-coli-outbreaks-europe. *See also* 2011 Review Report, *supra* note 166 (noting that no legal
      consequences follow if a country fails to explain why a more restrictive traffic and trade
      measure was adopted than those recommended by the WHO).

172   Hannah Murphy & Aynsley Kellow, *Forum Shopping in Global Governance: Understanding
      States, Business and NGOs in Multiple Arenas*, 4 GLOBAL POL'Y 139, 147 (2013) (noting that
      forum shopping may be beneficial since, for example, the TRIPS debate resulted in greater
      communication between the WTO and WHO on the intersection between international
      trade and health policy).

173   Jeremy Youde, *MERS and Global Health Governance*, 70(1) INT'L J. 119 (2014).

174   *Id.* at 120.

175   Lawrence O. Gostin & Devi Sridhar, *Global Health and the Law*, 370 NEW ENG. J. MED.
      1732, 1737 (2014).

operational."[176] But the lack of funding, which had been highlighted even in the 2011 Review Report, was seen as only one explanation for the continuing problem that many WHO members did not fulfill their basic surveillance and reporting obligations. In the case of MERS, it was suggested that states continued to be reluctant politically to suffer the economic and other consequences of reporting to the WHO that they faced a public health threat.[177]

But the biggest blow to confidence in the WHO and the 2005 IHRS arrived with the 2014 West African Ebola outbreak. The Ebola crisis, the "largest and most complex" on record,[178] had resulted in 11,261 deaths and 27,609 confirmed cases by July 2015.[179] As an Ebola Interim Assessment Panel, specially appointed to assess the WHO's response, concluded, that outbreak "exposed organizational failings in the functioning of WHO" and "demonstrated shortcomings" in the IHRS.[180] With respect to the 2005 IHRS, that panel drew three conclusions that would not have surprised anyone familiar with prior assessments by the organization or outside observers: (1) WHO member states had largely failed to implement the core capacities required; (2) nearly a quarter of states had instituted travel bans and other additional measures that the WHO had not required, were in violation of the IHRS, and significantly interfered with international travel; and (3) the WHO had unjustifiably delayed in declaring a PHEIC.[181] Echoing the 2011 Review Report's (unimplemented) recommendations in many respects, the Ebola Assessment Panel recommended consideration of: the establishment of a priority plan for financing technical assistance to help countries comply with the IHRS (perhaps in partnership with the World Bank), adoption of financial incentives to encourage states to

---

176   Youde, *supra* note 173, at 131. *See also* Gostin & Sridhar, *supra* note 175, at 1737.

177   Youde, *supra* note 173, at 134.

178   World Health Organization, *Report of the Ebola Interim Assessment Panel* 9 (2015), *at* http://www.who.int/csr/resources/publications/ebola/report-by-panel.pdf [hereinafter *Panel Report*].

179   World Health Organization, *Ebola Situation Report* (Jul. 8, 2015), *at* http://apps.who.int/ iris/bitstream/10665/179196/1/roadmapsitrep_8Jul2015_eng.pdf.

180   World Health Organization, *Panel Report, supra* note 178, at 5.

181   *Id. See also* World Health Organization, *IHR and Ebola: Special Session of the Executive Board on the Ebola Emergency*, EB136/INF./7 (Jan. 9, 2015), *at* http://apps.who.int/gb/ ebwha/pdf_files/EBSS3/EBSS3_INF4-en.pdf. It was not until August 8, 2014, four months after the threat of international spread first became apparent, at least to NGOs on the ground, that the WHO declared a PHEIC. Press Release, World Health Organization, *Statement on the 1st Meeting of the IHR Emergency Committee on the 2014 Ebola Outbreak in West Africa, Press Release* (Aug. 8, 2014), *at* http://www.who.int/mediacentre/news/ statements/2014/ebola-20140808/en/.

notify public health risks to the WHO, reliance on disincentives to discourage countries from adopting non-WHO endorsed control measures, and creation of an intermediate level of global health threat that would engage states at an earlier stage before a full-fledged PHEIC is declared.[182] Although the Ebola report sought to re-establish the WHO's pre-eminence as the lead IO on health, it also recommended that the UN Secretary-General's High-Level Panel on the Global Response to Health Crises should "identify procedures to take specific health matters to the United Nations Security Council and consider incentives and disincentives needed to improve global health security."[183] This recommendation, presumably intended to enhance the credibility of the IHRS' requirements by suggesting the threat of UN Chapter VII action,[184] also responded to the panel's worry of a growing gap between stakeholders invested in global health and those engaged in the UN's humanitarian system.[185]

The Ebola crisis may prove to be, unlike prior criticisms of the WHO, a milestone that leads to structural changes in the organization and the IHRS, and perhaps to a revolution in how the world deals with global health matters.[186] While the principal concern has been, of course, the fact that the WHO appeared to let a deadly virus spiral out of control through a delayed and fragmented response, Ebola has generated considerable introspection about whether the WHO is simply "overcommitted, overextended and in need of spe-

---

182 *Panel Report, supra* note 178, at 6. The Ebola Assessment Panel also highlighted as problems the WHO's reliance on voluntary funds, its adoption of zero growth budgeting, and the lack of a contingency fund to enable a rapid response to global health threats. *Id.* at 6–7.

183 *Id.*

184 Indeed, the Ebola Assessment Panel notes that during that crisis, some WHO members took action that made it impossible for health workers to reach the affected areas, and argues that in such cases "there should be a procedure to take this matter to the United Nations Security Council." *Id.* at 19.

185 *Id.* at 7. The Ebola Assessment Panel also suggested that global health threats should play a larger role when the UN General Assembly considers the Sustainable Development Goals. *Id.* at 9–10.

186 *See generally* Ilona Kickbusch & K. Srinath Reddy, *Global Health Governance—The Next Political Revolution*, 129 (7) PUB. HEALTH 838 (2015) (arguing that health crises generate a political drive for change and even to "cosmopolitan moments" that raise the imperative of health).

cific reforms"[187] or whether, more pessimistically, the WHO is no longer fit to serve its basic purpose.[188]

A more general criticism of the organization is that it suffers, like some other IOs, from a "democratic deficit" insofar as it is insufficiently responsive to its diverse members as well as to the substantial number of non-state concerns engaged in global health in forums like the Global Fund, UNAIDS, and the GAVI Alliance.[189] The perceived need for greater democratization generated proposals for a broader "feedback loop" involving businesses, foundations, the media, and other parts of civil society that would report on states' progress on monitoring or reporting.[190] Some have suggested borrowing from human rights regimes the idea of enabling such groups to issue "shadow reports" to accompany state official reports to the WHO.[191] Others have proposed establishing a new Committee C to the World Health Assembly comprised of a diverse group of non-state actors and other IOs to increase transparency, coordination, and engagement.[192] Others have argued for more specific reforms, including an emergency workforce within the organization to handle crises and enhanced attention to staffing regional offices with more independent officials willing to push back against the political desires of the states in which they are located. There are also differing views about whether the organization is sufficiently flexible to adapt to the rapidly changing health landscape in which the WHO is only one actor among many.[193] For some, the proposals now being pursued

---

187   Director-General, World Health Organization, The Future of Financing for the WHO: World Health Organization: Reforms for a Healthy Future, WHA Res. 64/4, ¶ 3 (May 5, 2011), at http://apps.who.int/gb/ebwha/pdf_files/WHA64/A64_4-en.pdf.

188   But see Kickbusch & Reddy, supra note 186, at 3 (arguing that the view that the WHO is an irrelevant global actor caught in a "gridlock and inertia is misguided").

189   See, e.g., Lawrence O. Gostin, Devi Sridhar, & Daniel Hougendobler, The Normative Authority of the World Health Organization, 129 (7) PUB. HEALTH 854, 858 & 860 (2015). See also R. van de Pas & L.G. van Schaik, Democratizing the World Health Organization, 128 (2) PUB. HEALTH 195, 196 (2014) (contending that "the BRICS [including their health ministers who regularly meet] have not yet spoken out en bloc at the WHA or EB, and rather focus their diplomatic efforts on the G20").

190   See e.g., Belinda Townsend et. al, Global Health Governance: Framework Convention on Tobacco Control (FCTC), the Doha Declaration, and Democratisation, 2 (2) ADMIN. SCI. 186 (2012).

191   See, e.g., Gostin, Sridhard & Hougendobler, supra note 189, at 5.

192   Id. at 8. See Ilona Kickbusch, Wolfgang Hein & Gaudenz Silberschmidt, Addressing Global Health Challenges Through a New Mechanism: The Proposal for a Committee C of the World Health Assembly, 38 (3) J.L. MED. & ETHICS 550 (2010).

193   For some the fact that the WHO has in general chosen to engage in de facto in lieu of formal constitutional amendment with respect to its core functions is part of the problem.

within the organization, while welcome, are too little too late and fail to address the WHO's deep structural problems.[194]

For those inclined to find more positive lessons even in crisis, the Ebola outbreak suggests a future of increasing and positive interactions among diverse IOs. Ebola produced responses, sometimes even coordinated, between the WHO and the UN Security Council and the General Assembly,[195] among other UN specialized organizations such as the International Civil Aviation Organization (ICAO) and the ILO, and even collaborations with the World Bank.[196] It marked, as noted, the first time in which the SC formally invoked its Chapter VII powers and declared a threat to global health "a threat to international peace and security," thereby moving the world a step closer to recognizing, rightly or wrongly, the "securitization" of health.[197] While the link between health and security was first made (like much else) in the prescient preamble of the WHO Constitution, the two concepts (now embedded

---

But see Gian Luca Burci, *Institutional Adaptation Without Reform: WHO and the Challenges of Globalization*, 2 INT'L ORG. L. REV. 437 (2005) (suggesting that this capacity for informal change is a strength not a weakness).

194   For the organization's own reform proposals, see, for example, World Health Organization Executive Board, *Ebola: Ending the Current Outbreak, Strengthening Global Preparedness and Ensuring WHO's Capacity to Prepare for and Respond to Future Large-Scale Outbreaks and Emergencies with Health Consequences*, WHA Res. BSSS3.R1 (Jan. 25, 2015), *at* http://apps.who.int/gb/ebwha/pdf_files/EBSS3/EBSS3_R1-en.pdf; Director-General, World Health Organization, *The Future of Financing for WHO: World Health Organization: Reforms for a Healthy Future*, A64/4 (May 5, 2011), *at* http://apps.who.int/gb/ebwha/pdf_files/WHA64/A64_4-en.pdf.

195   G.A. Res. 69/1, ¶ 2 (Sept. 19, 2014) (requesting "the Secretary-General to take such measures as may be necessary for the prompt execution of his intention" to establish the United Nations Mission for Ebola Emergency Response).

196   *See, e.g.*, World Health Organization & International Labour Organization, *Ebola Virus Disease: Occupational Safety and Health, Joint WHO/ILO Briefing Note for Workers and Employers*, (Aug. 25, 2014; update Sept. 5, 2014), *at* http://www.ilo.org/wcmsp5/groups/public/---ed_protect/---protrav/---safework/documents/briefingnote/wcms_304867.pdf; International Civil Aviation Organization, *ICAO and World Health Organization Collaboration on Ebola Outbreak* (Jul. 30, 2014), *at* http://www.icao.int/Newsroom/Pages/ICAO-and-World-Health-Organization-collaboration-on-Ebola-outbreak.aspx.

197   S.C. Res. 2177 (Sept. 18, 2014). *See also* Gian Luca Burci & Jacob Quirin, *Ebola, WHO, and the United Nations: Convergence of Global Public Health and International Peace and Security*, 18 (25) ASIL INSIGHTS (Nov. 14, 2014), *at* http://www.asil.org/insights/volume/18/issue/25/ebola-who-and-united-nations-convergence-global-public-health-and-.

in the wider notion of "human security")[198] were distant strangers for much of the WHO's and the SC's respective histories.[199]

4   The WHO's First Treaty: The Framework Convention on Tobacco Control

An examination of the WHO's legal impact would be incomplete without some attention to that organization's first (and so far only) deployment of its Article 19 authority to serve as a negotiating forum for treaties that then go to WHO members for ratification. The Framework Convention on Tobacco Control was adopted by the World Health Assembly in May 2003 as an annex to a resolution.[200] As of July 2015, 180 states have become parties to a treaty whose core objective is "to protect present and future generations from the devastating health, social, environmental, and economic consequences of tobacco consumption and exposure to tobacco smoke by providing a framework for tobacco control measures to be implemented by the Parties at the national, regional and international levels in order to reduce continually and substantially the prevalence of tobacco use and exposure to tobacco smoke."[201] As would be expected of an initiative that drew on the joint efforts of the WHO and the World Bank, the preamble of the FCTC draws on the links between the "tobacco epidemic" and global trade flows, the human rights of women, children, and indigenous peoples, and the right to sustainable development.[202] The FCTC is a traditional positivist treaty in form. It is a traditional treaty insofar as only states are permitted to ratify it, ratifications or accessions to it must be deposited with the UN Secretary-General as with respect to many other multilateral instruments seeking the benefits provided by Article 102 of the UN Charter, and, as anticipated by Article 19 of the WHO Constitution, those seeking to become parties,

---

198   *See* discussion of "human security" in Chapter II *supra*.

199   *See* Gian Luca Burci, *Health and Infectious Diseases, in* THE OXFORD HANDBOOK OF THE UNITED NATIONS 582, 587–588 (Thomas G. Weiss & Sam Daws eds., 2007) (noting that it was not until January 2000 that the Security Council first addressed a health crisis as a threat to international peace and security).

200   World Health Assembly, *Framework Convention on Tobacco Control*, WHA Res. 56.1 (May 21, 2003); WHO Framework Convention on Tobacco Control, May 21, 2003, 2302 U.N.T.S. 166, 42 I.L.M. 518 [hereinafter FCTC].

201   FCTC, *supra* note 200, art. 3.

202   *Id.* pmbl. *See also* ALVAREZ, *supra* note 155, at 354–357.

including WHO members, must each express their consent to be bound by it.[203] The FCTC is not a WHO regulation like the IHRs where WHO members must affirmatively opt out in order to avoid being bound. But, as commentators have pointed out, the legal duties imposed on state parties to the FCTC differ from positivist treaties such as the international sanitary conventions.

The structure of the FCTC is relatively simple.[204] It establishes a number of general "guiding principles" in Article 4 followed by open-ended "general obligations" in Article 5. Somewhat less vague duties on states intended to reduce demand for tobacco are imposed under Articles 6–14, while Article 15 covers measures to reduce supply. Article 16 requires states to "adopt and implement effective legislative, executive, administrative or other measures at the appropriate government level" to prohibit tobacco sales to minors; Article 17 requires parties to "promote, as appropriate" economically viable alternatives to growing tobacco; Article 19 requires states "to consider taking legislative action" to promote criminal and civil liability for the purpose of tobacco control; Article 20 requires states to develop and promote research, surveillance, and exchange information in the field of tobacco control; and Article 21 requires periodic reports to the conference of the parties (COP) established under Article 23. That COP gathers whenever it decides to meet; is capable of adopting protocols, annexes, and amendments (none of which are binding on a party to the FCTC absent its consent); and endeavors to operate on the basis of consensus.[205] As this suggests, the range of national measures of implementation anticipated (but not always required or clearly specified) under the FCTC is broad and, for a multilateral treaty, exceptionally intrusive with respect to matters that would otherwise be within states' domestic jurisdiction.

With the possible exception of the WHO Convention itself, no other public health treaty comes close in terms of comprehensiveness. The FCTC anticipates government intrusion with respect to exposure to second-hand smoke; tobacco taxes; sales to minors; the contents, packaging, advertising, and labelling of tobacco products; the relationship between the tobacco industry and government; educational and public awareness programs; tobacco smuggling; alternatives to tobacco farming; the liability of tobacco companies; and inter-

---

203   FCTC, *supra* note 200, arts. 34–35 (permitting WHO members as well as members of the
       UN to sign the treaty and limiting ratification or accession to such states); art. 36 (permitting entry into force only after the 40th state deposits its acceptance); art. 37 (establishing the UN as the depositary).

204   For a useful summary, see World Health Organization, *The WHO Framework Convention on Tobacco Control: An Overview* (Jan. 2015), *at* http://www.who.int/fctc/WHO_FCTC_summary_January2015.pdf.

205   FCTC, *supra* note 200, arts. 23, 28, 29 & 33.

national surveillance of the tobacco "epidemic." Moreover, thanks to an exceptionally proactive COP which has taken the reporting responsibilities assumed by treaty parties under Article 21 of the FCTC seriously, the FCTC has generated an unprecedented amount of information concerning how states are dealing with all these issues and about potential "best practices" associated with achieving (eventually) "tobacco free" societies around the world.[206]

How has such a treaty managed to attract so many states? Answer: it is not, based on its text, legally demanding. The FCTC does not establish a Tobacco Organization, does not require its parties to resort to the ICJ or any other form of binding dispute settlement, and, with some important exceptions, imposes minimal concrete obligations on its state parties.[207] While the FCTC includes, as noted, ostensible legal obligations, stating that parties "shall" undertake certain actions, most of these require only the establishment or designation of a particular government agency (e.g., "a national coordinating mechanism or focal points for tobacco control")[208] and impose only vague obligations (e.g., "shall develop ... comprehensive multisectoral tobacco control strategies").[209] When the duties on parties are more specific, they typically include language that accords states considerable (and sometimes self-judging) discretion as to whether, when, or how to comply (e.g., provisions suggesting that while provisions as to liability are an important aspect of tobacco control, they will be "determined by each Party within its jurisdiction"),[210] or numerous obligations that require action only "as appropriate,"[211] "in accordance with national law,"[212] "where approved by competent national authorities,"[213] or "in accordance with [a state's] capabilities").[214] Other FCTC provisions provide only for the exchange of information,[215] generally urge states to "cooperate,"[216] or contain mere expressions of desirable policy goals, such as Article 5.3's injunction that,

206 *See generally* World Health Organization, 2014 Global Progress Report on Implementation of the WHO Framework Convention on Tobacco Control (2014), *at* http://www.who.int/fctc/reporting/2014globalprogressreport.pdf.

207 The FCTC foresees that parties will handle interpretative disputes under that treaty through diplomatic channels and only suggests *ad hoc* arbitration when the disputing parties so agree. FCTC, *supra* note 200, art. 27.

208 *Id.* art. 5.2(a).

209 *Id.* art. 5.1.

210 *Id.* art. 4.5.

211 *See, e.g., id.* arts. 5.2(b), 5.5, 6.2, 7, 12, 13.4, 20.2, 21.1.

212 *Id.* arts. 5.3, 12(c), 15.2, 15.4, 15.6.

213 *Id.* art. 9.

214 *Id.* art. 5.2.

215 *See, e.g., id.* arts. 20–21.

216 *E.g., id.* Preamble, arts. 5, 17, 22.

in setting public health policies, states "act to protect these policies from commercial and other vested interests of the tobacco industry in accordance with national law."

As many commentators have noted, the FCTC is a prominent example of a relatively new kind of "managerial" multilateral treaty that some suggest is characteristic of the age of IOs.[217] Such treaties aspire to (and often achieve) universal or nearly universal participation, do so by imposing commitments that do not threaten sovereigns and that render reservations unnecessary, are not usually subject to binding dispute settlement, rely on consensus decision-making, and enable differentiated rights and obligations that are sensitive to differing states' capacities with respect to expected level of implementation or compliance. These managerial treaties are designed to attract states precisely because they do not do what real "law" typically does: they do not impose hard penalties for lack of compliance and indeed make judgments about whether a treaty "violation" has occurred (perhaps purposely) difficult. To the extent these treaties achieve their goals, they are said to do so because they rely, as do managerial approaches to compliance generally, on the "soft power" of convening states periodically to consider a specific topic (particularly one dominated by perceived experts), the persuasive role of repeated discourse among participants, and the prospect that "carrots," such as offers for technical assistance to enable states to change their laws and practices, can sometimes be as, or even more, effective than "sticks" in the form of hard disincentives such as authorized sanctions ordered by an IO organ or an international court.[218] It has been argued that, to a considerable extent, global human rights treaties that lack binding enforcement have these managerial qualities, as do a number of multilateral environmental agreements and the General Agreement on Tarrifs and Trade (GATT) (at least prior to its transformation into the WTO in 1994).[219]

Although the FCTC is sometimes dismissed as dealing with a "peripheral" subject or disparaged, given the discretion it accords to state parties, as a form of "á la carte multilateralism" where states get to do what they would have done in any case but can now justify their actions on the basis of treaty,[220] it deals with the leading cause of preventable death in the world.[221] It is the

---

217   See, e.g., ALVAREZ, supra note 155, at 329–331, 354–357.

218   Id. at 326–327.

219   Id. at 317–325.

220   See id. at 331.

221   See World Health Organization, An International Treaty for Tobacco Control, at http://www.who.int/features/2003/08/en/ (noting that there are 4.9 million tobacco-related deaths per year).

rare instance in which the WHO has initiated a process that addresses an endemic and perennial threat to health and literally the economic health of nations—and not a temporal or geographically limited crisis. It is also a case where it is possible to underestimate a treaty's impact if one only considers the treaty's original text—the framework for governance that it establishes— and not how that framework has been elaborated over the decade that the FCTC has been in place. The vague obligations contained in the FCTC have been elaborated considerably over time, thanks to eight sets of "Guidelines" that have since been issued by the FCTC's COP.[222]

Consider, for example, the Guidelines for implementation of Article 5.3, the provision requiring states to protect their policies from the interests of the tobacco industry. Those Guidelines, issued precisely in order to assist states in meeting their Article 5.3 obligations, begin by spelling out that they apply to "government officials, representatives and employees of any national, state, provincial, municipal, local or other public or semi/quasi-public institution or body within the jurisdiction of a Party, and to any person acting on their behalf."[223] They include relatively more precise "guiding principles" to guide this broad swath of regulators, such as the rule that "the tobacco industry should not be granted incentives to establish or run their businesses."[224] These are followed by a set of eight "Recommendations" for addressing the possibility of tobacco industry interference with public health policies, each of which is accompanied by even more precise sub-recommendations. The recommendation to be transparent with respect to interactions with the tobacco industry is followed, for example, by concrete examples of what this means: resort to public hearings, public notice, and disclosure of records of such transactions.[225] The recommendation to reject partnerships or non-binding agreements with the industry, means, among other things, refusing to accept any voluntary code of conduct or instrument drafted by the industry that is offered as a substitute for legally enforceable control measures and rejection of any proposed legislation drafted in collaboration with tobacco companies.[226] The Guidelines

---

222 *See* "Guidelines" for FCTC, arts. 5.3, 6, 8, 9, 11, 12, 13 & 14, available for download on the FCTC website, *at* http://www.who.int/fctc/guidelines/adopted/en/.

223 FCTC Conference of Parties, Guidelines for implementation of Article 5.3 of the WHO Framework Convention on Tobacco Control on the protection of public health policies with respect to tobacco control from commercial and other vested interests of the tobacco industry [hereinafter Article 5.3 Guidelines], ¶ 10, *at* http://www.who.int/fctc/guidelines/article_5_3.pdf?ua=1.

224 *Id.* ¶ 16 (Principle 4).

225 *Id.* ¶ 20 (Recommendation 2.2).

226 *Id.* ¶ 21 (Recommendations 3.3 & 3.4).

recommend requiring applicants for public office to disclose current or previous associations with the industry,[227] requiring government officials to divest themselves of direct interests in tobacco,[228] adopting effective measures to prohibit political contributions from the industry,[229] and banning any preferential tax exemptions for the tobacco industry.[230] The Article 5.3 Guidelines conclude by urging codes of conduct for all branches of government to encourage NGOs to serve as whistle-blowers in order to enforce the foregoing recommendations.[231]

The Guidelines for implementation of the FCTC's Article 11 on the packaging and labeling of tobacco products are, if anything, even more specific. Those Guidelines point out that larger warnings with pictures are "more likely to be noticed, better communicate health risks, [and] provoke a greater emotional response."[232] The Guidelines go further than does the Convention, which specifies that health warnings should be 50% or more of principal display areas on packaging but no less than 30%;[233] they recommend that states consider using warnings and messages that cover more than 50% of the principal display areas and "aim to cover as much of the principal display areas as possible."[234] Among other recommendations, the Guidelines urge using a range of health warnings and messages,[235] the inclusion of warnings in the various languages in use within a jurisdiction,[236] and that states consider plain packaging over the use of "logos, colours, brand images or promotional information," in part because "industry package design techniques . . . may suggest that some products are less harmful than others."[237]

While the FCTC Guidelines issued to date are not legally binding, there is some evidence that they are having normative effects.[238] The FCTC's Guidelines,

---

227   *Id.* ¶ 23 (Recommendation 4.5).

228   *Id.* (Recommendation 4.6).

229   *Id.* (Recommendation 4.11).

230   *Id.* ¶ 29 (Recommendation 7.3).

231   *Id.* ¶¶ 32–34.

232   FCTC Conference of Parties, Guidelines for Implementation of Article 11 of the WHO Framework Convention on Tobacco Control (Packaging and Labeling of Tobacco Products) ¶¶ 7; 14–16, *at* http://www.who.int/fctc/guidelines/article_11.pdf?ua=1.

233   FCTC, *supra* note 200, art. 11.1(b)(iv).

234   *Id.* ¶ 12.

235   *Id.* ¶¶ 23; 46.

236   *Id.* ¶ 28–29.

237   *Id.* ¶ 46.

238   *See generally* Sam Foster Halabi, *The World Health Organization's Framework Convention on Tobacco Control: An Analysis of Guidelines Adopted by the Conference of Parties,* 39

and not just the provisions of the FCTC itself, have now been cited or relied upon by some national courts in interpreting and upholding strong tobacco control measures and some courts appear to have been similarly inspired.[239] As a result, some states that have adopted some of the COP recommendations with respect to health warnings on cigarettes or that have required plain packaging now face challenges under the WTO and under the investor-state dispute settlement authorized by some investment protection agreements.[240] While decisions in those cases have not been issued to date, they illustrate the fact that the tobacco industry itself is now treating the vague generalities in the FCTC seriously and that states are doing the same with respect to some of the hortatory Guidelines.

The FCTC's COP has also deployed its power under Article 33 of the treaty to adopt protocols open to FCTC parties to accept. At its second session in 2007, the COP chose illicit trade in tobacco products, governed by Article 15 of the FCTC, to be the subject of its first protocol and established an Intergovernmental Negotiating Body (INB) for this purpose. Working off a template prepared by

---

GA. J. INT'L & COMP. L. 121 (2010). For a table listing national cases from across the globe illustrating the influence of international law on domestic health policy, see Gostin & Sridhar, *supra* note 175, Table 1 at 1738.

239 Monique E. Muggli et al., *Tracking the relevance of the WHO Framework Convention on Tobacco Control in legislation and litigation through the online resource, Tobacco Control Laws*, TOBACCO CONTROL (May 4, 2013), *at* http://tobaccocontrol.bmj.com/content/early/2013/05/03/tobaccocontrol-2012-050854.full.pdf. For examples of national court decisions that rely on the FCTC, *see* Canada (Attorney General) v. JTI-Macdonald Corp., [2007] 2 S.C.R. 610, 621 (Can.) ("Governments around the world are implementing anti-tobacco measures similar to and, in some cases, more restrictive than Canada's. The *WHO Framework Convention on Tobacco Control*... mandates a comprehensive ban on tobacco promotion, subject to state constitutional requirements... Domestically, governments now widely accept that protecting the public from second-hand smoke is a legitimate policy objective."); *BATSA v Minister of Health* (463/2011) [2012] ZASCA 107; [2012] (20 June 2012) at 13–14 ¶ 23 (S. Afr.) ("I do not think that it was open to the Minister and the legislature to ignore the Framework Convention when considering what steps to take to deal with the risks posed by tobacco use....This Court is therefore obliged, under the Constitution, to give weight to it in determining the question of justification or the limitation of the right to freedom of speech.").

240 For WTO disputes, see, for example, the WTO's summaries of DS441, *at* https://www.wto.org/english/tratop_e/dispu_e/cases_e/ds441_e.htm; DS467, *at* https://www.wto.org/english/tratop_e/dispu_e/cases_e/ds467_e.htm; & DS548, *at* https://www.wto.org/english/tratop_e/dispu_e/cases_e/ds458_e.htm. For investor-state disputes, see, for example, Philip Morris Asia Limited v. Australia, UNCITRAL, PCA Case No. 2012–12; Philip Morris Brands Sàrl v. Uruguay, ICSID Case No. ARB/10/7 (2010).

an expert body, the INB held five sessions between 2008 and 2012 attended by a large number of FCTC parties as well as representatives of civil society.[241] The COP adopted the Protocol to Eliminate Illicit Trade in Tobacco Products on November 12, 2012. The FCTC Protocol, which was open for signature on Jan. 10, 2013, had gathered 54 signatories but only 11 parties as of November 11, 2015;[242] it requires 40 states to enter into force.[243]

As indicated in its preamble, the Protocol, which is, of course, a treaty in its own right (albeit one limited to FCTC parties), stresses that illicit trade (that is production, shipment, possession, distribution, sale or purchase of tobacco products that are prohibited by law)[244] "undermines price and tax measures, designed to strengthen tobacco control...."[245] It also buttresses the need to address this topic by indicating that illicit trade, because it increases the accessibility and affordability of tobacco, has a disparate impact on younger and poor smokers, causes a loss of revenue to states, and is connected to transnational crime. As Jonathan Liberman has noted, the Protocol is "essentially a customs and law enforcement treaty born into a health institution."[246] Its key elements include establishing supply chain control mechanisms to better enable tracking of the supply chain and of suspicious transactions, requirements to make certain conduct unlawful or criminal, and establishing procedures for international cooperation with respect to the sharing of information on all the above.[247]

Notably, even though the criminal offenses intended to be reached by this Protocol overlap to some extent with the UN Convention Against Transnational Organized Crime (UNTOC),[248] the Protocol does not include a definitive list of the international crimes that its parties are agreeing to implement into

---

241   See FCTC website, Negotiations of the Protocol to Eliminate Illicit Trade in Tobacco Products, *at* http://www.who.int/fctc/protocol/about/inb/en/.

242   See United Nations Treaty Collection, *at* https://treaties.un.org/pages/ViewDetails .aspx?src=TREATY&mtdsg_no=IX-4-a&chapter=9&lang=en.

243   Protocol to Eliminate Illicit Trade in Tobacco Products [hereinafter FCTC Protocol] art. 45.1, Nov. 12, 2012, *at* http://apps.who.int/iris/bitstream/10665/80873/1/9789241505246_ eng.pdf?ua=1.

244   *Id.* art. 1.6 (Use of Terms).

245   *Id.* pmbl.

246   Jonathan Liberman, *The New WHO FCTC Protocol to Eliminate Illicit Trade in Tobacco Products—Challenges Ahead*, 16 ASIL INSIGHTS (Dec. 14, 2012), *at* http://www.asil.org/ sites/default/files/insight121214.pdf.

247   *Id.*

248   United Nations Convention against Transnational Organized Crime, Nov. 15, 2000, 40 I.L.M. 335 (2001). *See also* Gian Luca Burci, *Introductory Note to the Protocol to Eliminate*

their national law and enforce internationally. While an earlier draft of its text included a uniform agreed listing of core crimes, the revised text accords parties discretion to decide which of the many forms of conduct related to illicit trade in tobacco products should be treated as merely "unlawful," and which need to be treated as criminal offenses under national law.[249]

As Liberman points out, it remains to be seen how the WHO will implement this FCTC Protocol, should it come into force, within a dense governance field involving a number of related multilateral criminal conventions as well as the World Customs Organization, the International Criminal Police Organization (INTERPOL), the EU, and the UN Office on Drugs and Crime.[250] This may prove exceptionally challenging for the WHO because at least some of the other organizations, such as INTERPOL, engage with, expect close cooperation with, and even accept contributions from, the tobacco industry—a clear point of contention with respect to the FCTC, whose Article 5.3 and relevant Guidelines strongly discourage or ban such associations.[251] Indeed, to the extent the Protocol encourages its parties to treat counterfeit cigarettes, for example, as unlawful or even criminal offenses, it can be seen "as an instrument to enforce the intellectual property rights of the tobacco industry."[252] There is considerable irony if the first treaty adopted under the FCTC ends up treating its *bête noire*, the global tobacco industry, as a stakeholder.

While the FCTC is a work in progress, there are indications that it is achieving greater compliance than is the case with respect to the WHO's implementation of the IHRs. According to the 2014 FCTC Global Progress Report, implementation of the FCTC has progressed steadily since 2005.[253] The average implementation rate of its substantive articles approaches 60% (compared to over 50% in 2010), with 80% of the parties strengthening their existing

    Illicit Trade in Tobacco Products to the WHO Framework Convention on Tobacco Control, 52 I.L.M. 365, 366 (2013).

249 FCTC Protocol, *supra* note 243, art. 14.2 (providing that states shall "subject to its basic principles of domestic law, determine which of the unlawful conduct set out in [Art. 14.1] or any other conduct related to illicit trade in tobacco ... shall be criminal offences.").

250 Liberman, *supra* note 246.

251 *Id.*

252 Burci, *supra* note 248, at 367. This may explain why both Philip Morris International and British American Tobacco welcomed the adoption of the FCTC Protocol. *See, e.g.,* Liberman, *supra* note 246.

253 FCTC Secretariat, 2014 Global Progress Report on Implementation of the WHO Framework Convention on Tobacco Control, *at* http://www.who.int/fctc/reporting/2014globalprogres sreport.pdf?ua=1 [hereinafter 2014 Global Progress Report], at vii.

tobacco control laws after ratifying the FCTC.[254] Unlike comparable WHO reports on the IHRs, that report indicates progress over time with respect to the number of parties responding to implementation questionnaires and a steady increase in the average rate of implementation of comprehensive national strategies over time (from 49% in 2010, 59% in 2012, to 68% in 2014).[255] Most FCTC parties (113) reported in 2014 that they had established the required national focal point and two thirds had established a tobacco-control unit.[256] Progress over time was especially notable with respect to adoption of measures to prevent second-hand smoke, prevention of sales to minors, bans on tobacco advertising, and limitations on promotion and sponsorship; those FCTC provisions with specific timelines for implementation also showed relatively high levels of implementation.[257] That report also indicates considerable progress in many countries with respect to implementing the specific measures recommended in the FCTC guidelines, including those on Article 5.3.[258]

At the same time, the FCTC reports challenges to implementation that echo those facing implementation of the 2005 IHRs. As with respect to the latter, the lack of human and financial resources is a recurrent theme, as is the resistance of many legislators (in this instance due in part to the enormous clout of the tobacco industry).[259] As with respect to the IHRs, there is also considerable unevenness with respect to the level of implementation across distinct provisions of the treaty, with the level of implementation dropping off substantially when it comes to, for example, state measures to impose liability on tobacco manufacturers or efforts to support alternatives to tobacco farming.[260] There is also no guarantee that states will implement a measure merely because it is recommended in a FCTC Guideline.[261] More generally, one cannot be too sanguine about the progress of the FCTC when, despite its provisions and

---

254   *Id.* at vii and fig. 2.2.

255   *Id.* §§ 1, 3.1.

256   *Id.* § 3.1.

257   *Id.* § 2 ("Time-bound measures"). *See also id.* figs. 3.3., 3.9, 3.14.

258   *See, e.g., id.* § 2 ("Strong achievements and innovative approaches"), § 3.1.

259   *Id.* § 2 ("Priorities, needs and gaps, challenges and barriers to implementation"). *See generally* Townsend et al., *supra* note 189, at 190–192 (2012) (discussing the financial challenges facing developing countries seeking to implement the FCTC).

260   2014 Global Progress Report, *supra* note 253, fig. 2.1.

261   Thus, the 2014 Global Progress Report indicates that, despite a clear trend toward very large pictorial warnings on cigarettes, less than half of the reporting parties include warning labels that cover 50% or more of the display areas on the outside packaging of

Guidelines banning government association with the industry, the FCTC's own Guidelines on point tiptoe around the delicate problem of state-owned tobacco companies (such as China's) or the reliance by other governments on the vested interests of "Big Tobacco."[262] Another problem with drawing firm conclusions about the FCTC's relative "success" in implementation, whatever its implementation reports say, is an endemic cause-effect problem. As with respect to many multilateral treaties that are strongly supported by powerful Western states and that reflect national laws and practices already in existence in such states, it may be difficult to prove that the adoption of the treaty—or adoption of guidelines under it—instigated or caused high rates of domestic implementation. This is certainly not true of a state like Canada, whose existing tobacco control measures were highly influential on those ultimately incorporated in the FCTC,[263] but cause and effect may prove equally difficult to demonstrate in other cases, as where a state adopts tobacco control measures due to domestic or international pressure not connected to the FCTC or the WHO at all.

5   The WHO in Larger Context

The contemporary WHO is an organization that, like many others, has engaged in "mission creep."[264] Today's WHO has expanded its mission to encompass trade, intellectual property, peace and security, and human rights. Its 2005 IHRs engage the general health policies of nations and not merely their border controls over infectious diseases. Its first treaty, the FCTC, wrestles with long-debated questions concerning the proper scope of government power over private as well as public spaces and concerns itself with questions such

---

tobacco products. *Id.* § 2 ("Time-bound measures," "Strong achievements and innovative approaches").

262   *See, e.g.*, Article 5.3 Guidelines, *supra* note 223, ¶ 30 (Recommendation 8) (urging states to treat state-owned tobacco industries the same way they treat others). *See generally* Townsend et al., *supra* note 259, at 192–94 (discussing the influence on governments of the "vested interests" of the tobacco industry). Of course, to the extent governments gain income from the excise or other taxes imposed on (and encouraged by the FCTC) on tobacco, this too may undermine their interest in achieving the "tobacco-free societies" sought by the FCTC.

263   *See, e.g.*, Anne M. Lavack & Gina Clark, *Responding to the Global Tobacco Industry: Canada and the Framework Convention on Tobacco Control*, 50 CAN. PUB. ADMIN. 100 (2007).

264   *See generally* Jessica Einhorn, *The World Bank's Mission Creep*, 80 FOREIGN AFFAIRS 22 (2001).

as whether a privately owned shopping mall, restaurant, or any other place of public accommodation should ban smoking. That treaty and its ever-growing Guidelines intrude on the decisions of government officials at every level— from those serving on town councils to Presidents. To the extent the WHO adopts certain "democratization" proposals now being seriously considered,[265] that organization may soon be telling governments the types of stakeholders it needs to consult, when to do so, and with respect to which "health" issues. Fidler's "medical-technical" association is adapting the disease model that led to the eradication of smallpox to achieve the eradication of smoking. But that medical-technical group of experts is also expanding its expertise to tell media conglomerates the kind of advertising it should accept, sports teams the kinds of promotional support they can receive, and, of course, the public where and when it can smoke. Depending on the fate of the FCTC Protocol and the progress made on advancing the liability provisions of Article 19 of the FCTC, the WHO soon may be telling courts the types of civil and criminal liability they can impose. It is also inching closer to becoming an *aide de camp* to the P-5 if its officials (its Director-General and Emergency Committee) think that they need the enforcement credibility provided by the Security Council's Chapter VII authority in some cases.

The WHO's expansion of its mandate is not, of course, unique. Scholars of international organizations know that many intergovernmental organizations, including virtually all UN specialized agencies, have expanded their missions. Indeed, this phenomenon is an important reason why IOs and other international regimes are increasingly interacting with one another to address "regime complexes" that deal with, for example, the handling of plant genetic resources, rather than focusing on one organization or treaty regime.[266]

Consider the expanding mandate of another UN Specialized Agency, the International Civil Aviation Organization (ICAO). That association of a com-

---

265   *See supra* § 3.

266   Kal Raustiala & David G. Victor, *The Regime Complex for Plant Genetic Resources*, 58 INT'L ORG. 277 (2004). *See* Kal Raustiala, *Institutional Proliferation and the International Legal Order, in* INTERDISCIPLINARY PERSPECTIVES ON INTERNATIONAL LAW AND INTERNATIONAL RELATIONS: THE STATE OF THE ART 293, 300–301 (Jeffrey L. Dunoff & Mark A. Pollack eds., 2012). *See also* GOSTIN, GLOBAL HEALTH LAW, *supra* note 13, at 295–297 (describing the interaction of the IHRs and the Framework Convention on Tobacco Control with the trade regime); David P. Fidler, *The Challenges of Global Health Governance* (Council of Foreign Relations, Working Paper, 2010), *at* http://mercury.ethz .ch/serviceengine/Files/ISN/117105/ipublicationdocument_singledocument/4e384b66-04e9-4d23-a8dc-9f309a53253d/en/IIGG_WorkingPaper4_GlobalHealth.pdf (describing the current regime complex for global health governance).

parably narrow group of technical experts, in this instance aviation experts and aeronautical engineers, was supposed to focus on making international air transport services "safe and orderly."[267] Today, ICAO presides over a regulatory scheme consisting of Standards and Recommended Practices (SARPs) with 18 annexes that address, among things, environmental concerns (such as aircraft noise),[268] peace and security matters (such as requirements for machine-readable passports, passenger and luggage screening, and procedures for search and rescue),[269] trade and financial issues (such as the safe transport of certain goods and access to aviation facilities),[270] civil liability (such as the proper procedures for accident investigation),[271] and labor (such as the licensing and responsibility of pilots).[272] A number of SARPs relate to the spread of communicable disease through the aviation sector, including Annex 6 (operation of aircraft) and Annex 11 (which includes recommended on-board medical supplies); Annexes 11 (on air traffic services) and 14 (airports) were adjusted in light of the 2005 IHRs to incorporate the potential of a PHEIC in states' emergency plans.

ICAO also shares with WHO another characteristic: its regulatory activity, like the WHO's, blurs the line between legally binding and non-binding standards. Indeed, international aviation experts have long debated whether there is a difference, in this respect, between an ICAO "standard" and a mere "recommended practice." Their confusion is not surprising given the cryptic language of ICAO's Convention on point. Article 37 states that each ICAO member "undertakes to collaborate in securing the highest practicable degree of uniformity in regulations, standards, procedures ... in all matters in which such uniformity will facilitate and improve air navigation."[273] It thereby authorizes ICAO to adopt as may be necessary international standards and recommended practices on a wide number of matters but does not indicate their legal status. Article 38 only indicates that a member that finds it "impracticable to comply in all respects with any such international standard or procedure, or to

---

267   Convention on International Civil Aviation ("Chicago Convention"), Preamble, Dec. 7, 1944, 15 U.N.T.S. 295[hereinafter ICAO Convention]; *see also id.* art. 44(a).

268   International Civil Aviation Organization, Standards and Recommended Practices, Annex 16 ("Environmental Protection"). Annexes 1 through 18 are available *at* http://www .icao.int/safety/airnavigation/nationalitymarks/annexes_booklet_en.pdf.

269   *Id.* Annex 9 ("Facilitation"), Annex 17 ("Security: Safeguarding International Civil Aviation against Acts of Unlawful Interference"), Annex 12 ("Search and Rescue").

270   *See, e.g., id.* Annexes 6–8, 18.

271   *Id.* Annex 13.

272   *Id.* Annex 1.

273   ICAO Convention, *supra* note 267, art. 37.

bring its own regulations or practices into full accord . . . shall give immediate notification" to ICAO.[274] This provision resembles the opting out article in the WHO's Constitution with respect to WHO regulations discussed above,[275] except that it appears that ICAO has chosen not to presume agreement or compliance with its SARPs if it does not receive a notice from a ICAO contracting state.[276] While some of ICAO's internal documents suggest that only standards are binding, it is not clear that ICAO members or other stakeholders have acted as if there was any such clear distinction between a standard and a recommendation.[277] One of the leading commentators on ICAO, former ICJ Judge Thomas Buergenthal, has argued that the ambiguity concerning the legal status of SARPs is desirable and constitutes an improvement over the pre-ICAO regime. Under that scheme, as he explains, international aviation rules set by treaty, though clearly binding, did not gain the near universal participation desired to advance the harmonious rules that all agreed were necessary.[278]

As with the WHO, much of ICAO's "governance" activity comes in the form of guidelines issuable to ICAO members. These include, for example, ICAO Guidelines for States Concerning the Management of Communicable Disease Posing a Serious Public Health Risk.[279] These Guidelines are clearly inspired by the 2005 IHRs and include, under "general preparedness," recommendations that states establish a national aviation preparedness plan, with a clear contact point that provides a "reliable system for informing the public health authority of the pending arrival of a suspected case of a communicable disease."[280] ICAO

---

274   *Id.* art. 38.

275   *See* § 1 *supra.*

276   Frederic L. Kirgis, International Organizations in Their Legal Setting 261 (2d ed. 1993).

277   Thus, the ICAO Assembly has said that a standard is a rule that is regarded as "necessary" and "to which Contracting States will conform in accordance with the Convention," while a recommendation is a rule whose uniform application is "desirable" and to which Contracting States "will endeavor to conform." ICAO Assembly Res. A27-10, Appendix A, *in* Resolutions Adopted by the Assembly and Index to Documentation, 27th Sess., ICAO Doc. 9551, A27-RES, at 52 (1989). *But see* Kirgis, *supra* note 276, at 307–308 (summarizing the positions of commentators taking different views on the legal status of ICAO standards and recommendations).

278   Thomas Buergenthal, Law-Making in the International Civil Aviation Organization 119–122 (1969).

279   ICAO, *Guidelines for States Concerning the Management of Communicable Disease Posing a Serious Public Health Risk, at* http://www.icao.int/safety/aviation-medicine/guidelines/AvInfluenza_guidelines.pdf.

280   *Id.*

has also cooperated with the WHO in other respects. After excessive travel restrictions imposed by states in the wake of the H1N1 scare, the ICAO Council adopted a declaration emphasizing that aviation-related measures taken by ICAO members should be proportionate, non-discriminatory, and limited to health risks.[281]

As with the WHO, ICAO's approach to making and enforcing norms seems principally managerial. While the ICAO Convention, like the WHO's, permits contracting states to submit their aviation disputes to binding adjudication, this rarely occurs.[282] The enforcement of international aviation law relies, for the most part, not on actions taken by any court, national or international, but on the technical assistance, guidelines, and other tools of persuasion or socialization that reliance on "expertize" tends to generate. Yet resort to these "soft" tools should not be equated with the absence of implementation. The evidence that we have suggests that ICAO's SARPs achieve relatively high levels of state compliance and national implementation. This may be due to a number of factors, including the high level of self-interest states have in compliance, that ICAO rules are often incorporated by reference into national law or other treaties, and the routinized application of ICAO standards by market actors (such as airlines) which also have a strong economic interest in compliance.[283] As with respect to the WHO's IHRs and the obligations in the FCTC, the compliance and implementation efforts of ICAO rely on self-reporting by states and the resulting "mobilization of shame" imposed on states through the organization's own efforts. In the case of ICAO, these include, for example, safety audits, ICAO Council reports of members' infractions, or Council condemnations (such as in the use of force incidents noted below).[284] The managerial

---

281   See ICAO, *Annual Report of the Council: 2009*, 61, Doc. 9921 (2010). The report also includes discussion of ICAO-provided technical assistance provided to assist implementation of a harmonized regional and international approach for preparedness planning in the aviation sector to deal with the prevention of the spread of communicable diseases.

282   ICAO Convention, *supra* note 267, arts. 84–85. For some of the rare occasions when formal adjudication has occurred, see, for example, KIRGIS, *supra* note 276, at 443–468.

283   See generally Paul Stephen Dempsey, *Compliance and Enforcement in International Law: Achieving Global Uniformity in Aviation Safety*, 30 N.C.J. INT'L L. & COM. REG. 1 (2004). Note that market actors need to have ICAO-issued certificates of air worthiness under Art. 39 of the ICAO Convention. For an example of incorporation into a bilateral treaty, see, for example, Civil Aviation Security Agreement, U.S.-Cape Verde, Oct. 11, 1989, Art. III, TIAS 11705 (incorporating ICAO aviation security provisions by reference).

284   *See, e.g.*, ICAO Convention, *supra* note 267, art. 54(j) (permitting the Council to report infractions); Dempsey, *Compliance and Enforcement, supra* note 283, at 35 (commenting on Council audit procedures).

quality of ICAO SARPS—the "softness" of ICAO law—has also not prevented some scholars from suggesting that the aviation safety oversight function is now among the most fundamental responsibilities owed by states individually and collectively.[285]

This does not mean that ICAO does not rely on traditional tools of hard law, like treaties. While ICAO has not become a "treaty-machine" like the ILO, which has served as the venue for no less than 189 conventions and 6 protocols since 1919,[286] it has engaged in treaty-making on far more occasions than has the

---

285   See, e.g., Huang Jiefang, Aviation Safety, ICAO and Obligations Erga Omnes, 8 CHINESE J.
      INT'L L. 63 (2009).
286   As of July 2015, the ILO had adopted 189 Conventions, 6 Protocols to existing
      Conventions, and 204 Recommendations. See ILO, at http://www.ilo.org/dyn/normlex/
      en/f?p=NORMLEXPUB:1:0::NO::: (last visited Nov. 15, 2015). Many ILO recommendations
      are intended to serve functions that are comparable to those of the WHO's guidelines. ILO
      recommendations are often intended to be read alongside particular ILO conventions, to
      provide ILO treaty ratifiers greater context or detail with respect to the treaty obligations
      that they have assumed; ILO recommendations may also be intended to provide hortatory
      guidance even to non-ratifiers, perhaps with the intent of blazing a trail in favor of even-
      tual ratification. See generally KIRGIS, supra note 276, at 276–292. The ILO has used peri-
      odic Declarations, issued by the International Labor Conference or its Governing Body,
      to proclaim general principles and values for the organization as a whole. While neither
      ILO recommendations nor declarations are legally binding, these instruments have some-
      times had a greater normative significance for the organization and for international
      labor law generally than many of the ILO Conventions (some of which have not gathered
      widespread ratifications). The Declaration of Philadelphia (1944) is widely considered to
      have become a kind of de facto amendment to the ILO's original 1919 Constitution insofar
      as it emphasized the human rights nature of that organization, particularly with respect
      to elevating the freedom of association and expression. Constitution of the ILO, Annex,
      June 28, 1919, 15 U.N.T.S. 35; see, e.g., Eddy Lee, The Declaration of Philadelphia: Retrospect
      and Prospect, 133 INT'L LAB. REV. 467 (1994); Joseph Sulkowski, The Competence of the
      International Labor Organization Under the United Nations System, 45 AM. J. INT'L L. 286
      (1951). The Governing Board's Tripartite Declaration of Principles Concerning Multilateral
      Enterprises and Social Policy, from 1977, a voluntary code between governments, employ-
      ers and workers (the three interests represented in ILO organs), intended to guide mul-
      tinational business enterprises in applying international labor standards, has had a
      major influence on other efforts to clarify the relationship between MNCs and human
      rights, including on principles adopted by the UN General Assembly. See, e.g. Special
      Representative of the Secretary-General on the Issue of Human Rights and Transnational
      Corporations and Other Business Enterprises, Guiding Principles on Business and Human
      Rights: Implementing the United Nations "Protect, Respect and Remedy" Framework, U.N.
      Doc. A/HRC/17/31 (Mar. 21, 2011) (by John Ruggie), at http://www.ohchr.org/Documents/

WHO. Indeed, its treaty-making role helps to explain how ICAO transformed itself into a counter-terrorism security organization long before the WHO. When aircraft hijackings became a prominent feature of the international landscape in the 1970s, ICAO became the favored venue for negotiating what are now roughly a dozen aviation-related counter-terrorism conventions that enable the criminal prosecution or extradition of those who pose threats to planes or international airports.[287] Given the lengthy and, to date, inconclusive efforts at the UN General Assembly to negotiate a comprehensive convention against terrorism,[288] it is no surprise that states turned to the more technocratic, safety-oriented ICAO as the more promising place to conclude counter-terrorism conventions (albeit only those with a direct connection to aviation).

Today, ICAO continues to be a favored place to negotiate or amend international treaties deemed useful to the global "war" on terror. It was, for example, the venue for the negotiation of the Beijing Convention on the Suppression of Unlawful Acts Relating to International Civil Aviation.[289] That Convention, which builds on prior ICAO conventions on point, is a significant complement to Security Council Res. 1540 on weapons of mass destruction discussed

---

Issues/Business/A-HRC-17-31_AEV.pdf; Laurie E. Abbott, *Integrating the Ruggie Guiding Principles Into the International Economic Community*, 5 GEO. MASON J. INT'L & COMP. L. 261 (2014) (discussing, *inter alia*, the relationship between the Tripartite Declaration of Principles and the "Ruggie Principles"). A third example, the ILO declaration on Fundamental Principles and Rights at Work, from 1998, emphasized the importance of four core labor rights and suggests that the eight ILO Conventions that protect them are "fundamental." That Declaration is an important part of the ILO's tools to enhance monitoring and compliance. *See, e.g.*, Laurence R. Helfer, *Monitoring Compliance with Unratified Treaties: The ILO Experience*, 71 LAW & CONTEMP. PROBL. 193 (2008) (discussing ILO grants of authority to secure compliance even with respect to some unratified ILO conventions).

287 *See, e.g.*, Convention for the Suppression of Unlawful Seizure of Aircraft, Dec. 16, 1970, 860 U.N.T.S. 105; Convention for the Suppression of Unlawful Acts Against the Safety of Civil Aviation, Sept. 23, 1971, 974 U.N.T.S. 177; *see also* Paul Stephen Dempsey, *Aviation Security: The Role of Law in the War Against Terrorism*, 41 COLUM. J. TRANSNAT'L L. 649 (2003); Michael Jennison, *The Beijing Treaties of 2010: Building a "Modern Great Wall" Against Aviation-Related Terrorism*, 23 AIR & SPACE LAW. 9 (2011) (describing the development of the *aut dedere aut judicare* principal in ICAO conventions).

288 *See, e.g.*, G.A. Res. 67/99 (Dec. 14, 2012) (recommending the establishment of a working group to finalize a draft convention on international terrorism and recalling previous efforts at developing international legal instruments).

289 Convention on the Suppression of Unlawful Acts Relating to International Civil Aviation, *adopted* Sept. 10, 2010, DCAS Doc. No. 21 [hereinafter Beijing Convention].

in Chapter ɪɪ. It criminalizes the acts of using civil aviation for the purpose of causing death, serious bodily injury, or serious damage; using such aircraft to release or discharge any biological, chemical or nuclear (ʙᴄɴ) weapon to cause such harm; or using any ʙᴄɴ weapon on board or against civil aircraft.[290]

In addition, the ɪᴄᴀᴏ Council has condemned the use of force against civilian aircraft with respect to three high profile and highly politicized incidents: the Soviet's use of armed force against ᴋᴀʟ Flight 007 in 1983, the ᴜ.s. Vincennes' attack against Iran Air Flight 655 in 1988, and the destruction over Ukraine of Malaysia Flight MH17 in July 2014.[291] The first of these incidents led to a precedent-setting amendment, Article 3bis, to the ɪᴄᴀᴏ Convention.[292] Under Article 3bis ɪᴄᴀᴏ members "recognize that every States must refrain from resorting to the use of weapons against civil aircraft in flight and that, in case of interception, the lives of persons on board and the safety of aircraft must not be endangered."[293] Although the text of that amendment states that it "shall not be interpreted as modifying in any way the rights and obligations of States set forth in the Charter of the United Nations,"[294] Article 3bis has certainly alleviated doubts that the prohibition on use of force in Article 2(4) applies equally to civil aircraft.[295] The more recent aircraft incident over Ukraine led to a failed proposal at the ᴜɴ Security Council to establish an *ad hoc* tribunal (comparable to the Tribunal for Lebanon) to determine whether

---

290 *Id.* art. 1.

291 *See* ɪᴄᴀᴏ Council Resolution on Korean Airliner Incident, Mar. 6, 1984, 23 ɪʟᴍ 937 (1984); ɪᴄᴀᴏ Council Resolution on Iran Airbus Incident, Mar. 17, 1989, 28 ɪʟᴍ 898 (1989); ɪᴄᴀᴏ Council Resolution on Malaysia Airlines Flight MH17, Destroyed over Eastern Ukraine on 17 July 2014 (2014), *at* http://www.icao.int/Newsroom/NewsDoc2014/COUNCIL%20 RESOLUTION%20ON%20MALAYSIA%20AIRLINES%20FLIGHT%20MH17.pdf. *See also* S.C. Res. 2166 (July 21, 2014); ɪᴄᴀᴏ, ɪᴀᴛᴀ, ᴀᴄɪ, ᴄᴀɴsᴏ, Joint Statement on Risks to Civil Aviation Arising from Conflict Zones (July 29, 2014), *at* http://www.icao.int/newsroom/ pages/joint-statement-on-risks-to-civil-aviation-arising-from-conflict-zones.aspx (announcing Task Force to address civil aviation and national security and an ɪᴄᴀᴏ High-Level Safety Conference).

292 ɪᴄᴀᴏ Convention, *supra* note 267, art. 3bis (entered into force Oct. 1, 1988). For background on the ɪᴄᴀᴏ involvement with these incidents, including investigations of them under Art. 26 of the ɪᴄᴀᴏ Convention and sᴀʀᴘ Annex 13, see, for example, ᴋɪʀɢɪs, *supra* note 276, at 469–478.

293 ɪᴄᴀᴏ Convention, *supra* note 267, art. 3bis.

294 *Id.*

295 *See, e.g.,* Eric Edward Geiser, *The Fog of Peace: The Use of Weapons Against Aircraft in Flight During Peacetime,* 4 J. Iɴᴛ'ʟ Lᴇɢᴀʟ Sᴛᴜᴅ. 187 (1998).

crimes were committed.[296] These examples, as well as many others involving ICAO, suggest that, as with the WHO, it is probably unwise to dismiss that "technocratic" organization as one that achieves cooperation merely because it does not deal with "high politics."

The phenomenon of expanding institutional mandates is not limited to the UN, ICAO, and the WHO. As is well known, the World Bank and the International Monetary Fund (IMF) have also assumed many roles not envisioned by their creators. The World Bank, originally established to provide the financing for infrastructure projects in parts of Europe devastated by World War II, has become a multi-purpose development organization whose operational standards and procedures include guidance on such highly political or sensitive topics as the rights of indigenous peoples.[297] Bank standards and procedures deal, in ever more granular fashion, with a variety of government policies exposed to ever higher levels of transparency, the better to enable NGOs to complain either to host governments of Bank projects or the Bank about problems with particular development projects.[298] Like the WHO and ICAO, it too has become, in part, an environmental organization; indeed, the Bank now requires detailed environmental assessments prior to undertaking a project and has released detailed guidelines on what these assessments must

---

296   *See* Press Release, United Nations, Security Council Fails to Adopt Resolution on Tribunal for Malaysia Airlines Crash in Ukraine, Amid Calls for Accountability, Justice for Victims (July 29, 2015) (reporting that the draft resolution received 11 affirmative votes, 3 abstentions (Angola, China, and Venezuela), and one negative vote (Russia)).

297   *See* World Bank, Operational Manual, Operational Policy (OP) 4.10 (Indigenous Peoples), *at* http://web.worldbank.org/WBSITE/EXTERNAL/PROJECTS/EXTPOLICIES/EXTOPM ANUAL/0,,contentMDK:20553653~menuPK:4564185~pagePK:64709096~piPK:64709108 ~theSitePK:502184,00.html. The World Bank's policies might be compared to the rights contained in the ILO's Indigenous and Tribal Peoples Convention (International Labour Organization Convention, No. 169), June 27, 1989, *at* http://www.ilo.org/dyn/normlex/ en/f?p=NORMLEXPUB:12100:0::NO::P12100_ILO_CODE:C169. *See generally* Benedict Kingsbury, *Operational Policies of International Institutions as Part of the Law-Making Process: The World Bank and Indigenous Peoples, in* THE REALITY OF INTERNATIONAL LAW: ESSAYS IN HONOUR OF IAN BROWNLIE 323 (Guy S. Goodwin-Gill & Stefan Talmon eds., 1999); Galit A. Sarfaty, *The World Bank and the Internalization of Indigenous Rights Norms*, 114 YALE L.J. 1791 (2004).

298   *See generally* Laurence Boisson de Chazournes, *Policy Guidance and Compliance: The World Bank Operational Standards, in* COMMITMENT AND COMPLIANCE: THE ROLE OF NON-BINDING NORMS IN THE INTERNATIONAL LEGAL SYSTEM 281 (Dinah Shelton ed., 2000).

contain.[299] It is partly a human rights organization—but also one that, like the WHO, draws criticisms that it has not gone nearly far enough in that direction.[300]

The World Bank, along with the IMF, which was originally established to assist with fixed exchange rates, have become, along with the UN, ICAO, and the WHO, yet another set of institutional agents to promote and implement the "rule of law" in nation states. All are "good governance" institutions that are central pillars for those who study global administrative law.[301] Key governance Bank activities encompass requirements for financial practices that protect the Bank's resources, including rules for transparency and regulations consistent with democratic rule of law states seen as capable of detecting and penalizing corruption.[302] But the World Bank's activities today embrace reform agendas for recipients of its funds not mentioned in its Articles of Agreement that bear only an indirect connection to protecting Bank resources such as poverty reduction, population control, education and health promotion, the construction or protection of social safety nets, appropriate privatization procedures, general regulatory (as well as specific civil service) reforms, and judicial training.[303] It has also expanded its mission from project finance to include structural and sectoral adjustment programs, emergency recovery loans, hybrid loans that cover both adjustment and investment, free-standing environmental loans, debt service reduction loans, institutional reform loans,

299 See, e.g., World Bank, Operational Manual, OP 4.01 (Environmental Assessments), at http://web.worldbank.org/WBSITE/EXTERNAL/PROJECTS/EXTPOLICIES/EXTOPMAN UAL/0,,contentMDK:20064724~menuPK:64701637~pagePK:64709096~piPK:64709108~th eSitePK:502184,00.html.

300 For a discussion of how human rights considerations have penetrated the operational procedures of the World Bank and the IMF, see Laurence Boisson de Chazournes, *The Bretton Woods Institutions and Human Rights: Converging Tendencies, in* ECONOMIC GLOBALISATION AND HUMAN RIGHTS 210 (Wolfgang Benedek et al. eds., 2007). *See also* ALVAREZ, *supra* note 155, at 328; Roberto Dañino, *The Legal Aspects of the World Bank's Work on Human Rights: Some Preliminary Thoughts, in* HUMAN RIGHTS AND DEVELOPMENT: TOWARDS MUTUAL REINFORCEMENT 509 (Philip Alston & Mary Robinson eds., 2005). *But see* Galit A. Sarfaty, *Why Culture Matters in International Institutions: The Marginality of Human Rights at the World Bank*, 103 AM. J. INT'L L. 647 (2009).

301 *See generally* Benedict Kingsbury, Nico Krisch & Richard B. Stewart, *The Emergence of Global Administrative Law*, 68 L. & CONTEMP. PROBS. 15 (2005).

302 For a general introduction to the Bank's anti-corruption policies and practices, see Stuart H. Deming, *Anti-Corruption Policies: Eligibility and Debarment Practices at the World Bank and Regional Development Banks*, 44 INT'L LAW. 871 (2010).

303 *See generally* World Bank, Annual Report (2015), *at* http://www.worldbank.org/en/about/annual-report (describing scope of Bank's activities).

and economic reconstruction loans. The Bank now addresses a broad gamut of topics such as biodiversity, the rights of indigenous peoples, child labor, coastal and marine management, food security, varied environmental issues, poverty, disease and epidemics, education, tsunami and other natural disaster emergency relief, post-conflict reconstruction, money laundering, and terrorist financing.[304] Given this sweeping agenda, it too needs to interact (as do the WHO and ICAO) with numerous other IOs, including the Security Council (as in post conflict Iraq). Indeed, some scholars suggest that the Security Council has become an institutional enabler of the Bank's (and the IMF's) ever expanding mission creep since it has used both to advance its goals in Iraq, Afghanistan, and Kosovo.[305]

As with respect to other institutional products discussed here, the World Bank's legal tools do not fit comfortably within the traditional positivist sources of law: treaty, custom, or general principles. Some of the Bank's normative tools resemble ICAO's SARPs or the WHO's "soft law." The Bank's operational standards and practices are, for example, formally directed only at an internal audience. They instruct Bank's officials on how to do their job. But, as a number of commentators have suggested, many of these standards have a much wider normative bite and are having an impact on, for example, the human rights that might be owed to indigenous peoples, or the environmental assessments and notification and surveillance that states may owe one another under international environmental law.[306] Another group of scholars are now discussing the "governance" aspects of another one of the Bank's tools: the regularly updated rule of law indices issued by its International Finance Corporation (IFC).[307]

The IMF's most prominent "regulatory" tools are, of course, the conditions that it attaches to loans extended to countries. As is well known, IMF conditionality has been known to make highly intrusive and politically sensitive demands on those who receive IMF funds, including severe zero-deficit

---

304   *Id.*; *see also* Topics, World Bank (2015), *at* http://www.worldbank.org/en/topic.

305   *See, e.g.,* Kristen E. Boon, *Open for Business: International Financial Institutions, Post-Conflict Economic Reform and the Rule of Law,* 9 NYU J. INT'L L. AND POL. 513 (2007).

306   *See, e.g.,* Kingsbury, *supra* note 297; de Chazournes, *supra* note 298.

307   International Finance Corporation, World Bank, *Doing Business Report 2015: Going Beyond Efficiency* (2014), *at* http://www.doingbusiness.org/reports/global-reports/doing-business-2015. *See* GOVERNANCE BY INDICATORS: GLOBAL POWER THROUGH QUANTIFICATION AND RANKINGS (Kevin E. Davis, Angelina Fisher, Benedict Kingsbury & Sally Engle Merry eds., 2012); THE QUIET POWER OF INDICATORS: MEASURING GOVERNANCE, CORRUPTION AND RULE OF LAW (Sally Engle Merry, Kevin E. Davis & Benedict Kingsbury eds., 2015).

austerity demands on government budgets, the de-regulation of crucial sectors, reforms in the banking sector, and insistence that state-run industries be privatized.[308] The nature of IMF arrangements with states has led to controversy. Commentators are not in agreement about whether these agreements should be treated as mere contracts, state contracts that should be subject to *pact sunt servanda* no less than treaties, or treaties by another name.[309] But such positivist concerns seem less important than recognizing that IMF conditionality is itself a form of governance or law-making, whether or not it fits easily into Article 38 sources of law.

The IMF's approach to law-making or governance is a familiar one in places like the United States where, if the federal government wants to impose a rule on one of the fifty states of the U.S., it may resort to federal legislation (which may mean preempting activity formerly governed by state law). This may pose constitutional difficulties or may be politically difficult as it requires convincing the U.S. Congress to preempt state law in explicit fashion. The alternative is to do the same indirectly: through a mere appropriations measure that, for example, conditions the receipt of federal highway funds on U.S. states abiding by a 55 mph. speed limit on federal highways.[310] Law by appropriation—the conditioning of monies to satisfy a top down mandate—seems an apt description of how the IMF deploys its ability to demand that borrowing countries satisfy certain conditions. The legal, economic, and social impact of the IMF's turn to "conditionality" has generated a substantial literature, positive and negative.[311] Indeed, at least some of the resistance to the establishment of the Asian Development Bank rests on the fear that that new institution will fail to impose the "good governance" conditions that other international financial institutions require.[312]

---

308   See, e.g., Namita Wahi, *Human Rights Accountability of the IMF and the World Bank: A Critique of Existing Mechanisms and Articulation of a Theory of Horizontal Accountability*, 12 U.C. DAVIS J. INT'L L. & POL'Y 331 (2006) (critiquing conditionality as coercive); Sarah L. Babb & Bruce G. Carruthers, *Conditionality: Forms, Functions and History*, 4 ANN. REV. L. & SOC. SCI. 13 (2008) (assessing IMF conditionality in context of conditions imposed by other lenders historically).

309   See, e.g., Daniel Kalderimis, *IMF Conditionality as Investment Regulation: A Theoretical Analysis*, 13 SOC. AND LEGAL STUD. 103, at 117 (2004).

310   *Id.* at 105.

311   See, e.g., Wahi, *supra* note 308; see generally John W. Head, *Seven Deadly Sins: An Assessment of Criticisms Directed at the International Monetary Fund*, 52 U. KAN. L. REV. 521 (2004).

312   See generally Enrique R. Carrasco, Wesley V. Carrington & HeeJin Lee, *Governance and Accountability: The Regional Development Banks*, 27 B.U. INT'L L.J. 1 (2009) (assessing

10 comparisons inspire consideration about competing theories of international law compliance. Scholars, particularly, but not only, those who study international relations, have argued that international regimes prove most effective when they resort to (1) hard enforcement tools associated with national law (including "real" courts that can inflict financial damage or even arrest suspects); (2) persuasive techniques that convince states to comply voluntarily because compliance is in their self-interest; or (3) socialization or acculturation approaches where states are encouraged to follow "global scripts" or are encouraged to believe that continued status within an organization or a regime merits compliance.[313] Each of these compliance models or approaches leads to particular prescriptions, including establishing an institution capable of invoking economic sanctions or damage awards (whether an executive organ with such delegated power like the Security Council or an international court); the provision of technical assistance and training (including of national legislators who need to be convinced to implement the regime's rules into national law); or reliance on non-state actors (from NGOs to business interests) to encourage socialization or acculturation.[314]

These approaches and prescriptions tend to be advanced by different scholars who often treat the corresponding prescriptions for compliance as alternatives. But while it is tempting to draw a firm line between the World Bank's and IMF's approach to law-making and compliance and the techniques used at the WHO and ICAO, the temptation ought to be resisted. The international financial institutions have, to be sure, a potent financial stick—the threat to withhold funds—to enforce their operational standards or loan conditions. The same is true of the World Bank's anti-corruption regime, which may debar companies that engage in corruption from dealing with the Bank for set periods.[315] Yet, as is clear from the analysis of the WHO in this chapter, that organization also relies on financial resources to achieve its goals. Indeed, as noted, difficulties in securing compliance with the WHO's IHR or FCTC obligations are

---

charges that regional development banks, including the Asian Development Bank, are ineffective and undemocratic).

313   *See* Ryan Goodman & Derek Jinks, *How to Influence States: Socialization and International Human Rights Law*, 54 DUKE L.J. 621 (2004).

314   *Id.*

315   Indeed, because the World Bank's blacklisting of companies that have allegedly engaged in corruption resembles a sanction that ought to be imposed only after judicial review, the Bank has instituted reforms to improve the due process accorded those caught up its anti-corruption efforts. *See* Laurence Boisson de Chazournes & Edouard Fromageau, *Balancing the Scales: The World Bank Sanctions Process and Access to Remedies*, 23 EUR. J. INT'L L. 963 (2012).

often attributed, in substantial part, to the lack of resources needed for capacity building. In the case of the WHO, the technical assistance is seen largely as
a carrot; in the case of the IMF, it is mostly seen as a stick. The difference is a
matter of the broader context in which the funds are distributed.

On closer inspection, the stark divides sometimes suggested among the
three "distinct" approaches to compliance collapse in the face of the mix of
techniques actually in use by all of these IOs. Even the harder edged international financial institutions rely on a variety of soft law guidelines to achieve
their goals, and in most cases, they rarely invoke the sanction of refusing to
disperse promised funds.[316] Both market actors and states presume and rely
on the fact that most of those who borrow from the Bank and the Fund care
enough about their reputations that they will not default on monies or other
obligations owed to either.[317] On the other side, even the "managerial" WHO
and ICAO have recourse to some relatively hard remedies (and law). In both
cases, organizational soft law on health or aviation can be transformed to the
extent it is incorporated in national law, other treaties (or even custom or general principles), industry standards used by market actors (whether tobacco
companies or hospitals in the case of the WHO or airlines or pilot associations
in the case of ICAO), or, as will be addressed in the next chapter, to the extent
it is enforced by courts, national or international. The impact of an ICAO accident investigation about the causes of a fatal plane crash may not be limited to
a political condemnation of the underlying act by the ICAO Council, for example. To the extent that accident investigation becomes the subject of a case in
national court, it too can be transformed into hard law (and hard remedies)—
if it provides the basis for a judicial order compelling compensation from an
airline or imposing civil (or even criminal) penalties on the responsible actor.
This transformation is also obviously one of the primary goals of the FCTC's
Protocol on Illicit Tobacco Trade, an instrument that seeks to "harden" the
FCTC's Article 15 by turning illicit trade into a violation of civil or criminal
national law.

Another question usually raised when comparing IO regimes over time is
the relationship between the "mission creep" that IOs frequently experience
and positivist treaty interpretation. It is tempting here as well to oversimplify
matters and conclude that since all the organizations discussed have vastly
expanded their mandates over time, all must have treated their respective

---

316 For a description of the blurry lines between hard and soft law in the context of the World
    Bank Guidelines, see ALVAREZ, *supra* note 155, at 235–241.
317 *See generally* ANDREW T. GUZMAN, HOW INTERNATIONAL LAW WORKS: A RATIONAL
    CHOICE THEORY (2008).

constituent instruments as "living" constitutions subject to informal change without need for amendment.[318] On this view, the texts of the UN Charter, the WHO's and the ICAO's respective Constitutions, and the Articles of Agreement for the IBRD and the IMF must all have undergone highly teleological forms of interpretation that are inconsistent with the positivist rules of treaty interpretation in the Vienna Convention on the Law of Treaties (VCT).

It is true that the institutional practice of all of the IOs discussed here, including the practice of the SC in Chapter II and the GA in Chapter III, explains much about how each of the charters for these organizations has developed over time. It is also true that treating the subsequent practice of IO organs as the functional equivalent of the practice of the parties is not entirely consistent with the text of the relevant rule of the VCT.[319] But the ways in which, and the extent to which, the meanings of IO constitutions change over time vary with the organization in question. The underlying constituent instruments of IOs are not the same, and some contain more capacious language and corresponding objects and intents than do others.

In the case of the WHO and ICAO there are solid arguments for the proposition that much of what these organizations are now doing was anticipated in their respective charters from the outset. As discussed in section 1 of this chapter, the object and purpose of the WHO's Constitution (as expressed in its preamble) was to establish an organization that would take a holistic approach to "health" and was therefore given considerable powers to do so.[320] The expanding WHO mandates resulting from the 2005 IHRs and the adoption of the FCTC are, arguably, only belated efforts by that organization to assume the powers originally accorded to it. Indeed, for critics of the WHO, its shortcomings may be more about the organization's continued timidity, particularly its continued resistance to becoming the full-fledged advocate for the human right to health that it was meant to be.[321]

Much the same could be said about ICAO. ICAO's constitutional preamble indicates that that organization would deal with the abuse of access to civil

---

318   *See generally* GUY SINCLAIR, TO REFORM THE WORLD (forthcoming 2016).

319   *See* Vienna Convention on the Law of Treaties, art. 31(3)(b), *opened for signature* May 23, 1969, 1155 U.N.T.S. 331 (permitting consideration of "any subsequent practice in the application of the treaty which establishes the agreement of the parties regarding its interpretation") [hereinafter VCT].

320   *See supra* § 1.

321   The 2005 IHRs, for example, offer no recourse to those whose rights are violated by control measures.

aviation and its potential to become a "threat to the general security."[322] It also indicates that the organization would "avoid friction" and promote cooperation "on the basis of equality of opportunity" so that aviation could be "operated soundly and economically."[323] The 18 ICAO Annexes adopted to date, and the treaties drafted under its auspices, fit comfortably within a broad mandate that considers international civil aviation from a number of different frames, including as a tool of development, an engine for free trade and travel flows, and a weapon that can both buttress and threaten the security of nations. In the case of ICAO it is hard to argue as well that either its SARPs or its services as treaty negotiator exceeds the authorities conferred on it or its organs.

The Articles of Agreement of the World Bank and the IMF present different problems in this respect. Most observers agree that given the rapidly changing conditions in which these institutions have had to operate, both the Bank and the IMF have transformed themselves considerably and that their respective legal counsels have turned to teleological re-interpretations of the respective constituent instruments in order to do so.[324] These interpretations have not been subject to judicial review, at least not by an international court with binding authority. (But in the case of the World Bank, interpretations of World Bank internal policies, including its operational guidelines, have been subject to quasi-judicial interpretations issued by the World Bank's Inspection Panel that is charged with making the Bank more accountable to its stakeholders.)[325] The enabling principles of legal interpretation we have seen used in connection with the UN have been used by the legal counsels of these organizations. In the case of the IMF, its transformation from an entity focused on monetary policies, specifically the regulation of fixed exchange rates, to a broad ranging economic development agency has relied on a very expansive interpretation of one of its core purposes, namely Article I(v) of the Articles of Agreement.

Article I(v) of the IMF Articles of Agreement states that one of its functions is "[t]o give confidence to members by making the general resources of the Fund temporarily available to them under adequate safeguards, thus

---

322   ICAO Convention, *supra* note 267, pmbl.

323   *Id.*

324   On the World Bank, see SINCLAIR, *supra* note 318; on the IMF, see, for example, Kalderimis, *supra* note 309.

325   *See generally* Ellen Hey, *The World Bank Inspection Panel and the Development of International Law, in* INTERNATIONAL COURTS AND THE DEVELOPMENT OF INTERNATIONAL LAW: ESSAYS IN HONOUR OF TULLIO TREVES (Nerina Boschiero et al. eds., 2013).

providing them with opportunity to correct maladjustments in their balance of payments without resorting to measures destructive of national or international prosperity."[326] Although this article suggests that "adequate safeguards" means only conditions directed at ensuring repayment, the IMF has interpreted that term as a general license to impose an exogenous reform agenda that came to be associated, during the 1990s, with the "Washington Consensus," that is, a series of pro-market reforms that would encourage development through the promotion of free trade and capital flows by deploying decreasing levels of government regulation, reaffirm the protection of property rights (particularly the rights of foreign investors), and undertake, where possible, the privatization of government-owned economic sectors or industries.[327] For Sir Joseph Gold, who was, for a long time, the general counsel of the IMF, the license to apply "adequate safeguards" was sufficiently capacious to permit the IMF's undertaking this activity because

> [t]he content of conditionality has never been defined by the Articles or codified, beyond a few broad principles, by decisions of the Fund. The absence of a detailed code has enabled the Fund to develop and modify conditionality, as well as the form and content of stand-by and extended arrangements, to accord with changes in the world economy and with the special circumstances of individual members or classes of members.[328]

Sir Joseph also justified the IMF's expansive use of conditionality to address capital movements between nations on the basis that IMF conditionality did not impose a legal obligation under the IMF Articles since they were imposed pursuant to a separate arrangement that did not even amount to a treaty or a contract entailing a formal legal consequence for breach. "The practice of the IMF," wrote Gold, "must be taken to have affirmed the interpretation that as performance criteria are not obligations under the Articles or under a treaty or contract, they can include matters over which the IMF has no regulatory

326   Articles of Agreement of the International Monetary Fund, art. 1(v), July 22, 1944, 60 Stat. 1401, 2 U.N.T.S. 39, *at* https://www.imf.org/external/pubs/ft/aa/#art1.

327   In reaction to criticisms of IMF conditionality and its Western provenance, the IMF released a Statement of Principles Underlying the Guidelines on Conditionality, stressing the need for "national ownership" of such conditions. Statement of the IMF Staff: Principles Underlying the Guidelines of Conditionality, ¶¶ 2–3, rev'd Jan.9, 2006, *at* https://www.imf.org/external/np/pp/eng/2006/010906.pdf.

328   JOSEPH GOLD, *Financing: Conditionality, in* LEGAL AND INSTITUTIONAL ASPECTS OF THE INTERNATIONAL MONETARY SYSTEM: SELECTED ESSAYS, VOL. II, 436, 439 (1984).

jurisdiction if they have a bearing on the balance of payments and on the purposes of the IMF."[329] IMF conditionality, in other words, is not impermissible regulation over capital movements; it is simply a "mechanism of influence."[330]

Similarly, as a recent history that attempts to explain the transformation of the World Bank over time explains, the lawyers of the Bank were instrumental in transforming that institution from a financial institution that would arrange loans for the most useful and urgent reconstruction projects needed in postwar Europe into a worldwide development agency charged with promoting "good governance."[331] In this instance, this meant reinterpreting language in the Bank's Articles of Agreement that obliged the Bank to pay attention only to economic considerations in carrying out its work and prohibited it from interfering with or taking into account political issues.[332] The Bank's lawyers did not see this bar on "political" interference as an effective prohibition on the Bank's expanding activities. They got their way because under the Articles of Agreement, such questions of interpretation would go first to the Bank's Executive Directors and, if a member requested it, ultimately to the Board of Governors, whose decisions would be final.[333] By limiting authoritative interpretation to these two organs, the Articles endowed these entities with a remarkable degree of power *vis-á- vis* members. As Aron Broches would later put it, "when the Executive Directors exercise their power of interpretation, their activity has both judicial and legislative elements."[334]

Broches, who became the Bank's General Counsel in 1959, was instrumental in advancing the broad conception of the Bank's purposes and mandate. In a key legal interpretation, Broches relied on the Advisory Opinion issued by the

---

329 JOSEPH GOLD, INTERPRETATION: THE IMF AND INTERNATIONAL LAW 355 (1996), *quoted in* Kalderimis, *supra* note 309, at 117.

330 Kalderimis, *supra* note 309, at 117 (criticizing this view). *But see* Cynthia C. Lichtenstein, *International Jurisdiction over International Capital Flows and the Role of the IMF: Plus Ça Change...*, *in* INTERNATIONAL MONETARY LAW: ISSUES FOR THE NEW MILLENNIUM 61, 72 (Mario Giovanoli ed., 2000) (arguing that it is appropriate for the IMF to require capital controls if this contributes to a member's ability to repay the resources borrowed from the IMF).

331 *See* SINCLAIR, *supra* note 318.

332 International Bank for Reconstruction and Development: Articles of Agreement art. 4 § 10, Dec. 27, 1945, 2 U.N.T.S. 134, *at* http://siteresources.worldbank.org/BODINT/Resources/278027-1215526322295/IBRDArticlesOfAgreement_English.pdf.

333 *See, e.g.,* SINCLAIR *supra* note 318, at 359–360.

334 ARON BROCHES, *International Legal Aspects of the Operations of the World Bank, in* SELECTED ESSAYS: WORLD BANK, ICSID, AND OTHER SUBJECTS OF PUBLIC AND PRIVATE INTERNATIONAL LAW 3, 12 (1995), *quoted in* SINCLAIR, *supra* note 318, at 360.

ICJ in the Reparation for Injuries Case for the proposition that the Bank, like the UN, enjoyed "implied powers."[335] He argued that an operation or transaction did not have to be "expressly authorized or contemplated by a specific provision of the Articles" for the Bank to be able to carry it out and that a particular power "need not be shown to be necessarily or even reasonably implicit in any power given expressly by the Articles."[336] Rather, it was "enough that its exercise may further the achievement of the Bank's purposes, and that it is not prohibited by or inconsistent with the Bank's Articles of Agreement."[337] In this instance the Bank's charter seemed to have been read less like an ordinary treaty and more like a constitution.

As this brief summary of how constitutional empowerment has occurred demonstrates, some IOs, like ICAO and the WHO, have expanded their mandates merely by undertaking new tasks without much legal angst over whether these were legally authorized. Others, like the World Bank and the IMF, turned to their lawyers for permission. Yet others, like the SC and the GA discussed in earlier chapters, did a number of things. They expanded their mandate through subsequent practice, sometimes sought authorizing legal opinions from their legal secretariats, and, on rare but significant occasions, turned to international adjudicators for approbation or permission. In the next chapter we examine more closely, through select examples, how institutionalized international adjudicators are having an impact on international law.

---

335   SINCLAIR, *supra* note 318, at 360–361 (construing Reparation for Injuries Suffered in the Service of the United Nations, Advisory Opinion, 1949 I.C.J. 174 (Apr. 11)).

336   BROCHES, *supra* note 334, at 28, *quoted in* SINCLAIR, *supra* note 318, at 361.

337   *Id.*

The Main Functions of International Adjudication

1 Introduction

Chapter I introduced international courts and tribunals as part of the contemporary proliferation of institutions. In this chapter we look more closely at the legal impact of international adjudicators, including, but not only, the 24 permanent international courts that have been most closely examined by scholars.[1]

International judges and arbitrators are commonly portrayed in simple terms: as settlers of inter-state disputes that might otherwise lead to threats to the peace.[2] The idea that international adjudication serves to adjust or settle "international disputes or situations that might lead to a breach of the peace" is, of course, encouraged by Article 1(1) of the UN Charter, as well as by its Article 33, which identifies "judicial settlement" as one of the "peaceful means" by which disputes should be settled. Indeed, Article 38 of the Statute of the International Court of Justice (ICJ) affirms that the function of that body is "to decide . . . disputes as are submitted to it," and the same is true of the World Trade Organization's Dispute Settlement Understanding (DSU).[3]

The need to settle disputes in order to maintain peace, self-evident to those who established arbitral mechanisms at the turn of the nineteenth century, continues to be seen today as the principal (if not the only) function of

---

1 *See, e.g.*, Cesare P.R. Romano, *The International Judiciary in Context: A Synoptic Chart*, THE PROJECT ON INTERNATIONAL COURTS AND TRIBUNALS, *at* http://www.pict-pcti.org/publications/synoptic_chart.html; KAREN J. ALTER, THE NEW TERRAIN OF INTERNATIONAL LAW: COURTS, POLITICS, RIGHTS (2015). This chapter does not address a topic that has also been the subject of considerable scholarship, namely why such international courts and tribunals have proliferated over the past two decades. *See generally* Karen J. Alter, *The Evolving International Judiciary*, 7 ANN. REV. L. & SOC. SCI. 387 (2011).

2 *See, e.g.*, J.G. MERRILLS, INTERNATIONAL DISPUTE SETTLEMENT (2d ed. 1991).

3 *See, e.g.*, Understanding on Rules and Procedures Governing the Settlement of Disputes, Marrakesh Agreement Establishing the World Trade Organization Annex 2, art. 3.7, Apr. 15, 1994, THE LEGAL TEXTS: THE RESULTS OF THE URUGUAY ROUND OF MULTILATERAL TRADE NEGOTIATIONS 59 (1999), 1867 U.N.T.S. 493 [hereinafter DSU] ("The aim of the dispute settlement mechanism is to secure a positive solution to a dispute").

international courts.[4] This function is most clearly in evidence when ICJ judges are asked to determine a territorial or maritime boundary, or when international criminal courts are justified on the premise that without such courts the victims of mass atrocities and those who commit them would never find peace. Those who transformed the GATT into the WTO argued that the rule of law was needed to resolve inter-state frictions that could otherwise fester into breaches of the peace if left to the vicissitudes of power politics.[5] Similarly, those who negotiated the International Centre for Settlement of Investment Disputes (ICSID) Convention (now the most commonly used vehicle for settling investment disputes under international investment protection treaties) saw investor-state dispute settlement (ISDS) as the far more desirable alternative to the last resort once deployed under diplomatic espousal, namely "gunboat diplomacy."[6] Countless international judges and arbitrators have repeatedly affirmed that their role is to apply pre-existing rules to resolve the disagreement of the litigants before them.[7]

But settling *inter-state* disputes is not the only thing international judges and arbitrators do. "Interstate dispute settlement" does not really describe, for instance, the role of international criminal courts (which pit a prosecutor, usually portrayed as the embodiment of "the international community," against

---

4 *See, e.g.*, HERSCH LAUTERPACHT, THE FUNCTION OF LAW IN THE INTERNATIONAL COMMUNITY 59 (2011 ed.) (defining "international judicial settlement," including arbitration, to be "a method of settling disputes between States by a binding decision based upon rules of law"). *See also* Samantha Besson, *Legal Philosophical Issues of International Adjudication: Getting Over the Amour Impossible between International Law and Adjudication, in* THE OXFORD HANDBOOK OF INTERNATIONAL ADJUDICATION 413 (Cesare P.R. Romano, Karen J. Alter & Yuval Shany eds., 2013) [hereinafter OXFORD HANDBOOK]; Solomon T. Ebobrah, *International Human Rights Courts, in id.* at 225; Sean D. Murphy, *International Judicial Bodies for Resolving Disputes Between States, in id.* at 181; Tom Ginsburg, *Political Constraints on International Courts, in id.* at 483.

5 *See, e.g.*, JOHN H. JACKSON, THE WORLD TRADING SYSTEM 109–111 (2d ed. 1997) (describing the evolution of the WTO DSU as a shift from "power-oriented diplomacy" to "rule-oriented diplomacy").

6 *See, e.g.*, O. Thomas Johnson Jr. & Jonathan Gimblett, *From Gunboats to BITs: The Evolution of Modern International Investment Law, in* YEARBOOK ON INTERNATIONAL INVESTMENT LAW & POLICY 2010–2011 649 (Karl P. Sauvant ed., 2012).

7 *See, e.g.*, Armin von Bogdandy & Ingo Venzke, *The Spell of Precedents: Lawmaking by International Courts and Tribunals, in* OXFORD HANDBOOK, *supra* note 4, at 503, 506 (noting that it is important for international judges to "portray their decisions as firmly based on the law as it stands" and quoting Austin for the proposition that both jurists and judges need to resort to the "timorous fiction" that their statements of law are equivalent to statements of fact).

an individual), regional human rights courts (which consider whether states have abused individual rights *vis-à-vis* their own peoples), or ICSID arbitrations (which consider whether a state has abused the rights of a foreign investor). International adjudication, as much else in international law, no longer involves states as the only affected parties. Indeed, Alter's study of permanent international courts reveals that 16 of these (64%) have provisions that allow private actors to initiate litigation.[8] Of course, access to individual complaints is precisely the point of optional protocols permitting human rights complaints before the committees of the various UN human rights treaties. International adjudicative rulings triggered by an independent prosecutor, a human rights claimant, or a foreign investor involve non-state actors in the process of adjudicative law-making.[9]

In other instances, what judges do, even when this involves states or interstate entities such as international organizations, is not characterized even by the litigants themselves as involving "disputes." ICJ Advisory Opinions— whether dealing with the effects of UN sanctions against South African-controlled Namibia,[10] the extent to which "legal personality" can be attributed to the UN,[11] the extent to which the UN General Assembly can exercise its power of the purse,[12] the legality of nuclear weapons or the Israeli Wall,[13] or the effects of a declaration of independence by Kosovo authorities[14]—are generally not characterized as concrete "disputes," at least not by the entity requesting the opinion or by the majority of ICJ judges. Indeed, some argue

---

8   Karen J. Alter, *The Multiple Roles of International Courts and Tribunals: Enforcement, Dispute Settlement, Constitutional and Administrative Review, in* INTERDISCIPLINARY PERSPECTIVES ON INTERNATIONAL LAW AND INTERNATIONAL RELATIONS 345, 348, 363, Figure 14–5 (Jeffrey L. Dunoff & Mark A. Pollack eds., 2012).

9   *See, e.g.,* Ebobrah, *supra* note 4; Murphy, *supra* note 4; Christoph Schreuer, *Investment Arbitration, in* OXFORD HANDBOOK, *supra* note 4, at 295. *See generally* Paul B. Stephan, *Privatizing International Law,* 97 VA. L. REV. 1573 (2011) (seeing such non-state involvement as part of a larger trend towards "private" law-makers and enforcers).

10   Legal Consequences for States of the Continued Presence of South Africa in Namibia (South West Africa) notwithstanding Security Council Resolution 276 (1970), Advisory Opinion, 1971 I.C.J. 16 (June 21) [hereinafter Namibia Opinion].

11   Reparation for Injuries Suffered in the Service of the United Nations, Advisory Opinion, 1949 I.C.J. 174 (Apr. 11) [hereinafter Reparation Opinion].

12   Certain Expenses of the United Nations, Advisory Opinion, 1962 I.C.J. 151 (July 20) [hereinafter Certain Expenses Opinion].

13   Legal Consequences of the Construction of a Wall in the Occupied Palestinian Territory, Advisory Opinion, 2004 I.C.J. 136 (July 9) [hereinafter Wall Advisory Opinion].

14   Accordance with International Law of the Unilateral Declaration of Independence in Respect of Kosovo, Advisory Opinion, 2010 I.C.J. 403 (July 22).

that the ICJ should deploy its discretion and refuse to answer an advisory opinion that is in reality a disguised form of a dispute that is not otherwise subject to the contentious jurisdiction of the Court.[15] Moreover, even those ICJ advisory opinions that might plausibly be cast as involving a (disguised) dispute between states are at least equally directed at providing interpretations of organizational charters to organs needing guidance or providing advice to international civil servants seeking the same.[16]

ICJ Advisory opinions seem most effective when they render seemingly authoritative interpretations of the law (including the UN Charter) that are helpful to bureaucrats and least successful when they attempt to resolve an underlying inter-state dispute.[17] Characterizing efforts to seek the ICJ's advice on the law as principally or solely occasions for "dispute settlement" seems disingenuous. And it seems equally disingenuous to describe other instances—from the *Avena/LaGrand* line of contentious ICJ judgments[18] to any of a number of WTO panel and Appellate Body decisions—as principally or solely about "dispute settlement" when those bringing such cases appear to be seeking thoroughly reasoned (and therefore authoritative) legal rulings that can guide behavior going forward, and not merely a way to resolve a discrete dispute.[19]

---

15   *See, e.g.*, Namibia Opinion, *supra* note 10, ¶¶ 33–34 (carefully distinguishing a "dispute" between South Africa and the UN from advice sought by the Security Council). *But see* Legality of the Use by a State of Nuclear Weapons in Armed Conflict, Advisory Opinion, 1996 I.C.J 66 (July 8) [hereinafter WHO Opinion] (Oda, J., Dissenting Opinion) (suggesting that the advisory jurisdiction of the Court should be used only in cases involving real conflicts or disputes).

16   This is implicit in the pre-conditions for permissible advisory opinions suggested by the Court. *See, e.g.*, WHO Opinion, *supra* note 15, ¶¶ 10–15 (finding that the advisory jurisdiction of the Court is triggered when the agency requesting the opinion is duly authorized under the UN Charter to request such an opinion, where the opinion requested is a legal question, and where the question is one arising within the scope of the activities of the requesting agency).

17   *Compare* Reparation Opinion, *supra* note 11 and Certain Expenses Opinion, *supra* note 12 *with* Wall Advisory Opinion, *supra* note 13.

18   *E.g.*, LaGrand Case (Ger. v. U.S.), 2001 I.C.J. 466 (June 27); Case Concerning Avena and Other Mexican Nationals (Mex. v. U.S.), 2004 I.C.J. 12 (Mar. 31).

19   *See* Besson, *supra* note 4 (describing the "review" function); Carl Baudenbacher & Michael-James Clifton, *Courts of Regional Economic and Political Integration Agreements*, *in* OXFORD HANDBOOK, *supra* note 4, at 250 (describing how regional courts establish *sui generis* regimes); Murphy, *supra* note 4 (describing the gap-filling function of ICJ advisory opinions). *See generally* ANDREW T. GUZMAN, HOW INTERNATIONAL LAW WORKS: A RATIONAL CHOICE THEORY 26, 49–54 (2008) (discussing the general value

This chapter contends that like the IOs considered in the rest of this monograph, international courts and tribunals serve a multitude of functions.[20] It argues that whether and how adjudicators fulfill these functions depends on who the judges and arbitrators are, how the tribunals are structured, and what their jurisdiction is, as well as the broader institutional context in which they operate. Organizational structure affects substance, as it does with respect to the other IOs discussed in this monograph.

Part II of this chapter addresses the dispute settlement function. It contends that this is a convenient label for a far more complex reality that, depending on the context, may have adjudicators serving as the "agents" of states, as servants of the rule of law, as "triadic" mediators or conciliators for the disputing parties, or as "trustees" for a multitude of stakeholders beyond the litigants. Part III highlights that adjudicators are commonly expected to produce definitive findings of fact despite considerable obstacles and that they face considerable criticism when their findings prove defective. Part IV recognizes that those involved in international adjudication (from the litigants to the adjudicators and sometimes others) make law even when they claim that they are not doing so. Indeed, in a number of international regimes, adjudication is increasingly the principal vehicle for law elaboration and creation. Part V describes an increasing number of instances in which adjudicative law-making takes the form of "global governance," namely normative efforts to regulate third parties not involved in the underlying litigation, including non-litigating states, IOs,

---

of judicially determined "focal points" to guide the behavior of states). Indeed, some have seen recourses to the ICJ as efforts to exacerbate the political salience of a dispute, the very opposite of engaging in peaceful dispute settlement. *See, e.g.*, Shirin Sinnar, *Beyond "Whodunit": The Political Road to the Lockerbie Trial*, WASHINGTON REPORT ON MIDDLE EAST AFFAIRS July 2000, *at* http://www.wrmea.org/2000-july/beyond-whodunit-the-political-road-to-the-lockerbie-trial.html (characterizing the ICJ's 1998 decision to consider Libya's Lockerbie bombing case as "a political irritant for the U.S. and British position"); Andrew Apostolou, *A Court in The Service of Terrorism*, NATIONAL REVIEW, July 19, 2004, *at* http://www.nationalreview.com/article/211528/court-service-terrorism-andrew-apostolou (criticizing the General Assembly's recourse to the ICJ's advisory jurisdiction in the *Wall* case as "an act of political favoritism"); Alexander Orakhelashvili, *The International Court's Advisory Opinion on the UDI in Respect of Kosovo: Washing Away the "Foam on the Tide of Time*," 15 MAX PLANCK Y.B. U.N. L. 65, 70 (2011) (noting that the ICJ "also faced submissions as to potential political motives underlying the request for an Advisory Opinion" and explaining the Court's deflection of such concerns).

20   This chapter builds on a prior essay by the author, *What are International Judges For? The Main Functions of International Adjudication, in* OXFORD HANDBOOK, *supra* note 4, at 158.

individuals, or other non-state actors. This chapter contends that in undertaking these varied tasks, international adjudicators give particular emphasis to "judicial opinions" (mentioned only as a subsidiary evidentiary source (d) for the principal sources of international obligation contained in ICJ Statute Article 38(a)–(c)) and may sometimes apply sources of authority other than those enumerated in Article 38.

Some of the confusion over the functions of international adjudication stems from distinct observational standpoints.[21] States that establish an international tribunal, the adjudicators who serve on them and share an internal perspective, and scholars who evaluate the court from an external perspective may have very different perspectives on the "judicial role."[22] It is also the case that not every forum for international adjudication undertakes all the functions canvassed here.[23] These realities may explain the underlying scholarly disagreements.

Like blind persons who describe an elephant differently depending on which part of it they touch, observers of international courts differ depending on their own observational standpoint as well as which international adjudicators are being observed. Samantha Besson, for example, distinguishes the "law-identifying" from the "law-making" function, indicating that both occur in the course of settling disputes (which she re-labels as "law-enforcement").[24] She also identifies a distinct "review" function consisting of judicial control over executive action.[25] Von Bogdandy and Venzke, by contrast, describe four

---

21   This phrasing borrows a common emphasis from the "New Haven School" of legal theory. *See, e.g.*, Myres S. McDougal & Harold D. Lasswell, *Criteria for a Theory About Law*, 44 S. CAL. L. REV. 362 (1971) (describing the significance of observational standpoints).

22   For an examination of the systemic functions of international courts from the perspective of their state creators, see, for example, Murphy, *supra* note 4; Ginsburg, *supra* note 4; Baudenbacher & Clifton, *supra* note 19. For an account of judges' internal "communicative" practices in terms of their needs to explain their decisions to others, see, for example, von Bogdandy & Venzke, *supra* note 7. For an account that addresses the broader aspirational functions of human rights tribunals on the national and international rule of law, see, for example, Ebobrah, *supra* note 4.

23   Thus, many roles that, for example, Ebobrah attributes to human rights courts, such as to prevent relapse by subsequent governments, to show the world that a nation has nothing to hide, or to satisfy victims' need for justice by apportioning responsibility for reparation, are distinctive to such bodies, while others, such as to signal respect for international obligations, to resolve disputes, and to avoid situations that deteriorate into violations of the peace, are more generalizable. Ebobrah, *supra* note 4.

24   Besson, *supra* note 4, at 419–426.

25   *Id.* at 415, 432.

functions of international courts: "settling disputes," "stabilizing normative expectations," "making law," and "controlling and legitimating public
authority."[26] A distinctly academic stance is adopted by the political scientist
Karen Alter, who, in highlighting the "altered politics" produced by the operation of 24 permanent international courts, describes them as engaging in
"dispute settlement," "administrative review," "law enforcement," and constitutional review.[27] For their part, judges, national or international, are more reticent about acknowledging anything other their dispute settlement role. They
are not likely to proclaim in their judgments that they are going beyond the
application of the law—whether to "stabilize the expectations" of the disputants before them or in order to "legitimate public authority."

2   The Complex Dispute Settlement Function

The dispute settlement function, in its most traditional guise, is built on a
standard "rational actor" explanation for why states establish international
courts and tribunals. We are told that since states sometimes need to settle disputes between themselves, they establish systems to adjudicate such disputes
when this is in their interests. Under the strictest version of this functionalist
or "rational choice" account, binding dispute settlement emerges only when
states' needs to secure compliance with legal rules outweigh the reputational
or other costs associated with violating them.[28]

The simplest version of the rational actor account treats international
adjudication as a vehicle for securing the goals of the states that establish
the mechanism and that appear as disputants before it. This approach sees

---

26   *See, e.g.*, Armin von Bogdandy & Ingo Venzke, *On the Functions of International Courts:
      An Appraisal in Light of Their Burgeoning Public Authority*, 26 LEIDEN J. INT'L L. 49
      (2013). *Compare* Benedict Kingsbury, *International Courts: Uneven Judicialisation in Global
      Order, in* THE CAMBRIDGE COMPANION TO INTERNATIONAL LAW (James Crawford &
      Martti Koskenniemi eds., 2012), at 203 (describing the same as settling disputes, making
      commitments credible, governance, and producing legal knowledge).

27   ALTER, *supra* note 1.

28   *See, e.g.*, Andrew T. Guzman, *The Cost of Credibility: Explaining Resistance to Inter State
      Dispute Resolution Mechanisms*, 31 J. LEGAL STUD. 303 (2002) (arguing that dispute reso-
      lution clauses in treaties are most likely when rates of compliance with the treaty are
      already expected to be high, when the stakes are small, and when the adjudicator is inter-
      preting norms that both parties are equally likely to violate).

international adjudicators as the "agents" for state principals.[29] As a Weberian "ideal type," this principal-agent account has distinct implications. If international adjudicators are the agents of states, they owe their delegated powers to their principals and have no duties to non-litigating states or others, including the (ephemeral) "international community." Since the function of the adjudicating agent is to settle inter-state disputes preferably in an amicable manner such that the results are voluntarily accepted by the losing side, agent adjudicators should avoid exacerbating such disputes by undermining the often fragile agreement that led states to delegate settlement authority to them. Accordingly, adjudicators should not go beyond the jurisdictional consent given by the parties to address, for example, legal or factual matters not clearly anticipated in that consent. This means that agent adjudicators should ordinarily exercise the judicial (and judicious) "passive virtues," that is, they should deploy concepts of admissibility, standing, and mootness to narrow the dispute before them and increase the likelihood of successful settlement or eventual compliance with their ruling.[30] Agent-adjudicators should not take on legal or factual issues unless these are raised by the disputants, and they should probably resist third party interventions or court-initiated processes for fact-finding. They should avoid accusations of "judicial law-making" by rendering opinions that contain only as much reasoning as necessary and by applying canons of interpretation that are deferential to their state principals. Faithful agents of the litigating parties should, for example, adhere strictly to the "plain meaning" rule in the interpretation of treaties; find customary law only in express state practice paired with explicit *opinio juris*; and should otherwise avoid filling legal gaps in ways that would be perceived as exceeding the narrow delegation of power accorded to them by the state principals.

According to this ideal type, tribunals within discrete regimes, such as those concerned with international criminal law, trade, or investment, should consider only the regime-specific choice of law that they are licensed to apply. They should leave consideration of general public international law to those courts

---

29 *See, e.g.*, Eric A. Posner & John C. Yoo, *Judicial Independence in International Tribunals*, 93 CAL. L. REV. 1 (2005) (arguing that the only effective international tribunals are those that are "dependent," that is, *ad hoc* tribunals whose adjudicators are closely controlled by governments). *See generally* Daniel L. Nielson & Michael J. Tierney, *Delegation to International Organizations: Agency Theory and World Bank Environmental Reform*, 57 INT'L ORG. 241 (2003) (applying principal-agent theory to international organizations).

30 *See, e.g.*, Antonio F. Perez, *The Passive Virtues and the World Court: Pro-Dialogic Abstention by the International Court of Justice*, 18 MICH. J. INT'L L. 399 (1997); Ginsburg, *supra* note 4.

that are explicitly authorized to examine it (like the ICJ). Agent-adjudicators should avoid rulings that would otherwise surprise their state principals or that make the losing state party more reluctant to comply with them.[31] This interpretative stance is suggested by, for example, the text of the WTO's DSU, which provides that "[r]ecommendations and rulings of the DSB [Dispute Settlement Body] cannot add to or diminish the rights and obligations provided in the covered agreements."[32]

Posner and Yoo, among others, have argued that principal-agent theory best explains the institutional features of the most effective international courts and tribunals (meaning those leading to the most state compliance with their rulings).[33] They argue that this model explains why states attempt to protect themselves against rogue adjudicators, that is, agents who slip the confines of their delegated authority. In their view, the risks of such "agency slack" explain states' careful efforts to screen potential adjudicators to weed out those that might be inclined to engage in "judicial activism" as well as states' attempts to limit or monitor adjudicative decisions, to punish and reward faithful agents, and to build "checks and balances" on judicial action by requiring, for example, continued coordination between adjudicators and their state principals.[34] Principal-agent theory is also said to explain common institutional features of international courts that demonstrate states' reluctance to cede all control—as by continuing the tradition of state-appointed judges even for permanent courts like the ICJ,[35] restricting the jurisdiction of courts touted as "independent" (such as the jurisdictional limits imposed on the International Criminal Court (ICC)),[36] or retaining the capacity to resist enforcement of awards through sovereign immunity.[37]

---

31   The dispute settlement function is therefore viewed as consistent with efforts to encourage the disputing parties to settle their dispute through less formal methods such as negotiation, mediation, or conciliation. *See, e.g.*, U.N. Charter, art. 33; DSU, *supra* note 3, arts. 3.3–3.7, 4, 5, as well as provisions requiring negotiation or other methods of peaceful dispute settlement prior to resort to arbitration in a number of treaties.

32   DSU, *supra* note 3, art. 3.2.

33   Posner & Yoo, *supra* note 29.

34   *See generally* Ginsburg, *supra* note 4.

35   Statute of the International Court of Justice art. 4, ¶ 1, June 26 1945, 3 Bevans 1179, 59 Stat. 1055 [hereinafter ICJ Statute].

36   Rome Statute of the International Criminal Court, arts. 12–13, July 17, 1998, U.N. Doc. A/RES/54/109 [hereinafter Rome Statute].

37   *See, e.g.*, Dapo Akande, *International Law Immunities and the International Criminal Court*, 98 AM. J. INT'L L. 407 (2004). For another application of principal-agent theory

The compulsion to act as a faithful agent is said to be a mindset common to adjudicators even when they are delegated autonomous authority or extensive powers. It is said to explain why, for instance, the ICJ seems reluctant to exercise its powers to appoint its own fact-finders or to permit third party interventions or amicus;[38] why WTO panels have generally adhered to the so-called principle of "judicial economy;"[39] or why many ICSID arbitrators resist factual assertions or legal arguments not presented by the disputing parties.[40] The agency mindset may also tell us why, as noted, all or most international adjudicators routinely deny that they are engaging in any form of "law-making." At a more granular level, it may explain certain rulings by ICSID committees that defer to the interests of sovereigns even at the expense of the limits posed on annulment under the ICSID Convention,[41] particular shifts in ICJ jurisprudence over time,[42] as well as European courts' resort to judicially created innovations like the margin of appreciation or proportionality.[43]

---

in this context, see José E. Alvarez, *The Proposed Independent Oversight Mechanism for the International Criminal Court, in* UCLA School of Law Human Rights Project, HUMAN RIGHTS & INTERNATIONAL CRIMINAL LAW ONLINE FORUM, *available at* www.iccforum.com/oversight (enumerating the ways the ICC's Assembly of State parties continues to exert its influence over that court through financing, enforcement, and supervisory mechanisms).

38 *See, e.g.,* Military and Paramilitary Activities in and Against Nicaragua (Nicar. v. U.S.), Declaration of Intervention of the Republic of El Salvador, Order, 1984 I.C.J. 215 (Oct. 4) (denying El Salvador's attempt to intervene). On the ICJ's refusal to engage in its own fact-finding and discouragement of amicus, see *infra* text and note 79.

39 *See, e.g., United States—Measure Affecting Imports of Woven Wool Shirts and Blouses from India* ("*US—Wool Shirts and Blouses*"), WT/DS33/AB/R, WT/DS33/AB/R/Corr.1, adopted May 23, 1997 (applying the principle of judicial economy).

40 Glamis Gold, Ltd. v. United States of America, Award, 48 I.L.M. 1038 (NAFTA/UNCITRAL Ch. 11 Arb. Trib. June 8, 2009) (adopting the views of what constitutes custom urged by the United States as respondent and resisting the contention that prior arbitral rulings are relevant to finding custom) [hereinafter Glamis Gold].

41 *See, e.g.,* José E. Alvarez, *The Return of the State*, 20 MINN. J. INT' L. 223 (2011) (enumerating the ways that states are reasserting their voice and power in the international investment regime, including the impact of recent ICSID annulment committees).

42 *See, e.g.,* Edward Gordon, *The ICJ: On Its Own, in* PERSPECTIVES ON INTERNATIONAL LAW IN AN ERA OF CHANGE: FESTSCHRIFT IN HONOR OF PROFESSOR VED P. NANDA 74 (Anjali Nanda & Alissa Mundt eds., 2012).

43 *See, e.g.,* Ronald St. John Macdonald, *The Margin of Appreciation, in* THE EUROPEAN SYSTEM FOR THE PROTECTION OF HUMAN RIGHTS 83 (Ronald St. John Macdonald, Franz Matscher & Herbert Petzold eds., 1993).

But many of those who would defend the centrality of the dispute settlement function resist the principal-agent explanation for how international courts work or regard Posner's and Yoo's prescriptions for judicial behavior as simplistic.[44] Many scholars and not a few adjudicators refuse to treat the process of judging as puppetry subject only to the pull of states. Many contend that successful dispute settlement requires autonomous, impartial adjudicators who are *and are seen as* independent of states. The most prominent advocate of this perspective was Hersch Lauterpacht. In 1933, when the only sitting permanent international court in existence was the Permanent Court of International Justice (PCIJ), Lauterpacht accepted the premise that the function of that Court was to resolve disputes that could threaten the peace, but he saw its judges as autonomous actors and not the mere agents of the disputing state parties or of the states that established that Court.[45] His classic book on *The Function of Law in the International Community* (1933) sought to prove that there was no such thing as a "political" dispute not subject to legal scrutiny, notwithstanding the efforts of some states to restrict the jurisdiction of an international adjudicator through a clause purporting to prevent a tribunal from opining on a state's "essential interests" as decided by that state.[46] Such "self-judging" clauses reflected, in his view, a disreputable refusal to accord judges the respect they and the rule of law deserve.[47] For this reason he described states that purported to insert such clauses as in fact refusing to accept this

---

44   *See* Laurence R. Helfer & Anne-Marie Slaughter, *Why States Create International Tribunals: A Response to Professors Posner and Yoo*, 93 CAL. L. REV. 899 (2005) (challenging the rationales and prescriptions of principal-agent theory).

45   LAUTERPACHT, *supra* note 4, at 210. The views of Lauterpacht, who went on to serve on the ICJ himself, are relevant precisely because they are representative of a generation of international lawyers who went on to establish the ICJ and other contemporary courts and tribunals, to serve as lawyers to litigants before these tribunals, or to serve as adjudicators themselves. Martti Koskenniemi points out in his introduction to the new edition to Lauterpacht's text that, for Lauterpacht, international adjudicators were comparable to Ronald Dworkin's "Herculean" judge. Their impartiality is what enables legalized dispute settlement to succeed and why states turn to it in the first place. As Koskenniemi points out, in this conception there is no need for additional principal-agent constraints on the discretion of adjudicators since the legal rules that they apply are, themselves, sensitive to principles of proportionality, reasonableness, and other modes of "realist" adjustment. Martti Koskenniemi, *The Function of Law in the International Community: Introduction, in id.* at xxix, xli–xliii.

46   LAUTERPACHT, *supra* note 4. Koskenniemi's introduction characterizes this point as a primary motivation of Lauterpacht's work. Koskenniemi, *supra* note 45, at xxx.

47   Koskenniemi, *supra* note 45, at xxx.

mode of dispute settlement.[48] Lauterpacht argued that international judges were servants of the rule of law and not of states.[49]

For Lauterpacht, as for many others present at the creation of modern systems for institutionalized international adjudication, states resort to legalized international dispute resolution *because* it is an alternative to politicized dispute resolution by diplomats.[50] Whereas diplomats are perforce state agents, states turn to courts or arbitration when diplomacy will not suffice, that is, when they need to rely on a solution based on the application of recognized legal rules and not politics. Accordingly, Lauterpacht enumerated the many ways that international judges were entitled (indeed, as he saw it, duty bound) to engage in innovative or teleological treaty interpretations to avoid the degeneration of disputes into threats to the peace. The injunction against findings of *non-liquet* licensed, in his view, the use of creative analogies based on general rules, the recourse to general principles, applications of private law concepts, and forms of judicial "reconciliation" to balance competing principles—all capable of being deployed under a canon of "effectiveness" that would embrace the "larger needs of the international community."[51] Lauterpacht's prescient descriptions of the dispute settlement function help to explain the myriad departures from the principal-agent recipe book exhibited by contemporary courts of general jurisdiction or those operating within human rights, international criminal law, trade, or investment.[52]

A third account of what adjudicators do when they settle disputes originates with Martin Shapiro. Under Shapiro's account of the "triadic" dispute settlement function, effective adjudicators need to secure the cooperation of the losing party. Shapiro argues that the root concept involved in all adjudication is a triad. Two sides engaged in a conflict that they cannot resolve call upon a

---

48   *See, e.g.*, LAUTERPACHT, *supra* note 4, at 172 ("[I]t is the refusal of the State to submit the dispute to judicial settlement, and not the intrinsic nature of the controversy, which makes it political").

49   *See, e.g.*, LAUTERPACHT, *supra* note 4, at 93.

50   For more on the distinctions between forms of political dispute settlement and more legalized methods, see generally, Robert O. Keohane, Andrew Moravcsik & Anne-Marie Slaughter, *Legalized Dispute Settlement: Interstate and Transnational*, 54 INT'L ORG. 457 (2000).

51   LAUTERPACHT, *supra* note 4, at 118–119. *See also* von Bogdandy & Venzke, *supra* note 26, at 64–68 (enumerating examples of courts acting as "organs of a value-based international community").

52   *See generally* Murphy, *supra* note 4; von Bogdandy & Venzke, *supra* note 26; Schreuer, *supra* note 9; Baudenbacher & Clifton, *supra* note 19.

third party, a stranger to both and therefore impartial, to resolve it.[53] Shapiro focuses on how the third party in dispute settlement overcomes the basic instability of the triad. He emphasizes the need for the third party adjudicator to avoid delegitimizing his or her ruling by deflecting perceptions that the result is merely an arbitrary product of "two against one."[54] Like Lauterpacht, Shapiro accepts that triadic conflict resolution, even when based on pre-existing rules of law, inevitably involves "judicial lawmaking."[55] But unlike Lauterpacht, who urges that judges' legal gap-filling be undertaken explicitly, Shapiro argues that successful conflict resolution often requires third-party adjudicators to pretend or purposely obfuscate the extent to which they are making law in their rulings. Shapiro's triadic account explains why international adjudicators tend to mouth the same words as their national colleagues; why both affirm, along with Montesquieu, that they are but *bouches de la loi.*"[56] Successful triadic dispute resolution requires judges who act as if their interpretations are routine applications of the black letter of the law.[57]

This account of triadic dispute settlement explains why, as Shapiro puts it, judges lie: they do so to induce the losing party to comply without losing face. Note that this account of the dispute settlement function is consistent with, but does not require, the deployment of the so-called "passive virtues"—that is, judicial abstention doctrines such as mootness, ripeness, or principles of judicial economy. It accepts that third-party adjudicators may deploy different legitimizing strategies that vary with the institutional context. Of course, Shapiro's triad does not assume that states are necessarily the litigating parties or that the purpose of dispute settlement is to protect the rights of sovereigns; it can accommodate the possibility that ISDS, for instance, enforces the rights

---

53   MARTIN SHAPIRO, COURTS: A COMPARATIVE AND POLITICAL ANALYSIS 1 (1981).

54   *Id.* at 2; *see also* JOSÉ E. ALVAREZ, INTERNATIONAL ORGANIZATIONS AS LAW-MAKERS 528–529 (2006) (describing Shapiro's approach).

55   SHAPIRO, *supra* note 53, at 29 ("Because no human society has ever sought to set down an absolutely complete and particularized body of preexisting law designed exactly to meet every potential conflict, judicial 'discovery' must often of necessity be judicial lawmaking"). *See generally* von Bogdandy & Venzke, *supra* note 26.

56   MONTESQUIEU, THE SPIRIT OF THE LAWS, bk. XI, chap. 6, at 180 (Thomas Nugent trans., Batoche Books ed. 2001) (1748) ("[T]he national judges are no more than the mouth that pronounces the words of the law, mere passive beings, incapable of moderating either its force or rigour.").

57   Martin Shapiro, *Judges as Liars*, 17 Harv. J.L. & Pub. Pol'y 155 (1994). *See also* von Bogdandy & Venzke, *supra* note 26.

of investors as third-party beneficiaries and not merely of persons that continue to derive their rights from the states parties to an investment treaty.[58]

Like Shapiro and Lauterpacht, Karen Alter argues that international courts and tribunals are typically established to exercise relative autonomy (or what others call "bounded discretion") from the states that establish them or the particular litigants before them.[59] This explains why those who establish mechanisms for dispute settlement typically expend some effort to emphasize the adjudicators' independence. These efforts usually include rules precluding conflicts of interest for adjudicators and barring *ex parte* contacts and/or provisions enumerating professional qualifications for office and lengthy terms of judicial office for those serving on permanent courts. For these reasons, Alter argues that international adjudicators are more appropriately seen not as agents but as "trustees."[60] Her account, which might be seen as yet a fourth version of the dispute settlement function, builds upon both Lauterpacht and Shapiro's insights insofar as she identifies how, even when engaging only in dispute settlement, international adjudicators are not just the servants of the rule of law or triadic conciliators, but trustees for the underlying legal regime in which they operate. Her adjudicative trustees pay attention to community interests of the particular international regime and its national interlocutors (including national courts). The way that they dispose of particular disputes are attentive to the regime's wider stakeholders.

Alter's trustee account explains not only many of the characteristic institutional features of these tribunals but also why, contrary to the principal-agent ideal type, we increasingly expect international adjudicators to give reasoned opinions that have expansive potential to affect and guide the behavior of all the regime's participants (and not just the litigants before the court). It helps to explain why international adjudicators often seem engaged in proactively

---

58   Scholars continue to debate whether investors in ISDS approximate the position of individuals in human rights courts or remain in the posture of those who rely on their states' diplomatic espousal. *See, e.g.,* Zachary Douglas, *The Hybrid Foundations of Investment Treaty Arbitration,* 74 BRIT. Y.B. INT'L L. 151 (2003).

59   Karen J. Alter, *Agents or Trustees? International Courts in Their Political Context,* 14 EUR. J. INT'L REL. 33 (2008); Tom Ginsburg, *Bounded Discretion in International Judicial Lawmaking,* 45 VIRG. J. INT'L L. 631 (2004). *See also* Kenneth W. Abbott & Duncan Snidal, *Why States Act through Formal International Organizations,* 42 J. CONFLICT RESOL. 3 (1998) (arguing that states turn to international institutions, including courts, because they need tools for both centralization and independence); TAI-HENG CHENG, WHEN INTERNATIONAL LAW WORKS: REALISTIC IDEALISM AFTER 9/11 AND THE GLOBAL RECESSION 124–25 (2012) (discussing the value of "legalism" in justifying judicial action).

60   Alter, *supra* note 59.

settling or preventing future disputes and not only the case at hand. Her trustee account also helps to explain why international adjudicators of all stripes— from the ICJ to the WTO—respect and produce regime-specific precedent even without explicit authority from their principals;[61] why at least some of them adopt expansive notions of admissibility, standing, and mootness when these are seen, within particular regimes such as trade, as appropriate legitimizing strategies;[62] and why some adjudicators favor greater transparency or consider arguments raised by others beyond the litigants, as through amicus briefs in ICSID or authorization to consider the views of victims in the ICC.[63]

3   The Fact-Finding Function

All or most international adjudicators, like their national colleagues, engage in factual determinations. Although it is not often recognized as a distinct "function" of courts, the judicial finding of facts is as essential as the identification of the law.[64] Adjudicators need to establish "the truth" in order to determine which rules are applicable as well as to apply them accurately. Depending on the nature of the dispute and the regime, some international adjudicative mechanisms pay closer attention to the fact-finding function than others. Some contain specific rules for engaging in fact-finding, such as authorizations to appoint special masters for this purpose or to permit adjudicators to go onsite. Some, like the WTO, may reserve the fact-finding function to a "lower" chamber (i.e., WTO panels).[65] For some adjudications—such as international criminal trials, disputes over territory, or claims requiring calculations of damages—fact-finding assumes singular importance as judgments of guilt or acquittal, determinations of "effective occupation" or of "fair market value" are all based on factual evidence. Legal rulings in such cases may turn on

---

61   For an explanation of the appeal of precedent to international adjudicators that is consistent with triadic dispute settlement, see von Bogdandy & Venzke, *supra* note 7.

62   *See generally* Joost Pauwelyn, *The Role of Public International Law in the WTO: How Far Can We Go?*, 95 AM. J. INT'L L. 535 (2001).

63   Efforts to promote greater transparency and accountability within ICSID appear to be motivated by legitimacy concerns. *See, e.g.,* Benedict Kingsbury & Stephan Schill, *Investor-State Arbitration as Governance: Fair and Equitable Treatment, Proportionality and the Emerging Global Administrative Law, in* EL NUEVO DERECHO ADMINISTRATIVO GLOBAL EN AMÉRICA LATINA 221 (Benedict Kingsbury & Richard B. Stewart eds., 2009).

64   *Compare* Besson, *supra* note 4.

65   *See* David Palmeter, *The WTO Appellate Body Needs Remand Authority*, 32 J. WORLD TRADE 41 (1998).

whether the evidence demonstrates, for example, that a defendant was present at the scene of the crime, historic title was exercised, or a company's value was affected by the state's action.[66]

Adjudicative fact-finding has generated a number of controversies that need not be addressed here, including whether the fact/law distinction itself is always viable.[67] The distinction is illusive where, for example, international adjudicators, whether or not operating under a set of specific rules, have developed the law relating to the production, admission, and evaluation of evidence in the course of finding relevant facts.[68] Those who find facts may also be creating (perhaps from whole cloth), for example, legal rules on the burden and standards of proof, the propriety of drawing adverse inferences from a party's failure to produce evidence, or the weight to be given admissions against interest by a party.[69]

The fact-finding function enables adjudicators to exercise considerable discretion, even if the existence and scope of that discretion go unrecognized (particularly by the adjudicators themselves). Even international criminal judges—who in theory face the tightest constraints in terms of their delegated power to engage in fact-finding—necessarily engage in many subjective assessments, even while insisting that a defendant be proven guilty "beyond a reasonable doubt."[70] As Nancy Combs has explained, and as seems clear from the varying ways it has been described by judges and scholars, even this high standard of proof encompasses a broad range of probabilities.[71] Combs argues persuasively that judges evaluate the guilt of the defendant on the basis of individualistic tolerances for the likelihood of error; that is, the number of

---

66   Note that the dominance of facts in international criminal tribunals relates not only to determinations of the defendant's guilt. Fact-finding is also vital to producing the definitive history of atrocity in a region or country that is sometimes sought. *See* José E. Alvarez, *Rush to Closure: Lessons of the Tadić Judgment*, 96 MICH. L. REV. 2031 (1998) (discussing the tensions between such goals and the need to focus attention only on the factual allegations made against the defendant).

67   *See, e.g.*, Richard B. Bilder, *The Fact/Law distinction in International Adjudication, in* FACT-FINDING BEFORE INTERNATIONAL TRIBUNALS: ELEVENTH SOKOL COLLOQUIUM 95 (Richard B. Lillich ed., 1992).

68   *See, e.g.*, Keith Highet, *Evidence, the Court, and the Nicaragua Case*, 81 AM. J. INT'L L. 1 (1987); DURWARD V. SANDIFER, EVIDENCE BEFORE INTERNATIONAL TRIBUNALS (1939).

69   These are examples of adjudicative law-making that result from the adjudicative process itself. *See infra* § 4.

70   NANCY ARMOURY COMBS, FACT-FINDING WITHOUT FACTS 343–364 (2010).

71   *Id.* at 344–345.

wrongful convictions/acquittals that can be optimally accepted.[72] In making
these judgments, despite the single uniform standard of burden of proof that
formally applies, they may consider, for example, the seriousness of the charge
(e.g., manslaughter versus genocide), the perceived likelihood of recidivism
(e.g., a child molester versus a *genocidaire* who is not likely to have the opportunity to commit genocide again), the severity of the threatened punishment,
the punishment that the defendant has already suffered, or even more subjective "facts" such as any evidence of the defendant's remorse.[73] She argues that
those with a stake in international criminal tribunals accordingly tolerate a
relatively high level of fact-finding errors precisely because of the subjectivity
of such factual assessments.[74]

Of course, international adjudicators far afield from criminal law engage in
many efforts to determine facts that also involve assigning weights to uncertain factors or reliance on highly subjective assessments. This is perhaps most
evident when adjudicators as different as permanent judges on the European
Court of Human Rights (ECtHR) and ICSID arbitrators make regular recourse
to principles of proportionality or other forms of interest balancing, as with
respect to weighing the competing interests of property holders and government regulators.[75] In such cases, the substantive law itself, to the extent it
requires the balancing of competing interests, delegates discretion to those
who are charged with determining facts.

---

72   *Id.* at 345–346. According to Combs, efforts to quantify the "beyond a reasonable doubt"
       standard among U.S. studies of jury verdicts have ranged from a 90–95% probability of
       guilt to levels of certainty as low as 52.5%. *Id.* at 350.

73   *Id.* at 349–350. *But see* Joseph W. Doherty & Richard H. Steinberg, *Punishment and Policy
       in International Criminal Sentencing: An Empirical Study*, 110 Am. J. Int'l L. 49 (2016)
       (finding that only some of the factors that judges mention as being important actually
       seem to affect the types of sentences given in the International Criminal Tribunal for the
       former Yugoslavia (ICTY) and the International Criminal Tribunal for Rwanda (ICTR)).

74   Combs, *supra* note 70, at 353–355. More controversially, Combs contends that deci-
       sions regarding guilt at the ICTR, for example, reflect unstated assumptions concerning
       the likelihood that a particular ICTR defendant who was not shown to have commit-
       ted the specific offense charged may nonetheless have committed an equally punish-
       able offense in the context of mass killings, such as the genocide in Rwanda. She argues
       that underlying "balancing" factors—including fears of delegitimizing the underlying
       fledging enterprise of international criminal justice—make acquittals in high profile
       cases in international criminal tribunals less likely. *Id.* at 355–357.

75   *See, e.g.*, Alec Stone Sweet, *Investor-State Arbitration: Proportionality's New Frontier*, 4(1)
       L. & Ethics Hum. Rts. 47 (2010).

Judicial discretion with respect to fact-finding often involves discretion over the fact-finding rules themselves. For tribunals that do not operate under a set of detailed rules of procedure and evidence, such as the ICJ, the rules applicable to the fact-finding function are almost entirely judicially created.[76] These judge-made rules, particularly but not only those applied by the ICJ, exert a powerful influence on other tribunals faced with comparable questions having no default evidentiary rules of their own. Such rules, such as the weight to be given an admission against interest by a government, may be included as part of the "common rules of international procedure" or "general principles of international law applicable to arbitration."[77] Even when international courts or tribunals operate under detailed rules of procedure, their adjudicators often have considerable discretion to (re)interpret those rules that may have a considerable bearing on the issues raised in the underlying proceeding (and therefore on subsequent fact-finding). This includes discretion with respect to permitting third parties to intervene as amicus.[78]

There is considerable criticism of how international courts and tribunals have engaged in fact-finding and no shortage of suggestions for institutional or attitudinal reform. Some have contrasted the fact-finding that occurs in

---

76   *See, e.g.*, Keith Highet, *Evidence, The Chamber and the ELSI Case, in* FACT-FINDING BEFORE INTERNATIONAL TRIBUNALS, *supra* note 67, at 33; Highet, *supra* note 68.

77   *See, e.g.*, Trans-Pacific Partnership (TPP) 9.22.7, (not yet ratified) (indicating that investor claimant has the "burden of proving all elements of its claims, consistent with general principles of international law applicable to international arbitration") *at* https://ustr .gov/tpp/.

78   *See, e.g.*, Luigi Crema, *Testing* Amici Curiae *in International Law: Rules and Practice*, 22 IT. Y.B. INT'L L. 91 (2013) (discussing how the European Court of Human Rights, the Inter-American Court of Human Rights, the WTO's Appellate Body, and ISDS tribunals have developed considerable practice on identifying which persons or entities are permitted to intervene as amicus and subject to what conditions they may do so). For a specific example, see Methanex Corp. v. United States of America, Decision of the Tribunal on Petitions from Third Persons to Intervene as "Amici Curiae," (NAFTA/UNCITRAL Ch. 11 Arb. Trib. Jan. 15, 2001) (NAFTA ISDS arbitration deploying its discretion to permit amici subject to certain conditions that it imposes). Note that amici participation rules developed in *Methanex* strongly resemble those that were later adopted by the NAFTA Parties in their Free Trade Statement on Non-Disputing Party Participation Interpretation of Oct. 7, 2003 as well as in the revised UNCITRAL Rules on Transparency in Treaty-based Investor-State Arbitration art. 4 (2014). As Crema indicates, these decisions, and the trend in favor of permitting amici participation in most international courts and tribunals, transform bilateral disputes into polycentric "political forum[s]" and make more credible the claim, discussed *infra* in § V, that these adjudicative bodies are part of "global governance." Crema, *supra*, at 96.

national courts or arbitrations with that evident in ICJ opinions. It is said that, unlike ICSID arbitrations, for example, the ICJ too often relies on fact-finding undertaken by others, rarely deviates from the facts as presented in the written pleadings, fails to cross-examine witnesses or conduct on-site hearings, and discourages amicus from those who might have a different view of the relevant facts.[79] Some have suggested, more generally, that international adjudicators avoid engaging, to their detriment, with certain forms of facts, such as "scientific" facts requiring technical expertise or explicit reliance on probabilistic judgments.[80] The ICJ has been accused of being insufficiently proactive in deploying its own powers to find facts and of not, for example, appointing experts even when this seemed desirable. Perhaps as a result of these criticisms, in some recent cases the ICJ has taken modest steps to mollify its fact-finding critics.[81]

There is no shortage of reasons to explain the fact-finding difficulties faced by international adjudicators. International judges and arbitrators have to operate, after all, at a considerable geographic, cultural, and linguistic remove from the places and the persons implicated in the underlying crime or dispute. They are further handicapped by the absence of enforcement or subpoena powers to compel the production of evidence or to secure witnesses. International criminal tribunals faced with crimes committed in a zone of ongoing conflict face, in addition, formidable (and sometimes insurmountable) obstacles not usually faced by any national court. Fact-finding difficulties may also emerge from self-inflicted wounds—as when the states that establish these courts fail to select judges or arbitrators with relevant experience. It is hard to expect, for example, international criminal judges who have had no prior trial experience

79   *See, e.g.*, Thomas M. Franck, *Fact-Finding in the I.C.J.*, in FACT-FINDING BEFORE INTERNATIONAL TRIBUNALS, *supra* note 67, at 21 (criticizing the ICJ's avoidance of the facts and reliance on a paper trial in *Temple of Preah Vihear*, the Nicaragua Case, and its Advisory Opinion in *Western Sahara*). *See also* José E. Alvarez, *Are International Judges Afraid of Science?: A Comment on Mbengue*, 34 LOY. L.A. INT'L & COMP. L. REV. 81, at 83 (2011) (addressing Franck's arguments).

80   *Compare* Makane Moïse Mbengue, *International Courts and Tribunals as Fact-Finders: The Case of Scientific Fact-Finding in International Adjudication*, 34 LOY. L.A. INT'L & COMP. L. REV. 53 (2011) (making this claim) *with* Alvarez, *supra* note 79 (questioning Mbengue's premises and conclusions).

81   But these efforts have not mollified all the Court's critics. *See, e.g.*, JAMES DEVANEY, FACT-FINDING BEFORE THE INTERNATIONAL COURT OF JUSTICE (forthcoming 2016) (arguing that "the ICJ's current approach to fact-finding falls short of adequacy").

to be able to engage with the complex factual questions implicated in cases of mass atrocity involving hundreds of victims as well as alleged perpetrators.[82]

The extent and quality of judicial fact-finding is also heavily dependent on structural factors such as the tribunal's budgetary constraints, the availability of other institutional support, or the possibility of higher court review of the facts as well as the law. Ever since Nuremberg, it has been evident that the quality of the facts presented in international criminal courts, for example, is heavily dependent on the resources given to both prosecution and defense teams to mount a successful factual case on either side. The quality of adjudicative fact-finding may also vary depending on whether extra-judicial resources exist in the particular institutional context. Is a powerful state waiting in the wings to supply evidence to the ICC's prosecutor as needed? Is there a cadre of institutional bureaucrats—whether inside the WTO's secretariat, Interpol, or among other elements of civil society—to complement the fact-finding deficiencies of the judges or arbitrators operating within respective regimes?[83]

The extent and quality of adjudicative fact-finding may also be dependent on whether the particular adjudicative body is free to solicit or accept the views (including amicus briefs) of non-litigants. A tribunal that is open to amicus briefs or that, like the WTO or North American Free Trade Agreement (NAFTA) investment arbitrations, accepts the views of all state parties to the underlying treaty regime apart from the litigating parties, is no longer engaged in the pure triadic form of dispute resolution described by Shapiro in the prior section—or in the triadic form of fact-finding that more "bilateral" forms of adjudication anticipate.[84] An international court or arbitral body that can

---

82   See Bilder, *supra* note 67, at 98 (also suggesting that in some cases international courts' fact-finding difficulties are self-imposed insofar as they see decision-making based on analysis of legal principle as more prestigious or "weighty"); *see also* COMBS, *supra* note 70.

83   *See generally* Joost Pauwelyn & Manfred Elsig, *The Politics of Treaty Interpretation: Variations and Explanations across International Tribunals, in* INTERDISCIPLINARY PERSPECTIVES ON INTERNATIONAL LAW AND INTERNATIONAL RELATIONS, *supra* note 8, at 445, 460, Figure 18.1 (identifying various institutional factors); Helfer & Slaughter, *supra* note 44 (surveying the impact of diverse institutional constraints). Of course, the fact-finding approach of even established tribunals may change over time in response to internal or external pressures. *See generally* Maximo Langer & Joseph W. Doherty, *Managerial Judging Goes International but Its Promise Remains Unfulfilled: An Empirical Assessment of the ICTY Reforms*, 36 YALE J. INT'L L. 241 (2011).

84   Indeed, the tendency to accept amicus in international courts and tribunals stems from a growing recognition that these adjudicators have an impact on the making and application of public law and that therefore the wider public needs to be consulted.

receive the views of non-parties to the case before it is far more likely to engage in broader fact-finding than one that limits itself to the data supplied by the litigants. Accordingly, the increasing number of international courts and tribunals that now accept the views of amicus, including from NGOs, are, from the outset, forums that are far more likely to engage diverse perspectives with respect to finding relevant facts.[85]

At the same time, proposals for reforming or improving adjudicative fact-finding need to keep the institutional context in mind. Efforts to transplant procedures from one body to another may not produce the same results. For example, while some have suggested that international courts would do a better job on fact-finding if they appointed their own experts to go outside the four corners of what the litigants present to them, this assumes that this external recourse is always preferable or equally desirable for all adjudicative venues. Neither may be true. ICSID tribunals, for instance, may avoid the appointment of outside fact-finding experts because that forum remains tethered to the

---

See, e.g., Methanex v. USA, Amicus Curiae Submissions by the International Institute for Sustainable Development (Mar. 9, 2004).

85   On the increasing acceptance of amicus among international courts and tribunals, see, for example, Crema, *supra* note 78. *See also* International Criminal Court Rules of Procedure and Evidence, Rule 103(1), U.N. Doc. ICC/ASP/1/3 (2002), *at* http://www.icc-cpi.int; Rules of Procedure and Evidence of the International Criminal Tribunal for the Former Yugoslavia, Rule 74, UN Doc. IT/32/Rev. 49, *at* http://www.icty.org; Rules of Procedure and Evidence of the International Criminal Tribunal for Rwanda, Rule 74, U.N. Doc. ITR/3/Rev.19 (Apr. 10, 2013), *at* http://www.unictr.org/en/documents; The Internal Rules of the Extraordinary Chambers in the Courts of Cambodia, Rule 33(1) (Rev. 9), *at* http://www.eccc.gov.kh/sites/default/files/legal-documents/Internal_Rules_Rev_9_Eng.pdf; European Convention for the Protection of Human Rights and Fundamental Freedoms art. 36.2, Nov. 4, 1950, 213 UNTS 221, *at* http://conventions.coe.int/Treaty/en/Treaties/Html/005.htm; Rules of Procedure of the Inter-American Court on Human Rights art. 44, *at* https://www.cidh.oas.org/Basicos/English/Basic20.Rules%20of%20Procedure%20of%20the%20Court.htm; Rules of Procedure and Evidence of the Residual Special Court for Sierra Leone, Rule 74, *at* http://www.rscsl.org/Documents/RSCSL-Rules.pdf; Rules of Procedure and Evidence of the Special Tribunal for Lebanon, Rule 131, STL-BD-2009-01-Rev.7, *at* www.specialtribunalforlebanon.com/en/documents/stl-documents/rules-of-procedure-and-evidence; Regulation No. 2006/12 on the Establishment of the Human Rights Advisory Panel by the United Nations Interim Administration Mission in Kosovo § 13, U.N. Doc. UNMIK/REG/2006/12 (Mar. 23, 2006), *at* http://www.unmikonline.org/hrap/Documents%20HRAP/Regulations%20Eng/RE2006_12.pdf; Procedural Rules of the Court of Arbitration for Sport, Rule 41.4, *at* http://www.tas-cas.org/en/arbitration/code-procedural-rules.html; Rules of Procedure of the Administrative Tribunal of the International Monetary Fund, Rule XV, *at* https://www.imf.org/external/imfat/rules.htm.

model of commercial arbitration on which investor-state arbitration was constructed. Traditionally that species of arbitration is seen as the creature of the litigants who frame their dispute, consent to jurisdiction, and appoint its arbitrators. Fear of disrupting that model—and perhaps of running afoul of ICSID annulment—may constrain ICSID arbitrators' recourse to their own fact-finding experts or special masters. And it is not clear that ICSID fact-finding may require such external initiatives. Some have argued that ICSID arbitrators need no such external help insofar as they are drawn from the private bar or commercial practice and may be more comfortable with the handling of complex facts and the questioning of witnesses than, for example, the typical ICJ judge.[86] The fact that ICSID arbitrations typically involve well-funded litigants (at least on the side of investor claimants) who engage their own fact-finding experts and their own extensive presentation of witnesses and documents—as compared to the resources allocated to either side in international criminal courts, for example—obviously needs to be taken into account as well.

As the ICSID example suggests, the extent and quality of fact-finding may turn on the quality of the adjudicators themselves. Have they previously had experience in finding facts (as on a trial court) or has their judicial experience been limited to serving as appellate judges or perhaps worse still, been limited to writing about judges as scholars? Do they come from a legal tradition where judges, as opposed to advocates or litigants, are proactive in fact-finding? Although the difference between judges from Anglo-Saxon and the civil law have been overstated, it still remains the case that, as Durward Sandifer indicated long ago, judges from the Anglo-American tradition may approach the process of judging (at least non-criminal cases) less as a search for absolute "truth" than as a process that rewards the litigant who succeeds in presenting the most convincing evidence.[87] His or her approach may be quite different from someone trained in Germany, for example, where the judge is active even in the formulation of the factual issues and does not only rely on statements of fact submitted by the parties. As Sandifer notes, despite the fact that international adjudicators operate largely without formal rules restricting the admission of evidence, comparable to those that exist within national courts that are sensitive about the types of evidence that might go before a jury, an individual judge or arbitrator might still be inclined to emulate the practices of his or her own national court judges.[88] The relevance of these legal traditions may still

---

86   *See* Joost Pauwelyn, *The Rule of Law Without the Rule of Lawyers? Why Investment Arbitrators are from Mars, Trade Panelists from Venus* 109 AM. J. INT'L L. 761 (2015).

87   *See* SANDIFER, *supra* note 68, at 13 (rev. ed. 1975).

88   *Id.*

hold sway even in the context of today's international criminal courts, which have forged hybrid compromises concerning the receipt and handling of evidence (and determining facts) between the competing traditions.[89]

The relative embeddedness of a court within a larger regime also matters. Whether a court's assessment of the facts is likely to remain the last word within the specific legal regime in which it operates is likely to influence how (or even whether) that court engages in fact-finding. To the extent a court exists within a broader institutional framework that permits states parties to exercise their exit and voice,[90] this too will influence just how "proactive" on either law-making or fact-finding a judge or arbitrator is likely to be. Investor-state arbitral tribunals—which operate within a regime that permits states displeased with an arbitral outcome to resort to annulment proceedings, exercise civil disobedience by failing to pay arbitral awards, issue "interpretations" of the same treaties that the arbitrators are interpreting, or even exit from the underlying treaty regimes (such as ICSID or a particular bilateral investment Treaty (BIT))—may be more inclined to engage in active fact-finding than other tribunals.[91] As is true with respect to a court's ability to declare the law, a court's ability to assert itself with respect to the facts—and especially to present *sua sponte* factual issues that the litigants have ignored—may turn on whether the court thinks it can get away with such determinations or whether, alternatively, its own fragile legitimacy will be harmed by doing so.

To be sure, the institutional features or constraints of international courts or tribunals do not produce predictable consequences with respect to fact-finding. While it might be assumed that fiscal or temporal constraints will render adjudicators less able or willing to engage in proactive fact-finding, the opposite may be the case. As is well known, given the time and expense of the ICTY and ICTR, the UN resolved to force those tribunals to end all pending trials by a date certain.[92] This constraint appears to have inspired a more, not less, proactive judiciary with respect to fact-finding. Maximo Langer and Joseph Doherty argue that the pressure to quicken the pace of trials has encouraged a "managerial" approach to judging within those tribunals more akin to that found in some U.S. courts.[93] Similarly, the existence of some form of appeals mechanism may produce distinct results on fact-finding, depending on con-

---

89   *See, e.g.,* Daryl A. Mundis, *Improving the Operation and Functioning of the International Criminal Tribunals*, 94 AM J. INT'L L. 759, 765 (2000).

90   *See* ALBERT O. HIRSCHMAN, EXIT, VOICE AND LOYALTY 1–4 (1970).

91   *See generally* Alvarez, *supra* note 41.

92   *See, e.g.,* Langer & Doherty, *supra* note 83.

93   *Id.* at 242.

text. At one extreme, an international court's engagement with fact-finding may not have much to do with whether it exists within a structure permitting appellate review. Subject to narrow exceptions, the WTO's Appellate Body can only review findings of law, not fact, and it is not capable of remanding to a WTO panel to revisit factual findings.[94] An ICSID annulment process is even more restricted, at least according to Article 53 of the ICSID Convention; ICSID annulment committees are not supposed to undertake a full scale review of either legal or factual findings.[95] In both instances, despite these forms of "review," original fact-finding determinations may prove difficult to overturn. At the other extreme, the International Criminal Court operates within a hierarchical system that permits appeals from a trial chamber or pre-trial chamber; it also operates within a system that includes an Assembly of State Parties that might be inclined to "supervise" even the actions of that Court's "independent" prosecutor.[96]

We should not expect all our international tribunals, despite such differences in purpose, personnel, and structure, to approach fact-finding the same way. The institutional context in which international adjudicators operate, the constituencies that they affect, as well as the rules under which they operate, will all matter to how and what facts they will find.[97]

4   The Law-Making Function

As is evident to those who study, for example, human rights law, international criminal law, international trade law, or international investment law, these fields rely heavily on adjudicative caselaw as generated by regional human rights courts or UN human rights treaty bodies, international criminal courts, the WTO dispute settlement system, or ISDS, respectively. Anyone who wants to get an accurate sense of the contemporary meaning of the GATT covered agreements or the European Convention on Human Rights, for example, would

---

94   WTO, *Dispute Settlement System Training Module* § 6.5, *at* https://www.wto.org/english/
      tratop_e/dispu_e/disp_settlement_cbt_e/signin_e.htm.

95   Convention on the Settlement of Investment Disputes Between States and Nationals of
      Other States, arts. 50–53, Mar. 18, 1965, 575 U.N.T.S. 159, 17 U.S.T. 1270 [hereinafter ICSID
      Convention].

96   *See, e.g.*, Alvarez, *supra* note 37.

97   *See, e.g.*, Karen J. Alter, Laurence R. Helfer & Mikael Rask Madsen, *How Context Shapes the
      Authority of International Courts*, 79 L. & CONTEMP. PROBS. 1 (2016).

be foolish to look only at the original treaty texts.[98] Treatises on these topics consist almost entirely of adjudicative rulings examined not only for their effects on the specific litigants but for what they tell us the law is. International adjudicators make law, and not merely as an incidental or accidental adjunct to settling a particular dispute or resolving conflict. In some international regimes, a principal goal of its adjudicative mechanism is to enable the rendering of authoritative judgments on disputed points of law precisely because these are needed to guide all participants in the regime, and not only the parties to the concrete dispute being resolved.[99] The law-making function is one reason why international adjudicators are engaged in a more multilateral exercise than "triadic" dispute settlement implies.

Judicial gap-filling of the law is an inescapable by-product of the application of law to fact. It is also the by-product of certain communicative practices that appear endemic to the art of judging. International adjudicators are, as Bogdandy and Venzke contend, generally under the "spell of precedents."[100] As permanent international courts and tribunals have proliferated, so have their publically available rulings or awards. Through 2011, according to one study, the 37,236 legally binding judgments issued by such entities included: 18,511 by the European Court of Justice; 14,940 by the ECtHR; 239 by the Inter-

---

98   No one doubts that multilateral treaties that are accompanied by dispute settlement mechanisms, such as a human rights regional court or the WTO Dispute Settlement Body, incorporate a built-in mechanism for on-going legal (re)interpretations of the founding treaty. For an example involving the Inter-American Court of Human Rights, see, for example, Christina Binder, *The Prohibition of Amnesties by the Inter-American Court of Human Rights, in* INTERNATIONAL JUDICIAL LAWMAKING: ON PUBLIC AUTHORITY AND DEMOCRATIC LEGITIMATION IN GLOBAL GOVERNANCE 295 (Armin von Bogdandy & Ingo Venzke eds., 2012).

99   *See generally* Besson, *supra* note 4; von Bogdandy & Venzke, *supra* note 26. For examples within discrete regimes, *see* Murphy, *supra* note 4; Ebobrah, *supra* note 4; von Bogdandy & Venzke, *supra* note 7; Schreuer, *supra* note 9; Baudenbacher & Clifton, *supra* note 19. This reflects an instrumentalist or functionalist view of the legal impact of courts. There is, of course, a lengthy debate in jurisprudence, not discussed here but which we revisit in *infra* Chapter VI, concerning whether it is proper to see courts as having "constitutive" effects of their own or should only be seen as "declaring" the law made by the law-giver. As noted in *supra* Chapter I, to positivists the only law-giver in international law is the state.

100   Armin von Bogdandy & Ingo Venzke, *Beyond Dispute: International Judicial Institutions as Lawmakers*, 12 GERM. L.J. 979 (2011); Ingo Venzke, *Making General Exceptions: The Spell of Precedents in Developing Article XX GATT into Standards for Domestic Regulatory Policy*, 12 GERM. L.J. 1111 (2011). *See also* Pauwelyn & Elsig, *supra* note 83, at 456, 460 Table 18.1 (describing the ICJ, the WTO's Appellate Body, ISDS, the ECtHR, and the IACHR as examples of international adjudicators that are systemic followers of precedent).

American Court of Human Rights; 176 panel rulings and 108 Appellate Body rulings within the WTO; 77 by the ICJ; 93 judgments by the ICTY; 72 by the ICTR; and 17 rulings by the International Tribunal for the Law of the Sea (ITLOS).[101] These rulings have gained in significance and prominence insofar as they have become the basis for a body of "precedent" within international regimes (and sometimes across them) despite the absence of the principle of *stare decisis*.[102] The tendency for adjudicators to rely on other adjudicators has not been limited to today's permanent international courts. The phenomenon has also been evident with respect to quasi-judicial venues like UN human rights treaty committees and more *ad hoc* arbitral mechanisms.[103]

Even the non-legally binding views expressed by human rights treaty bodies, either in the course of examining individual complaints or in expressing "general views," have sometimes been cited by international courts or other adjudicative bodies, including national courts.[104] Thus, the ICJ addressed the legal status of the Human Rights Committee's interpretation of the International

---

101 ALTER, *supra* note 1, at 72–75, Figure 3.1. These numbers exclude advisory opinions and do not include rulings issued by the PCIJ or by GATT panels prior to 1994.

102 *See, e.g.*, ICJ Statute, *supra* note 35, art. 59 ("The decision of the Court has no binding force except between the parties and in respect of that particular case."). To be sure, none of the permanent international courts in existence operate under any rule rendering their decisions binding on others apart from the litigants in the case *sub judice*. Thus, even the ICC only indicates that its judges "*may* apply principles and rules of law as interpreted in its previous decisions." Rome Statute, *supra* note 36, art. 21(2) (emphasis added). The judicial preference for precedent discussed here refers to the trend to rely on prior adjudicative decisions rendered by either the same judicial body or others, national or international, not as binding authority but as "*jurisprudence constante*." The extent to which different international adjudicators rely on prior judicial decisions—the relative weight given to such authority—varies.

103 For an effort to explain why this occurs, see, for example, Patrick M. Norton, *The Use of Precedents in Investment Treaty Arbitration Awards*, 25 AM. REV. INT'L ARB. 167 (2014).

104 *See, e.g.*, Geir Ulfstein, *Law-Making by Human Rights Treaty Bodies, in* INTERNATIONAL LAW-MAKING: ESSAYS IN HONOUR OF JAN KLABBERS 249 (Rain Liivoja & Jarna Petman eds., 2013); David Weissbrodt, Joseph C. Hansen & Nathaniel H. Nesbitt, *The Role of the Committee on the Rights of the Child in Interpreting and Developing International Humanitarian Law*, 24 HARV. HUM. RTS. J. 115 (2011); Karin Oellers-Frahm, *Lawmaking Through Advisory Opinions?*, 12 Germ. L.J. 1033 (2011). *See also* Rosanne van Alebeek & André Nollkaemper, *The Legal Status of Decisions by Human Rights Treaty Bodies in National Law, in* UN HUMAN RIGHTS TREATY BODIES: LAW AND LEGITIMACY 356 (Helen Keller & et al. eds., 2012) (noting the impact of national law, including the existence of enabling legislation, as influencing the legal effect given to treaty bodies' views in national courts).

Covenant on Civil and Political Rights (ICCPR) in its ruling in the Diallo Case in 2010, noting:

> Since it was created, the Human Rights Committee has built up a considerable body of interpretative case law, in particular through its findings in response to the individual communications which may be submitted to it in respect of States parties to the first Optional Protocol, and in the form of its "General Comments". Although the Court is in no way obliged, in the exercise of its judicial functions, to model its own interpretation of the Covenant on that of the Committee, it believes that it should ascribe great weight to the interpretation adopted by this independent body that was established specifically to supervise the application of that treaty. The point here is to achieve the necessary clarity and the essential consistency of international law, as well as legal security, to which both the individuals with guaranteed rights and the States obliged to comply with treaty obligations are entitled.[105]

Anyone who examines the contemporary rulings or opinions issued by today's international adjudicators will find that a common source of authority cited, sometimes the most prevalent, are prior adjudicative decisions, often by the same adjudicative body. This reliance on prior rulings as persuasive authority, while not sanctioned by general international law or by the Statute of the ICJ in particular,[106] entails a number of consequences. It is the most prominent reason why many scholars posit that such courts engage in "law-making" insofar as their rulings have a legal impact beyond affecting the status of the parties before them.[107] It is also a key reason why international adjudication, even when modeled on arbitration mechanisms initially developed for the

---

105   Case Concerning Ahmadou Sadio Diallo (Republic of Guinea v. Democratic Republic of the Congo), Judgment, 2010 I.C.J. 639, ¶ 66 (Nov. 30). In that case, the Court also addressed the interpretations of regional human rights conventions by the relevant treaty bodies, noting that
       "Likewise, when the Court is called upon ... to apply a regional instrument for the protection of human rights, it must take due account of the interpretation of that instrument adopted by the independent bodies which have been specifically created, if such has been the case, to monitor the sound application of the treaty in question."
       Id. ¶ 67.

106   *See supra* note 102.

107   *See generally* von Bogdandy & Venzke, *supra* note 100; Venzke, *supra* note 100; Marc Jacob, *Precedents: Lawmaking Through International Adjudication, in* INTERNATIONAL JUDICIAL LAWMAKING 35, *supra* note 98.

handling of private (non-state) disputes, is commonly characterized as a form of "public" adjudication that produces "public law."[108] The production of public decisions that in turn rely on prior arbitral or judicial rulings is consistent with expectations for the rule of law; it is consistent with rule of law demands in favor of enhanced stability, predictability, and the protection of legitimate expectations. Reliance on this so-called *jurisprudence constante* promotes the harmonious or stable development of the law within particular international law regimes. Indeed, the absence of such reliance, the inability to render consistent interpretations within a particular regime, or the inability to deliver coherent jurisprudence across international law's various sub-regimes generates well-known anxieties about international law's "fragmentation."[109]

An international tribunal's reliance on its prior "caselaw" is a self-fulfilling phenomenon. The more that it happens, the more it increases expectations that this will and should occur. This is perhaps most clearly demonstrated by the production of *jurisprudence constante* even among *ad hoc* investor-state tribunals interpreting what are now over 3000 international investment protection treaties. The insistence, including by international civil society, that the relevant rules applicable to ISDS produce transparent proceedings and awards—leading to changes in the underlying rules governing ICSID or United Nations Commission on International Trade Law (UNCITRAL) arbitrations—has generated an increasingly visible ISDS "caselaw." The insistence on transparent awards has in turn generated an expectation that the role of investor-state arbitrators is not only to settle each dispute one at a time but precisely to engage in the production of consistent international investment law despite the lack of a single international investment treaty comparable to that which exists for international trade. This expectation, whether or not it is actually realized,[110] is now reflected in the statements made by some of the arbitrators

---

108 *See, e.g.*, Gus Van Harten & Martin Loughlin, *Investment Treaty Arbitration as a Species of Global Administrative Law*, 17 EUR. J. INT'L L. 121 (2006); GUS VAN HARTEN, INVESTMENT TREATY ARBITRATION AND PUBLIC LAW (2007). *See also* INTERNATIONAL INVESTMENT LAW AND COMPARATIVE PUBLIC LAW (Stephan W. Schill ed., 2010).

109 *See, e.g.*, Study Group of the International Law Commission, *Fragmentation of International Law: Difficulties Arising from the Diversification and Expansion of International Law*, U.N. Doc. A/CN.4/L.682 (Apr. 13, 2006) [hereinafter Fragmentation Study]; Gerhard Hafner, *Pros and Cons Ensuing from Fragmentation of International Law*, 25 MICH. J. INT'L L. 849 (2003).

110 *See* Andrea Bjorklund, *Improving the International Investment Law and Policy System, in* THE EVOLVING INTERNATIONAL INVESTMENT REGIME: EXPECTATIONS, REALITIES, OPTIONS 213, 220–221 (José E. Alvarez et al. eds., 2011) (criticizing investor-state arbitration

themselves.[111] This may explain why, according to statistical studies, investor-state arbitrators evince a marked preference for precedents,[112] and why at least ICSID awards have clearly become more self-referential over time.[113] This preference for precedents within ISDS also makes more credible the proposition

---

precisely on the basis that its arbitrators are not sufficiently deferential to prior rulings on point).

111   Indeed, the arbitrators in Saipem S.p.A. v. Bangladesh, a 2009 award, went so far as to suggest that they had a duty to consider prior awards:

"The Tribunal considers that it is not bound by previous decisions. At the same time, it is of the opinion that it must pay due consideration to earlier decisions of international tribunals. It believes that, subject to compelling contrary grounds, it has a duty to adopt solutions established in a series of consistent cases. It also believes that, subject to the specifics of a given treaty and of the circumstances of the actual case, it has a duty to seek to contribute to the harmonious development of investment law and thereby to meet the legitimate expectations of the community of States and investors towards certainty of the rule of law."

Saipem S.p.A. v. The People's Republic of Bangl., ICSID Case No. ARB/05/07, Decision on Jurisdiction and Recommendation on Provisional Measures, ¶ 67 (Mar. 21, 2007) (footnotes omitted). *See also* Stephan W. Schill, *System-Building in Investment Treaty Arbitration and Lawmaking, in* INTERNATIONAL JUDICIAL LAWMAKING 133, 162 n. 83, *supra* note 98 (noting "[v]irtually identical statements . . . in almost all cases in which Gabrielle Kaufmann-Kohler participated as an arbitrator"). *But see* Glamis Gold, *supra* note 40, at 1056–1059, ¶¶ 598–616 (declining to follow the precedent of awards interpreting treaties not specifically under consideration in this dispute); RosInvestCo UK v. Russ. Fed'n, Award on Jurisdiction, SCC Case No. V079/2005, ¶ 137 (doing the same and declaring "the primary function of this Tribunal to decide the case before it rather than developing further the general discussion . . .").

112   *See, e.g.*, Schill, *supra* note 111, at 153–156. Schill argues that the weight given to prior arbitral rulings in ISDS is such that these are more important than the texts of the underlying treaties or state practice. *Id.* at 163. Professor Fauchald found that prior arbitral case law was used as an "interpretive argument" in 92 out of 98 ICSID cases. Ole Kristian Fauchald, *The Legal Reasoning of ICSID Tribunals—An Empirical Analysis*, 19 EUR. J. INT'L L. 301, 335 (2008). Fauchald concludes that "most tribunals accept a strong presumption in favour of following longstanding and consistent case law." *Id.* at 337–338. Of course, real disagreements emerge even within an adjudicative system as devoted to *jurisprudence constante* as is ISDS. *See, e.g.*, JOSÉ E. ALVAREZ, THE PUBLIC INTERNATIONAL LAW REGIME GOVERNING INTERNATIONAL INVESTMENT 260–284 (discussing "The Inconsistent Argentina Cases"); Schill, *supra* at 165–169 (discussing judicial techniques for handling inconsistent awards).

113   One study, by Jeffery P. Commission, indicates that whereas in 1990, the average number of citations to prior ICSID awards was .33 per award; by 2006 it was 9.3, an increase of 2818%—vastly exceeding any jump that would have been predicted by the greater number of such awards over time. Jeffery P. Commission, *Precedent in Investment Treaty*

that there really is such a thing as an "international investment system" and not merely 3000 disparate agreements producing incoherent rulings.[114]

To be sure, those who establish international courts or tribunals do not explicitly delegate law-making power to their adjudicators. Like all actors who engage in contracting, states sometimes fail to anticipate the legal gaps or uncertainties in their agreements or the extent to which their adjudicators will need to fill them, and are often surprised when their judges or arbitrators make law.[115] It is unlikely that the 180 states that are now parties to international investment agreements anticipated that the arbitrators charged with settling disputes under these treaties would assume the role of producing *jurisprudence constante*—a result which means that even states that are not respondents to particular disputes will need to take into account those rulings since their interests could be affected by decisions in which they were not involved. Indeed, the spell cast by precedent, particularly in the investment regime, may explain at least some of the growing signs of backlash against ISDS generally. Not all states or stakeholders in the regime draw comfort from the possibility that the adjudication of investment disputes has become a key tool in building international investment law even without global agreement on a single multilateral investment treaty.[116]

But while states may be surprised by the attempt to produce *jurisprudence constante* across international investment treaties (and by comparable efforts by other international adjudicators), the reasons why many (if not all) international adjudicators tend to rely on what their predecessors have done are not mysterious. Some adjudicators are encouraged to do so by the specific expectations within a regime, such as trade and investment, for the production of predictable, and more or less stable, rules. Thus, while Article 3.2 of the WTO's DSU, as noted, stresses the function of dispute settlement and indicates that

---

Arbitration: A Citation Analysis of a Developing Jurisprudence, 24 J. INT'L ARB. 129, 148–150 (2007).

114   *See, e.g.,* Schill, *supra* note 111, at 140; Tai-Heng Cheng, *Is There a System of Precedent in Investment Treaty Arbitration?*, Address at the U.S. Council on International Business Young Arbitrators Forum (Oct. 22, 2006) *at* http://papers.ssrn.com/sol3/papers.cfm?abstract_id=1259943.

115   *See* DSU, *supra* note 3, art. 3.2 (barring rulings by the Dispute Settlement Body that "add to or diminish" rights in the covered agreements). *But see* Robert Howse, *Moving the WTO Forward—One Case at a Time*, 42 CORNELL INT'L L.J. 223, 227–228 (2009) (noting instances where WTO adjudicators advanced the law despite political deadlocks).

116   *Compare* THE BACKLASH AGAINST INVESTMENT ARBITRATION: PERCEPTIONS AND REALITY (Michael Waibel, Asha Kaushal, Kyo-Hwa Liz Chung & Claire Balchin eds., 2010) *with* Schill, *supra* note 111; Jacob, *supra* note 107.

WTO adjudicators should not "add to or diminish the rights and obligations provided in the covered agreements," it also indicates that this dispute settlement system is intended to provide "security and predictability." The predictability desired by consumers of WTO law is certainly enhanced by WTO panels' respect for WTO precedents, as well as the coherency generated by the WTO Appellate Body's own preference for its own precedents. Quite apart from the Rome Statute's explicit direction to its judges that they *may* consider that Court's previous decisions,[117] all other international criminal judges are encouraged to refer to prior relevant decisions by the ban on *nullum crimen sine lege* as well as the demand for strict interpretation of criminal law.[118] Concerns for the production and application of predictable law are also evident within the international investment regime. Thus, the 2012 U.S. Model Bilateral Investment Treaty, like its predecessor, indicates in its preamble that those who enter into that agreement are seeking a "stable framework for investment" to "maximize effective utilization of economic resources and improve living standards."[119]

But even without such direction, pragmatic rationales drive adjudicators' preference for precedents. Reliance on what other adjudicators have concluded in the past, particularly but not only within the same international regime, is a convenient source for the analogies which lie at the heart of most legal reasoning.[120] Reasoning by analogy reflects a preference for balancing the desire for the legal *status quo* with the need to respond to new situations and for increased precision over time; references to prior opinions are a key way to permit incremental change responsive to both. Of course, the spell of precedent may be all the more appealing to the extent those issuing the prior rulings share commonalities of thought and training; it may occur more readily within a common epistemic community with shared expertise.[121] Turning to prece-

117   Rome Statute, *supra* note 36, art. 21(2).

118   *Id.* art. 22, *but see infra* at text and notes 138–209 (discussing how international criminal courts nonetheless engage in law-making).

119   United States Department of State, *2012 U.S. Model Bilateral Investment Treaty* (*Treaty Between the Government of the United States of America and the Government of [Country] Concerning the Encouragement and Reciprocal Protection of Investment*) Preamble, *at* http://www.state.gov/documents/organization/188371.pdf. *See also* United States Department of State, 2004 U.S. Model Bilateral Investment Treaty Preamble, *at* http://www.state.gov/documents/organization/117601.pdf.

120   *See, e.g.*, Schill, *supra* note 111, at 157–158. *But see infra* at text and note 135 (discussing the constraints on the use of analogies in international criminal law).

121   At the same time, the absence of such commonalities may also help to explain sharp differences in how distinct international adjudicators engage in interpretation, including their relative recourse to precedent, as well as the absence of more evidence of trans-

dent, even if not binding, is also a convenient way to abbreviate the length of an arbitral or judicial opinion while still supplying the reasoned judgment that is usually expected.[122] Most obviously, it is a way to attempt to deflect charges of judicial law-making. A judge or arbitrator who concludes that the law provides x because other adjudicators have said the same spreads the blame for her interpretations, thereby stemming criticisms that she is engaged in "judicial activism."[123] This may encourage the voluntary state compliance that these usually fragile adjudicative mechanisms rely on. This is especially true to the extent prior opinions have the "lineage" or "pedigree" that Thomas Franck included in his conception of legitimacy.[124] For positivists, prior arbitral or judicial opinions, if accepted by states, might form part of the state practice and *opinio juris* that can be considered to establish custom.

There may also be more tactical reasons. Reliance on national judicial rulings may enable an international adjudicator to show deference to states. More cynically perhaps, given the increased number and variety of international rulings now emerging, the ability to select among these accords international adjudicators considerable discretion to pick those that are most sympathetic, consistent with what they want to achieve.[125]

These diverse rationales are not confined to entities envisioned as permanent bodies. Patrick Norton, writing in 1991 about the Iran-U.S. Claims Tribunal (a tribunal whose longevity was probably not anticipated by its creators), argued that the arbitrators before that Tribunal turned to prior arbitral awards as a way of legitimizing decisions that would otherwise lack unambiguously

---

judicial communications across the national-international divide. *Compare* Pauwelyn, *supra* note 86 (arguing that the differences in background between those who serve as adjudicators in ISDS and the WTO explains other features of those regimes' respective adjudications) *with* Anne-Marie Slaughter, *A Typology of Transjudicial Communication*, 29 U. RICH. L. REV. 99 (1994) (arguing that such communications are increasingly common and desirable).

122   *See, e.g.*, Schill, *supra* note 111, at 159–160.

123   Schill also argues that an adjudicator who prefers precedent "shifts the burden of argumentation by demanding a reasoned justification for departing from precedent." Schill, *supra* note 111, at 162. To the extent this is the case, the reliance on precedents may itself affect the burdens of proof.

124   THOMAS M. FRANCK, THE POWER OF LEGITIMACY AMONG NATIONS 91–100.

125   For discussion of the nuances among international courts even within those that express a preference for precedents, as between those that merely refer to their own prior rulings and those that appear to rely on them as if bound, see Tom Ginsburg, *International Judicial Lawmaking, in* INTERNATIONAL CONFLICT RESOLUTION 155 (Stefan Voigt, Max Albert & Dieter Schmidtchen eds., 2006).

authoritative sources.[126] He noted that prior arbitral awards—as compared to, say, lump sum settlements between the parties—appeared to be more impartial, contain a more fulsome form of reasoning, and were explicitly grounded in positive law. He also argued that reliance on such precedents deflected criticism since it enabled them to claim that they were only filling interstitial gaps in settled law.[127]

The appeal of prior precedents can also be explained by more general factors. To the extent that international judges abide by the injunction not to issue rulings of *non-liquet* (despite anomalies like the ICJ's opinion in the *Nuclear Weapons* Case),[128] rulings issued by their judicial or arbitral colleagues may be the only place to find the law needed to fill international law's many gaps. Some might also see recourse to such prior rulings as inherent to the rule of law, as reflected, for instance in Dworkin's emphasis on the integrity of the law and the need to treat like cases alike.[129] Recourse to arbitral or judicial rulings across international regimes—where, for example, ISDS rulings refer to, if not rely on, rulings issued by regional human rights courts—may be driven by the prevailing view (at least among scholars) that there is no such thing as a "self-contained" regime within international law.[130] Horizontal regime-crossing across international regimes, whether encouraged by the arguments presented by the litigants or (perhaps less commonly) produced at the initiative of the adjudicators themselves, is also a way to make sure that no self-contained regimes emerge; as such, it is a way to harmonize (and legitimize) the law produced by the world's diverse adjudicative mechanisms.[131] Similarly,

---

126   Patrick M. Norton, *A Law of the Future or a Law of the Past? Modern Tribunals and the International Law of Expropriation*, 85 AM. J. INT'L L. 474, 482–485, 499–500 (1991). *See also* Norton, *supra* note 103.

127   Norton, *supra* note 126, 499–500.

128   WHO Opinion, *supra* note 15, ¶¶ 95–97 (July 8) (finding a lack of "sufficient elements to enable [the Court] to conclude with certainty that the use of nuclear weapons would necessarily be at variance with the principles and rules of law ... in any circumstance").

129   *See* RONALD DWORKIN, LAW'S EMPIRE 225–275 (1986).

130   *See, e.g.*, Bruno Simma & Dirk Pulkowski, *Of Planets and the Universe: Self-contained Regimes in International Law*, 17 EUR. J. INT'L L. 483 (2006).

131   For one such effort, see Bruno Simma & Theodore Kill, *Harmonizing Investment Protection and International Human Rights: First Steps towards a Methodology, in* INTERNATIONAL INVESTMENT LAW FOR THE 21st CENTURY: ESSAYS IN HONOUR OF CHRISTOPH SCHREUER 678 (Christina Binder et al. eds., 2009) (proposing the use of Article 31(3)(c) of the Vienna Convention on the Law of Treaties (VCT) as a way to incorporate human rights standards and principles into ISDS). *See also* Jürgen Kurtz, *The Merits and Limits of Comparativism: National Treatment in International Investment Law and the WTO, in*

if one considers all or most forms of international adjudication as falling into the rubric of "public law," this perspective encourages a search for common forms of public law across international regimes, including allegedly public law principles of proportionality, other forms of "balancing," or general principles of "international procedure."[132] Looking to interpretations issued by other international adjudicators on, for example, the existence or meaning of customary international law is also a way to fulfill some of the "de-fragmentation" of interpretative rules suggested by the International Law Commission's (ILC) Study on Fragmentation.[133]

Are there exceptions to judicial law-making? The clearest potential exception, one would think, is international criminal law. International criminal judges, whether or not driven by reliance on prior precedent, are not supposed to be making up the law as they enforce it. International crimes are not supposed to be established in the course of applying the law. The reasons for

---

INTERNATIONAL INVESTMENT LAW AND COMPARATIVE PUBLIC LAW 243, *supra* note 108.

132 *See, e.g.*, Anthea Roberts, *Clash of Paradigms: Actors and Analogies Shaping the Investment Treaty System*, 107 AM. J. INT'L L. 45, 62 (noting that the "public international law paradigm" encourages "ongoing interactions between treaty parties (as law-givers) and tribunals (as law-appliers)"; *id.* at 66–67 (discussing cross-referencing of "public law" principles like proportionality); Venzke, *supra* note 100, at 1129–1131 (discussing recourse to the principle of "proportionality" in WTO caselaw); Benedict Kingsbury & Stephan W. Schill, *Public Law Concepts to Balance Investors' Rights with State Regulatory Actions in the Public Interest—The Concept of Proportionality, in* INTERNATIONAL INVESTMENT LAW AND COMPARATIVE PUBLIC LAW 75, *supra* note 108 (proposing recourse to the "proportionality" analysis as a remedy for investment tribunals' perceived inattention to public interests); Giacinto della Cananea, *Minimum Standards of Procedural Justice in Administrative Adjudication, in* INTERNATIONAL INVESTMENT LAW AND COMPARATIVE PUBLIC LAW, *supra* note 108, at 39 (discussing "minimum standards of procedure" including those stemming from "principles of natural justice").

133 Fragmentation Study, *supra* note 109 (arguing that treaty interpreters should have recourse to customary rules as the default rules, at least where the treaty does not explicitly provide to the contrary). For specific examples of cross-regime interpretative borrowing, see, for example, Cont'l Cas. Co. v. The Argentine Republic, ICSID Case No. ARB/03/9, Award (Sept. 5, 2008) (applying to the investor-state context the principles of "necessity" as applied in the WTO); Enron Corp. v. The Argentine Republic, ICSID Case No. ARB/01/3, Decision on the Application for Annulment of the Argentine Republic (July 30, 2010) (applying to the investor-state context the customary defense of necessity from the Articles of State Responsibility). For a commentary on these two efforts, see José E. Alvarez, *Beware: Boundary Crossings, in* BOUNDARIES OF STATE, BOUNDARIES OF RIGHTS: HUMAN RIGHTS, PRIVATE ACTORS, AND POSITIVE OBLIGATIONS (Tsvi Kahana & Anat Scolnicov eds., 2016).

this are well-known. As the leading international criminal scholar Antonio Cassese noted, at least since the development of international human rights and despite some differences between civil law and common law jurisdictions, international law has favored the application of the principle of "strict legality," that is, the doctrine that "a person may only be held criminally liable and punished if at the moment when he performed a certain act this act was regarded as a criminal offence under the applicable law."[134]

As articulated by Cassese, the principle of legality includes the principle of specificity (providing that criminal offenses must be as specific as possible with respect to both the objective elements of the crime and the requisite *mens rea*); the principle of non-retroactivity (so as to not cover acts performed prior to the enactment of the criminal law); the ban on the use of analogies to expand the scope and purport of criminal law to matters that were not regulated by the law (albeit subject to some exceptions); and a principle of construction favoring the accused (requiring judges facing conflicting interpretations of the law to favor a construction favorable to the accused).[135] These principles or rules of construction, including the all-important concept of *nullum crimen sine lege* (no crime without law), are justified on the basis that fairness and due process require individuals to be on notice that they are violating the criminal law and are subject to its harsh penalties. Moreover, they are needed because, to the extent the criminal law is about deterrence, this would not occur unless the law was clear from the outset. They are necessary as well to lessen the risk that the criminal law will be deployed by governments as a form of designed revenge against political opponents; that is, as an assurance against politicized criminal trials used to threaten and silence a government's political opponents.

Courts that violate the principle of legality de-legitimate themselves. The post-WWII convictions of Nazis at Nuremberg were criticized in part because the key linchpin for those prosecutions, "crimes against peace," arguably did not exist prior to the Allied Powers' discovery of it.[136] For this reason, those who establish contemporary international criminal tribunals—from the ICTY to today's hybrid courts and the ICC—take pains to ensure that such tribunals enforce only clearly established crimes under customary law or, to the extent

---

134 ANTONIO CASSESE, INTERNATIONAL CRIMINAL LAW 22 (3d ed. 2013).

135 *Id.* at 27–36.

136 *See, e.g., id.* at 25–26 (noting that the Nuremberg Tribunal's prosecution of "crimes against peace" was justified by a questionable theory of the crime's preexistence in international law). *But see* JORDAN J. PAUST, ET AL., INTERNATIONAL CRIMINAL LAW: CASES AND MATERIALS 591–672 (4th ed. 2013) (collecting sources for "offenses against peace" both before and after the Kellogg-Briand Pact of 1928).

such tribunals include jurisdiction over new crimes, do so only prospectively, once a treaty defining an international crime is in place and everyone is on notice that those treaty crimes exist.[137]

But despite these efforts, modern international criminal courts have continued to engage in law-making, with respect to both substantive international criminal law and procedural rules. Despite the claim that the statutes for the ICTY and ICTR adopted by the UN Security Council (UNSC) contain only clearly established international crimes presenting no problem under *nulle crimen sine lege*, it is now clear that those tribunals engaged in considerable legal innovations. Over the years, those tribunals have found, for instance, that war crimes that formerly applied only in the course of inter-state conflicts also apply with respect to internal conflicts, such as civil wars;[138] that all three categories of international crimes—genocide, crimes against humanity, and war crimes—include numerous offences targeting women as women (including mass rape, sexual violence, and rape to induce pregnancy as a form of genocide) even in the absence of prior state practice or clear treaty provision;[139] and that international criminal defendants can be convicted of engaging in a joint criminal enterprise or other forms of accomplice liability not contemplated at Nuremberg.[140] Indeed, the very first criminal tribunal of the modern age, the ICTY, developed the law of the UN Charter (and not just international criminal law) when it decided, in its very first jurisprudential ruling in the Dusko Tadić case, that it had the power to examine the legality of the UNSC's establishment of the ICTY itself.[141] The ICTY's Appeals Chamber suggested that the ICTY was legally constituted because, among other things, the tribunal incorporated international human rights standards.[142] As many commentators have noted, this decision appeared to exercise an implicit judicial review authority over the Security Council that the ICJ has taken pains to deny for itself, while also

---

137 *See, e.g.*, Rome Statute, *supra* note 36, arts. 22–24 (on the principle of legality), 30 (on the necessity of proper notice).

138 Prosecutor v. Tadić, Case No. IT-94-1-I, Decision on Defence Motion for Interlocutory Appeal on Jurisdiction, ¶¶ 65–137 (Int'l Crim. Trib. for the Former Yugoslavia Oct. 2, 1995) [hereinafter Tadić Jurisdiction Decision].

139 *See* Theodor Meron, *Rape as a Crime Under International Humanitarian Law*, 87 AM. J. INT'L L. 424 (1993).

140 *See, e.g.*, Prosecutor v. Delalić et al., Case No. IT-96-21T, Judgement, ¶¶ 325–329 (Int'l Crim. Trib. for the Former Yugoslavia Nov. 16, 1998) (on accomplice liability); *Tadić*, Case No. IT-94-1-A, Judgement, ¶¶ 185–229 (Int'l Crim. Trib. for the Former Yugoslavia July 15, 1999) (on "joint criminal enterprise" liability).

141 Tadić Jurisdiction Decision, *supra* note 138, ¶¶ 9–22.

142 *Id.* ¶¶ 45–48.

implying—along the way—that the Council's Chapter VII power was subject to at least some legal constraint.[143]

Some of these legal innovations pose challenges under the principle of legality. Consider the Special Tribunal for Lebanon. The Appellate Chamber of that body has opined that terrorism is a crime under customary international law.[144] This controversial decision, rendered in 2011, surprised many observers. It found an international crime of terrorism consisting of three elements:

> (i) the perpetration of a criminal act (such as murder, kidnapping, hostage-taking, arson, and so on), or threatening such an act; (ii) the intent to spread fear among the population... or directly or indirectly coerce a national or international authority to take some action, or to refrain from taking it; (iii) when the act involves a transnational element.[145]

This marked the first time that an international tribunal had affirmed the existence of this (allegedly) customary crime. That tribunal also suggested that customary law now permitted states to prosecute those who commit acts of terrorism—including acts of terrorism that fall within its definition but were not specially covered by the dozen or so multilateral counter-terrorism treaties,[146] such as, presumably, acts of cyberterrorism. Notably, that tribunal relied on UN General Assembly and Security Council resolutions, existing counter-terrorism conventions, decisions rendered by the ICTY and ICTR, and the views of scholars for the underlying evidence that customary law exists; there was little reference to state practice and *opinio juris* as these terms are traditionally construed.[147] That tribunal also relied on caselaw from the ICTY/

---

143 *See, e.g.*, José E. Alvarez, *Nuremberg Revisited: The* Tadic *Case*, 7 EUR. J. INT'L L. 245 (1996).

144 Interlocutory Decision on the Applicable Law: Terrorism, Conspiracy, Homicide, Perpetration, Cumulative Charging, Case No. STL-11-01/I (Special Trib. for Lebanon Feb. 16, 2011) [hereinafter Lebanon Decision on Applicable Law].

145 *Id.* ¶ 85.

146 *Id.* ¶ 105.

147 *Id.* ¶¶ 83–113. *See generally* Michael P. Scharf, *Special Tribunal for Lebanon Issues Landmark Ruling on Definition of Terrorism and Modes of Participation*, 15 ASIL INSIGHTS, Mar. 4, 2011; Ben Saul, *Legislating from a Radical Hague: The United Nations Special Tribunal for Lebanon Invents an International Crime of Transnational Terrorism*, 24 LEIDEN J. INT'L L. 677 (2011) (criticizing the decision for, among other things, relying on scant national practice and when doing so relying on some national laws that violate human rights law).

ICTR to affirm that, as a matter of customary law, international modes of liability, including joint criminal enterprise, now existed even when not affirmed by a treaty.[148]

The *Ayyash* decision by the Special Tribunal for Lebanon—rendered in 2012—suggests that judicial law-making can also occur through judicial inaction and the failure to rely on prior caselaw. Faced with a challenge to its jurisdiction comparable to that posed by the ICTY's first defendant, Dusko Tadić, the Appellate Chamber of that tribunal issued a decision directly at odds with the jurisdictional decision issued in response to Tadić's challenge noted above. Over a dissent by one judge, the Lebanon tribunal proclaimed that it had been delegated no power to engage in judicial review over the legality of how it was established by the Security Council.[149] The majority of that tribunal's judges accordingly refused to address the scope of the Council's power or whether the Council was subject to any legal limits, including human rights.[150] This decision, grounded in deference to positivist consent, rendered after a comparable UNSC-authorized tribunal had gone in the opposite direction, engaged in law-making of its own. By indicating that it could not review the actions of the Council because those were taken by a political body, the Special Tribunal for Lebanon renewed a lively debate about whether the Security Council was subject to either judicial review or to the constraints of law.[151] In seeking not to legislate from the bench, the majority of the *Ayyash* judges appeared to be suggesting that despite ICJ views to the contrary, there was such a thing as a "political question" doctrine in international law.[152] The *Ayyash* decision provides a

---

148 Lebanon Decision on Applicable Law, *supra* note 144, ¶¶ 236–249.

149 The Prosecutor v. Ayyash et al, STL-11-01/PT/AC/AR90.1 (Special Trib. for Lebanon Oct 24, 2012) [hereinafter Ayyash Decision] and *id.* at Separate and Partially Dissenting Opinion of Judge Baragwanath; *see also* José E. Alvarez, Tadić *Revisited: The* Ayyash *Decisions of the Special Tribunal for Lebanon* 11 J. INT'L. CRIM. JUST. 291 (2013).

150 Ayyash Decision, *supra* note 149, ¶ 35.

151 *Id.* ¶¶ 36–50. For the contours of the debate, see, for example, JAMES CRAWFORD, CHANCE, ORDER, CHANGE: THE COURSE OF INTERNATIONAL LAW, GENERAL COURSE ON PUBLIC INTERNATIONAL LAW 402–438 (2014) (suggesting that the Council is not subject to judicial review, at least not by the ICJ). For a somewhat different view, see José E Alvarez, *Judging the Security Council*, 90 AM. J. INT'L L. 1 (1996).

152 *See, e.g.*, Ayyash Decision, *supra* note 149, ¶ 41 (noting that it was not bound by the *Tadić* appeals decision that affirmed review authority despite the political or non-justiciable nature of the issues raised). *But see* Questions of Interpretation and Application of the 1971 Montreal Convention arising from the Aerial Incident at Lockerbie (Libya V. U.S.), Request for the Indication of Provisional Measures, 1992 I.C.J. 160, 166 (Feb. 27) (Weeramantry, J., Dissenting Opinion) ("[T]he fact that [the Court's] judicial decision based upon the law may have political consequences is not a factor that would deflect it

judicial imprimatur to those who argue that the Security Council is unbound by law, at least when it exercises its Chapter VII power.[153]

Or consider the law-making prowess of the Special Court for Sierra Leone (SCSL). That tribunal decided in Prosecutor v. Sam Hinga Norman, over the strong dissent by Justice Robertson, that the crime of conscripting or enlisting children under the age of 15 as soldiers existed as a customary international law crime at least by 1996, even before that act was criminalized in treaty law.[154] The majority in that case affirmed that both forcible and non-forcible recruitment of child soldiers was a recognized customary crime by that date, as required for the charges against Norman to be effective.[155] Like the Lebanon tribunal with respect to the alleged crime of terrorism, the majority in the Norman case took into account a variety of sources to make this determination, including statements by the President of the Security Council, other statements made at the General Assembly or by the Security Council (including its endorsements of a UNICEF report), and the widespread ratifications for the Convention on the Rights of the Child and its Optional Protocol, but was able to point to only a handful of states that had actually criminalized child enlistment by 1996.[156] As indicated by Justice Robertson in dissent, the majority could cite no evidence of widespread state practice as of that time.[157] As a result, he dissented from the affirmation of jurisdiction, concluding that though the law prohibits states from forcibly enlisting

---

from discharging its duties ..."); CRAWFORD, *supra* note 151, at 433 n. 1165 (quoting several authorities that reject the existence of a political question doctrine in international law).

153   Indeed, the majority in *Ayyash* explicitly states that "[b]eyond that notion of self-restraint ... there is nothing in the Charter that gives any of the other organs of the United Nations the power to review the Security Council's actions." Ayyash Decision, *supra* note 149, at ¶ 39. *See, e.g.*, Gabriël H. Oosthuizen, *Playing the Devil's Advocate: the United Nations Security Council is Unbound by Law*, 12 LEIDEN J. INT'L L. 549 (1999); CRAWFORD, *supra* note 151, at 437 (agreeing with Brownlie's contention that the "legal régime is primarily one of self-limitation" when it comes to the Security Council). *See also* Alvarez, Tadić *Revisited*, *supra* note 149. For an excellent summary of the ICJ's few interventions in this respect and scholarly views on both sides, see Rüdiger Wolfrum, *Judicial Control of Security Council Decisions (UNO)*, *in* INSTITUT DE DROIT INTERNATIONAL YEARBOOK 2015 (WORKS OF TALLINN SESSION), *at* http://justitiaetpace.org/annuaire_resultat.php?id=16. *See also* Alvarez, *Judging the Security Council, supra* note 151.

154   Prosecutor v. Sam Hinga Norman, Decision on Preliminary Motion Based on Lack of Jurisdiction, Case No. SCSL-2004-14-AR72(E), ¶¶ 8–27 (Special Ct. for Sierra Leone May 31, 2004) [hereinafter Norman Decision].

155   *Id.*

156   Colombia, Argentina, Spain, Ireland, and Norway. *Id.* ¶ 7(g).

157   Norman Decision, *supra* note 154, Dissenting Opinion of Justice Robertson, ¶¶ 42–43.

child soldiers (as a breach of Common Article 3 of the Geneva Conventions), the crime of non-forcible enlistment for those under 15, set out as an offense in the 2007 Statute of the Special Court, was not an offense cognizable under international criminal law as of 1996.[158] He concluded that prosecuting the defendant for this crime violated fundamental principles of criminal liability (primarily the requirement that prosecutions require a "clear statement of the conduct which is prohibited and a satisfactory requirement for the proof of *mens rea*").[159] To Justice Robertson, the crime of non-forcible enlistment of child soldiers became a war crime only when it was explicitly incorporated as a war crime in the Rome Statute for the ICC in 1998 and could only be legitimately prosecuted after that date.[160]

And what of the International Criminal Court? Many have assumed that given the extensive delineation of international crimes and elements of crimes in that tribunal's statute, that Court would not be accused of (or credited with) judicial law-making. The ICC's Rome Statute, after all, achieved an unprecedented level of detail with respect to defining the crimes under that Court's jurisdiction. No prior international tribunal had included the same catalogue of definitions for the crimes of genocide, crimes against humanity, or war crimes in both international and non-international armed conflict.[161] No other international tribunal had included the same extensive enumeration of "general principles of criminal law," encompassing such matters as *nullen crimen sine lege, nulla poena sine lege*, non-retroactivity, definitions of individual criminal responsibility (including forms of joint and accomplice responsibility), grounds for responsibility of commanders and other superiors, required mental elements, accepted defenses from responsibility, and definition of superior orders.[162] The Rome Statute was widely lauded as a massive achievement precisely because it had engaged in codifying (and progressively

---

158   *Id.* ¶¶ 35–50.

159   *Id.* ¶¶ 11–17, 36, 48.

160   *Id.* ¶¶ 40–47. Notably, even Justice Robertson accepts the idea that "there may be flash points at which it can be said that a new crime emerges in international law through general acceptance by States," *Id.* ¶ 24, and that the conclusion of the Rome Statute may have been such an occasion for what some might call "instant custom." Note the implication: subsequent decisions rendered by the ICC, at least with respect to what even the dissenting judge now sees as a customary crime, are not only interpretations of the Rome Statute. They are rulings elaborating a customary crime applicable even with respect to non-Rome Party states. Compare *infra* text and notes 300–308 (discussion concerning the meaning of certain ISDS rulings as interpreting customary law).

161   Rome Statute, *supra* note 36, arts. 5–8.

162   *Id.* arts. 22–33.

developing) concepts of international criminal law that had lain effectively dormant at least until the establishment of the ICTY and ICTR in the mid-1990s.[163]

Given the relatively few opinions issued by that Court to date, it is too early to draw definitive conclusions on the capacity for judicial law-making by the ICC, but the ICC's first full decision on the merits, the conviction by the trial chamber on March 14, 2012 of Thomas Lubanga on one count of conscripting, enlisting, and using child soldiers,[164] suggests that judicial law-making is very much alive in that court as well. That first trial, which took six years to complete, resulted in a number of interim decisions by the Court along the way to the trial chamber's conviction that required the Court to determine many legal issues of first impression. These included the legality or limits on the prosecutor's use of intermediaries in proving facts,[165] determinations concerning the respective rights of defendants and victims given the Rome Statute's innovative provisions in defense of the latter,[166] and findings concerning the respective powers of the Court and the Office of the Prosecutor on matters such as admissibility.[167] These legal determinations are likely to set precedents for the ICC and, given the prominence of that global court, quite possibly for general international criminal law.[168] Of course, these procedural and jurisdictional rulings are only the beginning; we can expect many more clarifications or elaborations of the underlying law through future decisions by the Court.

Nor was the law-making undertaken in the course of the *Lubanga* case limited to procedural or evidentiary issues. Lubanga was prosecuted under Article 8(2)(e)(vii) of the Rome Statute, which prohibits "conscripting or enlisting children under the age of fifteen years into armed forces or groups or using them to participate actively in hostilities." As is suggested by the *Norman* decision by the SCSL discussed above, a number of aspects of that crime remain to be clarified even after the entry into force of the Rome Statute. Lubanga's judges noted that the conduct proscribed under "conscripting" or "enlisting" children or "using them to participate actively in hostilities" was "not defined"

---

163   *See, e.g.,* Jerry Fowler, *The Rome Treaty for the International Criminal Court: A Framework for Justice, in* THE INTERNATIONAL CRIMINAL COURT: GLOBAL POLITICS AND THE QUEST FOR JUSTICE 131 (William Driscoll, Joseph Zompetti & Suzette W. Zompetti eds., 2004).

164   Prosecutor v. Lubanga, ICC-01/04-01/06, Judgment pursuant to Article 74 of the Statute (Mar. 14, 2012) [hereinafter Lubanga Decision].

165   *Id.* ¶¶ 183–484.

166   *Id.* ¶¶ 13–21, 485–502.

167   *Id.* ¶¶ 92–123.

168   *See, e.g.,* Alison Cole & Kelly Askin, *Thomas Lubanga: War Crimes Conviction in the First Case at the International Criminal Court,* 16 ASIL INSIGHTS, Mar. 27, 2012.

in the Rome Statute, but required the Court to define each of these terms using tools like the Vienna Convention on the Law of Treaties (VCT) as well as the jurisprudence of the SCSL, which had to interpret comparable terms.[169] Accordingly, the Court had to decide, for example, whether "using" child soldiers was a distinct offense from voluntary conscription or coercive enlistment. They found that it was indeed a distinct offense.[170] The *Lubanga* judges also considered what an "indirect" role in the underlying conflict entails and whether this could include the use of threat of sexual violence.[171] They also had to decide what was meant by criminal liability for co-perpetrating the crime of enlisting child soldiers since Lubanga was charged with coordinating with other senior leaders in the crime. On that point, the majority of the judges found that co-perpetration involves two objective elements: (i) the existence of an "agreement or common plan" between two or more persons embodying a sufficient risk that, if the events follow the ordinary course, the crime would be committed; and (ii) an "essential contribution" to the common plan by the accused.[172] The trial chamber in that case also had to clarify the *mens rea* or mental element needed to prove the underlying crime.[173] It found that it was necessary to prove

> (i) the accused and at least one other perpetrator meant to conscript, enlist or use children … to participate actively in hostilities or they were aware that in implementing their common plan this consequence "will occur in the ordinary course of events"; and (ii) the accused was aware that he provided an essential contribution to the implementation of the common plan.[174]

Whether or not any of these legal determinations implicate the principle of legality, they are significant judicial elaborations of the Rome Statute.

The capacity for law-making in the ICC is also suggested by the individual opinions issued in that case. Although the decision to convict Lubanga was unanimous, his judges did not all agree on the relevant law. Judge Fulford's separate opinion argued in part that there was no basis for the majority's theory

---

169   Lubanga Decision, *supra* note 164, ¶¶ 600–603.

170   *Id.* ¶ 620.

171   *Id.* ¶¶ 621–631.

172   *Id.* ¶¶ 980–1006.

173   *Id.* ¶¶ 1007–1016.

174   *Id.* ¶ 1013.

of co-perpetration as a distinct mode of liability under the Rome Statute,[175] while Judge Benito's separate and dissenting opinion expressed views on matters that the majority had expressly left unresolved, namely whether sexual violence could be considered as "using" children in armed conflict and whether "national armed forces" could include militia groups.[176] At the sentencing of Lubanga, Judge Benito also filed a dissenting opinion, expressing her "strong" disagreement with the majority decision to disregard "the damage caused to the child victims and their families" as a result of the harsh punishments and sexual violence inflicted upon them, pursuant to Rule 145(1)(c) of the Rules of Procedure and Evidence; as well as their decision to differentiate the sentences imposed for the distinct crimes of enlistment, conscription, and the use of child soldiers.[177]

As observers of national courts recognize, the potential for judicial lawmaking is enhanced when judges are authorized, as are the ICC's judges, to render individual signed opinions. While judges issue such opinions for different reasons (such as to avoid the overturning of a conviction on appeal), one reason for doing so is to influence the future path of the law, even when a majority of their colleagues go in a different direction in the case at hand. Even the brief separate opinions issued in the *Lubanga* case—none of which argued that the defendant should not have been convicted—suggest distinct paths for legal interpretation. They tell us that the Rome Statute's level of detail has not closed off the potential for judicial creativity even with respect to fundamental questions that affect the meaning and scope of its underlying crimes and that court's approach to sentencing. Of course, what all the judges said in *Lubanga*—both to clarify the Rome Statute and to suggest the Statute's continued ambiguities—put future defendants to that Court on notice for purposes of *nullum crimen sine lege* and *nullum crimen sine poene*.

The *Lubanga* rulings also contain dicta that predictably emerge from rule of law expectations for the issuance of "well-reasoned" decisions. Thus, the majority of the *Lubanga* judges suggested, by way of explaining the legitimacy of their decision of conviction for the crime of conscripting or enlisting child soldiers, that this crime already existed in customary law even prior to the entry

---

175   *Id.*, Separate Opinion of Judge Adrian Fulford, ¶¶ 13–18.

176   *Id.*, Separate and Dissenting Opinion of Judge Odio Benito, ¶¶ 14–21.

177   Prosecutor v. Lubanga, ICC-01/04-01/06, Decision on Sentence pursuant to Article 76 of the Statute, Dissenting Opinion of Judge Odio Benito ¶¶ 2–26. Judge Benito would have imposed the same sentence of 15 years for all 3 of these crimes since these emerged all from the "same plan," instead of the majority's lower sentences of 12, 13, and 14 years respectively for the crimes of enlistment, conscription, and use. *Id.* at 24–26.

into force of the Rome Statute.[178] This aside, consistent with the controversial *Norman* ruling discussed above, may affect the prospect of such prosecutions even for actions prior to the entry into force of the ICC's Statute elsewhere in national courts. This is an important dimension of judicial law-making: it may come to have a legal impact vertically, within national legal systems, and not just horizontally, on other international courts.

Other developments at the ICC suggest that that Court's Office of the Prosecutor (OTP) may also prove to be a formidable law-maker. By 2006, the OTP had developed over 130 draft policies, guidelines, and standard operating procedures,[179] and since then the Office has formally consolidated these into an "Operations Manual" and an internal "Code of Conduct."[180] The ICC's Prosecutor has issued policies interpreting specific terms in the Rome Statute, including the principle of complementarity (along with the concepts of whether a state is "unwilling or unable" to prosecute), the "interests of justice," and the "most serious crimes of concern to the international community as a whole."[181] The OTP has also issued policies concerning cooperation with states and other UN agencies; the handling and classification of security; source evaluation, evidence sampling, and management; crime scene investigation information management; impartial investigations and unique investigative opportunities; investigative best practices relating to interviewing practices and guidelines for different types of witnesses; guidelines to investigate sexual and gender crimes; guidelines for investigating child-related crimes and

---

178   Lubanga Decision, *supra* note 164, ¶ 542.

179   Office of The Prosecutor, Report on the Activities Performed During the First Three Years (June 2003–June 2006), Sept. 12, 2006, at 22–24, *at* https://www.icc-cpi.int/NR/rdonlyres/ D76A5D89-FB64-47A9-9821-725747378AB2/143680/OTP_3yearreport20060914_English .pdf [hereinafter OTP Three Year Report].

180   *See* Code of Conduct for the Office of the Prosecutor, Sept. 5, 2013, *at* https://www.icc-cpi .int/iccdocs/oj/otp-COC-Eng.PDF. The Operations Manual is not publicly available. *See* International Criminal Court, War Crimes Research Office, Legal Analysis and Education Project, Investigative Management, Strategies, and Techniques of the International Criminal Court's Office of the Prosecutor 9 (Oct. 2012), *at* https://www.wcl.american.edu/ warcrimes/icc/documents/ICCReport16.pdf.

181   *See* Office of the Prosecutor, Policy Paper on Preliminary Examinations ¶¶ 46–58, 59–71, 100–103, Nov. 2013, *at* https://www.icc-cpi.int/en_menus/icc/Pages/default.aspx [hereinafter OTP Preliminary Examinations Paper]. *See also* Office of the Prosecutor, Policy Paper on the Interests of Justice, Sept. 2007, *at* https://www.icc-cpi.int/NR/rdonlyres/772C95C9-F54D-4321-BF09-73422BB23528/143640/ICCOTPInterestsOfJustice.pdf.

questioning child witnesses; and exonerating circumstances and disclosure.[182] The OTP has also developed and implemented particular performance metrics to evaluate the processes and results of the Office's work.[183]

In the first ten years of the OTP's operation, that office, given the power to initiate investigations *proprio motu* and charged with making a number of preliminary determinations concerning admissibility, also had an impact on the meaning of the Rome Statute—and in all likelihood on the practices and procedures of others who attempt to prosecute international crimes. To be sure, nothing authorizes the OTP to render authoritative interpretations of the relevant Rome Statute provisions or its silences. But the same might be said with respect to the ICC judges—who are only authorized after all to render binding rulings with respect to particular defendants.[184] Neither they nor the OTP is given the power to issue authoritative or definitive interpretations of international criminal law for all time.

As with respect to other comparable action in other IOs—such as interpretations issued by the International Labour Organization's Labour Office, OTP Policy papers, and ICC rulings—might be characterized as institutional "soft law" or for those of a more positivist persuasion, as forms of treaty "subsequent practice."[185] In the case of the OTP, it is difficult to delineate with any precision the extent to which its pronouncements on prosecutorial strategy (including on specific investigations) and its efforts to indicate general goals constitute "policy" recommendations as opposed to more legalistic (or even binding) interpretations of the Rome Statute. Thus, for example, the OTP has described its Policy Paper on Preliminary Examinations as "a document reflecting an internal policy of the OTP" that "does not give rise to legal rights, and is subject to revision based on experience and in light of legal determinations by the Chambers of the Court."[186] But that same paper indicates that it was released "in the interest of promoting clarity and predictability" and to put perpetrators

---

182   *See* Office of the Prosecutor, Strategic Plan 2016–2018, Nov. 16, 2015, *at* https://www.icc-cpi .int/iccdocs/otp/EN-OTP_Strategic_Plan_2016-2018.pdf [hereinafter OTP Strategic Plan]; OTP Three Year Report, *supra* note 179.

183   OTP Strategic Plan, *supra* note 182, ¶¶ 103–109.

184   *See* Rome Statute, *supra* note 36, art. 25.

185   *See* ALVAREZ, *supra* note 54, at 217–257, 503–509, 599–600 (discussing adjudicative rulings as a species of soft law); Helen Keller & Leena Grover, *General Comments of the Human Rights Committee and Their Legitimacy, in* UN HUMAN RIGHTS TREATY BODIES 116, *supra* note 104 (noting that General Comments issued by human rights treaty bodies might be seen as either "authoritative interpretations" of the underlying treaties or "subsequent practice" for purposes of Article 31(3)(b) of the VCT).

186   OTP Preliminary Examinations Paper, *supra* note 181, ¶ 20.

on notice.[187] Only time will tell whether future ICC prosecutors will defer to these OTP pronouncements and treat them as that office's equivalent of *jurisprudence constante*.

The most politically salient role of the OTP to date involved Palestine's efforts to join the ICC. As is well known, when Palestine first approached the ICC in January 2009 with a declaration purporting to accept the Court's jurisdiction under the Rome Statute's Article 12(3), the OTP evaluated that request and ultimately demurred from making any final determination, suggesting that it was for the Assembly of States Parties, not the OTP, to decide whether to permit a declaration from an entity that was not a UN member and which at least some considered not to be a "state" for purposes of the Rome Statute.[188] Even that apparent exercise of self-restraint by the OTP in this high profile case was interpreted as having legal significance. The OTP made its determination only after first extensively considering the Palestinian request, thereby implying that the Prosecutor had the authority to decide at least which organ of the ICC is properly charged with accepting a potentially problematic Article 12(3) declaration. In the course of these deliberations, the OTP also stated that it would be guided by whether the practice of the UN indicated that Palestine should be considered a state.[189] That turned out to be an important and legally relevant conclusion that made the OTP and the ICC participants in the familiar game of turning to international organizations as *de facto* legitimators of would-be states.[190]

---

187   *Id.* ¶ 21.

188   Office of the Prosecutor, Situation in Palestine, Apr. 3, 2012, *at* https://www.icc-cpi.int/ NR/rdonlyres/C6162BBF-FEB9-4FAF-AFA9-836106D2694A/284387/SituationinPalestine 030412ENG.pdf [hereinafter Situation in Palestine]. Indeed, after Palestine's Article 12(3) declaration, the OTP went so far as to release a lengthy dossier of the submissions that it had received from various quarters directed at the legal merits of Palestine's declaration and whether it satisfied the ICC's statutory requirements. Office of the Prosecutor, Situation in Palestine: Summary of submission on whether the declaration lodged by the Palestinian National Authority meets statutory requirements, May 3, 2010, *at* https:// www.icc-cpi.int/NR/rdonlyres/D3C77FA6-9DEE-45B1-ACC0-B41706BB41E5/282852/ PALESTINEFINAL201010272.pdf.

189   Situation in Palestine, *supra* note 188, ¶ 6. The OTP was referring to the practice of the Treaty Section of the Office of Legal Affairs' Summary of Practice of the Secretary-General as Depositary of Multilateral Treaties, U.N. Doc. ST/LEG/7/Rev.1 ¶¶ 81–83 (1999) (noting the practice of the Secretary-General as affirmed by the General Assembly in 1973 that treaties open to participation by "all States" would be determined by the practice of the General Assembly), *at* https://treaties.un.org/doc/source/publications/practice/ summary_english.pdf.

190   *See* Chapter III *supra* (discussing the General Assembly's "gate-keeping" role, including with respect to Palestine).

After the General Assembly adopted its November 2012 resolution declaring Palestine an "observer State,"[191] and Palestine approached the ICC again in January 2015, with a new Article 12(3) declaration and an instrument of accession to the Rome Statute, the OTP accepted the General Assembly's action as having conclusive effect.[192] Just two weeks after the declaration and deposit of accession, the ICC's Prosecutor announced the opening of a preliminary investigation into the situation in Palestine.[193] These OTP actions affirmed a contestable proposition that had been originally advanced by the UN Office of Legal Affairs' Treaty Section on other occasions, namely, that the practice of the UN as an organization (including the practice of the Assembly which is normally charged only with recommendatory actions) is the decisive metric for permitting a state to join a treaty that permits "all states" to join it.[194]

Of course, the opening of the Palestine preliminary investigation is within the OTP's power to identify situations meriting such investigation *proprio motu*, provided the situation is covered by the ICC's jurisdiction.[195] The OTP had previously opened investigations into the situations in the Democratic Republic of the Congo (DRC) and Uganda because it found that these were, at the time, the "gravest admissible situations under the Statute's jurisdiction."[196] As this suggests, the OTP appears to have considerable discretion with respect to the opening of preliminary investigations; indeed, the OTP has claimed authority to consider factors not specifically enumerated by the Statute that may be relevant to the feasibility of initiating investigations into particular situations.[197] The OTP has also identified factors that it considers legally irrelevant, such as the alleged need for geographical balance.[198] In opening such investigations and in issuing policy papers on point, the OTP has begun to establish the legal

---

191   G.A. Res. 67/19 (Nov. 29, 2012).

192   Press Release, International Criminal Court, The Prosecutor of the International Criminal Court, Fatou Bensouda, opens a preliminary examination of the situation in Palestine, U.N. Doc. ICC-OTP-20150116-PR1083 (Jan. 16, 2015) ("The office examined the legal implications of [the General Assembly vote] for its own purposes and concluded ... Palestine would be able to accept the jurisdiction of the Court from 29 November 2012 onward ...").

193   *Id.*

194   *Id.* For a critique, see Nimrod Karin, *The Establishment of the International Criminal Tribunal for Palestine (Part I)*, JUST SECURITY, Jan. 21, 2015, *at* https://www.justsecurity .org/19272/establishment-international-criminal-tribunal-palestine-part-i/.

195   Rome Statute, *supra* note 36, art. 15(1).

196   OTP Three-Year Report, *supra* note 179, ¶ 11.

197   Paper on some policy issues before the Office of the Prosecutor 2, Sept. 2003, *at* http:// icc-cpi.int/NR/rdonlyres/1FA7C4C6-DE5F-42B7-8B25-60AA962ED8B6/143594/030905_ Policy_Paper.pdf.

198   OTP Preliminary Examinations Paper, *supra* note 181, ¶¶ 11, 29.

parameters needed for launching and conducting preliminary examinations into potentially admissible situations.[199] Of course, as noted in the governance section below, these examinations are of intense interest to states and may prompt legal actions within states—whether or not formal ICC full-fledged investigations and indictments ensue.[200]

The OTP is also currently developing rules to prioritize case selection within situations that are before the Court.[201] The OTP has suggested criteria for determining what are the "most serious" crimes or the most serious perpetrators worthy of allocation of the Court's limited resources.[202] Finally, it has adopted a policy of selecting cases involving a limited number of incidents and few witnesses to expedite the trial process.[203] As suggested by the charges against the ICC's first defendant, Lubanga, and as affirmed in policy statements, that office also prioritizes the prosecution of crimes against children and crimes involving sexual or gender-based violence.[204]

As is well known, the OTP's practice of having recourse to "intermediaries" to serve as liaisons between its investigators and witnesses on the ground has generated considerable interactions between the OTP and the Court.[205] Less well known has been the OTP's efforts to design and implement specific external relations strategies that it deems "crucial . . . if it is to succeed in its mandate."[206] Under this rubric, the OTP has asserted independent authority to enter into "State-specific agreements" with states and has established

---

199   *Id.* ¶ 19.

200   *Id.* ¶¶ 16, 100–103. *See also* Geoff Dancy & Florencia Montal, *Unintended Positive Complementarity: Why International Criminal Courts Investigations Increase Domestic Human Rights Prosecutions*, WORLD POL. (forthcoming) (contending that, while ICC preliminary investigations may inspire strategic behavior on the part of a target country's ruling coalition, the launch of formal ICC investigations triggers domestic prosecutions for human rights violations).

201   OTP Strategic Plan, *supra* note 182, ¶¶ 38–40.

202   OTP Preliminary Examinations Paper, *supra* note 181, ¶¶ 42, 59–66.

203   Office of the Prosecutor, Prosecutorial Strategy 2009–2012 ¶ 20, Feb. 1, 2010, *at* https://www.icc-cpi.int/NR/rdonlyres/66A8DCDC-3650-4514-AA62-D229D1128F65/281506/OTP ProsecutorialStrategy20092013.pdf.

204   OTP Strategic Plan, *supra* note 182, ¶¶ 39–40. *But see* Amy Senier, *The ICC Appeals Chamber Judgment on the Legal Characterization of the Facts in Prosecutor v. Lubanga*, 14 ASIL INSIGHTS, Jan. 8, 2010 (noting criticisms that the Lubanga indictment and trial omitted charges of rape and sexual violence).

205   *See* Lubanga Decision, *supra* note 164, ¶¶ 178–205. *See also* Caroline Buisman, *Delegating Investigations: Lessons to be Learned from the Lubanga Judgment*, 11 NW. J. INT'L HUM. RTS. 30 (2013) (criticizing the OTP's reliance on intermediaries in *Lubanga* and advocating comprehensive investigative policy reform).

206   OTP Strategic Plan, *supra* note 182, ¶¶ 78–83.

the Jurisdiction, Complementarity and Cooperation Division to manage such external relations.[207] Such external relations include cooperation efforts with international and regional organizations, such as Interpol and the World Bank's Integrity Vice Presidency (INT). In two memoranda of understanding, the OTP and INT have agreed to share information that would enable the OTP to trace money-laundering efforts that could lead to valuable evidence.[208] The OTP, in short, is also a treaty-maker.

As these examples suggest, adjudicative law-making is inevitable even where it is most contentious, namely, international criminal law. It occurs even with respect to a treaty, the Rome Statute, that delineates in unprecedented fashion the jurisdiction of the Court and the respective powers of the Trial and Appeals Divisions and the OTP. Even the Rome Statute leaves intended or unintended or unanticipated gaps in the law that need to be filled—and that can only be filled by those charged with prosecuting, judging, or defending the ICC's defendants or those representing victims. Further, as the ICC example indicates, judicial law-makers may be persons other than the judges or arbitrators themselves.[209]

5   The Governance Function

Adjudicators, including national judges, are sometimes expected to give meaning to, or endorse, public values, and what they decide with respect to a single case can have much broader effects on how states regulate themselves or others. This view of the task of judging, which sees judges as "regulators," has been propounded by U.S. scholars like Owen Fiss in the context of courts like the U.S.

---

207   OTP Three Year Report, *supra* note 179, ¶¶ 67, 83. *See also* Assembly of States Parties, Report of the Court on cooperation, ICC-ASP/14/27, Sept. 22, 2015, *at* https://www.icc-cpi .int/iccdocs/asp_docs/ASP14/ICC-ASP-14-27-ENG.pdf.

208   *See* Press Release, International Criminal Court, The Office of the Prosecutor of the International Criminal Court and the World Bank's Anti-Corruption Unit, INT, Strengthen Cooperation, ICC-OTP-20140624-PR1020 (June 24, 2014).

209   Another example may be those who are hired to assist judges or arbitrators in the course of their work. As is suggested by disclosure rules that require such individuals to demonstrate their independence and potential conflicts of interests, such persons may also influence the result and the law-making undertaken by such tribunals. *See, e.g.*, International Bar Association (IBA) Council, IBA Guidelines on Conflicts of Interest in International Arbitration, Explanation (b), *at* http://www.ibanet.org/Publications/ publications_IBA_guides_and_free_materials.aspx.

Supreme Court.[210] When extrapolated to the international level, it challenges the contention that international adjudicators are really only the "agents" of the state principals that establish international adjudicative mechanisms, including permanent international courts. It also challenges, as overly simplistic, Martin Shapiro's portrayal of "triadic" dispute settlement, and goes beyond the fact-finding and law-making/law-ascertainment functions described above.[211]

The governance function accepts the idea that judges and arbitrators, at the national and international levels, engage in autonomous normative action that has an impact on how states or international organizations regulate themselves.[212] It sees the governance or regulatory function of adjudicators not as violations of the rule of law but as part and parcel of it and of adjudication itself. It assumes that adjudicators are entitled (and may even be under a duty) to consider the broader policy implications of their rulings on third parties not before the court and that adjudicative law-making goes beyond filling those interstitial gaps in the law needed to render judgment in a particular case.[213]

The governance function sees adjudication as a polycentric, not merely triadic, enterprise.[214] From this perspective, international adjudications do not merely "complete" the treaty-contracts of states or make vague treaty standards relatively more precise one case at a time.[215] Strong proponents of this view, such as those who describe the "constitutionalization" of international law, see judges as super-legislators qualified and entitled to resolve conflicts between values that other international actors and sources of law dare not touch or fail

---

210   Owen M. Fiss, *Foreword: The Forms of Justice*, 93 HARV. L. REV. 1 (1979).

211   *See supra* §§ 3 and 4.

212   The governance function does not assume that judges or arbitrators can ignore legal constraints on their choice of law or jurisdiction but it assumes that, in applying those legal constraints, adjudicators consider the policy or governance implications of distinct interpretations of the law. *See, e.g.,* CHENG, *supra* note 59, at 124–131 (arguing that this is demanded by "specific morality" and suggesting that judges may need to suggest changes to unjust laws).

213   While this conception of the task of judging is most often propounded with respect to national judges operating within a constitutional scheme, Lauterpacht hinted at the governance function as early as 1933, when he urged judges to respond to the needs of the "international community" and not merely the parties before them. *E.g.,* LAUTERPACHT, *supra* note 4, at 131–135.

214   *See* ALVAREZ, *supra* note 54, at 535–536.

215   For contentions that the law-making (and governance) capacities of investor-state arbitrators are unusually ample because of the vagueness of the underlying treaties, see, for example, Schill, *supra* note 111, at 150–151.

to resolve.[216] Adjudicators come to the rescue when, at the international level, the efforts to achieve positivist consent fail, or when, nationally, the legislative and executive branches fail to produce a rule. Adjudicative governance occurs when the ordinary international "legislative" process—as reflected in *ex ante* agreement established via treaty or custom—does not succeed but authority, express or implied, has been delegated to adjudicators.

The contention that international adjudicators should function as supreme guardians of public virtue or general policy-makers, and not mere passive umpires calling legal "balls and strikes" between litigants, is, of course, controversial, even among U.S. Supreme Court judges.[217] But, while controversial, there is considerable evidence that the governance function is not a figment of the academic imagination. Many of those who serve on these tribunals see themselves as agents of the "international community" intent on pursuing "justice" broadly understood—as Lauterpacht would have described them.[218] Others see themselves at least as agents for de-fragmentizing international law by making sure that the rules generated within one international legal regime are not inconsistent with those produced in other such regimes or with general international law.[219] Further, adjudicative governance may emerge even when actors in courts and tribunals do not specially intend this result.[220]

Like the fact-finding and law-making functions, the governance function is sometimes explicitly embraced by those who establish international courts and tribunals, especially (but not only) by those who establish courts to advance political integration, as in Europe.[221] It emerges when judicial law-making becomes something more than incremental gap-filling to embrace more expansive normative concerns. It manifests itself, for example, in the strong trend towards accepting amicus briefs or other forms of third party participation within international courts, usually justified on the ground that

---

216   This view might be compared to Dworkin's defense of "Herculean" judges. Ronald Dworkin, 88 HARV. L. REV. 1057 (1975). *See also supra* note 45.

217   *See* Confirmation Hearing on the Nomination of John G. Roberts, Jr. To Be Chief Justice of the United States: Hearing Before the S. Comm. on the Judiciary, 109th Cong. 56 (2005) (statement of John G. Roberts, Jr., nominee) (suggesting that his job as Chief Justice of the U.S. Supreme Court would be to "call balls and strikes and not to pitch or bat"). *See generally* Jeremy Waldron, *The Dignity of Legislation*, 54 MD. L. REV. 633 (1995).

218   *See supra* note 45.

219   *See, e.g.*, Simma & Kill, *supra* note 131.

220   *See, e.g.*, Dancy & Montal, *supra* note 200 (describing the "unintentional positive complementarity" produced by the initiation of ICC investigations).

221   *See* Baudenbacher & Clifton, *supra* note 19.

when adjudication has an impact on more than the litigating parties, fairness and legitimacy dictates that others need to be heard.[222]

Consider the numerous functions that have been attributed to international criminal courts, from the ICTY to the ICC. Those present at the creation of such courts have argued that these bodies are necessary, not only to convict the guilty and absolve the innocent (including the collective), but also: to deter further violence; make atonement possible for perpetrators; honor the dead; serve the victims of mass atrocity by providing psychological relief, compensation, identification of remains, or restoration of lost property; re-channel the thirst for revenge at the national level where the atrocities occurred; assist in restoring the rule of law at the national level; affirm the Nuremberg Principles and the international rule of law; tell the truth of what occurred by providing an accurate historical record; and/or restore lost civilities in torn societies to achieve national reconciliation or "transitional justice."[223] These are grandiose goals for proceedings that might be seen, more simply, as providing fair trials to determine who should be punished—and making legal and factual determinations only as needed. While one can dismiss many of the goals above as rhetorical or suggest that many of these would be better allocated to non-judicial actors such as truth commissions, these policy goals have influenced those who work on these courts and the expectations of influential stakeholders who react to their rulings, many of whom have suggested that what is emerging is a new "system" for international criminal justice.[224] These broader governance concerns motivate scholars who devote considerable attention, for instance, to the question of whether post-Nuremberg tribunals contribute to "collective memory."[225]

Consistent with these diverse rationales, international criminal courts supply a number of examples of attempts to govern states. Since many international

---

222   *See generally* Crema, *supra* note 78.

223   *See, e.g.*, Alvarez, *supra* note 66, at 2031–2032. Many of these goals suggest an "expressive theory of trials" in which these are used to defend the rule of law over politics, particularly in pursuit of achieving "transitional justice." *See, e.g.*, David Luban, *Fairness to Rightness: Jurisdiction, Legality, and the Legitimacy of International Criminal Law, in* THE PHILOSOPHY OF INTERNATIONAL LAW 569, 574–577 (Samantha Besson & John Tasioulas eds., 2010).

224   *See, e.g.*, William W. Burke-White, *A Community of Courts: Toward a System of International Criminal Law Enforcement*, 24 MICH. J. INT'L L. 1 (2002).

225   *See, e.g.*, Robert R. Shandley, *Introduction to* UNWILLING GERMANS? THE GOLDHAGEN DEBATE 1 (Robert R. Shandley, ed., Jeremiah Riemer trans., 1998). For discussion (and critique) of the efforts in the ICTY's *Tadić* trial to produce an accurate account of history, see Alvarez, *supra* note 66, at 2054–2058.

crimes involve the actions, inactions, or compliance of states, it is widely assumed
that these courts deter governments from committing international crimes. This
is not just about deterring or punishing particular government actors. It is also
about persuading or convincing government actors to take affirmative measures
with respect to both government and non-state actors in their territory—such as
legislative action to enable domestic prosecutions, to remove or narrow amnesty
provisions, and to take all other measures that would make future convictions
of certain crimes less necessary and, should they still occur, more likely.[226] The
deterrence function of international criminal tribunals obviously includes
discouraging states from violating the obligations contained in the Torture
Convention, the Genocide Convention, and the Geneva Conventions—not only
by convicting those who commit violations of these treaties but by clarifying
what violations of these treaties are. It is hoped that the shadow of international
criminal prosecutions will persuade states to make modifications to their government manuals and disciplinary procedures to enable greater scrutiny over
their police, security forces, and national militaries to make sure such crimes—
and perhaps human rights violations more generally—are prosecutable.[227] In
the context of the ICC, such efforts, including assistance provided by the OTP,
have been characterized as attempts to engage ICC's "positive complementarity."[228]

The OTP's law-making efforts, noted above, are inextricably linked with that
office's governance effects, intended or not. That office's initial determina-

---

226   The ever-widening body of research on whether the ICC is achieving such goals includes
      Morten Bergsmo, Olympia Bekou & Anika Jones, *Complementarity After Kampala:
      Capacity Building and the ICC's Legal Tools*, 2 GOETTINGEN J. INT'L L. 791 (2010);
      Phil Clark, Law, Politics and Pragmatism: *The ICC and Case Selection in Uganda and
      the Democratic Republic of Congo, in* COURTING CONFLICT? JUSTICE, PEACE AND THE
      ICC IN AFRICA 37 (Nicholas Waddell & Phil Clark eds., 2008); SARAH M.H. NOUWEN,
      COMPLEMENTARITY IN THE LINE OF FIRE: THE CATALYSING EFFECT OF THE
      INTERNATIONAL COURT IN UGANDA AND SUDAN (2014).

227   While the Rome Statute, unlike, for example, the Convention Against Torture and Other
      Cruel, Inhuman or Degrading Treatment or Punishment (arts. 10–15, Dec. 10, 1984, 1465
      U.N.T.S. 85), contains no specific duties on Rome Statute parties to this effect, the hope is
      that the effect of preliminary and full scale investigations, indictments or trials, or even
      the sheer threat of any of these, will trigger pressure from civil society, including human
      rights NGOs, to force state action. *See generally* BETH A. SIMMONS, MOBILIZING FOR
      HUMAN RIGHTS: INTERNATIONAL LAW IN DOMESTIC POLITICS (2009).

228   By 2006, the OTP adopted this term to describe its prosecutorial strategy. *See* Office
      of the Prosecutor, Report on Prosecutorial Strategy ¶ 2, Sept. 14, 2006, *at* https://
      www.icc-cpi.int/NR/rdonlyres/D673DD8C-D427-4547-BC69-2D363E07274B/143708/
      ProsecutorialStrategy20060914_English.pdf; *see also* OTP Preliminary Examinations
      Paper, *supra* note 181, ¶¶ 100–103.

tions concerning whether complementarity precludes the admissibility of a particular case entail judgments as to whether a state is "unwilling or unable" to prosecute.[229] Most believe that this necessarily requires passing judgment on that state's ability to prosecute consistent with the human rights and other due process rights of the defendant.[230] A decision that a state is unwilling or unable to prosecute, standing alone, may be seen as a judgment on a state's compliance with both international criminal and human rights law. OTP decisions to open preliminary, and especially full, investigations and issue indictments of individuals, in addition, put considerable pressure on states to act. Such actions may drive governments or their national courts to open or pursue human rights prosecutions in national courts—which may extend beyond persons within the purview of the ICC itself.[231] Alternatively or cumulatively, the OTP may engage in collaborative efforts to facilitate state referrals to the ICC— as occurred in the situations of Uganda and the DRC or the failed effort to do so for the situation in Kenya.[232] These examples illustrate how, thanks in part to the ICC's first prosecutor, the ICC's complementarity regime is not merely a passive vessel funneling cases to that Court; it has been treated by the OTP as permission to seek to persuade or convince states to send situations to the Court or to take other internal governance actions that would make further ICC action unnecessary.[233] To be sure, the governance shadow of the ICC may not produce positive results. Perverse outcomes may emerge from ICC or OTP

---

229   Rome Statute, *supra* note 36, arts. 17–18.

230   *See, e.g.,* Amal Alamuddin, *Does Libya Have to Surrender Saif Al-Islam Gaddafi to the Hague?,* 1 MIZAAN: NEWSLETTER FROM LAWYERS FOR JUSTICE IN LIBYA, Apr. 2012, *at* http://www.doughtystreet.co.uk/documents/uploaded-documents/mizaan-newsletter-23rd-april-finalı.pdf.

231   *See* Dancy & Montal, *supra* note 200 (citing empirical evidence showing that the onset of an ICC investigation "is politically catalytic: it sets in motion strategic interactions among members of ruling groups, domestic courts, and local civil society organizations.").

232   *See* OTP Three Year Report, *supra* note 179, ¶¶ 2(b), 12 (on the Uganda and DRC referrals); Decision Pursuant to Article 15 of the Rome Statute on the Authorization of an Investigation into the Situation in the Republic of Kenya ¶¶ 52–54, ICC-01/09 (Mar. 31, 2010).

233   This vision was clear from the first ICC Prosecutor's first day on the job. *See* Luis Moreno Ocampo, Statement Made at the Ceremony for the Solemn Undertaking of the Chief Prosecutor of the International Criminal Court 3, June 16, 2003, *at* https://www.icc-cpi .int/NR/rdonlyres/D7572226-264A-4B6B-85E3-2673648B4896/143585/030616_moreno_ ocampo_english.pdf. ("The effectiveness of the International Criminal Court should not be measured by the number of cases that reach it. On the contrary, complementarity implies that the absence of trials before this Court, as a consequence of the regular functioning of national institutions, would be a major success.").

pressure.[234] A government's promises to prosecute consistent with human rights standards may turn out to be as empty as are the promises made by many governments when they ratify human rights treaties, for example.[235] The ICC's yielding of Saif Al-Islam Qaddafi to the jurisdiction of Libyan courts (or more accurately Libyan rebel groups) is seen by Qaddafi's lawyer at least as suggesting that human rights concerns fade from view once the ICC makes an initial determination that a state is willing and able to prosecute a defendant.[236]

When an international criminal tribunal renders a judgment that involves a government actor or a crime that could have been prevented by state action, that ruling, as von Bogdandy and Venzke contend, might be seen as an effort to "control[] and legitimate[e] public authority."[237] And when international criminal tribunals proclaim, as have the Special Tribunal for Lebanon and the Special Court for Sierra Leone, that certain acts constitute customary international law crimes,[238] such actions aspire to have global implications, whether or not these are actually achieved. The Lebanon Tribunal's affirmation that terrorism is another such crime, built on sporadic organizational precedents including Security Council resolutions, counter-terrorism conventions, the decisions of prior *ad hoc* tribunals, and the views of scholars,[239] appears to be directed at: encouraging states to ratify existing counter-terrorism conventions and fill gaps in the law left by these; spurring domestic courts and legislatures to criminalize such acts; providing an interpretative gloss for those Security Council resolutions that refer to but do not themselves define "terrorism";[240] or affecting the General Assembly's ongoing efforts to elaborate a general convention on the subject.[241]

---

234   *See, e.g.*, Jack Snyder & Leslie Vinjamuri, *Trials and Errors: Principle and Pragmatism in Strategies of International Justice*, 28 INT'L SEC. 5 (2003).

235   *See, e.g.*, Emilie M. Hafner-Burton & Kiyoteru Tsutsui, *Human Rights in a Globalizing World: The Paradox of Empty Promises*, 110 AM. J. SOC. 1373 (2005).

236   *See* Alamuddin, *supra* note 230.

237   Von Bogdandy & Venzke, *supra* note 26, at 57–59.

238   *See supra* § 4 (discussing the finding of a customary crime of terrorism in the Lebanon Decision on Applicable Law, *supra* note 144, and the finding of a customary crime of recruiting child soldiers in the SCSL's Norman Decision, *supra* note 154).

239   *Id.*

240   *See, e.g.*, S.C. Res. 1373 (Sept. 28, 2001).

241   *See, e.g.*, Scharf, *supra* note 147. Alternatively, this ruling might be seen as one that triggers sovereign backlash. *See, e.g.*, Saul, *supra* note 147 (criticizing the "poorly substantiated" opinion and noting that it is an excellent example of why the International Law Commission needs to refine the rules to "restrain haphazard analyses of custom such as this.").

Similarly, a central object of regional human rights courts is, of course, to discipline states for their actions, including national laws that violate individual rights. Innumerable decisions issued by the ECtHR and the Inter-American Court of Human Rights are directed at changing such laws or practices. Human rights courts are seen as instruments to make governments more rights compliant.[242] Like the WTO Dispute Settlement Body (discussed below) and international criminal courts, their function is, at least partly, to deter. This helps to explain why human rights venues, from regional human rights courts to UN human rights treaty bodies, have not always been focused on providing direct remedies, such as damages, to human rights victims.[243] For much of their early history, the Inter-American and European systems for human rights seemed most interested in issuing clarifications of the human rights obligations of their respective states parties.[244] The hope was that human rights adjudications, and the mobilization of elements of civil society that these venues empower, would steer states to greater human rights compliance.[245] Such efforts do not, of course, always succeed.[246] But although some regional human rights courts are, more recently, paying increased attention to victim

---

242   *See, e.g.*, SIMMONS, *supra* note 227. It is also argued that national domestic prosecutions of foreign leaders may have catalytic effects elsewhere. *See, e.g.*, Ellen Lutz & Kathryn Sikkink, *The Justice Cascade: The Evolution and Impact of Foreign Human Rights Trials in Latin America*, 2 CHIC. J. INT'L L. 1 (2001); NAOMI ROHT-ARRIAZA, THE PINOCHET EFFECT: TRANSNATIONAL JUSTICE IN THE AGE OF HUMAN RIGHTS (2005).

243   *See* Ebobrah, *supra* note 4. *See also* Thomas M. Antkowiak, *Remedial Approaches to Human Rights Violations: The Inter-American Court of Human Rights and Beyond*, 46 Colum. J. Transnat'l L. 351 (2008).

244   *See* Ebobrah, *supra* note 4.

245   *See supra* note 223 (discussing the "expressive theory of trials"). There is some evidence that national judges, such as those charged with interpreting international human rights standards, may also deploy their authority to advance domestic goals, that is, to exercise national governance. *See, e.g.*, Christopher McCrudden, *Why Do National Court Judges Refer to Human Rights Treaties? A Comparative International Law Analysis of CEDAW* 109 AM. J. INT'L L. 534 (2015). Note that there is evidence that in these cases, judges also downplay their law-making and governance roles. *Id.* at 540 (noting that while national judges play an active role in interpreting CEDAW, they prefer "to present this norm as top-down and [their] own role as somewhat passive"); *id.* at 547 (noting that Zimbabwean national courts employ principles of CEDAW "without direct acknowledgement" to avoid provoking sovereignty concerns).

246   *See, e.g.*, van Alebeek & Nollkaemper, *supra* note 104, at 359–371 (reporting estimates that perhaps as many as 70 percent of the views of the Human Rights Committee are not implemented, and adding that in some cases implementation is achieved only because of implementing legislation or through national court proceedings).

compensation, none of the prominent human rights adjudicative venues have abandoned their original core function of "mobilizing shame" against rights violators.[247] Despite the prevalence of individual complaints mechanisms, this regulatory goal remains key for UN human rights treaty bodies as well, including non-judicial or more political entities such as the Human Rights Council.[248]

Another example of adjudication that aspires to have a regulatory impact on states is, of course, the trade regime. The WTO's Dispute Settlement Understanding (DSU), although focused on settling discrete inter-state trade disputes, provides incentives for the monitoring of WTO members' compliance with their underlying WTO commitments. It establishes a system for deterring states from taking protectionist measures while also providing a mechanism that delivers on-going adjudicative interpretations of multilateral commitments that, especially given the existence of the Appellate Body, can be expected to affect the interpretation of those treaty commitments for all WTO parties and not only those involved in a particular dispute.[249] Of course, to the extent WTO adjudicators are also charged with applying and interpreting other soft law norms, such as the Codex Alimentarius (under the Agreement on the Application of Sanitary and Phytosanitary Measures (SPS) and the Agreement on Technical Barriers to Trade (TBT)), their governance function expands inso-

---

247   *See also* von Bogdandy & Venzke, *supra* note 26, at 57 (discussing the "vertical" governance function of both human rights courts and WTO dispute settlement bodies).

248   Indeed, the governance aspirations of the Inter-American Court of Human Rights, a court with an exceedingly broad advisory jurisdiction and an inclination to reach to human rights conventions outside Latin America, appears to be considerable. *See, e.g.*, Binder, *supra* note 98, at 312–313 (discussing that Court's jurisprudence as including references to global human rights treaties, the General Comments of the Human Rights Committee, and a number of soft law standards like the UN Guiding Principles on Internal Displacement).

249   *See, e.g.*, Venzke, *supra* note 100. This is one reason why non-litigating third party WTO members are permitted to be heard by WTO panels and to file written submissions. DSU, *supra* note 3, art. 10. Adjudicative law-making, when it involves the interpretation of a multilateral treaty that can be expected to affect, even if indirectly and not as a result of res judicata, the interests of other treaty parties, involves at least that governance element. For the same phenomenon under human rights adjudicators, see, for example, Binder, *supra* note 98 (discussing the impact of the Inter-American Court on amnesties in Latin America); Weissbrodt, Hansen & Nesbitt, *supra* note 104; Ulfstein, *supra* note 104 (characterizing the Views issued by UN human rights treaty bodies as law-making through the "dynamic ('evolutive') interpretation[s]" they enable of the underlying human rights conventions). *See also id.* at 252 (explaining the legal value of General Comments as a species of "subsequent state practice" since no state has protested the committees' issuance of such General Comments and these are within the "implied powers" of these committees, consistent with the ICJ's *Reparation* Opinion, *supra* note 11.

far as their interpretations of those standards may affect non-WTO parties to which the Codex applies.[250] Indeed, WTO rulings dealing with such standards may even indirectly affect the ways such codes are produced and by whom.[251] Innumerable WTO panel and Appellate Body decisions, from those that opined on the legality of the U.S. Trade Act to those concerning the timing of implementation measures in the protracted *Bananas* disputes, have constituted important steps in constructing trade governance.[252] For trade lawyers, the DSU is most successful when it has effects on third parties beyond the respondents to particular trade disputes, that is, when rulings issued in one case prevents other trade disputes from arising, or, as articulated by Andrew Guzman, when the information provided by its dispute settlers deters non-litigating states from engaging in trade practices that have been deemed illegal.[253] This is why the authorization of trade countermeasures by a WTO implementation panel to force a party to dismantle a protectionist measure is seen as a regrettable (and hopefully rare) event in a governance system that seeks to induce the disputing parties to settle their trade disputes and remove offending measures. The goal of the DSU, as is suggested by Article 3.7, is to avoid the "last resort" of authorized tit-for-tat trade retaliation. In fact, even proportionate tariff increases designed to convince a state to remove an offending measure undermine the free trade premises on which the WTO is built since it penalizes consumers through higher prices. From this perspective, the WTO regime, especially

250 WTO Agreement on the Application of Sanitary and Phytosanitary Measures, Apr. 15, 1994, 1867 U.N.T.S. 493; WTO Agreement on Technical Barriers to Trade, Apr. 15, 1994, 1868 U.N.T.S. 120. This is also true of the Inter-American Court of Human Rights. *See* Binder, *supra* note 98 (discussing Binder's point on the various sources of law applied by the Inter-American Court of Human Rights).

251 *See, e.g.*, Michael A. Livermore, *Authority and Legitimacy in Global Governance: Deliberation, Institutional Differentiation, and the Codex Alimentarius*, 81 N.Y.U. L. REV. 766 (2006) (discussing the effects on the Codex once it was incorporated into the SPS/TBT Agreements and enforced by WTO dispute settlement).

252 *See* Panel Report, *United States—Sections 301–310 of the Trade Act of 1974*, WT/DS152/R (Dec. 22, 1999); Appellate Body Report, *United States—Import Measures on Certain Products from the European Communities*, WT/DS165/AB/R (Dec. 11, 2000). *See generally* ALVAREZ, *supra* note 54, at 458–485.

253 GUZMAN, *supra* note 19, at 51–54. A complimentary perspective on how trade "governance" works is provided by those who focus on its effects within states. On this view, the shadow of WTO dispute settlement enables government elites to blame the WTO—or its dispute settlers—for their own inability to legislate the trade protectionist measures that may be sought by certain interest groups within the state. *See* John O. McGinnis & Mark L. Movsesian, *The World Trade Constitution*, 114 HARV. L. REV. 511 (2000).

its adjudicative centerpiece, is all about exercising trade "governance."[254] It is also a reason why some describe that regime as "constitutional" in its effects.[255]

The adjudicative governance function can also attempt to affect specific institutions. There are a number of examples where the ICJ's advisory opinions have been used, despite that Court's insistence that it does not have the power of "judicial review," as occasions for the exercise of the Court's governance function over the United Nations.[256] The Court's *Reparation* opinion, for example, established the UN's international legal personality and its implied power to present international claims for damages incurred by the organization itself and on behalf of family members of its agents; along the way, the Court opined that the organization had the capacity to engage in the functional equivalent of diplomatic espousal.[257] Its *Effect of Awards* opinion affirmed the General Assembly's power to create an independent tribunal to adjudicate claims by UN employees, under the Assembly's Article 22 authority to establish "subsidiary organs."[258] The *Certain Expenses* opinion found that the Assembly's power to approve the regular budget necessarily creates a duty on UN members to pay for those expenses,[259] while in its *Namibia* opinion, the Court controversially opined that the Security Council can take binding decisions under Articles 24 and 25, outside the context of Chapter VII, that such Council resolutions may be legally binding even if the Council fails to use the term "decision" and only declares a legal situation and "calls on" states to take actions, and

---

254 *See* Richard B. Stewart & Michelle Ratton Sanchez-Badin, *The World Trade Organization and Global Administrative Law, in* CONSTITUTIONALISM, MULTILEVEL TRADE GOVERNANCE AND INTERNATIONAL ECONOMIC LAW 457, 467 (Christian Joerges & Ernst-Ulrich Petersmann eds., 2d ed. 2011) (discussing how the WTO dispute settlement system has assumed a "regulatory and even an incipient administrative character").

255 *See, e.g.,* McGinnis & Movsesian, *supra* note 253; DEBORAH Z. CASS, THE CONSTITUTIONALIZATION OF THE WORLD TRADE ORGANIZATION: LEGITIMACY, DEMOCRACY, AND COMMUNITY IN THE INTERNATIONAL TRADING SYSTEM (2005).

256 *Compare* ALVAREZ, *supra* note 54, at 122–139 (discussing the effects of certain ICJ advisory opinions on the institutional law of the UN) *with* Namibia Opinion, *supra* note 10, ¶ 89 (affirming that the Court "does not possess powers of judicial review or appeal in respect of the decisions taken by the United Nations organs ...").

257 Reparation Opinion, *supra* note 11, at 187–188. For a characterization of the Court's ruling as a new power of diplomatic espousal, see *id.* at 197–198 (Hackworth, J., Dissenting Opinion) ("Certainly there is no specific provision in the Charter ... conferring upon the Organization authority to assume the role of a State, and to represent its agents in the espousal of diplomatic claims on their behalf.").

258 Effect of Awards of Compensation Made by the United Nations Administrative Tribunal, Advisory Opinion, 1954 I.C.J. 47, 57–58 (July 13).

259 Certain Expenses Opinion, *supra* note 12, at 157–167.

that the Assembly can render legally binding decisions such as terminating South Africa's mandate over Namibia.[260] The Court's opinion on the legality of the Israeli Wall followed earlier advisory opinions indicating that as far as the Court was concerned, the uncontested subsequent practice of UN organs can be treated as the equivalent of the subsequent practice of treaty parties for purposes of interpreting the UN Charter; in that instance it deployed institutional practice as permitting the Assembly to ask about the Wall, despite the constraints imposed on the Assembly under Article 12(1) (which directs the Assembly not to make recommendations with respect to disputes or situations before the Security Council, absent a request by the Council).[261] In all these instances the Court assumed the role of constitutional enabler of UN organs. It provided a judicial imprimatur to principles or doctrines that have facilitated the expanding power and mandates of the United Nations, such as the principle of effectiveness, the doctrine of implied powers, the canon of interpretation permitting the Charter to be read in light of the subsequent practice of UN organs, and a general presumption in favor of the legality of action taken by such organs.[262]

While the ICJ has never found any action taken by a UN organ to be *ultra vires* and has asserted that it does not engage in "judicial review" over UN organs, having not been given any such authority,[263] its advisory opinions have also suggested that some normative limits on the power of international organizations exist. This was perhaps clearest in the Court's refusal to answer the WHO's request for an opinion on the legality of the use of nuclear weapons, in which it suggested that UN specialized agencies were constrained by the "principle of speciality."[264] Notably the Court did so not in the exercise of its discretion to answer any particular advisory opinion posed to it but on the express premise that the WHO had no legal capacity to ask about the legality of nuclear weapons. The Court concluded that IOs do not possess "general competence" (as compared to states), that the implied powers of organizations are limited by the competences that are conferred on them under their constituent instruments, and that the UN "system" of organizations established by Article 63

---

260   Namibia Opinion, *supra* note 10, ¶¶ 96–103, 109–116.

261   Wall Advisory Opinion, *supra* note 13, ¶¶ 25–28. *See also* Reparation Opinion, *supra* note 11, at 180; WHO Opinion, *supra* note 15, ¶ 19; Namibia Opinion, *supra* note 10, ¶ 22.

262   *See* ALVAREZ, *supra* note 54, at 74–100. *See also* Oellers-Frahm, *supra* note 104, at 80–82.

263   *See, e.g.*, Namibia Opinion, *supra* note 10, ¶ 89.

264   WHO Opinion, *supra* note 15, ¶¶ 25–26. *See* EYAL BENVENISTI, THE LAW OF GLOBAL GOVERNANCE 89–144 (2014).

of the Charter anticipates that UN specialized agencies will not "encroach on the responsibilities of other parts of the United Nations . . ."[265]

In other advisory opinions, the ICJ has suggested that explicit terms of the Charter (and any express limits imposed on the power of UN organs) cannot be trumped by the subsequent practice of UN organs, the presumption of legality, or the principle of implied powers.[266] As Eyal Benvenisti has noted, the ICJ and other national and international adjudicators have affirmed that IOs (including those of the European Union) enjoy legal personhood that anticipates the existence of duties as well as rights;[267] have only limited powers as defined by their constituent instruments and not the general powers enjoyed by states (as with respect to their capacity to conclude only some types of treaties);[268] and that such organizations are subjects of and subjected to general international law.[269] Some courts have further opined that the state members of organizations may be directly accountable, procedurally and substantively, for human rights violations that they commit.[270]

And despite the absence of any explicit power in the Charter permitting the ICJ to judicially review the actions of UN organs like the Security Council, that Court's "governance" interventions have not been limited to its advisory

---

265   WHO Opinion, *supra* note 15, ¶¶ 25–26.

266   Thus, in 1950, when asked by the UN General Assembly whether that body could admit as a member a state without the prior recommendation of the Security Council, the Court responded that it could not do so in light of the explicit requirements for both organs to act under Article 4 of the UN Charter. Competence of the General Assembly for the Admission of a State to the United Nations, Advisory Opinion, 1950 I.C.J. 4 (Mar. 3). *See also* Conditions of Admission of a State to Membership in the United Nations, Advisory Opinion, 1948 I.C.J. 57, 64 (May 28) ("The political character of an organ cannot release it from the observance of the treaty provisions established by the Charter when they constitute limitations on its powers or criteria for its judgment. To ascertain whether an organ has freedom of choice for its decisions, reference must be made to the terms of its constitution. In this case, the limits of this freedom are fixed by Article 4 and allow for a wide liberty of appreciation.").

267   Reparation Opinion, *supra* note 11, at 182; Interpretation of the Agreement of 25 March 1951 Between the WHO and Egypt, Advisory Opinion, 1980 I.C.J. 73, ¶ 37. (Dec. 20). *See also* BENVENISTI, *supra* note 264, at 89–93.

268   BENVENISTI, *supra* note 264, at 93–96.

269   *Id.* at 99–144.

270   *Id. See also* International Law Commission, Draft Articles on the Responsibility of International Organizations, with Commentaries, U.N. Doc. A/66/10 52–172 (2011) (anticipating the existence of both primary and secondary rules for liability for internationally wrongful acts on both organizations and sometimes their members). *See also* Chapter VI *infra*.

jurisdiction. As indicated in Chapter II, that Court's interim decisions in the *Lockerbie* case, for example, while deferential to the Security Council, contained subtle forms of *de facto* judicial review, including the suggestion that at least Council actions taken under the UN Charter's Chapter VI and perhaps some aspects of Chapter VII decisions (other than the determination of what constitutes a threat or breach of the peace) might be subject to the Court's "powers of appreciation."[271] Other adjudicators have not been as discreet in asserting their review authority over the Council. The ICTY, in its jurisdictional decision in *Tadić*,[272] the European Court of Justice in the *Kadi* cases,[273] and even some national courts[274] have engaged in indirect forms of review over the Security Council.[275] These decisions have suggested that the Council needs to respect the procedural rights of individuals (as recognized under Article 14 of the ICCPR and the European Convention of Human Rights), at least if the Council wants its decisions (to establish a tribunal or to impose counter-terrorism sanctions on individuals) to be respected.[276] As these examples suggest, exercises in governance by international adjudicators need not be restricted to the particular regime in which the adjudicators operate and need not be directed solely at states.

Scholars associated with the Global Administrative Law (GAL) project have provided a framework for understanding the governance function as exercised by international adjudicative bodies. The extensive GAL literature catalogues and critiques various contemporary modes of regulating states (not only in their relations inter-se but internally). GAL scholars consider the efforts of transnational networks of government regulators, formal international organizations, and hybrid public/private bodies, but they also include as part of "global governance" the adjudicators that may be involved in these regimes.[277] To GAL scholars, investor-state arbitrators, tasked with settling disputes under investment protection treaties and providing compensation to foreign

271   See, e.g., Thomas Franck, *The "Powers of Appreciation": Who Is the Ultimate Guardian of UN Legality?*, 86 AM. J. INT'L L. 519 (1992); Alvarez, *Judging the Security Council, supra* note 151.

272   Tadić Jurisdiction Decision, *supra* note 138, ¶¶ 9–48.

273   Joined Cases C-402 & 415/05P, Kadi v. Council, 2008 E.C.R. I-6351 ¶¶ 248–330 [hereinafter Kadi I]; Joined Cases C-584/10 & 593/10P, Comm'n v. Kadi, 2013 E.C.R. I-0000 [hereinafter Kadi II].

274   See BENVENISTI, *supra* note 264, at 273–282.

275   See, e.g., von Bogdandy & Venzke, *supra* note 26 (describing international courts as weak systems of *horizontal* control and legitimation of authority).

276   See Tadić Jurisdiction Decision, *supra* note 138, ¶¶ 45–48; Kadi I, *supra* note 273, ¶ 344.

277   See, e.g., Stewart & Sanchez-Badin, *supra* note 254; Kingsbury & Schill, *supra* note 63.

investors, are as engaged in the "public" regulation of states as are WTO dispute settlement bodies or human rights adjudicative venues.[278]

If international criminal courts serve as an effective case study of judicial law-making precisely because they operate in a regime where this form of law-making is most contestable, ISDS proves an interesting example of the governance function even where there is no single international organization assigned the task of governance or a permanent court charged with interpretation under a multilateral treaty regime. The example of ISDS suggests that adjudicative governance can occur even when *ad hoc* panels of three arbitrators are appointed only to resolve a specific dispute between a host state of foreign direct investment (FDI) and a foreign investor.

The proposition that the seemingly chaotic "spaghetti soup mix" of international investment protection treaties and resulting investor-state arbitral awards are a form of global governance is counterintuitive. For this to be true, the motley collection of mostly bilateral investment treaties (BITs), regional investment chapters of free trade agreements (FTAs), and arbitral decisions emerging in their wake must first be "global." How can multilateral governance effects emerge from an essentially bilateral regime? Second, even if global rules were somehow to emerge from the combination of diverse treaties and *ad hoc* resolutions of investor-state disputes, how could a system designed merely to provide private investors with a more reliable remedy than old-fashioned diplomatic espousal possibly be a system for *regulating* how states govern themselves? To suggest that approximately 3000 BITs and FTAs operating without an investment organization, a single overarching treaty, or an independent civil service can be "global" and constitute "governance" would seem to stretch the common sense meaning of both terms.

Stephan W. Schill has provided six reasons for the international investment regime's global or "multilateral" effects.[279] Schill makes his case, first, by noting the common historic and multilateral pedigree of today's international investment treaties. He stresses the commonality of intent between today's (usually bilateral) investment treaties and prior multilateral instruments directed at capital flows, such as the 1967 Organization for Economic Cooperation and Development (OECD) Draft Convention on the Protection of Foreign Property, the Convention on the Settlement of Investment Disputes between States and

---

278   *See, e.g.*, Stephan W. Schill, *Enhancing International Investment Law's Legitimacy: Conceptual and Methodological Foundations of a New Public Law Approach*, 52 VA. J. INT'L L. 57 (2011); Kingsbury & Schill, *supra* note 63.

279   STEPHAN W. SCHILL, THE MULTILATERALIZATION OF INTERNATIONAL INVESTMENT LAW (2009).

Nationals of Other States (ICSID Convention), and the Convention Establishing the Multilateral Investment Guarantee Agency (MIGA Convention).[280] Second, Schill argues that BITs and FTAs are not *quid pro quo* bargains secured to extract purely bilateral concessions but are intended to produce multilateral effects. These treaties, he argues, are not contractual bargains; they advance common, universal interests, as David Ricardo's theory of comparative advantage requires.[281] Schill's third interlocking argument is that these agreements contain standard general guarantees that put all investors—or at least foreign investors—on the same plane.[282] His fourth contention in favor of "multilateralization" relies on one of these standard guarantees, namely the most-favored-nation (MFN) clause common to them and its generally expansive interpretation by investor-state arbitrators. Schill argues that MFN clauses ratchet up the level of investment protection, encouraging if not forcing the 180 states that have at least one BIT in place to enforce "the most favorable level of investment protection reached at one point of time and project this level into the future."[283] Fifth, Schill points outs how the broad definition of protected "investment" or "investor" in most of these treaties—which often extend to individual shareholders and not just to a company as a whole and may include entities incorporated in a BIT party even if this is a mere "paper" presence—has given them a more global ambit. These realities encourage treaty beneficiaries to engage in corporate restructuring to take advantage of the most investor-protective treaty available. Thanks to MFN guarantees and corporate restructuring (or "treaty-shopping"), BITs and FTAs have become vehicles for the protection of businesses far removed from those that the state parties to such treaties anticipated. Although ostensibly "restricted *ratione personae* to investors that have the nationality of the other contracting party in a bilateral relationship," in reality the third party beneficiaries of the investment regime are, according to Schill, in a comparable position to those who assert *erga omnes* or *erga omnes partes* obligations.[284]

Schill's final argument, the most relevant here, relies on the multilateralizing impact of ISDS. Granting investors direct access to arbitration becomes "an essential move away from bilateral inter-State compliance toward a multilateral ordering structure" because it "effectively removes the power of States

280   *Id.* at 25–49.
281   *Id.* at 88–117. *See* DAVID RICARDO, ON THE PRINCIPLES OF POLITICAL ECONOMY AND TAXATION (1817).
282   SCHILL, *supra* note 279, at 65–120.
283   *Id.* at 196.
284   *Id.* at 197–199.

to both unilaterally defect from investment treaties and bilaterally negotiate around the consequences of breaches of such treaties."[285] Schill points out that investor-state arbitral tribunals are empowered by investors' direct right of action, the limited influence of states on the arbitral process, the limited review of arbitral awards, and the effective provisions for enforcement of these awards.[286] He further argues that most investor-state arbitrators apply interpretative approaches consistent with a multilateral legal framework, that is, they tend to avoid reliance on treaty-specific negotiation history, privilege systematic over treaty-specific interpretations of commonly accepted treaty provisions, and make extensive use of arbitral precedents even if those do not concern the specific treaty at issue. He argues that despite divergent interpretations on some issues, there is an underlying "unity"[287] to the emerging arbitral caselaw, and that a "system"[288] of relatively stable, increasingly coherent, and predictable international investment law has emerged through arbitral interpretation. For Schill, these "multilateralizing" features are only encouraged by adjudicators' needs to fill gaps in the law to avoid findings of *non-liquet* and their need to provide convincing, reasoned opinions that resist national review or ICSID annulment.[289]

There are other reasons, apart from those advanced by Schill, for believing that the investment regime produces global and national regulatory effects. If, as Schill indicates, businesses other than those contemplated by BIT or FTA drafters are benefiting from such agreements, the realities of political economy encourage states to provide comparable benefits internally, even to national investors. Indeed, as would be predicted by Putnam's two-level game,[290] some states may have entered into BITs or FTAs due to internal pressures brought by their own national entrepreneurs. National companies may support such treaties, even if intended to protect their foreign competitors, if they believe that such rights will benefit them as well. This may be the case, for example, if a country's investment treaty commitments or particular arbitral awards drive improvements in national laws and administrative or judicial practices.[291]

---

285   *Id.* at 242.

286   *Id.* at 249.

287   *Id.* at 339.

288   *Id.* at 357.

289   *Id.* at 276–277. *See also* Kingsbury & Schill, *supra* note 63.

290   Robert D. Putnam, *Diplomacy and Domestic Politics: The Logic of Two-Level Games*, 42 Int'l Org. 427 (1988).

291   *But see* Tom Ginsburg, *International Substitutes for Domestic Institutions: Bilateral Investment Treaties and Governance*, 24 Int'l Rev. L. & Econ. 107 (2005) (providing

Moreover, if national entrepreneurs are, as is probable, attentive to the benefits conferred on foreign investors (including their competitors), the dynamic established by the combination of entry into investment protection treaties and ISDS caselaw may result in political pressures to expand the benefits of the rule of law to national and not only foreign investors.[292] MFN clauses and corporate restructuring are not, in short, the only reasons that make it difficult, in a post-BIT/FTA world, for countries to restrict those treaty benefits to only foreigners from certain treaty signatories. Once a country adheres to a BIT, for example, it may become less tenable to engage in an expropriatory act that results in less than fair compensation—even if the victim is its own national and not a foreign company—simply because it may be too politically costly to explain to local constituencies why only foreigners are entitled to property rights, the rule of law, or a politically neutral and effective adjudicative remedy when their rights are violated.

Guarantees extended to investors under these treaties such as umbrella clauses, treaty-based rights to assert claims in local courts, residual obligations to extend to the investor the "better of" national law or international legal obligations, customary law (as with respect to the international minimum standard, denial of justice, and full protection and security), assurances to provide "due process" and/or transparency, as well as rights to non-discrimination—*cumulatively or in combination* enhance the prospects for global and not merely bilateral rules. As is evidenced by UN Conference on Trade and Development's (UNCTAD) annual surveys of changes to national laws since 1992,[293] the proliferation of international investment treaties has been accompanied by changes to national laws in favor of business interests and liberal capital flows. And to the extent national laws and practices have changed in tandem with the rise of such treaties, it appears that most of these efforts do not differentiate between domestic and foreign enterprises; nor are these legislative changes typically limited to benefiting investors from particular treaty signatories. The evidence suggests that the proliferation of BITs and FTAs in the 1990s reflects and in turn

---

suggestive, but preliminary, evidence that investment treaties, by encouraging resort to ISDS, discourage national legal or judicial reforms).

292 But it is also possible that the perception that foreigners are receiving "special" benefits may produce, on the contrary, a reaction against such treaties.

293 *See, e.g.,* United Nations Conference on Trade and Development, World Investment Report 2015, Table III.1, U.N. Doc. UNCTAD/WIR/2015, *at* http://unctad.org/en/Publica tionsLibrary/wir2015_en.pdf (indicating the percentages of national regulatory changes that are both more and less welcoming to foreign investors as a share of national regulatory changes from 2000–2014).

encourages a global move in favor of the market, deregulation, and privatization—as proposed by the then influential "Washington Consensus"—and that, similarly, more recent investment treaties and arbitral decisions may reflect a move in favor of a "post-Washington consensus."[294]

There is another reason why BITs and FTAs have had global effects: the regulatory actions encouraged by such treaties have been aided and abetted by the actions of international financial institutions, particularly the International Monetary Fund (IMF). To the extent that all nations, especially least developed countires (LDCs), have been systematically reforming their laws in favor of liberal capital flows, they have been encouraged (or pressured) to do so by IMF structural adjustment conditions. The IMF is, to this extent, itself a global regulator of investment.[295] Governments have also been influenced (and their economies directly impacted) by the "doing business," "good governance," and other "rule of law" indicators applied by other institutions, like the International Finance Corporation and market actors.[296] As this suggests, the claim that the international investment regime as a whole lacks global institutions is a half-truth.[297] While the investment regime lacks a single overarching institution comparable to the WTO, it is assisted by a number of them—including the international financial institutions and the World Bank's ICSID.

The thesis that ISDS has a "global" impact draws support from interdisciplinary scholarship stressing the "network" or "systems" effects that regularly occur among state and non-state actors thanks to economic interdependence,[298] as well as from socio-legal analyses demonstrating how the interactions among

---

294   See, e.g., José E. Alvarez, The Evolving BIT, in 3 INVESTMENT TREATY ARBITRATION AND INTERNATIONAL LAW 1 (Ian A. Laird, Nina P. Mocheva & Todd J. Weiler eds., 2010); José E. Alvarez, Why Are We "Re-Calibrating" Our Investment Treaties?, 4 WORLD ARB. & MEDIATION REV. 143 (2010).

295   See Daniel Kalderimis, IMF Conditionality as Investment Regulation: A Theoretical Analysis, 13 SOC. & LEGAL STUD. 103 (2004).

296   For a critical review of some of these indicators, see Kevin E. Davis & Michael B. Kruse, Taking the Measure of Law: The Case of the Doing Business Project, 32 L. & SOC. INQUIRY 1095 (2007). See also GOVERNANCE BY INDICATORS: GLOBAL POWER THROUGH QUANTIFICATION AND RANKINGS (Kevin E. Davis et al. eds., 2015).

297   See, e.g., Beth A. Simmons, Bargaining over BITs, Arbitrating Awards: The Regime for Protection and Promotion of International Investment, 66 WORLD POLITICS 12, 14–16 (2013).

298   See generally Robert O. Keohane & Joseph S. Nye Jr. Introduction to GOVERNANCE IN A GLOBALIZING WORLD 1, 9–12 (Joseph S. Nye Jr. & John D. Donahue eds., 2000).

public institutions and businesses generate transnational law.[299] We are only beginning to understand how ISDS caselaw, which after all only emerged when claims were brought in the mid-1990s, complements the regulatory actions of international financial institutions and market actors. What seems clear is that the normative ripples of the investment regime—like those of human rights adjudications—extend beyond those who are immediately subject to an investor-state award.

As noted with respect to comparable efforts by international criminal tribunals who opine on customary crimes, the global impact of ISDS caselaw is all the more likely when the arbitrators appear to be passing on customary international law or general principles of law. As the author has argued elsewhere, this may occur where the underlying treaty guarantees are equated to customary law or where the arbitrators make explicit reference to such law, as with respect to ostensibly international rules "common" to arbitration.[300] Such recourse to general international law affects its evolution. As is further discussed below, the growing ISDS caselaw has probably had much to do with the finding, now common to a number of arbitral decisions, that the international minimum standard and conceptions of denial of justice entitle alien investors to better treatment now than at the beginning of the twentieth century.[301]

There are many examples of how investor-state arbitral awards regulate the world by elaborating global law, including custom and general principles, and not merely the interpretation of a particular investment treaty. Those searching for the contemporary meaning of international law governing expropriation and compensation for expropriation, as considered by the U.S. Supreme Court in its 1964 decision in *Banco Nacional de Cuba v. Sabbatino*, for instance, are now very likely to turn to investor-state caselaw for guidance. In that case,

---

299 *See, e.g.*, Gregory C. Shaffer, *How Business Shapes Law: A Socio-Legal Framework*, 42 CONN. L. REV. 147 (2009).

300 *See, e.g.*, NAFTA Free Trade Commission, Notes of Interpretation of Certain Chapter XI Provisions, July 31, 2001, *at* http://www.state.gov/documents/organization/38790.pdf (equating the "fair and equitable treatment" (FET) provision with the international minimum standard for the treatment of aliens). In the wake of that Commission statement, interpretations of the FET clause of the NAFTA by NAFTA arbitrators are seen as interpretations of customary law. *See generally* José E. Alvarez, *A BIT on Custom*, 42 N.Y.U. J. INT'L L. & POL. 17 (2009). *See also* Andreas F. Lowenfeld, *Investment Agreements and International Law*, 42 COLUM. J. TRANSNAT'L L. 123 (2003).

301 *See, e.g.*, Clayton/Bilcon v. Canada, Award on Jurisdiction and Liability ¶¶ 435–436 (NAFTA/UNCITRAL Ch. 11 Arb. Trib. 2015); Merrill & Ring Forestry L.P. v. Canada, Award ¶¶ 193 & 209–213 (NAFTA/UNCITRAL Ch. 11 Arb. Trib. 2010); Glamis Gold, *supra* note 40, ¶ 22, 1058 ¶¶ 612–613.

a majority of the Supreme Court found that customary law was so uncertain that it was impossible to conclude that an officially proclaimed nationalization in which the foreign government seized title to alien property and did so in a discriminatory fashion was an internationally illegal taking requiring the payment of compensation.[302]

Today, thanks to the proliferation of investment protection treaties and arbitral caselaw, most contemporary international lawyers would probably agree that contemporary customary law on point would:

(1)   Affirm that a state's denial of property rights to an alien (and possibly even to its own national under the customary law of human rights) is not purely a matter of national law or a state's sacrosanct "domestic jurisdiction" but is properly the concern of international law.

(2)   Accept that a state's denial of property rights to an alien triggers a number of procedural rights to due process or a fair and effective remedy, including, as is suggested by the *Kadi* decision of the European Court of Justice[303] and not only investor-state arbitral decisions, the right to judicial review and the ability to present one's case.

(3)   Consider the "property" of an alien that is subject to customary international law's limitations and constraints to include possessions beyond tangible real property, such as some forms of vested contractual rights and perhaps rights to some forms of intellectual property.

(4)   Require that when a direct expropriation occurs, the person or entity whose property has been taken or those claiming on that person's behalf be treated as having a right to compensation (that is, reparation under the rules of state responsibility) irrespective of whether the property was taken for a public purpose, whether or not it was discriminatory in its effect, and without regard to whether national law provides for such compensation. Today, far more than was true in 1964, as human rights advocates would acknowledge, the right to be compensated for permanent deprivations of one's property is protected under customary law. Moreover, it is widely assumed that custom would require that any such compensation should be commensurate with the value of the property actually taken—and not reflect merely its book value if that does not reflect the fair market value of the property when it was taken by the state.

---

302   Banco Nacional de Cuba v. Sabbatino, 376 U.S. 398, 427–437 (1964).

303   *See supra* notes 273, 276, and accompanying text.

(5) Include as an unlawful expropriation a taking of property resulting from a series of "creeping" measures taken by a state where these result in a total deprivation of the alien's property interest. It now seems less likely that customary law, and not just the law under a specific investment protection treaty, requires the state to issue a formal nationalization decree prior to a finding of an "unlawful" taking.

(6) Treat the duty to compensate for an expropriation as limited by states' general right to regulate in the public interest, as affirmed by the European Convention of Human Rights.[304] It is likely that the general law, and not only some contemporary investment treaties, would affirm for example that "except in rare circumstances, non-discriminatory regulatory actions by a Party that are designed and applied to protect legitimate public welfare objectives, such as public health, safety, and the environment, do not constitute indirect expropriations."[305]

Another example of the general governance impact of the ISDS rulings concerns the "international minimum standard." Most investor-state arbitral decisions have explicitly equated "fair and equitable treatment" (FET) treaty guarantees with the standards of customary law, have assimilated the two standards, or have suggested that an FET treaty guarantee needs to be informed by custom (as may occur under Article 31(3)(c) of the VCT). When this occurs, it is hard to disentangle FET rulings issued by investor-state arbitrators from decisions based on customary law. A number of tribunals have also suggested that the international minimum standard has "evolved" over time.[306] It appears that the international minimum standard is not quite the "minimum" that it used to be. This should hardly surprise in an age when tribunals are being asked to apply that standard in the context of treaties that demand that investors be treated "fairly" and "equitably."[307] It seems quite likely that the international minimum standard has evolved even since 1959 when Germany concluded its first BIT, and that the spread of BITs and FTAS, ISDS rulings, and

---

304 First Protocol to the Convention for the Protection of Human Rights and Fundamental Freedoms art. 1, Mar. 20, 1952, E.T.S. 9.

305 2012 U.S. Model Bilateral Investment Treaty, *supra* note 119, Annex B, ¶ 4(b).

306 For a typical example, see Clayton/Bilcon v. Canada, *supra* note 301, ¶¶ 427, 434–445 (relying heavily on ISDS caselaw to interpret the "evolving" content and contemporary meaning of the international minimum standard under customary international law).

307 *See, e.g.,* Glamis Gold, *supra* note 40, ¶ 22, 1058 ¶¶ 612–613 (finding that the standard articulated in the 1926 *Neer* case continues to apply to the meaning of FET under the NAFTA but suggesting that what is deemed "outrageous" or "shocking" evolves over time).

all that has accompanied the post-Cold War turn to the market has had a great to do with the expectations we now have of what "good governance" entails with respect to the treatment of aliens, including investors.

Today, most international lawyers would assert, at least in investor-state arbitrations, that the procedural rights enumerated above with respect to takings of property apply more generally. This means that a state needs to provide some access to an effective remedy, at least within its courts, if not through international arbitration, should it renege on a contractual commitment that it made to an investor; that a state cannot assert by way of a defense to such a claim a "secret" or wholly un-transparent law or agency process; that the mere absence of "bad faith" may not remove the taint of illegality from a state's actions; and that any process for adjudicating such a claim that a state provides needs to adhere to human rights law standards of fair process (and not merely principles drawn from the doctrine of state responsibility to aliens).

Thanks in part to ISDS, it is more likely today that custom or general principles of law would be interpreted to require a state to "ensure" some basic rights of all persons within its jurisdiction, including alien investors. This would include some duties to protect such persons through reasonable police protection from the actions of non-state parties, such as rioters—even in the absence of a specific "full protection and security" guarantee clause in an investment protection treaty (as where a treaty extends fair and equitable treatment or the protections of "international law").[308] This is certainly the case to the extent these rights are affirmed by the ICCPR as well as the Universal Declaration of Human Rights and affirm comparable rights for all persons, not merely foreign investors.

Investor-state arbitrators—along with other international adjudicators— are also applying *and therefore developing* such general principles of law as the meaning of "good faith," the concepts of "unjust enrichment" and "unclean hands," and the prohibition of a party benefiting from its own wrong or being a judge in its own cause.[309] Custom or general principles of law may also emerge

---

308   For a possible example, see the *Kadi* cases, *supra* notes 273, 276, and the accompanying text (finding that the implementation of UN counter-terrorist sanctions under European law violated individuals' rights to be heard and rights to non-interference with their property rights).

309   On the judicial contribution to the "clean hands" doctrine, see, for example, Ori Pomson & Yonatan Horvits, *Humanitarian Intervention and the Clean Hands Doctrine in International Law*, 48 ISR. L. REV. 219 (2015). Other international adjudicators not addressed here, such as the World Bank's Inspection Panel, may contribute to general international law to the extent such law is included in the Bank's internal guidelines, such as rules governing involuntary resettlement, environmental assessments, or the rights of indigenous peoples. *See, e.g.*, Ellen Hey, *The World Bank Inspection Panel and the Development of International Law,*

and be applied in such disputes to the extent a question arises as to whether state action respects "elementary requirements of the rule of law." ISDS and other adjudicative forums directed at state action also provide repeated occasions for considering and elaborating the Articles of State Responsibility—from its rules of attribution to its defenses from *pacta sunt servanda* (such as necessity).[310] While it may be true that these rules have long been established as customary, even the clearest rule develops once applied to concrete fact.

Among the general law that is being affected by ISDS as well as WTO caselaw are the ostensibly "common rules of international procedure" on which international adjudicators rely. We are now seeing considerable development within the trade and investment regimes concerning such matters as burdens and standards of proof, evidentiary standards more generally, and the precise meaning to be given to "equality of arms."[311] We are also seeing investor-state

---

     in INTERNATIONAL COURTS AND THE DEVELOPMENT OF INTERNATIONAL LAW: ESSAYS IN HONOR OF TULLIO TREVES 727, 737 (Nerina Boschiero et al. eds., 2013).

310   *See* International Law Commission, Draft Articles on Responsibility of States arts. 4–11 (on attribution), 25 (on the necessity defense), U.N. Doc. A/56/10 (2001). Investor-state claims against Argentina have now provided considerable fodder for considering the meaning of the customary defense of necessity, including such matters as which party bears the burden of proof or carries the burden of persuasion, and what the requisites of that defense—"grave peril," "only way," or "significant contribution"—mean. For discussion of the relevant cases, see José E. Alvarez & Kathyrn Khamsi, *The Argentine Crisis and Foreign Investors: A Glimpse into the Heart of the Investment Regime, in* YEARBOOK ON INTERNATIONAL INVESTMENT LAW & POLICY: 2008–2009, 379 (Karl P. Sauvant ed., 2009). Of course, repeated adjudicative consideration does not always result in greater clarity or enhanced consistency. One of the annulment rulings rendered in the course of the Argentina cases has raised additional questions, never previously addressed in the caselaw, with respect to the customary defense of necessity. *See* Enron Corp. v. The Argentine Republic, *supra* note 133, ¶¶ 385–393. *See* Alvarez, *Return of the State, supra* note 41, at 248–249; José E. Alvarez, *Beware: Boundary Crossings, supra* note 133. For an excellent elaboration of how human rights judicial and quasi-judicial bodies have deployed and, in turn develop, the rules of state responsibility, see Stefano Brugnatelli, *Human Rights Judicial and Semi-Judicial Bodies and Customary International Law on State Responsibility, in* INTERNATIONAL COURTS AND THE DEVELOPMENT OF INTERNATIONAL LAW 475, 485, *supra* note 309 (arguing that the jurisprudence of bodies like the ECtHR "constitutes, by far, the largest and most precious source of praxis… to assess how the customary rules on State responsibility shall be applied in case of violations of human rights obligations…").

311   *See* Thomas W. Wälde, *"Equality of Arms" in Investment Arbitration: Procedural Challenges, in* ARBITRATION UNDER INTERNATIONAL INVESTMENT AGREEMENTS: A GUIDE TO THE KEY ISSUES 161 (Katia Yannaca-Small ed., 2010).

arbitrators needing to resolve increased demands for provisional relief.[312] These demands are prompting rulings on matters such as whether provisional relief requires "irreparable harm" or can be issued merely to avoid aggravating the dispute. It would appear that the question of whether orders for such forms of interim relief are legally binding has migrated from the ICJ—and its rulings in the *Avena/LaGrand* line of cases that ICJ orders for provisional relief can indeed be binding[313]—to investor-state arbitrations.[314] It is likely that there will be continued two-way traffic among international courts and tribunals on such procedural questions.

The increased judicialization of international law, concerning the finding and application of general international law such as custom, suggests to some observers, more controversially, that the world's global judiciary is now changing the basic elements of what custom is or at least what it takes to prove its existence. On this view, the governance efforts of courts and tribunals extend to changing the basic understanding concerning the sources of international obligation.

The Sierra Leone tribunal's *Norman* decision, discussed above, illustrates the point. In that instance, the judges turned to a variety of sources to determine the existence of a customary crime. These included statements by the President of the Security Council, Reports of the UN Secretary-General, statements rendered by certain delegates to the Rome Conference for the ICC, statements made at the UN General Assembly or in regional organizations, prior rulings of the ICTY, the endorsement of a UNICEF Report by UN organs, the numbers of states that ratified the Rome Statute in 1998, and the Rights of the Child Convention and its Optional Protocol.[315] As the dissent points out in that case, very little evidence was presented to show actual state practice and *opinio juris*, with no evidence shown that significant numbers of states had, by 1996, actually made the underlying act criminal under either their national law or in any of their treaties, and that few had even articulated in any setting that such a crime existed as a matter of international law.[316] Perhaps

---

312   *See, e.g.*, INTERIM AND EMERGENCY RELIEF IN INTERNATIONAL ARBITRATION (Diora Ziyaeva et al. eds., 2015).

313   *See* LaGrand Case, *supra* note 18; Case Concerning Avena and Other Mexican Nationals, *supra* note 18.

314   *See generally* Robert Volterra, *Provisional Measures (Interim Measures) and Investment Treaty Arbitration under ICSID and UNCITRAL: Developments and Trends, in* 3 INVESTMENT TREATY LAW: CURRENT ISSUES: REMEDIES IN INTERNATIONAL INVESTMENT LAW, EMERGING JURISPRUDENCE OF INTERNATIONAL INVESTMENT LAW 17, (Andrew K. Bjorklund, Ian A Laird & Sergey Ripinsky eds., 2009).

315   Norman Decision, *supra* note 154, ¶¶ 1–7, 17–24.

316   *Id.*, Dissenting Opinion of Justice Robertson ¶¶ 42–43.

more striking was the fact that even the dissenting judge in that case was prepared to find that the crime of enlisting child soldiers was a customary crime
as of 1998, when the Rome Statute was only concluded but was not yet in force,
and when few states had engaged in any relevant actual state practice.[317] None
of the judges in that case, in other words, appeared to be faithful appliers of
the positivist definition of custom requiring sufficiently general state practice
accompanied by states' expression of accompanying *opinio juris*.

The *Norman* judges are not anomalous in disregarding the traditional requisites of custom. The editor of a recent collection of essays that extensively
surveys contemporary notions of custom concludes:

> While adjudicatory institutions often recite the standard conception of
> CIL, they do not actually seem to follow it. The ICJ, for example, often
> cites relatively little state practice in support of its claims about the con-
> tent of CIL. International criminal tribunals, too, seem to find rules of
> CIL through means other than the standard account. And the decisions
> of these international adjudicatory institutions, whether or not these rul-
> ings rely on traditional state practice and *opinio juris*, are in turn cited as
> evidence of the content of CIL.[318]

The increasing realization that international adjudicators are being "careless"
with custom helps to explain the ILC's current project to "identify" the elements of customary law.[319] This effort, led by Sir Michael Wood of the UK as
its rapporteur, is directed at instructing judges as to the proper way to identify custom. As Ben Saul, a critic of the Lebanon tribunal's recourse to custom

---

317   *Id.*, Dissenting Opinion of Justice Robertson ¶¶ 38–41.

318   Curtis A. Bradley, *Customary International Law Adjudication as Common Law Adjudication*,
      in CUSTOM'S FUTURE: INTERNATIONAL LAW IN A CHANGING WORLD 34, at 36
      (Curtis A. Bradley ed., 2016) (citations omitted). *See also* Stephen J. Choi & Mitu Gulati,
      Customary International Law: How Do Courts Do It?, *in* CUSTOM'S FUTURE 117, at 132,
      Figure 5.1 (survey of 175 findings of CIL in international tribunals demonstrating reliance
      on the following evidential sources in order of frequency: treaties, international tribu-
      nal cases, domestic cases, actions by states, academic articles and treatises, international
      committee reports, domestic statutes, UN/League resolutions...). As is documented
      throughout CUSTOM'S FUTURE, the principal evidentiary sources for custom relied upon
      by courts are not actual state practice and *opinio juris* but collective substitutes such as
      those relied upon in *Norman*, including multilateral treaties and various UN products, like
      General Assembly resolutions, as well as other judicial decisions.

319   Michael Wood, International Law Commission, Third Report on Identification of
      Customary International Law, U.N. Doc. A/CN.4/682 (Mar. 27, 2015), *at* http://legal.un.org/
      docs/?symbol=A/CN.4/682.

noted above, puts it, this ILC effort comes none too soon insofar as international lawyers are desperately in need of "refining the rules to restrain haphazard analyses of custom such as this."[320]

As will be addressed at greater length in Chapter VI, thus far, the ILC's draft conclusions suggest that it will indeed satisfy the clamor from some quarters for restoring state practice and *opinio juris* to their positivist pride of place.[321] The ILC is expected to generate conclusions and commentaries in some form but not a recommendation for conclusion of a treaty or other binding instrument. That its efforts, when completed, will successfully push back against what international courts and tribunals are doing in this respect seems extremely doubtful. As many scholars have indicated, the evidentiary, logistical, and linguistic challenges of undertaking the actual examination of state practice and *opinio juris* in a sufficiently wide swath of over 190 states are not likely to be overcome merely because the ILC disapproves of more collectivized "short cuts" to finding custom. Moreover, the assumption that the ILC appears to be making—that there was once a golden age when adjudicators actually did a good job of discerning the genuine general practice of states and that today's adjudicators just need to be reminded of what they should have learned in law school at the knee of their positivist professors—is likely to be wrong. In any case, at least until international adjudicators change their minds, it is plausible to suggest, as do a number of scholars, that the elements of custom are what judges and arbitrators make of them.[322] It is certainly the case, as was suggested

---

320   Saul, *supra* note 147, at 678. *But see* Chiara Ragni, *The Contribution of the Special Tribunal for Lebanon to the Notion of Terrorism: Judicial Creativity or Progressive Development of International Law?, in* INTERNATIONAL COURTS AND THE DEVELOPMENT OF INTERNATIONAL LAW 671, 682, *supra* note 309 (praising that Tribunal's approach as "consistent with the principles enshrined by the practice of other international tribunals, which, in assessing customary international law, have stated that uniformity in state practice is not required for the existence of the rule as such.").

321   *See, e.g.*, International Law Commission, Identification of Customary International Law: Text of the Draft Conclusions Provisionally Adopted by the Drafting Committee, Draft Conclusions 2–10, U.N. Doc. A/CN.4/L.689 (July 14, 2015), *at* http://legal.un.org/docs/?symbol=A/CN.4/L.869.

322   *See, e.g.*, Vassilis Tzevelekos & Kanstantsin Dzehtsiarou, *International Custom Making and the ECtHR's European Consensus Method of Interpretation* (forthcoming) ("Our argument is that, especially in the case of custom ... international courts act as a de facto substitute to the absence of a rule of recognition and, by identifying the customary rules that they apply for the purposes and in the context of cases brought before them, they also recognize the validity of those rules"); Peter Haggenmacher, *La Doctrine des deux éléments du droit coutumier dans la pratique de la Cour internationale*, 90 REVUE GÉNÉRALE DE DROIT INTERNATIONAL PUBLIC (RGDIP) 5 (1986) (arguing that *opinio juris* is essentially

in Chapter 1's discussion of the *Glamis Gold* arbitral ruling, that adjudicators' prior rulings—the ever-expanding and increasingly dense adjudicative decisions being rendered among various international regimes—and not actions by states are among the most prevalent evidentiary sources for determining the current content of custom.[323] Nor are international adjudicators' impact on the elements of custom the only instance in which these venues may exercise a constitutive effect on the sources of international obligation. Some of these adjudicators are also expected to determine, more generally, what an "international standard" is or, when such a standard exists at the national level, whether it ought to play a role within international adjudication.[324]

To be sure, attempts to govern states via adjudication through any of the methods identified above can generate resistance. Whether or not one agrees that the investment regime is both "global" and a form of "governance," there is little doubt that the governance aspirations of ISDS have encouraged a growing number of states to "re-balance" their model BITs, re-negotiate older, more investor-protective treaties, suspend future investment treaty negotiations, or attempt to narrow or even terminate their exposure to ISDS.[325] Increasing numbers of states are reacting to the governance aspects of this regime by attempting to exercise their exit and voice options. They are in effect "chafing at the BIT." This too is one kind of governance effect—albeit not the kind that adjudicators themselves expect or necessarily want. The backlash against ISDS is even apparent in the case of the United States, a state that has seen

---

made by interpreters). Those who argue the alternative—that irrespective of what international courts do and irrespective of whether states acquiesce in what they do the traditional two requisites for custom (state practice and *opinio juris*) remain unchanged—would appear to bear the burden of proof.

323 *See generally* von Bogdandy & Venzke, *supra* note 7.

324 *See, e.g.*, Joost Pauwelyn, Ramses A. Wessel & Jan Wouters, *When Structures Become Shackles: Stagnation and Dynamics in International Lawmaking*, 25 Eur. J. Int'l L. 733, 760–762 (discussing the WTO's finding that certain tuna labelling requirements were indeed such a standard, ISDS references to rules developed by the International Bar Association, and, in contrast, the refusal of an arbitration panel under the UN Convention on the Law of the Sea to consider the same IBA rules); Hey, *supra* note 309, at 735 (suggesting that the Inspection Panel may be "translat[ing] into law" the "requirements of international life" with respect to the relationship between development banks and individuals and groups in society, perhaps giving rise to "a new body of law or a new normative system, beyond classical international law.").

325 *See, e.g.*, United Nations Conference on Trade and Development, World Investment Report 2015 124–125, U.N. Doc. UNCTAD/WIR/2015, *at* http://unctad.org/en/PublicationsLibrary/wir2015_en.pdf (surveying these developments); Alvarez, *supra* note 41.

a considerable number of ISDS claims brought against it under the NAFTA's investment chapter.[326]

The governance implications of ISDS seems manifest from U.S. efforts over time to reduce, in successive Model BITs, the scope of virtually every investor guarantee contained in such treaties. This includes narrowing FET protections, eliminating the umbrella clause guarantee, reducing the scope of MFN clauses, and shrinking the definition of protected investment.[327] The U.S. has also attempted to narrow the discretion accorded to investor-state arbitrators in ways that Lauterpacht would have recognized: by enabling state parties to investment treaties to render interpretations of their treaties that are binding on investor-state arbitrators and by asserting a self-judging right for states to take actions they deem necessary to protect their "essential security."[328] These changes target those features of the regime that are most likely to produce regulatory effects on states. The state that once led the world in toppling the Calvo Clause is now a leader in attempting to "re-calibrate" both investment treaties and ISDS to secure greater sovereign "policy space." Some other leading BIT/FTA signatories, such as Canada and China, are following suit.[329]

Many of these changes seek to reduce the discretion of investor-state arbitrators to make law or exercise governance. They might be seen, in terms that Yoo and Posner would endorse, as efforts to bring adjudicators closer to functioning as state agents and not independent trustees.[330] The target of such re-calibrations is in part the regulatory model that some investment protection treaties and some investor-state arbitrators appear to endorse, namely, a model of good governance (and economic development) premised on deregulation and private party rights that has come increasingly under fire by some economists.[331] Much of the sovereign backlash against ISDS, in short, stems from the kind of governance that it is seen as advancing.

---

326   *See* Stephen Schwebel, *The United States 2004 Model Bilateral Investment Treaty: an Exercise in the Regressive Development of International Law*, 3 TRANSNAT'L DISP. MGMT. (2006); Alvarez, *Evolving BIT, supra* note 294.

327   *See, e.g.*, Kenneth J. Vandevelde, *A Comparison of the 2004 and 1994 U.S. Model BITs: Rebalancing Investor and Host Country Interests, in* YEARBOOK ON INTERNATIONAL INVESTMENT LAW & POLICY 2008–2009, 283, *supra* note 310.

328   *See, e.g.*, Alvarez, *Evolving BIT, supra* note 294.

329   *See, e.g., id.*; Organisation for Economic Co-operation and Development Secretariat, Novel Features in OECD Countries' Recent Investment Agreements: An Overview (Dec. 12, 2005), *at* http://www.oecd.org/investment/internationalinvestmentagreements/35823420.pdf.

330   *See supra* note 29.

331   *See, e.g.,* JOSEPH E. STIGLITZ, GLOBALIZATION AND ITS DISCONTENTS (2002) (criticizing the promulgation of the "Washington Consensus"); Dani Rodrik, *Growth Strategies, in*

The investment regime would not be the first instance in which treaty-makers suffer from buyers' remorse. The contemporary backlash against the investment regime may be a symptom of larger dialectical swings between historic periods in favor of "utopian market liberalism" followed by counter-movements in defense of greater governmental interventions in the economy.[332] More generally, efforts to promote global governance through adjudication are historically fragile since those that delegate authority to courts can change their mind by revoking their delegations of power or otherwise exercising their exit and voice.[333] Adverse reactions to the Inter-American Court of Human Rights' "judicial activism" with respect to amnesties or the death penalty, stemming from what some see as its judges' "radical[] monist understanding" of their powers,[334] and current reactions by individual African governments and the African Union to the ICC, provide other examples.[335] Sovereign backlash, with varying levels of success, has also emerged with respect to efforts by regional courts in West, East, and Southern Africa.[336] Resistance to international courts' law-making or governance efforts can take the form of lack of compliance with their decisions, whether or not one chooses to brand these acts of "civil disobedience."[337] States' responses can in turn prompt

---

1 HANDBOOK ECONOMIC GROWTH 967 (2005) (arguing that pursuit of the Washington Consensus model has not produced economic development as anticipated).

332 For an influential account of such a historical dialectic see KARL POLANYI, THE GREAT TRANSFORMATION (1944).

333 See, e.g., Nienke Grossman, *Legitimacy and International Adjudicative Bodies*, 41 GEO. WASH. INT'L L. REV. 107, 144–148 (2009) (arguing that international tribunals' legitimacy turns, among other things, on whether their interpretations are consistent with what states believe the law is or should be).

334 See, e.g., Binder, *supra* note 98, at 316. *See also* Laurence R. Helfer, *Overlegalizing Human Rights: International Relations Theory and the Commonwealth Caribbean Backlash against Human Rights Regimes*, 102 COLUM. L. REV. 1832 (2002).

335 See, e.g., Adam Branch, *Uganda's Civil War and the Politics of ICC Intervention*, 21 ETHICS & INT'L AFF. 179 (2007); Karen J. Alter, James T. Gathii & Laurence R. Helfer, *Backlash Against International Courts in West, East, and Southern Africa: Causes and Consequences*, 27 EUR. J. INT'L L. (forthcoming 2016).

336 See, e.g., Alter, Gathii & Helfer, *supra* note 335; Karen J. Alter, Laurence R. Helfer & Jacqueline R. McAllister, *A New International Human Rights Court for West Africa: The ECOWAS Community Court of Justice*, 107 AM. J. INT'L L. 737 (2013).

337 One important example is Argentina's purported failure to comply with ISDS awards. *See, e.g.*, Tsai-yu Lin, *Systemic Reflections on Argentina's Non-Compliance with ICSID Arbitral Awards: A New Role of the Annulment Committee at Enforcement?*, 5 CONTEMP. ASIAN ARB. J. 1 (2012); Charles B. Rosenberg, *The Intersection of International Trade and International Arbitration: The Use of Trade Benefits to Secure Compliance with Arbitral*

reactions by adjudicative actors, such as the decision by the ICC to terminate proceedings against Kenyan President Uhuru Kenyatta.[338] Such reactions by adjudicators faced with sovereign resistance are only one extreme; there is an extensive literature on subtler judicial techniques for handling or anticipating these, which are usually cast as addressing the perceived "democratic deficits" or the "democratic legitimation" of international (and national) law-making.[339] Efforts to engage in global governance via courts are historically contingent because the "altered politics" that they provoke, especially but not only within democracies, can be directed against such courts as well as in favor of them.[340]

6   Conclusions

The precise functions of international adjudicators are in the eye of the beholder. A determination by a chamber of the ICC that defendants retain certain rights even when presented by evidence produced by intermediaries used by the prosecution might be seen,[341] for instance, as (1) settling an interpretative dispute between the prosecutor and the defense, (2) assisting in furthering the truth of what actually occurred in a particular case, (3) providing an authoritative interpretation of that tribunal's rules, or (4) attempting to guide future prosecutors in the ICC or other international criminal courts on how to behave. That decision can, in short, be explained in terms of the dispute settlement, fact-finding, law-making, or governance functions described in this chapter.

There are other explanatory frameworks for what international courts and tribunals do. At a more general level, a rational choice perspective would explain that these adjudicators provide independent information that enables states to make decisions to pursue their individual interests. Andrew Guzman,

---

Awards, 44 GEO. J. INT'L L. 503, 510–515 (2012). *But see* Aloysius P. Llamzon, *Jurisdiction and Compliance in Recent Decisions of the International Court of Justice*, 18 EUR. J. INT'L L. 815 (2007) (finding substantial, though imperfect, compliance with the ICJ's decisions when cases are unilaterally initiated under that Court's compulsory jurisdiction and evidence of state consent to jurisdiction is challenged).

338   Press Release, International Criminal Court, Kenyatta case: Trial Chamber V(B) terminates the proceedings, U.N. Doc. ICC-CPI-20150313-PR1099 (Mar. 13, 2015).

339   *See, e.g.*, Armin von Bogdandy & Ingo Venzke, *On the Democratic Legitimation of International Judicial Lawmaking*, *in* INTERNATIONAL JUDICIAL LAWMAKING 473, *supra* note 98.

340   *See generally* ALTER, *supra* note 1, at 335–365.

341   *See supra* note 205 and accompanying text.

for example, explains that adjudicative findings of law or fact are essentially disinterested "information mechanism[s]" that guide state behavior and enable common understandings of what occurred.[342] This account is not inconsistent with the functions described here. Guzman's focal points enable the settling of disputes, increase the costs of violations of the law, and, by clarifying the law for others, assist in the governance of the particular regime as well as possibly others. More simply and concisely, we might see what international adjudicators do as efforts to "stabilize the normative expectations" of relevant actors.[343]

Categorizing the functions of international adjudicators is more than an exercise in semantics. For those engaged in the day-to-day business of judging, it matters how they see what they do. Adjudicators who identify as agents of states, third parties in a triad, or trustees for the international community or the rule of law, are likely to behave differently during proceedings and follow different interpretative scripts when drafting their opinions.[344] They may or may not apply the judicial "passive virtues," expand or narrow the factual or legal issues raised, engage in more or less creative interpretations of the relevant sources of law, join the majority for the sake of legitimizing consensus or file dissenting opinions, or consider or ignore broad policy considerations for the regime or for general international law. Adjudicators may act differently depending on whether they value (either generally or in a particular instance) one function over another. The functions described here may conflict, after all, and a particular court or adjudicative mechanism can morph over time, taking on one function over another.[345] The fact-finding function, for example, may be at odds with the dispute settlement function—as where a ruling that is based on a finding that a state's factual assertions are wrong may be more offensive than a decision based on the law. A court that opts for the first may make it less likely that a state will comply with a ruling, while one that chooses the second may incidentally make more law.[346] Or consider a case where

---

342   GUZMAN, *supra* note 19, at 51–54.

343   von Bogdandy & Venzke, *supra* note 26, at 54–55.

344   Such differences may reflect how the particular judges or arbitrators are selected, for example. It has been suggested that the party-appointed arbitrators involved in ISDS may be entitled to see themselves as advocates for the respective parties that appoint them. *See, e.g.,* Susan D. Franck, *International Arbitrators: Civil Servants? Sub Rosa Advocates? Men of Affairs? The Role of International Arbitrators,* 12 ILSA J. INT'L AND COMP. L. 499 (2006).

345   *See, e.g.,* Alter, *supra* note 8, at 355, Figure 14.3 (indicating the shifts of function in various international courts and tribunals over time).

346   *See, e.g.,* Bilder, *supra* note 67, at 98.

adjudicators avoid a ruling based on a finding of scientific fact lest it be undermined and prospects for compliance diminished by new or better technology.[347]

Adjudicators who insist on telling "the truth" about what occurred when that is inconsistent with what a state party says or who act as "trustees" in an institutional setting where they are expected to act as state "agents" may issue rulings that fail to resolve disputes because they are ignored. Those who prioritize the governance needs of "transitional justice," historic truth telling, or the needs of victims in judging international crimes may short-change defendants' needs for fair trials.[348] A failure to exercise the fact-finding function with sufficient rigor may foster overly expansive law-generation, and so on.[349] International adjudicators cannot always pursue or expect to achieve all the functions that their stakeholders want. Still, they have considerable discretion on whether and how to exercise them.

At the same time, "considerable discretion" is not *carte blanche*. As Joost Pauwelyn and Manfred Elsig have argued, adjudicators operate against a backdrop of extensive and distinct structural constraints that may change over time, along with the goals of the particular adjudicative scheme.[350] The extent to which judges and arbitrators can pursue the main functions of adjudication varies with the *ex ante* and *ex post* institutional constraints of each court, arbitral, or quasi-judicial setting.[351] These constraints, as well as the adjudicators' own views of their function, determine how judges and arbitrators exercise their discretion.[352]

As Pauwelyn and Elsig indicate, to the extent judges and arbitrators adhere to different views of their "dispute settlement" function, this may affect the hermeneutics of treaty interpretation—that is, the interpretative methods that they apply to resolve disputes before them or, more precisely, how judges or arbitrators choose to apply the rather open-ended rules for treaty interpretation contained in Articles 31–32 of the VCT.

---

347   Alvarez, *supra* note 79, at 94–95 (discussing why, in the *Methanex* ICSID ruling, it was important for that tribunal to answer a legal and not a purely factual question).

348   *See, e.g.*, Ruth Bettina Birn, *Fifty Years After: A Critical Look at the Eichmann Trial*, 44 CASE W. RES. J. INT'L L. 443 (2011); Christine Van den Wyngaert, *Victims Before International Criminal Courts: Some Views and Concerns of an ICC Trial Judge*, 44 CASE W. RES. J. IN'T L. 475, 487–488 (2011).

349   *See, e.g.*, Franck, *supra* note 79, at 31.

350   Pauwelyn & Elsig, *supra* note 83. *See also* Yuval Shany, *Assessing the Effectiveness of International Courts: A Goal-Based Approach*, 106 AM. J. INT'L L. 225 (2012).

351   *See* Ginsburg, *supra* note 4. *See also* Helfer & Slaughter, *supra* note 44.

352   *See, e.g.*, Helfer & Slaughter, *supra* note 44, at 955 (concluding that judges and arbitrators are not "lone rangers" untouched by "structural, political and discursive constraints").

International adjudicators face choices given the open-ended nature of the VCT. They can choose to adhere in positivist fashion, rigidly to text, party intent, and underlying objective as is suggested by Article 31(1) of the VCT. But even in this instance, adjudicators have interpretative space in determining how precisely to adhere to the "intent" of the treaty drafters. Is this best done by sticking to the text, by examining the original negotiating history of the treaty, or by looking to the treaty's "object and purpose?" Should achieving the goals of the treaty be privileged, even at the expense of its text or original negotiating history?[353] Even adjudicators inclined to follow the positivist tenets outlined in Chapter 1 face choices between original or evolutionary interpretations of text, context, and intent.[354] The extent to which they follow or ignore prior precedents vary. Tribunals and adjudicators within them differ on whether to interpret the regime in which they are operating as relatively self-contained or subject to more systemic interpretation.[355] Such decisions influence whether judges or arbitrators are praised for their judicial foresight or condemned for being "judicial activists."[356]

But the inclinations of individual adjudicators are not the only factors that influence how much interpretative discretion they exercise. The design or text of the treaties that they are interpreting obviously plays a substantial role. The "constructive ambiguities" of the UN Charter, for instance, such as the absence of definitions for crucial terms such as "self-determination," "human rights," "domestic jurisdiction," or even "armed attack" and "inherent" self defense, like imprecise terms in many other treaties, make it credible to claim that such treaties are "incomplete contracts" ripe for further clarification by adjudicators with jurisdiction.[357]

As Pauwelyn and Elsig explain, the institutional context in which adjudicators operate, in addition to other factors, also influences the "interpretation space" that judges and arbitrators have.[358] Institutional factors such as tribunal lifespan, its standing rules, the extent of its embeddedness in national system, or the existence of competing forums to hear comparable disputes all affect

---

353   *See* Pauwelyn & Elsig, *supra* note 83, at 450–452.

354   *Id.* at 452–454.

355   *Id.* at 457–459.

356   The extent of judicial activism has varied among tribunals and even within the same tribunal over time—as suggested by the examples in *id.* at 455.

357   For an elaboration of the concept of deliberately drafting "constructive ambiguities" into agreements, see, for example, Christine Bell & Kathleen Cavanaugh, *"Constructive Ambiguity" or Internal Self-Determination? Self-Determination, Group Accommodation, and the Belfast Agreement*, 22 FORDHAM INT'L L.J. 1345, 1356 (1998).

358   Pauwelyn & Elsig, *supra* note 83, at 459–468.

the law-making (or law-affecting) capacity of adjudicators.[359] A court like the Inter-American Court of Human Rights, alleged to have a "radical monist" understanding of international law and operating in a context where at least some Latin American countries have accorded constitutional rank to the rights in the American Convention on Human Rights, can be expected to have greater spill-over effects on national law than some other international courts.[360] All else being equal, a permanent court or body is more likely to encourage long-term or systemic legal interpretations, and provide opportunities for judicial activism than an *ad hoc* arbitral tribunal established just to resolve a specific dispute, whether as in ISDS or under an *ad hoc* criminal tribunal intended for only a fixed number of cases. The number of cases that a tribunal addresses is also an important aspect of its impact. Tribunals that provide standing to individuals and not just governments to file complaints are likely to generate a greater number of, and more systemic, rulings.[361] Courts like the Andean Court of Justice or the ECJ that are embedded in national judicial systems, that is, that demand interactions with national courts, may encourage private actors (and national judges) to engage in more disputes and enable more dynamic treaty interpretations.[362] Another relevant institutional factor is the degree to which the court or arbitral tribunal has competition from other forums. To the extent states or private claimants have choices on where to file their disputes, this discretion may weaken a particular court's ability to exercise its jurisdiction and may weaken its power to engage in dynamic or creative interpretations.

---

359   Such differences may exist even within a single regime. Non-ICSID investor-state arbitrators, for example, since they empower national courts to set aside awards, enable those courts to play a more significant role than occurs under ICSID. *See, e.g.,* Mexico v. Metalclad Corp., [2001] BCSC 644 (Can. B.C.) (partial set-aside of Additional Facility award by a Canadian court). Differences also exist with respect to the reasons national courts can give to resist enforcing ICSID and non-ICSID awards. *Compare* ICSID Convention, *supra* note 95, art. 55 (allowing general enforcement exception for "the law in force in any Contracting State") *with* Convention on the Recognition and Enforcement of Foreign Arbitral Awards (New York Convention) art. V(2)(b), June 10, 1958, 21 U.S.T. 2517, 330 U.N.T.S. 3 (recognizing only a more narrow "public policy" exception).

360   *See, e.g.,* Binder, *supra* note 98, at 314–324.

361   *See* Keohane, Moravscik & Slaughter, *supra* note 50.

362   *See* Karen J. Alter, Laurence R. Helfer & Osvaldo Saldías, *Transplanting the European Court of Justice: The Experience of the Andean Tribunal of Justice,* 3 AM. J. COMP. L. 629 (2012); J.H.H. Weiler, *The Transformation of Europe,* 100 YALE L.J. 2403 (1991).

CHAPTER VI

Three Challenges Posed by International Organizations

1   The IO Challenge to Legal Positivism

The actions of the contemporary Security Council, General Assembly, the World Health Organization (WHO) and the other international organizations considered in Chapters II through V challenge the basic tenets of legal positivism, the positivist sources of international law, and traditional understandings of the limited discretion accorded to those organizations under their constituent instruments. The law-making activities of these organizations cast doubt on propositions that international law is established only on the basis of the consent of states, emerges only from the three sources of obligation contained in Article 38 of the International Court of Justice (ICJ) Statute, can be easily distinguished on the basis of its clearly binding authority, and can be understood without the need to draw on non-legal disciplines such as sociology, political science, or economics. International law, or at least the part of it produced, interpreted, or enforced by global institutions such as those of the UN system, it turns out, is not a self-enclosed *legal regime*; understanding it requires drawing on the insights of those who study institutions, including those of national legal orders.[1] Contemporary international law cannot be fully appreciated or assessed without examining the sociology and political and economic motivations of IO bureaucracies, for instance.

Chapters II through V describe how the proliferation of international bureaucracies and international adjudicative venues has led to a density of legalization that makes it necessary to examine how IOs have contributed to the international legal process. These chapters illustrate through multiple examples why a focus on institutions and not only "sources" of law is essential. They highlight how the turn to IOs has made it more plausible than ever before to draw analogies from the national level, as is suggested by the many scholars

---

1   *Compare* Bruno Simma & Dirk Pulkowski, *Of Planets and the Universe: Self-Contained Regimes in International Law*, 17 EUR. J. INT'L L. 883 (2006) (arguing that discrete regimes of international law are not self-enclosed regimes).

who describe IOs as part of systems for "global governance."[2] The legal products discussed in those chapters—from Security Council resolutions to conditions imposed by the International Monetary Fund (IMF) on its loans to rulings issued by diverse adjudicators—also suggest the importance of "international law-makers" such as particular officials within IOs, the International Criminal Court's (ICC) Prosecutor, or other non-state actors whose participation in the international law-making process has been enabled by IOs. They highlight the legal impact of, for example, NGOs granted consultative or other status (such as labor unions and groups of business interests in the International Labour Organization (ILO), the aviation industry in the International Civil Aviation Organization (ICAO), or health professionals in the WHO).

The institutions examined here include global adjudicators, from courts to human rights treaty bodies. As indicated by Chapter V, these are not, as some positivists have suggested, mere settlers of inter-state disputes charged only with the mechanistic application of law to fact. They are law-making bodies, fact-finders, and purveyors of public values; they too are institutions for governance. Examining the internal operational aspects of these adjudicative bodies—and of individuals within them as law-making actors—is vital to understanding contemporary international law. A closer look at the internal structure of courts and the diverse roles of international adjudicators helps to explain how they affect the law. An international court or tribunal that permits non-state actors to have access to it or that permits its adjudicators to write individual opinions is more likely to engage in law-making than tribunals that permit neither of these things, for example. The governance capabilities of the "international judiciary" are another illustration of the gap between positivist understandings and the day to day law-making practices of IOs.

More generally, the study of international institutionalization casts doubt on the starting positivist premise that we live in a state of anarchy governed only by the dictates of states. It questions whether there are merely "islands of cooperation" consisting of sporadic international obligations that emerge only when inter-state consent coincides to produce either treaty or custom. Those attentive to the institutionally generated law discussed in this monograph might be more inclined to see the world as inter-locking regimes, subject to exceptional departures from these forms of governance by some states or

---

2   *See, e.g.,* THE POLITICS OF GLOBAL GOVERNANCE: INTERNATIONAL ORGANIZATIONS IN AN INTERDEPENDENT WORLD (Paul Diehl ed., 2001); David Gartner, *Beyond the Monopoly of States,* 32 U. PA. J. INT'L L. 595 (2010); Daniel C. Esty, *Good Governance at the Supranational Scale: Globalizing Administrative Law,* 115 YALE L.J. 1490 (2006).

regions. This starting point enables us to consider the characteristics of the law produced by these institutions, rather than beginning with a preconceived idea of what those obligations need to be and then attempting to fit the complex legal products of contemporary IOs within it. The law-making processes set in motion by the institutionalization and judicialization of international law challenge the core positivist tenets identified in Chapter 1, section 1.

1.1   *The Challenge to the Primacy of States and State Consent*

The elaboration, interpretation, and enforcement of international obligations are no longer confined to inter-state action. International legal obligations are now often partly created, interpreted, and enforced by non-state actors; sometimes they are intended to produce direct effects on non-state actors as well. This means that the consent of states as a basis for international law is increasingly attenuated, as where it is found that an IO is authorized to exercise an implied power nowhere indicated in its charter, where obligations on an IO member state result from the failure of that state to "opt out" of IO rules, where weighted voting within IOs or organs within them enables acts that are legally binding on all members despite minority opposition or inaction, or where informal modes of governance are preferred precisely because they sideline the need to secure states' consent.[3] The sidelining of state consent even occurs with respect to some kinds of international dispute settlement, as where, for example, ILO members that have not ratified ILO conventions on freedom of association are nonetheless exposed to ILO adjudicative mechanisms for resolving freedom of association complaints[4] or where the ICJ proceeds to provide an answer to a request for an advisory opinion that addresses what is in reality a contentious dispute that has not been submitted to that Court by the disputing parties.[5]

---

3 *See, e.g.*, Nico Krisch, *The Decay of Consent: International Law in an Age of Global Public Goods*, 108 AM. J. INT'L L. 1 (2014) (discussing specific examples where state consent is attenuated). *See also* Joost Pauwelyn, Ramses A. Wessel & Jan Wouters, *When Structures Become Shackles: Stagnation and Dynamics in International Lawmaking*, 25 EUR. J. INT'L L. 733 (2014) (arguing that informal international law-making may enable normatively superior benchmarks as compared "to the validation requirements of traditional international law" which they describe as demonstrating "thin state consent"). *See generally* INFORMAL INTERNATIONAL LAWMAKING (Joost Pauwelyn, Ramses A. Wessel & Jan Wouters eds. 2012).

4 Laurence R. Helfer, *Monitoring Compliance with Unratified Treaties: The ILO Experience*, 71 LAW & CONTEMP. PROBS. 193 (2008).

5 As was unsuccessfully argued by Israel in response to the General Assembly's request for an advisory opinion concerning the legality of the Israeli Wall. *See* Legal Consequences of

Moreover, even where inter-state consent is treated as an essential pre-condition for finding that an international obligation applies, in many institutional contexts that consent may be less than real. As repeatedly occurred with respect to the finding of customary law even before the rise of IOs,[6] such consent may be presumed on the basis of the inaction or silence of states. This is common practice where, for example, the failure to object to the practice of UN organs is deemed to evince their "acquiescence"—even when no institutional forum or real opportunity for the expression of state dissent exists. State consent with the action taken by an IO organ is also commonly assumed even when the legality of the underlying action taken by that organ is not clear or when states' delegation of authority to the organ is subject to contestation.[7] Of course, to the extent states are deemed to have consented to IO action because they have given their consent in advance—as where UN members have agreed in advance to abide by Security Council decisions under the Charter's Article 25—that consent was likely given long ago under very different circumstances.

In the case of the Security Council, those present at the creation did not foresee a Council that would take its license to define "threats to the international peace" or its authority to take all actions short of force under Article 41 as far as it has in the post-Cold War era. As Chapter II makes clear, a body originally intended to take UN police action against a specific target state that threatened the international peace has managed to transform itself, through a mix of institutional practice enabled by some ICJ advisory opinions, into a mechanism for the: contracting out of force to other states or groupings of

---

the Construction of a Wall in the Occupied Palestinian Territory, Advisory Opinion, 2004 I.C.J. 136 (July 9) [hereinafter Wall Advisory Opinion]. Of course, other ICJ advisory opinions have addressed matters that were of direct interest to a particular state and that would normally be the subject of contentious decision but for the absence of state consent. *See, e.g.,* Legal Consequences for States of the Continued Presence of South Africa in Namibia (South West Africa) Notwithstanding Security Council Resolution 276 (1970), Advisory Opinion, 1971 I.C.J. 16 (June 21) [hereinafter Namibia Opinion].

6   *See generally* MARTTI KOSKENNIEMI, FROM APOLOGY TO UTOPIA: THE STRUCTURE OF INTERNATIONAL LEGAL ARGUMENT 307–333 (2d ed. 2005) (describing the contradictory nature of contentions that the sources of international law rest on state consent).

7   Most recently, debates ensued, for example, over whether NATO's actions in Libya, including the actions that led to the death of Colonel Qadhafi, were truly authorized by the terms of Security Council Resolution 1973 (Mar. 17, 2011).

states,[8] resolving boundary disputes,[9] imposing environmental and other liabilities on an aggressor state,[10] reinstating a duly elected government,[11] forcing a state to extradite criminal suspects,[12] establishing international criminal
tribunals,[13] making general legal pronouncements intended to bind all states,[14]
authorizing the occupation of nations,[15] and imposing counter-terrorism sanctions directly on individuals and organizations.[16] While those who drafted the
Charter gave their consent to granting the Security Council seemingly unreviewable authority to take legally binding Chapter VII action, it seems doubtful
that they consented, back in 1945, to the increasingly varied menu of contemporary Council actions, and it is not clear that all or most UN members today
would agree that this newly self-empowered Council should remain unfettered
by law or by some form of judicial review (as arguably originally intended).[17]
The same considerations apply to other IOs whose mandates have vastly
expanded beyond original contemplation and whose basis in state consent is
similarly attenuated.

The complex interplay between non-state actors and the work of IOs,
particularly when the latter re-interpret states' other treaty obligations, also
diminishes the role or primacy of state consent. A considerable portion of
the activity of IOs—from General Assembly and ILO resolutions to projects
adopted by the International Law Commission (ILC) to rulings by international adjudicators—are intended to affect the interpretations of treaties
other than the constituent instruments of IOs. These IO processes, including

---

8   *See, e.g.*, S.C. Res. 678 (Nov. 29, 1990) (authorizing member States to intervene to protect
     Kuwait); S.C. Res. 940 (July 31, 1994) (authorizing intervention in Haiti); S.C. Res. 1973,
     supra note 7 (authorizing intervention in Libya); S.C. Res. 1816 (June 2, 2008) (authorizing
     intervention with respect to Somali pirates); S.C. Res. 1851 (Dec. 16, 2008) (same).

9   *See, e.g.*, S.C. Res. 687 (Apr. 8, 1991).

10   *Id.*

11   S.C. Res. 940, *supra* note 8.

12   S.C. Res. 731 (Jan. 21, 1992) & S.C. Res. 748 (Mar. 31, 1992) (imposing sanctions to encourage
     Libya to extradite Libyan suspects in the Lockerbie bombing).

13   S.C. Res. 827 (May 25, 1993) (ICTY); S.C. Res. 955 (Nov. 8, 1994) (ICTR); S.C. Res. 1315
     (Aug. 14, 2000) (SCSL); S.C. Res. 1757 (May 30, 2007) (STL).

14   S.C. Res. 1373 (Sept. 28, 2001); S.C. Res. 1540 (Apr. 28, 2004); S.C. Res. 2178 (Sept. 24, 2014).

15   S.C. Res. 1483 (May 22, 2003); S.C. Res. 1546 (June 8, 2004).

16   *See, e.g.*, S.C. Res. 1267 (Oct. 15, 1999), S.C. Res. 2087 (Jan. 22, 2013); S.C. Res. 2094 (Mar. 7,
     2013); S.C. Res. 2161 (June 17, 2014); S.C. Res. 2199 (Feb. 12, 2015); and S.C. Res. 2198
     (Jan. 29, 2015).

17   *See generally* JAMES CRAWFORD, CHANCE, ORDER, CHANGE: THE COURSE OF
     INTERNATIONAL LAW 402–438 (2014).

interpretations that result from the subsequent practice of IO organs, cannot be treated as the functional equivalent of state consent. As anyone who has seen the way a determination of "consensus" is reached within venues like the UN General Assembly can attest, a determination by that collective body to take a particular action merely because no member state within that body has objected does not mean that every UN member state has considered the question and acceded to it, much less to the action's implications. The same can be said of other IO efforts to (re)interpret treaties, whether produced by guidelines produced by the ILC or the ruling of an ICSID tribunal. And yet, today's treaties—at least when these are produced within IO venues—are more likely to take advantage of collective venues for ongoing interpretation, as when the UN General Assembly expresses its collective view concerning the interpretation of a particular human rights treaty. While, to be sure, Article 31 of the Vienna Convention on the Law of Treaties (VCT) anticipates that the subsequent practice of the parties to a treaty can influence the treaty's interpretation, it is quite a leap of judgment to treat collective venues like the general assemblies of IOs or expert bodies like the ILC or the Human Rights Committee as substitutes for expressions of state consent.

Prior chapters contain many examples of resort to the institutional collective interpretation of treaties. The ILO recommendations briefly addressed in Chapter IV, which are the product of that organization's tripartite membership and a key way that ILO conventions are (re)interpreted over time, for example, are not mere repositories for the desires of the government members of that organization. They are the product of unique compromises fashioned among the representatives of employer, employee, and government interests that participate in the ILO. These groupings of interests, which reach inside of states, help to explain interesting features of ILO treaties, such as the default rule barring treaty reservations and easy termination once ratification occurs.[18]

Similarly, the guidelines that give increasingly precise context to the original framework obligations issued by the meetings of the parties established under the WHO's Framework Convention on Tobacco Control, discussed in Chapter IV, result from complex institutional processes that incorporate the views of a number of state and non-state actors (from NGOs organized to promote tobacco control to groups of health care workers to those invested in

---

18   *See, e.g.*, Memorandum by the International Labour Office on the Practice of Reservations to Multilateral Conventions (Jan. 12, 1951), *in* 34 I.L.O. OFFICIAL BULL. 274, 287–288 (explaining that the special considerations applicable to possibility of reservations to ILO conventions include the need to respect the "unique tripartite composition" that give rise to the provisions of such treaties).

the business of tobacco production). Those guidelines, which set standards for "best practices" for treaty parties and reflect considerable input from a variety of state and non-state actors, cannot be reduced to the consensus views of all of the state parties to that treaty. The same can be said of other treaties whose meanings are defined over time through ongoing committees of the parties or meeting of the parties ("COPs" and "MOPs") which, despite the reference to parties, are open to the participation of diverse epistemic communities, national or international.

1.2   *The Challenge to the Article 38 Sources of Obligation*

The sources of international obligation identified in Article 38 no longer embrace all the rules and standards that international lawyers need to consult to advise their clients, including NGOs and multinational corporations (MNCs). Those sources include the binding rulings and non-binding "views" or advisory opinions produced by a variety of adjudicative mechanisms, including permanent international courts, human rights treaty bodies, and arbitral tribunals governed by rules produced by the World Bank's ICSID or the UN Commission on International Trade Law (UNCITRAL). An international lawyer would be charged with malpractice if she ignores, for example, IO generated codes of conduct for businesses; hortatory resolutions by the general assemblies of certain IOs; institutionally generated commission or expert reports (including those produced by UN special rapporteurs); or opinion letters issued by IO general counsels. Often treated as part of the "subsequent practice" of institutional organs or component parts of the internal "rules of the organization," the legal significance of these IO work products is not a simple matter of determining whether or not these are these are legally binding sources of international law under Article 38.

Contrary to a core positivist tenet, many of these IO legal products exist along a spectrum of legally binding authority and it is not always clear whether their violation is intended to be treated as an "international wrongful act" triggering state responsibility. Moreover, contrary to positivist expectations, some of these IO instruments—sometimes called (in violation of positivist ground rules) "soft law"—generate as much or sometimes greater compliance than formally binding sources of international obligation like treaties.[19]

---

19   *See, e.g.*, Martha Finnemore & Kathryn Sikkink, *International Norm Dynamics and Political Change*, 52 INT'L ORG. 887 (1998); Andrew T. Guzman & Timothy Meyer, *Soft Law*, in RESEARCH HANDBOOK ON THE ECONOMICS OF PUBLIC INTERNATIONAL LAW (Eugene Kontorovich ed., 2014). It is not always true that IO generated law that is formally legally binding, such as the WHO's 2005 International Health Regulations (World

And even those who believe that the ICJ's Article 38 continues to be an accurate description of the complete sources of international obligation can scarcely ignore the changes in those three sources produced by the turn to institutions. Today's treaties are often negotiated within IO venues. Even when that is not the case, IOs may be used for purposes of treaty implementation or enforcement. As a result, as Chapters II through V illustrate, international agreements as varied as those dealing with human rights, labor rights, or tobacco control differ fundamentally from the positivist compacts described in Chapter I section 1.1 in a number of respects.[20] The package deals that enable such treaties to be concluded, the procedural mechanisms enabling the participation of IO secretariats at critical junctures, the IO practices that have now been codified into voting rules that enable the finding of "consensus," and even the final clauses anticipating UN registration of treaty instruments have all affected their contents. The procedural mechanisms characteristic of institutionally embedded treaty-making processes impact the contents of such agreements. The institutionalization of treaties helps to explain why many of them have become *de facto* instruments to pursue the collective, and not merely bilateral, interests of states.[21]

The impact of institutionalization continues after treaties are concluded. As examples from Chapters II through V illustrate, treaties nestled in institutions are not interpreted in as static a fashion as the rules of treaty interpretation

---

Health Assembly, Revision of the International Health Regulations, Annex 2, WHA58.3 (May 23, 2005), *at* http://www.who.int/ipcs/publications/wha/ihr_resolution.pdf [hereinafter 2005 IHR]) are more likely to be implemented by states or be "effective" than are some examples of IO-generated soft law. It would appear, for example, that more states are in compliance with some of the guidelines issued under the WHO's Framework Convention on Tobacco Control (WHO Framework Convention on Tobacco Control, May 21, 2003, 2302 U.N.T.S. 166, 42 I.L.M. 518 [hereinafter FCTC]) than they are with respect to their legal duties to implement their core health capacities under the 2005 IHRs. See Chapter V *supra* § 3 and 4. *Compare* WHO, 2014 Global Progress Report on Implementation of the WHO Framework Convention on Tobacco Control (2014), *at* http://www.who.int/fctc/reporting/2014globalprogressreport.pdf *with* WHO, Summary of States Parties 2013 Report on IHR Core Capacity Implementation (2014), *at* http://www.who.int/ihr/publications/WHO_HSE_GCR_2014.10/en/. For another examples of relatively effective soft law, see, for example, CHRIS BRUMMER, SOFT LAW AND THE GLOBAL FINANCIAL SYSTEM: RULE MAKING IN THE 21ST CENTURY (2012).

20   *See* JOSÉ ALVAREZ, INTERNATIONAL ORGANIZATIONS AS LAW-MAKERS 273–400 (2005) (enumerating the ways the turn to IOs has changed the negotiation, interpretation, and enforcement of treaties).

21   *See generally* FROM BILATERALISM TO COMMUNITY INTEREST: ESSAYS IN HONOUR OF JUDGE BRUNO SIMMA (Ulrich Fastenrath et al. eds., 2011).

presume. The positivist understanding of how Articles 31–32 of the VCT are sup-posed to work, discussed in Chapter I, is no longer the dominant hermeneutic framework for the interpretation of all treaties. As illustrated by Chapters II through V, treaties embedded in IOs, particularly IO charters, are subject to more fluid, dynamic, or even teleological re-examination over time. This is par-ticularly (but not only) the case with respect to the UN Charter. As Chapters II and III make clear, thanks to the actions of the Security Council and the General Assembly, there are innumerable examples of the UN Charter's "evolv-ing" interpretations over time. Indeed, the perspective that the UN Charter is a "living" or "constitutional" instrument that responds to the needs of the "inter-national community" (and not necessarily the needs of individual member states or those whose views dominated the Charter's travaux) is the product of the age of IOs.[22]

Much the same can be said with respect to other institutionally grounded treaties, from older documents like the International Covenant on Civil and Political Rights (ICCPR) and more recent ones like the Rome Statute of the ICC, to those that respond to rapidly changing technological developments such as multilateral environmental treaties.[23] Although the interpretation of these instruments remains formally subject to Articles 31 and 32 of the VCT, their meanings are most likely to be affected not by the "subsequent practice" of their state parties (as anticipated by Article 31(3)(b) of the VCT) but by the practice of IO organs, international adjudicative bodies, or the actions and statements of IO officials.[24] In the case of the ICCPR, for example, that treaty's interpretation has been affected by the published "views" of its Human Rights Committee, including its general comments on such topics as permissible

---

22   *See generally* ALVAREZ, *supra* note 20, at 65–108 (discussing how the practice of
      UN organs has enabled the "constitutional" interpretation of the UN Charter). The propo-
      sition that IO constituent instruments are comparable to "living constitutions" was also
      encouraged by the work of IO general counsels like C. Wilfred Jenks, who recognized early
      on the transformative nature of opinions issued by the International Labour Office within
      the ILO. *See* C. Wilfred Jenks, *The Interpretation of International Labour Conventions by the
      International Labour Office*, 20 BRIT. Y.B. INT'L L. 132 (1939).

23   *See, e.g.,* FRANCESCA ROMANIN JACUR, THE DYNAMICS OF MULTILATERAL
      ENVIRONMENTAL AGREEMENTS (2013).

24   *See generally* Campbell McLachlan, *The Evolution of Treaty Obligations in International
      Law, in* TREATIES AND SUBSEQUENT PRACTICE 69 (Georg Nolte ed., 2013). *See also*
      Andrea Bianchi, *Law, Time and Change: The Self-Regulatory Function of Subsequent
      Practice, in id.* (arguing that reliance on subsequent practice with respect to treaties
      reflects the expectations of and demands made by collective groups of persons, including
      the "epistemic communities" that control specific regimes).

reservations; by invocations of that treaty by influential figures such as the
UN Secretary-General or Presidents of the Security Council; and by UN General
Assembly resolutions that purport to redefine that treaty's protections as new
circumstances develop.

As noted in Chapter III, the UN General Assembly, which has been the venue
for "declarations" that have become the leading human rights conventions,
has continued to exert a sense of ownership over these treaties. Assembly sessions have, time and again, periodically revisited many of those global human
rights conventions, suggesting, for example, re-definitions of the underlying
rights or focusing attention on how familiar rights can be adapted to benefit new categories of the disadvantaged (e.g., rural women, the disabled, or
NGO human rights defenders).[25] Human rights treaties, and the committees
to which states report under them, have also been affected by the Assembly's
more controversial efforts to condemn particular states for alleged human
rights violations.[26] The meaning and scope of treaties like the Convention
on the Elimination of All Forms of Discrimination Against Women (CEDAW)
or the Rights of the Child Convention have been impacted by perennial
re-visitations, not only by the UN General Assembly and international and
national adjudicators, but also by the incorporation or application of their
underlying rights by the World Bank and its Inspection Panel.[27]

---

25   *See, e.g.*, G.A. Res. 66/164 (Dec. 19, 2011) (indicating that states' duty to ensure human rights
      necessarily entails a duty to ensure the protection of human rights defenders, including
      civil society organizations).

26   *See, e.g.*, G.A. Res. 66/174 (Dec. 19, 2011) (invoking the ICCPR and other human rights trea-
      ties to condemn specific human rights violations alleged within the Democratic People's
      Republic of Korea).

27   *See, e.g.*, G.A. Res. 63/156 (Dec. 18, 2008) (re-interpreting states' duties to "respect" and
      "ensure" rights in these treaties to include duties to prevent and punish those respon-
      sible for trafficking in women and girls). Notably, that resolution re-defines trafficking,
      depending on the circumstances, as a cyber-security threat, as a form of child abuse, as
      evincing racial or other forms of discrimination, or as a type of forced labor. That resolu-
      tion also seeks to affect the underlying treaties' existing remedial schemes by "inviting"
      states to supplement their reporting obligations under the relevant treaties to include
      statistics on trafficking. It also "encourages" IOs who deploy peacekeepers and humani-
      tarian personnel to avoid conduct that facilitates trafficking. For another example, see
      G.A. Res. 66/140 (Dec. 19, 2011) (interpreting CEDAW and other human rights instruments
      as providing specific protections against discriminating against the girl child as with
      respect to access to education, nutrition, and health care). That resolution directs atten-
      tion at treaty interpretations that serve to protect the girl child from "various forms of
      cultural, social, sexual and economic exploitation and violence" such as female infan-
      ticide, child and forced marriages, and female genital mutilation. On the World Bank's

Even international criminal law, despite constraints imposed by the principle of legality,[28] has experienced considerable evolution as a result of the turn to institutions. As discussed in Chapter II, international criminal law would not have experienced a revival in recent times but for the Security Council's decisions to revive the expectations initially set at Nuremberg by establishing the International Criminal Tribunal for the former Yugoslavia (ICTY) and the International Criminal Tribunal for Rwanda (ICTR) in 1993 and 1994 respectively. Today's ICC is a creature of the age of institutions. Moreover, as discussed in Chapter V, the caselaw produced by those courts was critical to establishing the procedures followed by the ICC as well as its elements of crimes—the latter the most extensive effort to date to provide substantive content to the three core international crimes of genocide, crimes against humanity, and war crimes. While today many suggest that these core crimes, in all their detail, are now established as customary international crimes, to the extent this is true this would not have occurred but for the institutionalization produced by the Security Council and UN procedures for negotiating the Rome Statute. While formally the Rome Statute was the outcome of inter-state negotiations, important aspects of that treaty were the direct outcome of drafts initially proposed by the ILC and later compromises suggested by non-state actors and the UN's legal secretariat.[29]

Today, as illustrated by Chapter V, there is little doubt that international criminal law continues to be deeply influenced by the turn to institutionalized adjudication. Important terms in the Rome Statute continue to be elaborated and given ever more precision (not always without controversy) through the operation of the ICC, including its Office of the Prosecutor. While it is obvious that the ICC's judicial output contributes to the growing international criminal caselaw on point (no less than the decisions produced by the *ad hoc* tribunals established by Security Council fiat), the many policy papers drafted by that Court's office of the prosecutor are also helping to (re)define the Rome Statute,

---

Guidelines and their incorporation of human rights and other normative standards, see, for example, Laurence Boisson de Chazournes, *Policy Guidance and Compliance: The World Bank Operational Standards, in* COMMITMENT AND COMPLIANCE: THE ROLE OF NON-BINDING NORMS IN THE INTERNATIONAL LEGAL SYSTEM 281 (Dinah Shelton ed., 2000).

28   *See, e.g.,* ANTONIO CASSESE, INTERNATIONAL CRIMINAL LAW 139–158 (2003) (defining the elements of the principle of legality).

29   *See generally* THE STATUTE OF THE INTERNATIONAL CRIMINAL COURT: A DOCUMENTARY HISTORY (M. Cherif Bassiouni ed., 1998).

particularly with respect to significant procedural aspects.[30] Of course, that office's day to day choices with respect to evidence to present, positions to take on jurisdiction or admissibility or which charges to include in indictments—and reactions to these by the Court's judges—are also helping to redefine international criminal law in our time.

The ICC is only an example of a more general phenomenon: treaties that are subject to institutionalized mechanisms for interpretation, which include interpretations issued by the lawyers employed by IOs—from prosecutors to IO general counsels—are more likely to become dynamic instruments to achieve (changing) goals. These are not the static contracts that reflect the original intentions of their state parties, or that can change only when all their parties explicitly agree to do so, that positivists tend to describe.

As is discussed in Chapter V, the third Article 38 source, general principles of law, has also not emerged unscathed. To the chagrin of positivists who would relegate this source to the margins, general principles are seeing a renaissance in the age of IOs. As international adjudicators proliferate and interpreters' need to fill gaps in the law increases, there appears to be increasing resort to general principles.[31] Indeed, some public law scholars, anxious to draw closer domestic analogies between how international and national law permits states to engage in permissive regulation in the public interest, would make even greater use of these to elaborate a more closely integrated "public law" for states.[32]

---

30   *See, e.g.,* International Criminal Court, Office of the Prosecutor, Policy Paper on Preliminary Examinations (Nov. 2013), *at* https://www.icc-cpi.int/en_menus/icc/press%20and%20 media/press%20releases/Documents/OTP%20Preliminary%20Examinations/OTP%20-%20Policy%20Paper%20Preliminary%20Examinations%20%202013.pdf; International Criminal Court, Office of the Prosecutor, Policy Paper on the Interests of Justice (Sept. 2007), *at* https://www.icc-cpi.int/NR/rdonlyres/772C95C9-F54D-4321-BF09-73422BB23528/143640/ICCOTPInterestsOfJustice.pdf. The Court as a whole has also adopted significant guidelines with legal implications. *See, e.g.,* International Criminal Court, Guidelines Governing the Relation Between the Court and Intermediaries (Mar. 2014), *at* https://www.icc-cpi.int/en_menus/icc/legal%20texts%20and%20tools/ strategies-and-guidelines/Documents/GRCI-Eng.pdf.

31   For an example of increasing resort to general principles in the context of international criminal law, see Neha Jain, *Comparative International Law at the ICTY: The General Principles Experiment,* 109 AM. J. INT'L L. 488 (2015).

32   *See, e.g.,* Stephan W. Schill, *International Investment Law and Comparative Public Law—An Introduction, in* INTERNATIONAL INVESTMENT LAW AND COMPARATIVE PUBLIC LAW 3, 29–35 (Stephan W. Schill ed., 2010).

Chapters II through V provide abundant examples of the changes in conceptions of customary international law in the age of IOs. The role of custom has become more or less important depending on the institution (or institutions) presiding over a regime. In cases where the regime or IO avoids reliance on customary law and makes clear that its rules are *lex specialis*, custom may take a back seat or even disappear. This is arguably the case in the WTO where, except insofar as the Dispute Settlement Understanding incorporates the customary rules of treaty interpretation, only the GATT covered agreements are the subject of dispute settlement.[33] This explains why custom appears to be of decreasing relevance to trade specialists.[34]

Custom may, on the contrary, become even more important and experience a modern day renaissance in institutionalized settings where adjudicators are called upon to invoke it either as an independent source of obligation or because the relevant treaty or treaties incorporate custom.[35] In such cases, as discussed in Chapter V, customary law is likely to be identified and interpreted in ways that are not consistent with positivist premises. Thus, according to one study of the decisions issued by international courts, the leading evidentiary source for custom cited by today's judges is not the state practice/*opinio juris* favored by positivists but multilateral conventions, along with other authorities including, for example, General Assembly resolutions.[36] Notably, since even multilateral treaties rarely elicit the participation of all or most states and therefore require additional evidence to suggest that there is the more general

---

33   *See* Joel Trachtman, *The Obsolescence of Customary International Law* (2014), *at* http://papers.ssrn.com/sol3/papers.cfm?abstract_id=2512757.

34   *Id.*

35   *See, e.g.,* José E. Alvarez, *A BIT on Custom*, 42 NYU J. INT'L L. & POL. 17 (2009) (describing the impact on customary law of the spread of investment protection treaties and their interpretation in the course of investor-state arbitrations).

36   Stephen J. Choi & Mitu Gulati, *Customary International Law: How Do Courts Do It?*, *in* CUSTOM'S FUTURE: INTERNATIONAL LAW IN A CHANGING WORLD 117 (Curtis A. Bradley ed., 2015) (surveying a database of 175 CIL determinations by international tribunals, including the ICJ, and finding that the most frequently cited evidentiary sources used were (in order) treaties, other tribunal decisions, domestic judicial decisions, actions by states, academic articles and treatise, international committee reports, domestic statutes, IO resolutions, other IO materials, statements by state officials and agreements by states). Choi and Gulati conclude that judges generally do not turn to direct evidence of state practice and *opinio juris*, as positivists would predict, because this would require "superhuman research skills" that would be "impossible to collect, as a practical matter, unless one somehow assembled an extraordinary team of anthropologists, economists, historians, political scientists, and lawyers and lawyers that would then be able to spend decades excavating the historical record." *Id.*

acceptance to their terms deemed essential to finding custom, courts that turn to such treaties as evidence of custom are likely to supplement their analyses by resort to IO resolutions or IO generated reports. Chapter III enumerates some of the many examples—particularly dealing with human rights or the law regarding the global commons such as outer space—where the General Assembly has suggested that a treaty obligation is simultaneously a customary obligation binding on all states. As noted in Chapter V, even national courts called upon to find and apply international customary law often draw on a combination of multilateral treaties and IO legal products rather than laborious exercises to examine state practices or state by state exemplars of *opinio juris* evidenced by digests of state practice.[37] International and national adjudicators' reliance on such institutional "short-cuts" to finding custom are ever more influential because, over time, the proliferating publically known adjudicative decisions on point increasingly become the principal source of evidence for the existence and meaning of custom. Modern custom, accordingly, seems less reliant on the actual practice of states or states' explicit justifications for their actions and more dependent on organizational substitutes for these (including reliance on the views expressed by prior international courts or tribunals).[38]

1.3   *The Challenge to Bindingness*

The turn to IOs has enabled an even graver threat to positivist tenets. To the horror of traditional positivists, the binding force of international obligations—the key distinction between binding *lex lata* and *lex ferenada*—

---

37   For a prominent example in U.S. courts, see *Filartiga v. Peña-Irala*, 630 F.2d 876 (2d Cir. 1980) (relying on General Assembly resolutions and multilateral conventions that had not been ratified by the U.S. to prove that customary international law prohibits the use of torture).

38   *See, e.g.*, MICHAEL P. SCHARF, CUSTOMARY INTERNATIONAL LAW IN TIMES OF FUNDAMENTAL CHANGE: RECOGNIZING GROTIAN MOMENTS (2013); Jonathan I. Charney, *Universal International Law*, 87 AM. J. INT'L L. 529 (1993). *See also* Monica Hakimi, *Custom's Method and Process: Lessons from Humanitarian Law*, in CUSTOM'S FUTURE, *supra* note 36, at 148 (arguing that the positivist method for discovering the existence of CIL ignores the fact that the finding of custom is "deeply entangled with CIL-making" and ignores the "extremely influential" role of nonstate actors). While Art. 38(1)(d) of the ICJ's Statute recognizes the use of "judicial decisions" as an evidentiary source, in the modern age, thanks to the proliferation of international adjudicators and the increased inter-action among them, this evidentiary source has become far more significant, has embraced non-binding adjudicative opinions by international bodies and not just binding "decisions," and has overtaken reliance on the actual practice of states.

is no longer a reliable quality of "international law." The legally authoritative quality of much of international law in the age of IOs is now more likely to lie along a spectrum of bindingness. International law is not, as positivists would have it, subject to an "on/off" switch where something is or isn't law, thereby enabling a determination of whether or not its violation constitutes an "international wrongful act" in accordance with the Articles of State Responsibility. As is suggested by the concept of "soft law," some institutionalized generated norms or standards are "harder" or "softer" than others along a number of criteria, and they pose a number of distinct consequences or obligations on states and possibly other non-state actors. The usual positivist test—is this a rule that a judge could readily apply to a state to impose one of the remedies envisioned by the Articles of State Responsibility?—is no longer a reliable test for a lawyer to use in advising a client that asks, "Am I subject to any international law on point?"

Chapter III canvasses many examples of the most familiar legally ambiguous IO product, General Assembly resolutions. Faced with the reality that some of these resolutions appear to have legal effects—and have sometimes been relied upon for propositions of law by prominent national and international courts as well as scholars—positivists have tried, as noted, to pour the Assembly's products into the familiar vessels of treaty, custom, or general principles. They have suggested that influential (and often cited) Assembly definitions of the meaning of "aggression,"[39] "self-determination" and "interference in domestic jurisdiction,"[40] for example, should be seen as an effort to interpret those terms in the UN Charter, even though the Assembly is not explicitly charged with providing such authoritative Charter interpretations.[41] Alternatively, it has been suggested that some normative Assembly resolutions, including those that purport to "clarify" the interpretations of prominent human rights treaties such as the Convention on the Rights of the Child or CEDAW, should be seen as reflecting state practice or as efforts by the members of the Assembly to express their individual *opinio juris*, thereby suggesting that the Assembly

---

39   Declaration on the Principles of International Law Concerning Friendly Relations and Cooperation Among States in Accordance with the Charter of the UN, G.A. Res. 25/2625 (Oct. 24, 1970); Definition of Aggression, G.A. Res. 3314 (XXIX)(Dec. 14, 1974).

40   G.A. Res. 25/2625, *supra* note 39.

41   *See, e.g.*, RESTATEMENT (THIRD) OF THE FOREIGN RELATIONS LAW OF THE UNITED STATES § 103 Reporter's Note 2 (discussing the role of IO resolutions in providing "important evidence of law" and stating that resolutions by a principle organ interpreting the charter of an organization "may be entitled to greater weight").

is a forum for pronouncing rules of custom.[42] Others have argued that to the extent Assembly resolutions, such as its 1948 Universal Declaration of Human Rights, have since been incorporated into national laws, and even into national constitutions, we are entitled to see at least portions of that Declaration as reflecting general principles of law. Yet others have contended, more controversially but perhaps more candidly, that efforts to cabin the Assembly's diverse actions into the familiar Article 38 sources ignore the distinctive ways that this collective body affects the law. Chapter III identifies many examples of legally significant Assembly resolutions but also the diverse ways that the Assembly seeks to influence the law, as by attempting to influence the human rights committees charged with interpreting UN human rights conventions.

That chapter also illustrates the unique legitimacy the Assembly enjoys as the world's only "representative" deliberative body. For decades, positivists have struggled with the gap between UN Charter provisions that make clear that Assembly resolutions are only "recommendations" and the tendency of actors, including some states and national courts, to rely on the same "hortatory" Assembly resolutions to prove or support propositions of international law.[43] The text of the Charter does not provide a clear account of why some Assembly resolutions should be treated as legally binding on their own terms, as the ICJ itself has proclaimed. What is clear is that at least some General Assembly resolutions have had conclusive legal effects in some circumstances or with respect to some issues.[44]

---

42   *See generally* ROSALYN HIGGINS, THE DEVELOPMENT OF INTERNATIONAL LAW THROUGH THE POLITICAL ORGANS OF THE UNITED NATIONS (1963).

43   *See, e.g.,* Christopher C. Joyner, U.N. *General Assembly Resolutions and International Law: Rethinking the Contemporary Dynamics of Norm-Creation,* 11 CALIF. WESTERN INT'L L.J. 445 (1981); *see also* Rosalyn Higgins, *The Role of Resolutions of International Organizations in the Process of Creating Norms in the International System, in* INTERNATIONAL LAW AND THE INTERNATIONAL SYSTEM (William Butler ed., 1987)(discussing the normative impact of Assembly resolutions in their context, given their interactions with other manifestations of collective action).

44   *See, e.g.,* Namibia Opinion, *supra* note 5 (concluding that the General Assembly had the power to terminate South Africa's mandate over Namibia). The struggle to accommodate the resolutions of IOs given the wording of the ICJ's Art. 38 is clear from the following quotation from a prominent Chinese treatise: "[T]here are divergent opinions on the effect of the resolutions of the United Nations General Assembly. According to the provisions of the Charter of the United Nations, the function of the United Nations General Assembly is generally one of deliberation and recommendation. Except for resolutions relating to organizational and financial questions [which are legally binding], the resolutions of the

Ambiguity as to legal pedigree or with respect to legally binding status is characteristic of many other IO products discussed in prior chapters. The conditions that the IMF imposes as requirements for those seeking its long term financial assistance under its Articles of Agreement are not clearly "obligations under the Articles or under a treaty or contract."[45] It remains uncertain whether action by either a state or the IMF in violation of such commitments would constitute an international wrongful act entailing state (or IO) responsibility. If such IMF conditionality agreements are in fact treaties, these are compacts undertaken without explicit authorization in the IMF's Articles of Agreement and indeed, some might argue, in apparent disregard of the limits on the scope of that organization's authority.[46] Of course, like many commitments undertaken by IOs, such obligations are not subject to the compulsory jurisdiction of any binding national or international court and are therefore unlikely to be the subject of judicial consideration or attempt at enforcement that would clarify such matters to the satisfaction of positivists. Moreover, to the extent IMF conditionality, now firmly established in the practice of that organization, cannot be legally challenged, it is a tribute to the subsequent

---

General Assembly are in the nature of recommendations and do not possess legally binding force. However, one cannot infer from this fact that there would be no legal consequence of resolutions adopted by the General Assembly. Some resolutions of the General Assembly were adopted by unanimous or overwhelming majority votes of member states. Therefore, these resolutions not only have a certain binding force on those members who voted for their adoption, but also have general significance in international relations. In the meantime, some declarations included in certain resolutions may in whole or in part reflect existing or formative principles, rules, regulations or institutions of international law. Thus, these declarations undoubtedly become subsidiary means to determine principles, rules, regulations and institutions of international law. Consequently, one should consider resolutions of international organizations, especially certain kinds of resolutions of the United Nations, as parallel to judicial decisions and writings of publicists. [They have] become 'subsidiary means for the determination of rules of law,' though [these resolutions] are not direct sources of international law. Moreover, in view of their international character, their [priority as subsidiary means] should be higher than that of judicial decisions and writings of publicists." GUOJI FA (INTERNATIONAL LAW) 35 (Wang Tieya & Wei Min eds., 1981).

45   JOSEPH GOLD, INTERPRETATION: THE IMF AND INTERNATIONAL LAW 355 (1996) ("The practice of the IMF must be taken to have affirmed the interpretation that as performance criteria are not obligations under the Articles or under a treaty or contract, they can include matters over which the IMF has no regulatory jurisdiction if they have a bearing on the balance of payments and on the purposes of the IMF.").

46   See, e.g., Daniel Kalderimis, IMF Conditionality as Investment Regulation: A Theoretical Analysis, 13 SOC. & LEGAL STUD. 103 (2004).

practice of that organization, that is, the self-judging actions of the IMF and its legal counsel that enabled it. Conditionality is the product of legal interpretations issued by the IMF's general counsel authorizing such actions, as well as the approval of that organization's executive board. These interpretations have managed to involve the IMF in decisions relating to microeconomic polities adopted by states, despite the widely understood (if implicit) limits on that organization's ability to interfere in members' political affairs.[47] The binding authority and legal pedigree of IMF conditions are, in short, a matter of nuance, not positivism's on/off switch.

Nearly all the Standards and Recommended Practices (SARPs) produced within ICAO, which together constitute much of international aviation law, are characterized by ambiguous legal effect.[48] With the exception of ICAO's rules of the air (which are made explicitly binding under Article 12 of the Chicago Convention), SARPs are, under that Convention, subject only to a notification obligation.[49] Aviation lawyers have long been divided over the legal status of ICAO's SARPs; there is uncertainty over whether, for example, "standards" are more legally binding than are ICAO "recommendations" or whether, since both are subject to mere notification, no such distinctions can be made.[50]

Similarly, while the World Bank has endeavored to clarify that some of its operational policies are legally binding and others are not, in fact these policies are formally binding only on World Bank employees.[51] This is confirmed by the enforcement mechanisms in place to give them effect, including the World Bank's Inspection Panel. Inspection panel reports are intended to secure compliance by Bank employees with the Bank's operational policies and thereby correct costly mistakes in Bank projects.[52] Nothing in the operation of the Bank suggests that violation of the World Bank's own guidelines constitutes an internationally wrongful act for which the Bank can be held liable.

---

47   *Id. See also* EVA RISENHUBER, THE INTERNATIONAL MONETARY FUND UNDER CONSTRAINT at 50 (2001)(noting that while intervention in political affairs was not explicitly prohibited in the IMF's Articles, this was due to the fact that the founders of the IMF "never expected the Fund to have any microeconomic influence on national economies in the first place").

48   *See* Chapter IV § 5.

49   Under Article 33 of the Chicago Convention ICAO members only have to notify the organization should they opt not to comply with SARPs. Convention on International Civil Aviation, art 9, pmbl., Dec. 7, 1944, 15 U.N.T.S. 295 [hereinafter Chicago Convention].

50   For the classic study, see THOMAS BUERGENTHAL, LAW-MAKING IN THE INTERNATIONAL CIVIL AVIATION ORGANIZATION (1969).

51   *See* de Chazournes, *supra* note 27.

52   *Id.*

The Bank also has not indicated that its operational policies have any status as rules of international law binding on states. At the same time, as suggested by Chapter IV, it would be wrong to ignore the Bank's policies as irrelevant to general international law. Scholars and states alike have noted the broader legal impact of such World Bank products, as when World Bank guidelines incorporate (and give greater definition to) the rights of indigenous peoples or the constraints imposed by general principles of international environmental law.[53]

The legal impact of opinions issued by the general counsels of IOs, like those issued by the ILO's or the UN's respective lawyers, are also hard to ignore, even when these are not authoritative under the IO's charter and when the opinions themselves earnestly point this out.[54] Such opinions are often the grist for the subsequent practice of these organizations that, as noted, is usually the bedrock source for evolutionary interpretations of IO charters.

Strict positivists are also likely to have concerns with the various modes of legal impact described in Chapter V on international adjudicators. The ICJ's Article 38 accepts that "judicial decisions" are a source of evidence for what a treaty might mean, or whether a rule of custom or general principle of law exists. But the proliferation of international adjudicators, and the mounting level of their widely available "caselaw" has elevated the significance of judicial and arbitral opinions, not all of which can be seen as binding "decisions." Despite the absence of a formal doctrine of *stare decisis* in international law, the prior views of international (and some national) adjudicators have become—at least within some international law regimes such as trade, investment, and regional human rights—the principal source of legal authority for legal conclusions. When prior arbitral investor state opinions are, for example, the only source of authority for the conclusion reached by a subsequent investor-state tribunal, it is artificial to consider such rulings a mere "subsidiary" bit of evidence. The availability, depth of reasoning, and other benefits offered by adjudicative opinions have arguably turned these into yet another example of institutionally-generated "soft law"—that is, a source of

---

53   *See, e.g.*, Benedict Kingsbury, *Operational Policies of International Institutions as Part of the Law-Making Process: The World Bank and Indigenous Peoples*, in THE REALITY OF INTERNATIONAL LAW: ESSAYS IN HONOUR OF IAN BROWLIE 323 (Guy S. Goodwin-Gill & Stefan Talmon eds., 1999).

54   For examples, see Jenks, *supra* note 22, and GOLD, *supra* note 45. For a general description of the significance of legal opinions offered by the IMF's legal staff given the organization's resistance to "external" or "authoritative" forms of interpretations, see GOLD, *id.* at 579–583.

authority on which policy-makers (and judges) rely despite the fact that these are not legally binding outside the context in which the opinion was originally given.

Positivist international lawyers should, in theory, pay no heed to judicial or arbitral rulings provided in the course of a different case involving different litigants. Nor would the tenets of positivism suggest that any weight be given to the non-binding opinions or "views" issued by many of today's international adjudicators, from the ICJ when it acts pursuant to its advisory jurisdiction to human rights committees under the nine UN human rights treaties.[55] And yet, as Chapter V discusses, these opinions, along with rulings that are authoritative only with respect to the parties subject to them, have had a singular impact on the subjects of international law, states, and IOs. Indeed, as discussed further below, the law of international organizations can scarcely be understood without attention to key ICJ advisory opinions.

Even institutions or IO organs designed to produce legally binding obligations that positivists would respect and recognize have sometimes opted for more legally ambiguous products. As is well known, the WHO, an organization dominated by health professionals and not lawyers, for decades refused to exercise the power to conclude treaties included in constituent instrument, and was reluctant to issue the legally binding health regulations (also authorized) beyond the scope of those that preceded the establishment of that organization.[56] And even after that organization finally deployed the legal powers delegated to it and issued its path-breaking and ambitious International Health Regulations in 2005, it still continues to rely on "soft law" guidelines to clarify the meaning of those regulations and has abstained from seeking to enforce those ostensibly legally binding (and intrusive) regulations through anything more than a reporting scheme on WHO members.[57] To this day, the

---

55   On the impact of human rights treaty bodies, see generally Rosanne Van Alebeek & André Nollkaemper, *The Legal Status of Decisions by Human Rights Treaty Bodies in National Law, in* UN HUMAN RIGHTS TREATY BODIES: LAW AND LEGITIMACY 356 (Helen Keller & Geir Ulfstein eds., 2012) (discussing a number of factors that affect the legal status accorded the views of the Human Rights Committee within national legal orders).

56   Ironically, the WHO's refusal for many years to engage in formal law-making rendered that organization largely immune for a time to critiques that it threatened, like some other IOs, the exercise of "democratic self-governance." *See* Eric Stein, *International Integration and Democracy: No Love at First Sight*, 95 AM. J. INT'L L. 489 (2001).

57   *See, e.g.,* WHO, WHO Guidance for the Use of Annex 2 of the International Health Regulations (2005), WHO Doc. No. WHO/HSE/IHR/2010.4 (2008), *at* http://www.who.int/ ihr/revised_annex2_guidance.pdf. For a general introduction to the WHO's role in global

formally legally binding IHRs are treated more like political commitments.[58] Some of the same "softness" characterizes the ongoing development of the WHO's single treaty, the Tobacco Convention.[59]

A comparable refusal to engage with positivist law-making is suggested by the current agenda of the International Law Commission (ILC). There is unmistakable irony in the fact that the ILC, the UN's intended vehicle to pursue the positivist project to codify and develop the law through an ever-expanding network of multilateral conventions, has in recent times turned away from that core task. As is well known, the contemporary ILC has increasingly turned to the production of studies, guidelines, articles, and other legally ambiguous work products, only rarely proposing an inter-state negotiation for a treaty based on an ILC draft.[60] Interestingly, it has deployed these same soft tools even with respect to the (re)interpretation of treaties, in lieu of proposing formal treaty amendments or the negotiations of successor agreements.[61] It too seems to be engaging in shortcuts to the principal method for international law-making endorsed by positivism, namely inter-state treaty negotiations. While the ILC's work has always illustrated the difficulties of drawing firm lines between efforts to define *lex lata* from attempts to develop *lex ferenda*, its recent efforts to avoid treaty-making at all in deference to producing products whose legal pedigree and status are more challenging to define and do not engage a process for inter-state consent is hard to see as

---

health law, see Lawrence O. Gostin & Devi Sridhar, *Global Health and the Law*, 370 NEW ENG. J. MED. 1737 (2014).

58   This has been one source of criticism in the wake of that organization's failures to respond to the recent Ebola crisis. *See, e.g.*, WHO, IHR and Ebola, WHO Doc. No. EB136/UNF./7 (Jan. 9, 2015), *at* http://apps.who.int/gb/ebwha/pdf_files/EBSS3/EBSS3_INF4-en.pdf.

59   *See* Chapter IV *supra* § 1.3 (discussing the role of "soft" guidelines issued by the that treaty's meeting of the parties).

60   The one item on the ILC's current agenda that is specifically intended to result in a treaty is its project to codify the law with respect to crimes against humanity. *See, e.g.*, Sean D. Murphy, *Identification of Customary International Law and Other Topics: The Sixty-Seventh Session of the International Law Commission*, 109 AM. J. INT'L L. 822 (2016).

61   *See, e.g.*, International Law Commission, Report of the International Law Commission, 63d Sess., Apr. 26–June 3, July 4–Aug. 12, 2011, add. 1, U.N. Doc. A/66/10/Add.1; GAOR, 66th Sess., Supp. No. 10 (2011) (Guide to Practice on Reservations to Treaties); Georg Nolte, International Law Commission, First Report on Subsequent Agreements and Subsequent Practice in Relation to Treaty Interpretation, U.N. Doc. A/CN.4/660 ¶ 6 (Mar. 19, 2013) ("The materials and analyses which are contained in the present and future reports, as well as the conclusions of the Commission, should provide a common reference.").

anything other than a rejection of the fundamental tenets of legal positivism on which it was founded.[62]

And even when an IO organ is given the formal authority to adopt legally binding obligations on states, as is the case with the exceptional Security Council under Chapter VII of the UN Charter, that body has been known to avoid or deflect the rigors of positivism. For a considerable period of time, the Council has taken binding decisions that purport to apply to all "states" and not just UN members, despite positivism's insistence that treaties can bind only parties to them.[63] As noted in Chapter II, the Council has also produced resolutions that are legally ambiguous with respect to consequences. The most well-known instance is, of course, the example once cited for demonstrating that the Council can work as "intended," namely its actions in response to Iraq's invasion of Kuwait. As discussed in Chapter II, scholars and policymakers have long wrestled with the temporal limits on the authority to use force granted in Council Res. 678. Whether that resolution or subsequent Council actions dealing with Iraq continued to authorize the use of force measures deployed by the U.S. and UK to enforce the "no-fly zone" above Iraq in 1998 (under Operation Desert Fox), much less the 2003 invasion of Iraq despite the terms of Council Res. 1441, has provoked considerable controversy.[64] While the 2003 invasion is

---

62   Thus, even those who praise the ILC's pragmatic turn to non-treaty legal products, acknowledge that one advantage of this approach is precisely that it does not expose the ILC's product to direct state-to-state treaty negotiations that may derail that body's compromise formulations. Santiago Villalpando, *Codification Light: A New Trend in the Codification of International Law at the United Nations*, 8 (2) ANUÁRIO BRASILEIRO DE DIREITO INTERNACIONAL (BRAZILIAN Y.B. INT'L L.) 117 (2013).

63   *See, e.g.*, Security Council Res. 1373, *supra* note 14. As is well known, the UN Charter is less than clear with respect to its relationship to third parties given its Art. 2(6) (indicating that the organization "shall ensure that states which are not Members . . . act in accordance with these Principles so far as may be necessary for the maintenance of international peace and security.").

64   *See, e.g.*, Michael Glennon et al., *Legal Authority for the Possible Use of Force Against Iraq*, 92 ASIL PROC. 136 (1998) (addressing whether existing S.C. resolutions authorized Operation Desert Fox); Anthony H. Cordesman, *The Lessons of Desert Fox: A Preliminary Analysis* 18 (Center for Strategic and International Studies, 1999) (same). The literature on the legality of 2003 invasion of Iraq is extensive. For arguments for and against the U.S. government's attempt to argue that the 2003 action was authorized by prior Security Council resolutions, see Agora, *Future Implications of the Iraq Conflict*, 97 AM. J. INT'L L. 553 (July 2003). *See also* Alex J. Bellamy, *International Law and the War with Iraq*, 4 MELBOURNE J. INT'L L. 497 (2003). Note that some attribute the legal indeterminacy of this action to an initial ambiguity in Resolution 678—namely whether the Council was in that instance invoking the individual and collective self defense of Kuwait or its

regarded by most commentators and at least some courts as not authorized by the Council, the legality of the earlier actions by the U.S. and the UK remain fraught questions.[65]

The Council has also, notoriously, deployed its powers in legally uncertain ways in other instances. Its repeated affirmations, for instance, that

> criminal acts, including against civilians, committed with the intent to cause death or serious bodily injury, or taking of hostages, with the purpose to provoke a state of terror in the general public or in a group of persons or particular persons, intimidate a population or compel a government or an international organization to do or to abstain from doing any act, which constitute offences with the scope of and as defined in the international conventions and protocols relating to terrorism, are under no circumstances justifiable . . .

might be seen as restating the obligations owed by the parties to certain counter-terrorism conventions, re-interpretations of the duties owed by states under the UN Charter, or, alternatively, as was suggested by a decision of the Special Tribunal for Lebanon discussed in Chapter V, an affirmation that there now exists a customary international crime of terrorism.[66] Further, even when the Council is relatively precise in defining the scope of "all necessary measures" that it authorizes states to take under Chapter VII, as was the case in Council Resolution 1973 authorizing collective military action in the air space above Libya to save civilians under threat but not authorizing either regime change nor boots on the ground, its actions left considerable scope for discretion and disagreement.[67]

---

own Charter powers to authorize use of force under Article 42 in response to a threat to the international peace. *See, e.g.,* Oscar Schachter, *United Nations Law in the Gulf Conflict,* 85 AM. J. INT'L L. 452 (1991). The legality of that action and the meaning of the S.C. resolutions (including S.C. Res. 1441) played a substantial role in the official UK inquiry, known as the Chilcot Inquiry. *See* THE IRAQ INQUIRY, *at* http://www.iraqinquiry.org.uk/the-report/.

65   For an analysis of some of the national court cases discussing these issues, see Markus G. Puder, *The Construction of UN-System Law in Domestic and International Courts—The Second Gulf War as a Case Study,* 5 Revista OIDU 840 (2015).

66   *See, e.g.,* S.C. Res. 1566 (Oct. 8, 2004) and Interlocutory Decision on the Applicable Law: Terrorism, Conspiracy, Homicide, Perpetration, Cumulative Charging, Case No. STL-11-01/1 (Feb. 16, 2011) [hereinafter Interlocutory Decision on the Applicable Law].

67   *See* Chapter II *supra* § 3. *See generally* Sarah Brockmeier, Oliver Stuenkel & Marcos Tourinho, *The Impact of the Libya Intervention Debates on Norms of Protection,* 30 GLOBAL

Positivists' insistence that legal obligations, to be consistent with the rule of law, be clear as to binding authority as well as to underlying legal authority (pedigree) is at odds with the political realities facing the Council. As is suggested by Chapter II, the Council resorts to textual ambiguities are, in the typical instance, intentional concessions needed to secure the votes for passage of or to avoid vetoes with respect to particular resolutions. The Council constantly needs to straddle an uneasy (if pragmatic) line between the demands of politics and law.[68] It is sometimes hard to distinguish when the Council is acting as the world's policeman and when it is attempting to be its *de facto* legislator; that is, when it is making a political plea and when it is demanding that its subjects legally comply. While scholars from all parts of the political spectrum have criticized the proposition that the Council can be a legitimately, a law-maker,[69] there is no escaping the fact that the Council's actions have legal impacts on states. The Council itself has acknowledged this reality insofar as, on occasion, it seeks to indicate that a particular resolution does not intend to establish a legal precedent;[70] the implication is that some of its actions, like the practice of other IO organs and the caselaw produced by international adjudicators, assist in the ongoing (re)interpretation of the UN Charter (and other relevant law). As illustrated by Chapter II's description of the Council's

---

SOC'Y 113 (2015), *at* http://www.tandfonline.com/doi/full/10.1080/13600826.2015.1094029 (focusing on continued disagreements with respect to the responsibility to protect principle cited in Resolution 1973).

68   This is the case with respect to matters of procedure as well as substance. The Council may undertake procedural innovations for pragmatic reasons, without clarifying how its actions comport with the terms of the UN Charter or whether what it does is intended to respect any legal limits. Thus, S.C. Res. 2231 (July 20, 2015), which affirmed the terms of the "Iran Deal" with respect to the future of the Iran's nuclear program, includes an innovative provision which permits any one of the states that negotiated that deal (including non-P-5 member Germany) to notify the Council that in its view, Iran has violated the terms of the deal, thereby triggering the pre-existing Council sanctions against Iran to "snap back." Legal commentators are still debating whether this delegation of unilateral authority to in effect terminate one Security Council decision and re-activate others, is consistent with the voting provisions of the Charter or with any other implied limits on the Council's authority. *See, e.g.*, Jean Galbraith, *Ending Security Council Resolutions*, 109 AM. J. INT'L L. 806 (2015).

69   *See generally* Martti Koskenniemi, *The Politics of International Law—20 Years Later*, 20 EUR. J. INT'L L. 7 (2009) (focusing on the structural biases of international institutions to make the case against the increasing "managerialism" that favors using them for indeterminately defined forms of "governance").

70   *See, e.g.*, S.C. Res. 940, *supra* note 8, ¶ 2 (stressing the "unique" circumstances that prompted Chapter VII action to restore the elected government of Haiti).

controversial referrals of situations to the ICC,[71] this helps to explain why lawyers who draft Council resolutions often attempt to adhere to tried and true language used previously by the Council. They and other stakeholders recognize the broader normative effects of what the Council does.

Even more aggravating from a positivist perspective is the Council's penchant for avoiding, at least in some cases, a clear statement indicating the Charter basis for its actions. A number of Council actions, both before and after the end of the Cold War, simply "call upon" states to take certain actions without citation to relevant Charter authority, thereby failing to clarify whether the measures called for are legally binding decisions under Chapter VII or Article 25.[72] Council Res. 2249, adopted in 2015, is a clear example. That resolution "calls upon Member States that have the capacity to do so to take all necessary measures ... on the territory under the control of ISIL ... to redouble and coordinate their efforts to prevent and suppress terrorist acts committed specifically by ISIL ... and to eradicate the safe haven they have established over significant parts of Iraq and Syria."[73] While this resolution appears to authorize the most extreme action that the Council can take, namely the power to use military force, it does so without invoking either the words "decide" or "Chapter VII," unlike the Iraq resolutions discussed in Chapter II section 3.

For some, strategic ambiguity of this kind is a normatively desirable development given the "shackles" imposed by traditional positivist sources of law.[74] The shackles required of positivist treaties, which require explicit consent by national authorities including legislatures, help to explain why such sources are "stagnating" while recourse to "informal" types of law-making is rising.[75]

---

71   Thus, once the Council set the terms for its initial ICC referral in the case of the Sudan, it was predictable that it would turn to comparable language in its second ICC referral (in the case of Libya). *See* S.C. Res. 1593 (Mar. 31, 2005) and S.C. Res. 1973, *supra* note 7.

72   *See, e.g.*, Namibia Opinion, *supra* note 5, ¶ 116 (expressing the view that the Council was authorized to take legally binding action outside the context of Chapter VII so long as this was a binding "decision" under Article 25 of the Charter).

73   S.C. Res. 2249, ¶ 5 (Nov. 20, 2015). By calling ISIL actions "an unprecedented threat to international peace and security," this resolution invokes the language of Article 39 without actually citing to that UN Charter provision, In taking this rather unusual approach, the resolution invokes neither the Council's own Chapter VII authority nor that of states to take collective self-defense, unlike, for example, S.C. Res. 1373, *supra* note 14, adopted in the wake of 9/11, which invoked in its preamble the inherent right of individual or collective self-defense and also deployed the power of Chapter VII of the Charter.

74   Pauwelyn, Wessel & Wouters, *When Structures Become Shackles*, *supra* note 3.

75   *Id.* at 734. *See generally* Agora, *The End of Treaties?*, AJIL UNBOUND (April 18, 2014) *at* https://www.asil.org/blogs/end-treaties-online-agora.

Others are more apt to defend the continuing merits of positivism.[76] Few doubt that IOs have contributed to the trend towards "informality."

The challenge to the bindingness and clarity of international law extends to the definition of what constitutes an "international organization" (or "international legal person") capable of asserting rights and responsibilities in accord with the premises of the ICJ's Advisory Opinion in Reparation for Injuries.[77] Today, we are not quite certain which collectivities quality for this status. Scholars of global administrative law (GAL), for example, examine five forms of "globalized administrative regulation" by formal international organizations, by the collective action of transnational networks of national regulatory officials acting on national laws or regulations (e.g., the Basel Committee), by national regulators under a cooperation arrangement acting on issues of foreign or global concern (e.g., efforts on biodiversity conservation or greenhouse gas emissions), by hybrid inter-governmental-private arrangements (e.g., the Internet Corporation for Assigned Names and Numbers (ICANN), and by private institutions charged with regulatory functions (e.g., the International Standarization Organization (ISO)).[78] The inter-governmental global organizations that are the subject of this monograph and that positivists deem to be "international legal persons" capable of engaging with international law are only one of the actors producing GAL.

To the extent international lawyers are no longer of one mind with respect to who is an "international legal person," it is no surprise that what constitutes "international law" is also in dispute. Among those anxious to capture the reality of contemporary efforts to govern individuals, private association, enterprises, states, or other public institutions, are public law scholars based in Europe who aspire to examine all exercises of "international public author-

---

76   See, e.g., Jean D'Aspremont, Formalism and the Sources of International Law: A Theory of the Ascertainment of Legal Rules (2011). See also International Legal Positivism in a Post-Modern World (Jörg Kammerhofer & Jean D'Aspremont eds., 2014).

77   Whether COPs or MOPs established within certain treaty regimes, such as the Framework Convention on Tobacco Control and environmental treaties, constitute "international legal persons" for purposes of international law remains a contentious question. See, e.g., Alvarez, supra note 20, at 316–331 (describing "managerial forms of treaty-making" including the significance of COPs and MOPs). Indeed, the Institut de Droit International is, at this writing, embarking on a project to study that question.

78   Benedict Kingsbury, Nico Krisch & Richard B. Stewart, The Emergence of Global Administrative Law, 68 L. & Contemp. Probs. 15, 20–21 (2005).

ity," irrespective of whether these are encompassed by Article 38 sources.[79] Whether all such exercises of "international public law" should properly be considered part of "public international law" is one of the concerns of this literature.

1.4 Explaining How IO Charters "Evolve"

As Chapters II through IV suggest, in the hands of institutionally embedded actors, the constituent instruments of IOs have become blueprints for actions far beyond those that would have been predicted by their drafters. IOs have established a motley group of subsidiary bodies not contemplated by those "present at the creation." The actions taken by the Security Council and General Assembly, described in Chapters II and III, challenge the positivist state-centered understanding of the UN Charter as described in Chapter II, sections 1 and 2. The contention that the UN Charter was designed to protect sovereignty is difficult to reconcile with UN actions that appear to break with sovereignty or at least challenge its exercise. The positivist premise that the UN operates only to defend states from each other and does not disturb their "domestic jurisdiction" seems hard to reconcile with reality.

To be sure, the actions of the General Assembly and Security Council often seek to protect statehood and the concept of sovereignty. As Jacob Katz Cohen has argued, it is possible to explain many of the Security Council's efforts surveyed in Chapter II—to counter new forms of "threats to the peace" (including terrorist threats), to enable peacekeeping operations, and even to protect "human security"—as commitments to stabilize states and respond to state failure.[80] But, as Cohen himself recognizes, to achieve these goals the Council has deviated considerably from the text of the UN Charter and positivist understandings of the limits of the powers delegated by states to its organs.

As demonstrated by Chapter II, the Council no longer sees itself as only a tool for police action responding to inter-state threats. It has acted as *de facto* global legislator and even at times as global adjudicator. Its creative use of its authority to "contract out" the use of force—presumably under Article 42, even without the envisioned Article 43 agreements—has only been exceeded by its creative interpretation of the non-coercive tools at its disposal under

---

79   *See, e.g.*, Armin von Bogdandy, Philipp Dann & Matthias Goldmann, *Developing the Publicness of Public International Law: Towards a Legal Framework for Global Governance Activities*, 9 GERMAN L. J. 1375 (2008).

80   Jacob Katz Cogan, *Stabilization and the Expanding Scope of the Security Council's Work*, 109 AM. J. INT'L L. 324, 339 (2015).

Article 41 or its capacity to establish innovative "subsidiary organs" under Article 29. The Council, no less than the Assembly, has repeatedly interfered with the "domestic jurisdiction" of states, particularly in reaction to perceived violations of "human rights" with or without recourse to "enforcement action" as foreseen in Article 2(7).

In determining the legality of its actions, the Council and the Assembly have relied, as often as not, on their own institutional precedents. As Chapters II and III suggest, they have acted as if prior Council or Assembly actions were themselves a source of authority. Despite the absence of delegated treaty-making authority, the Council has intervened in the treaties that states may or may not conclude. It has not merely used its power to sanction states under Article 41 to trump states' existing treaties (as arguably foreseen by Article 103), it has also imposed agreements on states, supplemented existing multilateral agreements by enacting global legislation (not limited to UN member states but seemingly applicable to all states), and re-interpreted other inter-state agreements, including those that establish boundaries.[81] It has also sought to influence customary law, including the meaning or scope of international crimes, without waiting for its codification or progressive development as envisioned by Article 13(1).[82]

As is discussed in Chapter III, the UN General Assembly has also re-interpreted the UN Charter and other treaties, as well as customary law. In undertaking the last, it too has not always waited for the "scientific" codification or progressive development efforts of authorized sub-organs, such as the International Law Commission. Both the Council and the Assembly also have been proactive in affirming the rights of the organization as an international legal person, despite the fact that Articles 104 and 105 of the Charter address only the capacities of the organization in the "territories" of member states.[83] Both UN bodies have, like other IOs, produced or endorsed diverse legal products—from "declarations" to expert reports—that are ambiguous with respect to binding effect. Neither body has been particularly careful about distinguishing their "hortatory" efforts from those more authoritative effects, even though the text of the "positivist" Charter endorses such distinctions.[84]

The actions of the principal UN organs, aided and abetted by international adjudicators and non-state actors, have transformed the UN Charter, osten-

---

81   Chapter II *supra.*

82   Chapter II *supra* § 5 and Chapter V *supra* § 4.

83   *See* ALVAREZ, *supra* note 20, at 129–139.

84   *See* Chapters II and III *supra.*

sibly a conservative blueprint to defer "to the sovereign powers retained by states,"[85] into a mechanism that attempts to change the obligations of states and occasionally succeeds in doing so. A Charter that, by its text, delegated only limited police power to one organ, accorded another organ only the power to issue recommendations, refused to bind its members to any form of binding adjudication, and affirmed in the ICJ's Statute that the only legal obligations states have were those to which they give their consent, has created an institution whose own subsequent practice has become the most important source for re-interpreting the state-centric Charter itself. Along the way, the original delineation of functions between the Council and the Assembly, as well as among the "specialized" organizations of the UN system, has been subtly altered. Today, little remains of Article 12(1)'s supposed limits on the authority of the General Assembly to interfere with "disputes or situations" before the Security Council,[86] and the overlap between the activities of the UN and its specialized agencies has led to serious doubts about the continued viability of the "principle of speciality" as endorsed by the ICJ in its response to the WHO's request for an advisory opinion on the legality of nuclear weapons.[87] The "mission creep" of many of these organizations—which has enabled both the WHO and the Security Council, for example, to react to public health emergencies[88]—casts doubt on the ICJ's contention that the UN system consists of delimited spheres of influence with circumscribed delegations of authority.[89]

The expanding depth of UN peacekeeping, a concept which, as is well known, developed out of institutional practice and not the text of the Charter, provides a clear illustration of the evolving UN Charter and the shrinking domain in the

---

85   *See* Chapter II *supra* § 2 (describing the original positivist vision of the UN Charter). For an account of the role of the ICJ as enabling "informal" change with respect to the UN Charter, see Julian Arato, *Treaty Interpretation and Constitutional Transformation: Informal Change in International Organizations*, 38 YALE J. INT'L L. 289 (2013).

86   Chapter V *supra* § 5 (discussing the Palestine Wall case).

87   Chapter V *supra* § 5 (discussing the WHO advisory opinion).

88   See Chapter II *supra* § 10 and Chapter IV *supra* § 3.

89   It might be argued that given the expanding responsibilities for both intentional and unintentional threats to health for which WHO members are responsible under the revised IHRS (see Chapter IV *supra* § 3), that organization might now be entitled to ask for an ICJ advisory opinion concerning whether, for example, a WHO member that fails to develop core capacities to prevent access to chemical weapons within its territory is violating its WHO responsibilities. *Compare* Chapter V § 5 (discussing the WHO advisory opinion).

Charter rule barring interference with "domestic jurisdiction."[90] The growth in the numbers of UN Security Council mandated peace operations, and the intrusive administrative activities assumed by these, speaks volumes about the UN's current ambitions. Whereas in 1948, there was only one such mission, UNTSO (originally established to assist in supervising the observance of a truce in Palestine), in 1991, there were four such operations established: UNIKOM (to monitor a demilitarized zone along the Iraq/Kuwait boundary), MINURSO (to monitor a ceasefire and conduct a referendum in Western Sahara), UNAVEM II (to verify a peace agreement, monitor a ceasefire, and observe and verify elections in Angola), ONUSAL (to verify implementation of all agreements between El Salvador and the FMLN, including reform of the armed forces, creation of a new police force, reforms of the judicial and electoral systems, human rights, land tenure, other economic and social issues), and UNAMIC (to assist four Cambodian parties on a ceasefire and to initiate mine-awareness training).[91] Eight years later, in 1999, five more operations were established, two in East Timor and one in Kosovo, Sierra Leone, and the Congo.[92] At this writing, some 125,666 persons are involved in UN peace operations in roughly 16 countries.[93] While these peace operations once operated only at the borders of states—to protect them from each other—after the Cold War, more sovereign-intrusive missions have become the norm. Several, like UNMIK in Kosovo, have been charged with a wide spectrum of essential administrative functions covering matters such as health, education, banking and finance, postal services and telecommunications, and law and order.[94]

---

90   *See also* ALVAREZ, *supra* note 20, at 156–183 (surveying the impact of the Assembly and Council on Article 2(7)).

91   THE UN SECURITY COUNCIL: FROM THE COLD WAR TO THE 21ST CENTURY app. 1 (David Malone ed., 2004).

92   *Id.*

93   Peace-Keeping Fact Sheet, UNITED NATIONS PEACEKEEPING (Aug. 31, 2015), *at* http://www.un.org/en/peacekeeping/resources/statistics/factsheet.shtml.

94   The post-Cold War activity of the Security Council has included many more multilateral operations authorized to use force in the wake of the Council's actions with respect to Iraq in 1990 (discussed in Chapter II *supra*). *See, e.g.*, COLD WAR TO THE 21ST CENTURY, *supra* note 91, app. 2 (enumerating 14 occasions in which the Council authorized some form of multilateral operations from Nov. 1990 through Sept. 2003). Malone's Appendix 3 identifies the many Security Council mandated sanctions regimes, extending over 12 countries from 1966 to 2003. *Id.* As discussed in Chapter II *supra* § 7, these sanctions have evolved from comprehensive sanctions imposed on a target state to "smart sanctions" imposed directly on individuals and organizations within states.

How exactly did the UN Charter evolve to permit UN peacekeeping to become a mechanism for running states? Comparable questions can be posed with respect to the human rights activities of both organs as described in Chapters II and III. How did UN organs acquire the capacity to judge states on how they treat their own citizens? As noted, the Charter's provisions on human rights were vague and imposed minimal obligations on states in this respect; the Charter did not confer any specific power on the organization to enforce these non-defined rights. And yet the Security Council and General Assembly have become *de facto* agents of the human rights revolution—a revolution that, as led by the UN, has turned states "inside out." The only thing that precludes the Assembly's efforts to discover new rights, from privacy to the right to access to information, or to determine new categories of human rights beneficiaries, from the "girl child" to human rights defenders, is whether there are enough members of the Assembly to vote in support of either. The Security Council and UN peace operations now respond to threats to human security, and not merely inter-state frictions. Indeed, to the extent the Security Council fails to act or fails to authorize a UN peace operation, as in Syria, the claim is not that this is legally impossible but only that there is lack of sufficient political support within the Council to do so.

The Council's role in energizing international criminal law also requires some explanation. How has the Security Council evolved from the enforcer of the inter-state peace into a maker of courts? How has it been possible to interpret the UN Charter as enabling 15 of its members to compel states, such as Lebanon, to accept certain treaties and criminal jurisdiction? By what interpretative route has a Charter that held back from forcing members to accept any particular kind of peaceful dispute settlement mechanism (see Article 2(7)), been converted into an instrument for the most intrusive form of adjudication? How has the collective enforcer of the peace become a *de facto* agent for proclaiming new international crimes, sending suspects to the ICC or to *ad hoc* tribunals of its own making, or for directly imposing what appear to be criminal penalties on persons and organizations? By what warrant has the Council assumed the mantle of supervisor of sanctions committees charged with overseeing the bank accounts and travel bans of hundreds of individuals and agencies around the world? How did the Security Council acquire the power to undermine Libya's sovereignty by forcing it to extradite alleged terrorists, determine that its highest officials should be treated as criminals, and finally authorize what became regime change? How has the General Assembly, a body intended as a venue for states to vent hot air peacefully, become a place which determines whether Palestine, Kosovo, or Crimea are entitled to claim the benefits of statehood?[95]

This section provides a brief account of how the UN Charter and other IO charters have evolved to permit the expansion of their powers. Note that these changes have not resulted, as positivists would prefer, from formal charter amendment.[96] Resort to amendment, authorized under the UN Charter's Article 108, is politically difficult and, accordingly, rare. But it would be wrong to attribute the changes in the UN Charter to the triumph of politics over law. Remarkably, the evolutions of the UN Charter and other IO constituent instruments have occurred pursuant to the law and not in overt defiance of it, and with relatively few complaints by members of *ultra vires* action.[97]

The evolution of the UN Charter and other IO charters over time is the result of five general structural features that exist in uneasy tension with positivist tenets: these charters' "constructive ambiguities"; the VCT's own "constructive ambiguities"; the relative absence of clear charter limitations on IO powers; the reliance on the self-judging practice by IO organs; and the absence of formal judicial review. Examples using the UN Charter follow to illustrate these general points.

Although the UN Charter seems to give preference to preventing inter-state war as its primary purpose, its preamble's text and Article 1 indicate otherwise. Neither clearly prioritizes that state-centric goal. The second paragraph of the Charter's preamble, referring to "we the peoples," affirms "faith in fundamental human rights," while its fourth paragraph affirms the need for "social progress and better standards of life in larger freedom." The Charter does not define "sovereignty" or affirm that it is somehow a constraint on the UN's organs. While it mentions the "principles" of "sovereign equality," "equal rights," and "self-determination of peoples," along with the concept of "domestic jurisdiction," it defines none of those terms and, except for the ambiguous Article 2(7) discussed below, it does not say these are legal constraints on the delegation of powers to the organization. Further, as is well known, the Charter's drafters did not agree with proposals to give the ICJ or the General Assembly the power to issue authoritative interpretations of the Charter; it left these to be resolved by practice—which has meant in effect that it is up to members to object when a UN organ does something they deem to be *ultra vires*.[98] The text of the Charter seems, in short, open to the interpretation that when UN organs

---

95   *See* Chapter III *supra* § 4.

96   *See, e.g.*, Arato, *supra* note 85.

97   *See generally id.*

98   ALVAREZ, *supra* note 20, at 74–81.

and the Secretariat act, they are presumed to act legally, absent member objections. Since such objections rarely occur, in the usual case self-judging day-to-day decisions taken by UN organs and Secretariat officials are the final word.

The UN Charter's textual ambiguities enable its organs and adjudicative bodies with jurisdiction to consider the matter to reach for different hermeneutic frameworks for interpreting it. These legitimating (and sometimes divergent) modes of interpretation—which for illustrative purposes might be designated as: a consent-based model designed to protect sovereign equality, a minority protection model to shelter weaker states from the strong, a participation-based model seeking to ensure procedural protection in the making of decisions but not equal substantive outcomes, a teleological model grounded in achieving organizational goals at all costs, or a human rights-protective model—can each be justified based on distinct threads in the Charter's preamble and Article 1.[99]

Those seeking to interpret the Charter as an instrument for defending states' rights to be "left alone" would be disappointed by the ambiguities in Article 2(7). These come to the fore when we compare the text of that article to the comparable text in the League of Nations Covenant. The UN Charter's Article 2(7) provides that:

> Nothing...shall authorize the United Nations to intervene in matters which are essentially within the domestic jurisdiction of any state or shall require the Members to submit such matters to settlement under the present Charter; but this principle shall not prejudice the application of enforcement measures under Chapter VII.[100]

Article 15(8) of the League of Nations Covenant stated:

> If the dispute between the parties is claimed by one of them, and is found by the Council, to arise out of a matter which by international law is solely within the domestic jurisdiction of that party, the Council shall so report, and shall make no recommendation as to its settlement.[101]

Article 2(7) is broader than the League Covenant's comparable provision in some ways. The latter addressed only restrictions on the Council's ability

---

99   José E. Alvarez, *Judging the Security Council*, 90 AM. J. INT'L L. 1, 19 (1996) (adapting constitutional models initially suggested by Joseph Weiler in the EU context).

100   UN Charter art. 2(7).

101   Covenant of the League of Nations, Jan. 10, 1920, 1919 U.K.T.S. 4, art. 15(8) (amended 1924).

to intervene in disputes within members' domestic jurisdiction. On its face, Article 2(7) is a more comprehensive limit on all UN organs, not just the Council, and not just when they act in the course of settling a dispute. Indeed, Article 2(7) seems to impose a legal limit even for the Council—except when it applies "enforcement measures" under Chapter VII. But a closer look at the two provisions suggests some difficulties with treating Article 2(7) as a legal limit on the actions of UN organs. Unlike Article 15(8) on which it was presumably based, Article 2(7) contains no reference to "international law." This presumably intended departure from the text of the comparable provision in the League Covenant implies that "domestic jurisdiction" is a mere political principle, not a legal limit imposed and defined by international law. Another ambiguity is introduced by the use of the word, "essentially." For some this means that something really has to be "mostly" within a state's domestic jurisdiction for the Article 2(7) limitation to apply. Even if that is the case and "essentially" just signals the importance of some serious manifestations of domestic jurisdiction, this suggests that there exists a spectrum of sovereign actions that are "domestic." But, of course, if the limit contained in Article 2(7) applies only to the more serious domestic issues along that spectrum, some UN actions that nonetheless interfere with less serious domestic matters are by definition permitted. This plausible interpretation undermines the definiteness of the Article 2(7) limit. Interference with domestic jurisdiction becomes, in this view, a matter calling for judgment about the relative weight of a state's interest relative to the need to fulfill the collective's goals. This leaves the protections accorded to states up to majorities on the Assembly who may determine that the latter carry more weight in a particular case. This helps to explain why it is possible for one scholar to contend that "although the attempt is still made to define Article 2(7) in legal terms ... the conclusion seems inescapable that it is largely disregarded as an inconvenient potential limitation on UN action."[102]

The ambiguities of Article 2(7) are only exacerbated by the imprecision of the term "intervene"—also left undefined—and therefore calling for the exercise of judgment. For some only forcible UN "interventions" imposed without state consent—presumably short of enforcement action which, by definition, is not subject to the limits of Article 2(7)—are barred. Also left undefined is the term "domestic." If the scope of international law now embraces matters beyond those that engage states' foreign relations, this ambiguity is particularly significant. If, as most agree, international law now imposes limits even with respect to the rules that states apply to determine whether persons are

102   D.W. Greig, International Law 407 (2d ed. 1976).

entitled to claim their nationality, for example, what is left of "domestic jurisdiction" in terms of subject matter?[103] If Article 2(7) intends to demarcate
untouchable domestic matters based on whether international law applies to
them, that limit has steadily diminished as the coverage of international law
has expanded.

Article 2(7) objections are still heard, of course, at the UN and may still have
impact. They may lead, for instance, to more circumscribed language in an
Assembly resolution to secure its passage. This was the case, for example, in
the early days of UN election assistance when states reacted to an Assembly
resolution on the topic by insisting, based on Article 2(7) objections by some
states, that requiring language affirming that "no single political system or electoral method ... is equally suited to all nations" by UN election efforts "should
not call into question each State's sovereign right ... to choose and develop its
political, social, economic and cultural systems."[104] But Article 2(7) objections
by particular states targeted for Assembly criticism of their human rights practices have generally not prevented such condemnations and the imprecisions
of Article 2(7) itself help to explain why. The relative ineffectiveness of such
objections is also a product of the power of institutional practice. Once the
General Assembly began to "intervene" by criticizing members for their human
rights practices (as it did early in the life of the organization with respect to
Franco's Spain), it became harder to argue against the "institutional precedent"
that had been established and to which it members had "acquiesced."

Finally, Article 2(7) contains yet another loophole. While it permits the
Security Council to ignore domestic jurisdiction when that body takes "enforcement action under Chapter VII," such action is not defined or limited. As discussed in Chapter 11, the Council has used the ambiguities of Article 41, which
authorizes measures short of force but provides only a list of non-exhaustive
examples, as permission for everything from the imposition of smart sanctions to the creation of international courts. It has deployed the ambiguities of
Article 42 (which permits the Council to authorize force without restricting it
to UN forces authorized under Article 43 agreements) to "contract out" the use
of force to others. If all of these are "enforcement actions," this too has limited
the opportunities for applying the ostensible Article 2(7) limit.

Opportunities for expansive readings of what the Charter permit also follow from the absence of clear limitations on the triggers for Council action

103   *See, e.g.*, José E. Alvarez, *The "Right to be Left Alone" and the General Assembly* (ACUNS
       Reports and Papers, No. 5, 1994) 17 (concluding that "the domain of Article 2(7) appears to
       be shrinking fast, as is, presumably, sovereignty itself.").
104   *Id.* at 10–11 (citing the example of G.A. Res. 45/150).

under Article 39. While "aggression" was arguably defined at Nuremberg, neither a "threat" nor a "breach" of the peace was a legal term of art prior to the UN Charter. Accordingly, even international courts have been reluctant to suggest that anyone other than the Council can decide what these crucial licenses for Council action mean.[105] While Charter drafters may have intended to permit the Council to thwart WWII-type aggressors, the textual authority they accorded to the Council, to respond to whatever "threats" it decides may exist from time to time, was considerably broader. Further, nothing in Chapter VII explicitly connects the prohibition on inter-state resort to force in Article 2(4) to the Council's power to maintain or restore international peace and security in Chapter VII.[106] And even assuming that such a connection is made, this may hardly impose a real limit on the Council. Should anyone suggest that Council enforcement actions are limited to occasions when a state has threatened or used force against another state in violation of that state's territorial integrity or political independence, they would be met with the wider license in Article 2(4). That text bans the threat or use of force not merely when these target a state's territory or political independence but when these are deployed "in any manner inconsistent with the Purposes of the UN." Given the expansive purposes of the organization in Article 1, the Council would still be legally able to respond to a wide (and probably undefinable) spectrum of "threats."

Nor does the Charter appear to impose any real limits on when the Council can resort to the use of force. Although Article 42 anticipates that non-forcible measures under Article 41 need to be shown to be "inadequate," that determination (which is up to the Council to "consider" under the opening words of Art. 42) is apparently left to the Council to determine for itself.[107] As for what the Council is licensed to do under Chapter VII or for how long, here too the Charter gives the Council wide license. The Council may take whatever action is necessary "to maintain or restore international peace and security," a license that, as discussed in Chapter II, included under its Resolution 687 any actions

---

105   *See, e.g.*, Chapter II *supra* § 4 (discussing Lockerbie cases); Prosecutor v. Tadić, Case No. IT-94-1-I, Decision on Defence Motion for Interlocutory Appeal on Jurisdiction, ¶¶ 28–39 (Int'l Crim. Trib. For the Former Yugoslavia Oct. 2, 1995) [hereinafter Tadić Jurisdiction Decision]. *See also* Chapter V *supra* § 5.

106   This ostensible limit on Council action is further undermined to the extent the Council can take binding decisions under Article 25 of the Charter, as the ICJ has opined. *See* Namibia Opinion, *supra* note 5.

107   *See, e.g.*, Tadić Jurisdiction Decision, *supra* note 105, ¶¶ 29–30.

that the Council deemed necessary to "restore" the peace in the general area around Iraq and not merely around the boundaries between Iraq and Kuwait.

These are, of course, only some examples of the many textual ambiguities in the Charter. The UN Charter, like the constitutions of many states and IOs, provides numerous other examples of inconsistencies between distinct provisions (e.g., the Charter's affirmation of the principle of sovereign equality while at the same time according only some states permanent membership and the veto in the Security Council), loopholes (e.g., the absence of definitions for important paths to power such as what constitute "threats" to the peace or "human rights"), procedural gaps (e.g., the absence of concrete limits on how the General Assembly can take action, including the failure to specify what types of "important questions" require a super-majority vote), and mismatches between ostensible Charter rules and provisions for enforcing them (e.g., Charter provisions anticipating that ICJ contentious decisions are binding but providing only for Council action to enforce such rulings). Each of these provides ample opportunities for the exercise of discretion in Charter interpretation.

UN organs are encouraged to take interpretative leaps not only by gaps in the Charter's text and the sheer difficulties of Charter amendment under Article 108, but by the traditional rules for treaty interpretation. Articles 31–32 of the VCT, widely regarded as codifying the customary rules for treaty interpretation, are open-ended in many respects. Article 31's demand that interpreters adhere to a treaty's "object and purpose" leaves the term undefined. It permits recourse to the original intentions of the treaty's drafters (explicitly covered by Article 32) and/or the treaty's presumptive intent, as informed by treaty text and context. The ICJ, for its part, seems inclined to rely on the presumptive intent of the UN Charter and not its original *travaux*, even if reliance on the latter is licensed by the VCT's Article 32.[108] Article 31 is also ambiguous about the relative weight to be accorded its various component parts. It does not indicate whether the plain meaning of text and "other" context matters more than, for example, the subsequent practice of treaty parties in 31(3). The VCT rules do not preclude the alternative hermeneutic interpretations noted above.

The vagaries of the limits on UN action, apart from those suggested by Article 2(7), also encourage flexible Charter interpretation. While it is common to assert that consistent with the need to adhere to a treaty's "object and purpose" and UN Charter Articles 24(2) and 25, the UN cannot, as an organization, violate the "principles and purposes" of Articles 1 and 2, the slippery, imprecise,

---

108   *See* ALVAREZ, *supra* note 20, at 83–84.

and somewhat contradictory nature of those principles and purposes makes that limitation rather ephemeral. The contention that the General Assembly is limited to hortatory (non-legally binding) action, suggested by Article 11 (and particularly its attempt to distinguish Assembly "recommendations" from Council "action" under Article 11(2)), has had to wrestle with the Charter's contradictions in this respect, namely that this cannot be completely true insofar as the Assembly is also charged with taking "decisions" under Article 18, can determine the budget of the organization under Article 17, and can establish subsidiary organs under Article 22. All of these Assembly actions are presumably not hortatory and yet the outer limits of these delegations to the Assembly to take authoritative actions are not defined. The Charter does not provide a definitive list of types of Assembly "decisions;" its Article 18 only lists examples. Indeed, the ICJ has opined that the Assembly can in fact take some binding decisions not spelled out in the Charter,[109] and that this authority extends to establishing an independent tribunal capable of binding the Assembly itself.[110]

Similarly, no explicit legal limits are imposed on the Security Council. Article 36(3), sometimes cited for the proposition that the ICJ has exclusive jurisdiction over legal disputes, only indicates that in making "recommendations" the Council "should consider" that such disputes "should as a general rules be referred by the parties" to the ICJ. Such hedged language says nothing about the permitted scope of Council decisions, does not require the Council to refer legal disputes to the Court, and seems a bit inconsistent with Article 37's envisioned role for the Council in settling disputes, including its powers to recommend "terms of settlement."

Other legal limits that have been suggested on permissible UN action, such as the contention that the UN cannot interfere with states' inherent right to self-defense (under Article 51) or that, like all treaties, the UN Charter cannot impose duties on non-state parties, have not proven very effective in practice.[111] There are notorious difficulties with respect to defining the "inherent" rights of self-defense, particularly in an age when many such threats involve non-state actors or cyber-attacks, and the uncertainties are exacer-

---

109   See, e.g., Namibia Opinion, supra note 5.

110   Effect of Awards of Compensation Made by the United Nations Administrative Tribunal, Advisory Opinion, 1954 I.C.J. 47 (July 13) [hereinafter Effect of Awards Opinion].

111   One of the problems with such contentions is that these limits are usually based on customary international law or general principles of law and share the ambiguities or lack of precision of such sources. Those who argue that, for example, the Council cannot take a particular action because it would violate the *nemo iudex in causa sua* principle would need to provide some definitive contours to that equitable concept.

bated by the Council's failure to indicate when it is responding to a state's claim of self-defense as opposed to a collective threat to the peace.[112] While the VCT is clear that treaties only bind their parties, Article 2(6) of the Charter suggests that the organization can still "ensure" that non-UN members act in accordance with the Charter's principles as necessary for international peace. And even if one assumes that the UN can nonetheless only impose duties on parties to the Charter, the practice of the Council appears to have ignored this limit. As noted in Chapter II, the Security Council has directed some of its binding decisions at all "states" (including some international organizations) and not just UN members.

The contention that UN bodies cannot violate human rights is not apparent if one strictly applies the tenets of positivism. The UN, after all, cannot be a party to most human rights treaties; the fact that UN members are parties to such treaties (subject to particular reservations) says nothing about the particular duties that can be therefore attributed to their organizations, and even the conceptions of human rights in customary law are typically framed as rights against states, not IOs. Indeed, the easiest way to conclude that IOs are subject to human rights is to go beyond strict positivism and rely on the subsequent practice of IOs for this conclusion.[113] To the extent this is the route chosen, however, IOs would be under a duty to respect only those particular human rights that they have affirmed apply to their actions.

And even assuming that one were to find that some primary rules do limit the Council, how does one apply those limits given the Charter's Article 103, which, by its terms, assigns priority to UN obligations over those of other treaties? Notably, while that provision identifies only treaties and some have suggested that it is limited to enabling the Council to trump those treaties that stand in the way of its taking effective enforcement action, Article 103 is not so limited by its terms. The trumping power that it accords might apply to other UN organs and given the fact that there is no established hierarchy among the sources identified in the ICJ's Article 38—no reason why customary law as such is more important than a treaty—it may enable any such UN organ to

---

112 *See, e.g.,* OSCAR SCHACHTER, INTERNATIONAL LAW IN THEORY AND PRACTICE, 141–
     146 (1991) (discussing the indeterminacy of the legal limits applicable to invocation of
     self-defense).

113 *But see* ANDREW CLAPHAM, HUMAN RIGHTS OBLIGATIONS OF NON-STATE ACTORS,
     59–83 (2006) (proposing a number of distinct bases for determining that IOs have human
     rights responsibilities).

trump any international obligations, including those under custom, that stand in its way.[114]

For these reasons, the considerable expansion of the General Assembly's and the Security Council's respective powers to act, and the corresponding shrinkage of the limits imposed by Art. 2(7), has proceeded, not in spite of the law but *seemingly* in accordance with it.

The UN Charter's evolutions have also been the product of the limited jurisdiction of the ICJ and other international courts. As noted, the Charter does not provide the ICJ with "judicial review" authority and its contentious jurisdiction, limited to disputes between states, makes it unlikely that this Court would engage in such review except indirectly, in the course of considering an inter-state dispute that relates to the powers of a UN organ, as with the Lockerbie cases brought by Libya against the U.S. and the UK for their actions in the Council.[115] While, to be sure, the Court's Advisory Jurisdiction provides it with opportunities to issue at least non-binding opinions on such matters, the Court has, for reasons addressed in Chapter V, repeatedly denied that it engages in judicial review over UN organs.

While the ICJ has suggested, in its dicta, some limits on the powers of IOs,[116] it has most often been an enabler of what IOs have sought to do. The legal rules affirmed by the ICJ in the course of the relatively few advisory opinions that have been presented to the Court by IOs—the principle of effectiveness, the doctrine of implied powers, reliance on subsequent practice of IO organs, and the presumption of legality—have enabled the "mission creep" of not just the

---

114   But many assert that Art. 103 does not permit the organization to trump *jus cogens*. *See, e.g., id.* at 67–68 and 87–91. *See also* Application of the Convention on the Prevention and Punishment of the Crime of Genocide (Bosn. & Herz. v. Serb.), 1996 I.C.J. 433 (declaration of Judge *ad hoc* Lauterpacht); Joined Cases C-402 and C-415/05P, Kadi & Al Barakaat Int'l Found. v. Comm'n, 2008 E.C.R. I-6352 [hereinafter Kadi I] (argument of Advocate General Maduro). Even this seemingly obvious limitation remains speculative, however, particularly given the uncertainties with respect to the content of *jus cogens*. To the extent that the ban on states' use of force in the absence of self-defense is a *jus cogens* rule, for example, the Security Council would not be able to contract out the use of force to states, as it has, in cases involving threats to the peace not involving responses to self-defense.

115   *See* discussion of Lockerbie cases in Chapters II *supra* § 4 and V *supra* § 5.

116   As discussed in Chapter V *supra* § 5, the ICJ has suggested some limits on IO action. It has found that IOs, as international legal persons, are subject to (un-enumerated) duties as well as rights under general international law, have only limited powers as defined by their charters and the principle of speciality, do not enjoy the "general" powers enjoyed by states (such as the power to conclude any and all treaties), and cannot otherwise deploy implied powers that contradict the explicit terms of their charters.

UN itself but other IOs. The ICJ has given its imprimatur to many of the changes in the UN Charter addressed here and has not been an innocent bystander. It has affirmed the correctness of whatever the Security Council and the General Assembly have done whenever it has had an opportunity to do so and, by giving a reasoned opinion in justification of their acts, it has given considerable credence to these enabling principles.[117] And despite the proliferation of international courts addressed in Chapter V, with the exception of the European Court of Justice, which has the capacity to review the acts of the European Union, these other courts do not have jurisdiction to judicially review, with binding effect, the acts of international organizations. To the extent IOs have been subject to adjudicative review, this has occurred, as in the *Kadi* cases, indirectly, as when individuals have challenged the legality of laws designed to implement Security Council sanctions.[118]

2   The IO Challenge to Sovereignty

Does the IO challenge to state-centric legal positivism fundamentally challenge sovereignty? How have IOs changed what it means to be a sovereign today? IOs have not affected the "sovereignty" of all states equally. For a poor country like Haiti whose peace and security, and much else, has been in the hands of UN peacekeepers for decades, sovereignty is enjoyed in the form of trusteeship akin to what once existed under the League of Nations and the early decades of the UN Charter. That country has had its elections supervised by the UN, its military coup leaders toppled by the threat of Security Council action, and the health of its nationals apparently jeopardized by UN peacekeepers.[119] To some

---

117   This has been the effect in particular of the Reparation for Injuries Suffered in the Service of the United Nations, Advisory Opinion, 1949 I.C.J. 174 (Apr. 11); Effect of Awards Opinion, *supra* note 110; Certain Expenses of the United Nations (Article 17, paragraph 2 of the Charter), Advisory Opinion, 1962 I.C.J. 151 (July 20); Namibia Opinion, *supra* note 5; Questions of Interpretation and Application of the 1971 Montreal Convention Arising from the Aerial Incident at Lockerbie (Libya v. U.S.), Provisional Measures, 1992 I.C.J. 3 (Apr. 14); Questions of Interpretation and Application of the 1971 Montreal Convention Arising from the Aerial Incident at Lockerbie (Libya v. U.K.), Provisional Measures, 1992 I.C.J. 114 (Apr. 14); Wall Advisory Opinion, *supra* note 5. See *generally* ALVAREZ, *supra* note 20, at 122–145; Arato, *supra* note 85.

118   *See* Chapter V *supra* § 5.

119   *See, e.g.*, Yves Engler, *Minustah's Filthy Record in Haiti*, THE GUARDIAN (Sept. 11, 2011), *at* http://www.theguardian.com/commentisfree/cifamerica/2011/sep/11/haiti-united nations-minustah-cholera (critiquing the UN's response to the cholera outbreak); Jean-

human rights critics, the current Haitian government, which has refused to pursue the claims of its own cholera victims perhaps because it does not wish to offend its powerful UN benefactor, is really a UN occupation force.[120]

Or consider Iraq, an independent country to be sure, but one whose structure of government and numerous laws and institutions were radically transformed under a transformative occupation under U.S./UK auspices that was authorized by the Security Council. Much the same could be said for Libya, Kosovo, or to go further back in time, Namibia. These states owe their current forms of government, and in two of these cases, their very independence and claim to statehood to international institutions. Today, the state-in-being called Palestine also owes its growing legitimacy, and apparently its capacity to join international regimes like the ICC, to the actions of the General Assembly

---

Marc Biquet, *Haiti: Between Emergency and Reconstruction*, 4 INT'L DEV. POLICY (2013), *at* http://poldev.revues.org/1600. *See also* José E. Alvarez, *The United Nations in the Time of Cholera*, AM. J. INT'L L. UNBOUND (Apr. 4, 2014), *at* https://www.asil.org/blogs/united-nations-time-cholera. The criticisms of the international community's response, extends to the many NGOs that have been involved in Haiti. *See, e.g.*, Isabeau Doucet, *NGOs Have Failed Haiti*, THE NATION (Jan. 13, 2011), *at* http://www.npr.org/2011/01/13/132884795/the-nation-how-ngos-have-failed-haiti; Maura R. O'Connor, *Does International Aid Keep Haiti Poor?*, SLATE (Jan. 7, 2011), *at* http://www.slate.com/articles/news_and_politics/dispatches/features/2011/does_international_aid_keep_haiti_poor/the_un_cluster_system_is_as_bad_as_it_sounds.html.

120 Greg Grandin & Keane Bhatt, *10 Reasons Why the UN Occupation of Haiti Must End*, THE NATION (Sept. 26, 2011), *at* http://www.thenation.com/article/10-reasons-why-un-occupation-haiti-must-end/; Mario Joseph, Bureau des Avocats Internationaux, *The Fight Against UN Impunity and Immunity in Haiti: The Cholera Scandal*, *in* CIVICUS, STATE OF CIVIL SOCIETY REPORT 2014 (2014), *at* http://www.civicus.org/index.php/en/expert-perspectives/2018-the-fight-against-un-impunity-and-immunity-in-haiti-the-cholera-scandal ("Throughout the crisis, the government of Haiti has been notably silent in calling for UN accountability, in part due to the heavily interdependent relationship between the government and the UN."). Even back in the 1990s, the UN's involvement in Haiti was criticized for intruding into Haiti's domestic affairs and sovereignty by the governments of Brazil, China, and Cuba. U.N. SCOR, 49th Sess., 3429th mtg. at 6, U.N. Doc. S/PV.3429 (Sept. 29, 1994) ("[W]e think that whatever action is taken should be fully consistent with the Charter . . . and especially with the basic principle of non-intervention.") (statement by the Brazilian representative); U.N. SCOR, 49th Sess., 3413th mtg. at 5, U.N. Doc. S/PV.3413 (July 1, 1994) ("[T]he formulation that describes the situation in Haiti as a threat to regional peace and security . . . is new and removed from the precepts established by the Charter of the United Nations concerning the authority of the Security Council.") (statement by the Cuban representative); *id.* at 10 (indicating similar concerns by the Chinese representative).

and, less directly, UNESCO.[121] Other nations, like Somalia, stumble along in a state of *de facto* quasi-sovereignty with their security, both compromised and dependent on UN authorized actions on such vital matters as piracy and counter-terrorism.[122]

Or consider the relative sovereign rights enjoyed by a more developed state like Argentina. That state, which has defied the rulings of investor-state arbitrations under ICSID, is not quite the symbol of old-fashioned sovereignty that this suggests. Argentine nationalists would likely argue that much of recent Argentine history has been influenced if not dictated by the policies of institutions like the IMF, which they would argue, have encouraged government officials to adopt a disastrous fixed rate of exchange with the U.S. dollar along with a zero-deficit policy, deregulation, and privatization policies (the so-called Washington consensus model) that ultimately helped bring about the very economic emergency that led to the massive number of investor-state claims by foreign investors against that state.[123] Even if one disputes the claim that the IMF is actually to blame for Argentina's recent economic troubles, no one can question that the role of the IMF and ICSID has become a potent political issue within Argentina, and has had a huge impact on that country's respective political parties and leaders, that is, on its political independence. Of course, Argentina's defiance of ICSID decisions came with a price in the age of IOs: Washington denied GSP treatment to Argentina because of that defiance and its incoming capital flows plummeted, along with its rule of law rankings.[124]

And what about relatively rich and militarily powerful nations like China and the United States? Neither, it turns out, enjoy the mythical "absolute sovereignty" suggested by some legal positivists. Despite its power, the U.S. has not been immune from the density of IO-inspired legalization. Even U.S. law, which has been historically relatively impervious to international law, has been internationalized in the age of IOs. United States government practices have

---

121   *See* Chapter III *supra* § 4; Press Release, UNESCO, General Conference Admits Palestine as UNESCO Member (Oct. 31, 2011), *at* http://www.unesco.org/new/en/media-services/ single-view/news/general_conference_admits_palestine_as_unesco_member_state/#. VtNoRJMrJE4.

122   *See, e.g.,* Yaron Gottlieb, *The Security Council's Maritime Piracy Resolutions: A Critical Assessment,* 24 MINN. J. INT'L L. 1 (2015).

123   *See, e.g.,* Paul Blustein, *IMF Says Its Policies Crippled Argentina: Internal Audit Finds Warnings were Ignored,* WASHINGTON POST, July 30, 2004, at E01, *at* http://www .washingtonpost.com/wp-dyn/articles/A25824-2004Jul29.html (reporting on a critical report issued by the IMF's own internal audits unit).

124   Proclamation No. 8788, 77 Fed. Reg. 18,899 (Mar. 29, 2012).

undergone considerable human rights scrutiny by UN treaty bodies, which have criticized the Bush and Obama administrations particularly with respect to post-9/11 counter-terrorism policies involving "enhanced interrogation techniques," detentions in Guantanamo and beyond, and the use of drones, as well as with respect to the country's treatment of minorities, incarceration rates, and application of the death penalty.[125] Criticisms in the General Assembly and elsewhere compel the U.S. to explain why it refuses to ratify widely accepted human rights conventions such as CEDAW, the Rights of the Child Convention, and the Law of the Sea Convention. Pressures in IOs or by NGO observers within them help to explain the U.S.'s changing relationship with the ICC, from overt hostility to growing cooperation, as well as the U.S.'s inability to continue to secure exemption for UN peacekeepers from ICC jurisdiction.[126] As a litigant, the U.S. has also borne significant losses in WTO disputes and has needed to adapt its laws to adjust in response, and the continued reality and threats of investor-state claims under NAFTA has, as discussed in Chapter V, generated a new generation of U.S. BITs and FTAs that seek to better protect the U.S.'s regulatory sovereignty.

Even in the Security Council, the U.S. does not always get its way, not with respect to demanding action on Syria nor with respect to securing explicit UN authority for the use of force against Iraq in 2003. Although the Council is widely regarded as a tool for its veto-wielding hegemons, the requirement of consensus among those hegemons (including China and Russia) means that it is also sometimes a place where even U.S. hegemonic power is constrained

---

125   *See, e.g.*, UN Human Rights Committee, Concluding Observations on the Fourth Periodic Report of the United States of America, U.N. Doc. CCPR/C/USA/CO/4 (Apr. 2014); UN Human Rights Committee, Consideration of Reports Submitted by States Parties Under Article 40 of the Covenant: Concluding Observations of the Human Rights Committee: United States of America, U.N. Doc. CCPR/C/USA/CO/315 (Sept. 2006); UN Committee on the Elimination of Racial Discrimination, Concluding Observations on the Combined Seventh to Ninth Periodic Reports of the United States of America, U.N. Doc. No. CERD/C/USA/CO/7–9 (Sept. 25, 2014); UN Committee on the Elimination of Racial Discrimination, Consideration of Reports Submitted Under Article 9 of the Convention: Concluding Observations of the Committee on the Elimination of Racial Discrimination: United States of America, U.N. Doc. CERD/C/USE/CO/6 (May 8, 2008); UN Committee Against Torture, Concluding Observations on the Combined Third to Fifth Periodic Reports of the United States of America, U.N. Doc. CAT/C/USA/CO/3–5 (Dec. 19, 2014); UN Committee Against Torture, Consideration of Reports Submitted Under Article 19 of the Convention: Conclusions and Recommendations of the Committee Against Torture: United States of America, U.N. Doc. CAT/C/USA/CO/2 (July 25, 2006).

126   *See* Chapter II *supra* § 9.

or where at least a political price is extracted for the exercise of U.S. unilateral behavior.

Much the same can be said with respect to China. Indeed, Judge Xue Hanqin, in her Hague lectures on "Chinese Contemporary Perspectives on International Law," argues persuasively that the history of modern China is one of initial resistance followed by begrudging acceptance of "Western" international law, including the institutions of the UN system.[127] Indeed, there are considerable similarities with respect to the current postures of the U.S. and China with respect to the IOs addressed here. Like the U.S., China has had its share of abundant human rights criticisms at the General Assembly, before UN treaty bodies, and among NGOs that influence such bodies. The human rights of minorities in China, the rights of women (including especially the question of reproductive choice in rural areas during the period of the one child policy), the ability of Chinese citizens to access information, or to form independent labor unions or other associations have all generated complaints in diverse IO forums, including within the Human Rights Committee and in the ILO.[128] As with respect to the U.S., China has paid a political price in various IOs for its refusal to ratify or to fully implement some human rights treaties.

Chinese officials have undoubtedly been as surprised as have U.S. officials by the mission creep of some IOs or the types of claims filed against it before adjudicative forums. The Chinese government probably did not expect to be severely criticized by the ILO Committee on Freedom of Association in an opinion in 1990 in response to a complaint filed in that organization by the International Confederation of Free Trade Unions. In that opinion, the committee found that China's actions in response to the Tiananmen Square protests of June 3–4, 1989, especially the arrests of independent trade union activists, violated the rights to free association that are part of the membership obligations of all ILO members, whether or not the ILO member has ratified Conventions Numbers 87 and 98.[129] That body rejected China's claims that the complaint interfered with China's internal affairs.[130] In that instance, the ILO's

---

127   XUE HANQIN, CHINESE CONTEMPORARY PERSPECTIVES ON INTERNATIONAL LAW (2011).

128   *See generally* ANN KENT, CHINA, THE UNITED NATIONS AND HUMAN RIGHTS: THE LIMITS OF COMPLIANCE (1999); ANN KENT, BEYOND COMPLIANCE: CHINA, INTERNATIONAL ORGANIZATIONS AND GLOBAL SECURITY 181–219 (2007) (discussing China's interactions with the ILO and the Committee on Torture).

129   Complaint Against the Government of China Presented by the International Confederation of Free Trade Unions, ILO Committee on Freedom of Association, Case No. 1500 (1989), 73 I.L.O. OFFICIAL BULL. (ser. B), No. 1 at 99.

130   *Id.* ¶ 692.

reach to international labor law to address what China considered a national security question was comparable to the report issued by an ILO Commission of Inquiry responding to an international trade union's complaints against the actions of the government of Poland towards the Solidarity movement back in 1984.[131]

China's increasing engagement with virtually all the IOs addressed in this monograph is suggested by the fact that there are approximately 600 universities in China that now offer courses on international law, with 64 university law schools and legal institutes offering masters degrees in international and 16 offering doctorates.[132] China's growing enmeshment in IOs and some forms of international adjudication (like the WTO's) has led to many changes in its domestic law and institutions. China's accession to the WTO alone involved extensive legal reforms throughout China, including the amendment or repeal of over 3000 domestic laws to meet the needs of the market global economy and fulfill its WTO obligations.[133]

Like the U.S., China has also lost cases in the WTO dispute settlement system, including some involving sensitive questions that once would have been seen as within its "domestic jurisdiction."[134] Like U.S. officials, Chinese officials may find it difficult to comply with some of these rulings but, one way or the other, as Karen Alter, suggests, these decisions are likely to have political effects over the long term.[135] The global demands for rule of law, including transparency, are likely to be hard to resist for both countries.

---

131   Report of the Commission of Inquiry Instituted Under Article 26 of the Constitution of the International Labour Organization to Examine the Complaint on the Observance by Poland of the Freedom of Association and Protection of the Right to Organize Convention, 1948 (No. 87), and the Right to Organise and Collective Bargaining Convention, 1949 (No. 98), 67 I.L.O. OFFICIAL BULL. (ser. B), Special Supp., at 2 (1982).

132   Conversation with Prof. Cheng, Xiamen University.

133   Xue Hanqin & Jin Qian, *International Treaties in the Chinese Domestic Legal System*, 8 CHINESE J. INT'L L. 299, 308–309 (2009). *See also* Congyan Cai, *International Law in China's Courts*, AM. J. INT'L L. (forthcoming 2016)(enumerating the many changes in Chinese laws prompted by China's increased global connections and participation in international organizations).

134   *See, e.g.,* Appellate Body Report, *China—Measures Related to the Exportation of Various Raw Materials*, WT/DS394/AB/R (Jan. 30, 2012); *id.*, *China—Measures Affecting Trading Rights and Distribution Services for Certain Publications and Audiovisual Entertainment Products*, WT/DS363/AB/R (Dec. 21, 2009).

135   *See* KAREN ALTER, THE NEW TERRAIN OF INTERNATIONAL LAW (2014), 350–359 (discussing the "altered politics" brought about by international courts within democratic polities).

Moreover, even powerful countries with a proud attachment to sovereign values like China and the U.S. tend to comply eventually with their WTO obligations. Notably China appears to have fully implemented the first two cases in which its measures were found to be WTO inconsistent, China-Auto Parts and China-IP.[136] As one of the top exporting countries in the world, China, like the U.S., relies on the WTO to maintain an open trading environment for its products. Noncompliance with WTO decisions, even sensitive ones, would cost China political capital and could encourage protectionist trends elsewhere to the detriment of Chinese exports. Indeed, China's interest in maintaining the credibility of the WTO's dispute settlement system is suggested by its growing enthusiasm for bringing WTO claims of its own.[137]

China's approach to the international investment regime (discussed in Chapter V) appears, in some respects, to emulate the recent practices of the U.S. Some of China's most recent FTAs contain provisions to safeguard China's right to regulate and "re-balance" the rights of host states and foreign investors that are quite similar to those adopted by the U.S. government.[138] While China has not yet faced the wave of investor-state arbitrations that the U.S. has had under NAFTA, Chinese officials are reacting to the potential threat to regulatory autonomy posed by investment protection treaties through many of the same tools. But, like the U.S., China, as a leading exporter and importer of foreign capital with a strong economic interest in maintaining free incoming and outgoing investment flows, is not, unlike some countries, backing out of the investment regime or investor-state arbitration. Both countries remain supporters of the underlying institutions that support the trade and investment regimes.

China and the U.S. are also comparable in another respect: both have maintained a respectful distance from international courts and tribunals. Neither

---

136   *See* World Trade Organization, Dispute Settlement: Dispute DS342: China—Measures Affecting the Imports of Automobile Parts, *at* https://www.wto.org/english/tratop_e/dispu_e/cases_e/ds342_e.htm (last visited Feb. 29, 2016) (noting that China has notified the Organization of its compliance); World Trade Organization, Dispute Settlement: Dispute DS362: China—Measures Affecting the Protection and Enforcement of Intellectual Property Rights, *at* https://www.wto.org/english/tratop_e/dispu_e/cases_e/ds362_e.htm (same).

137   *See, e.g.*, Dan Wei, *Antidumping in Emerging Countries in the Post-Crisis Era: A Case Study on Brazil and China*, 16 J. INT'L ECON. L. 921 (2013).

138   *See, e.g.*, Stephan W. Schill, *Tearing Down the Great Wall: The New Generation of Investment Treaties of the People's Republic of China*, 15 CARDOZO J. INT'L & COMP. L. 73 (2007); Axel Berger, *Hesitant Embrace: China's Recent Approach to International Investment Rule-Making*, 16 J. WORLD INVESTMENT & TRADE 843 (2015).

state is a party to the ICC or to a regional human rights court. Neither is a party to the compulsory jurisdiction of the ICJ, although both have judges on that court. And yet, both countries are nonetheless subject to the possibility of diplomatic embarrassment through the actions of some of these courts and both have used their powers on the Security Council to both hinder and encourage actions by the ICC.[139] Neither can totally ignore the diverse functions of international courts canvassed in Chapter V.

Indeed, as indicated by China's recent decision not to participate in the jurisdictional stage of its dispute with the Philippines under Annex VII of the UN Convention on the Law of the Sea, sometimes the risks to "sovereignty" posed by international adjudication, and its uncertainties, are a step too far even for China, the second most powerful economy in the world.[140] This incident is reminiscent of the U.S.'s own mixed actions with respect to the ICJ. While the U.S. has been a frequent party to ICJ cases, it refused to participate at the merits stage after it lost its jurisdictional defense in the Nicaragua case, terminated its acceptance of the Court's compulsory clause after that case, resisted ICJ compulsory clauses in recent treaties, and failed to comply with the Court's high profile decisions regarding the Vienna Convention on Diplomatic Relations and withdrew its acceptance to ICJ jurisdiction with respect to that treaty.[141] It remains unclear whether China, like the U.S. in the Nicaragua Case, will discover that simply ignoring such tribunals when these have the power to continue proceedings and issue a judgment despite the absence of one party is not a good long-term strategy. China may find, as the U.S. did after its loss in the Nicaragua Case, that it is usually better to stay and fight than to cut and run, even when the litigation involves high profile issues that strike at the heart of national security such as China's claim that it has "indisputable sovereignty" over the South China Sea and islands within it. Whether this will prove to be the case depends on the reciprocal value of the rule of law and international adjudication as a tool to enforce it. Much

---

139   *See, e.g.*, Chapter II *supra* § 9.

140   *See* Julian Ku, *Why China Will Ignore the UNCLOS Tribunal Judgment, and (Probably) Get Away With It*, OPINIO JURIS (Nov. 4, 2015), *at* http://opiniojuris.org/2015/11/04/china-faces-its-nicaragua-v-united-states-moment/; *id.*, *China Manages to File—And Not File—a Legal Brief in the Philippines Arbitration*, OPINIO JURIS (Dec. 8, 2014), *at* http://opinio-juris.org/2014/12/08/china-manages-file-not-file-legal-brief-philippines-arbitration/

141   For an overview of the U.S.'s uneasy relationship with the ICJ, *see* Sean D. Murphy, *The United States and the International Court of Justice: Coping with Antinomies*, *in* THE UNITED STATES AND INTERNATIONAL COURTS AND TRIBUNALS (Cesare Romano ed., 2008).

depends on whether China perceives a need to stay involved in the UNCLOS adjudication system that it is defying.

For all these reasons, IOs have affected, sometimes dramatically, what it means to enjoy "sovereignty" today. But this does not mean, as some scholars have suggested, that "sovereignty" or "the state" is "withering away," "waning," is "in decline," "retreat," or is already dead.[142] The challenge IOs pose to sovereignty is far more complex than that.

To the extent "sovereignty" connotes uncontested power over all matters within one's territory, absolute freedom from outside interference, or the equivalent of a no-trespassing sign forbidding entry onto private property— that is, something like Greta Garbo's demand to be left alone—that kind of sovereignty, if it ever existed, is indeed in retreat. Today there is no such thing as the "absolute" sovereignty envisioned by philosophers like Jean Bodin and Thomas Hobbes.[143] Governments no longer control everything that happens within their territory whether as a matter of fact or of law. When the boundaries of states are as porous as they are today, no government alone, no matter how autocratic or powerful, has absolute control over what happens within them. Realization of that fact, as well as threats to the global commons, led to the establishment of IOs like the League of Nations and the ILO in the first place.

Governments today are hemmed in from all directions and not only by the treaties to which they have given consent. As critics of international law like to point out, today's state is less like Hobbes' Leviathan and more like Swift's Gulliver, who finds himself in Lilliput tied down by innumerable threads held by tiny captors each of which has little power but cumulatively exercise control.[144] There is also no doubt that *inter-national* law is no longer restricted to rules made by and for states. States no longer control the making, the interpretation, or the enforcement of all rules of international law. IO organs, officials within them, and entities that they create have become semi-autonomous actors capable of exercising implied and un-enumerated powers over states including over matters of "high politics." IOs and other

---

142   *See, e.g.,* Jose E. Alvarez, *State Sovereignty Is Not Withering Away: A Few Lessons for the Future,* in REALIZING UTOPIA: THE FUTURE OF INTERNATIONAL LAW 29 (Antonio Cassese ed., 2012) (citing a number of international law and international relations scholars who suggest this is the case).

143   JEAN BODIN, ON SOVEREIGNTY (Julian H. Franklin ed. & trans., 1992); THOMAS HOBBES, LEVIATHAN (1651).

144   *See generally* John R. Bolton, *Should We Take Global Governance Seriously?,* 1 CHI. J. INT'L L. 205 (2000).

non-state actors have become *de facto* law-makers or law-enforcers by subter-
fuge or fiat. International law is also becoming ever more privatized.[145] It is not
as *inter-governmental* as it once was.

As Chapter V illustrates, "inter-state dispute settlement" is not controlled
only by states and is not just about settling their disputes. Further, the "dispute
settlers" themselves exercise considerable autonomy and their rulings have normative effects beyond the litigating parties. This has been true for some time,
as even the ICJ, although open only to states for purposes of contentious cases,
has had considerable impact on the law thanks to requests for advisory opinions issued by IOs. Even when access to international adjudication remains
limited to states as disputants (as in the WTO), it is increasingly under pressure
to be transparent to others and to accept some form of non-state participation,
as through amicus briefs. International criminal courts, regional human rights
tribunals, and investor-state arbitrations are not as state-centric as the ICJ or
the WTO Dispute Settlement system. In these venues, independent prosecutors and private attorney generals capable of making claims against states play
significant roles, including as *de facto* law-makers.

Governments have been complicit in, even if sometimes surprised by, these
developments. As the Permanent Court of Justice indicated in *Wimbledon*,
when states make treaties, including those that establish IOs and courts, they
exercise, not diminish, their sovereignty.[146] That premise extends beyond
treaty-making. States have turned to IOs, including courts, in pursuit of their
short or long term self-interest. Whether the results are described as forms
of "global governance," "global administrative law," species of "global constitutionalism," "humanity's law," or new forms of "*ius gentinum*," there is little
doubt that today's governments secure benefits from, even while resisting,
aspects of institutionalization.[147]

---

145   *See, e.g.*, Fabrizio Cafaggi, *The Many Features of Transnational Private Rule-Making:
Unexplored Relationships Between Leges Mercatoriae and Leges Regulatoriae*, 36 U. PA. J.
INT'L L. 101 (2015).

146   *Case of the S.S. Wimbledon*, 1923 P.C.I.J. (ser. A) No. 1, at 25.

147   *See, e.g.*, Benedict Kingsbury, Nico Krisch & Richard B. Stewart, *supra* note 78 (describ-
ing forms of "global administrative law" and "*ius gentium*"); Ruti Teitel, *Humanity's
Law: Rule of Law for the New Global Politics*, 35 CORNELL INT'L L.J. 355 (2002);
DAVID SCHNEIDERMAN, CONSTITUTIONALIZING ECONOMIC GLOBALIZATION:
INVESTMENT RULES AND DEMOCRACY'S PROMISE (2008); Alec Stone Sweet &
Jud Mathews, *Proportionality Balancing and Global Constitutionalism*, 47 COLUMB.
J. TRANSNAT'L L. 73 (2008); *see also* THE EXERCISE OF PUBLIC AUTHORITY BY
INTERNATIONAL INSTITUTIONS: ADVANCING INTERNATIONAL INSTITUTIONAL LAW
(Armin von Bogdandy et al. eds., 2010).

Those who see in all of this "the end of the state" may be confusing a normative agenda with reality. To use "absolute sovereignty" as the starting point for measuring the "decline" of the modern state is to deploy an old myth to propagate a new one. Even Bodin never argued that sovereignty was absolute. He accepted the idea that sovereigns were bound by natural and divine law and that they had duties to respect property rights, for instance.[148] In the real world, sovereignty has always been measured by the capacity to deploy different tools of power subject to degrees of state control. No single description of what "sovereignty" means is likely to satisfy because the set of attributes that defines what it means to be a state changes over time and varies with the nation or government in question. Unlike the legal requisites for statehood, "sovereignty" remains a malleable concept around which people define themselves. Ever since Westphalia, sovereigns have pooled, shared, delimited, or delegated away some of their powers, even if nationality ties have retained a powerful hold over the identity of persons.

The dictum in *Wimbledon* reflects reality. Sovereignty and global governance are not binary oppositions or the products of a zero sum game. States may gain as much or more as they purportedly lose when they adhere to a treaty, join an international organization, or agree to binding international adjudication. Governments give their consent to such arrangements because, as Duncan Snidal and Kenneth Abbott point out, such arrangements enable them to secure the benefits of centralization and independence.[149] It is true that states' functionalist needs have steadily risen over time with globalization but we need to remember that states have had such needs for a long time. The drafters of the U.S. Constitution reconciled their desires for popular sovereignty with their equal demands that the new United States would fulfill promises to foreign nations (including the many foreign debtors at the founding). The U.S. founders discarded the myth of absolute sovereignty in the drafting of the U.S. Constitution. John Adams and Alexander Hamilton, for example, did not see international obligations as trespasses on sovereignty. They saw the duties imposed by the law of nations to be correlated with rights that would enable the U.S. to take its rightful place among independent nations. For them, as with today's rulers of the U.S. or China, the exercise of sovereignty requires fair, equal, and sometimes obligatory relationships. They recognized that a country with relatively few connections, like today's North

---

148   BODIN, *supra* note 143, at 44–45. But note that Bodin insisted that no human law could appeal to it.

149   Kenneth W. Abbott & Duncan Snidal, *Why States Act Through Formal International Organizations*, 42 J. CONFLICT RESOL. 3 (1998).

Korea, enjoys much less "sovereignty" than others. Those who established the United States devised a government of limited powers that would, for example, nonetheless respect the rights of foreign investors and be able to enter into binding inter-state agreements to secure their rights.[150]

Judge Xue Hanqin agrees. "Global governance and state sovereignty are the two sides of the same coin," she notes. "Without either of them, there would be no international law...There is no point in arguing about whether the Westphalian system is still functioning, or whether or not sovereignty remains a valid notion. From the inception of that system, there has been no absolute state sovereignty. From day one, when states engaged in relations with each other through law, they had to give up some of their sovereignty. A result of the development of international relations in recent decades is the expanding scope of international regulations and more restriction on sovereign rights."[151]

Statehood is not waning as a legal concept, any more than nationality is as a political one. What the "S" word empowers nations to do is evolving, as it always has. It is the rate of change in the evolution of sovereign powers that has changed as well as some of the agents for that change. States remain the primary engines of international law but other actors, including IOs, are now change agents as well. States retain considerable tools to keep IOs at bay, even if these are not purely the "agents" of the collective state principals that some like to think. The progressive narrative of ever-rising levels of "global gover-nance" that some self-identified "Grotian" international lawyers describe is something of a myth, at least to the extent it suggests a steady upward and one way flow of power from the local or national to the global. If the legal-ization (including judicialization) of the world has a narrative, it is, in all likelihood, something of a dialectical story, that is, an ever-shifting series of efforts to empower the global that encounters sovereign counter-reactions and adjustments, producing cycles back and forth.[152] Power in the age of IOs flows both ways: the global empowers the local and the local's view of what interna-tional rules mean influence the global. The international legal process is not

---

150 Daniel Hulsebosch, *Being Seen Like a State: The Constitution and Its International Audiences at the Founding* (unpublished manuscript).

151 Xue Hanqin, Remarks, *in Global Governance, State Sovereignty and the Future of International Law*, 107 ASIL PROC. 491 (2013).

152 *See also* KARL POLANYI, THE GREAT TRANSFORMATION (1944) (describing histori-cal cycles of "utopian market liberalism" followed by reactions to empower government regulation). *See also* the descriptions of developments in the investment regime in Chapter V *supra* § 5.

simply a top-down exercise dictating results to passive states; international law trickles up and not just down.

As states become aware of the scope of the powers that they have delegated, they re-calibrate their effects. As Eric Stein pointed out, the more an international regime exercises regulatory powers, the more likely sovereign backlash is likely to occur, as Grotian aspirations encounter complaints of "democratic deficits."[153] Indeed, the rise in the numbers of democracies in the world over recent decades makes such reactions more likely, as more polities are empowered to challenge the legitimacy of rule by "unaccountable" international elites (including judges or arbitrators).[154]

The backlash against the investment regime, including investor-state arbitral decisions described in Chapter v, is an example of the "return of the state" that may occur with respect to other international regimes or IOs.[155] In some quarters we are seeing disillusionment with the formulas for "good governance" pursued by international financial institutions as well as the European Union, for example. Similarly, the advice on offer by IMF experts is, particularly after the global economic crisis of 2008, viewed with considerable skepticism.[156] Those who pin their hopes for world order on the progress made within Europe to eclipse "national parochialisms" may be dismayed by how much those "parochial" sentiments continue to matter, even within Europe, where the citizens of the UK, Germany, Greece, and Italy, for example, do not always appear to be of one mind about following the dictates of European institutions or of EU officials. "Euro-skepticism," including about the value of internationalized "expert" rule extends beyond Europe.[157]

At the same time, sovereignty is not, and never has been, a one-size-fits-all proposition. International law's "sovereign equality" has always been narrow and formal, its operation largely confined to procedural rules such as "equality of arms" within international courts and tribunals. The capacity for states to resist the mission creep of IOs or the impact of the legal products they produce is not evenly distributed. Some sovereigns are far more constrained by "global

---

153   Eric Stein, *International Integration and Democracy: No Love at First Sight*, 95 AM. J. INT'L L. 489 (2001).

154   As recognized by Stein, *id.* at 492.

155   José E. Alvarez, *The Return of the State*, 20 MINN. J. INT'L L. 223 (2011).

156   *See, e.g.*, Blustein, *supra* note 123; *see generally* Katharina Pistor, *Global Network Finance: Institutional Innovation in the Global Financial Marketplace*, 37 J. COMP. ECON. 552 (2009).

157   *See, e.g.*, David Kennedy, *Challenging Expert Rule: The Politics of Global Governance*, 27 SYDNEY L. REV. 2 (2005).

governance" than others. There is no single recipe to meeting the challenge to sovereignty posed by IOs, and even when prescriptions exist not all states can effectively deploy them.

3   The IO Challenge to the Rule of Law

Particularly since the end of the Cold War, the UN system has repeatedly invoked the rule of law as justification for much of what it does. As discussed in prior chapters, IOs have turned to the rule of law (and often rule by lawyers, judges, and arbitrators) to respond to threats to the international peace, in reaction to abuses of state power (as with respect to human rights), to address pandemics, to harmonize civil aviation practices, to respond to terrorism, and to punish war criminals.

The IMF and the World Bank's pursuit of "good governance" embraces, as an important dimension, the improvement of the internal regulation of states, including the ways national courts enable private contracting and the establishment and operation of businesses. Promoting "justice and the rule of law" is, as noted in Chapter IV, a prominent feature of the World Bank's efforts to: improve the performance of judicial institutions; advise on criminal justice reform and security; support mediation and other accountability tools with respect to land, extractive industries, and urban development; promote reforms to improve the business and investment climate; enable legal empowerment (as with respect to NGOs); and secure transitional justice in "fragile" states or those emerging from periods of mass atrocity.[158] The World Bank's Integrity Vice Presidency, which attempts to discourage corruption among those with whom the Bank does business, is all about enforcing the rule of law.[159] The World Bank Group's annual "Doing Business Reports" provide extensive rule of law rankings for states, purporting to judge the progress states are making on everything from enabling the registration of property rights to the handling of construction permits.[160] These efforts are of a piece with many of the conditions that the IMF attempts to impose on recipients of its struc-

---

158   See, e.g., World Bank, Brief: Justice and the Rule of Law (Apr. 28, 2015), at http://www
        .worldbank.org/en/topic/governance/brief/justice-rights-and-public-safety.

159   For a description of the World Bank's anti-corruption regime, see Laurence Boisson
        de Chazournes & Edouard Fromageau, *Balancing the Scales: The World Bank Sanctions
        Process and Access to Remedies*, 23 EUR. J. INT'L L. 963 (2012).

160   See, e.g., World Bank, Doing Business 2016: Measuring Regulatory Quality and Efficiency,
        at http://www.doingbusiness.org/reports/global-reports/doing-business-2016.

tural adjustment loans. For its part, UNCTAD complements such efforts by, for example, producing annual "World Investment Reports" which keep track of changes in national laws and states' engagements with investment protection treaties.[161] As discussed in Chapter IV, the WHO's revised IHRs and Framework Convention on Tobacco, while reliant on "soft" forms of enforcement or normative development, resorts to the rule of law (and lawyers) to address matters once left almost entirely to health care professionals.

IOs have also relied on legal justifications to deal with security issues. Since 1999, some 250 Security Council resolutions, for example, have mentioned the "rule of law."[162] The rule of law paradigm is especially apparent with respect to UN peacekeeping. Since 2001, every UN mandated peacekeeping mission has been charged with a rule of law mandate, including tasks to promote, in the target state, judicial reform, constitutional reform, general law reform, enhanced rule of law compliance in public administration, greater legal awareness in the general population and greater access to justice, law enforcement reforms, or changes to policies pursued in places of detention, including prisons.[163] According to a 2009 report by the Secretary-General, rule of law programming included at that time 120 member states, from every region.[164] The UN's rule of law efforts have, inevitably, been bureaucratized. New UN bureaucracies have been established, such as the Rule of Law Coordination and Resource Group, amidst constant efforts to mainstream or harmonize such efforts as through "guidance notes" from the Secretary-General or instruments issued by the Office of the High Commissioner for Human Rights, UNICEF, and others.[165]

---

161 *See, e.g.*, United Nations Conference on Trade and Development, World Investment Report 2015, Table III.1, U.N. Doc. UNCTAD/WIR/2015, *at* http://unctad.org/en/PublicationsLibrary/wir2015_en.pdf.

162 Carolyn M. Evans, *Finding Obligation: Foundation for a More Accountable Security Council*, paper presented at Symposium: *International Organisations and the Rule of Law: Perils and Promise*, Victoria University of Wellington (Dec. 2015).

163 *See, e.g.*, Report of the Secretary-General, The Rule of Law at the National and International Levels, U.N. Doc. A/63/64 (Mar. 12, 2008); Report of the Secretary-General, Strengthening and Coordinating United Nations Rule of Law Activities, U.N. Doc. A/63/226 (Aug. 6, 2008); Report of the Secretary-General, Annual Report on strengthening and coordinating United Nations rule of law activities, U.N. Doc. A/64/298 (Aug. 17, 2009) [hereinafter Annual Report 2009]. *See also* Richard Zajac Sannerholm, *Looking Back, Moving Forward: UN Peace Operations and Rule of Law Assistance in Africa, 1989–2010*, 4 HAGUE J. ON RULE LAW 359 (2012).

164 Annual Report 2009 *supra* note 163, ¶ 3.

165 *See id.* ¶¶ 64–74. *See also* United Nations Development Programme, Guidance Note on Assessing the Rule of Law Using Institutional and Context Analysis, *at* http://www.undp

While, to be sure, the "good governance" efforts of these IOs include activities not directly related to the rule of law, such as improvements to the effectiveness or efficiency of governmental regulations, the core focus remains on seeking improvements in how states implement law internationally (as between themselves or between them and IOs) as well as nationally (as between a state's own nationals and businesses). This common goal cuts across the multiple tasks engaged by diverse international adjudicators described in Chapter V. States delegate authority to adjudicators to settle disputes, find facts, interpret and make law, and even engage in governance because of faith in the rule of law. The proliferation of international courts and tribunals reflects a hope that lawyers might resolve what politicians and diplomats alone cannot. From regional human rights courts to international criminal courts to the arbitration of trade and investment disputes, all are seen as enforcing the legal accountability of governments and/or individuals.

The proliferation and institutionalization of rule of law activity explains its prominence in the Millennium Declaration of 2000 and thereafter in the 2005 World Summit Outcome.[166] The General Assembly and its Sixth Committee have since debated the idea of the rule of law at both the national and international levels, leading to the High Level Declaration of 2012 affirming that "the rule of law applies to all States equally, and to international organizations, including the United Nations and its principal organs, and that respect for and promotion of the rule of law and justice should guide all of their activities and accord predictability and legitimacy to their actions."[167] The General Assembly has elevated rule of law promotion to UN Charter status on more than one occasion. Thus, in 2010, it proclaimed as follows:

> *Reaffirming* that human rights, the rule of law and democracy are interlinked and mutually reinforcing and that they belong to the universal and indivisible core values and principles of the United Nations,

---

.org/content/undp/en/home/librarypage/democratic-governance/access_to_justice-andruleoflaw/guidance-note-on-assessing-the-rule-of-law-using-institutional-a.html. Note that such Guidance Notes are yet another example of legally ambiguous "soft law" instruments.

166 General Assembly, United Nations Millennium Declaration, ¶¶ 9, 30, UN Doc. A/55/L.2 (Sept. 6, 2000); General Assembly, 2005 World Summit Outcome ¶¶ 11, 21, 24(b) 25(a), 119, 134, UN Doc. A/Res/60/1 (Oct. 24, 2005).

167 General Assembly, Declaration of the high-level meeting of the General Assembly on the rule of law at the national and international levels ¶ 2, U.N. Doc. A/67/L.1 (Sept. 24, 2012). *See also* Kenneth J. Keith, *The International Rule of Law*, 28 LEIDEN J. INT'L L. 403 (2015).

Reaffirming also the need for universal adherence to and implementation of the rule of law at both the national and international levels and its solemn commitment to an international order based on the rule of law and international law . . .

Convinced that the promotion of and respect for the rule of law at the national and international levels, as well as justice and good governance, should guide the activities of the United Nations and of its Member States . . .

4. *Calls upon* the United Nations system to systematically address . . . aspects of the rule of law in relevant activities, recognizing the importance of the rule of law to virtually all areas of United Nations engagement . . .[168]

The UN system's efforts to export the rule of law to states perceived as suffering from a governance deficit have been affirmed by UN officials at the highest levels. Consider the following statement by then-Secretary-General Kofi Annan:

[The rule of law] refers to a principle of governance in which all persons, institutions and entities, public and private, including the State itself, are accountable to laws that are publicly promulgated, equally enforced and independently adjudicated, and which are consistent with international human rights norms and standards. It requires, as well, measures to ensure adherence to the principles of supremacy of law, equality before the law, accountability to the law, fairness in the application of the law, separation of powers, participation in decision-making, legal certainty, avoidance of arbitrariness and procedural and legal transparency.[169]

As is suggested by these proclamations, the rule of law is widely seen as embracing procedural as well as substantive dimensions. According to the paradigm adopted by IOs (including international courts), the rule of law requires the equal application of law to all by neutral adjudicators but it also includes, substantively, extending to all individuals the protections of human rights. The rule of law as a principle of global governance draws significantly from the requisites for the national rule of law elaborated by legal philosophers

---

168   G.A. Res. 64/116 preamble and ¶ 4 (Dec. 16, 2009).

169   Report of the Secretary-General, The rule of law and transitional justice in conflict and post-conflict societies, ¶ 6, U.N. Doc. S/2004/616 (Aug. 23, 2004).

like Lon Fuller and Jeremy Waldron.[170] The concepts that Annan draws on—
the supremacy of the law, equality before the law, separation of powers, the
ostensible connections between democracy and the rule of law, the need to
avoid arbitrary and non-transparent actions—have their origins in national
law. The proposition that IO efforts to establish or strengthen the elements of
the national rule of law are themselves governance activities that require IOs
to satisfy the rule of law has been picked up by scholars, particularly those who
examine public law and seek to perfect it at the international level.[171]

This section addresses the disconnect between this aspiration and reality. It
argues that the challenges that IOs present to legal positivism and to states (sections 1 and 2) help to explain why it remains a daunting prospect to conceive of
or apply the "international rule of law." To be sure, there remain disagreements
over what are the core elements of the national rule of law. As a prominent
scholar has suggested, while everyone is for the rule of law, this posture is made
easier by the absence of a single definition of what it is actually is (even at
the national level), varying views about when it is relevant and to whom, and
by the hypocritical tendency to apply whatever we think the rule of law is to
others but not ourselves.[172] Such disagreements have fueled debates about
how or even whether IOs should be in the business of seeking to export the
rule of law. Simon Chesterman, for example, has warned against using the rule
of law to pursue normative agendas, and has queried when it is relevant and
to whom; he is troubled by the hypocritical tendency to derive specific human
rights and economic policies from the concept.[173] He urges restraint with
respect to how the rule of law is deployed, urging that it be treated as a tool "to
restrain sovereign power," rather than to define a status—such as the need to
establish a certain form of democracy on the model of some Western states—
that simply reflects an ideological agenda.[174] Waldron comes to a skeptical
conclusion as well, urging that the international rule of law not be seen as

---

170   *See, e.g.,* LON L. FULLER, THE MORALITY OF LAW (1964); Jeremy Waldron, *The Concept*
       and the Rule of Law, 43 GA. L. REV. 1 (2008).

171   *See, e.g.,* Richard B. Stewart, *Remedying Disregard in Global Regulatory Governance:*
       Accountability, Participation, and Responsiveness, 108 AM. J. INT'L L. 211, 220 (2014)
       (describing techniques of "disciplining administrative decision making, familiar in
       domestic law" at the global level "to limit decisions on the basis of power and expediency
       and to promote the rule of law"). *See also* EYAL BENVENISTI, THE LAW OF GLOBAL
       GOVERNANCE 89–99 (2014).

172   *See generally* BRIAN Z. TAMANAHA, ON THE RULE OF LAW: HISTORY, POLITICS,
       THEORY (2004).

173   Simon Chesterman, *An International Rule of Law?*, 56 AM. J. COMP. L. 331, 360 (2008).

174   *Id.* at 360–361.

benefitting sovereigns but as a set of prescriptions to prevent sovereigns from harming people, as well as to make IOs, to the extent they too exert power over individuals, accountable.[175]

At the same time, despite disagreements about the relative significance of various factors among leading rule of law scholars, many agree on its fundamental core elements at least at the national level. The difficulties of adhering to the suggestions made by the Security Council, the General Assembly, and Annan in the quotations above are made clear if we seek to apply these core elements to IOs.

Consider the six core elements of the rule of law as elaborated in a well-received book by Tom Bingham. According to Lord Bingham, the rule of law demands:

1. Equality; that is the equal application of the law;
2. Clarity, publicity, and judicial application; that is public law that is accessible, intelligible, clear and predictable and publicly administered by courts;
3. The exercise of legally bound discretion;
4. Good faith exercise of power in accordance with the purpose for which powers were conferred, without exceeding the limits of such powers;
5. The protection of fundamental human rights (including the principle of *nullem crimen* for criminal defendants and the right to a fair trial, along with rights to liberty, security, and property);
6. Effective remedies (the availability of other means to resolve civil disputes without prohibitive cost or delay).[176]

When we turn to IOs and their legal products, it is easier to find deviations from Bingham's six rule of law qualities than faithful compliance with them. While, to be sure, equality before the law (Bingham's first element) is respected procedurally before international courts, it is not a quality that we otherwise associate with many other aspects of IOs. Equality among states or their peoples is not a quality that comes to mind when we look at the voting procedures of the Security Council or of the executive boards of the World Bank or the IMF, much less with how the heads of those respective institutions are selected and by whom. Indeed, at this writing, the UN is debating whether the Security

---

175 *See, e.g.*, Jeremy Waldron, *Are Sovereigns Entitled to the Benefit of the International Rule of Law?*, 22 EUR. J. INT'L L. 315 (2011); Jeremy Waldron, *The Pre and Post UN Charter Order* (Nov. 1, 2015) (on file with author).

176 TOM BINGHAM, THE RULE OF LAW (2010).

Council will enable the General Assembly to have any choice with respect to possible candidates for the next Secretary-General, and no one knows when the Europeans and the u.s. will lessen their grip on the top posts at the IMF and World Bank, respectively.[177] While horizontal equity in the sense of "one state, one vote" is a quality associated with some organs of IOs, it is not a quality generally applicable to IOs that aspire to universal membership. As critical scholars like Antony Anghie have argued, a great deal of the law (hard and soft) issued by our governance institutions take the form of Western exports of law—often from countries that are already in compliance with its terms—to countries of the Global South who bear the brunt of adapting to the new regulatory needs expected of them, becoming the "rule-takers."[178] Anghie describes IO rule of law efforts themselves as contemporary examples of the "civilizing mission" initially pursued by colonial powers on those identified as "the other."[179]

IOs do not operate in the publicly accessible, transparent manner suggested by Bingham's second quality. Even if by "transparency" we mean open deliberation and participation by all state governments (rather than by the peoples within them), it is not a quality associated with either the UN Security Council or the conditionality decisions undertaken by the IMF, for instance. Bingham's third quality, legally bound discretion, is hardly achievable if, as discussed in section 1 above, there are doubts about whether IOs or organs or officials within them are subject to precisely demarcated legal limits on their actions, for example the principles and purposes stated in the UN Charter or the limitations on interfering in politics imposed on the IMF under its Articles of Agreement. And even assuming legal limits on IO actions exist, there are precious few international adjudicative venues for applying such limits—as anticipated by Bingham's second element—and therefore few examples of impartially applied (as opposed to self-judging) exercises of legally bound discretion in accord with his third element. While the ICJ might, if asked, provide an advisory opinion to clarify the scope of an IO's discretion, it would be rare indeed for a contentious case before it to result in a legally binding decision that questions the legality of an IO's action.[180] Moreover, if the implications of

---

177   See, e.g., Cara Anna, *UN cracks open secrecy on selecting next secretary-general*, Assoc. Press, Dec. 15, 2015, *at* http://bigstory.ap.org/article/c654f6790573475387eb62502806 bde9/un-cracks-open-secrecy-selecting-next-secretary-general.

178   *See generally* Antony Anghie, Imperialism, Sovereignty and the Making of International Law (2005).

179   *Id.* at 113–114.

180   While the *Lockerbie* cases resulting from Libya's claims against the UK's and the U.S.'s actions in the Security Council raised such questions, the ICJ deflected these and

Bingham's second and third elements are that judicial challenges to the legality of public law should be open to participation by the public, the restrictions placed on the ICJ's contentious jurisdiction—where those seeking to participate as either third parties or as amicus are often denied participation—make that highly unlikely.

As this suggests, Bingham's rule of law qualities anticipate the protection of persons, not governments. Waldron does the same. He argues that since the national rule of law is largely about protecting individuals from the abuse of state power, it would be odd indeed to suggest that when we apply the rule of law at the international level it ought to benefit states *inter se*.[181] He points out that ensuring that states are treated equally does not guarantee that their peoples are protected by the rule of law.[182]

There is also considerable room to question whether IOs that have seen remarkable mission creep—that is, most of them—are in compliance with Bingham's fourth element. If the rule of law requires the exercise of IO power to be justified on the basis of the original intent of those states that established today's IOs, or if it requires faithful and express consideration of whether all of an IO's current members would endorse what it is currently doing, much of the autonomous action of today's IOs would be subject to question. This much is clear from the explanation provided for evolving IO charters in section 1 above. Thanks in part to the practice of IO organs, in-house legal counsels issuing empowering office opinions, and enabling judicial opinions, IO constitutions have been dynamically interpreted as "living" constitutions whereby inquiries about the original intent of treaty drafters have given way to justifications for IO actions based on teleological charter interpretations, "implied powers," and deference to subsequent institutional practice based on a presumption of legality or the principle of effectiveness. These enabling precepts, endorsed by ICJ advisory opinions,[183] have enabled the ILO to transform itself into a technical assistance agency, the ICAO and the WHO to become institutional bulwarks against intentional terrorist threats to safe air travel and global health, respectively, the IMF to change from fixer of exchange rates to a decider of desirable macroeconomic policies generally, the World Bank to become a tool for good governance writ large and not mere funder of infrastructure projects, and the

---

implied that once the Council crosses the threshold of binding Chapter VII action, the prospects for judicial examination of its actions are considerably reduced. *See* Alvarez, *supra* note 99.

181   Waldron, *Are Sovereigns Entitled, supra* note 175.

182   *Id.* at 326.

183   *See supra* § 1; *see also* Arato, *supra* note 85.

Security Council to read its license to take police action as permission to establish "subsidiary bodies" that few would suggest were under contemplation back in 1945, including boundary demarcation bodies, claims commissions, "smart" sanctions bodies, and international criminal courts. All of these examples are dubious candidates for fulfilling Bingham's second, third, and fourth elements for the rule of law.

Of course the *Kadi* decisions in the European Court of Justice have put the Security Council's compliance with Bingham's fifth quality, which envisions human rights compliance by law-makers themselves, under the spotlight— and this is so even if we assume that the Council's counter-terrorism sanctions are not really criminal sanctions but civil penalties that require compliance with Bingham's less stringent conditions under his sixth rule of law element.[184] While the Council has, in response to *Kadi*-type challenges, established an ombudsperson procedure to address delisting claims under its Al-Qaida Sanctions Committee, it has not done so for its other sanctions programs.[185] Thus, even if we assume that the ombudsperson procedure is adequate to comply with Bingham's expectations for fair procedure for the "civil" claim of being denied access to one's money or the right to travel, it does nothing to satisfy rule of law expectations for the other sixteen Council sanctions programs that lack even that mechanism.

There are also serious questions about whether international criminal courts fully respect the *nullem crimen* principle included in Bingham's fifth rule of law element. Justice Robertson, dissenting in the Special Court for Sierra Leone's conviction of Norman based on the proposition that enlisting child soldiers was a crime back in 1996, argued that his co-judges violated that fundamental principle of legality.[186] Others have criticized as "radical" and "haphazard" the Special Tribunal for Lebanon's remarkable finding in 2011 that customary international law recognizes the crime of international terrorism and permits prosecuting individuals on the basis that they were conducting a joint criminal enterprise.[187] Interestingly, that tribunal, as did the majority of judges in the

---

184   *See* Chapter V *supra* § 5.

185   For a description of the ombudsperson innovation, see Grant L. Willis, *Security Council Targeted Sanctions, Due Process and the 1267 Ombudsperson*, 42 GEO. J. INT'L L. 673 (2011).

186   Prosecutor v. Sam Hinga Norman, Decision on Preliminary Motion Based on Lack of Jurisdiction, Dissenting Opinion of Justice Robertson, Case No. SCSL-2004–14-AR72(E) (Special Ct. for Sierra Leone May 31, 2004). *See also* Chapter V *supra* § 4 (discussing the decision and dissent at greater length).

187   Ben Saul, *Legislating from a Radical Hague: The United Nations Special Tribunal for Lebanon Invents an International Crime of Transnational Terrorism*, 24 LEIDEN J. INT'L L. 677 (2011). *See* Interlocutory Decision on the Applicable Law, *supra* note 66.

Norman case, drew considerably on IO evidentiary sources (including statements made by UN organs and UN officials) to prove that the relevant customary crimes existed.[188] This suggests that the some of the challenges that IOs pose to legal positivism, discussed at length in section 1 above, may explain the problems they confront in satisfying rule of law expectations.

The most noted rule of law failing associated with IOs concerns their inability to conform with Bingham's fifth and sixth elements when they themselves are responsible for inflicting harm on others. A combination of immunity from national court jurisdiction, uncertainty of applicable primary and (despite the ILC's efforts) secondary rules, and lack of cognizable international adjudicative venues with jurisdiction to consider claims against IOs has meant that many victims of IO malfeasance (with the possible exception of IO employees who may have access to administrative tribunals for this purpose) fail to find a forum to hear their complaints or to secure a legal remedy against the responsible organization. There is now a growing literature concerning the plight of victims of IO abuse—from children who have been subjected to sexual abuse by those engaged in UN peacekeeping operations to Haitian cholera victims who allege that the UN was responsible for spreading the disease—who have no judicial remedy to provide them with accountability as envisioned by Bingham's rule of law elements.[189]

Bingham and other rule of law scholars share, in addition, an assumption that the rule of law requires that law be minimally effective. A state whose laws, however well crafted, are disregarded, they would argue, is in no sense a rule of law state. Of course whether international law secures compliance has been debated for decades. Skepticism abounds about whether states abide by their international obligations, including those generated by IOs. There remains considerable doubt about whether Louis Henkin was right or just optimistic when he asserted that "almost all nations observe almost all principles of international law and almost all of their obligations almost all of the time."[190] Many scholars have argued that the widespread ratification of human rights treaties

---

188   *See* Interlocutory Decision on the Applicable Law, *supra* note 66.

189   *See generally* Waldron, the Pre and Post UN Charter Order, *supra* note 175 (noting that failures to confront the need for legal accountability for such failings undermines the UN's claim that it both promotes and is faithful to the rule of law). *See also* Bruce Rashkow, *Remedies for Harm Caused by* UN *Peacekeepers*, AM. J. INT'L L. UNBOUND, Apr. 2, 2014, *at* https://www.asil.org/blogs/remedies-harm-caused-un-peacekeepers; Alvarez, *supra* note 119.

190   LOUIS HENKIN, HOW NATIONS BEHAVE: LAW AND FOREIGN POLICY 47 (2d ed. 1979).

reflects the hypocrisy of states, not the effectiveness of law.[191] Others have suggested that even if Henkin is generally correct, those international rules that
appear not to generate widespread compliance—such as the duty to avoid the
use of torture—are so significant to the rule of law that it seems petty to point
out that indeed states do manage to comply with their duty to maintain most
of their export tariffs at the levels promised to the WTO, for example.

These two rule of law deficits, IOs' alleged accountability and compliance
gaps, have received considerable academic attention. Some have suggested
that neither is as serious as has been suggested. Keohane and Grant have
argued that since IOs are subject to no less than seven accountability mechanisms—hierarchical, supervisory, fiscal, legal, market-based, peer-to-peer, and
public reputational—IOs are in reality more "accountable" than are either
states or NGOs.[192] Some have pointed to hopeful signs that, while IOs remain
less subject to forms of legal accountability than even states (given the lack of
possible judicial venues and their enjoyment of sometimes absolute immunity
before national courts), the other six mechanisms enumerated by Keohane
and Grant result in political pressures that can, on occasion, enable forms of
legal recourse on behalf of those harmed by IO action.[193] Such optimism might
be justified based on examples of some cases where national courts have
punctured the IO veil and rendered IO members liable for acts performed on
behalf of an IO.[194] There are also some occasions where national courts have
interpreted the treaty-based immunities enjoyed by IOs narrowly and permitted actions directly against such organizations.[195] Some scholars have also

---

191   *See, e.g.*, Oona A. Hathaway, *Do Human Rights Treaties Make a Difference?*, 111 YALE L.J.
       1935 (2002).

192   Ruth W. Grant & Robert O. Keohane, *Accountability and Abuses of Power in World Politics*,
       99 AM. POL. SCI. REV. 29 (2005).

193   This is, of course, a common explanation for the Security Council's establishment of
       its ombudsperson procedure for the al-Qaida Sanctions Regime (as noted in Chapter II
       supra § 7), but it may also explain due process reforms to the World Bank's regime for
       sanctioning those charged with corruption. *See* de Chazournes & Fromageau, *supra*
       note 159. It may also help to explain some national courts' efforts to make inroads on the
       immunities enjoyed by some IOs in order to secure their greater accountability. *See, e.g.*,
       August Reinisch, *The Immunity of International Organizations and the Jurisdiction of their
       Administrative Tribunals*, 7 CHINESE J. INT'L L. 285 (2008).

194   *See, e.g.*, Kristen Boon, *Mothers of Srebrenica Decision: Dutch Court holds The Netherlands
       Responsible for 300 Deaths in 1995 Massacre*, OPINIO JURIS, July 17, 2014, *at* http://
       opiniojuris.org/2014/07/17/mothers-srebrenica-decision-dutch-high-court-holds-
       netherlands-responsible-300-deaths-1995-massacre/

195   *See, e.g.*, Reinisch, *supra* note 193.

defended international law's effectiveness. Thus, Teitel and Howse argue that traditional "compliance" inquiries are misdirected and the alleged compliance gap is not quite as large as has been suggested, once we pay greater attention to the complex legal processes set in motion by IOs and their interlocutors (such as NGOs).[196]

These rule of law challenges need to be considered in light of IOs' departures from the rigors of legal positivism discussed in section 1. As section 1 suggests, IOs have encouraged a broader trend towards "informal international lawmaking."[197] As noted above, that IOs have encouraged recourse to various forms of "soft law" is not, in itself, responsible for the possibility that international law is ineffective or may lack "compliance." As Howse and Teitel (among others) contend, soft law should not be equated with soft compliance.[198] But the fact that IO law-making is hard to reconcile with the tenets of legal positivism and poses challenges to traditional conceptions of the rule of law (including Bingham's) is still worth attention. How can we address questions about whether states or others "comply" with IO-generated law or whether IOs are accountable to those whom they harm if we are unclear about whether legally binding "obligations" exist to begin with?

Bingham, like most national rule of law scholars and legal positivists, assumes that the rule of law is about binding rules that can be distinguished from political or moral standards. This is essential to Bingham's second rule of law element: the need for clarity, publicity, and capacity for legal adjudication. These elements are necessary to the rule of law for reasons other than securing judicial enforcement. Rule of law scholars insist on the qualities of clarity and publicity because, they argue, stakeholders—and their legal advisors—need to know in advance and with reasonable clarity what the law prohibits, permits, or requires. The qualities of clarity and publicity are deemed essential because legal rules, by their very nature, require a certain level of constancy and predictability. Rule of law scholars, in short, assume, like legal positivists, that law is the product of authorized (and therefore foreseeable) law-makers—that law needs to be perceived as coming from legitimate legislative processes that enable the application of relatively constricted principles of legal interpretation premised on such processes, including recourse to legislative intent.

As this monograph repeatedly shows, these assumptions about the "inherent" qualities of law are difficult to satisfy at the international level

---

196   *See, e.g.,* Robert Howse & Ruti Teitel, *Beyond Compliance: Rethinking Why International Law Really Matters,* 1 GLOBAL POL'Y 127 (2010).

197   *See also* Pauwelyn, Wessel & Wouters, *When Structures Become Shackles, supra* note 3.

198   Howse & Teitel, *supra* note 196, at 134–135.

where "legislation" or "law-making" occurs through a variety of methods. If attainment of the international rule of law requires securing all the qualities suggested by Bingham's second element above, and in particular requires fulfilling these "inherent" qualities of law itself, this is a formidable obstacle in the age of IOs and "informal" law-making. Indeed, difficulties in extrapolating the basic values of the rule of law from the national to the international leads scholar (now ICJ judge) James Crawford to conclude that "we have only enclaves of the rule of law in international affairs."[199] To the extent IOs want to be judged, as Annan suggests, on the basis of their compliance with the rule of law and their successful promotion of it, they (and international legal scholars generally) may need to be come up with a better definition of what contemporary international law is—hard, soft, or in between. It is difficult to find out whether IOs are in fact contributing to the international rule of law if we remain uncertain what international obligations in the world of IOs are. While the informality of IO-generated law is not responsible for either the lack of IO accountability or the relative ineffectiveness of IO law, all three are inter-related.

One reason why it is difficult to make IOs accountable is that it is difficult to identify with precision the rules to which IOs are subject. This is one of the critiques of the ILC's recent effort to identify (or progressively develop) relevant secondary rules with respect to the responsibility of international organizations.[200] As noted, it is not clear what primary rules are applicable to IOs (or whether these include any and all human rights), much less secondary rules. There is relatively little practice with respect to both and, as the ILC itself acknowledges, considerable doubt about whether IOs share enough common traits as international legal persons to enable consistent secondary rules to apply to all of them. It is not clear that the same primary and secondary rules should apply to collective enforcers of the peace, institutionalized adjudicators, or global bankers, for instance—even if these are apt descriptors of the Security Council, the ICJ, and the World Bank, respectively.[201]

---

199   James Crawford, *International Law and the Rule of Law*, 24 ADEL. L. REV. 3, 12 (2003).

200   *See, e.g.*, José E. Alvarez, Keynote Address at the Canadian Council on International Law's 35th Annual Conference on Responsibility of Individuals, States and Organizations: International Organizations: Accountability or Responsibility?, Canadian Council of International Law (Oct. 27, 2006), *at* http://www.temple.edu/law/ils/CCILspeech.pdf.

201   International Law Commission, Draft Articles on the Responsibility of International Organizations (DARIO), with Commentaries, General Commentary ¶ 7, U.N. Doc. A/66/10 52–172 (2011). The ILC's DARIO have also been criticized with respect to how they deal with the accountability of IOs when they act jointly. *See* Laurence Boisson de Chazournes, *United in Joy and Sorrow: Some Considerations of Responsibility Issues under Partnerships*

The IO challenge to legal positivism is not the only reason for these uncertainties—but it helps to explain them. We simply do not have clear positivist sources of law (treaties or established custom) that give us a response to the question of whether IOs can be guilty of human rights violations no less than states. Given the differences among IOs, we are not sure whether there is a uniform correct response to that question. Even if we assume that some human rights obligations extend to IOs generally, we are not sure which duties apply or what criterion to use to make that determination. Since IOs are not parties to relevant human rights conventions, the answer is not clear—at least not without recourse to alternatives to positivist sources such as the "soft law" that the age of IOs has generated.[202] Similarly, no matter how sophisticated our theories of "compliance" are, there are times when it is important—indeed fundamental— to know whether a state does or does not have a legally binding obligation that it has failed to apply or to implement.[203] A state whose national suffers harm as a result of another state's lack of compliance with a guidance instrument under the 2005 IHRS, an ICAO standard or recommended practice, or a ruling by the UN Human Rights Committee or the ILO's Committee on Freedom of Association, and that raises such a complaint before a court with jurisdiction, is entitled to know whether the responsible state has committed an internationally wrongful act triggering a remedy under the Articles of State Responsibility. The response that no clear answer is possible because the underlying norms enjoy a spectrum of legal authority (consistent with section 1 above) or because the nature of state sovereignty is now too complex to be precisely demarcated (as suggested by section 2), is not one that a self-respecting lawyer wants to give.

---

among International Financial Institutions, in RESPONSIBILITY OF INTERNATIONAL ORGANIZATIONS: ESSAYS IN MEMORY OF SIR IAN BROWNLIE 211 (Maurizio Ragazzi ed., 2013).

202   See generally Jan Klabbers, The EJIL Foreword: The Transformation of International Organizations Law, 26 EUR. J. INT'L L. 9 (2015) (arguing that the predominant theory for IOs, functionalism, does not address the responsibilities of IOs to third parties and therefore produces no rules to address situations like those posed by allegations that the UN was responsible for the spread of cholera in Haiti).

203   For these and other difficulties emerging from the turn to "informal law-making," see Joost Pauwelyn, Is It International Law or Not, and Does It Even Matter?, in INFORMAL INTERNATIONAL LAWMAKING 125, supra note 3. These and other difficulties drive some scholars to the conclusion that it is a mistake to call all such phenomena "law." See, e.g., Jean d'Aspremont, From a Pluralization of International Norm-making Processes to a Pluralization of the Concept of International Law, in INFORMAL INTERNATIONAL LAWMAKING, supra, at 185 (praising the project of "IN-LAW" for refraining from labeling as "law" the norm-making activity of, among others, IOs).

The age of IOs, in short, presents a third rule of law challenge that is easier to state than to solve. IOs have challenged the fundamental framework
for international law—positivism—without replacing it with an alternative
agreed understanding of what international obligations are in the age of IOs.
They have challenged the Article 38 sources of law without creating a clear
alternative. Thanks to the creativity of IOs, we live in a time of proliferating
normative instruments and differing answers about which of them should
be considered "legal" or "authoritative" enough to be subject to the specialized use and skills of legal professionals.[204] We live at a time when public law
scholars, responsive to the informal forms of "law" produced by IOs (and other
actors apart from states, such as private entities like ICANN), suggest that all
such informal sources, to the extent they are intended to affect the public,
should be seen as part of global governance. They would include, to be sure,
Security Council "smart" sanctions under the Al-Qa'ida and Taliban Sanctions
Committee (despite claims that the Council does not and cannot "legislate"),
but also UNESCO's list of World Heritage sites, the OECD's Pisa rankings on
educational policies, or non-binding standards produced by the OECD, the
FAO, or other IOs.[205] For some, public law includes even the International
Finance Corporation's annual indices indicating the extent to which states
adhere to the rule of law noted above.[206] Some public law scholars suggest,
accordingly, that international lawyers should concern themselves with a new
category of "international public law"—to be distinguished from traditional
"public international law" while others argue that a more apt designation is
"global administrative law."[207]

Those of a more traditional positivist inclination criticize such efforts at
"deformalization" and await a counter-trend that would lead towards "resilient
formal law-ascertainment."[208] But if public law scholars have not yet generated

---

204   *See, e.g.,* d'Aspremont, *supra* note 203.

205   *See, e.g.,* von Bogdandy, Dann & Goldmann, *supra* note 79, at 1382 (citing these examples).

206   *See, e.g.,* THE QUIET POWER OF INDICATORS: MEASURING DEVELOPMENT,
       CORRUPTION, AND THE RULE OF LAW (Sally Engle Merry, Kevin Davis & Benedict
       Kingsbury eds., 2015). There is a rich irony that a tool intended to be used to promote the
       rule of law is itself treated as a kind of law, whether or not this is consistent with what the
       rule of law demands of "law."

207   *See generally* Benedict Kingsbury, *The Concept of "Law" in Global Administrative Law,*
       20 EUR. J. INT'L L. 23 (2009); von Bogdandy, Dann & Goldmann, *supra* note 79; THE
       EXERCISE OF PUBLIC AUTHORITY BY INTERNATIONAL INSTITUTIONS, *supra* note 147.

208   JEAN D'ASPREMONT, EPISTEMIC FORCES IN INTERNATIONAL LAW: FOUNDATIONAL
       DOCTRINES AND TECHNIQUES OF INTERNATIONAL LEGAL ARGUMENTATION 109
       (2015).

a widely acceptable definition for determining the content of "international public law," "global administrative law," or some other substitute for traditional Article 38 sources, the response that we should simply return to some (mythical?) golden age of legal positivism seems inadequate as well.[209]

The international rule of law would not necessarily be improved—even in terms of compliance—if we were to eliminate or reduce the pragmatic departures from legal positivism that are the subject of much of this monograph. What precisely is the alternative to Security Council resolutions that fail to provide clarity on which provisions are legally binding or that fail to identify the Charter provision on which the Council is relying?[210] Would it truly advance the rule of law to force the Security Council or its members to articulate why the "snap back" provisions in Council Resolution 2231 were legally authorized under the Charter? Would this have been a good idea if it had come at the expense of securing the Iran Deal in the first place?[211] Nor is it an easy call to suggest that Council Resolution 2249 on ISIS should not have been adopted absent greater clarity as to its legal foundation and binding effects.[212] Similarly, it is doubtful that the international rule of law would be improved if scholars and courts, national and international, were to come to the conclusion that, because of the demands of legal positivism or Bingham's second rule of law element, General Assembly resolutions should henceforth be treated as the mere hortatory measures that the Charter says that they are.[213] We may need the shortcuts to the laborious state-counting process for finding state practice/*opinio juris* that positivists prefer. The Security Council and General Assembly—as well as other IOs including international courts and tribunals—supply alternative forms of global law in response to the "shackles" imposed by Article 38 sources and the resulting gaps in the law.[214]

Attempts to "fix" the informal law-making of other IOs raise comparable difficulties. Commentators who have praised the wisdom of ICAO standards—as compared to the legally binding treaty alternatives pursued before ICAO was established—would certainly question the wisdom or efficacy of any effort to get ICAO to stop its awkward charade of pretending that states can merely opt out of SARPS.[215] It is not clear that international aviation law would be better

---

209   *See, e.g.*, Pauwelyn, *supra* note 203.
210   *See supra* § 1.
211   *See supra* note 68.
212   *See supra* note 73 and accompanying text.
213   *See supra* § 1.
214   *See, e.g.*, Pauwelyn, Wessel & Wouters, *When Structures Become Shackles, supra* note 3.
215   BUERGENTHAL, *supra* note 50.

off were we to direct that organization to make clear whether all or some of these standards are legally binding. It is also questionable whether attempts to clarify the extent to which COPs or MOPs in environmental treaties or the Framework Convention on Tobacco enjoy the rights and duties of other international legal persons would be worth the effort. Such collective entities, as noted with respect to the Tobacco Convention, may have secured greater state compliance in part because their powers and work products retain the virtues of flexibility.

Equally, the lack of clarity with respect to the product of many international "dispute settlers" may be a virtue rather than a flaw. To what end should we attempt to interfere with adjudicators' preference for precedents or force them to identify customary international law through only the licensed positivist forms of state practice and *opinio juris*, even if both of these hampers the development of the law and leads to rulings of *non-liquet*? Would it really be wise to tell national or international courts that the rule of law (or legal positivism) means that they should ignore the non-binding views of human rights treaty bodies or ILO adjudicative mechanisms, and that they need to wait for authoritative guidance on the interpretation of relevant treaties through a binding "judicial decision?"[216] Would not such counsel undermine efforts by quasi-judicial bodies like the Human Rights Committee to create a body of interpretative "precedent" and only encourage the fragmentation among international tribunals that frightens positivists themselves? What would be the point precisely of discouraging those national laws that now accord some of these non-binding products of international adjudication legitimacy or even binding authority? And, of course, it is unlikely that even a strict positivist would recommend the elimination of the advisory jurisdiction of the ICJ on the premise that the clarity of a binding decision by the Court would be more consistent with both positivism and the rule of law.

---

216   While the reception of the reports of the Human Rights Committee has not been widely embraced by national courts (at least in the absence of national laws making the Committee's view authoritative), see, for example, Van Alebeek & Nollkaemper, *supra* note 55, the ICJ has shown some deference to the Committee's views. *See also* Chapter v, *supra*, at note 105. *See also* Judgment No. 2867 of the Administrative Tribunal of the International Labour Organization upon a Complaint Filed against the International Fund for Agricultural Development, Advisory Opinion, 2012 I.C.J. 10, ¶ 39 (Feb. 1) (citing two General Comments of the Human Rights Committee as evidence of the evolution of the principle of equality of access to courts and tribunals). In these cases, it would appear that the Human Rights Committee's views have been elevated to the status of "judicial decisions" for purposes the ICJ Statute's Article 38(1)(d).

It would also be a mistake to suggest to IO general counsels that they should forgo giving legal advice when asked for it, at least until they are granted authority to issue clearly authoritative views in ostensible conformity with the requirements of the rule of law. Nor, despite abundant criticisms of "soft" ILC efforts, would it be a good idea to direct that body to produce only treaties subject to inter-state negotiation. Such a recommendation, would, after all, have prevented the finalizing of the Articles of State Responsibility, along with other useful, albeit informal, ILC products.

These efforts to rehabilitate legal positivism in conformity with the supposed needs of the rule of law would, in all likelihood, render less effective its alleged core function, namely to restrain sovereign and IO power that harms individuals. They would diminish the role of IOs—but also of international law and lawyers—in world affairs. We should be leery of how we "improve" the pragmatic compromises on which IO law is built, particularly if such improvements are built on the questionable assumption that the tenets of legal positivism or extrapolation of national rule of law elements from the national to the international level are necessary.

Mechanistic efforts to export the elements of the rule of law from the national to the international level should be resisted. While IOs have renewed the relevance of analogies to national governance, it is important to remember that these remain only analogies. Attempts to export the elements of the national rule of law to the international level require serious effort at "translation," no less than efforts to import international law into national law.[217] The requirements of the national and international rule of law differ and we are more likely to realize both if we recognize the differences.

Ameliorating the three rule of law gaps identified here—the challenge of accountability, the challenge of compliance, and the challenge of successfully defining what "law" is in the age of IOs—requires a different calculus for measuring success than that which we use to measure how national institutions

---

217   For considerations of the possible differences between conceptions of the national and international rule of law, see, for example, Simon Chesterman, *The UN Security Council and the Rule of Law: The Role of the Security Council in Strengthening a Rules-based International System: Final Report and Recommendations from the Austrian Initiative, 2004–2008*, U.N. Doc. A/63/69-S/2008/20 (May 7, 2008); Chesterman, *supra* note 173; Jeremy Waldron, *The Rule of International Law*, 30 Harv. J.L. & Pub. Pol'y 15 (2006); Keith, *supra* note 167. For the general proposition that international law needs to be "translated" for successful incorporation at the national level, see Karen Knop, *Here and There: International Law in Domestic Courts*, 32 NYU J. INT'L L. & POL. 501 (1999).

are accountable, how national laws are made effective, and even what "law" is at the national level.

While there is little doubt that IOs, particularly when they seek to export the rule of law to others, should themselves be subject to it—and should be accountable to those persons on whom they inflict damage—the methods and forms for accountability will (and probably should) differ from those found under national law.[218] Legal accountability for the victims of mass negligence may involve, under U.S. law, class actions in court. But accountability for the victims of cholera in Haiti, for example, may not require, to satisfy the international rule of law, depriving the UN of the immunity that it now enjoys in U.S. courts in order to make class actions there possible.[219] It is plausible to argue that Haiti's cholera victims could not reasonably have expected the substantial tort damages common to U.S. class actions—not in the face of treaty obligations that made such claims subject to a claims settlement commission established at the behest of the Haitian government and the UN.[220] But, in keeping with human rights principles that the UN and international tribunals have affirmed by their words and practice,[221] such victims should not be denied any effective remedy whatsoever, even if this emerges from a diplomatic settlement of their claims and a combination of a UN apology, modest individual compensation, and other forms of redress, including UN efforts to provide the infrastructure needed to supply clean water to all of Haiti.[222]

As this example suggests, while there is no question that all law needs to be at least minimally effective, the subjects of international law may be made to "comply" through a variety of mechanisms. International law's remedies

---

218   *See generally* Devika Hovell, *Due Process in the United Nations*, 109 AM. J. INT'L L. 1 (2016).

219   *See generally* Brett D. Schaefer, *Haiti Cholera Lawsuit Against the U.N.: Recommendations for U.S. Policy*, HERITAGE FOUND. BACKGROUNDER #2859, Nov. 12, 2013, *at* http://www .heritage.org/research/reports/2013/11/haiti-cholera-lawsuit-against-the-un-recommendations-for-us-policy (suggesting that maintaining immunity is needed to continue to encourage states to undertake UN peacekeeping).

220   Agreement between the United Nations and the Government of Haiti Concerning the Status of the United Nations Operation in Haiti ¶¶ 54–55, July 9, 2004.

221   *See, e.g.*, Universal Declaration of Human Rights, art. 10, G.A. Res. 217A (III) (Dec. 10, 1948) (access to "fair and public hearing" in determination of rights and obligations).

222   *See* Waite and Kennedy v. Germany, 1999-I Eur. Ct. H.R. 393 (finding no deprivation of fair trial right on the grounds of the legitimate aim of immunity for IOs and the availability of alternative means of legal redress). *See also* Amit R. Saksena, *The UN is at a Crossroads in Haiti*, INT'L POL'Y DIG., Jan. 7, 2015, *at* http://www.internationalpolicydigest.org/2015/01/07/ un-crossroads-haiti/; Hovell, *supra* note 218; Alvarez, *supra* note 119.

only rarely include a binding order issued by a court.[223] At the same time, the successful implementation of international law requires international lawyers, including within the Legal Counsel at the UN, who understand the need to make their clients aware that international obligations—even informal ones—require respect.[224]

Finally, just as differences exist between law and mere political or moral injunctions, gradations among legal obligations exist both at the national and international level. Analogies to the national rule of law need to be nuanced. We should look to and draw lessons from those *pockets* of national legal practice that most resemble IO practices and avoid those that do not.

Consider, for example, the significant role of institutional practice in the interpretation of IO charters highlighted throughout this monograph. That institutional practice may be the product of a series of General Assembly resolutions, accompanied by an occasional ICJ advisory opinion, paired with statements by the UN secretariat or opinions issued by its Legal Counsel. None of these are authoritative or binding in and of themselves and yet together these elements are, as noted, an essential way that IOs make law and even (re)interpret their charters. Are there comparable examples, compatible with common understandings of the rule of law, of national practices that are at once constitutive of law (or even a national constitution) *and* that are also capable of legally constraining law-makers?

In U.S. law an analogue to IO subsequent practice is presidential or executive practice, particularly with respect to foreign affairs. That practice, like IO practice generally, is not given authoritative effect in the U.S. Constitution and its binding force is a matter of conjecture. Moreover, that practice is rarely the subject of judicial review in U.S. courts, and when it is so examined, is often judged for consistency with prior presidential practice—as occurs when the ICJ examines the UN's practice. U.S. scholars Curtis Bradley and Trevor

---

223   *See* Howse & Teitel, *supra* note 196.

224   Indeed, perhaps because of the differences between the national and international rule of law, it may be that it is even more important for international lawyers to set an example with respect to maintaining high ethical standards in faithfully complying with the law in the advice that they provide. *See generally* Keith, *supra* note 167. The two-sentence response to the Haiti cholera complainants issued by the UN Legal Counsel, fifteen months after the organization was first notified of their claims, indicating that these were "not receivable" (Letter from Patricia O'Brien, Legal Counsel, United Nations, to Brian Concannon, Director, Inst. for Just. & Democracy in Haiti (Feb. 21, 2013), *at* http://opiniojuris.org/wp-content/uploads/LettertoMr.BrianConcannon.pdf) has been widely criticized for not satisfying that standard. *See* Waldron, *The Pre and Post UN Charter Order, supra* note 175; Alvarez, *supra* note 119.

Morrison have noted that the U.S. Supreme Court has recognized that the way in which the executive branch or the president has operated over time can provide a "constitutional gloss" on the scope of presidential power.[225] This determination is comparable to the ICJ's view in its *Reparation* Opinion that the subsequent practice of organs can be treated as the equivalent of the subsequent practice of states parties to a treaty and can therefore provide an interpretative gloss on the UN Charter.[226] The U.S. Supreme Court recognized this aspect of executive branch practice in its decision in *Youngstown Steel*, where Justice Frankfurter noted the legal significance of a "systematic, unbroken, executive practice long pursued to the knowledge of the Congress and never before questioned . . ."[227] When U.S. courts intervene, as they rarely do when the president's foreign affairs powers are involved, they accord significant deference to patterns of government practice.

In the U.S., and, one suspects, in at least some other countries, a pattern of comparable institutional practice can be constitutive of national constitutional law. Bradley and Morrison contend that this kind of "customary" law is also an important way that U.S. executive power is constrained. Indeed, they argue that presidential practice is itself a reason that it is untrue to say that the president of the United States is "unbounded by law" or is merely politically accountable.[228] They contend that in the absence of judicial review, the constraints on the ostensible "imperial presidency" are imposed by legal discourse itself—including the arguments proffering legal justifications for executive action issued by the Office of the General Counsel.[229] They acknowledge, as does Kenneth Keith, that the effectiveness of such legal constraints turns on the ethics and legal capacity of the executive's lawyers and, as is suggested by the infamous legal memoranda justifying "enhanced interrogation techniques" produced by executive branch lawyers during the administration George W. Bush, this is no guarantee that these constraints will be effective.[230] Bradley and Morrison accept the premise that such legal justifications must be open to public view and scrutiny and that the relative perceived strengths of legal arguments and the bases of authority cited matter, but they contend that legal

---

225   Curtis A. Bradley & Trevor W. Morrison, *Presidential Power, Historical Practice, and Legal Constraint*, 113 COLUM. L. REV 1097 (2013).

226   Reparation for Injuries, *supra* note 117.

227   Youngstown Co. v. Sawyer, 343 U.S. 579, 610–611 (1952) (Frankfurter, J., concurring).

228   Bradley & Morrison, *supra* note 225, at 1114–1128.

229   *Id.* at 1128–1131.

230   *Id.* at 1113. *See also id.* at 1120, 1132–1145; Keith, *supra* note 167, at 417.

discourse that relies on prior institutional practice to which other branches have deferred can be an effective legal constraint on executive discretion.[231]

Note that this account of the role of institutional or executive practice potentially prevents *ultra vires* action. It is not relevant only to *post hoc* justifications for what the executive has done. Bradley and Morrison, both of whom have served in the U.S. executive branch, argue that U.S. presidents and their lawyers tend not to make certain arguments if these are likely to be seen as weak; that is, that the executive sometimes avoids taking action because it would be unprecedented or because any possible legal justifications seem implausible.[232] The comparison to the Security Council failing to take specific exception to human rights—that is, refusing to state on the face of a resolution or in justification for its acts that it is simply exempt from human rights obligations—seems clear. Indeed, the Council's failure to make such claims provides a solid basis for a canon of interpretation that would posit that all Security Council resolutions should, absent any specific exception from fundamental human rights on their face, be interpreted not to violate such rights and be implemented to avoid such conflicts. Note that this restrictive canon of interpretation could emerge from the practice of the Council itself.

Bradley and Morrison contend that it is important to place any institutional or executive practice in context—to see if there was really any opportunity for others in the institution to object so that reliance on practice does not become a tautology comparable to U.S. President Nixon's infamous claim that "when the President does it, that means that it is not illegal."[233] They argue that this kind of legal discourse is more likely to be a real constraint when the actors have internalized the normative force of a legal rule or of prior practice; this of course requires that ethical lawyers play an important role in interpreting and applying the institutional practice. Legal discourse and reliance on institutional practice as constraint do not work if, for instance, law does not matter to Security Council members to begin with and lawyers are not consulted. Bradley and Morrison contend that the more lawyers are involved in executive practice—the more that their shared set of norms about what constitutes a good argument prevails—the more likely that a virtuous circle of law compliance will emerge.[234]

---

231   Bradley & Morrison, *supra* note 225, at 1132–1149 (citing a number of examples).

232   *Id.* at 1137–1140 (discussing the role of "external sanctions" on the legal advice offered to the executive branch) and 1140–1145 (discussing the significance of plausible legal justifications offered to justify executive action).

233   *Id.* at 1121.

234   *Id.* at 1133–1137.

There is much more that the comparison to u.s. (and others') executive practices may yield to those who study IOs. Bradley and Morrison argue, for example, that the lack of Austinian or formal enforcement mechanisms (including the relative absence of judicial review) is not an obstacle to their conclusions. Executives can be publicly shamed and other forms of backlash or public disapproval can also occur. "What makes a convention nonlegal," they write, "is not simply the unwillingness of courts to enforce it. Rather, it is that members of the relevant community do not understand its breach to be a violation of the law. . . ."[235] Bradley and Morrison argue that even rhetorical recourse to the rule of law—one can think here of Annan's and the General Assembly stances in favor of the rule of law quoted above—may have a "civilizing force," since the public invocation of legal principle can create pressure for respecting it.[236] In a related article, Morrison and Bradley consider other aspects of executive practice that would be of interest to students of IOs, namely its impact on legitimate expectations; its appeal to judges looking for predictability, consistency, and efficiency; or to judges looking to avoid charges of judicial legislation; its limits (e.g., practice cannot prevail against the explicit words of a constitution); its broader connections to common law constitutionalism and adaptability to changing circumstances, its strong connection to presumptions of legality; its relationship to appeals to expertise; and its capacity to correct a practice that has proven unworkable.[237]

Whether or not the analogy to u.s. presidential practice proves useful to IOs, the broader contention here is that those seeking to establish the international rule of law need to carefully consider which elements of the national rule of law—and which parts of national practice—provide relevant examples for the very different world of IOs. Finding the proper analogies to national law may assist in responding to legal positivist critiques, make IO practices more compatible with the practices of sovereigns, and enable more forms of IO accountability to emerge.

4   Conclusion

This chapter takes a broader, bird's eye view of the preceding parts of this monograph. It begins by revisiting the tenets of legal positivism described in

---

235   *Id.* at 1129.
236   *Id.* at 1143.
237   Curtis A. Bradley & Trevor M. Morrison, *Historical Gloss and the Separation of Powers*, 126 Harv. L. Rev. 411 (2012).

Chapter 1 and their relevance to 10-generated law. The ideal model of legal positivism shares a core of inter-related ideas. Positivism assumes the existence of delimited legal sources with binding authority grounded in state centricity and state consent. Under this view, 10s, since they have not been delegated such authority, are not "law-makers"; only states are. As the UN system turns seventy, it is becoming clear that global 10s, including institutionalized adjudicators, are producing a steady stream of norms whose legal impact does not easily comport with positivist tenets and whose significance is not made manifest by Article 38 of the Statute of the ICJ. Moreover, thanks to institutionalization, even the three basic sources of law under Article 38 have subtly changed.

Treaties, most often negotiated under the auspices of 10s, and ever more subject to interpretation by international adjudicators, are less likely to be the static contractual instruments of (original) state consent that positivists favor. Many treaties, including 10 charters, have become dynamic "living" instruments of governance that, particularly through the mechanism of evolving institutional practice coupled with rare but significant adjudicative (re)interpretation, change over time and become, as has the UN Charter itself, different compacts from those to which states gave their original consent.

Customary law is most often found not through laborious examination of the actual state practice and evidence of *opinio juris* of the UN's 193 member states but through resort to institutional shortcuts, including recourse to General Assembly resolutions, multilateral treaties with presumed general effect, or other 10 products such as judicial or arbitral decisions. This means, as is most clearly demonstrated by the determinations of custom made by national and international adjudicators, that customary international law may arise far more quickly than students of international law have been taught to expect, and that evidence of state consent may be inferred from something other than the direct practice and *opinio juris* of states—and indeed, that findings of particular rules of custom may arise from or be dependent on multilateral treaties increasingly negotiated under 10 processes and the *jurisprudence constante* of adjudicators themselves.

"General principles," once seemingly confined to a meager group of equitable concepts to which all states are presumed to have consented, are increasingly a more ample set of principles and practices, particularly as deployed by international courts and tribunals that have turned to these as part of their strategy to avoid determinations of *non-liquet*.

An even greater threat to positivism—a direct outcome of the complex institutional features highlighted in Chapter 1 sections 2.1–2.5—is posed by the informal effects of 10-generated norms. A great deal of international regulation exists along a spectrum of legally binding authority that is hard to reconcile either with Article 38 or with the traditional elements of the rule of law.

IO challenges to state-centric positivism have not made either positivism or states irrelevant to international law. One of the paradoxes of the age of IOs is how much they challenge legal positivism and its state centricity without doing away with either. Legal positivism remains the *lingua franca* of international lawyers.[238] This is suggested by continuing efforts to explain the legal effects of IO products, such as General Assembly resolutions, in terms of Article 38 sources. It is indicated by section 1.4 above, which reveals that the evolving legal interpretations of IO charters that have enabled IOs to challenge positivist assumptions are themselves the product of the (often ambiguous) texts of these charters and the positivist (but flexible) rules of treaty interpretation.

As demonstrated by section 2 above, IOs have challenged but hardly displaced states as the primary law-making actors. Some forms of IO law-making have enhanced the power of some states while other nations owe their sovereign powers or even their recognition as states to IOs. IOs, particularly the UN itself, have enabled many states to secure their independence and UN system organizations remain quite plausibly the most important strut for maintaining the power of states. But just as the sources of obligation have been transformed in the age of IOs, today's law-making actors, including states, have changed as well. The concept of, and the powers resulting from, sovereignty have been altered. All states, large and small, rich and poor, have been affected by the power of IOs and the shrinking domain of sacrosanct "domestic jurisdiction" that has accompanied the expanding domain of international law. At the same time, the generally implicit state delegations of power that have produced the growth of IO power and the corresponding contraction in the regulatory discretion that states retain are reversible phenomena subject to shifting tides. Sovereigns and IOs react to the powers exercised by each other and sometimes this reaction takes dialectical form.

The contradictory aspects of the age of IOs, introduced in the caveats mentioned in Chapter 1, section 3, include another irony: IOs purport to promote the rule of law but also pose formidable challenges to it. The elements most associated with the (national) rule of law—equality, clarity, limits on discretion, good faith exercise of power, protection of fundamental rights, and access to justice—are not easy to reconcile with the reality of IOs. Although IOs increasingly attempt to export the rule of law to states, and these efforts are increas-

---

238   For a rich account explaining the persistence of legal positivism, see MÓNICA GARCÍA-SALMONES ROVIRA, THE PROJECT OF POSITIVISM IN INTERNATIONAL LAW (2013).

ingly seen as a new paradigm for the entire UN system, rule of law attempts by everyone from UN peacekeepers to World Bank officials generate expectations that IOs themselves ought to be subject to the rule of law. These expectations are not always satisfied even as UN officials affirm that the accountability of all law-makers is fundamental to the rule of law. IOs are not exemplars for complying with the elements associated with the national rule of law that they seek to foster in others.

Much of the attention on the alleged rule of law failings of IOs has empha-sized two problems: IOs' failures with respect to making themselves legally accountable and their shortcomings in securing compliance with the norms that they produce. There are differences of opinion about how serious these two challenges are and many prescriptions on offer for improving the account-ability of IOs as well as the levels of and tools for "enforcement." The focus of section 3 above, however, is on a related, and perhaps even more formidable problem: the mismatch between the ways IOs engage in informal law-making and the ostensible requirement, under the rule of law, that all "law" emerges from duly designated legislators, needs to be clear and binding, and must be at least susceptible to judicial application.

Section 3 makes the case that the international rule of law requires a differ-ent calculus or basis of assessment than the national rule of law. It defends the turn towards the "informality" in law-making, law-makers, and the resulting "law" in which IOs have been complicit. It also suggests one promising basis of comparison: the role of executive branch practice within states. But these are advanced only as tentative justifications for the pragmatic compromises struck within IOs.

International law scholars have not yet provided a satisfactory and widely accepted test for determining when informal processes (involving either the IOs addressed in this monograph or a host of non-governmental actors) pro-duce something worthy of being called (and treated as) "international law." There is no single clear alternative to the listing of international obligations in Article 38 or to legal positivists' coherent (if outdated) explanation for why those sources make sense. Until public law scholars or others produce that alternative, positivism remains the *lingua franca* of the field by default. Until this rule of law challenge is adequately addressed, those who study IOs are likely to continue to have problems convincing people that the "law" produced by IOs is effective and that IOs can be held "accountable."

Selected Bibliography

Books

Aginam, Obijiofor. *Global Health Governance: International Law and Public Health in a Divided World*. Toronto: University of Toronto Press, 2005.

Alamuddin, Amal, Nidal Nabil. Jurdi, and David Tolbert. *The Special Tribunal for Lebanon: Law and Practice*. Oxford: Oxford University Press, 2014.

Alvarez, José E. *International Organizations as Law-makers*. Oxford: Oxford University Press, 2005.

Alvarez, José E. *International Organizations as Law-makers* 46 (2006).

Alvarez, José E., Karl P. Sauvant, Kamil Gerard, Ahmed, and Gabriela P. Vizcaíno, eds. *The Evolving International Investment Regime: Expectations, Realities, Options*. Oxford: Oxford University Press, 2011.

Alter, Karen J. *The New Terrain of International Law: Courts, Politics, Rights*. Princeton: Princeton University Press, 2014.

Amerasinghe, C.F. *The Law of the International Civil Service (as Applied by International Administrative Tribunals)*. 2d ed. Oxford: Clarendon Press, 1994.

Anghie, Antony. *Imperialism, Sovereignty, and the Making of International Law*. Cambridge: Cambridge University Press, 2005.

Benedek, Wolfgang, K. De Feyter, and Fabrizio Marrella, eds. *Economic Globalisation and Human Rights*. Cambridge: Cambridge University Press, 2007.

Benvenisti, Eyal. *The Law of Global Governance*. The Hague: Hague Academy of International Law, 2014.

Besson, Samantha and John Tasioulas, eds. *The Philosophy of International Law*. Oxford: Oxford University Press, 2010.

Bingham, Tom. *The Rule of Law*. London: Allen Lane, 2010.

Bjorklund, Andrea K. and August Reinisch. *International Investment Law and Soft Law*. Cheltenham, UK: Edward Elgar Pub., 2012.

Bogdandy, Armin Von. *The Exercise of Public Authority by International Institutions: Advancing International Institutional Law*. Heidelberg: Springer, 2010.

Boisson de Chazournes, Laurence, and Philippe Sands, eds. *International Law, the International Court of Justice, and Nuclear Weapons*. Cambridge: Cambridge University Press, 1999.

Boutros-Ghali, Boutros. *An Agenda for Democratization*. New York: United Nations, Dept. of Public Information, 1996.

Bowett, D.W. *The Law of International Institutions*. 4th ed. London: Stevens., 1982.

Bradley, Curtis A., ed. *Custom's Future: International Law in a Changing World*. Cambridge, UK: Cambridge University Press, 2016.

Brownlie, Ian. *Principles of Public International Law*. 8th ed. Oxford: Oxford University Press, 2012.

Brummer, Chris. *Soft Law and the Global Financial System: Rule Making in the 21st Century*. Cambridge: Cambridge University Press, 2012.

Buergenthal, Thomas. *Law-Making in the International Civil Aviation Organization*. Syracuse, NY: Syracuse University Press, 1969.

Cass, Deborah Z. *The Constitutionalization of the World Trade Organization: Legitimacy, Democracy, and Community in the International Trading System*. Oxford: Oxford University Press, 2005.

Cassese, Antonio. *International Law*. 2d ed. Oxford: Oxford University Press, 2005.

Cassese, Antonio, and Paola Gaeta. *Cassese's International Criminal Law*. 3d ed. Oxford: Oxford University Press, 2013.

Chayes, Abram, and Antonia Handler Chayes. *The New Sovereignty: Compliance with International Regulatory Agreements*. Cambridge, MA: Harvard University Press, 1998.

Chorev, Nitsan. *The World Health Organization Between North and South*. Ithaca: Cornell University Press, 2012.

Clapham, Andrew. *Human Rights Obligations of Non-State Actors*. Oxford: Oxford University Press, 2006.

Combs, Nancy A. *Fact-Finding Without Facts: The Uncertain Evidentiary Foundations of International Criminal Convictions*. Cambridge: Cambridge University Press, 2010.

Crawford, Adam, ed. *International and Comparative Criminal Justice and Urban Governance: Convergence and Divergence in Global, National and Local Settings*. Cambridge: Cambridge University Press, 2011.

Crawford, James. *Brownlie's Principles of Public International Law*. 8th ed. Oxford: Oxford University Press, 2012.

Crawford, James. *Chance, Order, Change: The Course of International Law, General Course on Public International Law*. Leiden: Brill–Nijhoff, 2014.

Cronin, Bruce and Ian Hurd, eds. *The UN Security Council and the Politics of International Authority*. London: Routledge, 2008.

D'Aspremont, Jean. *Epistemic Forces in International Law: Foundational Doctrines and Techniques of International Legal Argumentation*. Cheltenham: Edward Elgar Pub, 2015.

D'Aspremont, Jean. *Formalism and the Sources of International Law*. Oxford: University Press, 2011.

Danilenko, Gennady M. *Law-making in the International Community*. Dordrecht: M. Nijhoff, 1993.

Davis, Kevin E., Angelina Fisher, Benedict Kingsbury, and Sally Engle Merry, eds. *Governance by Indicators: Global Power Through Quantification and Rankings*. Oxford: Oxford University Press Institute for International Law and Justice, New York University School of Law, 2012.

De Wet, Erika, André Nollkaemper, and Petra Dijkstra. *Review of the Security Council by Member States*. Antwerp: Intersentia, 2003.

Devaney, James Gerard. *Fact-Finding before the International Court of Justice*. Cambridge, UK: Cambridge University Press, 2016.

Diehl, Paul F. *The Politics of Global Governance: International Organizations in an Interdependent World*. 2d ed. Boulder, CO: Lynne Rienner Publishers, 2001.

Dunoff, Jeffrey L., and Mark A. Pollack, eds. *Interdisciplinary Perspectives on International Law and International Relations: The State of the Art*. Cambridge: Cambridge University Press, 2012.

Dunoff, Jeffrey L., Steven R. Ratner, and David Wippman. *International Law: Norms, Actors, Process: A Problem-oriented Approach*. 3d ed. New York: Aspen Publishers, 2010.

Einsiedel, Sebastian Von, David M. Malone, and Bruno Stagno Ugarte, eds. *The UN Security Council in the Twenty-first Century*. Boulder 2015: Lynne Rienner Publishers.

Engle Merry, Sally, Kevin E. Davis, and Benedict Kingsbury. *The Quiet Power of Indicators: Measuring Governance, Corruption, and Rule of Law*. New York, NY: Cambridge University Press, 2015.

Evans, Malcolm D. *International Law*. 3d ed. Oxford: Oxford University Press, 2010.

Farrall, Jeremy Matam. *United Nations Sanctions and the Rule of Law*. Cambridge, UK: Cambridge University Press, 2007.

Farrall, Jeremy Matam and Kim Rubenstein. *Sanctions, Accountability and Governance in a Globalised World*. Cambridge: Cambridge University Press, 2009.

Fastenrath, Ulrich, Rudolf Geiger, Daniel-Erasmus Khan, Andreas Paulus, Sabine Von. Schorlemer, and Christoph Vedder, eds. *From Bilateralism to Community Interest: Essays in Honour of Judge Bruno Simma*. New York: Oxford University Press, 2011.

Fidler, David P. *International Law and Infectious Diseases*. Oxford: Clarendon Press, 1999.

Fidler, David P., and Lawrence O. Gostin. *Biosecurity in the Global Age: Biological Weapons, Public Health, and the Rule of Law*. Stanford: Stanford University Press, 2008.

Fox, Gregory H., and Brad R. Roth, eds. *Democratic Governance and International Law*. Cambridge, UK: Cambridge University Press, 2000.

Franck, Thomas M. *Fairness in International Law and Institutions*. Oxford: Clarendon Press, 1998.

Franck, Thomas M. *The Power of Legitimacy Among Nations*. New York: Oxford University Press, 1990.

Freeman, Marsha A., Rudolf, Beate, and C.M. Chinkin, eds. *The UN Convention on the Elimination of All Forms of Discrimination Against Women: A Commentary*. Oxford: Oxford University Press, 2012.

Fuller, Lon L. *The Morality of Law*. New Haven: Yale University Press, 1964.

Gaja, Giorgio, and Jenny Grote Stoutenburg, eds. *Enhancing the Rule of Law through the International Court of Justice*. Leiden: Brill Nijhoff, 2014.

García-Salmones Rovira, Mónica. *The Project of Positivism in International Law*. Oxford: Oxford University Press, 2013.

Genser, Jared, and Bruno Stagno Ugarte, eds. *The United Nations Security Council in the Age of Human Rights*. Cambridge, UK: Cambridge University Press, 2014.

Gold, Joseph. *Interpretation: The IMF and International Law*. London: Kluwer Law International, 1996.

Goodman, Neville M. *International Health Organizations and Their Work*. 2d ed. Edinburgh: Churchill Livingstone, 1971.

Gostin, Lawrence O. *Global Health Law*. Cambridge: Harvard University Press, 2014.

Grodin, Michael A., Daniel Tarantola, George Annas, and Sofia Gruskin. *Health and Human Rights in a Changing World*. 3d ed. New York, NY: Routledge, 2013.

Guzman, Andrew T. *How International Law Works: A Rational Choice Theory*. Oxford: Oxford University Press, 2008.

Henkin, Louis. *How Nations Behave: Law and Foreign Policy*. 2d ed. New York: Published for the Council on Foreign Relations by Columbia University Press, 1979.

Higgins, Rosalyn. *Problems and Process: International Law and How We Use It*. Oxford: Clarendon Press, 1994.

Higgins, Rosalyn. *The Development of International Law through the Political Organs of the United Nations*. London: Oxford University Press, 1963.

Hirschman, Albert O. *Exit, Voice, and Loyalty: Responses to Decline in Firms, Organizations, and States*. Cambridge, MA: Harvard University Press, 1970.

Hoof, Godefridos J.H. Van. *Rethinking the Sources of International Law*. Deventer, Netherlands: Kluwer Law and Taxation Publishers, 1983.

Inama, Stefano, and Edmund W. Sim. *The Foundation of the ASEAN Economic Community: An Institutional and Legal Profile*. Cambridge, UK: Cambridge University Press, 2015.

Jackson, John H. *The World Trading System: Law and Policy of International Economic Relations*. Cambridge, MA: MIT Press, 1997.

Joerges, Christian, and Ernst-Ulrich Petersmann, eds. *Constitutionalism, Multilevel Trade Governance and International Economic Law*. 2d ed. Portland: Hart Publishing, 2011.

Johnstone, Ian. *The Power of Deliberation: International Law, Politics and Organizations*. 2d ed. Oxford: Oxford University Press, 2011.

Keller, Helen, Geir Ulfstein, and Leena Grover, eds. *UN Human Rights Treaty Bodies: Law and Legitimacy*. Cambridge, UK: Cambridge University Press, 2012.

Kent, Ann E. *Beyond Compliance: China, International Organizations, and Global Security*. Stanford, CA: Stanford University Press, 2007.

Kent, Ann E. *China, the United Nations, and Human Rights: The Limits of Compliance*. Philadelphia: University of Pennsylvania Press, 1999.

Kirgis, Frederic L. *International Organizations in Their Legal Setting*. St. Paul: West Publ., 1993.

Klabbers, Jan. *An Introduction to International Institutional Law*. 2d ed. Cambridge, UK: Cambridge University Press, 2009.

Klabbers, Jan. *International Law*. Cambridge: Cambridge University Press, 2013.

Koskenniemi, Martti. *From Apology to Utopia: The Structure of International Legal Argument*. 2d ed. New York: Cambridge University Press, 2005.

Lauterpacht, Hersch. *International Law and Human Rights*. New York: F.A. Praeger, 1950.

Lauterpacht, Hersch. *The Function of Law in the International Community*. Oxford: Oxford University Press, 2011.

Macdonald, R. St.J. and Douglas M. Johnston, eds. *The Structure and Process of International Law Essays in Legal Philosophy, Doctrine and Theory*. Hingham: M. Nijhoff Publishers, 1986.

Mackenzie, Ruth, Kate Malleson, and Penny Martin. *Selecting International Judges: Principle, Process, and Politics*. Oxford: Oxford University Press, 2010. doi:10.1093/acprof:oso/9780199580569.001.0001.

Malone, David. *Decision-making in the UN Security Council: The Case of Haiti, 1990–1997*. Oxford: Clarendon Press, 1998.

Malone, David, ed. *The UN Security Council: From the Cold War to the 21st Century*. Boulder: Lynne Rienner, 2004.

Meron, Theodor. *The Making of International Criminal Justice: A View from the Bench: Selected Speeches*. Oxford: Oxford University Press, 2011.

Meron, Theodor. *War Crimes Law Comes of Age: Essays*. Oxford: Clarendon Press, 1998.

Merrills, J.G. *International Dispute Settlement*. 2d ed. New York: Cambridge University Press, 1991.

Nguitragool, Paruedee, and Jürgen Ruland. *ASEAN as an Actor in International Fora: Reality, Potential and Constraints*. Cambridge, UK: Cambridge University Press, 2015.

Nolte, Georg and Andreas Paulus. *The Charter of the United Nations a Commentary*. Edited by Bruno Simma and Daniel-Erasmus Khan. 3d ed. Oxford: Oxford Univ. Press, 2012.

Orford, Anne. *International Authority and the Responsibility to Protect*. Cambridge, UK: Cambridge University Press, 2011.

Polanyi, Karl. *The Great Transformation: The Political and Economic Origins of Our Time*. New York City: Farrar & Rinehart, 1944.

Popovski, Vesselin and Trudy Fraser, eds. *The Security Council as Global Legislator*. New York: Routledge, 2014.

Romano, Cesare P.R., Karen J. Alter, and Yuval Shany, eds. *The Oxford Handbook of International Adjudication*. Oxford: Oxford University Press, 2013.

Schachter, Oscar. *International Law in Theory and Practice*. Dordrecht, The Netherlands: M. Nijhoff Publishers, 1991.

Scharf. *Customary International Law in Times of Fundamental Change: Recognizing Grotian Moments*. Cambridge, UK: Cambridge University Press, 2013.

Schill, Stephan. *International Investment Law and Comparative Public Law*. Oxford: Oxford University Press, 2010.

Schill, Stephan. *The Multilateralization of International Investment Law*. Cambridge, UK: Cambridge University Press, 2009.

Schneiderman, David. *Constitutionalizing Economic Globalization: Investment Rules and Democracy's Promise*. Cambridge, UK: Cambridge University Press, 2008.

Schulte, Constanze. *Compliance with Decisions of the International Court of Justice*. Oxford: Oxford University Press, 2004.

Shapiro, Martin. *Courts: a Comparative and Political Analysis*. Chicago: University of Chicago Press, 1981.

Shapiro, Martin, and Alec Stone Sweet. *On Law, Politics, and Judicialization*. Oxford: Oxford University Press, 2002.

Shaw, Malcolm N. *International Law*. 6th ed. Cambridge, UK: Cambridge University Press, 2008.

Shelton, Dinah. *Commitment and Compliance: The Role of Non-binding Norms in the International Legal System*. Oxford: Oxford University Press, 2000.

Sievers, Loraine, and Sam Daws. *The Procedure of the UN Security Council*. 4th ed. Oxford: Oxford University Press, 2014.

Simmons, Beth A. *Mobilizing for Human Rights: International Law in Domestic Politics*. Cambridge: Cambridge University Press, 2009.

Sinclair, Guy. *To Reform the World: The Legal Powers of International Organizations and the Making of the Modern State*. Oxford: Oxford University Press, 2016.

Slaughter, Anne-Marie. *A New World Order*. Princeton: Princeton University Press, 2004.

Sloan, Blaine. *United Nations General Assembly Resolutions in Our Changing World*. Ardsley-on-Hudson, NY: Transnational Publishers, 1991.

Stiglitz, Joseph E. *Globalization and Its Discontents*. New York: W.W. Norton, 2002.

Sweet, Alec Stone. *The Judicial Construction of Europe*. Oxford: Oxford University Press, 2004.

Teitel, Ruti G. *Humanity's Law*. Oxford: Oxford University Press, 2011.

Tieya, Wang, and Wei Min, eds. *Guoji Fa (International Law)*. Beijing: Falu Chubanshe (Law Publ.), 1981.

Treves, Tullio, Nerina Boschiero, Tullio Scovazzi, Cesare Pitea, and Chiara Ragni. *International Courts and the Development of International Law: Essays in Honour of Tullio Treves*. The Hague: T.M.C. Asser Press, 2013.

Tzevelekos, Vassilis, and Kanstantsin Dzehtsiarou. "International Custom Making and the ECtHR's European Consensus Method of Interpretation." *European Yearbook on Human Rights* 16 (2016): 313-44.

Van den Herik, Larissa, and Nico Schrijver. *Counter-Terrorism Strategies in a Fragmented International Legal Order: Meeting the Challenges.* Cambridge: Cambridge University Press, 2013.

Venzke, Ingo. *How Interpretation Makes International Law: On Semantic Change and Normative Twists.* Oxford: Oxford University Press, 2013. doi:10.1093/acprof: oso/9780199657674.001.0001.

Verdirame, Guglielmo. *The UN and Human Rights: Who Guards the Guardians?* Cambridge, UK: Cambridge University Press, 2011.

Von Bogdandy, Armin, Rudiger Wolfram, Jochen Von Bernstorff, Philipp Dann, and Matthias Goldmann. *The Exercise of Public Authority by International Institutions: Advancing International Institutional Law.* Heidelberg: Springer, 2010.

Waibel, Michael, Asha Kaushal, Kyo-Hwa Liz. Chung, and Claire Balchin, eds. *The Backlash Against Investment Arbitration: Perceptions and Reality: Perceptions and Reality.* The Netherlands: Kluwer Law International BV, 2010.

Walzer, Michael. *Just and Unjust Wars: A Moral Argument with Historical Illustrations.* London: Allen Lane, 1978.

Wessendorf, Nikolai. The Charter of the United Nations: A Commentary 2137.

Woodward, Barbara K. *Global Civil Society in International Lawmaking and Global Governance: Theory and Practice.* Leiden: Martinus Nijhoff Publishers, 2010.

Xue, Hanqin. *Chinese Contemporary Perspectives on International Law: History, Culture and International Law.* The Hague: Hague Academy of International Law, 2012.

Zacher, Mark W., and Tania J. Keefe. *The Politics of Global Health Governance: United by Contagion.* New York: Palgrave Macmillan, 2008.

Journal Articles

Abbott, Kenneth W., and Duncan Snidal. Why States Act Through Formal International Organizations. *Journal of Conflict Resolution* 42, no. 1 (1998): 3. doi:10.1177/00220027 98042001001.

Agora. "Future Implications of the Iraqi Conflict." *American Journal of International Law* 97, no. 3 (2003): 553.

Akande, Dapo. "International Law Immunities and the International Criminal Court." *The American Journal of International Law* 98, no. 3 (2004): 407. doi:10.2307/ 3181639.

Alter, Karen J. "Agents or Trustees? International Courts in Their Political Context." *European Journal of International Relations* 14, no. 1 (2008): 33. doi:10.1177/ 1354066107087769.

Alter, Karen J. "The Evolving International Judiciary." *Annual Review of Law and Social Science Annu. Rev. Law. Soc. Sci.* 7, no. 1 (2011): 387. doi:10.1146/annurev-lawsocsci-102510-105535.

Alter, Karen J., Laurence R. Helfer, and Jacqueline R. McAllister. "A New International Human Rights Court For West Africa: The ECOWAS Community Court Of Justice." *The American Journal of International Law* 107, no. 4 (2013): 737. doi:10.5305/amerjintelaw.107.4.0737.

Alter, Karen J., Laurence R. Helfer, and Mikael Rask Madsen. "How Context Shapes the Authority of International Courts." *Law & Contemporary Problems* 79, no. 1 (2016): 1.

Alter, Karen J., Laurence Helfer, and Osvaldo Saldías. Transplanting the European Court of Justice: The Experience of the Andean Tribunal of Justice. *Am J Comp Law American Journal of Comparative Law* 60, no. 3 (2012): 629. doi:10.5131/ajcl.2011.0030.

Alvarez, José E. "A BIT on Custom." *New York University Journal of International Law and Politics* 42 (2009): 17.

Alvarez, José E. "Are International Judges Afraid of Science?: A Comment on Mbengue." *Loyola of Los Angeles International and Comparative Law Review* 34 (2011): 12.

Alvarez José E. "Beware: Boundary Crossings." NYU School of Law, Public Law Research Paper No. 14 (2014).

Alvarez, José E. "Crimes of States/Crimes of Hate: Lessons from Rwanda." *Yale Journal of International Law* 24 (1999): 365.

Alvarez, José E. "Hegemonic International Law Revisited." *The American Journal of International Law* 97, no. 4 (2003): 873. doi:10.2307/3133686.

Alvarez, José E. "International Organizations: Then and Now." *The American Journal of International Law* 100, no. 2 (2006): 324.

Alvarez, José E. "Judging the Security Council." *The American Journal of International Law* 90, no. 1 (1996): 1. doi:10.2307/2203749.

Alvarez, José E. "Nuremberg Revisited: The Tadic Case." *European Journal of International Law* 7, no. 2 (1996): 245. doi:10.1093/oxfordjournals.ejil.a015512.

Alvarez, José E. "Positivism Regained, Nihilism Postponed." Review of *Law-Making in the International Community*, by G.M. Danilenko. *Michigan Journal of International Law* 15, no. 3 (1994): 747.

Alvarez, José E. "The Return of the State." *Minnesota Journal of International Law* 20 (2011): 223.

Alvarez, José E. "Rush to Closure: Lessons of the Tadić Judgment." *Michigan Law Review* 96, no. 7 (1998): 2031. doi:10.2307/1290059.

Alvarez, José E. "Tadic Revisited: The Ayyash Decisions of the Special Tribunal for Lebanon." *Journal of International Criminal Justice* 11, no. 2 (2013): 291. doi:10.1093/jicj/mqt006.

Alvarez, José E. *"The 'Right to be Left Alone' and the General Assembly."* ACUNS Reports and Papers, No. 5 (1994).

Alvarez, José E. *"The United Nations in the Time of Cholera."* Am. J. Int'l L. Unbound, Apr. 4, 2014: https://www.asil.org/blogs/united-nations-time-cholera.

Alvarez, José E. "Why Are We 'Re-Calibrating' Our Investment Treaties?" *World Arbitration & Mediation Review* 4, no. 2 (2010): 143.

Arato, Julian. "Treaty Interpretation and Constitutional Transformation: Informal Change in International Organizations." *Yale Journal of International Law* 38, no. 2 (2013): 289.

Barnett, Michael N., and Martha Finnemore. "The Politics, Power, and Pathologies of International Organizations." *International Organization Int Org* 53, no. 04 (1999): 699. doi:10.1162/002081899551048.

Bederman, David J. "Collective Security, Demilitarization and 'Pariah' States." *European Journal of International Law* 13, no. 1 (2002): 121. doi:10.1093/ejil/13.1.121.

Bellamy, Alex J. "International Law and the War with Iraq." *Melbourne Journal of International Law* 4, no. 2 (2003): 497.

Bentekas, Ilias. "The International Law of Terrorist Financing." *American Journal of International Law* 97, no. 2 (2003): 315.

Benvenisti, Eyal. "Sovereigns as Trustees of Humanity: On the Accountability of States to Foreign Stakeholders." *The American Journal of International Law* 107, no. 2 (2013): 295. doi:10.5305/amerjintelaw.107.2.0295.

Blum, Gabriella. *Bilateralism, Multilateralism, and the Architecture of International Law*, 49 HARV. INT'L L. J. 323 (2008).

Blum, Gabriella. "Bilateralism, Multilateralism, and the Architecture of International Law." *Harvard International Journal of Law* 323, no. 2 (2008): 323.

Bogdandy, Armin Von, and Ingo Venzke. "On the Functions of International Courts: An Appraisal in Light of Their Burgeoning Public Authority." *Leiden Journal of International Law* 26, no. 01 (2013): 49. doi:10.1017/s0922156512000647.

Bogdandy, Armin Von, & Ingo Venzke. *On the Functions of International Courts: An Appraisal in Light of Their Burgeoning Public Authority*, 26 Leiden J. Int'l L. 49.

Boisson De Chazournes, Laurence, and Edouard Fromageau. "Balancing the Scales: The World Bank Sanctions Process and Access to Remedies." *European Journal of International Law* 23, no. 4 (2012): 963. http://ejil.oxfordjournals.org/.

Bolton, John R. "Should We Take Global Governance Seriously?" *Chicago Journal of International Law* 1, no. 2 (2000): 205.

Boon, Kristen E. "Open for Business: International Financial Institutions, Post-Conflict Economic Reform and the Rule of Law." *New York University Journal of International Law and Politics* 39, no. 3 (2007): 513.

Bradley, Curtis A. and Trevor M. Morrison. "Historical Gloss and the Separation of Powers." *Harvard Law Review* 126, no. 2 (2012): 411.

Bradley, Curtis A. and Trevor W. Morrison. "Presidential Power, Historical Practice, and Legal Constraint." *Columbia Journal of Transnational Law* 113 (2013): 1097.

Buergenthal, Thomas. "The Evolving International Human Rights System." *American Journal of International Law* 100, no. 4 (2006): 783.

Burke-White, William W. "A Community of Courts: Toward a System of International Criminal Law Enforcement." *Michigan Journal of International Law* 24, no. 1 (2002): 1–101.

Byers, Michael. "Terrorism, the Use of Force and International Law After 11 September." *International and Comparative Law Quarterly ICLQ* 51, no. 2 (2002): 401. doi:10.1093/iclq/51.2.401.

Cafaggi, Fabrizio. "The Many Features of Transnational Private Rule-Making: Unexplored Relationships Between *Leges Mercatoriae* and *Leges Regulatoriae*." *University of Pennsylvania Journal of International Law* 36 (2015): 101.

Caron, David D. and Brian Morris. "The United Nations Compensation Commission: Practical Justice, Not Retribution." *European Journal of International Law* 13, no. 1 (2002): 183. doi:10.1093/ejil/13.1.183.

Charney, Jonathan I. "Universal International Law." *American Journal of International Law* 87, no. 4 (1993): 529.

Charnovitz, Steve. "Two Centuries of Participation: NGOs and International Governance." *Michigan Journal of International Law* 18, no. 2 (1997): 183.

Chesterman, Simon. "An International Rule of Law?" *American Journal of Comparative Law* 56 (2008): 331.

Churchill, Robin R., and Geir Ulfstein. "Autonomous Institutional Arrangements in Multilateral Environmental Agreements: A Little-Noticed Phenomenon in International Law." *The American Journal of International Law* 94, no. 4 (2000): 623. doi:10.2307/2589775.

Clark, Roger S. "State Terrorism: Some Lessons from the Sinking of the 'Rainbow Warrior'." *Rutgers Law Journal* 20, no. 2 (1989): 393.

Cogan, Jacob Katz. "Stabilization and the Expanding Scope of the Security Council's Work." *The American Journal of International Law* 109, no. 2 (2015): 324. doi:10.5305/amerjintelaw.109.2.0324.

Collin, Jeff, Kelley Lee, and Karen Bissell. "The Framework Convention on Tobacco Control: The Politics of Global Health Governance." *Third World Quarterly* 23, no. 2 (2002): 265. doi:10.1080/01436590220126630.

Commission, Jeffrey P. "Precedent in Investment Treaty Arbitration: A Citation Analysis of a Developing Jurisprudence." *Journal of International Arbitration* 24, no. 2 (2007): 129.

Crema, Luigi. "Testing Amici Curiae in International Law: Rules and Practice." *The Italian Yearbook of International Law Online* 22, no. 1 (2013): 91. doi:10.1163/22116133–02201006.

DeLisle, Jacques. "Atypical Pneumonia and Ambivalent Law and Politics: SARS and the Response to SARS in China." *Temple Law Review* 77 (2004): 193.

Deming, Stuart H. "Anti-Corruption Policies: Eligibility and Debarment Practices at the World Bank and Regional Development Banks." *The International Lawyer* 44, no. 2 (2010): 871.

Dempsey, Paul Stephen. "Aviation Security: The Role of Law in the War Against Terrorism." *Columbia Journal of Transnational Law* 41, no. 3 (2003): 649.

Dempsey, Paul Stephen. "Compliance and Enforcement in International Law: Achieving Global Uniformity in Aviation Safety." *North Carolina Journal of International Law and Commercial Regulation* 30, no. 1 (2004): 1.

Doherty, Joseph W., and Richard H. Steinberg. "Punishment and Policy in International Criminal Sentencing: An Empirical Study." *American Journal of International Law* 110, no. 1 (2016): 49.

Douglas, Zachary. "The Hybrid Foundations of Investment Treaty Arbitration." *British Yearbook of International Law* 74, no. 1 (2004): 151. doi:10.1093/bybil/74.1.151.

Dugard, John. "Dealing With Crimes of a Past Regime: Is Amnesty Still an Option?" *Leiden Journal of International Law* 12, no. 4 (1999): 1001. doi:10.1017/s0922156599000515.

Einhorn, Jessica. "The World Bank's Mission Creep." *Foreign Affairs* 80, no. 5 (2001): 22. doi:10.2307/20050248.

Einsiedel, Sebastian von, David M. Malone, Bruno Stagno Ugarte. "*The UN Security Council in an Age of Great Power Rivalry.*" UN Univ. Working Paper Series, No. 4 (2015).

Falk, Richard A. "On the Quasi-Legislative Competence of the General Assembly." *The American Journal of International Law* 60, no. 4 (1966): 782. doi:10.2307/2196928.

Fauchald, Ole Kristian. "The Legal Reasoning of ICSID Tribunals—An Empirical Analysis." *European Journal of International Law* 19, no. 2 (2008): 301. doi:10.1093/ejil/chn011.

Fidler, David P. "Caught Between Paradise and Power: Public Health, Pathogenic Threats, and the Axis of Illness." *McGeorge Law Review* 34 (2004): 45.

Fidler, David P. "From International Sanitary Conventions to Global Health Security: The New International Health Regulations." *Chinese Journal of International Law* 4, no. 2 (2005): 325. doi:10.1093/chinesejil/jmi029.

Fidler, David P. "The Future of the World Health Organization: What Role for International Law?" *Vanderbilt Journal of Transnational Law* 31 (1998): 1079.

Fidler, David P. "The Globalization of Public Health: The First 100 Years of International Health Diplomacy." *Bulletin of the World Health Organization: The International Journal of Public Health* 79, no. 9 (2001): 842–49. http://www.who.int/iris/handle/10665/74977.

Fidler, David P. "Return of the Fourth Horseman: Emerging Infectious Diseases and International Law." *Minnesota Law Review* 81 (1997): 771.

Fidler, David P. "The UN and the Responsibility to Practice Public Health." *Journal of International Law & International Relations* 2 (2005): 41.

Fidler, David P. and Lawrence O. Gostin. "The New International Health Regulations: An Historic Development for International Law and Public Health." *The Journal of Law, Medicine & Ethics* 34, no. 1 (2006): 85. doi:10.1111/j.1748-720x.2006.00011.x.

Finnemore, Martha, and Kathryn Sikkink. "International Norm Dynamics and Political Change." *International Organization* 52, no. 4 (1998): 887. doi:10.1162/002081898550789.

Fiss, Owen. "Foreword: The Forms of Justice." *Harvard Law Review* 93, no. 1 (1979): 1.

Franck, Susan D. "International Arbitrators: Civil Servants? Sub Rosa Advocates? Men of Affairs? The Role of International Arbitrators." *ILSA Journal of International and Comparative Law* 12, no. 1 (2006): 499.

Franck, Thomas M. "The Emerging Right to Democratic Governance." *The American Journal of International Law* 86, no. 1 (1992): 46. doi:10.2307/2203138.

Franck, Thomas M. "The Powers of Appreciation: Who Is the Ultimate Guardian of UN Legality?" *The American Journal of International Law* 86, no. 3 (1992): 519. doi:10.2307/2203965.

Franck, Thomas M. "Terrorism and the Right of Self-Defense." *The American Journal of International Law* 95, no. 4 (2001): 839. doi:10.2307/2674629.

Franck, Thomas M. "The 'Powers of Appreciation': Who Is the Ultimate Guardian of UN Legality?" *The American Journal of International Law* 86, no. 3 (1992): 519. doi:10.2307/2203965.

Ginsburg, Tom. "Bounded Discretion in International Judicial Lawmaking." *Virginia Journal of International Law* 45 (2004): 631.

Ginsburg, Tom. "International Substitutes for Domestic Institutions: Bilateral Investment Treaties and Governance." *International Review of Law and Economics* 25, no. 1 (2005): 107. doi:10.1016/j.irle.2004.06.002.

Goodman, Ryan, and Derek Jinks. "How to Influence States: Socialization and International Human Rights Law." *Duke Law Journal* 54, no. 3 (2004): 621.

Gostin, Lawrence O. and Devi Sridhar. "Global Health and the Law." *New England Journal of Mecidine* 370 (2014): 1732. doi:10.1056/NEJMra1314094.

Gostin, Lawrence O., D. Sridhar, and D. Hougendobler. "The Normative Authority of the World Health Organization." *Public Health* 129, no. 7 (2015): 854. doi:10.1016/j.puhe.2015.05.002.

Gottlieb, Yaron. "The Security Council's Maritime Piracy Resolutions: A Critical Assessment." *Minnesota Journal of International Law* 24 (2015): 1.

Gowlland-Debbas, Vera. "The Limits of Unilateral Enforcement of Community Objectives in the Framework of UN Peace Maintenance." *European Journal of International Law* 11, no. 2 (2000): 361. doi:10.1093/ejil/11.2.361.

Grant, Ruth W., and Robert O. Keohane. "Accountability and Abuses of Power in World Politics." *Am. Pol. Sci. Rev. American Political Science Review* 99, no. 01 (2005). doi:10.1017/s0003055405051476.

Grossman, Nienke. "Legitimacy and International Adjudicative Bodies." *George Washington International Law Review* 41 (2009): 107.

Guzman, Andrew T. "The Cost of Credibility: Explaining Resistance to Interstate Dispute Resolution Mechanisms." *The Journal of Legal Studies* 31, no. 2 (2002): 303. doi:10.1086/340811.

Hafner, Gerhard. "Pros and Cons Ensuing from Fragmentation of International Law." *Michigan Journal of International Law* 25 (2003): 849.

Halabi, Sam Foster. "The World Health Organization's Framework Convention on Tobacco Control: An Analysis of Guidelines Adopted by the Conference of Parties." *Georgia Journal of International and Comparative Law* 39, no. 1 (2010): 121. doi:10.3390/admsci2020186.

Harrison, Mark. "Disease, Diplomacy and International Commerce: The Origins of International Sanitary Regulation in the Nineteenth Century." *Journal of Global History JGH* 1, no. 2 (2006): 197. doi:10.1017/s1740022806000131.

Harten, G. Van and Martin Louglin. "Investment Treaty Arbitration as a Species of Global Administrative Law." *European Journal of International Law* 17, no. 1 (2006): 121–50. doi:10.1093/ejil/chi159.

Hathaway, James C. "America, Defender of Democratic Legitimacy?" *European Journal of International Law* 11, no. 1 (2000): 121. doi:10.1093/ejil/11.1.121.

Hathaway, Oona A. "Do Human Rights Treaties Make a Difference?" *The Yale Law Journal* 111, no. 8 (2002): 1935. doi:10.2307/797642.

Helfer, Laurence R. "Monitoring Compliance with Unratified Treaties: The ILO Experience." *Law & Contemporary Problems* 71 (2008): 193. http://scholarship.law.duke.edu/faculty_scholarship/2223.

Helfer, Laurence R. "Overlegalizing Human Rights: International Relations Theory and the Commonwealth Caribbean Backlash against Human Rights Regimes." *Columbia Law Review* 102, no. 7 (2002): 1832. doi:10.2307/1123662.

Helfer, Laurence R. and Anne-Marie Slaughter. "Toward a Theory of Effective Supra-national Adjudication." *The Yale Law Journal* 107, no. 2 (1997): 273. doi:10.2307/797259.

Helfer, Laurence R. and Anne-Marie Slaughter. "Why States Create International Tribunals: A Response to Professors Posner and Yoo." *California Law Review* 93 (2005): 899.

Highet, Keith. "Evidence, the Court, and the Nicaragua Case." *The American Journal of International Law* 81, no. 1 (1987): 1. doi:10.2307/2202130.

Hovell, Devika. "Due Process in the United Nations." *American Journal of International Law* 109 (2016): 1.

Howse, Robert. "Moving the WTO Forward—One Case at a Time." *Cornell International Law Journal* 42, no. 2 (2009): 223.

Howse, Robert and Ruti Teitel. "Beyond Compliance: Rethinking Why International Law Really Matters." *Global Policy* 1, no. 2 (2010): 127. doi:10.1111/j.1758-5899.2010.00035.x.

Huber, Valeska. "The Unification Of The Globe By Disease? The International Sanitary Conferences On Cholera, 1851–1894." *Hist. J. The Historical Journal* 49, no. 2 (2006): 453. doi:10.1017/s0018246x06005280.

Hudec, R.E. *The New WTO Dispute Settlement Procedures: An Overview of the First Three Years*, 8 Minn. J. Global Trade.

Hudec, R.E. "The New WTO Dispute Settlement Procedures: An Overview of the First Three Years." *Minnesota Journal of Global Trade* 8, no. 1 (1999): 1.

Jain, Neha. "Comparative International Law at the ICTY: The General Principles Experiment." *The American Journal of International Law* 109, no. 3 (2015): 486. doi:10.5305/amerjintelaw.109.3.0486.

Jenks, C. Wilfred. "The Interpretation of International Labour Conventions by the International Labour Office." *British Yearbook of International Law* 20 (1939): 132.

Jia, Bing Bing. "The Crime of Aggression as Custom and the Mechanisms for Determining Acts of Aggression." *The American Journal of International Law* 109, no. 3 (2015): 569. doi:10.5305/amerjintelaw.109.3.0569.

Johnstone, Ian. "Legislation and Adjudication in the UN Security Council: Bringing down the Deliberative Deficit." *American Journal of International Law* 102, no. 2 (2008): 275. doi:10.2307/30034539.

Joyner, Christopher C. "U.N. General Assembly Resolutions and International Law: Rethinking the Contemporary Dynamics of Norm-Creation." *California Western International Law Journal* 11 (1981): 445.

Jurdi, Nidal Nabil. "The Subject-Matter Jurisdiction of the Special Tribunal for Lebanon." *Journal of International Criminal Justice* 5, no. 5 (2007): 1125. doi:10.1093/jicj/mqm071.

Kalderimis, Daniel. "IMF Conditionality as Investment Regulation: A Theoretical Analysis." *Social & Legal Studies* 13, no. 1 (2004): 103. doi:10.1177/0964663904040194.

Kennedy, David. "Challenging Expert Rule: The Politics of Global Governance." *Sydney Law Review* 27 (2005): 2.

Kennedy, David W. "The Move to Institutions." *Cardoza Law Review* 8, no. 5 (1987): 841.

Keohane, Robert O., Andrew Moravcsik, and Anne-Marie Slaughter. "Legalized Dispute Resolution: Interstate and Transnational." *International Organization* 54, no. 3 (2000): 457. doi:10.1162/002081800551299.

Kickbusch, Ilona, and K. Srinath Reddy. "Global Health Governance—The Next Political Revolution." *Public Health* 129, no. 7 (2015): 838. doi:10.1016/j.puhe.2015.04.014.

Kickbusch, Ilona, Wolfgang Hein, and Gaudenz Silberschmidt. "Addressing Global Health Governance Challenges through a New Mechanism: The Proposal for a Committee C of the World Health Assembly." *The Journal of Law, Medicine & Ethics* 38, no. 3 (2010): 550. doi:10.1111/j.1748-720x.2010.00511.x.

Kingsbury, Benedict. "The Concept of 'Law' in Global Administrative Law." *European Journal of International Law* 20, no. 1 (2009): 23.

Kingsbury, Benedict, and Lorenzo Casini. "Global Administrative Law Dimensions of International Organizations Law." *International Organizations Law Review* 6, no. 2 (2009): 319. doi:10.1163/157237409x12670188734311.

Kingsbury, Benedict, Nico Krisch, and Richard B. Stewart. "The Emergence of Global Administrative Law." *Law & Contemporary Problems* 68 (2005): 15. http://scholarship.law.duke.edu/lcp/vol68/iss3/2.

Klabbers, Jan. "The EJIL Foreword: The Transformation of International Organizations Law." *European Journal of International Law* 26, no. 1 (2015): 9. doi:10.1093/ejil/chv009.

Klabbers, Jan. "Clinching the Concept of Sovereignty: Wimbledon Redux." *Austrian Review of International and European Law* 3, no. 3 (1998): 345.

Klabbers, Jan. "The Relative Autonomy of International Law or the Forgotten Politics of Interdisciplinarity." *Journal of International Law & International Relations* 1 (2005): 35. doi:10.1057/9781137318107.0008.

Knop, Karen. "Here and There: International Law in Domestic Courts." *New York University Journal of International Law and Politics* 32 (1999): 501.

Knop, Karen. "Here and There: International Law in Domestic Courts." *New York University Journal of International Law and Politics* 32 (2000): 501.

Koh, Harold Hongju, and Todd F. Buchwald. "The Crime of Aggression: The United States' Perspective." *The American Journal of International Law* 109, no. 2 (2015): 257. doi:10.5305/amerjintelaw.109.2.0257.

Koskenniemi, Martti. "The Politics of International Law—20 Years Later." *European Journal of International Law* 20, no. 1 (2009): 7. doi:10.1093/ejil/chp006.

Koskenniemi, Martti. "The Fate of Public International Law: Between Technique and Politics." *Modern Law Review* 70, no. 1 (2007): 1. doi:10.1111/j.1468-2230.2006.00624.x.

Koskenniemi, Martti. "The Police in the Temple: Order, Justice and the UN: A Dialectical View." *European Journal of International Law* 6, no. 1 (1995): 325. doi:10.1093/ejil/6.1.325.

Koskenniemi, Martti and Päivi Leino. "Fragmentation of International Law? Postmodern Anxieties." *Leiden Journal of International Law* 15, no. 3 (2002): 553. doi:10.1017/s0922156502000262.

Krisch, Nico. "The Decay of Consent: International Law in an Age of Global Public Goods." *The American Journal of International Law* 108, no. 1 (2014): 1. doi:10.5305/amerjintelaw.108.1.0001.

Krisch, Nico and Benedict Kingsbury. "Introduction: Global Governance and Global Administrative Law in the International Legal Order." *European Journal of International Law* 17, no. 1 (2006): 1. doi:10.1093/ejil/chi170.

Lavack, Anne M. and Gina Clark. "Responding to the Global Tobacco Industry: Canada and the Framework Convention on Tobacco Control." *Canadian Public Administration* 50, no. 1 (2007): 100. doi:10.1111/j.1754–7121.2007.tb02005.x.

Lewis, Grant L. "Security Council Targeted Sanctions, Due Process and the 1267 Ombudsperson." *George Washington International Law Review* 42 (2011): 673.

Llamzon, Aloysius P. "Jurisdiction and Compliance in Recent Decisions of the International Court of Justice." *European Journal of International Law* 18, no. 5 (2007): 815. doi:10.1093/ejil/chm047.

Lobel, Jules and Michael Ratner. "Bypassing the Security Council: Ambiguous Authorizations to Use Force, Cease-Fires and the Iraqi Inspection Regime." *The American Journal of International Law* 93, no. 1 (1999): 124. doi:10.2307/2997958.

Lowenfeld, Andreas F. "Investment Agreements and International Law." *Columbia Journal of Transnational Law* 42 (2003): 123.

Lutz, Ellen, and Kathryn Sikkink. "The Justice Cascade: The Evolution and Impact of Foreign Human Rights Trials in Latin America." *Chicago Journal of International Law* 2, no. 1 (2001): 1.

Mack, Erick. "The World Health Organization's New International Health Regulations: Incursion on State Sovereignty and Ill-Fated Response to Global Health Issues." *Chicago Journal of International Law* 7, no. 1 (2006): 365. http://chicagounbound .uchicago.edu/cjil/vol7/iss1/18.

Mbengue, Makane Moïse. "International Courts and Tribunals as Fact-Finders: The Case of Scientific Fact-Finding in International Adjudication." *Loyala of Los Angeles International and Comparative Law Review* 34 (2011): 53. http://digitalcommons.lmu .edu/ilr/vol34/iss1/4.

McCrudden, Christopher. "Why Do National Court Judges Refer to Human Rights Treaties? A Comparative International Law Analysis of CEDAW." *The American Journal of International Law* 109, no. 3 (2015): 534. doi:10.5305/amerjintelaw.109 .3.0534.

McDougal, Myres S. and Harold D. Lasswell. "Criteria for a Theory About Law." *California Law Review* 44 (1971): 362.

McGinnis, John O., and Mark L. Movsesian. "The World Trade Constitution." *Harvard Law Review* 114, no. 2 (2000): 511. doi:10.2307/1342574.

Meron, Theodor. "Rape as a Crime Under International Humanitarian Law." *The American Journal of International Law* 87, no. 3 (1993): 424. doi:10.2307/2203650.

Mortenson, Julian Davis. "The Travaux of Travaux : Is The Vienna Convention Hostile To Drafting History?" *The American Journal of International Law* 107, no. 4 (2013): 780. doi:10.5305/amerjintelaw.107.4.0780.

Mundis, Daryl A. "Improving the Operation and Functioning of the International Criminal Tribunals." *The American Journal of International Law* 94, no. 4 (2000): 759. doi:10.2307/2589804.

Murphy, Sean D. "Terrorism and the Concept of 'Armed Attack'" in Article 51 of the UN Charter. *Harvard International Law Journal* 43, no. 1 (2002): 41.

Nielson, Daniel L., and Michael J. Tierney. "Delegation to International Organizations: Agency Theory and World Bank Environmental Reform." *International Organization* 57, no. 2 (2003). doi:10.1017/s0020818303572010.

Norton, Patrick M. "A Law of the Future or a Law of the Past? Modern Tribunals and the International Law of Expropriation." *The American Journal of International Law* 85, no. 3 (1991): 474. doi:10.2307/2203108.

Norton, Patrick M. "The Use of Precedents in Investment Treaty Arbitration Awards." *American Review of International Arbitration* 24, no. 2 (2007): 129.

O'Connell, Mary Ellen. "Dangerous Departures." *The American Journal of International Law* 107, no. 2 (2013): 380. doi:10.5305/amerjintelaw.107.2.0380.

Oellers-Frahm, Karin. "Lawmaking Through Advisory Opinions?" *German Law Journal* 12, no. 5 (2011): 1033. http://static1.squarespace.com/static/56330ad3e4b0733dccoc8495/t/56b70de6cf80a12820a591aa/1454837223050/GLJ_Vol_12_No_05_OellersG%C3%87%C3%89Frahm.pdf.

Oosthuizen, Gabriël H. "Playing the Devil's Advocate: The United Nations Security Council Is Unbound by Law." *Leiden Journal of International Law* 12, no. 3 (1999): 549. doi:10.1017/s0922156599000278.

Orakhelashvili, Alexander. "The International Court's Advisory Opinion on the UDI in Respect of Kosovo: Washing Away the "Foam on the Tide of Time." *Max Planck Yearbook of United Nations Law Online* 15 (2011): 65.

Palmeter, David. "The WTO Appellate Body Needs Remand Authority." *Journal of World Trade* 32, no. 1 (1998): 41.

Paust, Jordan J. "Ten Types of Israeli and Palestinian Violation of the Laws of War and the ICC." *Connecticut Journal of International Law* 31 (2016).

Pauwelyn, Joost. "The Role of Public International Law in the WTO: How Far Can We Go?" *The American Journal of International Law* 95, no. 3 (2001): 535. doi:10.2307/2668492.

Pauwelyn, Joost. "The Rule of Law Without the Rule of Lawyers? Why Investment Arbitrators Are from Mars, Trade Adjudicators from Venus." *The American Journal of International Law* 109, no. 4 (2015): 761. doi:10.5305/amerjintelaw.109.4.0761.

Pauwelyn, Joost. "The Transformation of World Trade." *Michigan Law Review* 104 (2005): 1.

Pauwelyn, Joost, R.A. Wessel, and J. Wouters. "When Structures Become Shackles: Stagnation and Dynamics in International Lawmaking." *European Journal of International Law* 25, no. 3 (2014): 733. doi:10.1093/ejil/chu051.

Pellet, Allain. "Can a State Commit a Crime? Definitely, Yes!" *European Journal of International Law* 10, no. 2 (1999): 425. doi:10.1093/ejil/10.2.425.

Perez, Antonio F. "The Passive Virtues and the World Court: Pro-Dialogic Abstentio by the International Court of Justice." *Michigan Journal of International Law* 18 (1997): 399.

Plotkin, Bruce. "Human Rights and Other Provisions in the Revised International Health Regulations (2005)." *Public Health* 121, no. 11 (2007): 840. doi:10.1016/j.puhe.2007.08.001.

Plotkin, Bruce Jay. "Mission Possible: The Future of the International Health Regulations." *Temple International and Comparative Law Journal* 10, no. 2 (1996): 503. http://hdl.handle.net/10822/895940.

Posner, Eric A., and Miguel F.P. De Figueiredo. "Is the International Court of Justice Biased?" *The Journal of Legal Studies* 34, no. 2 (2005): 599. doi:10.1086/430765.

Posner, Eric A., and John C. Yoo. "A Theory of International Adjudication." *California Law Review* 93 (2005).

Powell, Catherine. "Libya: A Multilateral Constitutional Moment?" *American Journal of International Law* 106 (2012).

Putnam, Robert D. "Diplomacy and Domestic Politics: The Logic of Two-Level Games." *International Organization* 42, no. 3 (1988): 427. doi:10.1017/s002081830 0027697.

Quigley, John. "The Privatization of Security Council Enforcement Action: A Threat to Multilateralism." *Michigan Journal of International Law* 17 (1996): 249.

Rashkow, Bruce. "*Remedies for Harm Caused by UN Peacekeepers.*" Am. J. Int'l L. Unbound, Apr. 2, 2014: https://www.asil.org/blogs/remedies-harm-caused-un-peacekeepers.

Raustiala, Kal and David G. Victor. "The Regime Complex for Plant Genetic Resources." *International Organization* 58, no. 2 (2004): 277. doi:10.1017/s00208183 04582036.

Reisman, W. Michael. "The Constitutional Crisis In The United Nations." *American Journal of International Law* 87, no. 83, (1993) 399. doi:10.1163/ej.9780792323181.13–496.69.

Roberts, Anthea. "Clash Of Paradigms: Actors And Analogies Shaping The Investment Treaty System." *The American Journal of International Law* 107, no. 1 (2013): 45. doi:10.5305/amerjintelaw.107.1.0045.

Rosand, Eric. "Security Council Resolution 1373, the Counter-Terrorism Committee, and the Fight Against Terrorism." *The American Journal of International Law* 97, no. 2 (2003): 333. doi:10.2307/3100110.

Rosand, Eric. "The Security Council as 'Global Legislator': Ultra Vires or Ultra Innovative?" *Fordham International Law Journal* 28, no. 3 (2004): 521–90.

Ruys, Tom. "The Meaning of 'Force' and the Boundaries of the Jus Ad Bellum: Are 'Minimal' Uses of Force Excluded from UN Charter Article 2(4)?" *The American Journal of International Law* 108, no. 2 (2014): 159. doi:10.5305/amerjintelaw.108.2.0159.

Sapsin, Jason W. et al. "SARS and International Legal Preparedness." *Temple Law Review* 77 (2004): 155.

Sarfaty, Galit A. "Why Culture Matters in International Institutions: The Marginality of Human Rights at the World Bank." *American Journal of International Law* 103 (2009): 647.

Sarfaty, Galit A. "The World Bank and the Internalization of Indigenous Rights Norms." *Yale Law Journal* 114 (2004): 1791.

Saul, Ben. "Legislating from a Radical Hague: The United Nations Special Tribunal for Lebanon Invents an International Crime of Transnational Terrorism." *Leiden Journal of International Law* 24, no. 3 (2011): 677. doi:10.1017/s09221565 11000203.

Scharf, Michael. "The Letter of the Law: The Scope of the International Legal Obligation to Prosecute Human Rights Crimes." *Law and Contemporary Problems* 59, no. 4 (1996): 41. doi:10.2307/1192189.

Scheffer, David J. "Beyond Occupation Law." *The American Journal of International Law* 97, no. 4 (2003): 842. doi:10.2307/3133684.

Schill, Stephan W. "Enhancing International Investment Law's Legitimacy: Conceptual and Methodological Foundations of a New Public Law Approach." *Virginia Journal of International Law* 52, no. 1 (2011): 57.

Schill, Stephan W. "Tearing Down the Great Wall: The New Generation of Investment Treaties of the People's Republic of China." *Cardozo Journal of International & Comparative Law* 15, no. 1 (2007): 73.

Shaffer, Gregory C. "How Business Shapes Law: A Socio-Legal Framework." *Connecticut Law Review* 42, no. 1 (2009): 147.

Shany, Yuval. "Assessing The Effectiveness Of International Courts: A Goal-Based Approach." *The American Journal of International Law* 106, no. 2 (2012): 225. doi:10.5305/amerjintelaw.106.2.0225.

Shapiro, Martin. "Judges as Liars." *Harvard Journal of Law and Public Policy* 17 (1994): 155.

Shkabatur, Jennifer A. "A Global Panopticon? The Changing Role of International Organizations in the Information Age." *Michigan Journal of International Law* 33 (2011): 159. http://repository.law.umich.edu/mjil/vol33/iss1/508.

Silva, Mario. "Somalia: State Failure, Piracy, and the Challenge to International Law." *Virginia Journal of International Law* 50, no. 3 (2010).

Simma, Bruno. "Self-contained Regimes." *Netherlands Yearbook of International Law* 16 (1985): 111. doi:10.1017/s0167676800003482.

Simma, Bruno and Andreas L. Paulus. "The Responsibility of Individuals for Human Rights Abuses in Internal Conflicts: A Positivist View." *The American Journal of International Law* 93, no. 2 (1999): 302. doi:10.2307/2997991.

Simma, Bruno and Dirk Pulkowski. "Of Planets and the Universe: Self-contained Regimes in International Law." *European Journal of International Law* 17, no. 3 (2006): 483. doi:10.1093/ejil/chl015.

Simmons, Beth A. "Bargaining over BITs, Arbitrating Awards: The Regime for Protection and Promotion of International Investment." *World Politics* 66, no. 1 (2013): 12. doi:10.1017/s0043887113000312.

Slaughter, Anne-Marie. "Judicial Globalization." *Virginia Journal of International Law* 40 (2000): 1103.

Stahn, Carsten. "The Ambiguities of Security Council Resolution 1422." *European Journal of International Law* 14, no. 1 (2002): 85. doi:10.1093/ejil/14.1.85.

Stahn, Carsten. "Responsibility to Protect: Political Rhetoric or Emerging Legal Norm?" *American Journal of International Law* 101, no. 1 (2007): 99.

Stein, Eric. "International Integration and Democracy: No Love at First Sight." *American Journal of International Law* 95, no. 3 (2001): 489.

Stephan, Paul B. "Privatizing International Law." *Virginia Law Review* 97 (2011): 1573.

Stewart, Richard B. "Remedying Disregard In Global Regulatory Governance: Accountability, Participation, And Responsiveness." *The American Journal of International Law* 108, no. 2 (2014): 211. doi:10.5305/amerjintelaw.108.2.0211.

Sweet, Alec Stone. Investor-State Arbitration: Proportionality's New Frontier. *Law & Ethics of Human Rights* 4, no. 1 (2010). doi:10.2202/1938-2545.1044.

Sweet, Alec Stone. "Judicialization and the Construction of Governance." *Comparative Political Studies* 32, no. 2 (1999): 147.

Sweet, Alec Stone, and Jud Matthews. "Proportionality Balancing and Global Constitutionalism." *Columbia Journal of Transnational Law* 47 (2008): 68.

Szasz, Paul C. "The Complexification of the United Nations System." *Max Planck Yearbook of United Nations Law Online* 3, no. 1 (1999): Xxi. doi:http://dx.doi.org/10.1163/187574199X00018.

Szasz, Paul C. "The Security Council Starts Legislating." *The American Journal of International Law* 96, no. 4 (2002): 901. doi:10.2307/3070686.

Taft IV, William H. and Todd E. Buchwald. "Preemption, Iraq, and International Law." *American Journal of International Law* 97, no. 3 (2003): 557.

Talmon, Stefan. "The Security Council as World Legislature." *The American Journal of International Law* 99, no. 1 (2005): 175. doi:10.2307/3246097.

Taylor, Allyn L., T. Alfven, D. Hougendobler, S. Tanaka, and K. Buse. "Leveraging Non-binding Instruments for Global Health Governance: Reflections from the Global AIDS Reporting Mechanism for WHO Reform." *Public Health* 128, no. 2 (2014): 151. doi:10.1016/j.puhe.2013.08.022.

Trachtman, Joel P. "The Crisis in International Law." *Case Western Reserve Journal of International Law* 44 (2011): 407.

Townsend, Belinda et. al. *Global Health Governance: Framework Convention on Tobacco Control (FCTC), the Doha Declaration, and Democratisation*, 2 (2) ADMIN. SCI. 186 (2012).

Venzke, Ingo. "Making General Exceptions: The Spell of Precedents in Developing Article XX GATT into Standards for Domestic Regulatory Policy." *German L* 12, no. 5 (2011): 1111.

Villalpando, Santiago. "Codification Light: A New Trend in the Codification of International Law at the United Nations." *Anuário Brasileiro De Direito Internacional Brazilian Yearbook of International Law* 2 (2013): 117.

Voeten, Erik. "The Impartiality of International Judges: Evidence from the European Court of Human Rights." *Am. Pol. Sci. Rev. American Political Science Review* 102, no. 4 (2008): 417. doi:10.1017/s0003055408080398.

Von Bogdandy, Armin, Phillipp Denn and Matthias Goldman. "Developing the Publicness of Public International Law: Towards a Legal Framework for Global Governance Activities." *German Law Journal* 9 (2008): 1375.

Von Bogdandy, Armin, and Ingo Venzke. "Beyond Dispute: International Judicial Institutions as Lawmakers." *German Law Journal* 12, no. 5 (2011): 979.

Von Bogdandy, Armin, and Ingo Venzke. *On the Functions of International Courts: An Appraisal in Light of Their Burgeoning Public Authority*, 26 LEIDEN J. INT'L L. 49 (2013).

Wahi, Namita. "Human Rights Accountability of the IMF and the World Bank: A Critique of Existing Mechanisms and Articulation of a Theory of Horizontal Accountability." *University of California Davis Journal of International Law and Policy* 12 (2006): 344.

Waldron, Jeremy. "Are Sovereigns Entitled to the Benefit of the International Rule of Law?" *European Journal of International Law* 22, no. 2 (2011): 315–43. doi:10.1093/ejil/chro31.

Waldron, Jeremy. "The Concept and the Rule of Law." *Georgia Law Review* 43, no. 1 (2008): 1.

Waldron, Jeremy. "The Rule of International Law." *Harvard Journal of Law and Public Policy* 30, no. 1 (2006): 15.

Weil, Prosper. "Towards Relative Normativity in International Law?" *The American Journal of International Law* 77, no. 3 (1983): 413. doi:10.2307/2201073.

Weiler, Joseph H.H. "The Transformation of Europe." *Yale Law Journal* 100, no. 8 (1991): 2403.

Weisburd, Arthur Mark. "The War in Iraq and the Dilemma of Controlling the International Use of Force." *Texas International Law Journal* 39, no. 4 (2004): 521.

Weissbrodt, David, Joseph C. Hansen, and Nathaniel H. Nesbitt. "The Role of the Committee on the Rights of the Child in Interpreting and Developing International Humanitarian Law." *Harvard Human Rights Journal* 24 (2011): 115. http://harvardhrj.com/wp-content/uploads/2009/09/115-154.pdf.

Weston, Burns H. "Security Council Resolution 678 and Persian Gulf Decision-Making: Precarious Legitimacy." *The American Journal of International Law* 85, no. 3 (1991): 516. doi:10.2307/2203110.

Willis, Grant L. *Security Council Targeted Sanctions, Due Process and the 1267 Ombudsperson*, 42 Geo. J. Int'l L. 673 (2011)

Wippman, David. "The Costs of International Justice." *American Journal of International Law* 100, no. 4 (2006): 881.

Xue, Hanqin., and Qian Jin. "International Treaties in the Chinese Domestic Legal System." *Chinese Journal of International Law* 8, no. 2 (2009): 299. doi:10.1093/chinesejil/jmp007.

Youde, Jeremy. "MERS and Global Health Governance." *International Journal* 70, no. 1 (2014): 119.

Zacklin, R. "The Failings of Ad Hoc International Tribunals." *Journal of International Criminal Justice* 2, no. 2 (2004): 541. doi:10.1093/jicj/2.2.541.

Zidar, Andraž. "WHO International Health Regulations and Human Rights: From Allusions to Inclusion." *The International Journal of Human Rights* 19, no. 4 (2015): 505. doi:10.1080/13642987.2015.1045340.

Book Chapters

Alter, Karen. "The Multiple Roles of International Courts and Tribunals." In *Interdisciplinary Perspectives on International Law and International Relations: The State of the Art*, edited by Jeffrey L. Dunoff and Mark A. Pollack. Cambridge: Cambridge University Press, 2012.

Alvarez, José E. "Beware: Boundary Crossings." In *Boundaries of State, Boundaries of Rights: Human Rights, Private Actors, and Positive Obligations*, edited by Tsvi Kahana and Anat Scolnicov. Cambridge, UK: Cambridge University Press, 2016.

Alvarez, Jose E. "The Evolving BIT." In *Investment Treaty Arbitration and International Law*, edited by Laird, Ian A., Nina P. Mocheva, and Todd J. Weiler. 3d ed. Huntington: Juris Publishing LLC, 2010.

Alvarez, José E. "State Sovereignty Is Not Withering Away: A Few Lessons for the Future." In *Realizing Utopia: The Future of International Law*, edited by Antonio Cassese. Oxford: Oxford University Press, 2012.

Alvarez, José E. "What Are International Courts For? The Main Functions of International Adjudication." In *The Oxford Handbook of International Adjudication*, edited by Cesare P.R. Romano, Karen J. Alter, and Yuval Shany. Oxford: Oxford University Press, 2013.

Alvarez, José E., and Kathryn Khamsi. "The Argentine Crisis and Foreign Investors: A Glimpse into the Heart of the Investment Regime." In *International Courts and the Development of International Law: Essays in Honour of Tullio Treves*, edited by Nerina Boschiero, Tullio Scovazzi, Cesare Pitea, and Chiara Ragni. The Hague: T.M.C. Asser Press, 2013.

Besson, Samantha. "Sources of International Law." In *The Philosophy of International Law*, edited by Samantha Besson and John Tasioulas. Oxford: Oxford University Press, 2010.

Bianchi, Andrea. "Law, Time and Change: The Self-Regulatory Function of Subsequent Practice." In *Treaties and Subsequent Practice*, edited by Georg Nolte. Oxford, 2013: Oxford University Press.

Bilder, Richard B. "The Fact/Law Distinction in International Adjudication." In *Fact-finding before International Tribunals: Eleventh Sokol Colloquium*, edited by Lillich, Richard B. Ardsley-on-Hudson, NY: Transnational Publishers, 1992.

Binder, Christina. "The Prohibition of Amnesties by the Inter-American Court of Human Rights." In *International Judicial Lawmaking: On Public Authority and*

Democratic Legitimation in Global Governance, edited by Armin Von Bogdandy and Ingo Venzke. Heidelberg: Springer, 2012.

Boisson de Chazournes, Laurence. "Policy Guidance and Compliance: The World Bank Operational Standards." In *Commitment and Compliance: The Role of Non-Binding Norms in the International Legal System*, edited by Dinah Shelton. Oxford: Oxford University Press, 2000.

Boisson de Chazournes, Laurence. "United in Joy and Sorrow: Some Considerations of Responsibility Issues under Partnerships among International Financial Institutions. In *Responsibility of International Organizations: Essays in Memory of Sir Ian Brownlie*, edited by Maurizio Ragazzi. Leiden: Martinus Nijhoff Publishers, 2013.

Broches, Aron. "International Legal Aspects of the Operations of the World Bank." In *Selected Essays: World Bank, ICSID, and Other Subjects of Public and Private International Law 3, 12* (1995).

In *International Legal Aspects of the Operations of the World Bank*. Leiden: Martinus Nijhoff Publishers, 1995.

Collins, Richard. "Classical Legal Positivism in International Law Revisited." In *International Legal Positivism in a Post-modern World*, edited by Jörg Kammerhofer and Jean D'Aspremont. Cambridge: Cambridge University Press, 2014.

D'Aspremont, Jean. "From a Pluralization of International Norm-making Processes to a Pluralization of the Concept of International Law." In *Informal International Lawmaking*, edited by Joost Pauwelyn, Ramses A. Wessel, and Jan Wouters. Oxford: Oxford University Press, 2012.

Dañino, Robert. "The Legal Aspects of the World Bank's Work on Human Rights: Some Preliminary Thoughts." In *Human Rights and Development: Towards Mutual Reinforcement*, edited by Philip Alston and Mary Robinson. Oxford: Oxford University Press, 2005.

Franck, Thomas M. "Fact Finding in the I.C.J." In *Fact-finding before International Tribunals: Eleventh Sokol Colloquium*. Edited by Richard B. Lillich. Ardsley-on-Hudson, NY: Transnational Publishers, 1992.

Gold, Joseph. "Financing: Conditionality." In *Legal and Institutional Aspects of the International Monetary System: Selected Essays, Volume II*. Washington D.C.: International Monetary Fund, 1984.

Guzman, Andrew T., and Timothy Meyer. "Soft Law." In *Research Handbook on the Economics of Public International Law*, edited by Eugene Kontorovich. Cheltenham: Edward Elgar Publishing, 2014.

Hey, Ellen. "The World Bank Inspection Panel and the Development of International Law." In *International Courts and the Development of International Law: Essays in Honour of Tullio Treves*, edited by Nerina Boschiero, Tullio Scovazzi, Cesare Pitea, and Chiara Ragni. The Hague: T.M.C. Asser Press, 2013.

Higgins, Rosalyn. The Role of Resolutions of International Organizations in the Process of Creating Norms in the International System. In *International Law and the International System*, edited by William Elliott Butler. Dordrecht: M. Nijhoff, 1987.

Hood, Anna. "The United Nations Security Council's Legislative Phase and the Rise of Emergency International Law-Making." In *Legal Perspectives on Security Institutions*, edited by Hitoshi Nasu and Kim Rubenstein. Cambridge, UK: Cambridge University Press, 2015.

Jacobs, Marc. "Precedents: Lawmaking Through International Adjudication." In *International Judicial Lawmaking: On Public Authority and Democratic Legitimation in Global Governance*, edited by Armin Von Bogdandy, Ingo Venzke, and Bruno Simma. Heidelberg: Springer, 2012.

Johnson, Jr., O. Thomas, and Jonathan Gimblett. "From Gunboats to BITs: The Evolution of Modern International Investment Law." In *Yearbook on International Investment Law & Policy*, edited by Karl P. Sauvant. Oxford: Oxford University Press, 2012.

Kingsbury, Benedict. "International Courts: Uneven Judicialisation in Global Order." In *The Cambridge Companion to International Law*, edited by James Crawford and Martti Koskenniemi. Cambridge: Cambridge University Press, 2012.

Kingsbury, Benedict. "Operational Policies of International Institutions as Part of the Law-Making Process: The World Bank and Indigenous Peoples." In *The Reality of International Law: Essays in Honour of Ian Brownlie*, by Guy S. Goodwin-Gill and Stefan Talmon. Oxford: Clarendon Press, 1999.

Kingsbury, Benedict and Stephan Schill. "Investor-State Arbitration as Governance: Fair and Equitable Treatment, Proportionality and the Emerging Global Administrative Law." In *El Nuevo Derecho Administrativo Global En América Latina*, edited by Benedict Kingsbury and Richard B. Stewart. Buenos Aires: Ediciones Rap, 2009.

MacDonald, Ronald St. John. "The Margin of Appreciation." In *The European System for the Protection of Human Rights*, edited by Ronald St. John Macdonald, Franz Matscher, and Herbert Petzold. Dordrecht: Martinus Nijhoff Publishers, 1993.

McLachlan, Campbell. "The Evolution of Treaty Obligations in International Law." In *Treaties and Subsequent Practice*, edited by Georg Nolte. Oxford: Oxford University Press, 2013.

Murphy, Sean D. "The United States and the International Court of Justice: Coping with Antinomies." In *The Sword and the Scales: The United States and International Courts and Tribunals*, edited by Cesare P.R. Romano. Cambridge, UK: Cambridge University Press, 2009.

Pauwelyn, Joost. "Is It International Law or Not, and Does It Even Matter?" In *Informal International Lawmaking*, edited by Joost Pauwelyn, Ramses A. Wessel, and Jan Wouters. Oxford: Oxford University Press, 2012.

Pauwelyn, Joost, and Manfred Elsig. "The Politics of Treaty Interpretation: Variations and Explanations across International Tribunals." In *Interdisciplinary Perspectives on International Law and International Relations: The State of the Art*, edited by

Jeffrey L. Dunoff and Mark A. Pollack. Cambridge, UK: Cambridge University Press, 2012.

Ragni, Chiara. "The Contribution of the Special Tribunal for Lebanon to the Notion of Terrorism: Judicial Creativity or Progressive Development of International Law?" In *International Courts and the Development of International Law: Essays in Honour of Tullio Treves*, edited by Nerina Boschiero, Tullio Scovazzi, Cesare Pitea, and Chiara Ragni. The Hague: T.M.C. Asser Press, 2013.

Raustiala, Kal. "Institutional Proliferation and the International Legal Order." In *Interdisciplinary Perspectives on International Law and International Relations: The State of the Art*, edited by Jeffrey L. Dunoff and Mark A. Pollack. Cambridge: Cambridge University Press, 2012.

Schill, Stephan W. "International Investment Law and Comparative Public Law—An Introduction." In *International Investment Law and Comparative Public Law*, edited by Stephan Schill. Oxford: Oxford University Press, 2010.

Schill, Stephan W. "System-Building in Investment Treaty Arbitration and Lawmaking." In *International Judicial Lawmaking: On Public Authority and Democratic Legitimation in Global Governance*, edited by Armin Von Bogdandy, Ingo Venzke, and Bruno Simma. Heidelberg: Springer, 2012.

Simma, Bruno. "Consent: Strains in the Treaty System." In *The Structure and Process of International Law: Essays in Legal Philosophy, Doctrine, and Theory*, by Ronald St. John Macdonald and Douglas M. Johnston. The Hague: Martinus Nijhoff, 1983.

Simma, Bruno, and Theodore Kill. "Harmonizing Investment Protection and International Human Rights: First Steps Towards a Methodology." In *International Investment Law for the 21st Century: Essays in Honour of Christoph Schreuer*, edited by Christina Binder and Christoph Schreuer. Oxford: Oxford University Press, 2009.

Tzanakopoulos, Antonios. "Domestic Court Reactions to UN Security Council Sanctions." In *Challenging Acts of International Organizations before National Courts*, edited by August Reinisch. Oxford: Oxford University Press, 2010.

Ulfstein, Geir. "Law-Making by Human Rights Treaty Bodies." In *International Law-making: Essays in Honour of Jan Klabbers*, compiled by Rain Liivoja, edited by Jarna Petman. London: Routledge, 2014.

Van Alebeek, Rosanne, and André Nollkaemper. "The Legal Status of Decisions by Human Rights Treaty Bodies in National Law." In *UN Human Rights Treaty Bodies: Law and Legitimacy*. Edited by Helen Keller and Geir Ulfstein. Cambridge, UK: Cambridge University Press, 2012.

Voeten, Erik. "International Judicial Behavior." In *The Oxford Handbook of International Adjudication*, edited by Cesare Romano, Karen J. Alter, and Yuval Shany. Oxford: Oxford University Press, 2014.

Voeten, Erik. "International Judicial Independence." In *Interdisciplinary Perspectives on International Law and International Relations: The State of the Art*, edited by Jeffrey L. Dunoff and Mark A. Pollack. Cambridge: Cambridge University Press, 2012.

Voeten, Erik. "Politics, Judicial Behavior, and Institutional Design." In *The European Court of Human Rights between Law and Politics*, edited by Jonas Christoffersen and Mikael Rask. Madsen. Oxford: Oxford University Press, 2011.

Von Bogdandy, Armin, and Ingo Venzke. "The Spell of Precedents: Lawmaking by International Courts and Tribunals." In *The Oxford Handbook of International Adjudication*, by Cesare P.R. Romano, Karen J. Alter, and Yuval Shany. Oxford: Oxford University Press, 2014.

Von Bogdandy, Armin, and Ingo Venzke. "On the Democratic Legitimation of International Judicial Lawmaking." In *International Judicial Lawmaking: On Public Authority and Democratic Legitimation in Global Governance*, edited by Armin Von Bogdandy and Ingo Venzke. Heidelberg: Springer, 2012.

Von Einsiedel, Sebastian. "Introduction." *The UN Security Council in the Twenty-first Century*. Edited by Sebastian von Einsiedel, David M. Malone, and Bruno Stagno Ugarte. Boulder: Lynne Rienner Publishers, 2016.

Yasuaki, Onuma. "The ICJ: An Emperor Without Clothes? International Conflict Resolution, Article 38 of the ICJ Statute and the Sources of International Law." In *Liber Amicorum Judge Shigeru Oda*, edited by Shigeru Oda, Nisuke Andō, Edward McWhinney, and Rüdiger Wolfrum. Leiden: Brill–Nijhoff, 2002.

Other

Waldron, Jeremy. *The Pre and Post UN Charter Order*. Speech, Nov. 1, 2015: https://its .law.nyu.edu/eventcalendar/index.cfm?fuseaction=main.detail&id=42235.

Restatement (Third) of the Foreign Relations Law of the United States (1987).

About the Author

Biographical Note

José Enrique Alvarez, Born on March 3rd, 1955 in Habana, Cuba. Emigrated to the United States in 1961.

Education: Harvard Law School (Cambridge, MA) J.D. *Cum Laude* (1981); Magdalen College, Oxford University (Oxford, England) B.A., First Class (highest honors) in Jurisprudence (1979); Harvard College (Cambridge, MA), A.B. *Summa Cum Laude* (1977).

Academic positions: Herbert and Rose Rubin Professor of International Law; Director, LLM Degree in International Legal Studies, New York University School of Law (2009 to present); Hamilton Fish Professor of International Law & Diplomacy (as of 2005), Columbia Law School; Director, Center on Global Legal Problems (1999–2008); Professor, University of Michigan Law School; Director, Center for International and Comparative Law (1994–1999); Associate Professor, George Washington University School of Law (1989–1993).

Other professional activities: *American Journal of International Law*: Editorial Board (1997–2007), Co-Editor in Chief (April 2013 to present); U.S. Department of State, Advisory Committee on Public International Law (1994–fall 2008) and (from Dec. 2009 to present); Institut de Droit International, Elected Associé (September 2013); National University of Singapore, Member of International Advisory Panel of the Centre for International Law (Feb. 2013 to present); International Criminal Court, Office of the Prosecutor: Special Adviser on Public International Law (May 2010–June 2012); Institute for Transnational Arbitration, Academic Council (elected as of 2010); *Journal of International Criminal Justice*: Board of Editors (2003–2007), Advisory Board (2007 to present); American Society of International Law: Chair, International Institutions Interest Group (1993–1994), Nominating Committee (1999) and (2000), Executive Council (1995–1998), Executive Committee of Executive Council (1995–1996); Co-Chair, 1997 Annual Meeting; Research Committee (1998–2000), President's Interest Group Committee (2000), Vice President (2002–2004), Centennial Committee (2005–2006), President (2006–2008), Chair, Nominating Committee (2009), Counselor (2013 to present); Center for the Study of Human Rights, Columbia University, Advisory Board (2000–2004); Center on Reproductive Rights, Board (2009–2016), chair, Strategic Planning Committee (2012–2013); Council on Foreign Relations: Member (since 1994); American Bar Association: Co-Chair, International Institutions

Committee (1992–1993), Council, International Law Section (1994–1997), member, Task Force on the International War Crimes Tribunal for the Former Yugoslavia (1993–1996); American Law Institute: Member (1999 to present), Adviser, Project on Principles of Trade Law: The World Trade Organization (2002–2006); International Affairs Fellow, Council on Foreign Relations and Resident Associate, Carnegie Endowment of International Peace (1989–1990); Attorney-Adviser, Office of the Legal Adviser, U.S. Department of State (1983–1988); Adjunct Professor, Georgetown Law Center (1983–1988); Attorney, Shea & Gardner (1982–1983); Law clerk, The Honorable Thomas Gibbs Gee, U.S. Ct. of Appeals (1981–1982).

Publications

Books

(1) *The Public International Law Regime Governing International Investment* (AIL-Pocket Books, 2011) (also at 344 *Recueil des cours* 195 (2011))

(2) *The Evolving International Investment Regime: Expectations, Realities, Options* (edited) (with Karl Sauvant, Kamil Gérard Ahmed and Gabriela del P. Vizcaíno) (Oxford University Press 2011)

(3) *International Organizations as Law-Makers* (Oxford University Press 2005; paperback 2006); (also in Chinese translation, 2011)

(4) *The American Contribution to International Investment Law* (edited) (forthcoming Brill 2016)

Published Lectures and Keynote Addresses

(5) "Crossing the Public/Private Divide: *Saipem v. Bangladesh* and other 'Crossover' Cases," in Albert Jan Van den Berg, ed., *International Arbitration The Coming of a New Age?*, ICCA Congress Series No. 17, 400 (2013)

(6) "The Paradoxical Argentina Cases," (with Gustavo Topalian), 6 *World Arbitration & Mediation Review* 491 (2012)

(7) "Is the International Investment Regime a Form of Global Governance?," ICCA Congress Series No. 16, 50th Anniversary Conference, Geneva, 19–20 May 2011

(8) "The Return of the State," 20 *Minnesota Journal of International Law* 223 (2011); keynote address, ASIL/International Economic Law Interest Group Biennial Conference, Nov. 2010

(9) "MacKinnon's Engaged Scholarship," 46 *Tulsa Law Review* 25 (2011); originally presented at the annual meeting of the American Association of Law Schools, Plenary Session, Jan. 7, 2005

(10) "Why are We 'Re-Calibrating' Our Investment Treaties?," 4 *World Arbitration & Mediation Review* 143 (2010); originally presented at the annual Institute for

Transnational Arbitration (ITA)-American Society of International Law (ASIL) Conference, Mar. 2010

(11) "Are Corporations 'Subjects of International Law'?," 9 *Santa Clara Journal of International Law* 1 (2011); originally presented as a keynote address at the University of Santa Clara Law School, Mar. 2010

(12) "But is it Law?," Presentation at Annual Meeting of the American Society of International Law, 2009, Proceedings of the Annual Meeting 2010

(13) "The Evolving BIT," Luncheon Address, April 2009, Washington, D.C., published in *Transnational Dispute Management*, June 2009; also in Ian A. Laird and Todd Weiler, eds., *Investment Treaty Arbitration and International Law* 1 (2010)

(14) "Three Responses to 'Proliferating' Tribunals," 41 *N.Y.U. Journal of International Law and Politics* 991 (2009)

(15) "Contemporary International Law: An 'Empire of Law' or the 'Law of Empire'?," Annual International Law Lecture, American University, Sept. 2008, published in 24 *American University International Law Review* 811 (2009); also published in Spanish in 4 *Bajo Palabra, Revista de Filosofía* (2009)

(16) "Contemporary Foreign Investment Law: An 'Empire of Law' or the 'Law of Empire'?," Meador Lecture, 60 *Alabama Law Review* 943 (2009)

(17) "Speech: The Internationalization of U.S. Law," 47 *Columbia Journal of Transnational Law* 537 (2009), originally presented as luncheon address, International Law Weekend, Oct. 2008

(18) "The Future of Our Society" and "Fifty Ways International Law Hurts Our Lives," Presidential Address, American Society of International Law, Annual Meeting, April 2007, President's Speech; reprinted in *American Society of International Law, Proceedings of the 102nd Annual Meeting* 499 (2008)

(19) "Governing the World: International Organizations as Law-Makers," 31 *Suffolk Transnational Law Review* 591 (2008)

(20) "The Schizophrenias of R2P," Presented at 2007 Hague Joint Conference on Contemporary Issues of International Law: Criminal Jurisdiction 100 Years After the 1907 Hague Peace Conference, The Hague, The Netherlands on June 30, 2007; reprinted in Philip Alston & Euan MacDonald, eds., *Human Rights, Intervention, and the Use of Force* (2008)

(21) "A Tribute to Louis Sohn," 39 *George Washington International Law Review* 643 (2007)

(22) "Institutionalized Legalization and the Asia-Pacific Region," 5 *New Zealand Journal of Public and International Law* 9 (2007)

(23) "International Organizations: Accountability or Responsibility?," Luncheon Address, Canadian Council of International Law, Proceedings of the Annual Meeting, 2007

(24) "Torturing the Law," 37 *Case Western Journal of International Law* 175 (2006)

(25) "A Conversation with Secretary of State Condoleezza Rice," (Moderated by Gwen Ifill) *American Society of International Law, Proceedings of the 100th Annual Meeting* 1 (2006)

(26) "Do States Socialize?," 54 *Duke Law Journal* 961 (2005)

(27) "Commemorating Oscar Schachter, The Teacher," 104 *Columbia Law Review* 556 (2004)

(28) "The Closing of the American Mind," Luncheon Address, Canadian Council of International Law, October 2003, Proceedings of the Annual Meeting, 2004 "International Organizations as Law-Makers," in Proceedings of the Sixth Hague Joint Conference held in The Hague, The Netherlands, 3–5 July 2003, 11–20 (Asser Press 2004) (Keynote Address); also presented in modified form as opening lecture in the Challenges in International Governance Speaker Series, Columbia Law School, Sept. 24, 2003 as "The Promise and Perils of International Organizations" (available as archived webcast at www.law.columbia.edu)

(29) "The UN's 'War on Terrorism,'" 31 *International Journal of Legal Information* 238 (2003)

(30) "Measuring Compliance," *American Society of International Law, Proceedings of the 96th Annual Meeting* 209 (2002)

(31) "The New Treaty Makers," XXV *Boston College International & Comparative Law Review* 213 (2002) (Keynote Address at Festshrift in Honor of Cynthia Lichtenstein on "Globalization and the Erosion of Sovereignty")

(32) "How *Not* to Link: Institutional Conundrums of an Expanded Trade Regime," VII *Widener Law Symposium Journal* 1 (2001) (Keynote Address for symposium on "The World Trade Organization and the Structure of Global Governance")

(33) "Interliberal Law: A Comment," *American Society of International Law, Proceedings of the 94th Annual Meeting* 249 (2000)

(34) "Post-ICC Challenges," Australia/New Zealand Society of International Law, Proceedings of the Annual Meeting (2000)

(35) "Lessons from the Akayesu Judgment," *ILSA Journal of International & Comparative Law* (1999)

(36) "Genocide: Then and Now," *Law Quad Notes*, University of Michigan Law School (Summer 1998)

(37) "Seeking Legal Remedies for War Crimes: International Versus National Trials," 6:1 *International Institute Journal*, University of Michigan (Fall 1998)

(38) "A Conversation with Professors Louis Henkin and Louis Sohn," *American Society of International Law, Proceedings of the 92nd Annual Meeting* (1999)

(39) "A New Nuremberg," *Law Quad Notes*, University of Michigan Law School) (Fall/Winter 1997)

(40) "Critical Theory and the North American Free Trade Agreement's Chapter Eleven," 28 *Inter-American Law Review* 303 (Winter 1996–97) "International Law: Some Recent Developments," 46 *Journal of Legal Education* 557 (1997)

(41) "The Likely Legacies of Tadic," 3 *ILSA Journal of International and Comparative Law* 612 (1997)

(42) "The United States Financial Veto," *American Society of International Law, Proceedings of the 90th Annual Meeting* 319 (1997); modified version published as "Dollars as Discipline: The U.S. and the U.N.," *Law Quad Notes* (University of Michigan Law School) (Spring 1997)

(43) "Theoretical Perspectives on Judicial Review by the World Court," *American Society of International Law, Proceedings of the 89th Annual Meeting*, 85 (1995)

(44) "Expanding the Security Council: Are There Checks to Provide Balance?," *Law Quad Notes* (University of Michigan Law School) (Fall 1994); modified version published as "The Security Council and Peacemaking: Too Little, Too Late or Too Much, Too Soon?" in 14 *The UN University* (June 1995)

(45) "Researching Legal Issues in the United Nations" in *Introduction to International Organizations* (L. Louis-Jacques & J.S. Korman, eds. 1996)

(46) "Who's Afraid of the 'New World Order'?" *Law Quad Notes* (University of Michigan Law School) (Spring 1996)

(47) "Organizational Insights," *American Society of International Law, Proceedings of the 87th Annual Meeting*, 400 (1993)

(48) "Article 2, Paragraph 7 Revisited," *Academic Council on the United Nations System (ACUNS), Reports and Papers, No. 5* (1994)

(49) "The Development and Expansion of Bilateral Investment Treaties," *American Society of International Law, Proceedings of the 86th Annual Meeting* (1992)

Articles, Book Chapters, and Book Reviews

(50) "Is Investor-State Arbitration 'Public'?" *Journal of Internatioanl Dispute Settlement* (forthcoming 2016)

(51) "Is the Trans-Pacific Partnership's Investment Chapter the New 'Gold Standard'?" NYU IILJ Working Paper Series 2016/3 (MegaReg Series), available at http://www.iilj.org/research/MegaReg.asp

(52) "'Beware: Boundary Crossings'—A Critical Appraisal of Public Law Approaches to International Investment Law," 17 *Journal of World Investment & Trade* 171 (2016)

(53) "International Organizations and the Rule of Law," NYU IILJ Working Paper Series, 2016/4 (GAL Series), available at http://www.iilj.org/documents/GAL20164.pdf

(54) "International Organizations and the Rule of Law: Challenges Ahead," in Chia-Jui Cheng, ed., *The New International Legal Order* (forthcoming 2016)

(55) "Global Judicialization Revisited" (Book Review Essay), 109 *American Journal of International Law* 677 (2015)

(56) "Foreword: The Hard and Soft Power of the Security Council," Vesselin Popvski & Trudy Frasier, eds., *The Security Council as Global Legislator* xiv (2014)

(57) Book Review of Jean L. Cohen's Globalization and Sovereignty, 107 *American Journal of International Law* 697 (July 2013)

(58) "Limits of Change by Way of Subsequent Agreements and Practice" in Georg Nolte, ed., *Treaties and Subsequent Practice* 123 (OUP 2013)

(59) "Tadić Revisited: The Ayyash Decisions of the Special Tribunal for Lebanon" 11 *Journal of International Criminal Justice* 291 (2013).

(60) "What Are International Judges for? The Main Functions of International Adjudication," in Cesare Romano, Karen J. Alter, & Yuval Shany, eds., *The Oxford Handbook on International Adjudication* (OUP 2013)

(61) "State Sovereignty is Not Withering Away: A Few Lessons for the Future," in Antonio Cassese, ed., *Realizing Utopia—The Future of International Law* 26 (OUP 2012)

(62) "Are International Judges Afraid of Science?: A Comment on Mbengue," 34 *Loyola of Los Angeles International and Comparative Law Review* 81 (2012)

(63) Book Review of Stephan W. Schill's The Multilaterialization of International Investment Law, 105 *American Journal of International Law* 377 (2011)

(64) "Foreword," in Richard Collins & Nigel D. White, eds., *International Organizations and the Idea of Autonomy: Institutional Independence in the International Legal Order* (2011)

(65) "Revisiting the Necessity Defense in the Argentina Cases" (with Tegan Brink) Yearbook of International Investment Law & Policy 319 (2010–2011)

(66) "The Argentine Crisis and Foreign Investors: A Glimpse into the Heart of the Investment Regime," (with Kathryn Khamsi) in Karl P. Sauvant, ed., *Yearbook of International Investment Law & Policy* 379 (2008–2009); available as a pdf at http://www.vcc.columbia.edu/pubs/

(67) "The Rise of Emerging Market Multinationals: Legal Challenges Ahead," in Karl Sauvant, Wolfgang Mascheck & Geraldine McAllister, eds., *Thinking Outward: Global Players in Emerging Markets* 425 (2010)

(68) "Sovereign Concerns and the International Investment Regime," in Karl P. Sauvant, Lisa Sachs, & Wouter P.F. Schmit Jongbloed, eds., *Sovereign Investment: Concerns and Policy Reactions* (OUP 2012)

(69) "The Once and Future Foreign Investment Regime," in Mahnoush Arsanjani, Jacob Katz Cogan, Robert D. Sloane & Siegfried Wiessner eds., *Looking to the Future: Essays on International Law in Honor of W. Michael Reisman* 607 (2010)

(70) "Alternatives to International Criminal Justice," in A. Cassese, ed., *The Oxford Companion to International Criminal Justice* 25 (2009)

(71) "A BIT on Custom," 42 N.Y.U. Journal of International Law & Politics 17–80 (2009), (published in Portuguese translation as a chapter in M.R. Ribeiro, ed., *Direito Internacional Dos Investimentos* (2014))

(72) "Foreword: Progress in International Law?," in Russell A. Miller & Rebecca M. Bratspies, eds., *Progress in International Law* 3 (2008)

(73) "Implications for the Future of International Investment Law," in Karl P. Sauvant, ed., *Appeals Mechanism in International Investment Disputes* 29 (Oxford 2008)

(74) "The Factors Driving and Constraining the Incorporation of International Law in WTO Adjudication," in Merit Janow, ed., *The WTO at Ten: Governance, Dispute Settlement, and Developing Countries* 611 (2008)

(75) Book Review of Gus Van Harten's Investment Treaty Arbitration and Public Law 102 *American Journal of International Law* 909 (2008)

(76) Book Review of Dan Sarooshi's International Organizations and Their Exercise of Sovereign Powers; 101 *American Journal of International Law* 674 (2007)

(77) "Introducing the Themes" (Introduction to Symposium on "Democratic Theory and International Law"), 38 *Victoria University of Wellington Law Review* 159 (August 2007)

(78) "Legal Perspectives," in T. Weiss & S. Daws, eds., *The Oxford Handbook on International Organizations* 82 (OUP 2007)

(79) "The NAFTA's Investment Chapter and Mexico," in R. Dolzer, M. Herdegen, & B. Vogel, eds., *Foreign Investment Its Significance in Relation to the Fight against Poverty, Economic Growth, and Legal Culture* 241 (Konrad Adenauer Stiftung 2006) (also published in German and available at http://www.kas.de/wf/de/33.8989/)

(80) "The Dark Side of the UN's War on Terrorism," in András Sajó, ed., *Abuse: The Dark Side of Fundamental Rights* 163 (Eleven International Publishing 2006)

(81) "International Organizations: Then and Now," Centennial Essay, 100 *American Journal of International Law* 324 (2006), reprinted in E. Kwakwa, ed., *Globalization and International Organizations* (2011)

(82) "Between Law and Power" (Review Essay of Erika de Wet's The Chapter VII Powers of the UN Security Council and David M. Malone's The UN Security Council from the Cold War to the 21st Century) 99 *American Journal of International Law* 459 (2005)

(83) "Trying Hussein: Between Hubris and Hegemony," 2 *Journal of International Criminal Justice* 319 (2004)

(84) "Foreword: The Ripples of NAFTA," Foreword to *NAFTA Investment Law and Arbitration: Past Issues, Current Practice, Future Prospects* xxi (Todd Weiler, ed. 2004)

(85) "Legal Unilateralism," in Margaret Crahan, John Goering, & Thomas G. Weiss, eds., *Wars on Terrorism and Iraq: Human Rights, Unilateralism, and U.S. Foreign Policy* (2004)

(86) "Hegemonic International Law Revisited," 97 *American Journal of International Law* 873 (2003)

(87) "Introduction, Symposium on The Regulation of Foreign Direct Investment," 42 *Columbia Journal of Transnational Law* 1 (2003)

(88) "The Security Council's War on Terrorism: Problems and Policy Options," in Erika de Wet & André Nollkaemper, eds., *Review of the Security Council by Member States* 119 (2003)

(89) "The New Dispute Settlers: (Half) Truths and Consequences," 38 *Texas International Law* Journal 1 (2003) (reprinted in Paul Berman, ed., *The Globalization of Justice* (2005))

(90) "Foreword" and "The WTO as Linkage Machine," Symposium on "The Boundaries of the WTO," 96 *American Journal of International Law* 1–4, 146–158 (José E. Alvarez, ed.) (2002)

(91) Book Review of Sands and Klein's Bowett's Law of International Institutions, 13 *European Journal of International Law* 552–557 (2002)

(92) "Do Liberal States Behave Better?: A Critique of Slaughter's Liberal Theory," 12 *European Journal of International Law* 183–246 (2001)

(93) Book Review of Hilary Charlesworth and Christine Chinkin's The Boundaries of International Law, 95 *American Journal of International Law* 459–464 (2001)

(94) "Constitutional Interpretation in International Organizations," in *The Legitimacy of International Organizations* 104 (Jean-Marc Coicaud & Veijo Heiskanen, eds. 2001)

(95) "Multilaterialism and its Discontents," 11 *European Journal of International Law* 393–411 (2000)

(96) Book Review of Philip Gourevitch's We Wish to Inform You that Tomorrow We Will Be Killed with Our Families, 93 *American Journal of International Law* 738–740 (1999)

(97) Book Review of Les Nations Unies et le Droit International Humanitaire/The United Nations and International Humanitarian Law, 10 *European Journal of International Law* 465–468 (1999)

(98) "Crimes of States/Crimes of Hate: Lessons from Rwanda," 24 *Yale Journal of International Law* 365–483 (1999) (reprinted in Gerry Simpson, ed., *War Crimes Law* (Vol. I) (2003))

(99) "Accounting for Accountability" (Review of Abrams and Ratner's Accountability for Human Rights Atrocities in International Law), 37 *Columbia Journal of Trans. Law* 1003–1014 (1999)

(100) "Rush to Closure: Lessons of the Tadić Judgment," 96 *Michigan Law Review* 2031–2112 (1998)

(101) "Foreword: Why Nations Behave," 19 *Michigan Journal of International Law* 303–317 (1998)

(102) Book Review of A Critical Study of the International Tribunal for the Former Yugoslavia, 8 *European Journal of International Law* 198–200 (1997)

(103) "Foreword: What's the Security Council For?," 17 Michigan Journal of International Law 221–228 (1996)

(104) "Nuremberg Revisited: The Tadić Case," 7 *European Journal of International Law* 245–264 (1996)

(105) "Judging the Security Council," 90 *American Journal of International Law* 1–39 (1996)

(106) "Legal Issues," in *A Global Agenda: Issues Before the 50th General Assembly of the United Nations* (John Tessitore & Susan Woolfson, eds. 1995)

(107) "The Once and Future Security Council," 18 *Washington Quarterly* 5–20 (1995), reprinted in *Order and Disorder after the Cold War* (Brad Roberts, ed. 1995)

(108) Book Review of United Nations, Divided World, About Face? The United States and the United Nations, and Financing an Effective United Nations, 88 *American Journal of International Law* 827–831 (1994)

(109) "Legal Issues," in *A Global Agenda: Issues Before the 49th General Assembly* (J. Tessitore & S. Woolfson, eds. 1994)

(110) "Financial Responsibility of Members," in volume 2, *The United Nations and the International Legal Order* 1091–1119 (O. Schachter & C. Joyner, eds. 1995); revised for paperback edition (1997)

(111) "Positivism Regained, Nihilism Postponed," Review Essay of Danilenko's Law-Making in the International Community, 15 *Michigan Journal of International Law* 747–784 (1994)

(112) "Burdens of Proof," Review Essay of Fact-Finding Before International Tribunals, 14 *Michigan Journal of International Law* 399–427 (1993)

(113) "Legal Issues," in *A Global Agenda: Issues Before the 48th General Assembly* (J. Tessitore & S. Woolfson, eds. 1993)

(114) "Legal Issues," in *A Global Agenda: Issues Before the 47th General Assembly* (J. Tessitore & S. Woolfson, eds. 1992)

(115) "The Quest for Legitimacy," Review Essay of Thomas M. Franck's The Power of Legitimacy Among Nations, 24 *N.Y.U. Journal of International Law and Politics* 199–267 (1991)

(116) "Legal Remedies and the UN à la Carte Problem," 12 *Michigan Journal of International Law* 229–311 (1991)

(117) "Promoting the 'Rule of Law' in Latin America: Problems and Prospects," 25 George Washington Journal of International Law & Economy 281–331 (1991); also published in Spanish, as "El Estado de Derecho en Latinoamérica: Problemas y Perspectivas," in *Estudios Especializados de Derechos Humanos* (T. Buergenthal & A. Cançado Trindade, eds. 1996)

(118) Book Review of Global Companies & Public Policy: The Growing Challenge of Foreign Direct Investment, 24 *George Washington Journal of International Law & Economics* 235 (1991)

(119) "Legal Issues," Chapter in *A Global Agenda: Issues Before the 46th General Assembly* (J. Tessitore & S. Woolfson, eds. 1991)

(120) "Legal Issues," in *A Global Agenda: Issues Before the 45th General Assembly* (J. Tessitore & S. Woolfson, eds. 1990)

(121) "Political Protectionism and U.S. International Investment Obligations: The Hazards of Exon-Florio," 30 *Virginia Journal of International Law* 1 (1989)

(122) Recent Development: "Refugees—United Nations Meeting on Refugees and Displaced Persons," 21 *Harvard International Law Journal* 290 (1980)

On Line Commentary

"To Court or Not to Court," NYU IILJ MegaReg Forum, 2016/2, available at http://www.iilj.org/research/MegaReg.asp

"The UN in the Time of Cholera," *AJIL Unbound* (Apr. 4, 2014), available at http://www.asil.org/blogs/united-nations-time-cholera

"The Proposed Independent Oversight Mechanism for the International Criminal Court," in UCLA Human Rights & International Criminal Law Online Forum, available at http://uclalawforum.com/

Guest Columns, *Opinio Juris* (Sept. 27–29, 2010), available at http://opiniojuris.org/2010/09/27/what-i-did-on-my-summer-vacation-part-i-the-transparency-of-the-international-investment-regime/

Monthly columns published as President of the American Society of International Law, from 2006–2008, available at http://www.asil.org/ilpost/president/index.html and quarterly newsletter columns at http://www.asil.org/newsletter/president/preso71226.html

"The Democratization of the Invisible College," (ASIL Presidential Column), reprinted at 6 *Transnational Dispute Management* Issue 1 (Mar. 2009)

Lectures on Video

"International Organizations as Law-Makers," (53 minute lecture), available at the UN's Audiovisual Library of International Law, at http://www.un.org/law/avl/

"An Introduction to the Evolving International Investment Regime," (3 lectures,
    75 minutes), available at the UN's Audiovisual Library of International Law, at
    http://www.un.org/law/avl/
A number of the publications listed in this CV are available for downloading as pdfs at
    http://www.law.nyu.edu/faculty/facultyprofiles/jalvarez/pubsfordownload/index
    .htm

Index

Printed in the United States
By Bookmasters